HOW TO DESIGN & BUILD YOUR OWN HOUSE

HOW TO DESIGN & BUILD YOUR OWN HOUSE

Lupe DiDonno & Phyllis Sperling

ALFRED A. KNOPF, NEW YORK, 1978

THIS IS A BORZOI BOOK PUBLISHED BY
ALFRED A. KNOPF, INC.

Library of Congress Cataloging in Publication Data
DiDonno, Lupe [date]
How to design & build your own house.
Includes index.
1. House construction. I. Sperling, Phyllis,
joint author. II. Title.
TH4811.D48   690'.8'64   77–20352
ISBN 0–394–40228–6
ISBN 0–394–73416–5 pbk.
Manufactured in the United States of America
First Edition

Grateful acknowledgment is made to the following for permission
to reprint previously published material:

Anderson Corporation—brochures courtesy Anderson Corporation,
Bayport, Minnesota.
Canadian Wood Council—span table courtesy Canadian Wood Council,
Ottawa, Ontario.
McGraw-Hill Book Company—tables and diagrams from *Time Saving
Standards* by John Hancock Callender, Copyright © 1974 by McGraw-Hill, Inc.
Used by permission of McGraw-Hill Book Company.
Slant/Fin Corporation: excerpts from Publications M-10 and 30-10 courtesy
Slant/Fin Corporation, Greenvale, New York.

To the City of Pergammon,
where it all began,
and to Anna and Sharon

Contents

PART THREE: CONSTRUCTION

ACKNOWLEDGMENTS

We would like to thank the following people for their help and advice in the writing of this book.

* Harry Carey, teacher, Middlebury, Vt.

* Frederick Defenthal, electrician, Miller Place, N.Y.

* Andrew DiDonno, numerical control manager, New Britain, Conn.

* Vito DiDonno, contractor, New Britain, Conn.

  Ronald DiDonno, architect, Brooklyn, N.Y.

* Rocco Ferrara, Jr., mason, New Britain, Conn.

  Y. S. Lee, engineer, Ardsley, N.Y.

  Samuel Lomask, engineer, New York, N.Y.

* Peter Neilsen, contractor, St. James, N.Y.

  Enio Rizzi, engineer, New York, N.Y.

  Herman Sands, architect, New York, N.Y.

  Arthur Spaet, engineer, New York, N.Y.

  Leonard Weiss, engineer, New York, N.Y.

* Built their own homes.

Introduction

For most people not in the construction trades, the idea of designing and building your own house is at once exciting, frightening, and overwhelming. For some it enters the realm of romantic fantasy. Yet each year more and more people are making the decision to construct their own living environment—or at least to take an active part in the design or interior finishing of their home.

There are, of course, a number of very good rational and emotional reasons for you to attempt to design and build your own house. The pros include the ability to customize your environment when designing the building. For a number of people, an individualized, expressive house is a high priority and worth the trial and tribulation ahead. For others, the attraction is the work itself, the need to provide for themselves, and the subsequent pride of accomplishment. Yet another motivation is the need to obtain housing within a tight budget; a great deal of money can be saved by providing one's own labor.

On the debit side of the ledger is the commitment of time involved. Not everyone is willing to give up weekends and vacations to the long, sometimes solitary hours of hard work that lie ahead. For most people building a house is a gamble. Few home repairers and not many do-it-yourself types, no matter how accomplished, feel confident enough to undertake such a project. The work involved is so enormous, the time commitment so great, that at the outset of the undertaking it is essential to ponder the comparative merits and sacrifices involved. Questions regarding talent, motivation, money, and commitment must be asked and answered before land is purchased and ground broken. The following pages attempt to help you ask and answer these and other questions.

Not everyone who will read these pages will make the decision to do it all himself. It is our feeling that you need not take on the entire responsibility of designing and building in order to reap the psychological and financial rewards of a custom-designed, custom-built house. Your home will feel every bit as good to you if you have taken a somewhat more limited role in its development.

The idea of designing your own home is tantalizing for a number of reasons. Neither the city apartment nor the suburban development house has turned out to be a totally satisfying living environment. Such a place is little more than the bedroom to which we commute, the place to which we have our mail sent, and the rooms in which we store our earthly possessions. In spite of ambitious attempts to landscape around it, redecorate and individualize it, the house remains very much like the one next door. Houses throughout the country tend to resemble each other to such an extent that a family moving anywhere in the United States can be sure of finding a house almost identical to the one they left behind.

An analysis of what people look for in a home will perhaps help to explain why many of us are not completely satisfied with the choices of dwelling places available to us. First, a home should satisfy our psychological need for security. In the past a family occupied the same house for many generations. This created a sense of stability. In our highly mobile society, houses are anonymous and interchangeable. When we first move to a house, little about it distinguishes it as our own. It sometimes takes years of living (children's handprints on the wallpaper and wear marks on the rug) to make us feel that this house is where we belong.

Second, a house should be functional. It should provide us with protection from the weather and space in which to cook, eat, wash, and sleep. Furthermore, it should be sizable and convenient enough so that we may go about these activities without constantly getting in one another's way.

Third, a house should provide an aesthetically pleasing setting for living. Each of us, of course, has a different idea of what constitutes a "house beautiful." Beauty, after all, is not easy to define. It is a combination of what fashion dictates and what we have been taught to admire. Yet, we do know what makes us feel comfortable and what makes us feel uncomfortable. Perhaps we should rely on these instincts when determining for ourselves what constitutes an aesthetic environment.

The average family in the market for a home can easily find one that is the right size, has an efficient working plan, and is pleasing to look at. On the other hand, it is much more difficult to find a house in which they feel as if they really belong. Although it is impossible to find a house with the buyer's family history already built in, it is possible to design and construct a house for a family that will reflect its particular personality and life style. A tailor-made suit looks, fits, and wears better than one designed and constructed for all those who happen to wear the same size. Similarly, a house can be tailored to the needs and tastes of the individuals who will make it their home. It can be as spacious or as small as required. It can be formal or relaxed, busy or unrushed, boisterous or subdued. Its inner spaces can differ in mood—large, open spaces for the times we feel expansive, small, cozy spaces for the times when we need to retreat.

A house can be designed around specific interests or hobbies. A family that enjoys cooking could make the kitchen their playroom and might decide to make it the largest and most comfortable room in the house. The home of an artist or musician might have the studio as its focal point. This area could be centrally located in the house or could be removed and secluded from the general living space.

A well-designed house should be able to adjust to change. A family that intends to grow should design a home that is easily expandable. A couple whose children will soon be leaving home would do well to consider a plan that is flexible. For example, it is possible to design a house that functions as one complete living unit for a large family, but later can be subdivided into two living units. The smaller apartment may be used by a member of the family who chooses to live alone, or might be rented for extra income.

A house that reflects the personality of the individuals who live in it will very likely be the most comfortable and secure environment for them. A highly organized person would be most comfortable in an efficient and orderly home. A person who hates to clean could create an almost maintenance-free house. An exuberant, active person might be happiest in a house with an open plan, one that has many interconnecting levels and ladders instead of stairs.

Moreover, a home can be designed and built for the varied living arrangements that are becoming more common. The tract developer does not build for the commune. Nor does he design houses for two or more families who prefer to live together. Such special housing situations demand specialized design.

In addition to the many reasons for wanting a home whose design reflects your own needs, there is a strong appeal in the idea of building that house by yourself. In our highly industrialized society, most of us have been trained to perform limited technical tasks and to depend on the skills of others for everything else we need. This dependence on others for essentials such as food and shelter is sometimes alarming because we can't be sure of the quality of what we are getting. Many people have already turned to growing their own vegetables and sewing their own clothes. The knowledge that we can provide for our own needs, even partially, makes us feel somehow more complete as human beings.

There are also good economic reasons for doing it yourself. First of all, you save money by substituting your own work for paid labor. Secondly, you can economize by deciding exactly which rooms and appliances you really need and want, and which you could well do without. Much of the money that goes into a standard house is spent on cosmetic frills that are not utilitarian and often not to the purchaser's taste. A third way to economize is to build a minimal house of good quality that is programmed to expand in stages, and to add to the house at the rate you can afford.

Having established the reasons for wanting to design and construct your own house, the question "Can I?" looms large. Some do-it-yourself construction manuals have suggested all that is required to do the job is putting your mind to it. We seriously question this attitude. A number of skills must necessarily be mastered to succeed at building a house. If you are going to make a serious attempt to design a building or direct its construction, you are going to have to learn to read plans and drawings—a very different skill from reading the morning paper. Plan reading requires a certain feel for spatial relations and an understanding of visual symbols. What you are doing is feeding your mind two-dimensional images and asking it to come up with a three-dimensional perspective. If you can put together a child's toy or a piece of patio furniture by following the manufacturer's diagrams you will probably have no problem following the directions given in this book. If, on the other hand, you have difficulty reading road maps and other diagrammatic drawings that use visual symbols, you will most likely need assistance in planning your home.

In addition, you should have some minimal ability with tools and enjoy working with them if you are actually going to do most of your own labor. This talent comes under the broad heading of manual dexterity, and entails not only the ability to drive a nail and saw a board but also means being able to take careful measurements and do precise work.

The third requisite could loosely be termed motivation. We caution those who have *some* desire to build a house, *some* ability in reading plans, and *some* talent with tools not to plunge right into the project. Having the necessary technical talents does not make an architect-construction worker. Building a house is a long-range project, with many months of hard work and a large investment of capital between your initial concepts and completion. Anyone seriously contemplating either the design or construction of his own home would be wise to read the whole book through to obtain an overall picture of what is involved and then decide if he has the stamina to see the project through.

One final word on ability. The talents required for house building are not sex-linked. Many women who have never lifted a hammer are likely to have developed the technical skills required in construction. Knitting instructions and architectural details differ in subject only. Following sewing patterns requires the same talent as reading architectural plans; all that is needed to transform one skill into the other is the inclination to do so.

This point can be illustrated by an example where the reverse kind of transfer of training occurred. A friend of ours, a male architect, was surprised to receive a sewing machine for his birthday. His wife, who presented him with the gift, cleverly reasoned that if he could read construction plans, he could read complicated dress patterns; and if he could so painstakingly cut and glue architectural models, he would be able to carefully cut out those patterns and sew the pieces of cloth together. She was right. In the first two months he curtained the windows, upholstered the couch, and clothed his family.

Most of the labor required in construction does not involve lifting great weights. We, therefore, are convinced that most women possess the strength and stamina called for to complete most building tasks.

We have prepared this book for the beginner. A good deal of the technical information included in the following chapters may appear redundant or oversimplified to those who have had some experience in design and construction. Most laymen, however, will need the step-by-step instructions we provide.

The book is divided into three major parts. The first section covers what architects call the schematic and preliminary design phases. In it you will find instructions on how to attack the problem of designing the house from the inside (functional planning and the organization of elements) to the outside (how the house is to relate to the environment and to the neighborhood). In addition, it will offer advice on what to look for and what to avoid when buying property. It is unusual for a "how-to" book to devote so many of its pages to design. We have become convinced, after having perused almost every available volume on the subject and having seen many owner-built homes, that such information is sorely needed. We have discovered that too much effort has been spent in building poorly designed, mediocre houses. It seems to us a shame that a family of workers should devote energy and sweat to constructing a box similar to one they could purchase from any land developer. The chapters on design serve, at the very least, as consciousness-raising material. Should you decide to hire an architect to design the house (and we recommend it), our discussion of design will provide you with a rich vocabulary to communicate what you want in your home. If you decide to buy a stock plan from a magazine, you will be able to evaluate what you have purchased with an educated and critical eye.

Part Two of the book deals with translating preliminary plans into working drawings. Before you begin construction yourself—or hire a contractor—it is absolutely necessary to have established the exact dimensions of everything in the house and to have specified exactly where each window, toilet, and electrical receptacle is to go. We will also instruct you on how to choose and specify those parts of the house (windows, doors, furnace, hardware) that can be purchased prefabricated and ready to install. Included in this section is a chapter on how to evaluate the cost of what you have designed and specified, and how to make peace with the local building department. We will also try to enlighten you on the financial help (or hindrance) you may expect from the banking establishment.

Part Three is devoted to construction. Chapter by chapter we will teach you how to build your own home, from the excavation to the finished walls. Each chapter covers a complete division of the work or "trade." In addition, there will be a discussion of how the materials are sold and what tools are needed. Detailed, step-by-step instructions are given on how to build the particular section of the house covered by each chapter and how to integrate it into what has been previously built. Running alongside the text are insets on basic skills. These insets are included for those who have had no experience in that segment of construction. In Chapter 20, Foundations, for example, we will instruct you in how to mix concrete and lay

block. In Chapter 21, Floor Framing, we will teach you how to toe in a nail.

We have organized this book so that you can do everything by yourself: design, drawings, and construction. We do not recommend that you do all of it without professional help. We *strongly* advise you to consult an architect while in the planning stages. The architect will review your plans, fill in the gaps, or show you how you might do the same thing more cheaply or with less effort. In some communities the question of whether or not to consult a professional is moot. Some ordinances require that plans for any building over a specified size must bear the seal of a registered architect or engineer.

As with any single volume that attempts to cover a vast territory, there are likely to be individual circumstances that are not covered. Chapters 21, 22, and 23, covering framing, instruct you on how to frame doors, windows, and stairs. They do not provide detailed diagrams to cover all the framing situations you may encounter. Thus, we have included a bibliography that you are advised to consult for additional information on any particular construction item. Most of these books are popular and will be on the shelves at your local library.

Perhaps your most pressing question at this point is, "Will it all be worth it?" This you will have to answer for yourself; it is a very private decision. Aside from the fact that you will save money by doing most of the work yourself, house building is very much a labor of love. Those people who have designed and/or constructed their own home have derived deep satisfaction from their work. Their feeling of pride and comfort in the house is not found in other homeowners. Most of the house builders enjoyed the work itself and profited enormously from the experience. They feel that the results were well worth the great effort expended. We think you will agree.

Lupe DiDonno
Phyllis Sperling
OCTOBER 1977
NEW YORK, N.Y.

PART ONE: THE PROBLEM– AN APPROACH

1
Functional Space Planning

The most important thing that a house can offer is the good feeling you get as you open the door and walk inside. If it is your house, you feel that you are home and within the embrace of your own private world. If you are a guest, you immediately feel welcomed and tempted to share in the charm and warmth of the house. No matter how many times you cross the familiar threshold, the feeling should be there. If anything, it should grow more intense with time.

A house, like a person, should have its own mystique. It engages you, grows on you, endears itself to you in its own way. One kind of house is immediately familiar and open. You can stand at its entrance and from that one vantage point take in the whole experience it offers. The space you are in may be large, well lit, and open to other rooms, levels, and the outdoors. Such a house seems to bubble over with excitement. Another type of house has an aura of mystery at first. You learn a little about it when you enter; its experiences unfold as you walk through it from room to room. Each pleasure is small, yet the overall effect is rich and harmonious. It is a house that never overwhelms.

THE FAMILY

Achieving the proper mood for a house is an intangible necessity in good design. Most builders pay considerable attention to the tangibles—room layout, economic plumbing arrangements, window size and placement—but give little consideration to what is potentially a house's most important asset, its personality. The personality of your house should reflect the personality of your family. A home's environment should mirror the life styles of its inhabitants. Your family is the starting point when designing your own house. What they need in a living environment is the major criterion in its design.

The needs of a family fall into three, often overlapping, categories: 1. psychological needs —that which makes us feel comfortable and secure; 2. functional needs—that which allows us to carry out household activities efficiently; and 3. aesthetic needs—that which pleases and enlivens us. It is our feeling that when the psychological needs of a family are determined, analyzed, and incorporated into a design, the functional needs of that family will automatically be satisfied. Furthermore, a solution that successfully harmonizes psychological and functional requirements will need few frills to be aesthetically pleasing.

An Individual's Need for Privacy

The family* consists of individuals who sometimes need to be together and sometimes want

* We are using "family" as a generic term incorporating any number of combinations of people who live together on a permanent basis, the most common unit being the nuclear family consisting of mother, father, and children. Our use of "family" includes the extended family and people who, although not related, choose to live communally.

Some spaces are dynamic and open. In this multilevel house space flows freely while still allowing various activities to take place independently. A quiet reading area on a balcony with access to the outdoors sits directly over the living space and overlooks the dining area. The use of angled walls, the simple exposed structure, the light and window openings all contribute to the visual excitement. Architect, Neski Associates; photographer, William Maris

Traditionally there is a definite distinction between the interior of a house and the outdoors. In this case only very subtle barriers separate the inside from the outside of the house, and the two blend. The dining room is constructed of industrial greenhouse components. The paving material and the interior wall finishes are extended outside to complete the feeling of continuity. Architect, Peter K. Woerner; photographer, Robert Perron

to be alone. They need to be alone to have quiet, to study or work, or they need privacy in order to think. All people, children included, need to withdraw occasionally to put together the events of the day or to ponder a decision. The place a person chooses for this private contemplation is a room or area that he feels is his own. The bedroom is the most likely candidate. Most people seem to have a particular attachment for the place where they sleep. Perhaps we shed our inhibitions when we take off our clothes.

The bedroom need not be the only bastion of privacy in the house. The kitchen, when the rest of the family has deserted it, is another choice; so is the study or the porch. Each member of the family should feel that he has at least one spot in which he may be alone and undisturbed.

Communal Activities

Most of the activities of a family are communal. It is not only more efficient to cook and eat together, it is more pleasant. The shared spaces of the family—the living room, dining room, kitchen, and playroom—are the places in which to share ideas, experiences, and love. These areas should have a warm and comfortable environment, conducive to such exchange. Shelves laden with books create a comfortable surrounding for a family that enjoys reading. It may seem too stuffy, however, for a family not intellectually oriented. A family that loves the outdoors is likely to feel happiest in a room that embraces the outside.

Special demands are often made on the com-

Functional
Space Planning

3

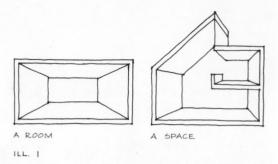

A ROOM   A SPACE

ILL. 1

Space can be defined by visual rather than physical boundaries. In this house one space is separated from another by a change in level, ceiling height, or plane. A continuous flow between spaces is maintained by the use of the same floor, wall, and ceiling materials throughout. Architect, F. Tomsick; photographer, Jeremiah O. Bragstad

T.V., and feed the kids. Other families do not feel the need for as rigid a space hierarchy. They choose to live and entertain informally and do not want these independent areas. It is all a matter of life style.

Moods are also a part of the spatial needs. There are rainy days when we feel miserable and want to crawl into a hole somewhere. But there are other times when the sun is shining and we feel good; we almost want to open up our house and let every ray of sunshine in. If we are so inclined, we might divide our communal space into a small, windowless area and another that has glass everywhere.

Each family has its own ideas on how to make best use of its space—it is the *quality* and not the *quantity* that is vital to good design.

THE SPACE

Thus far we have used the terms "rooms" and "space" almost interchangeably. A "room" is usually defined by physical boundaries such as walls, doors, floors, and ceilings. A "space" can be defined as an area in which a specific activity is likely to take place. For example, an area near the kitchen can be set aside for eating. It need not be a room surrounded by walls. It could be a corner of the living room or kitchen, a balcony overlooking the family room, or the center of a greenhouse. Any number of locations are possible as long as the original criterion of being close to the kitchen is maintained (Ill. 1).

Spaces are defined by visual rather than physical boundaries. These boundaries are provided by light, texture, color, materials, furniture, changes in floor level or ceiling height, and so on. A space can be partially enclosed by low walls or it may be totally free from them. The ceiling above it can be raised or lowered. It can be dramatically lit with a skylight. A free-standing fireplace or a "floating" bookshelf can partially enclose it. All of these elements manipulated in various ways set this space aside from any other space in the house, giving it a different use or setting a different mood.

Space Relationships

A house should be thought of as a relationship of spaces, not a collection of rooms. Achieving

munal spaces of our homes. Many families differentiate between formal and informal areas. They want a formal living and dining room, in which to entertain non-family members, in addition to informal spaces, in which to relax, watch

the proper space interaction to satisfy your family's needs is what constitutes a successful house. The spaces can relate directly or indirectly to each other. Sometimes they even overlap. For example, the need for privacy and sound control will determine the distance that the bedrooms should be located from the noise-producing areas of the house. Functional criteria will place the kitchen in close proximity to the eating spaces. A need for supervision will locate a workroom, where an adult plans to spend a lot of time, directly adjacent to a children's playroom.

A bubble diagram for space analysis is an excellent technique to use while planning space relationships. It is constructed by drawing a simple circle for each room or space that you will include in your house. The circle need not in any way reflect the square footage of the actual room, but it is often helpful to make somewhat larger circles for the bigger rooms (such as the living room) and smaller circles for the smaller rooms (bathrooms). The organization of these circles on paper should reflect the functional organization of the spaces within the house. Rooms that must relate to one another (such as the kitchen to the dining room) are depicted by drawing their circles in close proximity to one another. The need for a direct physical relationship is emphasized by connecting the circles with an arrow (Ill. 2).

With the aid of this technique, you can begin with basic relationships and gradually progress to more detailed diagrams. Once a diagrammatic ideal has been established, a plan with dimensions can be laid out. After designing the actual house, you may find that all the relationships in the bubble diagram could not be incorporated in the actual plan. In such a case the bubble diagram as originally drawn can serve as a checking device for the criteria that were originally set, and corrections of the house plans can be made.

A house, most simply, is divided into three parts: private, communal, and service areas. A tiny ski cabin might have only one room and a bathroom. That room, however, must be able to accommodate these three spatial needs even if it is not able to satisfy them all at the same time. It might serve as a boisterous communal space during the day but by necessity convert to a quiet private space at night so that people can sleep. At other times a table may be unfolded so that the occupants can eat. Here the activities

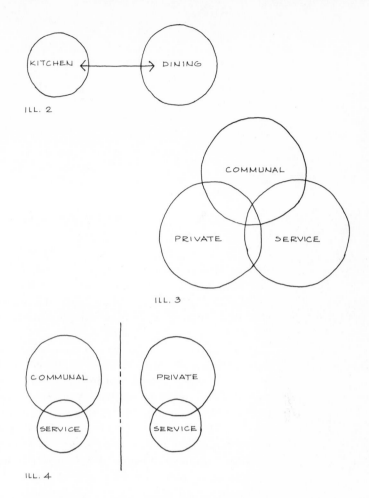

ILL. 2

ILL. 3

ILL. 4

are differentiated temporarily (in terms of time). In a larger house, we have the luxury of defining them spatially.

The private spaces in a house generally consist of those areas assigned to sleeping, resting, and studying (in addition to the bathroom, which overlaps as a service area). Areas used for family gathering and interaction such as eating, talking, and playing are obviously in the category of communal spaces. Service areas make up the third group—the kitchen, bath, laundry room, garage, closets, and so on.

There are a variety of ways in which the private, communal, and service spaces can be arranged. They can overlap, allowing private and communal areas to come in contact with each other in addition to sharing service areas, or they can be completely segregated (Ills. 3 and 4). The traditional four-story urban townhouse was a good example of segregated spaces. Its two lower levels were divided into service and communal spaces. The ground floor contained a large kitchen and a workroom. The parlor floor above had a dining room in the back of the house. The top two floors housed the bedroom

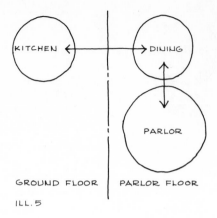

GROUND FLOOR | PARLOR FLOOR

ILL. 5

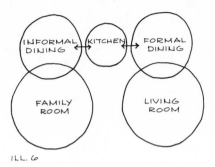

ILL. 6

suites. This very formal approach was considered efficient in an era when most buyers could afford the servant power necessary to run food and laundry up and down flights of stairs (Ill. 5).

It is still popular today to segregate the communal and service areas within a house to allow for separation of formal and informal activities such as family eating as distinguished from dinner parties. These duplicate dining spaces, however, must both relate directly to the kitchen since the average middle-class American family no longer employs full-time kitchen help (Ill. 6).

More and more families are choosing to eliminate formality from their homes and with it the need for these parallel spaces. Some are combining the family and living rooms into one space and are incorporating additional rooms such as a studio, workshop, or library. Others are making one room, such as the kitchen, the focal point of the family's activities. Such a kitchen would contain a handsome, well-organized area for the preparation of food, an eating area, a sitting area, and perhaps a fireplace.

Communal Spaces

Most of the activities of a family are concentrated in and around the communal areas of the house. Special attention should therefore be focused on the design of these areas. What kinds of activities take place in the communal spaces of your house and what kinds of experiences do you hope to have in these rooms?

Families gather to talk and argue, watch T.V. or the fire, read out loud or to themselves, prepare food, eat, gossip, fight, listen to music, work, and play. The activities to be housed in these communal areas will be as varied as the age groups within the family. Play areas will

accommodate activities that may at times be unharmonious such as a quiet game of chess and a noisy Ping-Pong match. Work areas might be used by someone preparing an elaborate term paper while someone else is creating a giant sculpture. Eating areas could include as many eating styles as quick snacks, children's feeding, around-the-table dining, and formal dinners.

The communal areas of the house are also used to entertain friends, making additional demands on already limited space. Entertaining can range from having a few friends for drinks to throwing a large party and inviting half the neighborhood. It also includes birthday and slumber parties for children, community group meetings, teen dances, and card parties.

Once you have established the activities or combination of activities that are to take place in these areas, you must determine the type of environment that should surround them. Your family may find that they usually interact with family and non-family members alike on a small, intimate scale. To them a large space with ballroom dimensions would be useless and feel uncomfortable. Perhaps a house with a small living-dining area would satisfy all the family and entertaining needs.

Another family might find that they want a large open space exclusively for adult gatherings. The younger family members would like to have a similar space for themselves and their friends, a place where they could play and have parties without being continually scolded. In addition, they all agree that a range of smaller spaces is necessary to house activities such as small study groups, piano lessons, reading, and one-to-one conversation.

With an unlimited budget all these spaces can easily be accommodated. Unfortunately, expectations are generally far greater than budgets and compromises must be made. One way to go

```
      I                          II
1. SMALL CONVERSATIONAL      1. BRIGHT, OPEN, SPACIOUS,
   GROUPINGS                    DYNAMIC
2. T.V. WATCHING             2. NOISY, BOISTEROUS
3. LARGE OPEN SPACE FOR      3. INTIMATE, WARM, PROTECTED
   PARTIES                   4. FORMAL
4. GROUP STUDY AREA          5. QUIET
5. PLAYROOM                  6. STRONG OUTDOOR FEELING
6. FORMAL DINING ROOM
7. QUICK EATING AREA
8. PLACE TO RAISE PLANTS
9. PLACE FOR STRING
   QUARTET PRACTICE
```

POSSIBLE OVERLAPS

BRIGHT, OPEN, SPACIOUS, DYNAMIC FEELING
- BIG PARTIES
- STRING QUARTET PRACTICE

Need badly!

CHILDREN COMMUNAL NOISY BOISTEROUS
- BIG PARTIES
- STRING QUARTET PRACTICE
- PLAYROOM FOR TODDLERS
- QUICK EATING AREA

Future

INTIMATE, WARM, PROTECTED
- T.V. WATCHING
- SMALL CONVERSATIONAL GROUPING
- DINING

Want very much

FORMAL
- SMALL CONVERSATIONAL GROUPING
- BIG PARTIES
- FORMAL DINING ROOM

Activities overlap other spaces. We can't afford it. OMIT!

QUIET
- STUDY

Children can have desk space in bedroom OMIT!

STRONG OUTDOOR FEELING
- DINING
- RELAXING
- PLANT RAISING

Want very much

ILL. 7

about setting up priorities is to make a list of all those functions or activities you wish to incorporate in the design. A second list is then drawn up—this time, however, only noting the various environments you would like to see in the house. The functional needs of the first list must then be matched to the psychological needs of the second. A number of different activities often require the same kind of atmosphere. For instance, reading, sewing, and quiet conversation might be comfortably accommodated in a room that feels intimate and cozy. Quite a different kind of environment might be desired for a cocktail party, club meeting, or piano practice. A set of priorities is established, distinguishing those spaces that are essential from those that although attractive are not imperative. Perhaps the latter can be incorporated at a future date (Ill. 7).

Your family may find after studying these long lists that a large communal area will be sufficient to accommodate all your entertainment and most of the family's activities. This particular area will not only house large groups but it will also let in lots of sunshine and air. It can be used for communal functions in addition to providing a place to be when feeling exuberant and wishing to be in close contact with the outdoors. The rest of the communal needs will be answered by a quiet space where reading and more intimate interchange can occur. This space can be designed to be sheltered and warm and could double as a private place to retreat on gray winter days or when feeling miserable.

At this stage in the planning process, it is important to begin to visualize these spaces. Most likely, you have a picture in your mind as to what form these particular spaces are to take. You might envision a room with a strong outdoor feeling, such as a greenhouse for year-round use or a simple screened porch for summer evenings. A "large, bright" room could be seen as more than one story in height with large glass walls as well as a skylight above. An "intimate" space, on the other hand, might be pictured as a tiny alcove off the dining room, perhaps a step or two below floor level, having continuous built-in sofas that face a stone hearth and fire.

Mental images such as these are helpful in designing a house. We are not, after all, designing in a vacuum. We have all been in other people's homes and have seen photographs of well-designed houses in magazines. While it is helpful to have strong mental images of what to incorporate into the design, don't be misled into choosing elements that are merely stylish. Think carefully about the kinds of space you want to live with and construct them from materials you like. Research the subject by familiarizing yourself with various floor plans and design schemes developed by contemporary architects. Browse through magazines that specialize in residential architecture and see how cleverly certain professionals manipulate space. Study books on old colonial houses and French chateaus and get an understanding of the underlying concepts behind these houses. There is a good deal to be learned from the Mediterranean house, which is organized around a courtyard, and the Japanese house, in which spaces are separated with sliding screen walls. Soon you will begin to see and evaluate the merits of designs in terms of their conceptual structure rather than style.

Facing page: *a quiet, intimate retreat can be incorporated into an expansive, open area. Three different experiences are part of the same space: a forest-like environment in the planted area; a light, open expanse on the balcony surrounded by glass and treetops; and a darker, cave-like area in the lower space. Note the juxtaposition of materials, the use of greenhouse glass, and the exposed mechanical ductwork. Architect, John Johansen; photographer, Norman McGrath*

ILL. 10

ILL. 8

ILL. 9

ILL. 11

Private Spaces

The private areas of a house call for the same type of careful planning as the communal areas. Do you need any private areas? If so, what functions should they encompass and how many do you need? All of us need a place to sleep and dress, to gather our thoughts, to retreat and feel alone. Private space or spaces can be large or small, bright or dark, open or closed. To some people a space of their own represents a place in which to spend the first few hours of the day using the phone, working, and reading. Others might use this space exclusively for sleeping or when ill. They would prefer to spend most of their time in the communal areas. The functional and psychological requirements to be met by these two spaces will be vastly different. The first will demand a large area for sitting, working, and sleeping and should have a bright and cheerful feeling, while the second could be as basic as a sleeping cell.

Traditionally, private spaces in a house have been separated into separate spaces for adults and children. Adult privacy is provided by the master bedroom, which is larger in area and has direct access to a private bathroom. The secondary bedrooms become the children's spaces and are generally smaller, sharing a common bathroom (Ill. 8).

Although this arrangement has proven efficient for many families it must not necessarily become the model for every family. A family whose foremost concern is flexibility rather than segregation can be happiest by providing a large area that can be segmented into any number of smaller spaces. This space can be divided in accordance with changing needs (Ill. 9).

Another family may find that an adult private and communal area totally isolated from children's private and community areas is essential. The adult area might be a single space that accommodates sleeping, relaxing, working, and grooming in a group of spaces. The children may prefer to play and work together but do not wish to share sleeping spaces. Their private space could be a large communal play- and workroom with sleeping cells and bathroom facilities closely related (Ill. 10).

Yet another family with a different attitude toward sleeping and working could choose a communal sleeping arrangement directly related to a series of private working and relaxing alcoves (Ill. 11). The possibilities are innumerable. The main concern is that your family's needs are answered.

Service Spaces

We can now consider the supportive spaces of a house: the service areas. They are the garage, kitchen, bathrooms, laundry, and storage areas. Because of their supportive nature they are generally located in the most efficient relationship to the areas they serve.

Kitchens are most convenient when located adjacent to the dining and eating areas serving both the indoors and outdoors. The bathrooms are used by both members of the family and their guests. They are consequently situated not only in the private areas of the house but also in areas easily accessible to visitors. Considerations of weather, terrain, and functional relationship to the house affect the location of the garage. If the house is to be built in a climate where there is frequent rain and snow, a garage directly connected to the house is highly desirable. In drier, warmer areas physical proximity is not imperative. Similarly in terms of terrain, a garage can be easily built into a steep slope underneath the house and become an accessible although inconspicuous element.

Storage areas fall into the categories of private storage for personal items such as clothing, books, documents, and so on, and communal storage for group possessions such as unused furniture, equipment, and tools. Accordingly, private storage should relate to private areas and communal storage to communal areas. Keep in mind ease of access when providing storage for bulky items.

Organizational approaches to service areas vary according to need and economy. One of the most efficient labor- and money-saving approaches is the central service core. This concept integrates the kitchen, bathrooms, and laundry areas by locating them adjacent to each other, thus necessitating minimum plumbing and resulting in considerable economy. The service core's central location within the house provides easy accessibility from all areas (Ill. 12).

Where maximum economy is not imperative, a more flexible approach is feasible, with the location of kitchen, bathrooms, and other service areas being influenced by other criteria such as light, spaciousness, and openness.

CIRCULATION

Up to this point, we have been concerned with the three major categories of spaces within a house and the relationship among them. We must now begin to think in terms of integrating a circulation system into and between these spaces.

The house is punctured by points of access and departure. Family members, guests, and strangers will enter and leave the house from these points. Access could be from a yard, main road, play area, garage, or other point. These entrances and exits become buffer zones between the inside and outside. When access is from a yard or play area, you will probably need a transitional space to provide for the disposal of heavy clothing, muddy boots, and bundles. Another access point could occur adjacent to the main road and be generally used by visitors. This would become a place of welcome before entering other areas of the house.

Once people have been greeted or have taken off their muddy boots, what happens next? How do they get to where they are going or where you are leading them? Circulation within the house is of prime importance. While developing a plan, bear in mind the circulation or traffic flow among the various rooms. A diagonal walk from an entrance through one or two rooms to get to the kitchen could be very nice if you are taking a tour of the house. On the other hand, it could be back-breaking if all you are trying to do is dump your groceries on the kitchen counter. Similarly, the formality of a dinner party would be shattered if your guests were led to the dining room via a messy kitchen.

Although these examples might sound like exaggerations, you will be surprised how easy it is to forget the obvious when confronted with such an engaging project as the design of a house.

We stress the importance of these exercises as a means of ascertaining and affirming the spatial requirements and functional arrangements you wish to incorporate into the design. Be sure to

SERVICE CORE
ILL. 12

give time and consideration to the internal functioning of the house before proceeding further. When you are satisfied with one or more schemes you can begin to study the house's external environment, and its relationship to it.

Hold on to these early diagrams until the design of the house has been finalized. They will be valuable as a reminder of your earliest design requirements before the necessary compromises had to be made.

2
Environmental Planning

The house should ideally blend in with and acknowledge its surroundings, whether they are an established residential neighborhood or a forest. A glass-and-steel house (which might be elegant sited in a heavily wooded area) can be a sore spot in an old Victorian town where the houses are rich in wood detailing. On the other hand, by blending in we don't mean re-creating the house next door. Today, although we still admire the beauty of the Victorian-style homes that were constructed around the turn of the century, building their replicas nearly one hundred years later would seem absurd if not impossible.

Life styles have changed and new ways of organizing the household have brought about new approaches to house design. The turn-of-the-century family who could afford to live in these elegant mini-mansions could afford to employ the cheap labor needed to clean, polish, and repaint the house's intricate detailing. The modern family cannot afford the necessary "staff." A style is a product of its time and cannot, therefore, be re-created.

We can, however, re-create those spatial elements of a Victorian house that are attractive and compatible with present life styles. The spaciousness of a parlor floor can be attained by designing large and airy living areas with very high ceilings. Furthermore, we can render a contemporary version of the precise hierarchy of public to private spaces identified with this style by articulating the progression of spaces moving from stoop to porch to parlor, dining room, master bedroom suite, and sleeping alcoves.

Just as it is unthinkable to rebuild the rich-in-detail Victorian house, it is also preposterous to consider leveling a hilly, wooded site to construct a house that is unsuitable for such a location. Clearing most of the vegetation for purposes of displaying your new house to the world will most likely diminish the beauty of the setting (and inspire the wrath of every nature lover in the area). If your concept of siting is clearing most of the land and planting a lawn, you might do a lot better by buying a piece of farm land. An empty field offers the designer the freedom to explore the house's sculptural form.

It is not feasible to copy the style of a hundred years ago or build in a forest without touching a single tree. We can, however, take into consideration such things as siting, scale, height, texture, and vegetation, which make up the fabric of the area, so that the house we build will blend and harmonize with its environment.

A degree of harmony with the existing houses or landscape can be achieved by continuity in the use of existing materials and scale and proper siting. We can best illustrate what we mean by harmony, or "succession," by citing examples where it is lacking. A neighborhood that features streets lined with magnificent stone houses will be destroyed by even one house clad in slick aluminum siding. Stone is a natural material, rich in texture and having deep earthy colors. If building in stone proves to be impossible for the owners of the property, a better choice might be another natural material such as wood. The wood siding can be left to

Left: *a house can either blend into its environment or act as a counterpoint to it. In this case the house stands as a sculptural form in the field, not blending with but nonetheless complementing the open space. Architect, Robert Whitton; photographer, Esto Photo Graphics*

Below: *this house, set in a rugged environment, relates to and complements its site in a very sophisticated way. The roughly textured concrete vertical supports echo the texture and mass of the nearby boulders. The more delicate horizontal structural members are similar in tactile quality and color to the trees surrounding the house. Architect and photographer, C. Blakeway Millar*

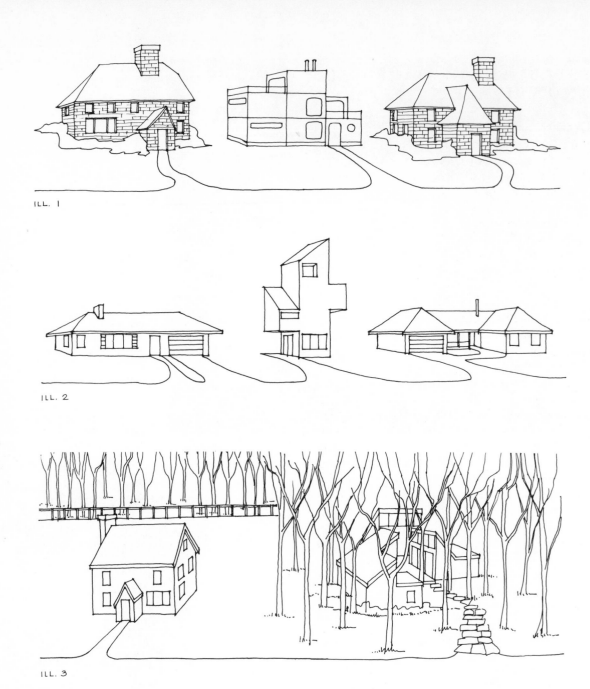

ILL. 1

ILL. 2

ILL. 3

weather naturally to its own earthy patina. An alternative choice would be brick, which has a texture similar to stone (Ill. 1).

Lack of succession in scale is exemplified by the building of a four-story tower in a neighborhood of low-lying ranch houses (Ill. 2). (In most cases the height of the house will be regulated by zoning laws.) Lack of succession in siting and vegetation would occur if someone purchased a piece of land in a forest, where most of the houses can barely be seen, and treated it as if it were a potato field (Ill. 3). In all of these examples both the new house and its surroundings would have benefited from an awareness of

the relationship a house must have to its environment.

When we talk about continuity, we presuppose that a fabric or texture of some kind is already established in the community. Obviously, when dealing with the tightly knit fabric of a turn-of-the-century neighborhood such as Society Hill in Philadelphia or the French Quarter in New Orleans, maintaining the continuity of these established patterns becomes crucial to the design of an individual house. In a new and expanding area the succession is less important since the houses most likely vary in their design approaches.

ESTABLISHING SEMIPUBLIC AND PRIVATE AREAS

Openness within the house itself is limited by every individual's occasional need for privacy from the family's communal activities. Similarly, the openness of the house to the street is affected by the family's need for privacy from the neighbors.

A transition from public to private space is a necessary element in the design of a house. Older houses show more evidence of this concern than their newer counterparts. As you walk through older towns and neighborhoods, you will find many houses with front porches. (By the way, the "sitting porch," or veranda, is considered by historians to be an American invention.) These porches serve as buffer zones between what is public and what is private. Someone sitting on his front porch becomes a part of the street life while still being in his separate, semiprivate domain. Obviously, this does not occur when a person sits on a sidewalk. With the advent of the automobile and the era of riding by instead of walking by, the front porch has become all but extinct. Its modern counterpart, the front lawn, cannot be said to accomplish what its predecessor did. It is not a successful buffer between public and private areas. Strangers are aware that the lawn is private property. Yet someone sitting or relaxing on his front lawn is a conspicuous element in the streetscape. Generally, he will prefer sitting in the back yard, where there is more likelihood of privacy (Ill. 4).

By defining exterior spaces in terms of how they are to be used you will be likely to utilize the site more fully. Let's examine the type of activities that could take place out of doors. One member of the family is an enthusiastic flower gardener while the rest of the group raises vegetables. The horticulturist takes pride in his flowers and enjoys displaying them. The rest of the group is happy to share their produce. It seems logical, then, when planning the landscape design, to locate the flower beds on that portion of the property that is most public. The vegetable garden can be located in a secluded portion near the back of the site. The family as a whole, although not particularly interested in raising flowers, admires the rich display of color in late spring and summer. They might choose to locate the family room adjacent to the flower beds and to construct a deck reaching out from this room into the garden. The garden and the

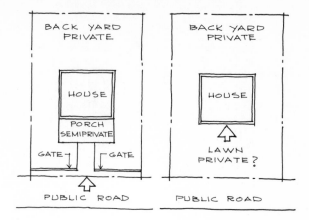

ILL. 4

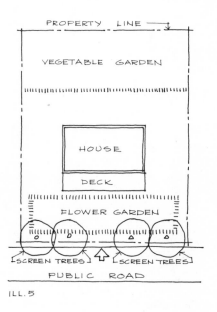

ILL. 5

deck become extensions of the family's activities into the neighborhood (Ill. 5).

An exterior eating area is another feature that the family might want to include in the overall design. The most logical place for this activity is directly outside the food preparation area. Other possible areas for outdoor activities are a place for sun bathing, a private swimming pool, children's gyms, goldfish ponds, formal gardens, and mini-basketball courts.

THE HOUSE AND ITS NATURAL ENVIRONMENT

When we talk about the house and its natural environment, we mean the relationship of the house to the sun, to the view (if there is one), to the topography of the site, and to the climate of the area. Consideration of all these factors will

Environmental
Planning

15

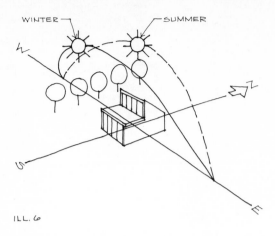

WINTER   SUMMER

ILL. 6

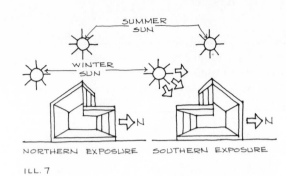

SUMMER SUN

WINTER SUN

NORTHERN EXPOSURE   SOUTHERN EXPOSURE

ILL. 7

deliver a better house in terms of beauty, comfort, and economy.

Following the Sun

Sunlight adds immeasurably to the beauty of an interior space. How much sun is desirable, how it is allowed to enter the room and at what time of day are important design questions. We are all aware that the sun rises in the east and sets in the west. In northern parts of the United States and Canada the sun follows a different path in the sky depending on the season. In the winter the sun stays low in the southern sky. It rises in the southeast and sets in the southwest. In summer (because of the tilt of the earth in relationship to the position of the solar disk) the sun appears to follow an arch-like pattern, rising in the northeast and setting in the northwest (Ill. 6).

A room with large expanses of glass that has a direct northern exposure will almost never have the sun's rays pierce the glass (the exception will be in late June, when the rays of the rising sun in the northeast will shine through the windows in the early morning, as will the setting sun on late June evenings).

A room with a southern exposure, on the other hand, will be joyously lit with bright sunlight. The room's occupants will be further rewarded by the warmth of the sun's radiant heat on their bodies. During the summer months that same room is protected from the glare of the sun in midday by the fact that the noonday sun in summer is directly overhead, casting its oppressive rays onto the roof and not through the windows (Ill. 7).

North light, we should note, is far from un-

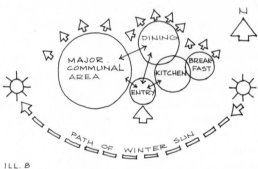

VIEW

MAJOR COMMUNAL AREA

DINING

BREAK FAST

KITCHEN

ENTRY

N

PATH OF WINTER SUN

ILL. 8

desirable. A room with large windows facing north can be brightly lit with *reflected* light. Artists have traditionally preferred their studios to be naturally lit with northern light.

The location of the rooms within the house should take into consideration the sun's path in the sky. If a brightly lit breakfast room in the morning is considered desirable, that room should be located on the east side of the house. People who find that the sun's rays piercing through the windows at 5 a.m. drive them to distraction should consciously locate their bedrooms on the west side of the house to avoid the sunrise. A western exposure in the living areas often causes problems. Since the sun sets low in the western sky a room unprotected from the sun's glare by either shades or screens can be hot and uncomfortable.

The View

Design, as we have said before and will say again, is a series of compromises. You may have analyzed the needs of the family members in

Situated spectacularly on a mountainside in the Caribbean, this house was designed to embrace the view. The placement of the windows and the roof overhang artfully maximize the view and minimize the glare. Architect, Ronald DiDonno; photographer, Alex Nitkin

relationship to the sunlight and decided that a house with the communal spaces open to the south is desired. If your property has an ocean view and that ocean is "south" of the property, you are in luck. On the other hand, if the ocean is "north" of the site, you will have to make some compromises. A main living space on the north side of the house will have the view but no direct sunlight. One on the south side gets the light but misses the view. A clever solution to the problem, if possible, is to locate this important room at the end of the house so that it can take advantage of both natural assets (Ill. 8).

It would be a pity to turn your back on the view if you are lucky enough to have one. Surprisingly, a goodly number of people (most of them land developers) have exhibited enormous insensitivity in this area. Very often a builder who constructs a house for speculative purposes (he builds it first and then tries to sell it) will take a stock house plan and plunk it down on the site. His only consideration regarding the house's orientation is that the front door face the street. A number of such houses feature large picture-windowed living spaces facing

homely streets while another side of the house that is left windowless faces a spectacular view.

We can even document a case in which some friends of ours actually constructed their own house without any regard to a spectacular view. They purchased a set of construction plans before selecting a site. The site that they eventually bought was on the crest of a hill overlooking a beautiful valley; the view is uninterrupted for miles. As presently built, the house has a two-story living room with a cathedral ceiling, a dining room, and a porch facing a pleasant grove of trees. Only one small bathroom window offers a glimpse of the valley below.

A house built on a site with a view should exploit it to the fullest. Decks, large glass areas, porches, overhangs, and so forth can all be used to embrace the view and make it an important asset to the house.

Topography

Topography is another important criterion to which a house should respond. The easiest sites

The magnificent view of the valley beneath this house can be enjoyed through the clear expanse of glass. A feeling of complete openness is obtained by the continuation of the ceiling and flooring materials to the terrace outside and by the elimination of mullions between the sheets of glass. Architect, Robin Molny; photographer, Marc Neuhof

vary and so should the houses located on them. A house sitting on a hillside can be designed as a series of levels crawling up the hill. As the rooms climb, terraces can be located on the roofs of the ones below. This design solution would be more difficult to create and inappropriate for a flat site (Ill. 9).

The hanging houses in the Spanish city of Cuenca offer an excellent example of buildings that are strongly influenced by topography (Ill. 10). The city lies in a mountainous area, with sheer rocky cliffs leaving little room for house building. Many of the houses are literally attached to the cliffs and cantilevered from them. This housing type could never have been developed in the Southwest prairies of the United States, where ranch houses are the common dwelling type.

Climate

A house's orientation is closely tied to climate. Exposures that are desirable in cold climates could prove terribly uncomfortable in hot ones. In cold areas plenty of sun and protection from winter winds are of primary importance. In hot and humid locations protection from the sun and openness to cool breezes become the rule. A good example of responsiveness to climate is New England's colonial house. Having to deal with extremely cold winters, the colonists adopted heat conservation as the critical design factor. To minimize heat loss to the outside, windows were few and small and all the rooms were wrapped around a central chimney. In addition, any large openings occurred to the south, while the northern facade (where the prevailing winter winds came from) remained nearly unbroken (Ill. 11).

Conversely, in hot and humid areas, houses are heavily sheltered from the sun and remain wide open to receive cool breezes. Long, wide overhangs, particularly on the western and eastern facades, act as barriers against the intense sunshine. The shape of the house becomes narrow and elongated, allowing for maximum outdoor exposures. Air is permitted to circulate underneath the structure by elevating the house from the ground. Walls become merely screens to further facilitate the air flow (Ill. 12). The different treatment given to these two types of houses is evidence of how design can influence the heating and ventilation.

to work with are those with a gentle slope. Construction is simplified since excavation and backfilling are minimal. Drainage problems are also simplified. You will not have to deal with the problems of excess runoff water from nearby steep slopes, which will need to be diverted and require a sophisticated (read, expensive) drainage system. This does not imply, however, that sites with unusual characteristics are not desirable. On the contrary, unusual sites often offer possibilities for exciting design solutions.

A site with a steep slope does not call for a design similar to that used for a perfectly flat site. The physical configurations of the sites

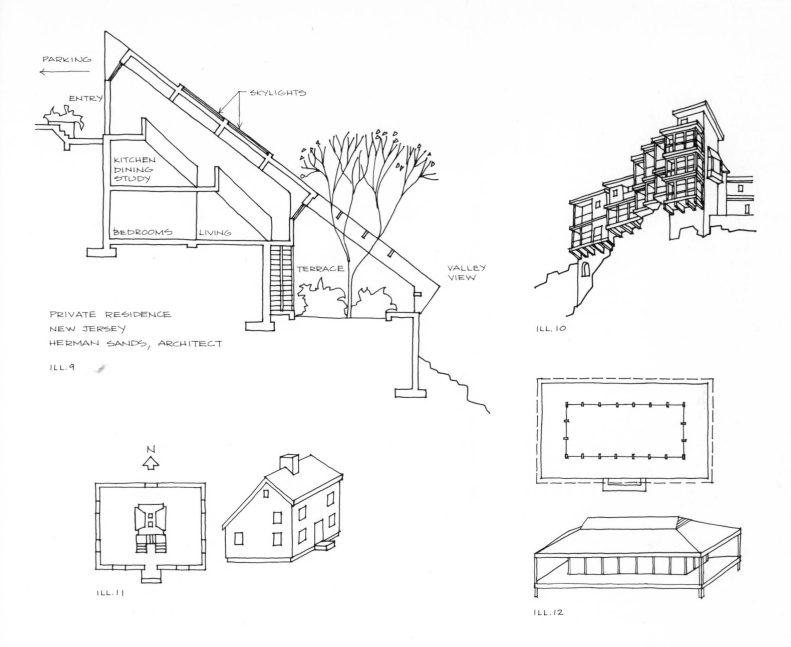

PARKING

ENTRY

SKYLIGHTS

KITCHEN
DINING
STUDY

BEDROOMS   LIVING

TERRACE

VALLEY
VIEW

PRIVATE RESIDENCE
NEW JERSEY
HERMAN SANDS, ARCHITECT

ILL. 9

ILL. 10

N

ILL. 11

ILL. 12

Heat Transfer

Heat is gained or lost through those surfaces of a house that come into direct contact with the outside. Exterior walls, roofs, and floors control much of the heat transfer and, therefore, become critical factors in the concept of energy conservation. A row house in the city has a smaller heating bill than a detached house in a suburb. The suburban house has four exterior wall exposures, while the row house has only two. In cold climates a conventional two-story house with a minimum of openings ranks very high in heat conservation and, therefore, in energy savings. The two-story house has fewer

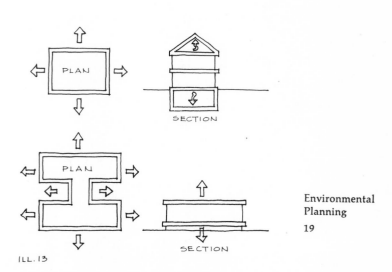

PLAN

SECTION

PLAN

SECTION

ILL. 13

Environmental
Planning
19

Many contemporary designers have done away with the attic in favor of the room with an exposed roof structure. By eliminating the attic the designer has utilized what he considers lost space and has added spaciousness and interest to the room. The structure of the roof, the beams and wooden planks, can be left exposed and unpainted to become integral parts of the room.

For the practical minded, an additional attraction of the one-part roof and ceiling is the elimination of having to construct both ceiling and roof. Although there are slightly less work and materials involved, the cost of the exposed roof will be the same as the roof with an attic. The exposed beams and planks will have to be of better quality than gypsum-board rafters and ceiling joists.

There is a disadvantage to this otherwise attractive design solution. Heat rises. In a room with a high, peaked ceiling the heat tends to be concentrated in the upper reaches of the space, far away from the room's occupants. Consequently, a good bit of the fuel dollar is spent to heat the peak of the roof. Furthermore, it is difficult to properly insulate this type of construction from heat gain in summer and heat loss in winter.

Most of the beautiful old houses that dot the landscape have attics between the bedroom floor and the peak of the roof. The attic space serves as a device to control heat gain and loss through the roof. The environmental justification for the attic is particularly obvious in the summer in houses with properly ventilated attics. The heat of the house rises up through the floors into the attic. A stream of outside air is directed through the attic space that removes the heat. This cool stream of air also removes the heat that is being absorbed by the roof from the sun overhead. The house remains surprisingly cool even on the most brutally hot days. In the gable without an attic, insulation and reflecting materials are used to ward off the heat gain from the summer sun and to conserve the mechanically generated heat in winter. Although methods of insulation are constantly improved, the cost of heating and cooling an exposed, high-ceilinged peaked roof is likely to be greater than for a house with an insulated attic.

peripheral walls and roof and floor areas than its one-story counterpart of the same size. Heat loss is reduced by minimizing the surface areas in contact with the outdoors, and heat is also transferred to its various levels (Ill. 13).

Other important considerations in heat transmission are buffer zones such as attics, basements, and enclosed porches, which are sandwiched between the indoors and the outdoors and become mixing boxes of heat exchange. In winter cold air is trapped in the attic and mixed with the warmer air within the house. In summer the reverse takes place. The magnitude of heat transmission between inside and outside temperatures is thus reduced. The same can be said of basements, enclosed porches, and any other buffer areas (Inset I).

The number of openings in the walls together with the walls' materials are also influential in conserving energy. Various materials exhibit different insulating qualities (see Chapter 13, Environmental Systems). A heavily insulated brick wall will prevent heat from being lost to or gained from the outside. A glass sheet, on the other hand, has little insulating value. Should the brick wall be punctured repeatedly to accommodate window openings, the insulating value of the wall will be greatly diminished. The more openings and the greater the use of glass, the greater the heat loss. (The manufacturers of prefabricated windows have been working on this problem for years and have come up with what they call "insulated glass," which is two thin sheets of glass separated by a vacuum, or dead-air space. Although this system reduces the transmission of heat, it by no means has the same insulating value as a solid wall.)

Maximum energy savings might not always take precedence when designing a home. A family might choose a one-story house because one of the family members has difficulty climbing stairs, even though such a house is less efficient in terms of heat loss. If reducing energy expenditures is imperative (as it should be to every conservation-minded citizen), a multi-leveled house could prove more efficient (see Chapter 13). In compromise cases the greatest possible energy conservation can be achieved by controlling the orientation to the sun and wind. In northern climates you might orient the house so that north walls have few or no windows. Heat-producing areas such as the kitchen can also be located to the north. These elements will become the shelter against winter winds. Generous openings to the south and east will allow the sunlight, with its radiant heat, to flow into the rooms. Deciduous trees (those that lose their leaves in winter) can be planted near the western facade to protect the walls from the hot summer sun while allowing the heat of the sun to penetrate full strength during the winter months, when it is most needed. In warmer climates the house can be oriented to welcome the prevailing breezes. The walls can be designed literally to open up and let the wind blow through. Overhangs may appear on the western and southern facades, preventing the sun's radiation from heating the walls.

Once a hierarchy of criteria has been established, the rest of the design will fall into place. We reiterate, design is a constant process of adjustment and compromise.

Operational Checklist

1. Meshing with the neighborhood fabric

   Is the continuity of the neighborhood maintained in the materials selected for the new house?

   In the scale of the house?

   In the landscaping of the property?

2. Establishing semipublic and private areas

   What are the family activities that will occur outdoors? Possibilities include outdoor cooking, dining, dancing, entertaining, swimming and sunbathing, tennis or other sports, gardening, street watching, or snoozing.

3. Evaluating the natural environment of the house

   A. Sunlight

      What spaces require or desire sunlight?

      Where will these rooms be located to maximize sunlight?

      Where will compromise be necessary?

   B. The view

      Is there a view?

      If so, how can it be used to best advantage?

4. Topography

   What is the slope of the site?

   How should the topography influence the house's design?

5. Climate

   What are the climatic conditions of the area?

   What is the direction of the prevailing winds?

   How can the house be best protected from the severity of the weather?

6. Heat transfer

   How does the shape of the house influence heat transmission?

   How do the house's materials influence heat transmission?

   What kinds of compromises will have to be made in terms of the amount of desired glass and the house's shape in consideration of heating efficiency?

   How do buffer zones help and where can they be located?

3
Site Selection

You should feel good about the place you choose to live in. The most beautiful house in the world will be diminished if its residents hate the neighborhood. People who live on the most romantic-looking islands will learn to despise their homes if they are bored by the lack of social life. Conversely, even the most magnificent Manhattan duplex apartment becomes a jail for the man who finds that city life jangles his nerves. The first decision to make is where you want to live: in an urban environment, a rural area, or a suburban community. Be careful in making this decision; it is a very important one. Many people have been misled by myths about suburban living. They have left what they considered to be the urban jungle ("for the sake of the children") to purchase a house in the "nearby" suburbs. Years later they finally admit that they are bored to death, they can no longer afford the taxes, the commute to work is exhausting, and they dream of retiring to the vital life they used to live in the city.

Having made the initial decision of what type of community to live in you are advised to choose a neighborhood in which you feel you can make an easy adjustment. This, too, is often overlooked when people go out to buy a house or land. "Community" is of vital importance. Very often a family will look for a split-level house in the suburbs and purchase one if it is the right price, without ever investigating the neighborhood. They might find later that the other residents of the area are all retired. These older people, most of whom are living on pen-

sions, are not at all interested in the school system and have continuously voted down all school improvement bills (not because they hate kids; school construction often means higher taxes in purely residential villages). Moreover, they don't like the idea that the family that has just moved in has three noisy children and two dogs. The older residents may also resent the idea that the new people have uprooted the rose garden and replaced it with a black-topped basketball court. The new residents might be surprised to learn that their friendly "hellos" are answered with coolness.

If you have children, you must ask a number of important questions. Will there be children nearby for your kids to play with? Are the kids generally nice or do they hang out in gangs in front of the supermarket at night because the community offers no recreation alternatives? Ask the neighbors (those with kids of their own) if they are satisfied with the schools. One very good way of determining how the local school ranks is to call the education department of the local state college or university. They place their students in the local schools for practice teaching and have a good idea of how effectual each of the local school systems is.

If the adults of the family are active in community affairs or politics, it is important to determine whether the community shares these interests. A woman who has been active in women's rights for years may find herself alone in a community of women who consider "liberation" a dirty word. This woman might consider the community an excellent challenge for proselytizing or she might be miserable without a supportive group.

Among other considerations are the following: If you are even nominally connected with a religious group, make sure that there is a place of worship in the area. It is a good idea that there be some sort of "affinity group" for your children and that religious education, if desired, can be provided for without having to travel miles.

Check the crime rate of the neighborhood. Is it increasing disproportionately? Will this be a factor if you might someday have to sell the property? How respected and efficient is the police department? How well organized is the fire department? Are the streets maintained well? Who pays for their maintenance? Is the snow plowed in the winter?

What additional amenities are provided in the community? Is there a free library system? Are there parks and playgrounds? Is the mail delivered or must you pick it up daily at the post office? Does the community provide for garbage disposal, or must you take your own trash to the dump?

What is the tax rate in the area? In some neighborhoods where most of the houses are very old the community levies disproportionately high taxes on new construction. A house that is fifty years old and worth $75,000 on the open market might pay only $800 in taxes annually. The new house next door, although of similar size and worth the same amount of money, may be taxed three times as much.

There are other things to consider that determine whether a neighborhood has a high tax structure or a low one. Generally, older communities that are not undergoing expansion have adequate schools, libraries, and sewage facilities. Their operational budgets include such items as teachers' salaries and maintenance of facilities. Newer, growing communities, on the other hand, have to construct school buildings, sewage systems, fire houses, and so on. These capital expenditures, even if the repayment of loans is spread over many future years, add considerably to the financial burden of each community resident.

Another factor that affects the tax structure is the amount of industry in the area. Very often a non-noxious industrial plant benefits the community greatly by providing jobs for residents and customers for stores and, most significantly,

by carrying a large part of the community's taxes.

Study the streets of the neighborhood and see how well the other houses are maintained. Very often you can get a bargain in a neighborhood on the upswing (one that had deteriorated but is now being revitalized). On the other hand, you may pay a premium price for a piece of land in an area that for one reason or another will be on a downslide in future years (for example, if a highway is slated to slice through the neighborhood).

PHYSICAL CHARACTERISTICS OF THE SITE

Some very important questions should be asked about the utilities that are available. Most urban sites are supplied with city water and sewage systems. Rural areas, very often, have neither. Suburban property sometimes has only one. If there are no public water mains, you will have to supply your own drinking, bathing, washing, and sprinkling water. This means that you will have to dig a well. Ask your future neighbor how deep he had to dig for water. If fresh drinking water is close to the surface, the well will cost less money. If the drilling company must dig a hundred or more feet, the proposition can easily exceed a thousand dollars and will, therefore, add to your budget.

The sewer system is another important factor. If there is no sewer line in the front of the property, you will have to dispose of your wastes *on* the property. This item is covered in greater detail in Chapter 14. Keep in mind that cesspools and septic tanks cost a great deal and will require some future maintenance. (If there are water and sewers in the streets, you are not home free either. Two trenches must be dug from the house to the street and the lines must be connected by a licensed plumber.)

The slope of the site is also important. Never plan to build a house in a hole. If you build your house at the bottommost part of a valley, you will end up in a puddle of rain water more often than not. Flooded living rooms are no one's idea of a pleasant home environment.

A site with a gentle slope is the cheapest to build on for a number of reasons. First, the gentle slope allows rain water to run off the property, instead of puddling on it. This avoids the expense of a drainage system. In addition, building on a nearly flat site simplifies excavation and, therefore, construction. A steep site may require fancy machinery for excavation and elaborate underpinnings. Another point to consider in terms of slope is warmth from the sun and protection from winds. A piece of land located on a high slope remains warmer than one on a lower slope, since warm air, being lighter than cold air, rises. A southern-sloping site will receive more of the sun's radiation than a flat one.

It is also helpful to find out the direction of the prevailing winds. A piece of land located near the crest on the windward side of a hill will receive high-speed winds. On the other hand, land situated on the leeward slope will be subject to less turbulent winds. You should also get an idea of how the sun travels the site. Many times sites in urban areas receive sunshine only a few hours of every day because of shadows cast by high-rise buildings nearby. Similarly, a rural or suburban site may be in the shadow of a nearby mountain or cliff and may not receive direct sunlight during most of the day in the winter months.

Be sure to choose a site with ready access. A piece of property high in the mountains may provide an excellent view and a great deal of privacy. If this privacy is maintained by the fact that the nearest dirt road is a four-mile hike away, you might decide against the purchase. How will you get machinery and materials to the site for construction of the house? Even if you manage to get something built there, you will have to hike the four miles carrying groceries and other purchases. Don't buy the property on the assumption that you will build a road to your home site. Even the crudest road costs a small fortune to construct. Trees must be cleared, the terrain must be leveled, and earth must be hauled. The road will no doubt cost much more than the house.

Check with the neighbors to determine if there are land-erosion problems on the particular site you are considering, or if the area tends to get flooded in severe storms. Many magnificent pieces of property on high cliffs, commanding marvelous views, are losing inches of land each year to the sea. However, if the price is right and the erosion is slow, you may be getting a good deal in spite of the diminishing land. (Make sure you build far from the eroding end.) Many people with eroding land have come to

the conclusion that they will be dead and buried long before the erosion becomes a threat. Meanwhile they are reaping the benefits of a magnificent waterfront view.

Soil conditions are a major consideration. First, you should find out what type of soil is on the site. If there are large boulders underneath the topsoil, excavation will be an expensive problem. The level of water below ground, called the water table, should be determined as well. If the water table is high (a foot or two below the surface), your basement will have a tendency to be flooded periodically.* Most high water tables are in lowlands or marsh areas. Find out if your property has been land-filled. If you are very close to purchasing a piece of property, it may be a good idea to have a surveyor or soil-analysis lab test the soil. (At this point have the drinking water tested if you have a well.) He will take soil samples at various points of potential construction on the site. The composition of the soil is important and is determined at the site by "impact testing" and is analyzed more thoroughly in the laboratory.

Soils are classified in terms of their permeability and strength. Permeability is the property which permits seepage of water through the soil's voids and determines its ability to absorb rain water and sewage effluent. Percolation tests are made to determine the permeability of the soil and its suitability as a leaching field for sewage effluent. The strength of the soil determines its bearing capacity. (If the soil is weak, the foundations must be enlarged at added cost or they will suffer settlement cracks.) In cases of poor bearing soils, an elaborate foundation must be dug, piles† must be driven into the soil, or both. (More information on these deviations appears in Chapter 11, Foundation Design.)

If you are lucky, the soil tests will show compacted sand and gravel or sand-clay. Both of these are excellent foundation beds, absorb liquids easily, and are simple to excavate. Wet clays, noncompacted sands, and silt are not as easy to deal with. Clay not only does not allow for the quick absorption of water (which will cause puddling, if not flooding), it also tends to swell and increase in volume when heavily watered. A foundation built on such clays may

---

* A "well point" to measure water-table fluctuations can be installed at a nominal cost at the same time that percolation tests, borings, etc., are taking place.
† Piles are heavy stakes that are driven into the ground as foundations. These stakes, often tapered, rot-treated telephone poles, work on the principle of friction.

heave when the clay is wet. When the clay dries, it will shrink, causing the heaved foundation to fall. This will eventually weaken the foundations and jeopardize the house built upon them.

There are things to look for as well as to look out for when choosing a site. We have mentioned the asset that a view contributes to the house and to the site. We have not mentioned the great benefits of trees. Mature trees on the site provide natural shade, help significantly in preventing topsoil erosion, provide privacy from the neighbors and supports for hammocks. A wooded site is a many splendored thing. A non-wooded site is ideal for the vegetable grower and the lawn lover.

ZONING LAWS, EASEMENTS, AND COVENANTS

Zoning laws are designed primarily as a legal expedient to protect the community from unpopular growth or "mixed use," which occurs when various types of buildings—houses, factories, gas stations, offices—are built together without regard for the impact these buildings could have on each other.

Zoning laws, for the most part, try to maintain the scale of a neighborhood (that is, by not allowing anyone to build over a certain height) and to divide the community into residential, commercial, and industrial zones. They also establish a house's minimum distance from the road and adjacent neighbors' homes. These minimum distances are the "set-back" lines and govern the dimensions of all yards. If the front-yard set-back is determined by the zoning ordinances to be 40', you cannot build the house within 40' of the front property line. Similarly side-yard and rear-yard limitations are set by ordinance. If the site is irregular in shape, you may find that you will not have enough room for the house once all of these set-backs are satisfied. Check to see if there is enough room for a future expansion, an elevated deck, a pagoda, or a toolshed.*

In most areas of the United States where residential construction is currently under way,

the local community or town has a building department and possibly a planning board as well. The local department of buildings deals basically with the use of approved materials and techniques of installation, and conformance to minimum standards for plumbing, heating, electrical wiring, etc. The planning board is responsible for interpreting zoning, granting variances (exceptions to the zoning laws), and supervising the orderly development of the town. (In the absence of such an agency, the building department is usually charged with the responsibility of enforcing zoning restrictions dealing with specialized uses, signs, set-backs, side yards, height restrictions, and so on, which the town or community may have established by covenant for all property within its boundaries.)

A covenant is an agreement made between the seller and the purchaser. Some covenants, for example, stipulate that all the houses in the neighborhood must be kept painted white. This kind of covenant is legally binding. Other types of covenants, for instance, one stipulating that the owner is not permitted to sell his home to a member of a particular ethnic group, are not legal. In some neighborhoods, of course, unwritten covenants are in force.

Another term you should be familiar with before buying or building a house is easement. This is a clause written into a deed giving the right to another party (the government, a utility company, a landowner, etc.) to make use of your property. For example, the town may have an easement on your property for the maintenance of a water main. This means that you can use the land in any way you choose as long as it does not interfere with the access necessary for maintenance of the water main.

A visit to your prospective community's town clerk will be very rewarding. This office will be able to provide you with a copy of the community's zoning ordinance and usage map or a fact sheet explaining the covenants or easements that affect its growth. From the zoning ordinance map you will be able to determine exactly what you can and cannot do with your property and whether your immediate neighbors are residential, commercial, or industrial.*

---

* Be careful to note whether the site fronts on more than one street. In such cases the site might be deemed as having more than one "front yard," thereby making the buildable parcel smaller and rendering the construction of a pool or a tennis court on this "front yard" property illegal.

* A word of caution: residential usage is generally divided into density or concentration of population. The least dense usage is single-family occupancy, which is usually called R1. Usages can range up to R12, in which case you might find yourself in a mixed zone, a veritable grab bag, composed of noisy industry and congested commerce.

One often-ignored stipulation of most zoning ordinances is the determination of the *minimum* allowable size of a house built in that area. One of the authors was about to purchase a one-acre site in a rural area. She found out, well along the way of negotiations, that the community had stipulated by law that the minimum size of that house had to be 3,000 square feet. The author did not want a house that big, nor could she have afforded to build one if she did. The community had, in effect, "zoned out" everyone except the very rich.

A further note on that very same community. Most small communities in lovely, desirable areas have legal restrictive zoning. By "legal" we mean that by law the community cannot discriminate against a family on the basis of race, religion, or color, but they can discriminate against people who have chosen to deviate slightly from the middle-class norm by living in extended families or communes. The village previously mentioned took to court a small group of university professors living together in a large house on the grounds that the people occupying the house were not related to each other. The court ruled in favor of the village. Now, no more than four unrelated people are allowed to live together under the same roof in that township.

It might be helpful to check with your local planning board or city officials to determine if there have been any recent amendments to the zoning laws that affect development in and around your property. You do not want to discover too late that an airport has recently been approved for construction in the area. Your hearing, nerves, and pride would suffer as a result of a major gap in your information. Be cautious in selecting and purchasing property. Our best advice to you is to seek counsel before committing yourself.

Operational Checklist

1. Where do you desire to live—in the country, the city, or the suburbs?

2. Amenities of the community
   Who lives in the community?
   What are the children like?

Is there an active political and community consciousness?

What is the crime rate?

How good is the police department?

What about the fire department?

What about religious institutions?

Is there a library? parks? free mail service?

How good are the schools?

How high are the taxes?

Are the other houses in the neighborhood well-maintained?

What development plans are on the books for the future?

Is the community building new schools, a state penitentiary?

3. Physical properties of the site
   What utilities are available and what are the costs to plug into them?

   If no public utilities are available, how much will it cost to dig a well and install a septic tank?

   What is the slope of the site and how will it affect the drainage?

   How will the location of the site affect the amount of sunshine and wind?

   Will the sun be blocked off by nearby buildings, mountains?

   How difficult will it be to excavate the site?

   What access is there to the site? Will you have to build a private road?

   What are the amenities of the site? Are there trees, a pond, does it afford a view?

   Are there any soil-erosion problems? Flooding problems?

   What are the soil conditions? Is the soil type favorable to drainage? excavation? bearing of the foundations?

   Will you have expensive problems?

4. Zoning
   What is the site zoned for? Is it in a prime residential area?

   Can you build the kind and size of house that suits you, or do the zoning and covenants rule it out?

   Do you have enough room on the site to build what you need?

   Will your privacy be protected by shrubs, trees, and exterior walls?

   Is there room on the site for planned future expansion?

4
Economy Through Design

We have discussed in detail why designing your own house can result in a more functional plan and a more successful relationship to the surrounding environment. There are, however, other advantages to personalized house building besides functional or aesthetic ones. Careful planning and design can bring about high economic returns on the investment of your time and money.

In a well-designed house that must also meet the requirements of a tight budget, maximum aesthetic use should be made of every structural, functional, and decorative element. These elements include staircases, fireplaces, windows, as well as the use of color and the texture of various materials. Very exciting design solutions can be obtained at no extra cost by the creative manipulation of these elements.

Other essential criteria in the design of an economical house are the careful selection of a structural system, finishing materials, and standardized, prefabricated parts. Again we stress the importance of building only what is needed. Provision for future needs in the planning of the present house is yet another crucial form of economy.

LIGHT

The least expensive means of adding visually to the house is in harnessing the energy of the sun. Sunlight, as yet free and untaxed, is available in most parts of the world during most times of the year. We discussed earlier that sunlight has the almost magical ability to make most people feel good. In addition to this psychological benefit, the use of natural light can make a space *look* better.

Large windows expand the space by letting in the outdoors. (See the photograph on page 18.) Variations in room lighting can set a space apart from the rest, giving it a distinct feeling or character. One room may be lit by a clearstory (Ill. 1). The light in that space would come from above. An adjacent space might have large panes of glass allowing in great splashes of light (Ill. 2). Windows high on a wall can subtly light a room without obstructing the placement of furniture (Ill. 3). A single point in a room (above an object of art or a special plant, for example) can be highlighted by a small skylight (Ill. 4). This one item will be made to stand out against the subtly lit background.

Not all the rooms in the house, of course, need to have special treatment in terms of lighting. It is enough to select only those spaces in which a different visual quality is desired. Other rooms can be planned with conventional windows, which can be selected from the local merchant or building-supply house. The placement and arrangement of stock windows should receive the same care as the specialty items discussed above. They should be located with an eye to how they will best serve the interior of the house as well as how they will look on the outside of the building (Ill. 5). More information

In this house, walls of inexpensive industrial windows were used to open the outdoors to the indoors. An uncluttered interior space is achieved by the use of built-in couches and tables, while flexibility of seating can be obtained by using the steps leading into the living room as a miniature amphitheater. Architect, Peter Bohlin; photographer, Joseph W. Molitor

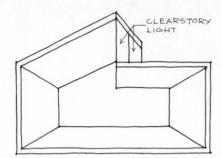

CLEARSTORY LIGHT

ILL. 1

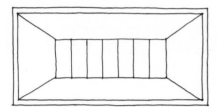

ILL. 2

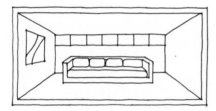

ILL. 3

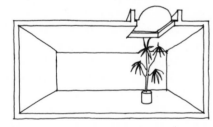

ILL. 4

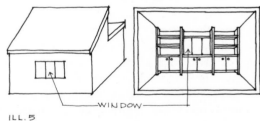

WINDOW

ILL. 5

about window sizes and proportions is included in Chapter 12.

FIREPLACES

A fireplace not only provides warmth and light in winter, it serves as a room's focal point during the entire year. This design element can be used in a number of ways. In a room with a sloping ceiling, or in a space with one portion of the ceiling higher than the other, the fireplace can be located at the point of maximum ceiling height, so that the long chimney flue expresses the verticality of the space (Ill. 6). Additionally,

it will define space if it is free-standing between two areas (Ill. 7). A roughly textured fireplace can add richness to an otherwise stark room (Ill. 8). The visual play between solid and void is emphasized when a fireplace is placed on an exterior wall and is flanked at both sides by planes of glass (Ill. 9).

The Problem—
An Approach
28

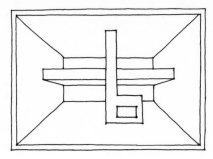

ILL. 6

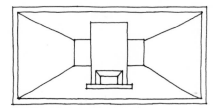

ILL. 7

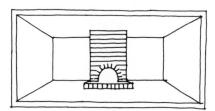

ILL. 8

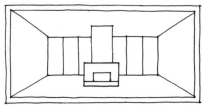

ILL. 9

A fireplace can serve as a free-standing sculptural form and/or define space. This one opens into two rooms, its round flue emphasizing the verticality of the space and the contrast between solid and voids. Architect, Neski Associates; photographer, William Maris

Fireplaces are expensive and difficult to build. Not only must the firebox be constructed but a chimney must also be built to house a flue so that hot gases can escape to the outside. (The expense of a second chimney can be eliminated if the fireplace flue can share a chimney with the boiler or furnace flue. See Chapter 16.) Although a handmade stone or brick fireplace is a tremendous asset to a house, a much less expensive means to the same end can be obtained by using prefabricated metal units These units are available in a large selection of models, some of which are complete and ready for installation. This type is generally brightly colored and rather sculptural in shape. Other models provide you with the interior fireplace components, which are later encased in any number of finishing materials (see Chapter 16).

GREENHOUSES

A greenhouse can be integrated into the design plans of those people who enjoy raising house plants or gardening. (See the photograph on page 3.) Greenhouses can be used as extensions of spaces in a playroom or dining area (Ill. 10). This all-glass area lets in light and serves as a means of bringing the outdoors in. A greenhouse might be used in place of a corridor to connect two spaces (Ill. 11). A skylit atrium

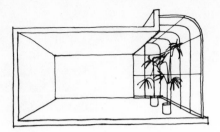

ILL. 10

ILL. 11

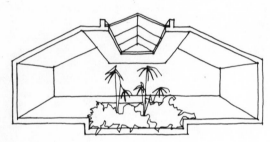

ILL. 12

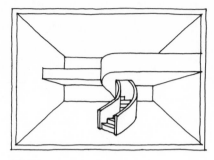

ILL. 13

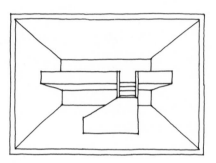

ILL. 14

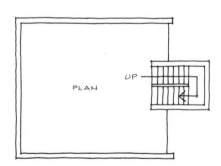

ILL. 15

(not quite a greenhouse, but serving the same function) can be the central highlight of a house plan (Ill. 12). Ready-assembled greenhouses and skylights are available from various manufacturers or can be framed in with the rest of the house.

STAIRCASES

If you are designing a two-story house, you will have to include a staircase to get from one level to the other. Since this is a functional requirement, it is the most easily justifiable decorative element in the house. It would be a pity to keep this potential piece of sculpture enclosed between two walls. The staircase is better used when expressed as a design element. One of the ways this might be achieved is by emphasizing the shape of the stair, for example, by making it spiral around a support (Ill. 13), by opening

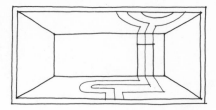

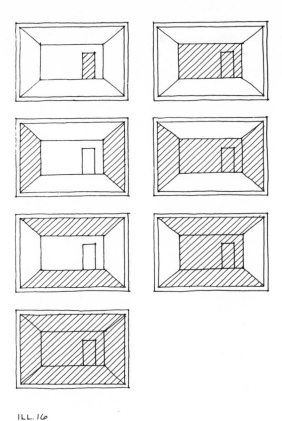

ILL. 16

the risers, or by using an unusual material such as slate or cast iron. The stair will become a sculptural element, be it straight or U-shaped, if it is freed entirely from the surrounding walls and allowed to stand alone in the space. A free-standing stair can serve as a space definer between two rooms much as a fireplace can (Ill. 14). A staircase can add interest to the outside of the house as well if its form is expressed on the outside wall (Ill. 15). More on the design of stairs follows in Chapter 16.

COLOR

The use of color is probably the least expensive way to manipulate a space. We are all sensitive to certain colors. The place where you now live probably exhibits your preferences. However, most of us could learn to use color more effectively. If every room displays the same intensity

of color, called hue, the change in color becomes meaningless. The result is as ineffective as using no color at all. We recommend the use of a wide range of colors and tones. A room used as a study could be treated with a soft, quiet color; a playroom could be enlivened with a bright and intense tone.

Color is not limited to wall surfaces. A room can be treated as a cube of space and all of its surfaces—walls, doors, window frames, cabinets, etc.—can be the same color. On the other hand, you might choose to emphasize one element within a room, such as a single wall or door, and treat it with an extravagant color (Ill. 16). It is common for architects to paint the interior of houses all in white. This facilitates the use of color in selected areas such as a particular wall or ceiling surface, a free-standing element such as a stair, a low partition or a fireplace, and sometimes even a pipe, duct, or railing.

Another way to use color is in supergraphics —the continuation of graphic patterns on various surfaces occurring on the same or different planes (Ill. 17). This is a simple and playful way in which to accomplish interesting spatial effects and optical illusions with a minimum of financial investment. Supergraphics used in any room in the house can be exciting (and easily changed when desired).

TEXTURE

Texture can also be manipulated to add visual variety to an area. It is not uncommon to visit a house and be surrounded by "sameness." By sameness we mean the same wall, ceiling, and floor texture. Wallpaper alone cannot substitute for a range of different materials. A number of varying materials used effectively in one or more areas of the house will provide the space with richness of texture. The finishing materials

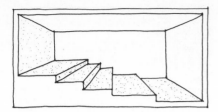

ILL. 18

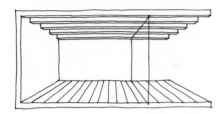

ILL. 19

The imaginative juxtaposition of a number of finishing materials makes this an especially handsome interior space. Rough-textured boards are diagonally mounted on the walls, the ceiling material continuing the pattern. The cloth wall hangings and the white plastered balcony accent the walls. Architect, William Morgan; photographer, Creative Photographic Service

wood planks, quarry tile, ceramic tile, stone, brick pavers, etc., that can be used both on the interior and the exterior. Always keep in mind the activities that take place in an area before deciding the material for the floor. (See Chapter 17.) Ceiling surfaces or structural members can also flow from exterior spaces to interior spaces (Ill. 19).

BUILT-IN FURNITURE AND CABINETRY

Where maximum adaptability is not a requirement, built-in furniture can be a design asset and a space saver. Cleverly designed sleeping, sitting, working, and storage areas can be integrated into the overall house design. For instance, if a guest room, study, T.V. room, and sewing area must be made out of the same small space, a storage wall might be designed incorporating all of these diverse elements. The "wall" might contain a hidden, fold-down Murphy-type bed, a fold-out desk and typewriter table, a hidden entertainment area, in addition to the usual bookshelves and record cabinets (Ill. 20).

If flexible space is desired, modular wall-closet units on lockable casters can be built and rolled to where they are needed. These portable closets can be used in rows or groupings to act as elements that divide large spaces into smaller ones (Ill. 21).

most commonly used for this purpose are carpeting and wood flooring. Even these familiar materials can be given new meaning if used in unusual ways. Carpeting may be used on the floor of a small sitting area, carried over built-in, cushioned platforms (to be used for lounging), and laid right onto the walls of the room (Ill. 18).

Brick, stone, or wood walls carried from an exterior to an interior space not only enhance the room and set it apart from the rest of the house, but also allow the space to flow continuously from outside to inside. Floor materials and patterns can also be carried from a deck or courtyard into a living or family room. There are numerous floor materials available, such as

Finishing materials can be used to establish a continuity between interior and exterior spaces. In this house, the balcony overlooking the living and dining areas is projected through the glass to the outside, where it becomes a deck. The redwood siding is used both inside and outside the house. In the interior, it is contrasted with quarry tile, rough brick, and large expanses of glass. Architect, Walter Blum; photographer, Ronald DiDonno

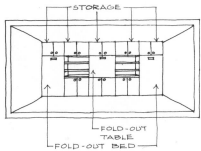

ILL. 20

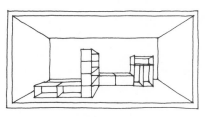

ILL. 21

The structure of a house may be completely enclosed or, as in this case, partially exposed. The spaces between the studs are bridged with shelves to display small knickknacks and plants. Architect, William Turnbull; photographer, Morley Baer

STRUCTURE

Displaying the "bare bones" of a design scheme can be another point of interest. If the available construction materials and craftsmanship are of good quality, you might choose to leave the skeleton of the house partially exposed (Ill. 22). Uncovered pipes, rafters, and wall studs add considerably to a space (as long as there are no code restrictions that prohibit this design approach).

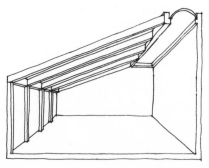

ILL. 22

STRUCTURAL ECONOMY

The design and structure of a contemporary house are intertwined to the degree that it is impossible to think of one without the other. The structure of the house dictates the design concept or the design approach, and vice-versa: the design of the house often predetermines the structural system. For instance, if you choose to build your house of masonry load-bearing walls, the design of the interior spaces will reflect this decision. The openness of the house's plan will be somewhat restricted by the need for load-bearing interior partitions to support the weight of the floors and roof above, unless wooden or steel columns are introduced into the structural scheme.

A house plan that tries to achieve a great deal of openness between the spaces and various levels of the house dictates that the building be constructed with columns and beams instead of load-bearing walls. In residential construction this almost always indicates wood-frame construction. The wood-frame structure allows the designer a greater opportunity to open spaces by using columns in place of walls. It is very important that the structural system of the building work with rather than against the design approach.

Standardization

Aside from the larger conceptual design and structural approaches, the integration of structural design, construction practices, and economics is important even in small design decisions. For example, lumber is sold in standardized lengths, with increments of 2'. This means that the lumber used in floor joists (the row of mini-beams that directly support the floor system) is sold in lengths of 10', 12', 14', 16', etc. We could design a room that is to be 14½' wide if we so desired. The floor joists could be supported on either side by walls or beams. In constructing the floor we would have to purchase the joists in lengths of 16' (14' lumber is obviously too short). We would then have to cut 1½' from each joist. Joist lumber is expensive and is sold by the foot. Unless we have a definite structural use for all of those 1½' pieces, we would be wasting a lot of expensive material. In addition to the money thrown out, we would have to measure and cut each joist,

wasting much time and energy. It would have been considerably easier to have designed the supporting elements for the joists at either 14' or 16' apart in order to use standardized, pre-sawed lumber.

It is a good idea, in general, to design for those elements that are most readily available. Lumberyards and supply houses keep large stocks of certain popular items and the most called-for sizes. Familiarize yourself with what is available. Custom items (that is, those windows, doors, tiles, and pieces of structural lumber that have to be ordered from the mill, made special, or imported) will undoubtedly take a long time to arrive and be more costly than standardized, readily available items. Besides, if most companies manufacture sliding glass doors that are 6'-4" wide, does it make a great deal of sense to design for one that is 6'-8" wide? Are you making a conscious design decision when you choose this size, or are you specifying it out of ignorance of stock sizes? It is, of course, possible to have a door of this width made up if you are willing to pay a premium price for it.

The best advice we can offer is to become acquainted with the products presently on the market. Inquire of the supplier about the product's local availability and its cost, durability, and performance rating. Manufacturers have a wealth of information on their products and are generally eager to forward any literature you might request (see Chapter 17, Inset I).

MATERIAL ECONOMY

Economy can also be effected in the realm of finishing materials. The most successful house is not the one that employs the most gimmicks or cosmetic frills, but one that most honestly reflects its overall plan and space concept. Expensive finishing materials are not necessarily the key to a good house. A brick fireplace can have the same visual interest as one encased in marble. Similarly, a wall covered with paint in an interesting color can be as decorative as one covered in expensive wallpaper. A costly wallpaper can be purchased to cover only one wall of a room. The other walls and the ceiling can be painted in a color complementing the paper. The effect can be as beautiful (perhaps more so) as if you had plastered the expensive wallpaper on every surface of the room. Conversely, if the price of a material is very low, you may choose to be extravagant in its use, thereby effecting some highly unusual results. (One of the authors purchased many yards of brightly colored striped linen at the throwaway price of $.50 per yard. She covered three walls of a bedroom—and the ceiling—with the fabric, made curtains out of it, and sewed what remained as a bedspread. The room was, to say the least, eye-catching, but was balanced nicely by the almost spartan simplicity of the rest of the house.)

One method used to evaluate the comparative economies of finishing materials is to consider initial cost in comparison to maintenance costs. Insulated window sashes are more expensive than window sashes containing plain glass. The expense, however, would most likely be offset in later fuel-oil savings. A masonry house is more difficult and expensive to build than a wooden one. Brick walls, on the other hand, are almost maintenance free as opposed to wood-clad walls.

THE ECONOMY OF LONG-RANGE PLANNING

The most important economy that can be made in the design and construction of a house (or any building, for that matter) is in the planning. The cost of construction materials is steadily increasing. It might make good sense to build a huge house now, because the cost of that extra room in the future will be greater than it is today. This philosophy makes sense if you have the available capital. Most people today have small savings accounts (if they have any at all) and high day-to-day living expenses. Most of us cannot afford to build what we don't absolutely need. Unless the house builder has money to burn, this "think practical" philosophy will have to be his guiding principle. No one, not even the very rich, can fulfill every fantasy. We hope that this fact is consolation for a somewhat pared-down version of the dream house.

It is possible, however, to build a smaller house in anticipation of someday expanding it. Often a couple with a small child will build a two-bedroom house and plan to add bedrooms and a playroom as the family grows. An amateur photographer might put off the construction of an elaborate darkroom facility for a few years. The dreams need not be completely abandoned, only temporarily postponed. Through careful planning an "expanding" or "growing" house can be designed. In actuality, the plan for the expanded house is developed at the same time as the plan for immediate construction. The expanded portion of the plan should not look tacked on to the house as an afterthought but should be designed as an integral part of the original functional plan. The following illustrations should be helpful in understanding the concept of planning for future expansion.

The family in house no. 1 (Ill. 23) purchased a home from a local builder. The three-bedroom house comfortably met their needs at the time. The house itself had a neat, if typical, plan. The bedrooms were segregated from the communal spaces of the house; the living-dining room worked well in relationship to the kitchen. The addition of two new children made the family feel cramped. They decided to expand the house but ran into numerous difficulties. The additional bedrooms could not be built without cutting down the size of the master bedroom considerably. The playroom could be added onto the kitchen, but natural light in the dining room would be sacrificed. The couple could not build out from the living room because of the side-yard limitations. Aside from the awkwardness of the expanded plan, the exterior of the house would suffer aesthetically. The couple is faced with the choice of living with these less-than-perfect spaces, or moving.

The family who built house no. 2 (Ill. 24) was on a very tight budget but acknowledged the need for growth in their plan. A master plan was developed, which provided for future expansion. Two bedrooms, one bath, a playroom, a one-car garage, and a shop were later incorporated into the house proper. The expanded portion of the house did not disturb its original functioning, nor is the original design concept (separation of sleep areas and communal areas) altered. The expanded section, in fact, enhances the house aesthetically.

The following items are crucial in the development of a master plan. In anticipating expansion it is important to keep in mind that the source of natural light for the room should not be disturbed. If a second story is planned for, it is important to build in the structural capability for it in the initial design. Needless to add, make sure there is enough "legal" room on the site for the anticipated expansion.

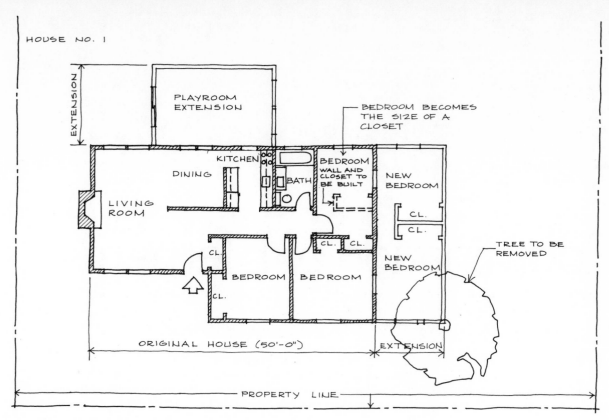

HOUSE NO. 1

PLAYROOM EXTENSION

EXTENSION

BEDROOM BECOMES THE SIZE OF A CLOSET

KITCHEN

DINING

BATH

BEDROOM WALL AND CLOSET TO BE BUILT

NEW BEDROOM

LIVING ROOM

CL.

CL.

CL.

CL.

NEW BEDROOM

BEDROOM

BEDROOM

CL.

TREE TO BE REMOVED

ORIGINAL HOUSE (50'-0")

EXTENSION

PROPERTY LINE

ILL. 23

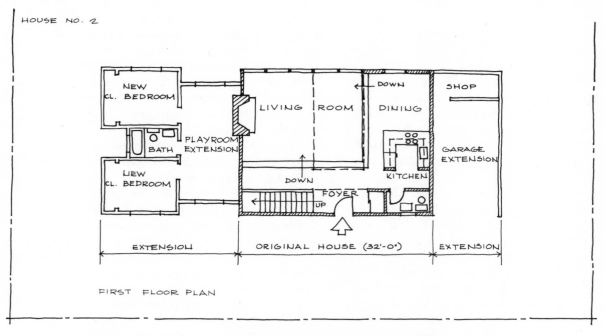

HOUSE NO. 2

NEW CL. BEDROOM

BATH

PLAYROOM EXTENSION

NEW CL. BEDROOM

LIVING ROOM

DOWN

DINING

SHOP

GARAGE EXTENSION

KITCHEN

DOWN

FOYER UP

EXTENSION

ORIGINAL HOUSE (32'-0")

EXTENSION

FIRST FLOOR PLAN

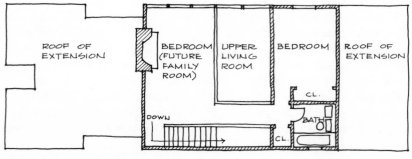

ROOF OF EXTENSION

BEDROOM (FUTURE FAMILY ROOM)

UPPER LIVING ROOM

BEDROOM

ROOF OF EXTENSION

CL.

DOWN

CL.

BATH

ILL. 24

SECOND FLOOR PLAN

5
Coordination of Elements

Design is a process of integration. The isolated elements of function, structure, and environment must be tied together into a scheme, a plan for the house. The planning process is not an easy one, but can be made less frightening if approached in a series of rational steps. The following section attempts to demystify the design process by devising a sample family and having them create a house of their own. The example starts with functional analysis and concludes with plans and preliminary elevations for the proposed house. It would be helpful to keep in mind while perusing this section that there is no fixed, clearly defined process of design. We can only attempt to explain the creative process by illustration.

At this point we introduce the sample family. The Harris-Banks's are a couple in their early thirties. June Harris is an editor of a local newspaper. Murray Banks is a novelist who works at home. The couple has a two-year-old son. June, Murray, and their child feel cramped in their small two-bedroom apartment and have been toying with the idea of investing part of the royalties from Murray's newest book in the down-payment on a house of their own. They have explored the local suburbs and have thus far not found anything that is completely satisfactory. The houses that they have been shown are either too large for their present needs, or are entirely unaffordable. Although the couple found a few houses pleasant enough and relatively adaptable to their life style, they are unhappy about having to shoehorn their pattern

of living into some developer's idea of the typical American family.

The Harris-Banks's feel that although they do not have a great deal of money to spend, they want to invest it in a house that meets their needs directly. They would probably be able to find use for the two additional bedrooms in a four-bedroom house, and for the basement and rumpus room as well. They cannot, however, afford the luxury of superfluous space. In addition, the houses that they have been shown lack "specialness," visual excitement, and personality. Mortgaging themselves for thirty-five years to a house that neither meets their functional needs nor reflects their personal life style seems rather absurd to them.

Their functional needs are not altogether typical. Murray writes at home and needs a space in which to work that is isolated from the main activities of the house. Furthermore, he plays the cello with a local string quartet. He needs a quiet space in which to practice alone, and a large space in which to rehearse with the group. June raises house plants. Her collection of tropical plants is large and her tallest specimens are outgrowing the 8' ceiling height of the present apartment. She would like a tall space for her floor plants as well as a small greenhouse for the hanging pots. Both adults like to cook and entertain. They want a living area that is large enough to accommodate a lot of people and yet intimate enough for a group of six dinner guests. A large and efficient kitchen in which to feed their son is a must. They prefer a formal setting for dinner, but would like a breakfast space in the kitchen as well.

The family at present needs a minimum of two sleeping rooms, one for the adults and one for the child. As they expect their family to grow, they anticipate a future need for at least one more bedroom and a guest room. Should their family increase to include two more children, they would like to provide a play-work room in their plans. As far as service areas are concerned, the couple has decided that a minimum of one and a half bathrooms would be adequate to meet their present needs. They decide to forgo a garage, and to economize further they decide to build the house without a basement.

More important to our sample family than their functional needs is their emotional "program." June has always lived in apartment buildings with small cubicle rooms connected by corridors and she hungers for a house with a feeling of spaciousness and expansiveness. She would be pleased with a wall-less house that is entirely open in feeling. Sunshine, and lots of it, has a special appeal to both adults. At odds with their desire for openness and light is their need for intimacy and privacy. Both envision a small womb-like corner or retreat (perhaps with a fireplace), in which to read or quietly sip brandy at the end of the day.

The toughest decision they face is whether to commit themselves to the design and construction of their own house. They talk to other couples who have built homes from scratch or added extensions onto their existing houses, and decide that although the task seems formidable, they will undertake the challenge. The next step is to speak to an architect, who agrees to help them out of the trouble spots they might encounter in the design procedure, and who will review their plans before they become finalized. Having lined up this professional consultant, they initiate the land search.

The most logical and convenient place to begin the hunt is in the small city in which June works. Although the urban character of the city's neighborhoods is attractive, the price tags on available in-town properties are beyond their means. Likewise, suburban lots are high in price. Their search takes them beyond the suburban line into a semirural area about a forty-minute drive from downtown. Here they purchase a heavily wooded four-acre site featuring a view of a pond to the southeast (Ill. 1).

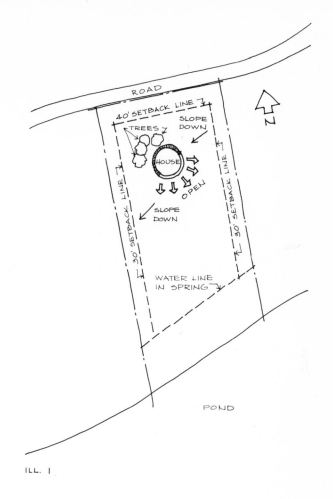

ILL. 1

OUTLINING NEEDS: DEVELOPING A PROGRAM

Murray and June were advised to begin by drawing up a space "program." They did this by listing the spaces they felt they both wanted and needed to include in the house and describing the functions for these areas. Adjacent to each space listed they attempted to describe the atmosphere they had in mind for it (Ill. 2). In counting up the listed areas they found that they were programming for a house that was much too big. The living, lounging, and dining areas were considered essential to the family's life style. So, of course, were the two bedrooms, the bathrooms, and the kitchen. The playroom, on the other hand, could wait until the family grew larger. (Rehearsal space for the quartet could be found by moving around some furniture in the living room.) The guest room and the potting shed would have to be deferred to a future time (a sleep sofa could be used in the study to accommodate an occasional guest). The

Coordination of Elements

39

ROOM	FUNCTION	FEELING
LIVING SPACE	ENTERTAINING, EXHIBIT FOR PLANTS	BRIGHT, OPEN, SPACIOUS
LOUNGING AREA	CONVERSATION, READING, FIRE-WATCHING	INFORMAL, WARM, ENCLOSED, HOMEY
DINING AREA	SEMIFORMAL DINING	BRIGHT DURING DAY, WARM AT NIGHT (FIREPLACE?)
STUDY AREA	QUIET, WRITING, CELLO PRACTICE	ISOLATED, "INSPIRING"
PARENT'S BEDROOM	SLEEPING, SITTING	BRIGHT, SPACIOUS, "UNUSUAL", (FIREPLACE?)
CHILD'S BEDROOM	ENOUGH ROOM FOR BUNK BEDS AND PLAY SPACE	"PLAYFUL"
GUEST ROOM (?)	SMALL	PRIVATE
PLAYROOM (?)	REHEARSAL FOR QUARTET, T.V. WATCHING	RUSTIC, INDOOR OUTDOORSY, ROOM
SHOP-POTTING SHED (?)	FOR PUTTERING	
KITCHEN	COOKING	EFFICIENT, MODERN
SERVICE: HALF BATH FULL BATH WITH TUB LAUNDRY ROOM PANTRY CLOSETS		

ILL. 2

LOWER LEVEL

UPPER LEVEL

ILL. 3

house had now shrunk to seven distinct spaces, not counting the bathrooms and utility room. The Harris-Banks's decided to include all of these in the plans for the house that was to be built immediately, and at the same time to design an extension that could be added at a later date.

The next step in programming involved the relationship of these spaces to one another. (The couple found it easier to deal with the first stage of the house by itself. Once they had established the desired internal workings of stage one, they would relate the extension to it.) June and Murray wanted a compact house with minimal circulation and corridor space. They had a mental image of a multileveled house, with spaces opening out into each other both horizontally and vertically. Murray's writing area would be the exception. This space had to be isolated from the sleeping and communal areas of the house.

The kitchen and dining areas had to be adjacent to one another by the nature of their interdependent operations. The main living room should have a close relationship to the dining room. A fireplace was desired in both the dining room and the lounge area. Since fireplaces are expensive, it occurred to the couple that they could use one and make it visible from both spaces. According to June's original concept of open, flowing space, the three areas could be one large space subdivided into distinct functional areas by something other than walls. (A slight change in levels, perhaps?) The main entrance to the house should serve the living room primarily, and should also afford a direct route to the kitchen (Ill. 3).

The bedroom areas of the house could be separated from the communal areas, perhaps a floor above. The sleeping rooms should be near each other and the bathroom. A laundry space could be near the bedrooms or close to the kitchen; either solution would be acceptable. The study area should be isolated from the noise of the house, but should allow supervision of the child's bedroom at night.

Having established the program and the desired relationship of the spaces, the couple then attempted to incorporate the necessary environmental factors. Their site is heavily wooded and since they did not wish to upset the natural environment unduly, they chose a compact plan for the house rather than a rambling one. The most interesting view from the site is to the pond

The Problem—
An Approach

40

in the southeast, and they want to capitalize on this view as much as possible. Access to the site is from the north. Since this is a public road, it will be necessary to screen the internal workings of the house from the public eye. The desire to open the house to the southeast and close it to the northwest, luckily, conforms to the most logical rules of heat conservation. Placing most of the windows on the southern wall takes advantage of the radiant heat of the low winter sun. By minimizing the penetrations on the east, west, and especially on the north walls, heat loss is minimized.

Before drawing any site plans, the couple visited the local building department to determine the zoning laws in effect for their property. They learned that there is no limitation on the size of the house. There is, however, a mandatory 40′ front-yard set-back (not at all difficult to maintan on a site as large as theirs) and a 30′ side-yard limitation. The height of the house is restricted to a maximum of 35′.

The other houses in the area are, for the most part, traditionally designed two- and three-storied Victorian, colonial, and nondescript old farm houses. Scattered about are a few contemporary houses; which integrate well with the rural fabric. The material most often used is clapboard and naturally aged shingles. Most of the houses have steeply pitched roofs, which seems to be the only consistent characteristic of the area's domestic architecture.

After discussing the various options, the couple established that they would have the large living area and the dining room face the view to the southeast. They easily agreed to have the kitchen and breakfast area face the east to take advantage of the morning sun. June would like to attach a small prefabricated greenhouse to the east wall of the breakfast room. The retreat, however, needed to be inward in feeling, perhaps at the core of the house without any windows whatsoever. The Harris-Banks's also decided that it would be pleasant to place the bedrooms on the east to allow the morning sun to penetrate. The study could be oriented westward to catch the sunset (Ill. 4).

As you can probably see even in these early stages, there are a number of successful ways of accommodating the program. The two bedrooms (one of them opening up to the living room) could be on an upper floor, while the communal areas and the study can be arranged on the floor below. At this point, the couple hit on an orga-

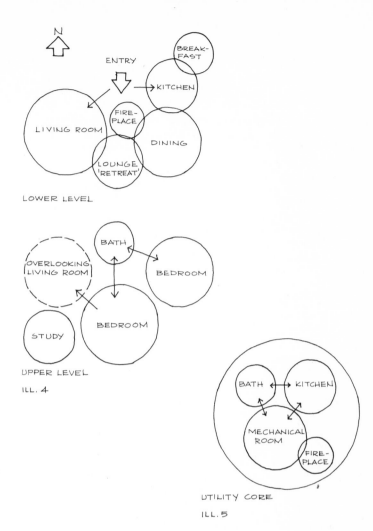

nizational concept. They decided to organize the house around an efficient and economical utility-mechanical core, which would simplify the plumbing (Ill. 5). The bathrooms neatly stack one on top of the other. The mechanical equipment (the boiler and hot-water heater) could be placed adjacent to the half-bath on the first floor. The laundry could be placed adjacent to the bathroom on the second floor.

As an additional stroke of economy, it was reasoned that the same chimney that would carry the flue of the fireplace could be used to exhaust the waste gas of the burner. Money could be saved by not having to construct two separate chimneys.

With this design concept in mind, the Harris-Banks's organize the bubble diagram around a utility core (Ill. 6). The first floor seems to fall into place easily. The spaces flow in a continuous circle around the core: each a unique, defined space but part of a larger area. The

Architects seldom use rulers, T-squares, and triangles to lay out the schematic floor plans of a simple house. Instead, they quickly draw freehand sketches of these plans. They have repeated this procedure so often that they have a feel for the room sizes and good working relationships between spaces. The amateur designer, however, will most likely have to stick closely to traditional mechanical layout methods.

The easiest way to draw a preliminary floor plan is on graph paper. Find a pad of graph paper based on a ⅛" grid (the lines on the paper mark off ⅛"). Assign a foot to each square: a room measuring 15' by 20' will equal 1⅞" × 2" on the graph paper. The second most valuable aid is a roll or pad of tracing paper. With it you can make changes to the house merely by taping another layer of paper onto a drawing.

For these earliest sketches graph paper, cheap tracing paper, pencils, erasers, and drafting tape (masking tape will serve) will suffice. For the more advanced drawings you will need more sophisticated equipment. All of these items can be acquired in any art supply store and in some stationery stores.

DRAFTING EQUIPMENT

An architect's scale (not an engineer's scale) that has ⅛" and ¼" demarcations on it.

A T-square

A triangle (Although an adjustable triangle is the most versatile, a 30–60-degree or 45-degree triangle can be bought very cheaply and will serve adequately.)

A pencil with a medium-hard lead, or a drafting pencil with F (or 2H) lead will do. (There is no need to invest in a lead sharpener; a sandpaper pad—although messy—will do.)

A square-edged table with a smooth surface, or a drawing board

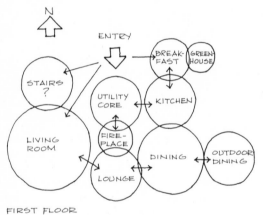

FIRST FLOOR

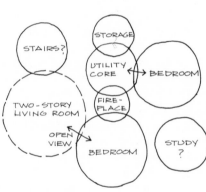

SECOND FLOOR

ILL. 6

second floor creates more problems. By putting the study in the southeast corner, it captures the maximum view, but is too close to bedroom areas. In spite of the problem with the study, enough progress has been made in programming to go on to the schematic design stages, which add dimensions to the bubbles (Insets I and II).

DEVELOPING A SCHEMATIC PLAN

With the bubble diagrams for reference, graph paper, tracing paper, and furniture cutouts on hand, the Harris-Banks's begin to translate conceptual relationships into realistic spaces.* The first step is to orient the house geographically; the corner of the paper is given a north arrow. Almost all architectural drawings are drawn with north up and south at the bottom of the paper. The couple knows that the areas which are to be provided with a view of the pond will

* The following method should be used by new designers who may have trouble moving directly from the bubble diagrams to floor plans. First, determine the approximate sizes of all the spaces outlined in the bubble diagram. Draw each room separately as a rectangle or square at ⅛" scale, i.e., ⅛" = 1'. Cut out the rectangles and arrange them following the organization of the bubble diagrams. This procedure should give you a rough plan. The proportions and sizes of the rooms can be modified to "clean up" the plan.

The Problem—
An Approach

42

Coming to grips with dimensions is a common problem many people face. What does your friend mean when he says that his house is 4,000 square feet? Is it a large house or a small one? How big is a room that measures 15' × 20'? Perhaps the simplest way to get a feeling for dimensions is by taking a tour of your own house or apartment and measuring the rooms you now live in. Find out exactly how big that living room which feels so spacious is, or that bedroom which is not big enough. The second step is to measure a few pieces of furniture. Get acquainted with the sizes of pieces that you own: dining table, sofa, beds, and chairs. Finally, study the spaces between the furniture. For example, are the spaces separating the furniture in conversational areas large enough? Do you feel uncomfortably close to the people sitting opposite you, or too distant from them? Similarly, look at the circulation spaces around the furniture and between the rooms. Are they sufficiently spacious or are they tight? Measure these spaces and find out their actual dimensions. Soon you will begin to associate dimensions with space.

Service areas also require dimensional study. The largest kitchens and bathrooms are not necessarily the ones that work best. The patterns in which these areas are utilized should be analyzed. A small kitchen could prove extremely efficient if designed around the family's usage. On the other hand, a spacious one could be awkward if the space is provided in the wrong areas. Similarly, a large bathroom might be inefficient if all the facilities within it—the tub, sink, and toilet—are part of the same space. Perhaps a smaller one with spatial differentiation between these areas could be more successful by providing privacy, enabling more members of the family to use the bathroom at the same time. The most successful layouts are designed through a study of the family's usage. Take note of the sequence in which the fixtures, appliances, counter and storage spaces are used. Measure those appliances and fixtures you now have and find out the dimensions of those you plan to get. Sizes together with utilization patterns will allow the planning of efficient layouts.

Once you get a feeling for dimensions required to satisfy the program, "large" and "small" spaces can be translated into square feet. Each room or space will then become 15' × 20' or 20' × 30'. What started as a bubble diagram of spatial relations now becomes a plan.

When shaping and sizing the bubbles to make realistic rooms out of them, be sure to keep in mind the proportions of the spaces and possible furniture layouts. A good rule of thumb on proportions is *not* to make a room's length more than twice its width. Corridors, of course, are the exception. To experiment with furniture layouts, cut out small pieces of paper to the same scale as the drawing, representing the sizes of furniture, appliances, and fixtures. (You can trace the most commonly found household items off the drawing in figure below. They have been drawn to ⅛" scale.) Place the pieces of furniture in the spaces drawn to quickly determine whether the room sizes and shapes are compatible with the objects to be placed in them.

COMMON SIZES, WIDTHS, AND LENGTHS

Entry: The minimum size for greeting a guest and taking his coat is 5' × 5'. A gracious entry foyer can be as large as 10' × 10'. Be sure to provide a coat closet adjacent to the entry.

Closets: The minimum depth of a closet is 2'. The length can be whatever you want. A walk-in closet should be about 7'-0" wide to allow for clothing to be hung on both sides. The doors to a closet can be hinged (swinging out), sliding, or louvered.

Sliding doors interfere least with furniture placement in the room because they take up no space when they are opened.

Hallways: A hall can be as narrow as 2½' if it is very short (2' to 3'). It can be as narrow as 3', if it is not longer than 6' or 8'. The hall should be about 4' wide if it is to run more than 10'. Reasons of practicality and proportion dictate the dimensions of halls. It is difficult for two people to cross each other in a hallway that is 2½' wide. Also, a long, skinny hall seems to be oppressive, while the same hall a few feet wider is more comfortable in feeling. In addition, the wider hallway can be better lit and can be used to hang objects of art.

Doors: The front door of a house is usually 3' wide. Doors to bedrooms, kitchens, or studies are generally 2'-6" wide. The door to the bathroom is preferably 2'-6", but could be 2'-0" if absolutely necessary. The same holds true for closets. All doors are 6'-8" in height.

Ceiling heights: The height of the ceiling can vary between 7' (in the old colonials) to 12' to 14' (in the old townhouses). New houses are usually built with ceilings of a minimum of 8' for living areas, and a minimum of 7½' for bedroom areas. The structure between floors can take up anywhere between 1' and 2½'. Ceiling height,

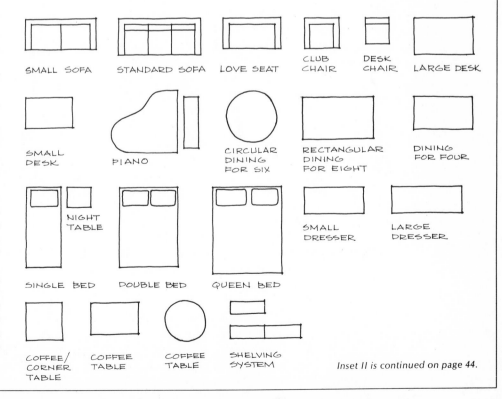

SMALL SOFA STANDARD SOFA LOVE SEAT CLUB CHAIR DESK CHAIR LARGE DESK

SMALL DESK PIANO CIRCULAR DINING FOR SIX RECTANGULAR DINING FOR EIGHT DINING FOR FOUR

NIGHT TABLE SMALL DRESSER LARGE DRESSER

SINGLE BED DOUBLE BED QUEEN BED

COFFEE/CORNER TABLE COFFEE TABLE COFFEE TABLE SHELVING SYSTEM

Inset II is continued on page 44.

Continued from page 43

like anything else in design, is dependent on a sense of proportions. A room that is 5′ × 5′ would probably look preposterous with a ceiling height of 10′. A living room 30′ × 20′ would have no sense of grandness if the ceiling height were kept to 8′ (it would look as if someone were sitting on it).

Wall thicknesses: The exterior walls of a house constructed from wood are about 6″ thick; the interior partitions, approximately 5″ thick. Masonry walls (brick or stone) are about 10″ thick. These are *design* dimensions, to allow you to reserve enough room on the plans for wall thicknesses; they are not the actual thickness of the walls. Actual thicknesses can be determined by the methods outlined in Chapter 10, Vertical Supports: Walls and Columns.

Kitchens: The stove and sink usually are designed to protrude 2′ from the wall. For this reason kitchen counters are usually 2′ deep so that they end flush with the appliances. Overhead cabinets are generally 1′-0″ deep. The door of the refrigerator often extends another 1″ or 2″ past the counter.

be on the lower side of the paper, the kitchen and the breakfast room on the right-hand side of the paper, and the front door close to the road, which is off the top of the sheet.

The most logical place to start this particular scheme is with the mechanical core. (Had the couple not hit on this organizational scheme, they would most likely have chosen the front entry or the main living space as the starting point.) They guess the mechanical space at about 8′ × 5′. (It is to accommodate the boiler and a hot-water heater.) The half-bath can be beside it (about 5′ × 5′). The fireplace fits in nicely in the leftover space (Ill. 7). This 8′ × 10′ area becomes the core of the house. The kitchen (about 8′ × 10′) is placed on the east side of the core, with the sink and dishwasher backing onto the core wall. The dining area (ample but not extravagantly sized at about 14′ × 10′) is placed to the south of the kitchen. The breakfast area (as yet undetermined in size) will go to the north of the kitchen. The living room (15′ × 20′) can go either to the left (west) of the core or to the south of it. The western position is chosen so that the entry from the north can be adjacent to it. The lounge area is depressed about 12″ or so below the main floor level and is located between the living room and the dining space so that the fireplace can be seen from both areas (Ill. 8).

After quickly drawing the first-floor plan, a number of obvious errors and omissions were caught. First, the breakfast area would be much too small. Even if space could be found for a table, there would be no room to walk around it. Second, the door to the mechanical room would be an ugly scar on the living room wall. It could just as easily be placed on the wall of the corridor. Similarly, there is no reason why the half-bath should open into the kitchen. Its door, too, could be placed on the north wall of the core.

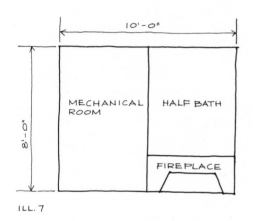

ILL. 7

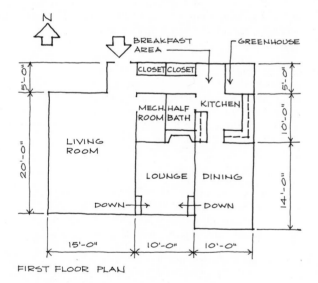

FIRST FLOOR PLAN

ILL. 8

That decision freed valuable wall space in the kitchen for badly needed counter space. Next, it was decided that the short stubs of wall between the kitchen and dining area could be modified to open the spaces to each other. If it was later determined that they were needed structurally, they could be put back into the plan. Visual separation between eating and cooking areas could be made with hanging cabinets and plants. The most obvious omission was the staircase that would lead to the upper floor. It was decided to square out the missing corner to the northwest with a U-shaped stair (Ill. 9). This would put the stair near the entrance.

Now for the second floor. A piece of tracing paper was placed over the revised plan of the first floor. The couple had decided to have a high-ceilinged living room, so they marked off an "X" on the second floor to indicate that there would be no floor in that area. The staircase was next drawn and the outline of the first floor's outer walls and the walls of the mechanical core traced. To be sure they did not forget the chimney coming through the floor going to the roof, they traced it.

The most obvious indication was to draw a corridor from the stair, around the mechanical core, to the southeast quarter of the house. This would divide the area into two bedrooms, one 7' × 10', the other 10' × 11', and a study, 10' × 12' (Ill. 10). This plan at first seemed to satisfy the program, but on further investigation was found wanting. The 7' × 10' bedroom seemed too small. Murray felt that the study, instead of being isolated from the noise of the house, was now at the very center of it. When June shaded in the circulation area, she discovered that it was excessive. The long, twisted corridor reminded her of halls she had seen in boarding houses. Since the second-floor plan did not satisfy the couple, it was rejected.

The second attempt (Ill. 11) proved to be more promising. A balcony was drawn around the west side of the core, creating a passage directly from the stair to what was previously called the study area. They then switched those two spaces around. Access to the study was through the bedroom-sitting room. The balcony widened the parents' room by 3', and the elimination of the east-side corridor widened the child's room to 10'. However, there were problems with this new plan as well as improvements. The laundry area had to be switched from the east side to the west side of the core, which placed it on the balcony overlooking the living room—tolerable, but not ideal.

The couple was very happy with their efforts thus far and decided to see how the house "massed." There are a number of ways to approach the way a house will look. One is to

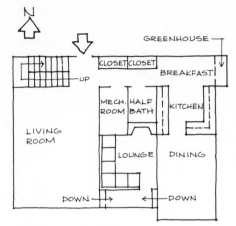

FIRST FLOOR PLAN

ILL. 9

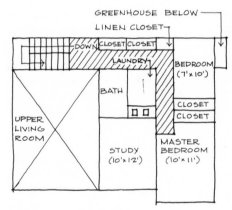

SECOND FLOOR PLAN

ILL. 10

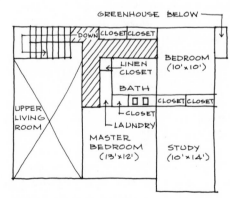

SECOND FLOOR PLAN

ILL. 11

build a model of the house (even in its most schematic stages). The other is to draw sections and elevations of the house. An elevation is a picture of the outer walls. There are four views, or elevations of a house, one for each point of the compass. We suggest that you follow both procedures: make a model and draw sections and elevations before finalizing the plans and going on to the next stage.

STUDYING THE HOUSE IN SECTION

A section is an imaginary slice through the house that allows you to study and visualize the relationships among different levels and spaces (not very different from slicing a fruit to discover its underlying structure). In drawing the section, you first determine which part of the plan you wish to investigate. You then draw a line through the floor plan at that point and at the same point on all the other floors. The levels are then drawn on top of each other in much the same way you would draw an elevation, or vertical view (Ill. 12).

The Harris-Banks's first investigate an east-west cut made through the utility core (Ill. 13). On the first floor, from left to right, the spaces that appear on the section are the living room, the utility core, and the kitchen. On the second floor, the living room extends through the second-floor structure, the balcony railing shows the balcony itself, the laundry room, the bathroom, and the child's bedroom. The couple decided to cap the house with a sloped roof: first, to conform to the other houses in the area and, second, to simplify the construction and waterproofing of the roof were it flat. The roof slopes low over the living area and peaks at the east wall of the core. Special precautions were taken to ensure that there was sufficient headroom over the balcony (about 7').

The couple was content with the shape of the roof. It reminded them of the old colonial salt-boxes, an example of which still stood in the neighboring village. What disturbed them was the unnecessary space over the mechanical core at the point at which the roof peaked. There was no reason for the ceiling height in the bathroom to be 15'. The room would look awkward, the heat would rise and stay there, and dust would collect high up on the walls.

ILL. 12

The problem was solved by drawing a ceiling across the mechanical core and laundry room, leaving the roof over the bedrooms and living room sloped (Ill. 14). June suggested that the low-roofed space could be reached by ladder from the second floor and could be utilized for storage. Murray said that the area probably would command the best view from the house since it extended above the tree line and looked westward toward the city skyline. It would be a pity, they agreed, to relegate the area for dead storage. Would it be possible, they wanted to know, to make some active use out of the space on the third floor? They knew that the maximum house height for their area was 35', and so they were still within the limit. The ceiling of that third-floor attic was not quite high enough for a legally habitable space, but if they arranged the slopes of the roofs differently, they could get sufficient headroom and a window to the west (Ill. 15). The room, it was decided, could be used as a study, since it not only commanded a sensational view and faced the western sunset but was by far the most isolated space in the house, being reached only by ladder.

Somewhat excited by their newest idea, the Harris-Banks's started building a study model (Inset III) of the house so that they could better understand its shape and the slope of the roof. Essential to the construction of the model were an additional two sections taken through the house—east-west through the lounge, and north-south through the mechanical core and the study loft (Ill. 16). Laying a clean sheet of tracing paper over the plan for the second floor,

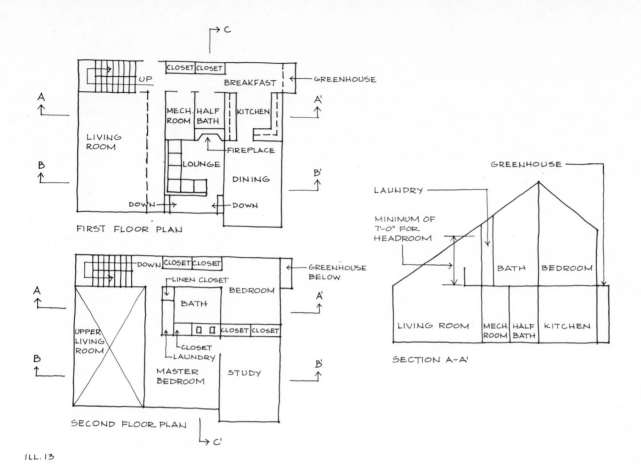

FIRST FLOOR PLAN

SECOND FLOOR PLAN

SECTION A-A'

ILL. 13

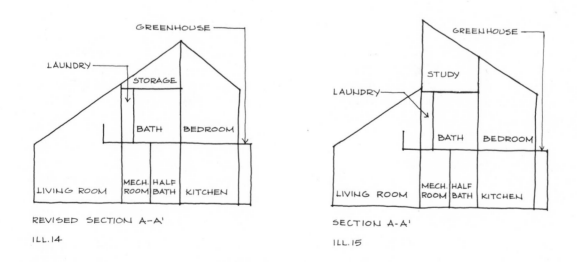

REVISED SECTION A-A'

ILL. 14

SECTION A-A'

ILL. 15

the couple then drew the plan for the third floor, the study loft (Ill. 17). They were not too happy with the long, narrow space divided by the chimney flue, but decided that they would probably find some use for the space. With the study moved to a different floor, they found themselves with additional space on the second floor to enlarge the master bedroom and include a deck (Ill. 18). June and Murray found the model very helpful in understanding the roof slopes.

Coordination of Elements

47

INSET III / CONSTRUCTING THE MODEL

Because framing (and particularly roof framing) is difficult, the design of the house (particularly of the roof) should be as simple as possible. Let the master carpenter build the house of the seven gables; you should abstain from anything that ambitious. Developing the final form of the house is a difficult procedure. To help you make certain critical decisions you must build a cardboard model of the house—not just after you have finalized its design, but at the very earliest stages of the design phase, while the house is taking shape.

With cardboard (the kind that used to come with laundered shirts, or chipboard, or matte board, or illustration board), matte knife, and glue (Elmer's) in hand, begin by building the first floor at a scale of 1/4" = 1'-0" or at 1/8" = 1'-0" if that is the scale of your schematic drawings. Cut and glue the outer walls surrounding the first floor and the load-bearing partitions. (Make them about 9'-0".) Similarly, construct the second floor and its partitions above that. If there is a third level, a change in level, a balcony, or a cantilever, be sure to include it in the model. Designing the roofing system is a matter of studying how the different placement of pieces of cardboard representing the roof affects the spaces within the building while at the same time achieving an interesting outside form.

Once some understanding of the form and the spaces that are created is determined, go back to the drawing board to work out the precise elevations of the house. From the elevations and sections you will get the exact dimensions for completing the model.

There is always more than one way to roof a house. Try a few, change the interior of the rooms if it is warranted, rethink the ceiling heights, the positions and shapes of the windows. Keep modifying the model and the elevations. If no solution pleases you, you might wish to redesign the entire house. Be assured that most architects have similar problems. The design of a simple one-family house might require the building of five or six study models and many more schematic sketches.

One final note: Remember that houses are not built out of cardboard and glue. All of those roof planes must be supported by either columns or walls. It is, therefore, imperative that you keep structural considerations in mind while developing the form. It is at this stage of design-development that the services of an architect are most valuable.

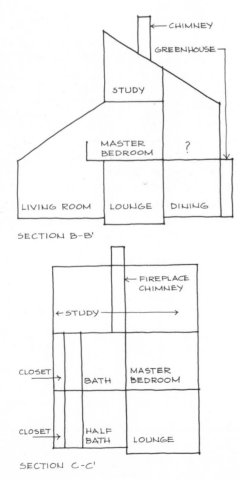

SECTION B-B'

SECTION C-C'

ILL. 16

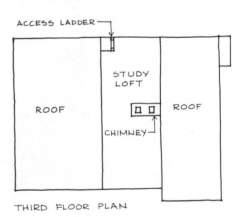

THIRD FLOOR PLAN

ILL. 17

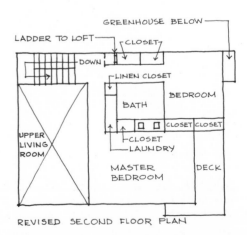

REVISED SECOND FLOOR PLAN

ILL. 18

The Problem—
An Approach

48

PREPARING THE PRELIMINARY DRAWINGS

Satisfied and excited with the plans, sections, and model of the house, the Harris-Banks's sought consultation with the architect. She reviewed their schematics and agreed that they had what might prove to be a very exciting house. She made a few recommendations as well. The loft could be cut in half and the sections of the roof changed to obtain a continuous-sloping ceiling from the living room into the master bedroom (Ill. 19). The construction of the house would prove to be simpler and more economical if it could be fitted into a rectangular floor plan, specifically on some sort of module. A modular plan is one that uses a pre-established size as the determinant for the sizes of the rooms and/or the heights of the walls. The most efficient module in a wood-frame house is a 4' module. Almost all of the building components—plywood sheathing, flooring, etc. —come in 4' or 8' sizes. Almost all lumber, likewise, is sold in 2' increments. The architect recommended that the couple lay out a 4' grid and try to adapt their plans to it. In addition, she suggested that perhaps only a portion of the lounge area be sunken to allow for a level passage between the dining and living areas. The step could provide the seat of the sofa that would be facing the fireplace. She also reminded them that walls had thicknesses, which means that all of the rooms they had laid out would become smaller to allow for the area taken up in the thicknesses of the walls (see page 43, Inset II).

The Harris-Banks's went home, laid out a grid, and made the plans conform to the module. These schematic drawings were later developed into the final plans for the house (Ill. 20). Before finalizing these plans the couple designed the possible extensions that could be added later.

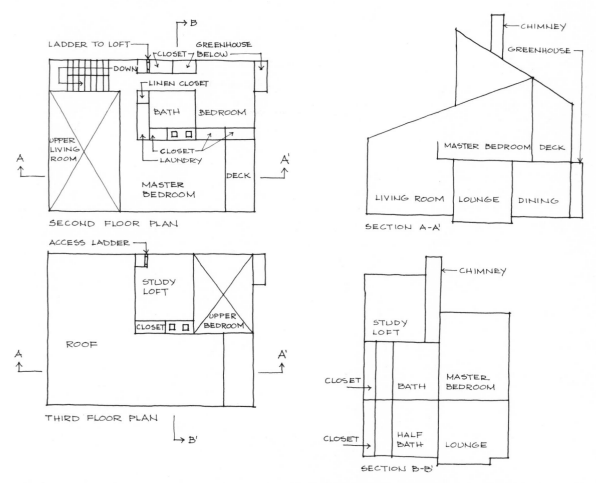

ILL. 19

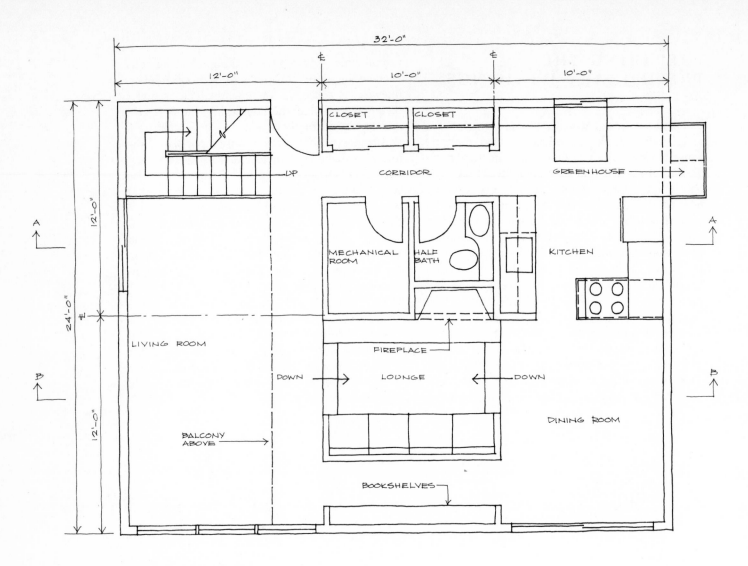

32'-0"

12'-0"   10'-0"   10'-0"

12'-0"

24'-0"

12'-0"

A

B

A

B

CLOSET   CLOSET

CORRIDOR   GREENHOUSE

UP

MECHANICAL
ROOM   HALF
BATH   KITCHEN

LIVING ROOM

FIREPLACE

DOWN   LOUNGE   DOWN

DINING ROOM

BALCONY
ABOVE

BOOKSHELVES

FIRST FLOOR PLAN

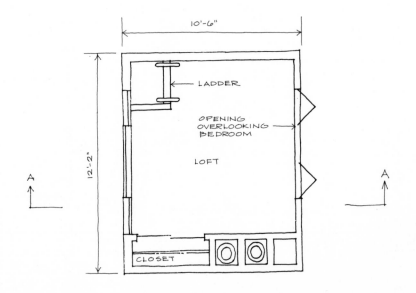

10'-6"

12'-2"

A   A

LADDER

OPENING
OVERLOOKING
BEDROOM

LOFT

CLOSET

ILL. 20

LOFT PLAN

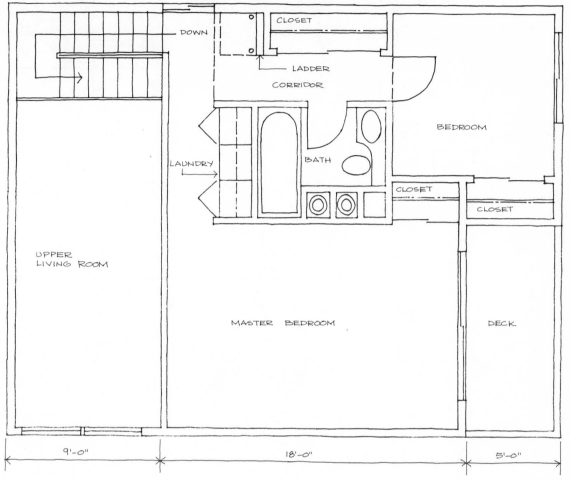

DOWN

CLOSET

LADDER

CORRIDOR

BEDROOM

BATH

LAUNDRY

CLOSET

CLOSET

UPPER
LIVING ROOM

MASTER BEDROOM

DECK

|← 9'-0" →|← 18'-0" →|← 5'-0" →|

SECOND FLOOR PLAN

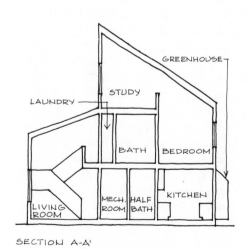

GREENHOUSE

LAUNDRY

STUDY

BATH

BEDROOM

LIVING
ROOM

MECH.
ROOM

HALF
BATH

KITCHEN

SECTION A-A'

ILL. 20

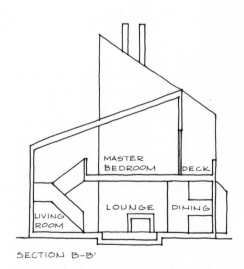

MASTER
BEDROOM

DECK

LIVING
ROOM

LOUNGE

DINING

SECTION B-B'

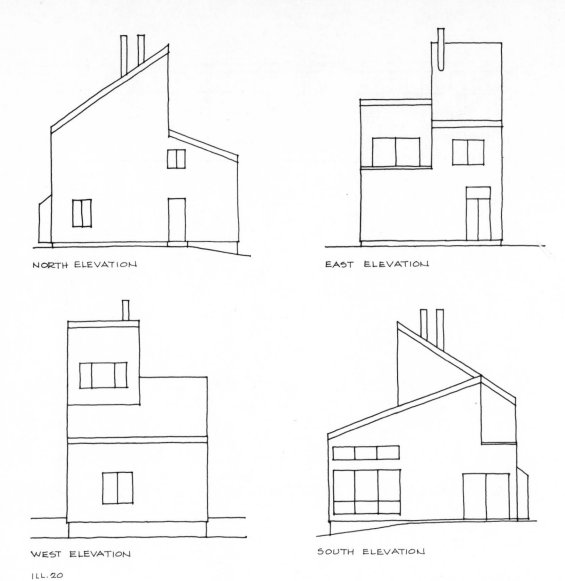

NORTH ELEVATION

EAST ELEVATION

WEST ELEVATION

SOUTH ELEVATION

ILL. 20

MASTER PLANNING THE EXTENSION

The house that Murray and June designed has a number of extension possibilities and limitations. It would make no sense, for instance, to expand the house to the south. The windows to the view would be cut off by such an extension, which would mean a major change in the character of the house. On the other hand, having the corridor to the north allows an extension to be added on this side that would not disturb the circulation of the existing house or the sources of light. The extension possibilities to the north are explored in Illustration 21. A potential extension to the northwest, which includes a two-car garage, two additional bedrooms, a potting shed, a full bathroom, and a large family room, is shown in Illustration 22. This more ambitious extension takes advantage of the slope of the site and joins the house at the half level—in other words, the garage and potting shed are a half level (or about 4½′) below the level of the living room floor. The staircase is extended down to that level. The bedrooms and family room, about 8′ above the level of the garage floor, are on a level between the first and second landings. They are joined to the house by the middle landing in the U-shaped stair. The roof over the living area extends at the same angle to cover the extension. The extension makes good use of the natural slope of the land and provides for a direct route between the road and the garage.

With these two alternate extensions master planned, the Harris-Banks's go on to the next

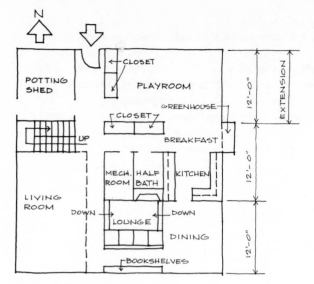

FIRST FLOOR PLAN

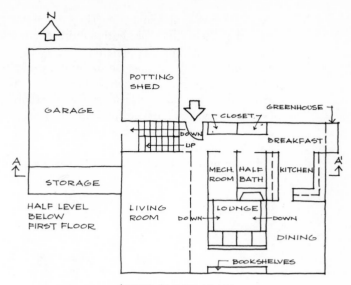

FIRST FLOOR PLAN

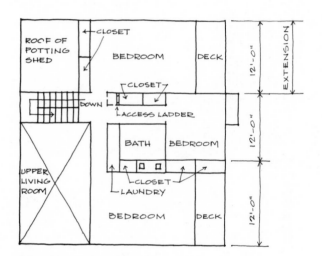

SECOND FLOOR PLAN

ILL. 21

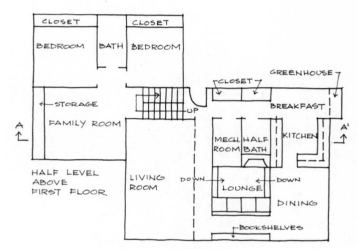

FIRST FLOOR PLAN

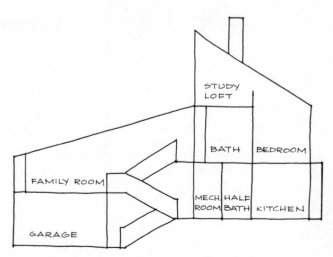

SECTION A-A'

ILL. 22

stages of house development. They must translate the lines that presently represent their house into building components. Structural and mechanical systems must be designed, building materials chosen, construction methods evaluated, and financial and legal problems resolved in order for the plans and elevations to become a real building. These subjects are discussed in Part Two of this book.

Please note that not all amateur designers will hit on the final plans for their house as quickly as our sample family did. Design is sometimes a trial-and-error procedure. A great deal of patience is needed until satisfactory results are seen. The importance of careful preliminary planning cannot be overemphasized. It is far better to correct a serious mistake with an eraser or scrap of cardboard than to have to alter your house after construction has begun.

This is a rendered interior section of the Harris-Banks's house as they have conceived it thus far. The bedroom space opens to the living room; the lounge is sunk in about 1', separating the living room from the dining area. Although few people can draw in such detail and with such facility, it is important that the designer have a complete understanding of the spaces being created and their visual interrelationships. Architects, Lupe DiDonno and Phyllis Sperling; rendering by Herman Sands

PART TWO: DESIGN DEVELOPMENT

6
Structural Principles

We have found that most people have only a vague idea of what makes a house stand up. Some think that the nailing or cementing of one member to the other is the most essential structural necessity. Others are of the opinion that buildings should be constructed of thin floor slabs and massive columns and walls. Although most of us have the rudiments of structural knowledge, the more or less sophisticated structural sensibilities required for putting together a house require additional education.

The structure of a simple house employs the same basic principles as the megastructure of a skyscraper. In the attempt to gain insight into how any building works, it is more valuable to think of the structural components as working together to transfer loads downward to the ground, rather than to consider them as holding something up.

When dealing with buildings, one of the essentials to keep in mind is structural continuity. This kind of continuity applies to human anatomy as well. Our body skeleton carries the weight of our various organs and tissues from one bone to the other, until the entire load is transferred through our feet to the ground. Similarly, the loads on a building, both inherent (dead loads: the weight of materials) and applied (live loads: people, furniture, and snow), must be transferred through the various horizontal, vertical, and diagonal structural members to the foundation and from there to the ground.

A house (or for that matter any building)

consists of four main parts: the *roof*, which protects from the weather and carries the load of its structure plus the weight of snow, wind, and rain to the *vertical supports* (walls, load-bearing partitions, and columns), which enclose the house and transfer the weight of the roof and floors downward; the *floors*, which directly receive the weight of people and furniture and transfer that weight to the vertical supports; and the *foundations*, which transfer the total house loads and secure it to the earth (Ill. 1).

In our analysis of how loads are transferred through the body of the house, we divide the structure into two supporting systems: the horizontal supporting system (the floors, slabs, flat or slightly sloped roofs) and the vertical supporting system (the walls, foundations, bearing partitions, columns). There is a practical reason for such a division: the structural components of each system work differently in transferring the loads (Ill. 2).

THE VERTICAL SUPPORTS

There are basically three ways to structure any building: you can frame it with columns and beams, you can use load-bearing walls to support the floors, or you can construct the building using light-frame construction methods, which in essence combine the other two systems. The Empire State Building in New York City is of steel-frame construction. In that

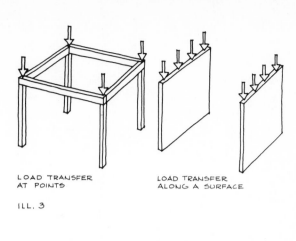

ROOF:
LIVE LOAD: WEIGHT OF RAIN,
         WIND AND SNOW
DEAD LOADS: WEIGHT OF
         STRUCTURAL
         MATERIALS

VERTICAL SUPPORTS:
(WALLS, PARTITIONS, AND
 COLUMNS)
WEIGHT OF ROOF + FLOOR

FLOORS:
WEIGHT OF VERTICAL SUPPORTS
+ WEIGHT OF PEOPLE AND
FURNITURE

FOUNDATIONS:
WEIGHT OF TOTAL HOUSE

ILL. 1

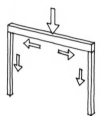

LOAD TRANSFER
AT POINTS

LOAD TRANSFER
ALONG A SURFACE

ILL. 3

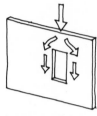

BEARING WALL

POINT SUPPORT

ILL. 4

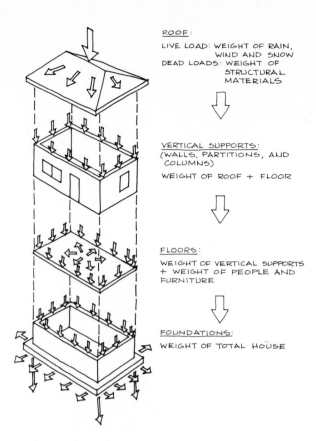

SUBFLOOR

JOISTS

PLATES

STUDS

SOLE PLATE
HEADER
SILL

FOUNDATION

FOOTING

EARTH

ILL. 2

structure and in thousands like it of smaller stature, the loads of the building are transferred through the steel frame downward, much as a person's weight is carried to the ground by the body's skeleton. The floor loads are transferred through beams to girders to columns and down through the columns to the foundations. The walls act to enclose the building, are nonstructural, and are referred to as curtain walls. A small house could be constructed using exactly the same principles if framed with lightweight steel components or lumber, a method known as post-and-beam construction (Ill. 3).

A small warehouse with masonry walls is structured on the principle of the load-bearing wall. The walls of this building do more than enclose space for reasons of privacy and help retain mechanically provided heat in winter. These walls and partitions transfer the weight of the floors and roof to the foundation all along the length of the wall (Ill. 3). The brick or masonry-block house is based on this principle. Since the wall acts as a unit to transfer the loads, there is a certain limit to the number of openings that can be placed in it. When the penetrations in a wall become so large that the wall can no longer act structurally as load-bearing, alternate arrangements are needed for the transfer of the weight. In such cases, the loads are distributed through beams, which transfer them to point supports, that is, columns (Ill. 4).

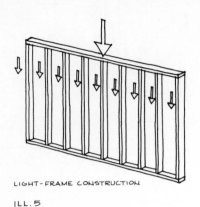

LIGHT-FRAME CONSTRUCTION

ILL. 5

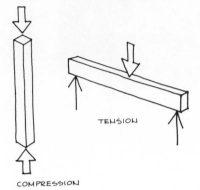

TENSION

COMPRESSION

ILL. 6

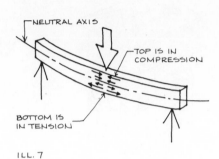

NEUTRAL AXIS

TOP IS IN COMPRESSION

BOTTOM IS IN TENSION

ILL. 7

In a building of light-frame construction the house is framed using slim structural members spaced closely together. The floor consists of joists (mini-beams) spaced 12″, 16″, or 24″ apart instead of heavier beams spaced 4′ to 8′ apart. The walls consist of studs (mini-columns), which are spaced at the same short intervals. By positioning the studs so close together and connecting them with sheathing for bracing (usually sheets of plywood), the wall is converted into a load-bearing wall (Ill. 5). If all the walls and partitions are constructed in this way and the penetrations for the doors and windows are limited and small (narrower than 6′), there is no need for any columns to support the floors or roof above. If the interior space is large, or if the partitions are inconveniently placed for load-bearing purposes, columns can be used to support the structure above (Inset I).

THE HORIZONTAL SUPPORTS

In the vertical support system of the house, especially in walls and short columns, loads are transferred through compression (Ill. 6). The molecules or fibers in the column are being compressed or squeezed together. Most structural materials are strong in compression, meaning that they can carry a great deal of load while being squeezed, but to varying degrees are weak in tension (stretching). These stresses occur when a structural member is positioned horizontally (Ill. 6). When a beam is placed between two supports and is loaded, it is said to be subjected to "bending" stresses. The beam gives, or deflects, under the weight.

Bending is a combination of compression

(squeezing) and tension (stretching). If we concentrate on what is happening somewhere in the middle of the beam, we will see that the uppermost molecules in the member are being compressed, whereas the lower molecules are being stretched, or placed in tension (Ill. 7). The tension stresses are greatest at the *bottom* of the section and decrease toward the center. The compression stresses are greatest at the *top* of the beam and decrease toward the center. The centermost molecules (those running along an imaginary line called the neutral axis) are not subjected to any stresses at all. Because of the dual stresses (tension and compression) that occur in horizontal structural members when subjected to bending, they require different structural analysis than do short vertical supports, which are only subject to compressive stresses.

Let us suppose that a hiker has to cross a stream that is 4′ or 5′ wide. He would know that a long twig about 2″ in diameter would not support his weight across the gap. (We are assuming, of course, that he is a tightrope walker.) He would probably decide that a tree trunk 4″ in diameter would do the trick (Ill. 8). Were the gap increased from 5′ to 15′, he might question whether a 4″ log (assuming he was able to find one that long) would be able to support his weight across the longer span (Ill. 9). Presented with this problem he would probably turn around and look for a log thicker than 4″. He suspects, correctly, that the 4″ log would bend too much or perhaps would even snap in two if he attempted to walk on it.

Whether we realize it or not, most of us have some basic knowledge of the tenets of structural design. In the example just given the hiker knew that the dimensions of the structural member required to bridge the gap were dependent on

Originally, wood-frame construction consisted of heavy timbers spaced at wide intervals with thick planks spanning between them for the floor and the roof. The joints connecting these timbers were carefully hand-cut and connected by wooden or metal pegs. This method of construction was a modification of the methods used in Europe in the seventeenth century. Erection was costly, time consuming, and required the strength of many men to lift the timbers into place and join them. The advent of the sawmill in the mid-seventeenth century and the invention of the manufactured nail in the 1830's revolutionized house building by allowing the development of the balloon frame.

The balloon frame, a new framing method that first appeared in a Chicago church, utilized a number of lightweight wood sections spaced inches apart instead of heavy timbers spaced many feet from one another. The home builder, stocked with slender square-cut pieces of wood, an apron pocket full of iron nails, and a handsaw, could raise the house himself (or with the help of a neighbor) in a few weeks. Although not as rigid as the heavy timber frame, and less fire-resistant, the balloon frame soon became the chief means of constructing the then popular two-story house.

Currently, two light-framing methods are used for residential construction: the balloon frame, and the platform (or western) frame, the latter being the most popular of the two.

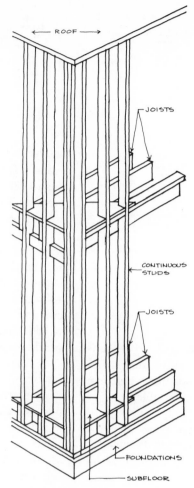

THE BALLOON FRAME

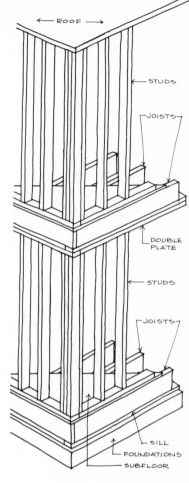

THE PLATFORM FRAME

THE BALLOON FRAME

The predominant characteristic of the balloon frame is the use of 2″ × 4″ mini-columns (studs) that run vertically from the foundation to the roof. The frame is not rigid in itself (it will not be able to stand up at right angles in a wind storm) but requires the addition of diagonal bracing or plywood sheathing to keep it from sway-

ing under pressure. This method of construction is still being used today for two-story houses faced with masonry or stucco (above).

THE PLATFORM FRAME

The simplest method of wood-frame construction is the platform frame. In this method, the builder constructs the entire

subfloor before beginning the walls. In doing so, the worker has a flat and safe surface on which to build the wall sections. These sections are usually constructed horizontally on the floor and then tilted up into place, temporarily braced, plumbed straight, and nailed to the subfloor. This system is the easiest to construct and will be the one discussed throughout the rest of this book.

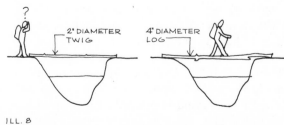

ILL. 8

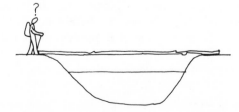

ILL. 9

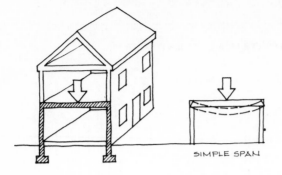

ILL. 10

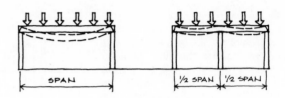

ILL. 12

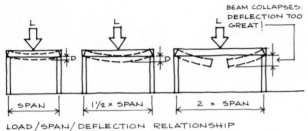

LOAD / SPAN / DEFLECTION RELATIONSHIP

ILL. 11

the length of the span and the loads to be supported. In fact, even highly sophisticated structural problems that involve spanning between supports can be reduced to four variables:

1. *The span*—the distance between the supports, and how the member is connected to its supports.

2. *The loads* to be carried—how much weight, where it is concentrated, and for how long.

3. *The cross-sectional dimensions* of the structural member—the thickness and shape of the cross section of the member.

4. *The material* being used*—its strength, characteristics, ability to withstand the stresses it is being subjected to.

The Span

The word "span" means the distance between supports. The most common span in residential architecture is the "simple span." This refers to a horizontal member (a plank, joist, beam, or girder) that is supported at both its ends by either walls or columns (Ill. 10). The ends may be secured to the supports in some way, but the connection is not rigid enough to prevent slight

* We'll be primarily discussing wood as the spanning material.

movement (or rotation). When a simple span is loaded (that is, when weight is put on the beam), it tends to give somewhat under the weight. This giving, or bending (the combination of tension and compression), causes the beam to become slightly distorted. We use the term "deflection" to describe the amount of distortion. In the case of the hiker, the distance between the supports was increased from 5' to 15' without any increase in the thickness of the cross section of the log, or in the load that it would have to bear. This increase in the span would cause the member (the log) to deflect even more (under its own weight). Were you to further increase the span (without changing the cross-sectional dimensions of the spanning member), the beam would eventually fail (Ill. 11).

Since these variables (the span, the loads, and the cross-sectional dimensions of the beam) are interdependent, an increase in one of them (in this case, the span) would require either an increase in the cross section of the member or a reduction of the load. Supposing that these alternatives are impractical, the obvious thing to do is divide the long span into shorter ones. This can be done by bridging all of the shorter spans with one long continuous beam, or by erecting a number of short beams, each bridging one span, or by making the connections to the supports rigid ones (Ill. 12).

The continuous beam across more than one span will do the job better—that is, with less deflection—than would the discontinuous beams. (The continuity of the member over the supports tends to reduce the overall bending.) It is difficult, however, to obtain a very long beam or girder. (About the longest lumber you will be able to get without special order is 22'.) The simply spanned beam, one that spans from one support to the other, is commonly used in residential architecture and is perfectly adequate in most cases (Ill. 13).

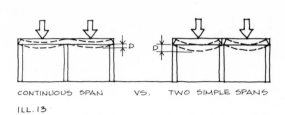

CONTINUOUS SPAN VS. TWO SIMPLE SPANS

ILL. 13

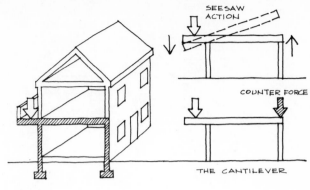

SEESAW ACTION

COUNTER FORCE

THE CANTILEVER

ILL. 14

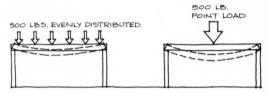

500 LBS. EVENLY DISTRIBUTED

500 LB. POINT LOAD

EVENLY DISTRIBUTED LOAD VS. CONCENTRATED LOAD

ILL. 15

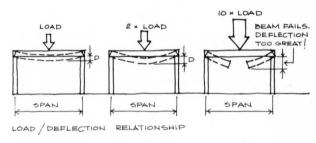

LOAD

2 × LOAD

10 × LOAD

BEAM FAILS. DEFLECTION TOO GREAT!

SPAN   SPAN   SPAN

LOAD / DEFLECTION RELATIONSHIP

ILL. 16

THE CANTILEVERED SPAN: There are instances where the design of a house calls for an overhang or a balcony, eliminating the end support of the beam. In this situation the beam is cantilevered. The structural member will have two supports, but only one of these will occur at the end. The other support occurs somewhere along the length of the beam. When the end of the cantilevered portion is loaded, the effect is like a seesaw (Ill. 14). The upward motion at the cantilevered portion must be opposed by a downward force at the beam's opposite end. A wall or other similarly heavy weight applied at the noncantilevered end will act to balance the beam. Otherwise, the connection between the beam and its end support will have to be made very strong.

The Loads

A beam's primary function is to carry the loads applied along the length of its span to its supports. Three crucial questions about the loading of a beam must be answered: How much weight must the beam carry? For how long? Is the load concentrated at any one point or is it evenly distributed along the beam's length? If the load is evenly distributed along the length of the span, every inch of the member is put to work supporting the weight applied to it, in addition to transferring the weight to the nearest support. The same total load applied at a single point causes different problems. If the load is applied at or near midspan, the bending and consequent deflection will be greater (Ill. 15).

The length of time the load will be sustained is an important consideration as well. A wood member might be fine to support an enormously heavy load for a few minutes or even as long as a week. It will bend a bit under the load and deflect to some extent, but if the load is removed

it will come back to its original shape. If the load is kept there for as long as a year, strange as it may seem, the material gets tired. When the load is removed, the member will not assume its original shape.

The magnitude of the loads to be carried is the decisive factor in the design of a beam. The greater the load on a beam, the greater the bending stresses, and the greater the danger of the beam failing. If the loads are too great for the beam it will collapse (Ill. 16). Presented with a large load and a fixed span, the only variable left is the cross-sectional dimensions of the structural member.

Cross-Sectional Dimensions

The cross section of a structural member refers to the shape and area of a cut perpendicular to its length. When we speak of cross-sectional

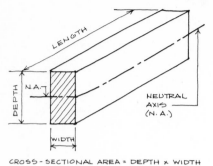

CROSS-SECTIONAL AREA = DEPTH × WIDTH

ILL. 17

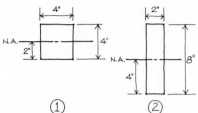

① ②

BOTH SECTIONS 1 AND 2 HAVE A CROSS-
SECTIONAL AREA OF 16" SQUARE.
THE 2"×8" IS MORE EFFICIENT SINCE
IT PLACES MORE MATERIAL FURTHER
AWAY FROM THE NEUTRAL AXIS.

ILL. 18

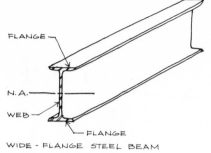

WIDE-FLANGE STEEL BEAM

ILL. 19

area, we refer to the *amount* of material in the cross section. In a rectangular section this would be the width times the depth of the cross section. If we speak of the *shape* of the section, we are talking about its position and proportions (Ill. 17). It is a fact that a rectangular member when placed on its edge (long side vertical) will be able to span a longer distance and support a larger load than if it were placed on its flat side. Actually, the strength of a structural member is not so much dependent on the *amount* of material in the cross section as it is on the *depth* of the section. The most efficient section has most of its material (cross-sectional area) furthest away from its neutral axis (Ill. 18). In doing this it is putting the most resistance where the stresses (compression and tension) are the greatest, at the top and the bottom of the section. Where the stresses are at their smallest (near the neutral axis), there is need for little material.

The wide-flange steel beam economically responds to this basic principle (Ill. 19). The member is designed in such a way as to put the most steel where it is needed, at the top and the bottom, to counter the bending stresses. The same principles apply to wood, but it is wasteful and expensive to cut wood in the wide-flange shape. Instead, wood is cut into rectangular sections of narrow width and large depth. Were timber to become as precious and costly a resource as steel, we might see lumbermills cutting more economically designed spanning members.

In conclusion, we have learned of the interrelationship between span, load, and the structural member's cross-sectional dimensions. In the design of joists, beams, and girders, all of these factors must be juggled to produce a satisfactory, economical structural solution.

THE ROOF STRUCTURE

A flat roof acts exactly like a floor and is structurally designed as a horizontal component system. Sloped roofs, on the other hand, present their own problems. If the slope of the roof is steep (over 20 degrees), it begins to differ from a strictly load-transferring horizontal component. The sloped roof transfers the load diagonally. This diagonal thrust must be broken down into a vertical and horizontal component in order to design for its proper support. The vertical component is supported by the walls (or beams to columns). The horizontal component, or lateral thrust, must be accounted for as well; otherwise there is a tendency for the roof to push out the walls (Ill. 20).

This outward thrust could be accommodated by placing a buttress against the outer walls. (That is the way the lateral thrust of the nave in the gothic cathedrals was countered, Ill. 21.) Buttressing, however, is clumsy and unwieldy. The thrust could be countered by tying the rafter ends together using a steel chain or a piece of timber. This section is in tension, that is, it is being pulled or stretched. The most common solution in houses is to use a wood section as a collar beam or as ceiling joists to tie the rafter ends to each other, thereby countering the thrust (Ill. 22).

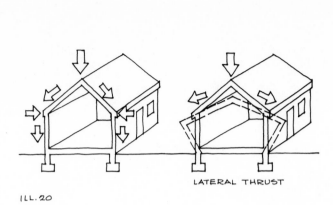

LATERAL THRUST

ILL. 20

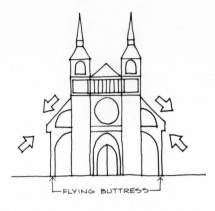

FLYING BUTTRESS

ILL. 21

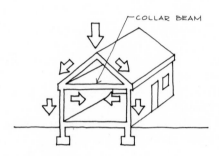

COLLAR BEAM

ILL. 22

7
Building Materials

One of the most important decisions affecting both the aesthetics and structure of your home is the selection of appropriate materials. A thorough understanding of materials readily available such as wood, stone, brick, concrete, and concrete block is essential before making such a decision.

WOOD

Because of the availability of timber in most parts of the country, the most popular choice in the United States has always been wood-frame construction. Approximately 80 percent of the homes built are structured in wood. Houses of timber were built when this country was in its infancy and many of these houses—now more than 200 years old—still stand. Today, both traditional and daring contemporary houses are constructed of this handsome, durable, and relatively inexpensive building material. Wood is not only used structurally as the support of the house (its "frame") but is used in siding, in the window frames, and often as roofing. Wood, being easily worked by a beginner and readily available, is the recommended choice of the authors. A house constructed of this material is easily repaired, altered, and expanded; its component parts are lightweight and combine easily. (On the debit side, however, is its combustibility and its edibility—by termites, that is.)

How Wood Works

Wood is almost always cut from the tree lengthwise, parallel to its long, sinuous fibers. It is strongest in this direction. Standing upright on a slim trunk, the living tree carries the weight of its branches, leaves, fruit, and the added loads of snow and wind (Ill. 1). Wood is very strong in compression, which means that it can carry a lot of weight. Long vertical pieces of lumber act as columns or mini-columns (called studs) and carry the entire weight of the second floor and the roof down to the foundation (Ill. 2).

Very often the tree is subjected to high winds, which cause it to bend. Wood's ability to bend (and not to break under pressure), to regain its original shape when the pressure is removed (its elasticity), and to resist completely succumbing to the bending forces (its stiffness) makes it a very good material to use horizontally as well as vertically. When a board is placed on its narrow side and made to span two supports, it is subjected to such bending stresses. The long sinews in wood, its fibers, resist these stresses (Ill. 3).

The living tree consists of about 55 percent moisture. When the tree is cut down (thus becoming deadwood), it loses its natural juices and shrinks. Often, the moisture content of the lumber is removed artificially by the mills in drying ovens called kilns. Ideally, the moisture should be about 19 percent for wood that is to be used structurally. Why is the moisture content so important? If the lumber is used "green" (straight from the tree without being dried

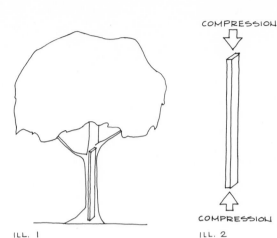

ILL. 1

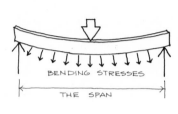

COMPRESSION

COMPRESSION

ILL. 2

BENDING STRESSES

THE SPAN

ILL. 3

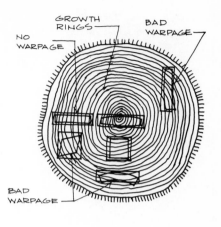

GROWTH RINGS

NO WARPAGE

BAD WARPAGE

BAD WARPAGE

ILL. 4

out), it will dry in time, and in doing so will shrink quite a bit, while other building materials such as tile, glass, masonry, gypsum board, etc., will not. Joints that were previously tight will become loose. Nails will become exposed, doors and windows will leak air. At the other extreme, if wood were oven-dried to remove all of its water, it would then have the tendency to thirstily absorb moisture from the air in great quantities. The swollen wood would cause doors and windows to stick in hot, humid weather. Wood swells and shrinks perpendicular to its grain, and in relation to how it is sliced from the tree trunk (Ill. 4).* Wood shrinks only slightly parallel to its grain (in its length).

Lumber

"Boards" usually refer to pieces of wood that are less than 2″ in depth, whereas "lumber" is wood cut into standard structural sizes and is generally over 2″ in depth. The "nominal" (rough) size is what it is called in the yard and on architectural drawings (2 × 4, 2 × 6). The actual, dressed dimensions of the lumber you take home are smaller. (A 2 × 4 will be ½″ smaller in two dimensions.) The reduction in

size of the lumber dimensions is justified as part of the milling process that standardizes lumber sizes by planing all four surfaces to a smooth, uniform product. You pay for the nominal size, but buy the actual member. Kiln-drying—which also plays a part in diminishing the size of the lumber—reduces the shrinkage that may take place in the finished house. The reductions in dimensions have been standardized, so that a 2 × 4 will always be exactly 1½″ by 3½″, and a 1 × 12 will always measure 25/32″ × 11¼″. Inset I gives the actual dimensions of the most common nominal sizes. The length of the board, by the way, is not affected. When you buy a 14′ long board it should measure 14′.

Lumber is sold in lengths up to 24′. Although you can have lumber cut to any size (under 24′), it is more efficient to use it in the standard lengths in which it is sold—less waste, less labor. Yard lumber is commonly sold in lengths of 8′, 10′, 12′, 14′, and 16′. Lumber longer than 16′ may be difficult to find in all areas and/or more costly. Lumber longer than 24′, whether cut from one piece or laminated,* is very expensive and should not be needed for residential construction. It is a good idea to plan the joists in modules of 2′ so that you will not have to cut longer sections down.

TYPES AND GRADES OF LUMBER: Many kinds of wood are used for construction pur-

---

* Warpage depends on the original moisture content of the wood and where in relationship to its annual rings the cut was made. In purchasing lumber you cannot examine each piece to check the annual ring pattern. You can, however, avoid excessive warping by buying kiln-dried (preshrunk) lumber.

* Laminated means several thin layers of wood being bonded together to form one solid piece.

INSET I / NOMINAL AND DRESSED SIZES OF SOFTWOOD LUMBER

(These are the "actual" dimensions for the following "nominal" sizes. When you purchase a 2 × 4, the actual lumber you go home with is 1½″ × 3½″.)

		Nominal	Actual (dry)	Green
Boards	(up to 12″ wide)	1″	¾″	
		1¼″	1″	
		1½″	1¼″	
Lumber	(thickness: 2″, 3″, 4″;	2″	1½″	1⁹/₁₆″
	width: up to 12″	3″	2½″	2⁹/₁₆″
	and over)	4″	3½″	3⁹/₁₆″
		6″	5½″	5⅝″
		8″	7¼″	7½″
		10″	9¼″	9½″
		12″	11¼″	11½″
		over 12″	less ¾″	less ½″
Timbers	(5″ thick and over)	5″ and larger	less ½″	less ½″
Decking	(tongue-and-groove boards)	2″ (thick)	1½″	
		3″	2½″	
		4″	3½″	

NLGA RULE
NO. 1
S-GRN
HEM-FIR N

ILL. 5

poses and each variety of tree is divided further into grades depending on the quality of the sample cut. Wood is classified as either softwood or hardwood (misleading terms, because they have absolutely nothing to do with the strength of the timber). Hardwoods are cut from deciduous trees (trees that lose their leaves in the winter) and are used primarily in the making of furniture and for fine interior trim. Softwoods refer to lumber cut from conifers, or trees that have needles. This wood is used for structural framing. Examples of softwoods are southern pine, Douglas fir, and hem-fir.

Each type of wood (named after the tree from which it is cut) is further divided into grades. The building code writers and the lumber industry carefully grade the lumber on criteria of strength, usage, and imperfections. Reading through the lists is much like reading the guidelines from the Internal Revenue Service. What complicates matters further is that you will be buying lumber from a small retail dealer, who will most likely stock only one variety of mixed or unknown grade.

Lumber is classified into two major grade categories: stress-graded lumber—used in larger buildings for long spans; and yard lumber—used for light framing, one-family houses, etc.

You will not generally find stress-graded lumber in the lumberyard; it is usually ordered specially. Yard lumber is divided into the following subcategories: *select-structural*—the best of the yard lumber—will be clear, that is, without knotholes, bark, splits, or other defects; *construction* (also called no. 1); *standard and better* (no. 2); and *utility* (no. 3). No. 1 lumber is used for horizontal purposes, no. 2 is used vertically. Lumber sold in the yards bears the stamp of the manufacturer, indicating the tree from which it was cut, its grade, and its moisture content (Ill. 5). Sometimes the stamp may indicate the suggested usage as well, such as "stud" (Insets II and III).

MASONRY

Parallel to the development of wood-frame houses was that of masonry houses. The Georgian-style house became popular in the South, where red clay soil is abundantly found for the manufacturing of bricks. In areas where stone could be easily quarried, the wealthy commissioned mansions built of cut rock. Its enormous durability and beautiful texture have made

LUMBER CUT FOR HORIZONTAL USE

Joists: Usually 2″ (nominal) in thickness used to directly support floor or ceiling, and supported in turn by a larger horizontal member (beam or girder) or a bearing wall. Joists are generally spaced at small, regular intervals, such as 12″, 16″, or 24″ on center.

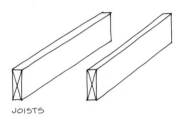

JOISTS

Beams: Larger (in cross section, not necessarily in length) than joists. Used to support joists and transfer their loads to vertical supports (or to girders).

Girders: Similar to beams, only larger in cross section.

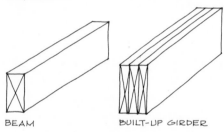

BEAM   BUILT-UP GIRDER

Planks: 2″ in thickness (could be 3″ or 4″). Used as flooring, roofing, or decking, directly over and supported by beams.

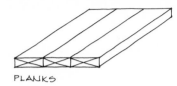

PLANKS

LUMBER CUT FOR VERTICAL USE

Posts: Vertical supports, usually short.

Columns: Vertical supports, longer than posts. Used to transfer horizontal loads down to the foundations.

Studs: Mini-columns. A series of slender structural members placed at small, regular intervals as the supporting elements in load-bearing wood walls and partitions.

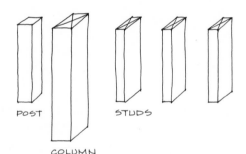

POST   STUDS

COLUMN

LUMBER CUT FOR DIAGONAL USE

Bracing: A piece of lumber applied to the frame on the diagonal to stiffen the structure.

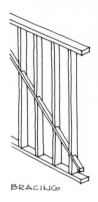

BRACING

Bridging: Used in an "X" pattern between the joists to stiffen the floor.

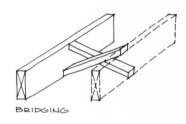

BRIDGING

---

stone and brick the choices of the builders of some of America's finest homes. Masonry construction is guaranteed not to burn, rot, or require periodic painting. Its handsome exterior is virtually maintenance free. If you are considering building a house of masonry, there are a number of important disadvantages to consider as well. First, brick and stone are more expensive than wood; second, masonry skills are more difficult to master than simple carpentry; and third, building in masonry is generally more time consuming. For those of you who still dream of a house constructed of brick (or for those who are contemplating building a masonry fireplace or wall) we include this section.

Masonry refers to natural materials such as stone, and man-made materials such as brick, concrete, clay, and other cast or poured materials that are bonded together with mortar.

Stone

Although stone is one of civilization's oldest and most beautiful building materials, it would be irresponsible of us to recommend your undertaking so massive a project as building a stone dwelling. The material is hard to find, expensive to buy, back-breaking to quarry, tricky to cut, heavy to haul, and time consuming to lay. For those of you who require further discouragement, we repeat a story told to us by a friend about a friend in Vermont. This ambitious person decided to quarry the stone on his property and build a small house out of it. Now,

Building Materials

67

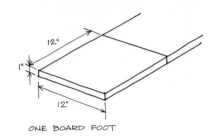
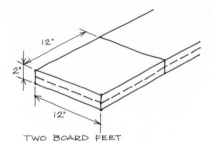
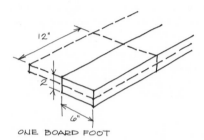
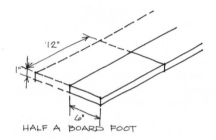
two years later, and only half finished, he regrets that decision. He expected the work to be time consuming and difficult. He expected the back pain and the bruises. What he did not expect was the unrelieved tedium of the project. He may not continue.

Brick

There are many types of brick. Some are marketed for great strength, some for unique color, and others for unusual size. Bricks are made out of clay that is either dug from underground tunnels or stripped from the surface of the earth. Essentially, the raw clay is dried, crushed into a fine powder, and mixed with water to a mud consistency. The clay is then molded into units, dried in ovens, and finally baked in high-temperature kilns. This is the age-old procedure for manufacturing the bricks you might come into contact with.

Bricks are named according to the clay they are manufactured from (fire clay or otherwise), the kind of method used in shaping the units (sand or water struck), the care taken in the manufacturing procedure (face brick or common), the built-in strength, or the finish applied to the face after the initial firing (glazed brick).

Common brick is made from surface clays and shales. Although the standards for color and texture are not particularly rigorous, common brick is graded into three categories. The first grade, SW (severe weather), is for brick that is to be used for exterior construction in climates that combine wetness with temperatures below freezing. The second grade, MW (moderate weather), is for exterior use in dry climates that might possibly be subject to freezing temperatures. The third classification, NW (no weather), is for interior use.

Face brick is similar to common brick but is manufactured with greater care given to color and texture. Most important civic or commercial buildings would be constructed of face brick of one kind or another.

Fire brick is constructed of fire clay, which is mined underground. The clay itself has an enormous resistance to heat, and fire brick is used exclusively in areas of high heat intensity, such as fireplaces and furnace rooms.

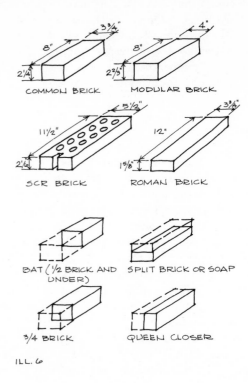

COMMON BRICK   MODULAR BRICK

SCR BRICK   ROMAN BRICK

BAT (½ BRICK AND UNDER)   SPLIT BRICK OR SOAP

¾ BRICK   QUEEN CLOSER

ILL. 6

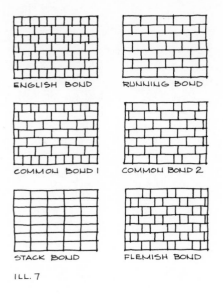

ENGLISH BOND   RUNNING BOND

COMMON BOND 1   COMMON BOND 2

STACK BOND   FLEMISH BOND

ILL. 7

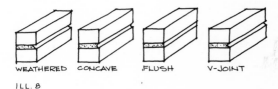

WEATHERED   CONCAVE   FLUSH   V-JOINT

ILL. 8

Glazed brick is fire brick coated with a ceramic glaze and then kiln-baked. The resulting brick might have a glossy or matte finish. A wide range of color possibilities is available in glazed brick.

Brick comes in many sizes and shapes (Ill. 6). The standard brick size (which includes the bricks described above) is 2¼″ high × 3¾″ wide × 8″ long. The term "red brick" covers a surprisingly large range of shades from palest pink to oxblood. Brown brick bonded with dark mortar is becoming increasingly popular.

Included in the aesthetic decisions to b̶ ̶a̶d̶ before choosing a particular build̶ ̶ ̶ ̶ ̶ its texture and the method in which ̶ ̶ ̶ ̶ be bonded together into a wall (Ill. 7). Other considerations include the type of bonding material, its color, the width of the joints, and the method that will be used by the mason to "strike" the joints (Ill. 8).

Brick, although very strong in compression, is weak in tension. Because it is an inelastic material and cannot resist bending stresses, brick cannot be used as a beam. It may, however, be made to span as an arch, where it is acting purely in compression.

All of the above is but a brief introduction to the material. Consult the Bibliography for further references if more information is desired.

BRICK CONSTRUCTION METHODS: There are more ways to build a brick wall than there are to skin a cat. Brick may be used as the building's structural material (its load-bearing walls and piers being the sole support for the floors and the roof), or it might be used as an enclosing material to flesh out a skeleton constructed of wood or steel. In residential construction both methods are used. Brick is often used in conjunction with a balloon-frame skeleton in a one-family house (Ill. 9). When used as a load-bearing material, the brick wall is most often constructed of 8″ of solid brick, or of concrete block backing one layer of brick (Ills. 10 and 11).*

* Very often the professional bricklayer will construct what is called a "cavity" wall. The cavity wall has a wythe (layer) of brick and one of concrete block behind it. In between the layers is an air space of about 2″. This space acts dually as an insulator and to prevent the penetration of water into the interior space. We will not dwell on this type of construction any further since the construction of the cavity wall is a difficult skill to master.

Building
Materials

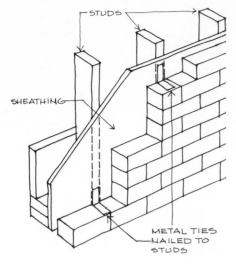

STUDS

SHEATHING

METAL TIES
NAILED TO
STUDS

ILL. 9

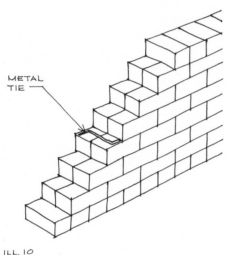

METAL
TIE

ILL. 10

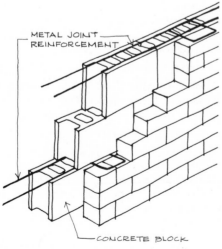

METAL JOINT
REINFORCEMENT

CONCRETE BLOCK

ILL. 11

Although the structure and the exterior finish of the aforementioned walls are one and the same, the interior of the wall will have to be further treated for waterproofing and for insulating in temperate or more severe climates. See Chapter 13 for insulation details.

Concrete

The whole house or its foundations can be constructed of stone, wood, or concrete. The most commonly used materials for foundations are concrete and its manufactured products such as concrete block. Concrete can best be described as a shapeless man-made stone. It has all the durability and compressive strength of stone plus the additional advantage of being suitable for casting into any number of shapes, a property which makes concrete a very versatile building material.

Concrete is made up of four components: fine aggregates (sand), coarse aggregates (crushed stone), Portland cement (see Inset IV), and water, which are mixed to form a paste. The chemical reaction between the cement and water causes concrete to harden into a rock-like material. Portland cement triggers the process of hardening (known as hydration), when it is mixed with the water. The coarse aggregates are usually crushed stone or gravel of varying sizes. Sand is used to fill in the voids in the mixture. Water is added, not only to react with the cement but also to increase the workability of the mixture. Care must be taken in adding water, however, since the more water added, the less strong the concrete. Proportions and mixtures of concrete vary according to the nature of the job to be performed. In other words, the concrete mixture required for concrete beams may be different from that used for foundation walls and footings.

Mixing concrete is a skill learned through experience and not by formulas. Since the mixing of concrete is learned largely through trial and error, it may take a long time before you come up with the correct mixture. Instead of experimenting with the material, it may prove wisest to purchase mixed concrete, ready to be poured from the spout at the rear of the supplier's mixer-truck.

Ready-mixed concrete has a number of other benefits besides sparing you a tedious job. First, the manufacturing process assures you a mixture of uniform quality. When you mix small batches of concrete by yourself, there are many variables and openings for error. One batch may be fine, another unworkable, and yet a third, too wet. On the other hand, when you purchase concrete already mixed, you order the exact mixture you require from the supplier. He will in turn provide you with concrete of the specified strength, for example, the recommended mixture for footing and foundation work. (It is not a bad idea to request a written guarantee stating that the concrete mixture delivered to you is of the specified strength and quality.) Secondly, ordering from a supplier allows you to pour the concrete evenly without having to worry about mixing new batches before the first pour sets (dries up). Look in the Yellow Pages or inquire at your local lumberyard for companies in your area that offer this service. Make sure to check that they sell the quantities you need. (See page 72, Inset V.)

Concrete, like stone and brick, is very strong in compression but weak in tension. It can manage the compressive stresses by itself but does not hold up too well under stretching and bending forces (tension). To compensate for this, concrete is often combined with steel to withstand bending and produce a more efficient and much stronger material—reinforced concrete. Steel bars are imbedded in the concrete. The concrete then carries the compressive load while the steel (an excellent material in tension) takes care of the tensile stresses. Reinforcing steel bars are placed in the area where there is tension (Ill. 12). Reinforcement is almost always placed specifically in the lower portion of the simply supported horizontal beam, where most of the "stretching" occurs.

One of the major advantages of concrete is also one of its drawbacks: having to be molded and shaped by forms. Erecting formwork is not easy. It involves lots of carpentry work and great care. Forms have to be well constructed. They must be tight, rigid, and strong enough to sustain the weight of the concrete. In addition, they should be easy to remove from the dried concrete (see Chapter 20). The construction of formwork for continuous foundation walls might take the beginner many days of work. The cost of lumber for the forms is an additional deterrent. The professional contractor will use old lumber over and over again in formwork. The new home builder usually does not have a garage full of old lumber to be recycled for forms. He must purchase new wood and will probably have to discard the material after he peels it off the solidified concrete.

An option to wood formwork is prefabricated metal forms. These forms are available commercially and are simpler and faster to erect than wood ones. The cost of renting them should be compared to the cost of lumber formwork both in terms of time and materials. The Yellow Pages or the manufacturers of ready-mixed concrete can probably tell you whether prefabricated formwork is available locally.

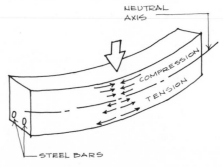

ILL. 12

Building Materials

71

INSET V / HOW TO ESTIMATE QUANTITIES OF CONCRETE

Concrete is sold by the cubic yard. In order to estimate the amount of concrete you need, multiply the length of the wall or pier (in feet) × its width (in feet) × its height or depth (in feet or inches), and then divide the result by 27 (3' × 3' × 3') to convert cubic feet to cubic yards. (If one of the figures is in inches, don't forget to divide that figure by 12 to convert into feet.) To illustrate the procedure we will use our sample house. Let's assume that the footings are 12" deep and 24" wide.

The foundation walls are 12" wide and 4'-0" high. In addition, we have two piers, each of which is 12" square and 4'-0" high, sitting on footings which are 24" square and 12" high.

FOOTINGS:
$$33'\text{-}0'' \times 2'\text{-}0'' \times 1'\text{-}0'' = 66 \text{ cu. ft.} \times 2 = 132 \text{ cu. ft.}$$
$$20'\text{-}0'' \times 2'\text{-}0'' \times 1'\text{-}0'' = 40 \text{ cu. ft.} \times 2 = \underline{80 \text{ cu. ft.}}$$
$$212 \text{ cu. ft.}$$

To convert into yards:

$$\frac{212}{27} = 7.85 \text{ cu. yds. required for footings}$$

FOUNDATION WALLS:
$$32'\text{-}0'' \times 4'\text{-}0'' \times 1'\text{-}0'' = 128 \text{ cu. ft.} \times 2 = 256 \text{ cu. ft.}$$
$$23'\text{-}0'' \times 4'\text{-}0'' \times 1'\text{-}0'' = 92 \text{ cu. ft.} \times 2 = \underline{184 \text{ cu. ft.}}$$
$$440 \text{ cu. ft.}$$

To convert into cubic yards:

$$\frac{440}{27} = 16.3 \text{ cu. yds. required for foundation walls}$$

PIERS:
$$4'\text{-}0'' \times 1'\text{-}0'' \times 1'\text{-}0'' = 4 \text{ cu. ft.}$$
$$2'\text{-}0'' \times 2'\text{-}0'' \times 1'\text{-}0'' = \underline{4 \text{ cu. ft.}}$$
$$8 \text{ cu. ft.}$$

There are 2 piers = 8 cu. ft. × 2 = 16 cu. ft.

To convert into cubic yards:

$$\frac{16}{27} = .59 = .6 \text{ cu. yd. required for piers}$$

Add all parts:
footings	=	7.85 cu. yds.
foundation wall	=	16.3 cu. yds.
piers	=	.6 cu. yd.
		24.75 cu. yds.

Allow 10 percent for waste:
Total cu. yds. = 24.75 + 2.4 = 27.2 cu. yds.

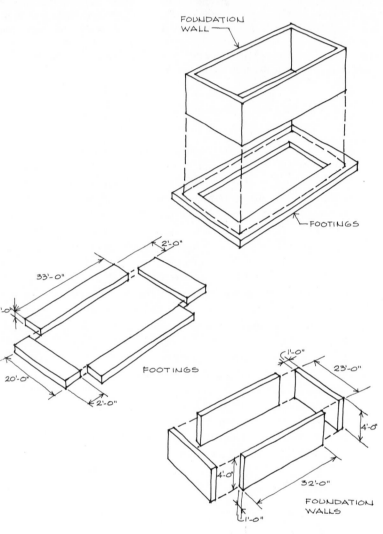

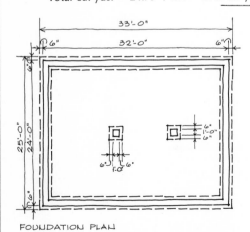

FOUNDATION PLAN

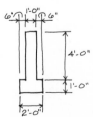

FOUNDATION WALL SECTION

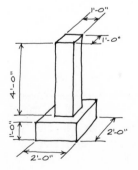

The American Society for Testing Materials (ASTM) has classified concrete block into the following categories: NI, NII, SI, SII. The letters "N" or "S" denote the block's resistance to frost action. Grade "N" units are to be used in areas subject to freezing, thawing, and with direct exposure to moisture (that is, walls above and below grade). Grade "S" units should be used only in walls that are not exposed to weather. The designations "I" and "II" are indicators of the moisture content of the block. Type "I" units have a low maximum moisture content and are intended for use in areas with a low relative humidity (such as desert regions). Type "II" units have no specified moisture content and can be used where relative humidity is average to high (most of the United States).

Concrete Block

Concrete block is a newcomer to residential construction. For this reason, there's been a tendency to cover the block's surface with other, more traditional materials like brick or stone. People still feel that concrete block is part of the warehouse aesthetic, and are reluctant to use it as the material for their house. They are surprised to find out that concrete block comes in a great variety of textures and colors, which when left "natural" can be interesting. (It is not unusual to paint concrete block, and there are special paints available for this purpose. Painting will, of course, add to the block's future maintenance.)

Concrete block is a manufactured product made up of the same components as concrete. The mix proportions and the curing process are closely regulated, resulting in a product of uniform quality. Concrete block is both quicker to erect and less expensive than stone, brick, or poured-in-place concrete, while at the same time offering their durability and low maintenance. Among the many shapes and sizes in which concrete block is available, the stretcher block is the most popular.

The stretcher is an all-purpose block with nominal dimensions of 8″ × 8″ × 16″ (actual: 7⅝″ × 7⅝″ × 15⅝″). A corner and double corner (or pier block) are used in conjunction with the stretcher block for end conditions (Ill. 13).

When you go to buy block, you will find that the material is divided into four classifications. These categories have been created by the American Society for Testing Materials to be used as a guide when purchasing masonry. They deal with resistance to frost action and moisture content (Inset VI).

Concrete block is also rated according to strength, ranging from solid load-bearing block

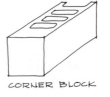

STRETCHER BLOCK   CORNER BLOCK   DOUBLE CORNER OR PIER BLOCK

ILL. 13

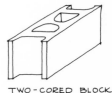

THREE-CORED BLOCK   TWO-CORED BLOCK

ILL. 14

for jobs where heavy compressive strength is required, to hollow non-load-bearing block for use as non-load-bearing partitions. The most commonly used block, however, is the hollow load-bearing block, since it offers a great range of uses and is most readily available. It has a good capacity for carrying compressive stresses, in addition to being lightweight and coming in a wide range of shapes and sizes.

One further breakdown of blocks is into two- and three-cored units, each with slightly different physical properties. Two-cored units have larger holes than three-cored ones, thereby containing less concrete and consequently being lighter and slightly cheaper. Because of the larger air space, they have better insulating qualities. Three-cored blocks, on the other hand, have more concrete mass, greater compressive strength, and more bearing surface. Three-cored blocks are a better choice for jobs where compressive stresses are coming directly from above (such as would be required for foundation walls and piers). Two-cored blocks would be best suited for regular walls and partitions (Ill. 14).

Concrete-block walls are laid up in a running pattern similar to brick (see Chapter 20).

Building
Materials
73

INSET VII / WHICH SIDE OF THE CONCRETE BLOCK SHOULD FACE UP?

Because the cores in the block are tapered, one face has smaller cavities than the other and, therefore, more concrete bearing surface. In order to get maximum bonding with the mortar, the side with the smaller cores should always face up.

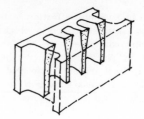

INSET VIII / HOW TO ESTIMATE QUANTITIES OF CONCRETE BLOCK

If you are using 8" × 16" concrete block, you will need approximately 110 blocks for every 100 square feet of wall area. For example, if you are building a wall 8'-0" high and 30'-0" long, the wall area is 240 square feet:

$$\frac{240}{100} = 2.4$$

110 blocks × 2.4 = 264 blocks

8
Floor Systems

The next series of design decisions is governed by structural determinants rather than by aesthetic ones. The first decision is whether the floor will be of wood-frame construction or of cast-in-place concrete.

The use of concrete is limited to the first floor of a basementless house. The advantage of the slab in a one-story house is that all the pipes and plumbing lines can be laid out in advance and the concrete poured over them. Its disadvantages are that it is difficult to moisture-proof and very tricky to construct properly. Since we do not recommend that you attempt this labor on your own, this book does not contain instructions on pouring the slab. If you wish to construct a slab on grade, contact a professional.

A wood platform floor (Ill. 1), on the other hand, is simple to construct and can be used on any level of the house, above a basement, or over a crawl space.*

It is easier to understand the design of the floor system if one first has a clearer understanding of how the floor works. Simply stated, each component of the floor acts to transfer the weight placed on it to the earth on which the house stands. The floorboards receive the live loads and transfer that weight plus their own weight to the joists. The joists add their own structural weight and transfer the loads to the girders or beams, which in turn transfer the loads to the vertical supports or directly to the foundations. Eventually all of the live and dead loads are transferred by the foundation's footings to Mother Earth herself. The trick is to get the loads transferred *evenly* to the ground without putting undue stress on any of the components.

THE PLATFORM FLOOR

In our discussion of the walls used in platform-frame construction we mentioned that one of the advantages of this framing method is that the walls and the floor are constructed separately. The platform floor is exactly that, a platform. It consists of a subfloor (the finished floor is laid much later, after the danger of its being ruined by rain, cement drippings, paint, etc., has passed), which is nailed to the floor joists. The subfloor is usually made of sheets of plywood. The floor joists are long, slender horizontal members spaced either 12", 16", or 24" apart.*

---

* The only place it would not be used is in a garage.

* Why the 16", 12", or 24" spacing? This spacing is used for studs, floor joists, and roof rafters. It is a modular unit derived from the fact that most sheathing materials come in 4' × 8' units. 4 feet = 48". Forty-eight inches divided by 16" = 3 even spacings, 48" divided by 24" = 2 spacings, 48" divided by 12" = 4. This ensures that the sheathing or subfloor or interior panels or exterior siding (all of which come in the modular 4' width) has a nailing surface on both of its long sides (see Ill. 2).

For similar reasons the distances between structural components are measured "on center," abbreviated o.c. A 16" o.c. designation for the joists means that there is a 16" distance between the center line of one joist and the center line of the next.

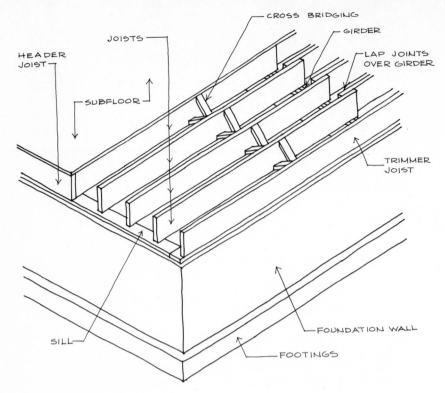

HEADER JOIST

JOISTS

CROSS BRIDGING

GIRDER

LAP JOINTS OVER GIRDER

SUBFLOOR

TRIMMER JOIST

FOUNDATION WALL

SILL

FOOTINGS

ILL. 1

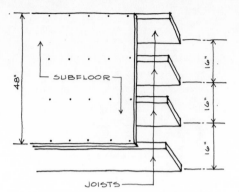

48"

SUBFLOOR

16"

16"

16"

16"

JOISTS

ILL. 2

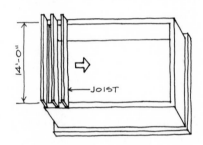

14'-0"

JOIST

ILL. 3

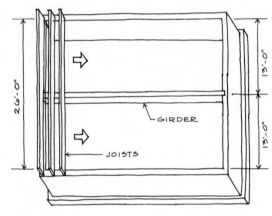

26'-0"

13'-0"

13'-0"

GIRDER

JOISTS

ILL. 4

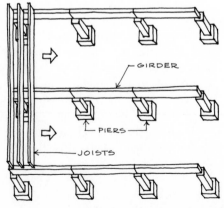

GIRDER

PIERS

JOISTS

ILL. 5

These joists span between supports. Both supports could be continuous foundation walls (Ill. 3). More likely the joists will span between a foundation wall and an intermediate girder (Ill. 4). If the foundations are not continuous, the joists will span from a perimeter girder to an intermediate girder (Ill. 5).

In a house with continuous foundation walls the joists frame into a member called the header (Ill. 1). If the house sits on piers, the joists frame either into a header or directly into the girder. The header is usually the same size (the same cross-sectional dimensions) as the joists. It is used as a nailing surface for the joists (giving them added rigidity) and also serves to enclose the space and to keep out unwanted animals and drafts. The end joist that sits on the foundation wall parallel to the run of the joists is called the trimmer joist. It closes off those ends of the house and carries the end load of the floor and the wall (Ill. 1).

Both the headers and the trimmers sit on a mud sill (pressure treated to resist rot and insects), a wood board generally 2" × 6" or 2" × 8", which lies directly on top of the foundation wall and is bolted to it with anchor bolts (Ill. 1). The remaining structural element of the floor system is the bridging. The cross bridging or solid bridging helps make the floor more rigid.

The bridging holds the joists in straight, reducing the potential movement in the floor (Ill. 1). A well-designed and constructed floor should not creak. Although a tiny bit of resilience is tolerable, if not actually desirable, a creaky floor is not.

As we discussed in Chapter 6, the design of the floor system is determined by the loads on the floor, the distance the beams and joists must span, and the strength of the lumber you are going to use. Knowing all of these factors you can specify the dimensions, spacing, and length of the joists and beams.

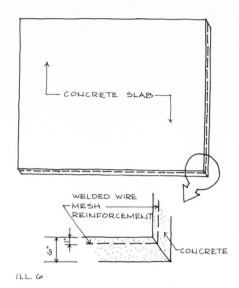

ILL. 6

LOADS

The building code in most regions of the United States has established 40 pounds per square foot (from now on referred to as 40 psf) as the live load you must allow for on the first floor of a one-family residence (30 psf may be used for the second floor, if there are to be only bedrooms there, and for the attic). Forty psf means that you *must* design the floor with the ability to carry forty pounds on every square foot of space. If that does not sound like much to you, picture a room 10' by 10' with one hundred five-year-old kids crammed into it. Our design charts (Tables A and B) incorporate these design load requirements. The loads cover normal household furniture such as bookshelves and pianos. If you intend to install a heavier piece of equipment (for example, an industrial-sized printing press), visit your local building department for special load tables. The garage must be designed for 50 psf live load. Most houses, whether designed for a concrete-slab floor or a wood-frame floor, use a minimum of 6" thick concrete slab for the floor of the garage, reinforced with welded wire fabric placed 1" below the top of the slab (Ill. 6).

SPANS

The design span is determined by the floor plan of the building. If the house is to be less than 18' or 20' wide, you may be able to span from foundation wall to foundation wall without needing any intermediate supports (Ill. 3). If the house is to be over 24' wide, you will need an intermediate support, which will reduce the span in half (Ill. 4). There are borderline cases. For instance, if the house plan is 20' wide, you could specify floor joists that are 20' long. These joists will be able to carry the load without fear of failure. It may turn out, however, that your floor will have too much bounce to it (the needle of the phonograph might bounce up every time someone crosses the room). For the borderline cases we recommend breaking the span in two. In addition, lumber over 14'-0" might be difficult to come by. The length of the joists might be determined by the lengths available in the local lumberyard.

JOIST DESIGN

The design of the floor joists is relatively simple. The reason for its simplicity is the availability of joist charts, which have compiled all the mathematical calculations onto one page. All that is left for you to do is to feed the charts the required span of the joists and the type of lumber you will be using. The chart spits out the cross-sectional dimensions of the appropriate structural member.

Let us use, as an example, a house 24' wide. We decide that the 24' span will be broken into two spans of 12' each. Therefore, the joist span is 12'. Our first choice for the lumber is Douglas fir, a long-time favorite of architects and contractors. After visiting the lumberyard, we discover that Douglas fir is in short supply this season. We are advised to use hem-fir, which is

TABLE A: FLOOR JOISTS—40 PSF LIVE LOAD*

		Joist size (inches)							
		2 × 6		2 × 8		2 × 10		2 × 12	
Species	Grade	Joist spacing (inches)							
		12	16	12	16	12	16	12	16
		Maximum allowable span (feet and inches)							
Coast sitka spruce	select structural	10-11	9-11	14-5	13-1	18-5	16-9	22-5	20-4
	no. 1 & appearance	10-11	9-9	14-5	12-10	18-5	16-4	22-5	19-11
	no. 2	10-3	8-11	13-7	11-9	17-4	15-0	21-1	18-3
	no. 3	7-9	6-9	10-3	8-11	13-1	11-4	15-11	13-9
Douglas fir-larch (north)	select structural	11-2	10-2	14-8	13-4	18-9	17-0	22-10	20-9
	no. 1 & appearance	11-2	10-2	14-8	13-4	18-9	17-0	22-10	20-9
	no. 2	10-11	9-11	14-5	13-1	18-5	16-9	22-5	20-4
	no. 3	9-3	8-0	12-2	10-7	15-7	13-6	18-11	16-5
Eastern hemlock-tamarack (north)	select structural	10-0	9-1	13-2	12-0	16-10	15-3	20-6	18-7
	no. 1 & appearance	10-0	9-1	13-2	12-0	16-10	15-3	20-6	18-7
	no. 2	9-6	8-7	12-6	11-4	15-11	14-6	19-4	17-7
	no. 3	8-7	7-5	11-3	9-9	14-5	12-5	17-6	15-2
Hem-fir (north)	select structural	10-6	9-6	13-10	12-7	17-8	16-0	21-6	19-6
	no. 1 & appearance	10-6	9-6	13-10	12-7	17-8	16-0	21-6	19-6
	no. 2	10-3	9-4	13-6	12-3	17-3	15-8	21-0	19-1
	no. 3	8-3	7-2	10-11	9-5	13-11	12-0	16-11	14-7
Ponderosa pine	select structural	9-9	8-10	12-10	11-8	16-5	14-11	19-11	18-1
	no. 1 & appearance	9-9	8-10	12-10	11-8	16-5	14-11	19-11	18-1
	no. 2	9-6	8-7	12-6	11-4	15-11	14-5	19-4	17-7
	no. 3	7-7	6-7	10-0	8-8	12-10	11-1	15-7	13-6
Red pine	select structural	10-0	9-1	13-2	12-0	16-10	15-3	20-6	18-7
	no. 1 & appearance	10-0	9-1	13-2	12-0	16-10	15-3	20-6	18-7
	no. 2	9-9	8-6	12-10	11-2	16-5	14-3	19-11	17-4
	no. 3	7-5	6-5	9-10	8-6	12-6	10-10	15-3	13-2
Spruce-pine-fir	select structural	10-6	9-6	13-10	12-7	17-8	16-0	21-6	19-6
	no. 1 & appearance	10-6	9-6	13-10	12-7	17-8	16-0	21-6	19-6
	no. 2	10-0	8-8	13-2	11-6	16-10	14-8	20-6	17-9
	no. 3	7-7	6-7	10-0	8-8	12-10	11-1	15-7	13-6
Western cedars (north)	select structural	9-6	8-7	12-6	11-4	15-11	14-6	19-4	17-7
	no. 1 & appearance	9-6	8-7	12-6	11-4	15-11	14-6	19-4	17-7
	no. 2	9-2	8-4	12-1	11-0	15-5	14-0	18-9	17-0
	no. 3	7-9	6-9	10-3	8-11	13-1	11-4	15-11	13-9
Western white pine	select structural	10-3	9-4	13-6	12-3	17-3	15-8	21-0	19-1
	no. 1 & appearance	10-3	9-4	13-6	12-3	17-3	15-8	21-0	19-1
	no. 2	9-8	8-4	12-9	11-0	16-3	14-1	19-9	17-1
	no. 3	7-5	6-5	9-10	8-6	12-6	10-10	15-3	13-2

*To be used for activity floors.

a bit cheaper than Douglas fir, not as strong, but readily available. The lumber agent is stocked with both no. 1 grade and no. 2 grade. He informs us, off the record, that most of the local building contractors are using no. 1 hem-fir for all the horizontal members, such as joists and beams, and no. 2 (a lower grade) for the wall studs. That seems good enough for us. We de-

cide to specify no. 1 hem-fir for the joists and girders.

Going to the simplified joist table, designed specifically for a live load of 40 psf (Table A), we read down the left-hand column and find hem-fir (north) no. 1. The numbers in the boxes are the span designations in feet and inches. Reading across the line from left to right we

TABLE B: FLOOR JOISTS—30 PSF LIVE LOAD*

		Joist size (inches)							
		2 × 6		2 × 8		2 × 10		2 × 12	
Species	Grade	Joist spacing (inches)							
		12	16	12	16	12	16	12	16
		Maximum allowable span (feet and inches)							
Coast sitka spruce	select structural	12-0	10-11	15-10	14-5	20-3	18-5	24-8	22-5
	no. 1 & appearance	12-0	10-10	15-10	14-4	20-3	18-3	24-8	22-3
	no. 2	11-6	10-0	15-2	13-2	19-4	16-9	23-6	20-5
	no. 3	8-8	7-6	11-6	9-11	14-8	12-8	17-9	15-5
Douglas fir-larch (north)	select structural	12-3	11-2	16-2	14-8	20-8	18-9	25-1	22-10
	no. 1 & appearance	12-3	11-2	16-2	14-8	20-8	18-9	25-1	22-10
	no. 2	12-0	10-11	15-10	14-5	20-3	18-5	24-8	22-5
	no. 3	10-4	9-0	13-8	11-10	17-5	15-1	21-2	18-4
Eastern hemlock-tamarack (north)	select structural	11-0	10-0	14-6	13-2	18-6	16-10	22-6	20-6
	no. 1 & appearance	11-0	10-0	14-6	13-2	18-6	16-10	22-6	20-6
	no. 2	10-5	9-6	13-9	12-6	17-6	15-11	21-4	19-4
	no. 3	9-7	8-3	12-7	10-11	16-1	13-11	19-7	16-11
Hem-fir (north)	select structural	11-7	10-6	15-3	13-10	19-5	17-8	23-7	21-6
	no. 1 & appearance	11-7	10-6	15-3	13-10	19-5	17-8	23-7	21-6
	no. 2	11-3	10-3	14-11	13-6	19-0	17-3	23-1	21-0
	no. 3	9-3	8-0	12-2	10-6	15-6	13-5	18-10	16-4
Ponderosa pine	select structural	10-9	9-9	14-2	12-10	18-0	16-5	21-11	19-11
	no. 1 & appearance	10-9	9-9	14-2	12-10	18-0	16-5	21-11	19-11
	no. 2	10-5	9-6	13-9	12-6	17-6	15-11	21-4	19-4
	no. 3	8-6	7-4	11-3	9-9	14-4	12-5	17-5	15-1
Red pine	select structural	11-0	10-0	14-6	13-2	18-6	16-10	22-6	20-6
	no. 1 & appearance	11-0	10-0	14-6	13-2	18-6	16-10	22-6	20-6
	no. 2	10-9	9-6	14-2	12-6	18-0	15-11	21-11	19-5
	no. 3	8-4	7-3	11-0	9-6	14-0	12-2	17-0	14-9
Spruce-pine-fir	select structural	11-7	10-6	15-3	13-10	19-5	17-8	23-7	21-6
	no. 1 & appearance	11-7	10-6	15-3	13-10	19-5	17-8	23-7	21-6
	no. 2	11-0	9-9	14-6	12-10	18-6	16-4	22-6	19-11
	no. 3	8-6	7-4	11-3	9-9	14-4	12-5	17-5	15-1
Western cedars (north)	select structural	10-5	9-6	13-9	12-6	17-6	15-11	21-4	19-4
	no. 1 & appearance	10-5	9-6	13-9	12-6	17-6	15-11	21-4	19-4
	no. 2	10-1	9-2	13-4	12-1	17-0	15-5	20-8	18-9
	no. 3	8-8	7-6	11-6	9-11	14-8	12-8	17-9	15-5
Western white pine	select structural	11-3	10-3	14-11	13-6	19-0	17-3	23-1	21-0
	no. 1 & appearance	11-3	10-3	14-11	13-6	19-0	17-3	23-1	21-0
	no. 2	10-10	9-4	14-3	12-4	18-2	15-8	22-1	19-2
	no. 3	8-4	7-3	11-0	9-6	14-0	12-2	17-0	14-9

*To be used for sleeping rooms exclusively.

pass 10'-6", 9'-6", 13'-10", and stop at 12'-7". We look up that column to discover that the structural member made out of no. 1 hem-fir that can span 12'-7" with a live load of 40 psf on the floor is a 2 × 8 spaced 16" on center. If we continue reading across the line, we will find that the other span lengths are either too long or too short. We had skipped over the span length of 13'-10" previously. The same 2 × 8 could span the distance of 13'-10" if it were spaced 12" o.c. We would not specify such close joist placement since the 16" o.c. spacing for the same joists is perfectly adequate for the job.

Let us say that Douglas fir was available in a lumberyard in the next town. (Don't believe everything a merchant tells you!) The dealer is

It is not necessary to frame the house completely in lumber. Steel beams and girders can span longer distances with less chance of bending than can wood beams, and are therefore often used in place of heavy wooden girders in the framing of floor systems. A 6″ deep steel section can substitute for a wooden member 14″ deep, thus saving headroom. The table gives the allowable loads for steel beams and it indicates two types of steel sections. The well-known I-beam is designated on the table as an S section. The W designation refers to a steel section with wider flanges than the 1 section (Ill. I-1). Illustration I-2 shows framing details.

TABLE I-A: SAFE LOADS (IN POUNDS) FOR STEEL BEAMS AND GIRDERS

	Spans					
Shapes	10′	12′	14′	16′	18′	20′
S 6 × 2.5	8,700	7,300	6,200			
S 6 × 17.25	10,400	8,700	7,400			
S 7 × 17.5	13,300	11,100	9,500	8,300		
S 8 × 18.4	17,100	14,200	12,200	10,700	9,500	8,400
S 8 × 23	19,300	16,100	13,800	12,000	10,700	9,600
W 8 × 17	21,000	17,000	15,000	13,000		
W 10 × 21	33,000	28,000	24,000	21,000	18,000	15,000

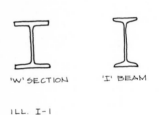

'W' SECTION   'I' BEAM

ILL. I-1

SCAB TO MAINTAIN JOIST CONTINUITY

MINIMUM ½″ SPACE BETWEEN STEEL GIRDER AND SCAB TO ALLOW FOR SHRINKAGE

NAILING PLATE BOLTED TO FLANGE, SAME THICKNESS AS PERIMETER PLATE

1. DIRECT BEARING

NAILING PLATE BOLTED TO FLANGE, SAME THICKNESS AS PERIMETER PLATE

2. LEDGER BEARING

ILL. I-2

anxious for business and informs us that he will sell us the Douglas fir at the same price as the other dealer wants for the hem-fir. What's more, he will deliver it the twenty or so miles at no extra charge. To determine exactly how much stronger the Douglas fir is, find it on the left-hand side of Table A (Douglas fir, larch, north). A 2 × 8 of Douglas fir spaced 16″ o.c. can span 13′-4″. (Remember that the 2 × 8 of hem-fir was only good for 12′-7″.) If we specify the Douglas fir 2 × 8 we will be overdesigning slightly (there is never any harm in overdesigning, and actually it is safer) but at no additional cost to us. Either joist is acceptable. We might choose lumberyards by other considerations. The owner of lumberyard A lives in our town and is a neighbor. He has offered to throw the nails into the deal. He has given us much worthwhile advice and has dealt with us with a great deal of patience and so on.

Design Development

GIRDER DESIGN

Floor joists are the lightweight horizontal members that carry the subfloor. Joists are easily differentiated from beams in that they are always spaced closely together. Beams and girders are heavier structural members and are harder to tell apart. Generally, a girder is heavier than a beam, meaning that it either spans a wider gap or carries a heavier load or supports beams. In buildings that have joists, beams, and girders, the joists carry the direct floor loads, transferring these loads to the beams, which transfer the loads to the girders, which transfer the loads to the vertical supports or to the foundations. Few house designs require both beams and girders. We will call the intermediate support for the joists, the "girder." The girder must be strong enough to carry the weight of the joists, which carry the weight of the floor system.

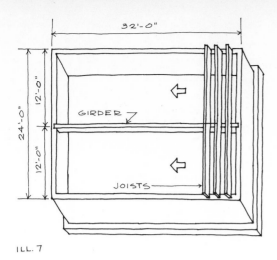

ILL. 7

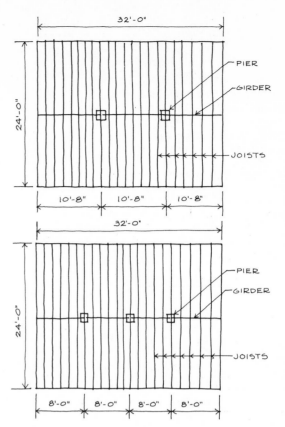

ILL. 8

Let us make some tentative design decisions based on a simplified version of our sample house. (Professional structural designers work in the same trial-and-error way. They will make tentative design decisions and then test them out by calculation.) The width of the house is 24'. We divide the span into two parts of 12' each; the joists will span this 12' distance (see Ill. 7). The length of the house is 32', much too long for a light-frame wood girder to span. (For information on the steel-girder alternative, see Inset I.) In fact a rule of thumb in wood-girder design has established 10' as the maximum practical span length for a girder. Anything longer than 10' and the cross-sectional dimension of the girder gets too heavy. Since design requirements dictate spans for girders and beams of greater length, we recommend a comfortable maximum of 12' for the girder spans.

We can divide the girder span into three parts of 10'-8" each, or four parts of 8'. How we divide the girder's span will determine how many foundation piers must be constructed, two or three, respectively (Ill. 8). First we must determine which portion of the floor will be supported at the perimeter of the house and which must be supported by the girder. We have illustrated our potential floor framing plan in Illustration 9. Under it is a section through that plan at the point indicated by the lines with the arrows at the ends. (The letter A-A' identifies the section and shows exactly where on the plan the cut is taken.) We will analyze the requirements for four spans of 8' each.

Since the joists are spanning the north-south direction, it is obvious that the east and west perimeters of the building must only support the weight of the walls above them (except for the spot on which the ends of the girders rest). The center girder supports half the weight of

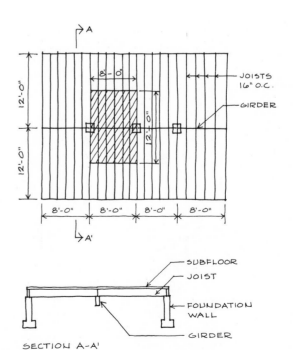

SECTION A-A'

ILL. 9

Floor Systems
81

TABLE II-A: DEAD LOADS

When calculating loads, both live loads and dead loads must be accounted for. Table 11-A gives the weights of various building materials and composite structural items. Most of the listings are per square foot, which means that if you are trying to determine the weight of a 2 × 4 stud wall with ½″ gypsum-board walls on both sides of the studs, you would multiply the weight of the wall per square foot (8.2 lbs.) × the dimensions of the wall (let us say, 8′ high by 12′ long) = 787.2 lbs.

		Pounds per square foot
Walls	wood stud wall: ½″ gypsum board, both sides	8.2
	4″ lightweight concrete-block wall	20.0
Floors	plyscore	1.5
	hardwood flooring	4.0
	joists with hardwood floor and plyscore subfloor	
	2 × 6	10.5
	2 × 8	11.5
	2 × 10	12.0
	2 × 12	12.5
Roofing	shingles:	
	wood	2.5
	asphalt	2.4
	asbestos-cement	2.6
	plywood sheathing	1.5
Windows	For windows and sliding glass doors constructed of wood frame and double glazing (insulating glass) use 3.5 psf for approximating purposes	3.5
Ceilings	½″ gypsum board	2.1
Roof Plank	2″ thick	5
	3″ thick	8

(The following are *not* in pounds per square foot):

		Pounds per linear foot
Beams and Girders	4 × 8	7.2
	3 × 10	6.6
	4 × 10	9.1
	4 × 12	11.0
	6 × 10	13.8
	4 × 14	13.0
	6 × 12	16.7
Stairs	Weight for a complete simple stair about 3′-0″ wide: 300 lbs.	

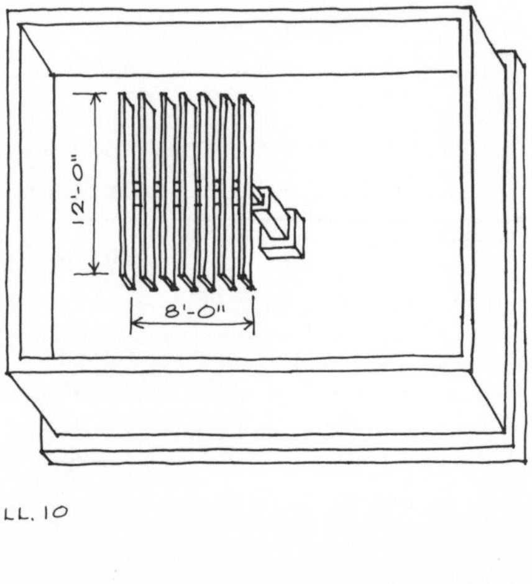

ILL. 10

the floor joists as indicated on the framing plan (Ill. 9) by the shaded portion. If the total floor is 24′ wide and the girder is placed midway between the north and south perimeters of the building, the girder will be supporting half of each of the 12′ spans, that is, a total of 12′ of width. If we isolate (for calculation purposes) the part of the floor system directly supported by the girders, we can add up the loads that will be placed on it (Ill. 10).

Live loads are the first consideration. Since we are designing the first floor of the house, we are required to design for a minimum of 40 psf. The dead loads (the weight of the materials in the joists, subfloor, finished floor, etc.) are about 10 psf. The total L.L.'s and D.L.'s are 50 psf, 50 psf × 12 feet × 8 feet = 4,800 lbs.

If there are load-bearing partitions that either rest on the girder or on the section of floor that the girder supports, these loads must be considered too as they will be taken on by the girder (see Inset II). The next calculation requires us to guess the weight of the girder itself. Since we don't know what the girder will be, we have no idea of its weight. We guess the girder to be a 4 × 10. (This is an educated guess on our part. The joists are 2 × 8's, we assume that the girder will have a larger cross-sectional area.) We consult Table II-A for the weights of the various structural members. The 4 × 10 weighs 9 lbs. per linear foot (9 lbs. × 8 ft. = 72 lbs.).

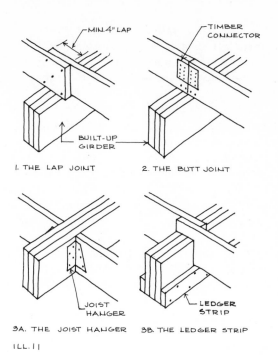

1. THE LAP JOINT 2. THE BUTT JOINT

3A. THE JOIST HANGER 3B. THE LEDGER STRIP

ILL. 11

Calculations

L.L. + D.L.	= 4,800
D.L. of the girder (9 lbs. × 8')	= 72
Loads for the load-bearing partition: 4,800 lbs. for the floor above (assume a second story) that it is supporting and 500 lbs. for the weight of the wall itself	= 5,300
D.L. of non-bearing partition	= 500
Total L.L. and D.L.	10,672

Table C will give us the proper girder for the given loads. We find that a 4 × 14 will support 10,900 lbs. for an 8'-0" span. An alternate would be a 6 × 12, which would allow more headroom. Or we could consider using a steel beam. Table I-A has spans greater than 10'. However, the I beam, designated as S 6 × 17.25, can support 10,400 lbs. for a span of 10', so we can assume it will be good for 10,600 lbs. for the smaller span of 8'.

We wish there were an easier way to design the girders. We know of none. We will give you this advice. When designing joists use the charts and stick closely to them. When designing the girders, overdesign! The bit of extra lumber (or steel) you throw into the girder comes to pennies when compared to the cost of the house.

JOIST CONNECTIONS

There are three ways to frame the joists into the girder and to each other. The method chosen

TABLE C: SAFE LOADS (IN POUNDS) FOR WOOD BEAMS AND GIRDERS

				Spans			
Size	6'	7'	8'	9'	10'	11'	12'
4 × 8			4,250	3,780	3,400	3,090	2,830
4 × 10			6,820	6,060	5,450	4,960	4,540
6 × 10	11,357	10,804	9,980	8,887	7,997	7,520	6,890
6 × 10 built-up	10,068	9,576	8,844	7,878	7,086		
6 × 12			13,300	12,900	12,100	11,000	10,100
8 × 12			18,100	17,500	16,500	15,000	13,800
4 × 16			13,300	12,600	12,100	11,700	11,500
4 × 14			10,900	10,400	10,100	9,840	9,180

usually depends on the framing situation. The first method is to lap the joists over the girder, nailing the joists to each other and to the girder (Ill. 11). This would be used in a house with a basement or a crawl space for framing the first floor. (As an alternative to using a wood beam, you might consider using steel as described in Inset I.) It is easy to construct the lapped joint since the joists do not require absolutely precise measuring and cutting. However, if you were to use the lapped method to frame the second floor, you might have problems with headroom

(Ill. 12). If you had specified a beam 10″ in depth and a joist of 8″, the total depth of the floor structure (from the ceiling of the first level to the floor of the second) could come to almost 2′!

The second method is to butt the joists end to end over the girder and use metal ties to connect them to each other (the joists are then nailed to the girder, Ill. 11). This simplifies the planning of the joist layout to some extent by allowing the joists to line up in straight rows across multiple spans. This method does nothing, however, to solve the headroom problem outlined above.

If it is desirable for the joists and the girder to lie approximately on the same plane (for headroom reasons) the joists can be "hung" from the girder (the third method) either by using joist hangers designed and sold for this purpose, or by resting the joists on a "ledger strip," which is nailed to the girder (Ill. 11).

Framing the joists into a continuous foundation wall is accomplished by nailing the ends of the joists to both the mud sill and to the header (Ill. 13). The intermediate girder is supported on its extreme ends by the foundation wall (if there is to be one). It is desirable to have the girder at the exact height of the sill, so that the joists can rest on the top of the girder (lapping over it) and span to the top of the mud sill. To get the girder at this height it cannot be supported on top of the foundation wall, but must be lowered into the wall. This is accomplished by constructing a "pocket" in the foundation wall prior to pouring the concrete. This pocket will be discussed further in Chapter 20 (see Ill. 14).

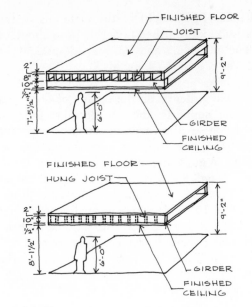

ILL. 12

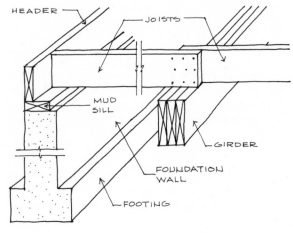

ILL. 13

FRAMING AN OPENING

You might have gotten the idea, so far, that all floor joists are evenly spaced underneath the floor and lie there like cots in a barracks. Unfortunately, the regular spacing of the joists will most likely be disturbed by one or more special conditions. The first is the need for openings to accommodate stairs coming up from the floor below. The fireplace foundations must be accommodated by framing an opening for them, too. In addition, the neat row of joists is upset by the need to increase the support under the floor that carries a partition. We will deal with the openings first.

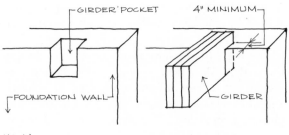

ILL. 14

There are two ways in which an opening can disturb a row of joists—first, when the opening's length runs parallel to the joists, and second, when the opening's longer side is perpendicular to the run of the joists (Ill. 15). In

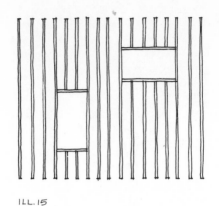

ILL. 15

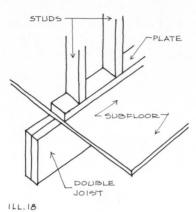

STUDS

PLATE

SUBFLOOR

DOUBLE JOIST

ILL. 18

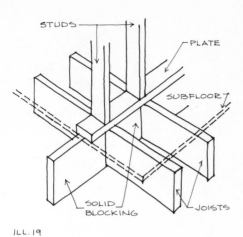

STUDS

PLATE

SUBFLOOR

SOLID BLOCKING

JOISTS

ILL. 19

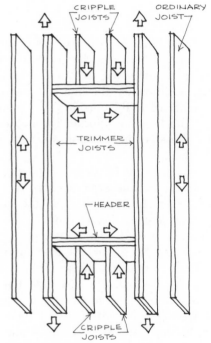

CRIPPLE JOISTS

ORDINARY JOIST

TRIMMER JOISTS

HEADER

CRIPPLE JOISTS

ARROWS INDICATE HOW THE LOADS ARE TRANSFERRED

ILL. 16

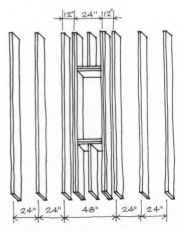

12" 24" 12"

24" 24" 48" 24" 24"

ILL. 17

both cases the joists will have to be cut somewhere along their span. This, in effect, "cripples" the joists. A new series of members must be added to maintain some sort of structural continuity. Usually, what is done is to butt the crippled joists up against a header that frames the opening. (The header will be of the same cross-sectional dimensions as the ordinary joists.) The two full-length joists that straddle either side of the opening (the trimmer joists) are doubled as well. (They must bear the loads of the headers which are carrying the weight of the crippled joists, as shown in Illustration 16.)

The opening is thus framed by a box made of doubled headers and trimmers. If the opening does not line up with the spacing of the joists, it might even be necessary to throw in an extra joist or two. This is easier than reorganizing the joists or relocating the stairs to conform more readily to the framing plan (Ill. 17).

FRAMING UNDER A PARTITION

The floor under a partition must be reinforced in order to carry the continually added load of the wall. When the partition runs parallel to the run of the joists, the joists are simply doubled beneath it (Ill. 18). Joists should also be doubled up underneath bathtubs. If the partition runs perpendicular to the joists, there is no need for added reinforcement. Some conservative carpenters recommend solid blocking between the joists directly beneath the partitions. Others argue that every other joist beneath a load-bearing partition should be doubled (Ill. 19).

Floor Systems
85

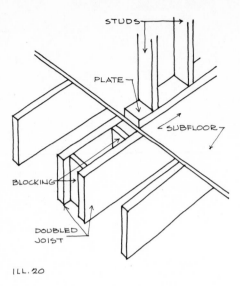

ILL. 20

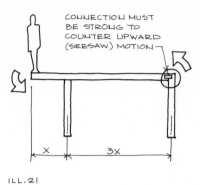

ILL. 21

If a partition running parallel to the joists is to carry plumbing, it is necessary to create a space through which these lines will pass. The floor joists are doubled and separated a few inches (they are placed to straddle the plate of the partition above). Solid bridging is nailed between them every 16" so that the two joists will act in unison (Ill. 20).

FRAMING A CANTILEVER

A cantilevered (overhung) floor area, such as a balcony, presents a special problem—easily solvable in residential construction. Although a cantilever should be calculated mathematically, we need not go to the trouble if the length (the distance out from the support) is short. One helpful rule of thumb is to be sure that the cantilevered structural member is continuous with the span next to it. The part that overhangs the support should not be longer than one-fourth the length of the adjacent (fully supported) part (Ill. 21). The noncantilevered end must either be counterweighted or firmly anchored to its support to counter the upward tendency that comes about when a load is placed on the overhang.

If the cantilever occurs parallel to the run of the joists, this rule is easily applied. The regular joists are merely extended so that they span the length between the supports and also the cantilevered length. A header is placed at the end of the projection to supply rigidity to the joists. The joists on either end of the projected portion are referred to as trimmers, and they are

doubled. Solid blocking (short pieces of lumber) are constructed between the joists (over the support) to maintain the structural integrity of the beam. Additionally, the ends of the joists are rigidly connected to the outside girder with joist hangers. The hanging "pocket" is put on top since the stress is sometimes upward, or gravitational (Ill. 22).

In a case where the joists are running perpendicular to the cantilevered portion, a special problem arises. In order to use the rule of thumb noted above (the overhung joists must be counterbalanced by an extension at least three times the length of the overhang), it is necessary to cut into the joists running perpendicular to the overhang (Ill. 23). Essentially, we have a condition similar to framing an opening, in that we are left with crippled joists. The solution to the framing problem is shown in Illustration 23. If you are going to design a cantilever that is perpendicular to the joists, don't make it longer than 5' or 6'.

BRIDGING

The joists, when nailed into place at both ends of the span, are further stabilized by diagonal pieces of lumber nailed between them, called "bridging." The bridging not only helps to stabilize the joists, but aids in the distribution of a concentrated load, such as a refrigerator, to the other members of the floor system. Cross bridging (Ill. 24) joins the joists by means of two diagonal pieces of wood, usually 1 × 2's that cross each other in an "X" pattern. Solid

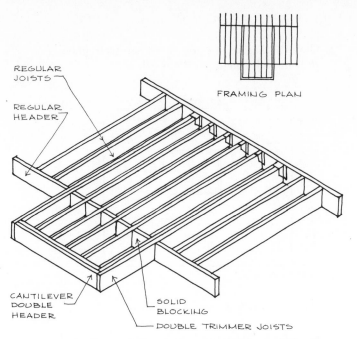

REGULAR JOISTS

REGULAR HEADER

CANTILEVER DOUBLE HEADER

SOLID BLOCKING

DOUBLE TRIMMER JOISTS

FRAMING PLAN

CANTILEVERED PORTION IS PARALLEL TO THE RUN OF THE JOISTS

ILL. 22

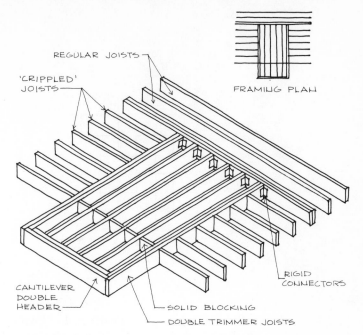

REGULAR JOISTS

'CRIPPLED' JOISTS

CANTILEVER DOUBLE HEADER

SOLID BLOCKING

DOUBLE TRIMMER JOISTS

RIGID CONNECTORS

FRAMING PLAN

CANTILEVERED PORTION IS PERPENDICULAR TO THE JOISTS

ILL. 23

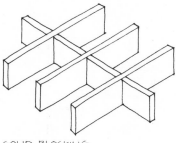

SOLID BLOCKING

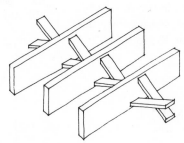

CROSS BRIDGING

ILL. 24

bridging uses pieces of lumber the same dimensions as the joists. The pieces are measured, cut, and nailed solidly into place. It is obvious that cross bridging, which relies on lumber of more slender dimensions than the type used for solid bridging, uses wood more efficiently. A row of bridging joins the joists every 6' to 8' (Ill. 25).

SUBFLOORING

The final floor of the house will have two layers—the subfloor, or the rough floor, and the finished floor, which may be of wood planks, parquet squares, tile, or carpet. The subfloor is constructed immediately after the joists are secure and the bridging in place. The subfloor, bridging, and joists are nailed tightly together to

JOISTS

6'-0"

6'-0"

6'-0"

BRIDGING

BEAM

ILL. 25

form a structural unit that acts to resist stresses and transfer loads. In addition, the subfloor acts as a platform on which the wall units may be constructed. The finished floor is not installed until much later.

Floor Systems

87

1. Draw a diagram of the first-floor plan only, showing full-height partitions (Ill. 27).

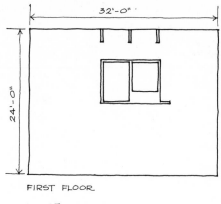

FIRST FLOOR

ILL. 27

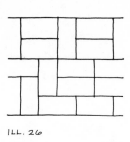

ILL. 26

Subflooring may be constructed of boards ¾″ thick and 6″ or 8″ wide. The boards would be laid diagonally (at a 45-degree angle to the line of the joists) for added stability. Diagonal subflooring, however, is hardly ever used anymore. Plyscore (a form of plywood made for subflooring) has taken its place. The plyscore comes in 4′ × 8′ panels and is arranged on the joist bed in a basket-weave pattern (Ill. 26).

FRAMING THE SAMPLE HOUSE

The sample house presents some difficult framing problems. The framing plans for the first and second floors of the house incorporate all of the deviations you may come across in the design of your own residence: cantilevers, decks, openings, load-bearing partitions, and load-bearing columns. If your house plan is very simple and straightforward, you may find this section overly complicated and of little value to you. If so, skip it. The information provided earlier in this chapter should be sufficient for the design of simple floors.

For those of you who venture with us to develop the framing plans for the sample house, be sure that you understand the basic principles explained in the first part of the chapter. We are going to draw heavily on that information. In the first part of this section we will show the step-by-step formulation of the framing plan itself. Having determined the framing plan, we will proceed with the mathematics to size the sections.

2. In order to determine which partitions on the first floor must serve as load-bearing for the floor above, we draw a diagram of the second floor only, showing full-height partitions. Leave an opening for the two-story living room (Ill. 28).

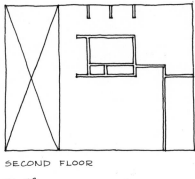

SECOND FLOOR

ILL. 28

3. Looking at both the first- and second-floor plans, we can see that there are not enough walls to serve as intermediate supports for the floor joists. We would have to run the second floor's joists the full 24′ width (Ill. 29).

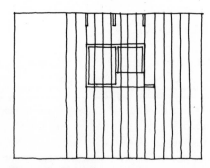

SECOND FLOOR

ILL. 29

4. A distance of 24'-0" between supports is excessive. We cut it in half by providing girders running the length of the house. The girders are supported at points A and B by columns within the core walls (represented here as dots). Girder BC is no problem. Girder BD, however, requires a cantilevered portion (AD) to provide support for the joists framing the balcony. This is a difficult framing condition (Ill. 30).

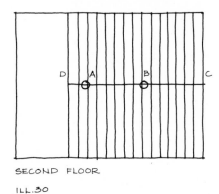

SECOND FLOOR

ILL. 30

5. Instead, we try running the girders on the second floor the width of the house. (We will keep the columns at A and B.) There are now four girders, all 12' long. The joists run perpendicular to the girders and are either 10' or 13' long. The 13' joists handle the balcony. The 3':10' ratio of that cantilevered portion satisfies the 1:3 requirement for cantilevers. The second-floor framing is now complete (Ill. 31).

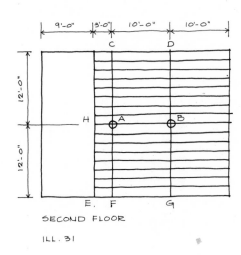

SECOND FLOOR

ILL. 31

6. Back now to the first floor. We take into account the second-floor structural requirements and locate columns A and B, which carry the loads from the second floor (Ill. 32).

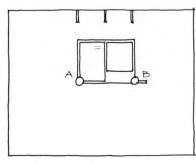

FIRST FLOOR

ILL. 32

7. We need an opening in both floor plans to allow for the fireplace foundation, on floor 1, and the chimney flue, on floor 2. (The heavy bricks need a foundation of their own. It is not conceivable that the wood floor can carry that weight.) We draw that opening (Ill. 33).

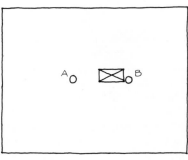

FIRST FLOOR

ILL. 33

8. After locating the fireplace opening, we realize that it is impossible to run a girder between points A and B. We, therefore, run the girders the width of the house (Ill. 34).

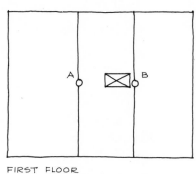

FIRST FLOOR

ILL. 34

Floor Systems

89

9. The joist rests on girders CA, DB, AF, and BG running east-west. Their lengths are 12', 10', and 10'. We now recognize the problem of the sunken conversation pit. We had intended to drop the pit about a foot. This, however, is not a fixed dimension (Ill. 35).

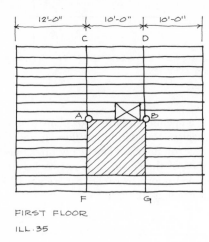

FIRST FLOOR

ILL. 35

10. The framing system we had planned to use for the first floor is the lap joint of joist and girder. (The joists overlap each other and rest *on* the girder.) The solution to the conversation pit is to hang the pit joists to the girders with joist hangers. We should have a difference of about 10″ or 12″ between the first-floor level and the level of the floor in the pit by using this framing detail (Ill. 36).

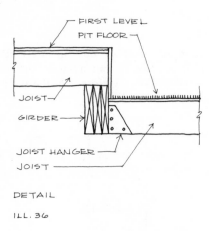

DETAIL

ILL. 36

11. Now that we have the first- and second-floor framing plans, we draw a structural section through the house. We can readily see that we will have a large ceiling-to-floor depth because of the cantilever on the second floor. We can also begin to make some structural decisions about the roof. We should be able to use columns A and B for the roof support (Ill. 37).

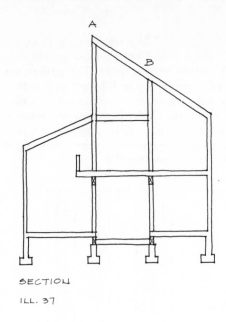

SECTION

ILL. 37

JOIST AND GIRDER CALCULATIONS

1. We begin with the second-floor joists (Ill. 31). The joists run east-west. The length from H to B and E to G is 13'. We use one piece of lumber 13'-0″ long. The span, however, is only 10'-0″ (A to B and F to G). Refer to Table A.* Although a Douglas fir no. 1, 2″ × 6″ joist spaced every 16″ o.c. can span 10'-2″, we feel it is a bit close to the actual span. We can choose instead a 2″ × 6″ spaced every 12″ o.c. or go to a 2″ × 8″ spaced at 16″ o.c. We choose the 2″ × 8″ at 16″ o.c. since it will prove more economical. We will use this joist for the other span on the second floor as well.

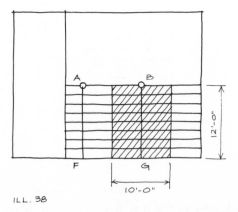

ILL. 38

* We will use Table A (live load 40 psf) rather than Table B (live load 30 psf) because when the house is expanded, the master bedroom will be converted into a family room.

2. Now for the second-floor girders (Ill. 38). Girder BG must be designed to support the part of the floor crosshatched in the diagram. The area to be supported is 10′ × 12′ = 120 sq. ft.

L.L. (40 psf) + D.L. (11.5 psf for floors and joists) = 51.5 psf × 120 sq. ft. = 6,180.

Load-bearing partitions: none
(the columns will carry the roof load)

Non-load-bearing partitions:
12′ long × about 12′ high
materials: glass
Table II-A: glass weighs approx 3.5 lbs./sq. ft.
3.5 lbs. × 12′ × 12′ = 504

The weight of the girder: an 8 × 14 weighs about 25 lbs./linear ft. = 300 lbs.

Total loads = 6,180 + 504 + 300 = 6,984

We specify a 4 × 14 or a 6 × 12. We prefer the 6 × 12 because of the headroom problem. For purposes of uniformity, we will specify the same section for girder AF as well, even though there is less load on it. We design the other girders on the second floor in the same way.

3. The same procedure is used to design the first-floor joists and girders.

4. The first- and second-floor framing plans and details are shown in Illustration 39.

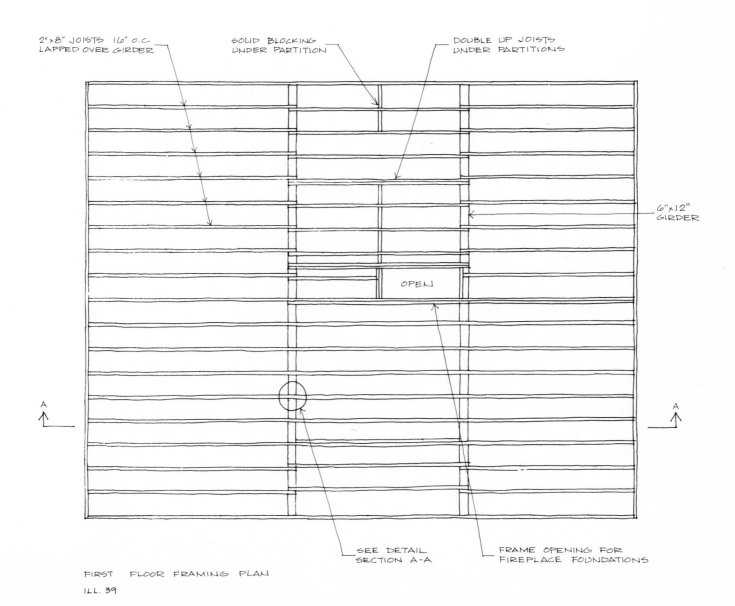

2"×8" JOISTS 16" O.C. LAPPED OVER GIRDER

SOLID BLOCKING UNDER PARTITION

DOUBLE UP JOISTS UNDER PARTITIONS

6"×12" GIRDER

OPEN

A

A

SEE DETAIL SECTION A-A

FRAME OPENING FOR FIREPLACE FOUNDATIONS

FIRST FLOOR FRAMING PLAN

ILL. 39

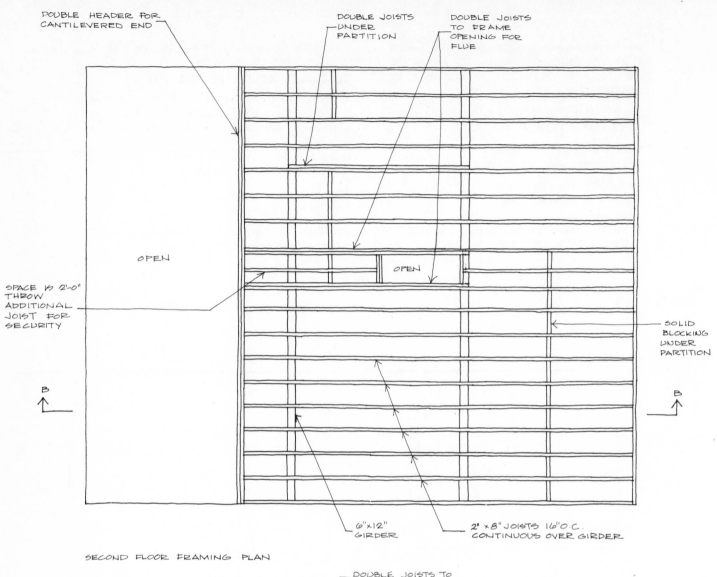

DOUBLE HEADER FOR
CANTILEVERED END

DOUBLE JOISTS
UNDER
PARTITION

DOUBLE JOISTS
TO FRAME
OPENING FOR
FLUE

OPEN

SPACE IS 2'-0"
THROW
ADDITIONAL
JOIST FOR
SECURITY

OPEN

SOLID
BLOCKING
UNDER
PARTITION

B

B

6"x12"
GIRDER

2" x 8" JOISTS 16" O.C.
CONTINUOUS OVER GIRDER

SECOND FLOOR FRAMING PLAN

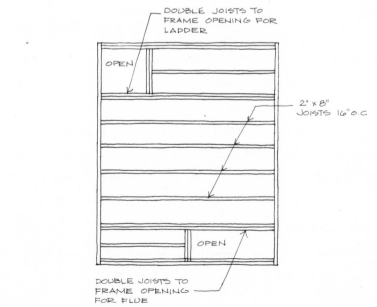

DOUBLE JOISTS TO
FRAME OPENING FOR
LADDER

OPEN

2" x 8"
JOISTS 16" O.C

ILL. 39

OPEN

DOUBLE JOISTS TO
FRAME OPENING
FOR FLUE

LOFT FRAMING PLAN

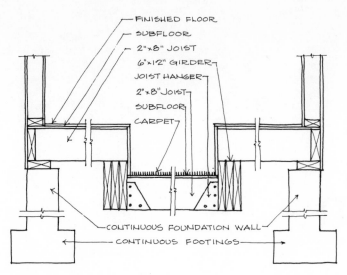

FINISHED FLOOR
SUBFLOOR
2"×8" JOIST
6"×12" GIRDER
JOIST HANGER
2"×8"JOIST
SUBFLOOR
CARPET

CONTINUOUS FOUNDATION WALL
CONTINUOUS FOOTINGS

SECTION A-A' : FIRST FLOOR

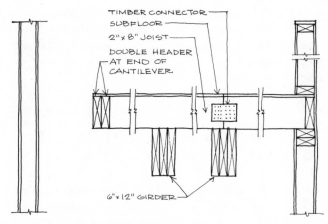

TIMBER CONNECTOR
SUBFLOOR
2"×8" JOIST
DOUBLE HEADER
AT END OF
CANTILEVER

6"×12" GIRDER

SECTION B-B' : SECOND FLOOR

ILL. 39

9
Roof Design

The approach to the structural design of the roof is much the same as to the floor systems. Loads and the transfer of loads from structural member to member is the most important consideration, even though the loads on a roof are substantially lighter. In addition to its own structural weight, the roof is expected to bear the pressures of a driving rain, a powerful wind force, and the weight of piled-up snow. In most northern climates the snow loads are the greatest and, therefore, govern the roof's design. In many areas of the northern United States the design loads for roofs will vary from 20 to 30 psf depending on the slope of the roof. If the roof is very steep, the snow will tend to slide off it. If the roof has a more gentle slope, the snow will remain where it is, piling weight onto the roof structure. The design load for gently sloping roofs is, therefore, greater than for those that are more steeply pitched.

The slope of the roof can be analyzed by comparing the rise to the run (Ill. 1). If the run of the rafter is 10 feet horizontally and the rise is 5 feet vertically, then the slope is 1 to 2, or expressed in inches, 6 to 12. The flat roof will have a design load based on the climate and whether or not the surface is to be used for human traffic or recreation. Check the local building codes for these figures.

Although there are many attractive roof shapes used by the contemporary designer, space limitations force us to confine our discussion to the framing of only three kinds: the gable roof with an attic, the gable or shed roof without an attic (used in the sample house), and the flat roof.

Whatever the roof design, you must draw a roof framing plan (similar to the one in Illustrations 15 and 17) showing all structural members. This plan should be drawn to a scale of at least ½" = 1'-0".

THE GABLE ROOF WITH AN ATTIC

The pitched roof with an attic is the most commonly used roof and is a continuation of the light-frame construction used to build the floors and walls. The elements used in this kind of framing, the ceiling joists, the rafters, and the ridge, are shown in Illustration 2. The design of the roof framing system is similar to that of the flooring system in that the rafters and joists are lightweight and are spaced at 12", 16", or 24" intervals. The roof framing plan is laid out in much the same way as the floor framing plan.

Design Procedure

Draw both a plan and a section of the roof and ceiling at ½" scale. Draw the plan of the top floor of the house showing the double plates of the supporting (load-bearing) walls and partitions. Next draw a section through the designed roof and measure its exact pitch. (The "de-

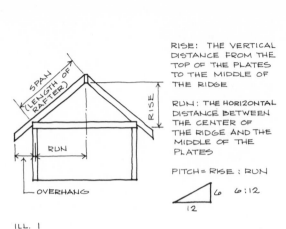

RISE: THE VERTICAL DISTANCE FROM THE TOP OF THE PLATES TO THE MIDDLE OF THE RIDGE

RUN: THE HORIZONTAL DISTANCE BETWEEN THE CENTER OF THE RIDGE AND THE MIDDLE OF THE PLATES

PITCH = RISE : RUN

6 : 12

ILL. 1

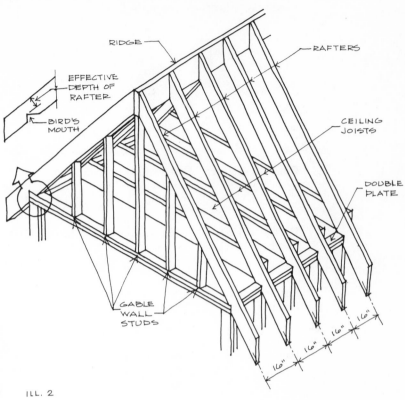

ILL. 2

signed" roof is the product of the preliminary sections described in Chapter 5.) This section will help you determine the actual length of the piece of lumber to be used as a rafter (the span of the rafter plus the overhang). You might modify the pitch so as to use the lumber lengths more economically. (Remember that joist-rafter stock is sold in increments of 2'.)

Select the ceiling joists. These are usually framed at the same spacing as the rafters, to simplify the marking and nailing. If the attic is not designed for either storage or human traffic the loads are usually light. Most building codes only require a design live load of 10 psf. (Consult your code before designing the ceiling or, for that matter, any element of the house.) We suggest that you design the joists for heavier loads. If the attic is designed for heavy storage or as an activity space, you will have to use the same design loads required for the second story of the house (usually 30 psf). Table A covers these design requirements for joist selection.

Rafters

The selection of the rafter sections is dependent on two criteria, the climate (the amount of snowfall) and the pitch of the roof. The steeper the roof, the lower the design load. Tables B and C cover the design of roofs with pitches of over and under 3 in 12, respectively. The procedure for rafter selection is exactly the same as that outlined for joists in detail in Chapter 8. In this

case, however, the "span" is the *actual length* of the rafter between supports (that is, between the plates on one side and the ridge on the other).

The Ridge

The ridge itself is usually constructed of a 2" thick section that is about 2" deeper than the rafter sections to simplify framing. (The ridge is nonstructural since it does not carry the weight of the rafters. The rafters are buttressing each other and are actually supporting the ridge. For this reason, the length that the ridge spans is not an important structural consideration.)

Gable Ends

The triangular walls at the ends of the gable are constructed out of studs in much the same way as the wall sections outlined in Chapter 10 (Ill. 2). In platform framing the gable ends can be built as continuations of the floor below or as separate tilt-up sections.

Roof Design
95

TABLE A: JOISTS—30 PSF LIVE LOAD

		Joist size (inches)							
		2 × 6		2 × 8		2 × 10		2 × 12	
Species	Grade	Joist spacing (inches)							
		12	16	12	16	12	16	12	16
		Maximum allowable span (feet and inches)							
Coast sitka spruce	select structural	12-0	10-11	15-10	14-5	20-3	18-5	24-8	22-5
	no. 1 & appearance	12-0	10-10	15-10	14-4	20-3	18-3	24-8	22-3
	no. 2	11-6	10-0	15-2	13-2	19-4	16-9	23-6	20-5
	no. 3	8-8	7-6	11-6	9-11	14-8	12-8	17-9	15-5
Douglas fir-larch (north)	select structural	12-3	11-2	16-2	14-8	20-8	18-9	25-1	22-10
	no. 1 & appearance	12-3	11-2	16-2	14-8	20-8	18-9	25-1	22-10
	no. 2	12-0	10-11	15-10	14-5	20-3	18-5	24-8	22-5
	no. 3	10-4	9-0	13-8	11-10	17-5	15-1	21-2	18-4
Eastern hemlock-tamarack (north)	select structural	11-0	10-0	14-6	13-2	18-6	16-10	22-6	20-6
	no. 1 & appearance	11-0	10-0	14-6	13-2	18-6	16-10	22-6	20-6
	no. 2	10-5	9-6	13-9	12-6	17-6	15-11	21-4	19-4
	no. 3	9-7	8-3	12-7	10-11	15-1	13-11	19-7	16-11
Hem-fir (north)	select structural	11-7	10-6	15-3	13-10	19-5	17-8	23-7	21-6
	no. 1 & appearance	11-7	10-6	15-3	13-10	19-5	17-8	23-7	21-6
	no. 2	11-3	10-3	14-11	13-6	19-0	17-3	23-1	21-0
	no. 3	9-3	8-0	12-2	10-6	15-6	13-5	18-10	16-4
Ponderosa pine	select structural	10-9	9-9	14-2	12-10	18-0	16-5	21-11	19-11
	no. 1 & appearance	10-9	9-9	14-2	12-10	18-0	16-5	21-11	19-11
	no. 2	10-5	9-6	13-9	12-6	17-6	15-11	21-4	19-4
	no. 3	8-6	7-4	11-3	9-9	14-4	12-5	17-5	15-1
Red pine	select structural	11-0	10-0	14-6	13-2	18-6	16-10	22-6	20-6
	no. 1 & appearance	11-0	10-0	14-6	13-2	18-6	16-10	22-6	20-6
	no. 2	10-9	9-6	14-2	12-6	18-0	15-11	21-11	19-5
	no. 3	8-4	7-3	11-0	9-6	14-0	12-2	17-0	14-9
Spruce-pine-fir	select structural	11-7	10-6	15-3	13-10	19-5	17-8	23-7	21-6
	no. 1 & appearance	11-7	10-6	15-3	13-10	19-5	17-8	23-7	21-6
	no. 2	11-0	9-9	14-6	12-10	18-6	16-4	22-6	19-11
	no. 3	8-6	7-4	11-3	9-9	14-4	12-5	17-5	15-1
Western cedars (north)	select structural	10-5	9-6	13-9	12-6	17-6	15-11	21-4	19-4
	no. 1 & appearance	10-5	9-6	13-9	12-6	17-6	15-11	21-4	19-4
	no. 2	10-1	9-2	13-4	12-1	17-0	15-5	20-8	18-9
	no. 3	8-8	7-6	11-6	9-11	14-8	12-8	17-9	15-5
Western white pine	select structural	11-3	10-3	14-11	13-6	19-0	17-3	23-1	21-0
	no. 1 & appearance	11-3	10-3	14-11	13-6	19-0	17-3	23-1	21-0
	no. 2	10-10	9-4	14-3	12-4	18-2	15-9	22-1	19-2
	no. 3	8-4	7-3	11-0	9-6	14-0	12-2	17-0	14-9

The advantage of the attic in the summer to dissipate the heat trapped in it from the sun's rays beating on the roof and from the rising heat from the living spaces is purely dependent on the ventilation of this buffer zone. Most houses have small louvers at the ends of the gables. These skinny louvers (supposedly closed in winter and opened in the summer) are insufficient to ventilate an attic of any size. It is recommended that large louvers or windows be planned for the gables and that a large ventilating fan be installed in the attic to facilitate air flow through the space. Additional discussion of insulation and condensation protection follows in Chapter 13.

Plywood roof sheathing (exterior grade), ⅝" or ¾", is recommended. Finished roofing will be covered in Chapter 12.

TABLE B: RAFTERS, HIGH SLOPE (OVER 3 IN 12) WITH NO FINISHED
CEILING—20 PSF LIVE LOAD, 7 PSF DEAD LOAD

		Joist sizes (inches)							
		2 × 4		2 × 6		2 × 8		2 × 10	
		Joist spacing (inches)							
		12	16	12	16	12	16	12	16
Species	Grade	Maximum allowable span (feet and inches)							
Coast sitka spruce	select structural	11-1	10-0	17-4	15-7	22-11	20-6	29-2	26-2
	no. 1 & appearance	11-1	9-9	16-5	14-2	21-7	18-9	27-7	23-11
	no. 2	10-3	8-10	15-0	13-0	19-10	17-2	25-3	21-11
	no. 3	7-8	6-8	11-4	9-10	15-0	12-11	19-1	16-6
Douglas fir-larch (north)	select structural	11-3	10-3	17-8	16-1	23-4	21-2	29-9	27-1
	no. 1 & appearance	11-3	10-3	17-8	16-1	23-4	21-2	29-9	27-1
	no. 2	11-1	10-0	17-4	15-4	22-11	20-2	29-2	25-9
	no. 3	8-11	7-9	13-6	11-9	17-10	15-5	22-9	19-8
Eastern hemlock-tamarack (north)	select structural	10-1	9-2	15-11	14-5	20-11	19-0	26-9	24-3
	no. 1	10-1	9-2	15-11	14-5	20-11	19-0	26-9	24-3
	no. 2	9-7	8-8	15-0	13-8	19-10	18-0	25-3	22-11
	no. 3	8-4	7-3	12-5	10-9	16-5	14-3	20-11	18-2
	appearance	10-1	9-2	15-11	14-5	20-11	19-0	26-9	24-3
Hem-fir (north)	select structural	10-7	9-8	16-8	15-2	22-0	19-11	28-0	25-5
	no. 1 & appearance	10-7	9-8	16-8	15-0	22-0	19-10	28-0	25-3
	no. 2	10-4	9-3	15-8	13-7	20-8	17-11	26-5	22-10
	no. 3	7-11	6-10	12-1	10-5	15-11	13-9	20-4	17-7
Ponderosa pine	select structural	9-10	8-11	15-6	14-1	20-5	18-6	26-0	23-8
	no. 1 & appearance	9-10	8-11	15-6	13-11	20-5	18-4	26-0	23-6
	no. 2	9-7	8-8	14-6	12-6	19-1	16-6	24-4	21-1
	no. 3	7-5	6-5	11-1	9-7	14-8	12-8	18-8	16-2
Red pine	select structural	10-1	9-2	15-11	14-5	20-11	19-0	26-9	24-3
	no. 1 & appearance	10-1	9-2	15-8	13-7	20-8	17-11	26-5	22-10
	no. 2	9-10	8-6	14-3	12-4	18-10	16-3	24-0	20-9
	no. 3	7-5	6-5	10-10	9-5	14-4	12-5	18-3	15-10
Spruce-pine-fir	select structural	10-7	9-8	16-8	15-2	22-0	19-11	28-0	25-5
	no. 1 & appearance	10-7	9-7	16-1	13-11	21-2	18-4	27-0	23-5
	no. 2	10-0	8-8	14-8	12-8	19-4	16-9	24-8	21-4
	no. 3	7-6	6-6	11-1	9-7	14-8	12-8	18-8	16-2
Western cedars (north)	select structural	9-7	8-8	15-0	13-8	19-10	18-0	25-3	22-11
	no. 1 & appearance	9-7	8-8	15-0	13-8	19-10	18-0	25-3	22-11
	no. 2	9-3	8-5	14-7	12-8	19-2	16-9	24-6	21-4
	no. 3	7-6	6-6	11-4	9-10	15-0	12-11	19-1	16-6
Western white pine	select structural	10-4	9-5	16-3	14-6	21-6	19-1	27-5	24-5
	no. 1 & appearance	10-4	9-3	15-8	13-7	20-8	17-11	26-5	22-10
	no. 2	9-7	8-3	14-1	12-2	18-7	16-1	23-8	20-6
	no. 3	7-3	6-3	10-10	9-5	14-4	12-5	18-3	15-10

THE GABLE OR SHED ROOF WITHOUT ATTIC

The structure of a pitched roof without an attic can be built of light-frame construction or can be designed for plank-and-beam (also called post-and-beam) construction (Ill. 3). Plank-and-beam construction differs from its light-frame cousin in that it consists of structural members that are heavier than studs and joists and can, therefore, be spaced at greater intervals. A large wood-frame building, such as a church, will most likely be constructed of columns (posts) and beams. It is possible to mix the two systems. For example, a house with platform-frame construction floor and walls might have plank-and-beam construction for the roof.

TABLE C: RAFTERS, LOW SLOPE (3 IN 12 OR LESS)·WITH NO
FINISHED CEILING—30 PSF LIVE LOAD

		Joist size (inches)							
		2 × 6		2 × 8		2 × 10		2 × 12	
		Joist spacing (inches)							
		12	16	12	16	12	16	12	16
Species	Grade	Maximum allowable span (feet and inches)							
Coast sitka spruce	select structural	13-9	12-6	18-2	16-6	23-2	21-1	28-2	25-7
	no. 1 & appearance	13-6	11-8	17-9	15-5	22-8	19-7	27-7	23-10
	no. 2	12-4	10-8	16-3	14-1	20-9	18-0	25-3	21-11
	no. 3	9-4	8-1	12-4	10-8	15-8	13-7	19-1	16-6
Douglas fir-larch (north)	select structural	14-1	12-9	18-6	16-10	23-8	21-6	28-9	26-1
	no. 1 & appearance	14-1	12-9	18-6	16-10	23-8	21-6	28-9	26-1
	no. 2	13-9	12-6	18-2	16-6	23-2	21-1	28-2	25-7
	no. 3	11-1	9-8	14-8	12-8	18-8	16-2	22-9	19-8
Eastern hemlock-tamarack (north)	select structural	12-7	11-5	16-7	15-1	21-2	19-3	25-9	23-5
	no. 1 & appearance	12-7	11-5	16-7	15-1	21-2	19-3	25-9	23-5
	no. 2	11-11	10-10	15-9	14-3	20-1	18-3	24-5	22-2
	no. 3	10-3	8-10	13-6	11-8	17-2	14-11	20-11	18-1
Hem-fir (north)	select structural	13-3	12-0	17-5	15-10	22-3	20-2	27-1	24-7
	no. 1 & appearance	13-3	12-0	17-5	15-10	22-3	20-2	27-1	24-7
	no. 2	12-11	11-2	17-0	14-9	21-8	18-9	26-5	22-10
	no. 3	9-11	8-7	13-1	11-4	16-8	14-5	20-3	17-7
Ponderosa pine	select structural	12-3	11-2	16-2	14-8	20-8	18-9	25-1	22-10
	no. 1 & appearance	12-3	11-2	16-2	14-8	20-8	18-9	25-1	22-10
	no. 2	11-11	10-3	15-8	13-7	20-0	17-4	24-4	21-1
	no. 3	9-1	7-11	12-0	10-5	15-4	13-3	18-8	16-2
Red pine	select structural	12-7	11-5	16-7	15-1	21-2	19-3	25-9	23-5
	no. 1 & appearance	12-7	11-2	16-7	14-9	21-2	18-9	25-9	22-10
	no. 2	11-9	10-2	15-5	13-5	19-9	17-1	24-0	20-9
	no. 3	8-11	7-9	11-9	10-2	15-0	13-0	18-3	15-9
Spruce-pine-fir	select structural	13-3	12-0	17-5	15-10	22-3	20-2	27-1	24-7
	no. 1 & appearance	13-2	11-5	17-5	15-1	22-2	19-3	27-0	23-4
	no. 2	12-0	10-5	15-10	13-9	20-3	17-6	24-8	21-4
	no. 3	9-1	7-11	12-0	10-5	15-4	13-3	18-8	16-2
Western cedars (north)	select structural	11-11	10-10	15-9	14-3	20-1	18-3	24-5	22-2
	no. 1 & appearance	11-11	10-10	15-9	14-3	20-1	18-3	24-5	22-2
	no. 2	11-7	10-5	15-3	13-9	19-5	17-6	23-7	21-4
	no. 3	9-4	8-1	12-4	10-3	15-8	13-7	19-1	16-6
Western white pine	select structural	12-11	11-9	17-0	15-6	21-9	19-9	26-5	24-0
	no. 1 & appearance	12-11	11-2	17-0	14-9	21-8	18-9	26-6	22-10
	no. 2	11-7	10-0	15-3	13-2	19-5	16-10	23-8	20-6
	no. 3	8-11	7-9	11-9	10-2	15-0	13-0	18-3	15-9

The plank-and-beam roof may, of course, have a ceiling beneath the roof concealing its structure. It would be a shame, however, not to take advantage of its potential to enhance the rooms below it, since the heavier structural members can be quite handsome. If the planks are to be exposed to the interior space, a means of insulating the roof from above must be devised. Many designers, it should be noted, con-

sider the 2", 3", or 4" thick planking to be insulation enough. In cold climates the 2" planking should be beefed up with 1" or more of rigid insulation. (If you use thicker insulation board, you will have to use very long roofing nails, not always immediately available.) The finished roofing is applied above the insulation (Ill. 4).

One major structural problem must be surmounted when using this kind of construction

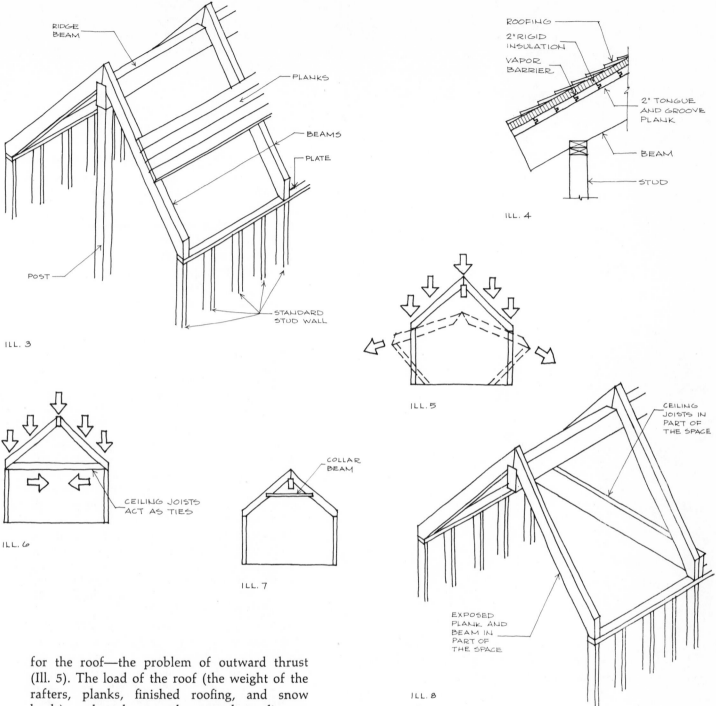

ILL. 3

RIDGE BEAM

PLANKS

BEAMS

PLATE

POST

STANDARD STUD WALL

ILL. 4

ROOFING

2" RIGID INSULATION

VAPOR BARRIER

2" TONGUE AND GROOVE PLANK

BEAM

STUD

ILL. 5

ILL. 6

CEILING JOISTS ACT AS TIES

ILL. 7

COLLAR BEAM

ILL. 8

CEILING JOISTS IN PART OF THE SPACE

EXPOSED PLANK AND BEAM IN PART OF THE SPACE

for the roof—the problem of outward thrust (Ill. 5). The load of the roof (the weight of the rafters, planks, finished roofing, and snow loads) pushes down and outward, tending to flatten the roof and push out the walls at the point of roof support. This problem is not encountered in framing a roof with an attic, because the ceiling joists act as ties to connect the opposite supporting walls and counter the outward thrust (Ill. 6). Since we have eliminated the ceiling (and therefore its joists), we must seek some other remedy for this nonstatic condition. The rafters may be tied together at the top with collar beams that become part of the exposed roof (Ill. 7). Another solution is to ex-

pose only part of the roof structure and to construct a ceiling on the rest of that roof (Ill. 8). The end and side walls of the house with the ceiling will help to balance the outward thrust and stabilize the house. Alternates are to use columns in the side walls or to construct small buttresses.

The critical difference between this framing and the one with ceiling joists is that in this

Roof Design
99

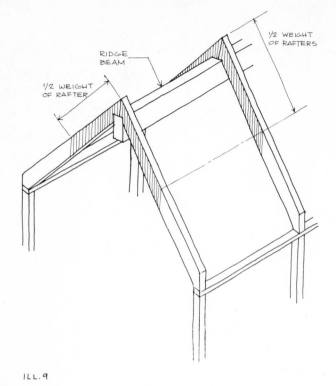

ILL. 9

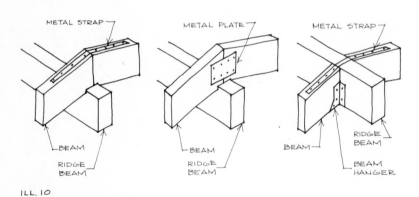

ILL. 10

the loads that they carry (Ill. 9). Special care must be taken to connect the rafters to each other and to the ridge beam. Details are outlined in Illustration 10.

Structural Design for Plank-and-Beam Construction*

1. Frame the roof: Use a large-scale (1½" = 1'-0") drawing. Be sure that loads are transferred to the foundation by means of load-bearing walls or partitions, beams, and columns.

2. Make sure that the spans are not excessive. Limit the span of the rafters to 18' or 20', the span of the ridge beam to 16'.

3. Determine the slope by drawing the section beneath the plan. The "span" of the rafter can be determined by scaling the drawing or by using the right-triangle method ($a^2 + b^2 = c^2$).

4. Determine the live load requirements by checking the building code for your locality.

5. Decide on the rafter spacing. This depends on the thickness of the planks to be used.
   2" plank will span up to 8'-0"
   3" plank "   "   " 15'-0"
   4" plank "   "   " 20'-0"
   Rafter spacing might be determined by the aesthetic effect on the interior space. If the room is 18'-0" long, you might choose to space the rafters every 6' on center to create three even spaces on the ceiling, even though the 2" plank you are using can span up to 8'.

6. Select the rafter using Table D. Before using the table, determine the stress capabilities of the lumber you are designing with. If you are using eastern hemlock of common structural grade (f = 1,100), you will have to use the f = 900 designation on the table.

7. Select the ridge beam according to Table E. This table has been greatly simplified for the purposes of this book and is keyed to Table D. Since we have limited the spacing of the rafters to either 6' or 8', these are the only spacings considered in Table E. The ridge beam will either have a span of 12' or 16' unsupported. If you wish a longer span,

* In this chapter we have attempted to streamline the design procedure by eliminating much of the sophisticated structural theory and compiling tables instead of explaining the mathematical formulas. The net effect of this simplification is to make the design procedure seem less complex than it actually is. Since the structural design of the house is so important to the future safety of its occupants, we strongly advise that you hire a structural engineer or an architect to design the roof framing plan and specify the rafters and beams. At the very least, have a professional check your design before proceeding with construction.

instance the ridge member must be structurally designed to be self-supporting like a beam and to carry the weight of its rafters. The design of the ridge is tricky. Any errors in its calculations can seriously affect the overall structural soundness of the house. For this reason, we *strongly* recommend that you consult an architect or a structural engineer, while still in the design stages. In the roof with an attic the ridge member does not have to be structurally designed since it relies on the self-buttressing effect of the rafters. In the case of a roof without ties, the ridge is designed as a girder spanning between two walls or columns. It must not only be counted on to carry its own weight, but also must bear the weight of half the rafters and

Plank spacing	10' — 6'-0"	10' — 8'-0"	12' — 6'-0"	12' — 8'-0"	14' — 6'-0"	14' — 8'-0"	16' — 6'-0"	16' — 8'-0"	18' — 6'-0"	18' — 8'-0"	20' — 6'-0"	20' — 8'-0"
For L.L. of 20 psf or less												
Stress grade												
f = 900	4 × 8 2/2 × 8	3/2 × 8 2/2 × 10	3/2 × 8 2/2 × 10		2/2 × 12 3/2 × 10	4/2 × 10 2/3 × 10 6 × 10	2/3 × 10 6 × 10	8 × 10 3/2 × 12	4/2 × 10 3/2 × 12		6 × 12 2/4 × 12	
f = 1200	3 × 8 2/3 × 6	4 × 8 2/2 × 8	3 × 10 4 × 8	3/2 × 8 2/3 × 8	2/2 × 10 4 × 10	3/2 × 10 2/2 × 12	3/2 × 10 3 × 12	6 × 10 2/3 × 10	3/2 × 10 4 × 12	4/2 × 10 3/2 × 12	3/2 × 12	6 × 12
f = 1500		3 × 8 2/3 × 6	2/2 × 8	3 × 10	3 × 10	2/2 × 10	2/2 × 10 4 × 10	2/2 × 12 3/2 × 10	2/2 × 12	6 × 10 2/3 × 10	4 × 12	3/2 × 12
For L.L. of 20–30 psf												
Stress grade												
f = 900	3/2 × 8 2/2 × 10	2/4 × 8	2/4 × 8 3/2 × 10	2/3 × 10	2/3 × 10 6 × 10	2/4 × 10	2/4 × 10 3/2 × 12	4/2 × 12	4/2 × 12 2/4 × 12	5/2 × 12	2/3 × 14 2/4 × 12	10 × 12 4/3 × 12
f = 1200	4 × 8	3/2 × 8 2/2 × 10	2/2 × 8	3/2 × 10 2/4 × 8	3/2 × 10	6 × 10 2/3 × 10	4 × 12 6 × 10	2/3 × 12 3/2 × 12	4/2 × 10 3/2 × 12	4/2 × 12 2/4 × 12	8 × 12 6 × 12	8 × 12 2/4 × 12
f = 1500	3 × 8 2/3 × 6	4 × 8	2/2 × 8	2/3 × 8 2/2 × 10	2/2 × 10	3/2 × 10	3/2 × 10 2/2 × 12	6 × 10 4/2 × 10	2/3 × 10 4 × 12 6 × 10	2/3 × 12 3/2 × 12 8 × 10	3/2 × 12	2/3 × 12 6 × 12 4/2 × 12

we advise you to consult an architect or engineer, as the section you will need might be a massive one and may present construction as well as deflection problems.

Instructions in the Use of Table D

See illustrations on page 102.

The above table is designed to simplify the selection of beams or rafters to be used in flat-roof framing (post-and-beam) or for pitched-beam roofs (as rafters).

SPAN: Considered to be from support to support. If the roof is flat, it is the horizontal distance between supports. If the roof is pitched, it is the actual length of the section between supports.

SPACING: Either 6'-0" or 8'-0" is the dimension between the beams (rafters). It is the span of the planks.

L.L.: Either 20 psf or less, or between 20 and 30 psf should cover most code requirements.

F: The fiber stress in bending for the particular wood being designed for.

Douglas fir	no. 1 select	f = 900
	no. 2 construction	f = 1,500
	no. 3 standard	f = 1,200
hemlock, eastern	no. 1 select structural	f = 1,300
	prime structural	f = 1,200
	common structural	f = 1,100
	utility structural	f = 950
hemlock, west coast	select structural	f = 1,600
	construction	f = 1,500
	structural	f = 1,200

Deflections were not considered in compiling this table. Since there are hardly any stiff wall-finishing materials (for example, plaster) in common use today, deflections of only fractions of an inch would not be harmful to the building or its inhabitants.

For rafter lengths of less than the 2' increments use the higher span. That is, if you have a span of 10'-11", use the span tables for 12'-0".

For ridge spans of either 12' or 16'

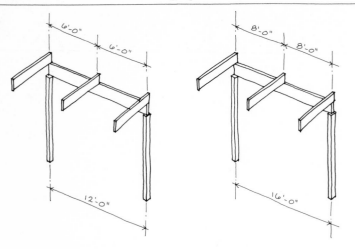

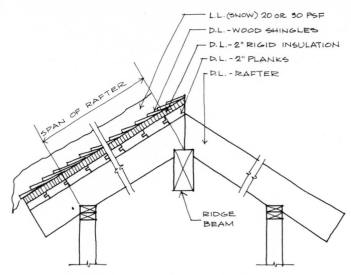

RIDGE BEAM SECTIONS FOR PLANK AND BEAM CONSTRUCTION

For L.L. of 20 psf

Span of rafter	Ridge span = 12'-0"		Ridge span = 16'-0"	
	f = 1200	f = 1500	f = 1200	f = 1500
10'	3-2 × 10	4 × 10	8 × 12	6 × 12
	4 × 12		6 × 14	
	6 × 10			
12'	4 × 12	4 × 12	10 × 12	4 × 16
	3-2 × 10			
	6 × 10			
14'	4 × 14	4 × 12	10 × 12	8 × 12
		6 × 10		6 × 14
16'	4 × 14	6 × 10	12 × 12	10 × 12
	8 × 10		6 × 18	
18'	6 × 12	4 × 14	6 × 18	10 × 12
		8 × 10	10 × 14	6 × 16
20'	4 × 16	4 × 14	10 × 14	6 × 18

For L.L. of 30 psf

10'	4 × 14	4 × 12	8 × 12	6 × 12
12'	4 × 14	6 × 10	10 × 12	4 × 16
			6 × 16	
14'	4 × 16	4 × 14	6 × 16	10 × 12
			8 × 14	
16'	4 × 16	4 × 14	6 × 18	10 × 12
	6 × 14			6 × 16
18'	8 × 12	4 × 16	6 × 18	6 × 16
	6 × 14			8 × 14
20'	6 × 14	4 × 16	8 × 16	6 × 18

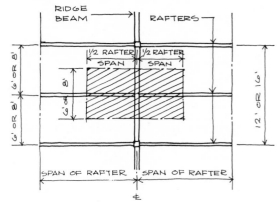

FRAMING PLAN

FLAT ROOFS

The word "flat" in the case of a roof is often a misnomer. Roofs (even the ones that are used for decks) are, in most cases, not designed or constructed perfectly flat. A small pitch is usu-ally an integral part of the design to facilitate the removal of water from the roof. Without a pitch, water and ice tend to build up on the roof. If the roofing membrane is undamaged, the puddling will cause no harm. But if there is even the tiniest of cracks in that membrane, there is a great chance of leakage. (The storm drainage system, discussed in Chapter 14, must be well-designed and periodically checked and cleaned to avoid heavy water and snow loads. The roof might not be designed to handle these extra loads.)

There is a good deal of variety in the design of flat roofs. They may or may not have an overhang. They may be constructed out of posts and beams or out of closely spaced joists. They may or may not sport an "exposed" ceiling. The

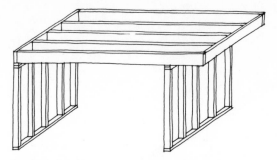

JOISTED FLAT ROOF SUPPORTED BY STUD WALLS

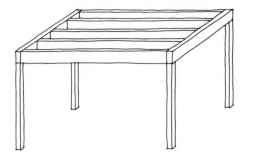

JOISTED FLAT ROOF SUPPORTED BY POST AND BEAM

ROOF BEAMS SUPPORTED BY POST AND BEAM

ILL. 11

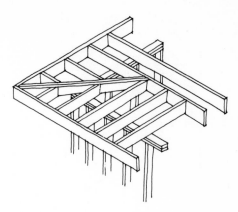

FLAT ROOF FRAMING CORNER DETAIL

ILL. 12

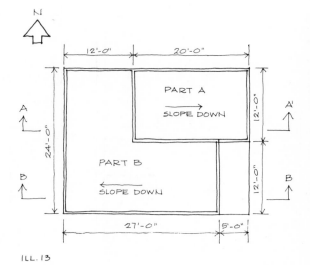

ILL. 13

various framing patterns are shown in Illustration 11.

The joisted flat roof is structured like a floor. Building codes must be checked for the design loads on the roof. Because the roof is flat, and must support snow loads, the ceiling, the built-up roofing, and whatever mechanical pipes and ducts are hung from it, the loads are not as small as those used for pitched roofs. The depth of the joists will be dependent on the design loads and on the spans. Use the joist tables in Chapter 8 to select the members. Check Illustration 12 for framing the overhangs.

For post-and-beam construction the methods outlined for the use of Table E must be followed to select the beams. Choose 2″, 3″, or 4″ plank as outlined in step 5 of the method to design for plank-and-beam construction, page 100. Bear in mind that this table is designed for live loads of 20 and 30 psf respectively.

STRUCTURAL DESIGN OF THE ROOF OF THE SAMPLE HOUSE

The sample house roof is designed for plank-and-beam construction. There are two separate roof plans (see Illustration 13)—Part A and Part B. We begin our analysis with the smaller one, Part A.

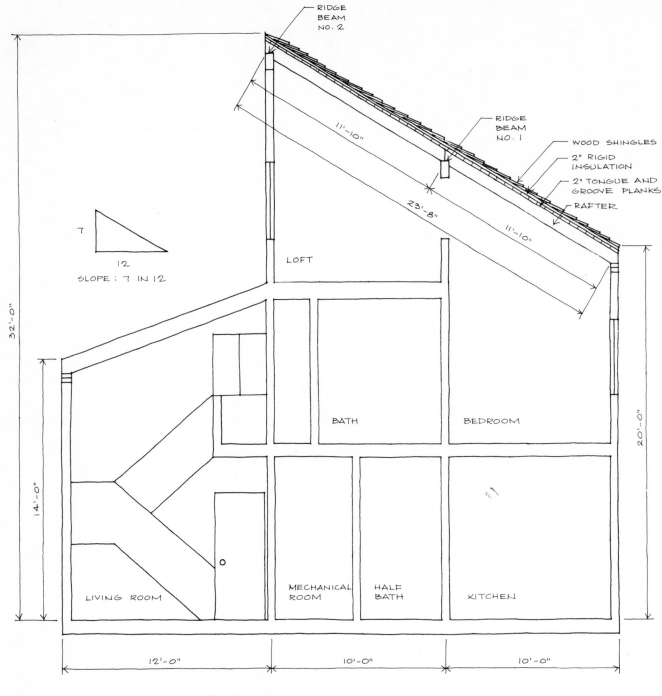

RIDGE BEAM NO. 2

RIDGE BEAM NO. 1

WOOD SHINGLES

2" RIGID INSULATION

2" TONGUE AND GROOVE PLANKS

RAFTER

11'-10"

23'-8"

11'-10"

SLOPE : 7 IN 12

32'-0"

14'-0"

20'-0"

LOFT

BATH

BEDROOM

LIVING ROOM

MECHANICAL ROOM

HALF BATH

KITCHEN

12'-0"

10'-0"

10'-0"

SECTION A-A: PART 'A' OF ROOF

ILL. 14

Part A

In a large-scale drawing determine the spans* of the rafters. In this case (Ill. 14) we have a potential rafter length of over 23', which we will

* See definition of "span" for pitched roofs on page 95.

break up into two lengths, each 11'-10". We measure the slope and find it to be 7 in 12.

Decide on the rafter spacing. The 2" thick tongue-and-groove planks can span up to 8'. We could divide the 12'-0" distance from the fireplace wall to the north wall with three spans of 4' each or two spans of 6' each. The two

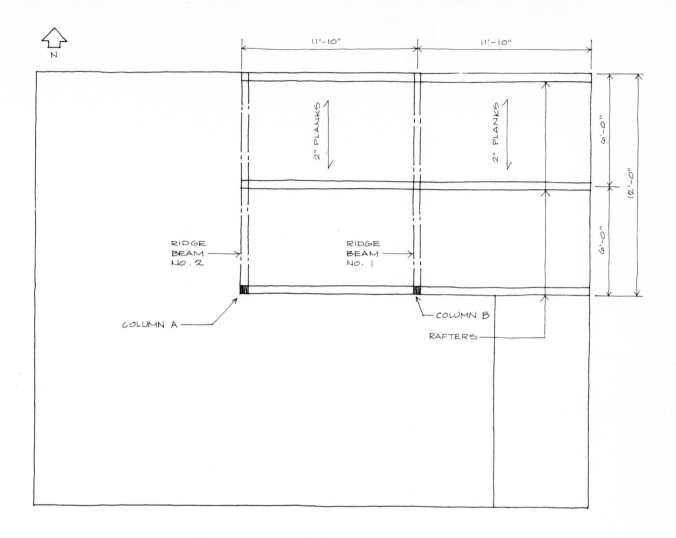

PART 'A' - ROOF FRAMING PLAN

ILL. 15

spaces of 6′ each would make better use of the spanning potential of the roof planks. We choose 6′ spacings (Ill. 15).

From the slope of the roof (7 in 12) and from the building code, we determine the required design live load. In this case it is 20 psf (for a slope of more than 3 in 12).

Choose rafters using Table D. The spans of our rafters are 11′-10″ each. We use the 12′ designation on the table for rafter span. The rafters will be spaced at 6′. We are planning to use $f = $ 1,200 lumber or better (hem-fir). We, therefore, choose a 4 × 8 rafter. (We would have headroom problems with the 3 × 10.) To increase the

structural continuity we will endeavor to obtain the rafter lumber in 23′ lengths to cover both spans. If this proves impossible, we will strap the two rafter sections together at their adjoining ends.

In selecting the ridge beams, begin with RB no. 1 (Ills. 14 and 15). The span of the ridge beam is 12′; the rafter span is almost 12′. We will use $f = $ 1,200 lumber or better. The L.L. is 20 psf. Use Table E, and select three 2 × 10′s. (The composite beam is easier to find and cheaper to buy than a solid section.) Although the loads on RB no. 2 are smaller, we will use the same ridge section for ease of framing.

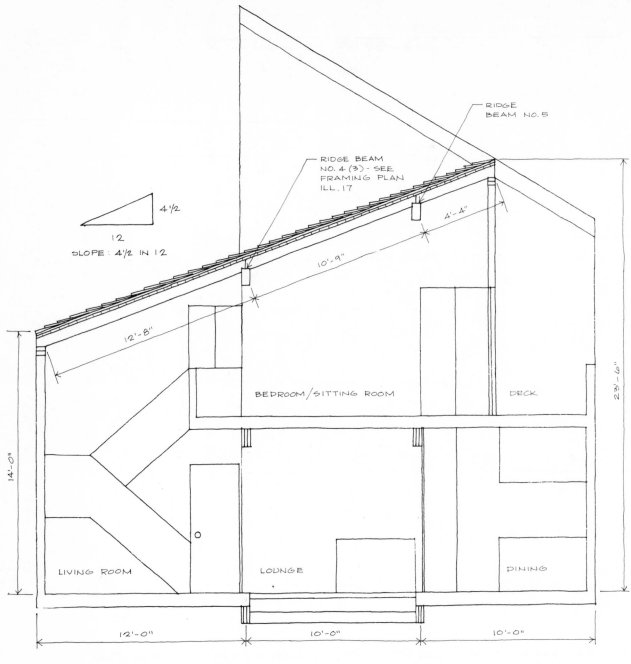

RIDGE
BEAM NO. 5

RIDGE BEAM
NO. 4 (3) - SEE
FRAMING PLAN
ILL. 17

4½

12

SLOPE: 4½ IN 12

4'-4"

10'-9"

12'-8"

23'-6"

BEDROOM/SITTING ROOM

DECK

14'-0"

LIVING ROOM

LOUNGE

DINING

12'-0"

10'-0"

10'-0"

SECTION B-B: PART 'B' OF ROOF

ILL. 16

Part B

Determine the span of the rafters (Ill. 16). The span of the rafters will be 12'-8" on the west side of the house over the living room. The span of the rafters over the master bedroom will be 10'-9" with a cantilevered portion of 4'-4". (Al-though we will design the rafters for the 10'-9" span, we must choose a piece of lumber that is at least 15'-1".) The slope is 4½ in 12.

Decide on the rafter spacing. To be consistent with Part A we choose the 6' spacings. The rafters over the living room will be spaced 6' on center and there will be one at each end (north

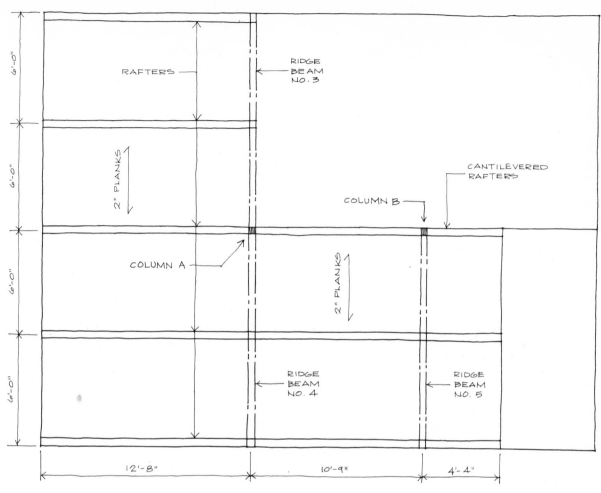

N

RAFTERS ← → RIDGE BEAM NO. 3

2" PLANKS

6'-0"

6'-0"

6'-0"

6'-0"

CANTILEVERED RAFTERS

COLUMN B

COLUMN A

2" PLANKS

RIDGE BEAM NO. 4

RIDGE BEAM NO. 5

12'-8"   10'-9"   4'-4"

PART 'B'- ROOF FRAMING PLAN

ILL.17

and south) and three intermediate rafters (Ill. 17).

The slope is more than 3 in 12 and from the building code we determine that the L.L. is 20 psf.

Choose rafters using Table D. The span of the rafters is 12'-8" for the living room. We will have to consult Table D for the 14' spans. Lumber is $f = 1,200$, spacing is 6'-0".

We choose two 2 × 10's. We may decide to use a single 4 × 10 in place of the two 2 × 10's if we can find a good-looking piece of lumber. (Remember, these rafters are to be exposed to the living room.)

For the cantilevered rafter of 15'-1" long (but only 10'-9" in design span) we consult Table D at 12'. We can use a 15'-1" length of 4 × 8 or one of 3 × 10. Since this member is to cantilever over 4', it might be a good idea to overdesign. Also, for aesthetic purposes, the rafters should be the same dimensions of those used over the living room going into the bedroom-sitting room. The rafters should appear to soar upward and look as if they are continuous. We will, therefore, use the same section (4 × 10) as we chose for the first span.

Now for the ridge beams. Ridge beams support half of two spans (Ills. 16 and 17). We begin with RB no. 4 because it presents a special problem. Since it will be supporting the cantilevered rafter to the east of it, we will have to be careful to secure the rafters to the ridge beam using reversed joist hangers to counter the upward seesaw tendencies. The span to the west of the beam is 12'-8" and to the east 10'-9" totaling 11'-8½". Consult Table E using the 12' rafter span designation. We select a 6 × 10 or three 2 × 10's. RB no. 3 has only half the loads on it, but for ease of framing we will select the same section. The same for RB no. 5.

10
Vertical Supports: Walls and Columns

The vertical components of the house deserve a chapter of their own since they fulfill quite different structural and aesthetic functions than the floors or roof. The floor system, be it of wood frame or of concrete, is designed on strictly mathematical criteria based on spans, loads, and deflection limits. The walls and partitions, on the other hand, do not serve only as structural components but also weatherproof the house and provide its "public face."

Although the structural criteria are not critical in the design of walls and partitions, we will consider them first. The walls, partitions,* and columns of the house transfer the roof and floor loads down to the foundations. Theoretically, these components are stressed only in compression. Different materials act differently under the various stresses. Unreinforced concrete is very strong in compression but extremely weak in tension, as in bending. Wood, on the other hand, although not as strong as concrete in compression, can assume a great deal of bending stress. For the most part, load-bearing walls are constructed of reinforced concrete, rammed earth, adobe, brick, concrete block, or stone. A variation on the load-bearing theme is the wood-frame stud wall. Because the size of this book is limited, we cannot pursue the design and construction of walls in all of these materials. We will limit our discussion to the wood-frame wall

and the concrete-block wall (see Chapter 11 on foundations). Refer to the Bibliography for specific references to other books that outline construction in the remaining materials.

Since all of the above materials have large reservoirs of compressive strength, their structural design is not a major problem. As a matter of fact, load-bearing walls for the one-family house are usually not structured mathematically at all. A 6" concrete-block wall, or a double-thick wall of brick, or even a load-bearing frame wall (consisting of 2 × 4 studs and ½" thick sheathing*) is usually considered overdesigned structurally.

WALLS AND PARTITIONS

The load-bearing stud walls used in platform-frame construction are built after the floor below has been completed. The walls are simple to fabricate since almost all the components are of uniform size. The wall units can be built in long sections on the platform floor itself, or can be prefabricated in smaller units off-site and erected later.

The wall frame consists of 2 × 4 studs running approximately 7½' long vertically between the sole plate (a 2 × 4 positioned horizontally)

* Partitions are interior walls, whether they are load-bearing or not. The word "walls" is reserved for the exterior of the building, again, whether load-bearing or not.

* For sheathing under vertical siding you must use ¾" thick plywood since the siding is not nailed directly into the studs.

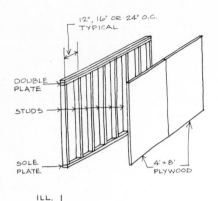

ILL. 1

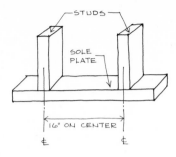

ILL. 2

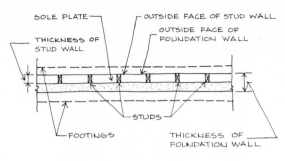

ILL. 3

on the bottom and the double plates on the top (Ill. 1). Because we do not notch the studs to let in bracing (as is done in the braced frame), we must rely on the plywood sheathing to add rigidity to the frame. The plywood sheathing panels (sold in 4′ × 8′ sheets) nailed to the studs act dually as bracing and sheathing.

Studs are traditionally spaced 16″ on center (o.c.). "On center" means that the distance between them is measured from the center of one piece to the center of the other (Ill. 2). Studs can be spaced 12″ o.c. or 24″ o.c., depending on the loads above. Experience has taught that the 16″ spacing for the studs works most efficiently in almost all cases. Architects, carpenters, and contractors nearly always design the wall with stud spacing every 16″ o.c.

The space between the studs is filled with insulating materials in climates that require it. Until recently the thickness of the insulation was specified at 2″. The energy crunch of the 1970's, however, has made 4″ thick insulation standard today. Insulation is sold in a number of types and sizes. The most commonly used is a blanket insulation available in rolls 15″ wide (to fit snugly in between the studs). More on the subject follows in Inset I, Chapter 13.

Wall Design

To determine the thickness of the exterior walls and the interior partitions (in order to draw them to scale on the plan) simply add up the items in the wall section. Beginning in the interior, the gypsum-board wall is ½″ thick, the 2 × 4 studs are 3½″ thick (see the table on nominal and dressed sizes in Chapter 7), the insulation, being in between the stud spaces, doesn't add to the thickness of the wall, the

sheathing is ½″, ⅝″, or ¾″ thick, and the outside siding can be anywhere from ½″ thick (for plywood panels) to 2″ thick for hand-split shakes. The wall, therefore, adds up to approximately 5″ to 6″ in thickness. When drawing the wall on the plan, line the outside face of the wall studs with the outside face of the foundation wall (Ill. 3). Thus the wall (the sheathing and the exterior siding are outside of the foundation wall line) is drawn at 4″.

The interior partitions, consisting only of 3½″ studs and two gypsum-board faces of ½″ each, measure 4½″. All plumbing lines and electrical wires, by the way, are run between the studs. The plan for our sample house incorporates decisions on the walls and is drawn as shown in Illustration 4.

COLUMNS

When the designer of a building wants to open one space into another and eliminate the need for a partition, he will use a beam spanning between two columns to support the floor joists above (Ill. 5). The columns might be designed to stand free and unattached in the expanded space or might be "masked" as part of an adjacent partition. See the plans for the sample house (Ill. 4); note how the columns are hidden in the "core" partitions. Columns are generally constructed out of wood, steel, reinforced concrete, or are lally columns, which are hollow steel shafts filled with concrete. In private residential construction, wood is by far the most popular choice.

Columns must be calculated much like beams and girders because they are inadvertently subjected to bending stresses (refer to Chapter 6).

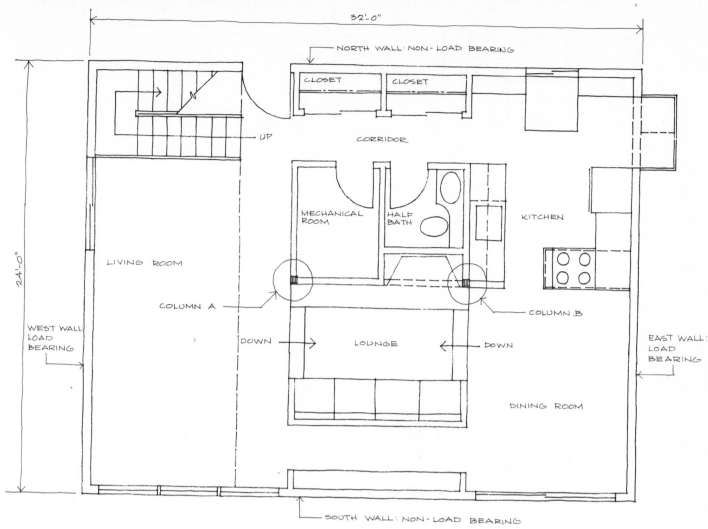

32'-0"

NORTH WALL: NON-LOAD BEARING

CLOSET   CLOSET

CORRIDOR

UP

24'-0"

LIVING ROOM

MECHANICAL ROOM

HALF BATH

KITCHEN

WEST WALL: LOAD BEARING

COLUMN A

COLUMN B

EAST WALL: LOAD BEARING

DOWN

LOUNGE

DOWN

DINING ROOM

SOUTH WALL: NON-LOAD BEARING

FIRST FLOOR PLAN

ILL. 4

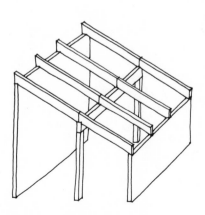

ILL. 5

Wood is weaker in bending than it is in compression. Bending, therefore, becomes the critical design factor. If the load on the column is applied centrally (along its neutral axis) and evenly, the stresses on that column are purely compressive. If the loads are applied off-center or unevenly (even as little as a quarter of an inch) the column will bend or "buckle" slightly (Ill. 6). In wood-frame construction it is very difficult to control the loading and subsequent bending on the column. Even if the builder is very careful to center the load on the column, the lumber itself might contain an invisible defect which unbalances its load-carrying capacity. Because of the likelihood of the column's bending we must consider the tensile strength of the material and its elasticity.

Vertical Supports: Walls and Columns

111

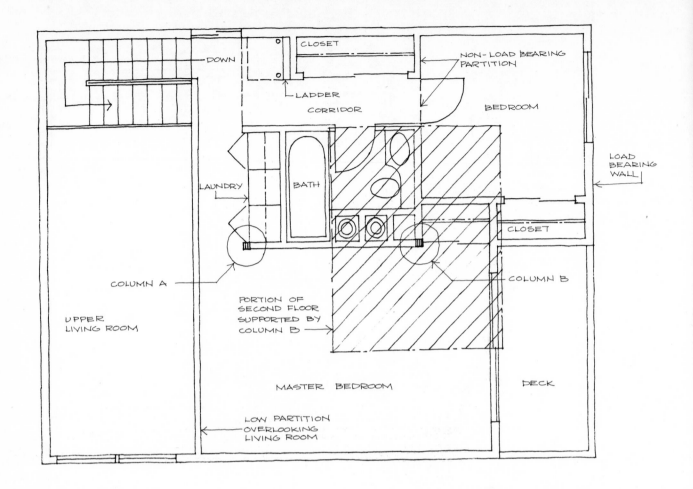

SECOND FLOOR PLAN

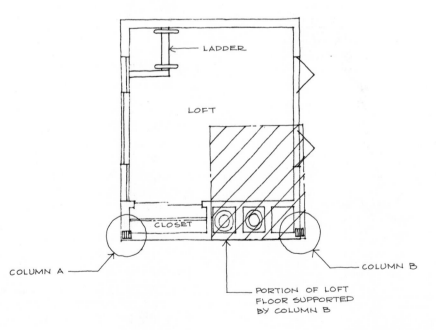

ILL. 4   LOFT PLAN

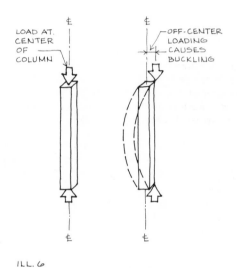
INSET I / CRITERIA FOR COLUMN DESIGN

FOR COMPRESSION

The load (P) divided by the cross-sectional area (A) of the column section must equal the allowable compressive stress of the particular lumber you will be using (f):

$$\frac{P}{A} = f$$

FOR BUCKLING

The length in inches (L) of the column divided by the depth in inches (d), the smallest dimension in its cross section, must not be allowed to exceed 50—a figure developed by structural analysts based on mathematics and experience:

$$\frac{L}{d} < 50$$

If the column is a 4 × 8 (actually 3½" × 7½"), d is 3½". If the length is 14', L is 14' × 12" = 168". The $\frac{L}{d}$ = 48, which is just less than 50. Therefore, the maximum height of a nominal 4" deep column (no matter how small the load) cannot exceed 14'.

Even if the slenderness ratio $\left(\frac{L}{d}\right)$ is less than 50, the load that the column is able to support is reduced as its height increases. For instance, a column 8' high that is 4 × 4 can support a total load (P) of 9,890 lbs. The same section at 10' high can only support 6,330 lbs. These calculations are compiled in Table A, page 117.

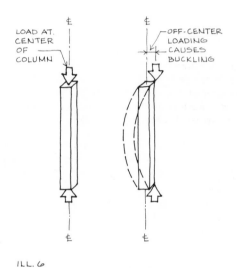

ILL. 6

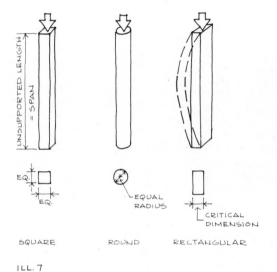

ILL. 7

As in designing beams, the span of the column must be considered, since span is one of the variables that determines the amount of bending. In the design of a column, its *unsupported length* (or height) is equivalent to the span of a beam. It is the length that is left free to move or buckle. The column will tend to buckle along its slimmest axis. For this reason it is most practical to design a round column since all the radii are equidistant from the neutral axis. A square column is a good choice as well. Often, however, we are unable or unwilling to select a square or round column but prefer to choose one that is rectangular in cross section. (A 6 × 6 square column is difficult to conceal in a partition, whereas a 4 × 8 column is quite simple to mask.) In the case of the rectangular column its slimmest dimension is the critical one (Ill. 7).

Columns are designed following very specific rules and formulas. Two major criteria are critical to the design of these slender vertical structural members: First, the column must be able to hold up the load. That is, it must be strong enough to resist the compressive stresses applied to it. Second, the column must also have adequate thickness to withstand possible buckling. If a load is not applied dead center on top of the column or if the column section has a minute flaw (even if not visible to the eye), there is a strong tendency for it to buckle under a substantial load (Inset I).

Vertical
Supports:
Walls and
Columns

113

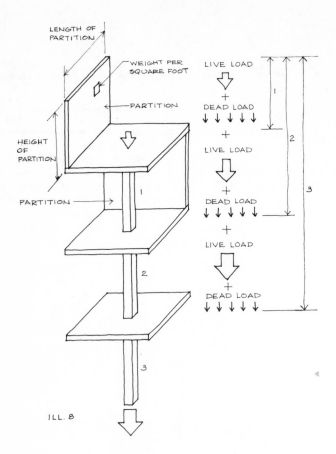

ILL. 8

Column Design

Remember when designing columns that the loads are cumulative. That is, if you want to design the column on the lowest floor you must begin to calculate loads from the top of the building, the roof, and work your way down (Ill. 8). It seems to be simpler to start at the top of the house and design the uppermost columns first before considering the ones on the ground floor. There is, however, a good reason to begin with the lower columns and to proceed upward. The bottom column in the series will be receiving the largest load and will most likely be the thickest of the columns.* Having determined the heaviest column we might choose to use that same size section for the columns above it or below it (even if that large size may not be structurally needed) so as to simplify our calculations and the actual construction process without adding significantly to the cost.

* Because the free-standing length of the column and not only the loads it is subjected to determines its cross-sectional dimensions, it will not necessarily be the thickest column.

1. Determine the location of all columns. Be sure that they are continuous and are supported by foundations and footings.

2. Establish all loads on each section (floor to floor) of each column separately. Include the live load (L.L.) as established in the code times the floor area supported by the column. For the dead load (D.L.) include the weight of the materials used in the flooring system (joists, subfloor, finished floor) plus the weight of the partitions. (Length of partition times its height times its weight per square foot of surface, Ill. 8.) Refer to Chapter 8, Inset II, for dead loads.

3. Working from the top down, determine the loads accumulated on the lowest column section. (Add all the floor loads.) This gives you P, the axial load in pounds. Go to Table A, maximum allowable axial loads for columns, page 117, look under the heading corresponding to the height of the column for that section of column only—not for the whole length from basement to roof; you want the unattached length only. Read down until you come to a number greater than your load P. Read left to determine the nominal dimensions and the cross section. Make sure that the P/A for the chosen section and column height is *less* than that recorded in the table.

EXAMPLE: Axial load P for lowest section of column on two-and-a-half-story house is 15,000 lbs.; the column height is 14'-0". Check Table A. Read down under P in 14' column. Stop at 17,100, which is the first figure that is larger than 15,000 lbs. Look to the left. Nominal size of section is 6 × 6. The area of the 6 × 6 is 30.25. Check:

$$P/A = \frac{15,000}{30.25} = 496$$

Check against the maximum P/A allowed (just to the left of the maximum allowable load for that height column), which in this case is 568.

$$496 < 568*\quad \text{Use a } 6 \times 6.$$

DESIGN OF THE SAMPLE HOUSE

1. Determine the location of all columns. Be sure that they are continuous and are supported by foundations and footings.

2. Establish all loads on each column separately. Begin with column B (Ill. 9).

* < means is less than.

Loads Due to Roof (Part A)

See Illustrations 9, 10, and 11.

L.L. × area = total L.L. on Part A of roof. Notice that the roof slopes. The length of the rafters is more than the 10′ length seen in the plan. To calculate the actual length, create a right triangle, with the rise as the vertical leg and the run as the horizontal leg. The formula for determining the hypotenuse $(a^2 + b^2 = c^2)$ will yield the actual length.

$$(6.5)^2 + (10)^2 = 42 + 100 = \sqrt{142} =$$
$$11.9′ \ (11′\text{-}10″)*$$

Live loads:
30 psf for low slope (3 in 12 or less)
20 psf for steep slope (over 3 in 12)

$$20 \text{ psf} × 11.9′ × 6′ = 1{,}428 \text{ lbs.}$$

Dead loads: see Chapter 8, Inset II.
For the weight of the roof:

2.5 psf for wood shingles
$\underline{+ \ 5.0 \text{ psf for 2″ plank}}$
7.5 psf × 11.9′ × 6′ = 535 lbs.

For the weight of the structural members in the roof (the ridge beam and the rafters), consult the roof framing plan (Chapter 9, Ill. 15) and Chapter 8, Inset II. Note that this segment of the roof supports half the weight of the center E–W rafter and all of the weight of the rafter that frames into the column. The column also supports half the 12′ length of RB no. 1. The 6′ length of RB no. 1 (designated in the previous chapter as three 2 × 10′s) weighs 13.8 pounds per linear foot.

$$13.8 \text{ lbs. per linear foot} × 6′ = 83 \text{ lbs.}$$

The rafters are designated as 4 × 8′s. The structural weight of the rafter sections that are supported by this column is 7.2 lbs. per linear foot.
7.2 lbs. per linear foot × 11.9′ = 85.7 lbs.
per rafter

85.7 lbs. per rafter × 1.5 rafters = 128 lbs.

128 lbs. for the rafters
$\underline{+ \ 83 \text{ lbs. for the ridge beam}}$
211 lbs.

Total L.L. + D.L. = 1,428 + 535 + 211 =
2,174 lbs.

* Slope on 7:12 is translated into decimals (6.5:10) for calculation purposes.

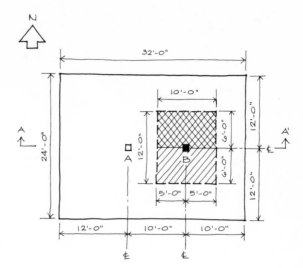

ILL. 9

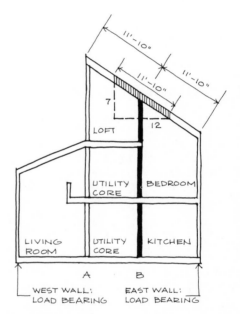

SECTION A-A′

ILL. 10

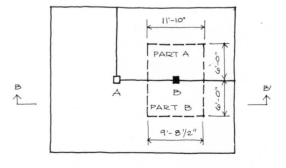

ILL. 11

Vertical Supports: Walls and Columns

115

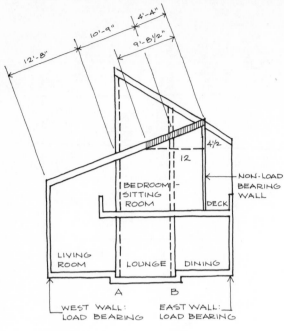

SECTION B –B'

ILL.12

Loads Due to Roof (Part B)

See Illustrations 11 and 12.
L.L. × area:
The slope is $4\frac{1}{2}$ in 12.
Therefore, use 20 psf for L.L.
The length of the roof segment is 9'-8½" (about 9.6') and the width is 6'.

$$20 \text{ psf} \times 9.6' \times 6' = 1,152 \text{ lbs.}$$

$$\text{D.L.: 7.5 psf for the weight of the roof} \times 9.6' \times 6' = 432 \text{ lbs.}$$

For the weights of the rafters and ridge beam we again consult the roof framing plans and Chapter 8, Inset II. RB no. 5 is designated as a 6 × 10 weighing 13.8 lbs. per lineal foot.

A 6' long portion of its length is supported by column B.

$$13.8 \text{ lbs.} \times 6' = 83 \text{ lbs.}$$

The rafters are 4 × 10's and weigh approximately 9 lbs. per lineal foot. About 1½ rafter lengths are supported by column B for a portion of 9.6'.

$$9 \text{ lbs.} \times 1.5 \times 9.6' = 130 \text{ lbs.}$$

$$\begin{array}{r} 130 \text{ lbs. for the rafters} \\ + \quad 83 \text{ lbs. for the ridge beam} \\ \hline 213 \text{ lbs.} \end{array}$$

$$\text{Total L.L.} + \text{D.L.} = \\ 1,152 + 432 + 213 = 1,797 \text{ lbs.}$$

Total Loads of Parts A + B of Roof

$$2,174 + 1,797 = 3,971 \text{ lbs.}$$

Loads Due to Loft Floor

See Illustration 13.
L.L. (30 psf) + D.L. (approximately 10 psf for materials and joists) = 40 psf

The section of floor supported by column B is 5' × 6'.

$$40 \text{ psf} \times 5' \times 6' = 1,200 \text{ lbs.}$$

There are two partitions:
Partition no. 1 is about 6' tall and 6' long.
The partition weighs 8.2 lbs. per sq. ft.

$$6' \times 6' \times 8.2 \text{ psf} = 295 \text{ lbs.}$$

Partition no. 2 is 5' long and its height averages about 8'.

$$5' \times 8' \times 8.2 \text{ psf} = 328$$

$$\text{Total L.L.} + \text{D.L.} = 1,200 + 295 + 328 = \\ 1,823 \text{ lbs.}$$

Loads Due to Second Floor

See Illustration 14.
L.L. + D.L. = 40 psf
$40 \text{ psf} \times 10' \times 12' = 4,800 \text{ lbs.}$

Partitions:
1. 6' long × 8' high = 48 sq. ft.
2. 5' long × 12' high (aver.) = 60 sq. ft.
3. 5' long × 8' high = 40 sq. ft.
4. 5' long × 12' high (aver.) = 60 sq. ft.
   $$\underline{\phantom{208 \text{ sq. ft.}}}$$
   208 sq. ft. × 8.2 psf
   = 1,705 lbs.
5. Is a glass wall, therefore 6' long × 12' high × the wt. of glass (see Chapter 8, Inset II), which is approximately 3.5 psf.
   6' × 12' × 3.5 psf = 252 lbs. However, half of this load will go to the east load-bearing wall: 252/2 = 126 lbs.

$$\text{Total L.L.} + \text{D.L.} = 4,800 + \\ 1,705 + 126 = 6,631 \text{ lbs.}$$

Total Loads on Column B

parts A and B of roof =	3,971
loft floor =	1,823
second floor =	6,631
	12,425 lbs.

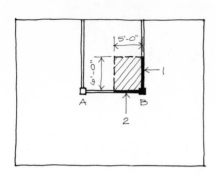

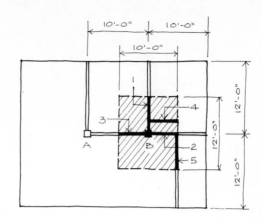

ILL. 13   ILL. 14

TABLE A: MAXIMUM ALLOWABLE AXIAL LOADS FOR COLUMNS

P = Maximum allowable axial load in pounds
P/A = Allowable axial stress for buckling in psi (pounds per square inch)

Nominal size	A sq. in.	8' P/A	8' P	9' P/A	9' P	10' P/A	10' P	11' P/A	11' P	12' P/A	12' P	13' P/A	13' P	14' P/A	14' P
4 × 4	13.14	752	9,890	595	7,820	482	6,330	398	5,230	335	4,400	286	3,750	246	3,230
4 × 6	19.94	752	15,000	595	11,900	482	9,610	398	7,940	335	6,670	286	5,680	246	4,900
4 × 8	27.19	752	20,500	595	16,200	482	13,100	398	10,800	335	9,100	286	7,750	246	6,680
4 × 10	34.44	752	25,900	595	20,500	482	16,600	398	13,700	335	11,500	286	9,820	246	8,470
4 × 12	41.69			595	24,800	482	20,100	398	16,600	335	13,900	286	11,900	246	10,200
4 × 14	48.94					482	23,600	398	19,500	335	16,400	286	14,000	246	12,000
4 × 16	56.19					482	27,100	398	22,400	335	18,800	286	16,000	246	13,800
6 × 6	30.25							917	27,700	806	23,300	655	19,900	568	17,100
6 × 8	41.25									806	31,800	655	27,100	568	23,300

At this point it would be best to calculate the loads on column A to see which column carries the greater load. It might be easiest to specify the same columns for A and B to simplify the carpentry. Let us assume here that column B carries the greater load.

To specify column B (and column A), add the weight of the column (this is also a guesstimation). We will guess a 4 × 8, which weighs 7.2 lbs. per linear foot. The column is about 23' high.

$$7.2 \text{ lbs. per linear foot} \times 23' = 165 \text{ lbs.}$$

$$\text{Total load} = 12,590 \text{ lbs. or } 12,600 \text{ lbs.}$$

Check Table A.
The unsupported lengths of the column are

9'-0" first to second floor
8'-0" second floor to loft
7'-0" loft to roof

The 9' length governs since it is the longest.

A 4 × 8 can support 16,200 lbs., considerably more than the total load. Even if we made minor errors in our calculations, we can safely assume that this column will be strong enough. Also its width, a nominal 4" (actual 3½"), will fit in with the 3½" wide stud partition.

Check: P/A = 12,600/27.19 sq. inches = 463

Check the table: the allowable P/A for a 4 × 8 column with an unsupported length of 9' is 595. The total, 463, is less than the maximum allowable. We are o.k.

Use a 4 × 8.

Vertical Supports: Walls and Columns

117

11
Foundation Design

The foundation is the structural element of a house that transfers all the loads (including the structural weight of the house) to the surrounding ground, giving the house stability and permanence. It literally roots the house to the soil (Ill. 1). This is well illustrated historically where entire buildings have been destroyed, leaving the foundations behind as the only clue to what and where they were.

Foundations can take many forms. Early colonial buildings were constructed on top of a few flat stones, which served to isolate the building from the ground and prevent the wood from rotting. The settlers soon learned that this method did not provide them with a stable house. Bad storms and uneven settling either ripped the house from the ground or the walls were destroyed by rotting. Very few, if any, of these houses remain. Another type of foundation is seen in fishermen's houses in New England's coastal towns; these homes are built over the water resting on wooden piles—the only way in which a house could be secured to the underwater bedrock.

Because foundations are a crucial component of the structure continuum, it is important to study how they transfer the house loads into the surrounding ground. There are two basic types of loading conditions: point loads and uniformly distributed loads. A pole vaulter making his jump clearly illustrates both these principles. While preparing to jump, he runs, grabs on to the pole, and places his entire weight on it. His weight is being transmitted to the ground at only one point. Once he completes the jump, he comes to rest lying flat on a mat. The ground now receives his weight at many points along this mat; it is being transmitted uniformly (Ill. 2). Similarly, foundations can transmit loads to the ground at points or uniformly.

In addition to the type of loading, the design of foundations and the selection of materials are determined by the type of soil on which the house is to be built, the topography of the site, the nature of the superstructure (whether it is a year-round house as opposed to a vacation cabin), and the availability of materials. The kinds of foundations used in contemporary construction may be classified into three basic types: continuous foundations, piles, and piers.

The most durable of the three is the continuous foundation wall. The wall, completely or partially buried in the earth beneath the house, follows the perimeter of the house and rests on a continuous base called the footing. The loads of the walls, floors, and roof are uniformly distributed along the foundation walls. These walls, in turn, evenly transfer all the loading to the surrounding earth. Continuous foundation walls are most usually built of concrete poured into formwork or concrete blocks (Ill. 3).

Piles and piers are essentially fingers gripping the ground, holding the structure in place. These fingers transmit the loads to the ground at various points. Piles (used mostly for construction in wetlands or marshes) are driven, or hammered, into the earth. They are most commonly

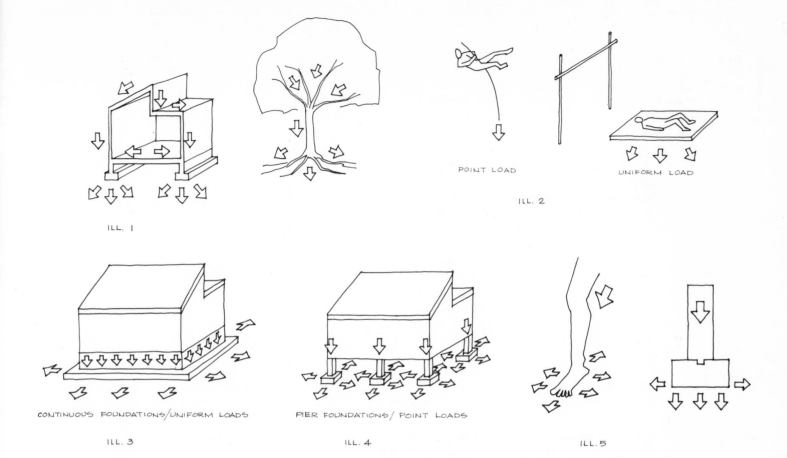

ILL. 1

POINT LOAD   UNIFORM LOAD

ILL. 2

CONTINUOUS FOUNDATIONS/UNIFORM LOADS

ILL. 3

PIER FOUNDATIONS/ POINT LOADS

ILL. 4

ILL. 5

made out of chemically treated tree trunks. Piers, on the other hand, are built on normal soils and are cast or laid in place rather than driven. They are usually constructed of poured concrete or masonry block (Ill. 4).

FOUNDATION TYPES

Continuous Foundations

Continuous foundation walls are the best choice in the majority of cases. (They are suited to all soil types and terrains with the exception of marshlands, bodies of water, and very steeply sloping land.) Continuous foundations assure you that the loads are evenly distributed to the earth, giving you a longer-lasting structure—a fact that might prove helpful when dealing with lending institutions. In addition, foundation walls help insulate the floor from drafts and serve to hide the "life-support systems" (the electric, heating, plumbing, and gas lines). Another important benefit derived from continuous

foundation walls is of particular importance in those parts of the world bothered by termites. The concrete walls tend to isolate the wooden structure from the earth (where the nests are), and (if constructed perfectly) successfully protect the wooden frame.

Continuous foundations are built in two separate stages: first the footing, and then the wall. The footing (like its namesake) spreads the weight of the wall over a wider square-foot area. The spreading of the foundation at the bottom puts more earth directly under the weight, which offers more resistance to the downward push (Ill. 5). Footings are constructed out of poured-in-place concrete. The foundation wall rests on the footing. It may be constructed of poured concrete or concrete block. The height of the wall itself is determined by the depth of the frost line (see Inset I) and by the decision whether or not to include a basement or simply build over a crawl space.

The choice between poured concrete or concrete-block foundation walls is contingent on whether the house is to have a full basement or a crawl space. Poured-in-place concrete, con-

Foundation
Design
119

INSET I / FROST LINE

Frost line is the depth to which frost penetrates and freezes the ground. Foundations placed above this line are in danger of cracking as the ground beneath them expands and moves due to freezing. Local codes will advise you of the depth of frost penetration in your particular area. The National Building Code requires foundations to be located at a minimum of one foot below the frost line.

structed properly, will give you a stronger wall with less likelihood of cracks and leakage. The work and expense, however, are considerable drawbacks. Concrete block is much easier to work with than poured concrete and, in addition, is less expensive. It is not as strong as poured-in-place concrete, and is more difficult to waterproof. If you are not considering a full basement, block is the best choice. For a house that is to have a basement with a living space, the choice is more difficult. In any case we recommend the addition of steel reinforcement in footings and concrete-block walls.

Pier Foundations

An alternative to the costly and time-consuming methods described above is pier construction. Pier foundations save time, labor, and money. They are particularly suitable for steeply sloping terrain or where excavation should be kept to a minimum. A word of caution: In cold or temperate climates the exposed plumbing lines underneath the floor are in danger of freezing. In addition, the heat loss through the floor is staggering. Unless you are building a house to be used only during summer months (so that plumbing lines are drained of water during the winter), we advise the use of pier footings only in warm areas not subject to freezing temperatures. The other problem of pier footings is uneven settling. All piers must rest on a similar soil bed to avoid uneven settling and subsequent cracks in the structure of the house (Ill. 6).

Piers are most commonly constructed of treated wood, poured concrete, or concrete block, and vary in shape from a simple column to a column resting on a footing (Ill. 7). Treated wood piers are good for light frame buildings such as bungalows or tool houses. They are not as durable as masonry piers and eventually will have problems of rot and decay. Many building codes do not allow their use for house construction. We do not recommend them. Masonry

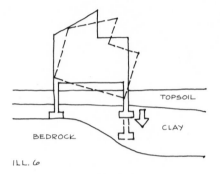

TOPSOIL
CLAY
BEDROCK
ILL. 6

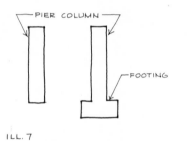

PIER COLUMN
FOOTING
ILL. 7

piers, on the other hand, whether constructed of poured concrete or concrete block, offer more stability and are not subject to rotting.

Poured-in-place concrete piers are stronger than their concrete-block counterparts. This is due to the homogeneity of concrete as a material. They do, however, require more labor and are more expensive. The expense is due to purchasing both the lumber and the ready-mixed concrete.

Of all the alternatives, concrete-block piers are the easiest and cheapest to build. Blocks are easy to handle and can be stored on the site, eliminating the problem of having to build all piers on the same day (as in the case of poured concrete). The skills required are similar to those used in laying brick. Building with concrete block can be a one-person job. To get a much stronger pier, we suggest that you reinforce the pier with steel bars and fill the holes in the block with cement.

If you are building piers with footings, you will have to purchase and pour concrete. (Check

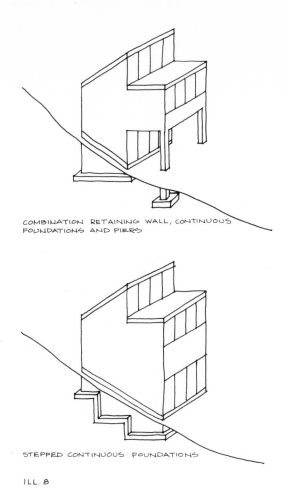

COMBINATION RETAINING WALL, CONTINUOUS
FOUNDATIONS AND PIERS

STEPPED CONTINUOUS FOUNDATIONS

ILL. 8

driving or casting piles is not an easy one and requires heavy machinery to drive the wood or precast concrete piles into the ground or to drill the holes for pouring concrete. If your house requires such a foundation, hire a professional.

Variations

We have limited our discussion to simple pier, pile, and continuous foundations. There are, of course, numerous variations and combinations of these (Ill. 8). For example, a house can have a partial full basement to enclose the boiler while the rest of the building sits on a crawl space or piers. Continuous foundations can be stepped when built on sloping ground to facilitate excavation. Combinations of continuous and pier foundations are also possible. On steeply sloping sites, one of the foundation walls might have to also serve as a retaining wall. (This involves a more complex design procedure. We suggest that, if faced with this condition, you consult a professional as an insurance against costly errors.) Always keep in mind while making design decisions the benefits and drawbacks of each type of foundation. Try to keep the design and the construction work as simple as possible.

to see if the company sells that small a quantity of concrete.) The formwork for footings, however, is very simple. Although this type of pier requires more work than a simple column pier, it will give you a considerably better distribution of loads and consequently a stabler house. Your job can be simplified by pouring the footing and then building the pier itself out of concrete block.

Pile Foundations

Piles are particularly effective for building on marshlands or on water. They can be constructed of treated wood, poured concrete, or precast concrete. (In large-scale construction, steel beams are used, but this is far too sophisticated for small-scale residential work.) Treated wood piles are widely used in beach-house building. Poured or precast concrete piles are also used but although more durable they are considerably more expensive. The process for

SIZING THE FOUNDATIONS

The size and depth of the foundations are directly related to the bearing capacity of the soil, the house loads, the underground water table, and, in cold and temperate climates, the frost line. The loads on residential design are light and therefore foundation sizes are rarely determined mathematically. In many areas, the local building code will tell you the sizes required depending on the house design and the type of soil you are dealing with.

In the event that your local code has no requirements for foundation sizes, or you are building in an area with no code, here are some helpful guidelines. Since the width of the foundation wall is related to the wall directly above, it would vary from approximately 8" to 12". For instance, in wood-frame construction, the outside walls will generally be 6" wide; therefore a width of 8" will be adequate for the foundation wall. In the case of a brick-bearing wall, which

Foundation
Design
121

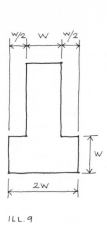

ILL. 9

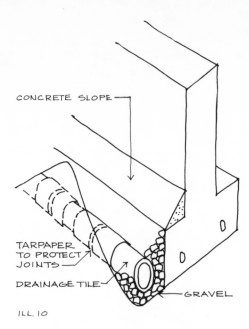

CONCRETE SLOPE

TARPAPER TO PROTECT JOINTS

DRAINAGE TILE

GRAVEL

ILL. 10

will be about 8" wide, you will most likely need a 10" or 12" foundation wall.

A good rule of thumb for sizing footings is to make the footing width twice the width of the foundation wall and its depth the same as the width of the foundation wall. For example, if the foundation wall is 12" wide, the footing should be 24" wide and 12" deep (Ill. 9). (In poor load-bearing soils such as clay, footings carrying heavy loads may have to become wider in order to spread the load over a larger area.)

Foundation depth is a variable of whether you have a basement or a crawl space, the distance to suitable bearing soil, the frost line, and the underground water table. The bottom of the footing should be above the water table to avoid leakage problems and at least 1' below the frost line. (Consult your local code.)

If your particular site or house design presents any unusual problems, do not hesitate to consult an architect. Professional help will save you a lot of headaches later on in the building process.

WATERPROOFING

A few words should be said about waterproofing techniques. If your building sits on piers or piles, you don't need to concern yourself with waterproofing. Houses sitting on crawl spaces are also generally exempted from the headaches of waterproofing, unless they happen to rest on soils of such wetness that the local codes or general local practice demands it. When the house sits over a full basement, however, you have no choice but to deal with waterproofing (particularly if the foundation walls are built of concrete block or fall below the ground water table).

In average soil conditions, black asphalt, tar, or pitch, or one of a variety of other bituminous compounds (usually referred to by trade names) is applied on the exterior of the foundation walls. Although this does not offer a complete guarantee against leakage, it will undoubtedly help. Another technique is membrane waterproofing. This type is used in very wet soils and consists of alternate layers of hot pitch (tar or asphalt) and felt, which are carefully lapped to the exterior of the foundation wall. (See page 249, Inset VI.) Membrane waterproofing offers more protection than any of the rolled-on types.

In addition to either of the above techniques, footing drainage pipes are placed adjacent to the footing and following the perimeter of the house. A layer of gravel or crushed stone is placed all around the pipe (Ill. 10). These pipes may be of porous cylindrical clay (without hubs) or perforated black plastic. Their function is to collect all the excess water accumulated around the footing's perimeter and divert it (generally to a storm sewer, a drywell, or another location on the site), thus preventing water pressure from building up next to the foundations. (See pages 171 and 253 for more details.)

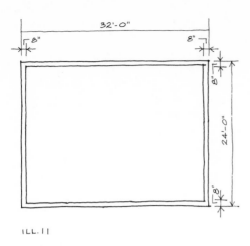

ILL. 11

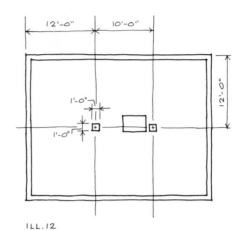

ILL. 12

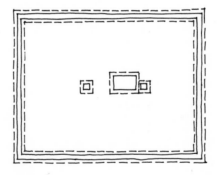

ILL. 13

Consult the local codes for recommendations or requirements in your particular area. Don't forget, however, that the effectiveness of any waterproofing method is directly proportional to the thoroughness of its application.

LOCATING THE FOUNDATIONS OF THE SAMPLE HOUSE

The sample house has exterior stud walls of approximately 6″ and sits on a crawl space that is 4′ high. The decision to build a crawl space was made to minimize excavation, construction, backfilling, and waterproofing problems and yet provide a stable and uniform base.

1. Because the exterior walls are 6″, the foundation walls will be 8″ thick and 4′ high, resting on 16″ wide and 8″ deep footings.

    We draw the perimeter of the house and indicate the foundation wall thickness (Ill. 11).

2. The piers for columns coming from the first and second floors, in addition to the fireplace foundation, are located next.

    It is apparent that the proximity between the fireplace foundation and one of the piers may pose a problem. Further study of the fireplace is needed (Ill. 12).

3. With a dotted line, we outline the 4″ projection of all footings (Ill. 13).

4. Openings are indicated in the foundation walls for ventilation purposes.

5. The final foundation plan is shown in Illustration 14, page 124.

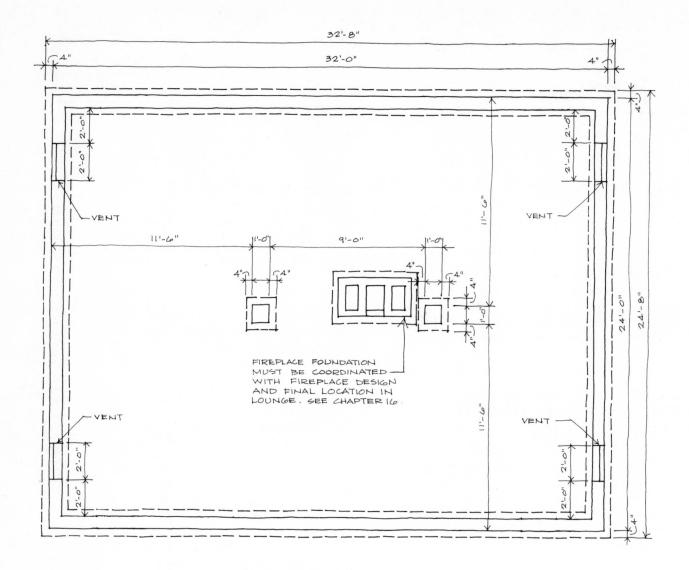

FOUNDATION PLAN

ILL. 14

12
Completing the Exterior

Some people get so carried away by the process of construction that they fail to remember their original purpose for building. It is like failing to see the forest for the trees. A friend of ours purchased a magnificent piece of property in the mountains of northern California. The site offered a number of stunning and restful views. The owner had dreamed for years of building his house near the top of the hill so that he could see the morning mist settling into the valley below him. He began building two years ago and has since successfully poured hundreds of yards of concrete and has nailed what seem to be thousands of studs and joists. Unfortunately, he hastily planned and purchased the windows for the house and, as a consequence, has only partial access to his view. When we questioned him about the size (small), the location (indiscriminately chosen), and quality (poor) of his windows, he claimed to know little about the subject, having bought the only windows (double-hung, aluminum) in stock at the local lumberyard. It seemed a shame that this man, who had researched the intricacies of earthquake design and who could quote chapter and verse from the electric code, did not know the difference between a casement window and one that is double-hung, and had never heard of hermetically sealed glazing.

In the case of this home builder, we think the trouble was that he had reached a saturation point in the planning and research stage of house design and was anxious to get on with the building itself. This is not an uncommon prob-lem in projects that require a great deal of time and effort. In house building (as opposed to rug weaving or totem-pole carving) hasty planning in the initial stages leads to expensive and long-lasting blunders, some of which cannot easily be corrected. The moral of this short sermon is to convince you not to lose patience with the design stages and skip over Chapters 12 through 18 but to be steadfast in continuing to research carefully and plan all aspects of the house that will later affect your safety, comfort, finances, and future pleasure in your home.

COMPLETING THE EXTERIOR WALLS

Once the structural elements of the exterior walls are completed (the studs and the sheathing), the finishing material is applied for reasons of appearance and weatherproofing. There are many ways in which the exterior walls may be finished. Exterior finishing materials may be categorized into natural and "others." The authors must admit a strong prejudice to natural materials, which include all of the wood products, stone, and brick, over "others" which include aluminum and vinyl-coated metal siding. This prejudice stems from the fact that the natural materials look like what they are supposed to be. That is, wood boards look like wood boards, brick looks like brick, and so on. The other products disguise themselves as something

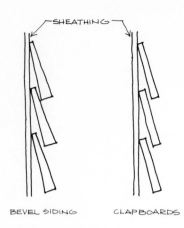

BEVEL SIDING   CLAPBOARDS

ILL. 1

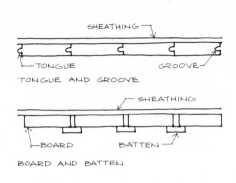

TONGUE AND GROOVE

BOARD AND BATTEN

ILL. 2

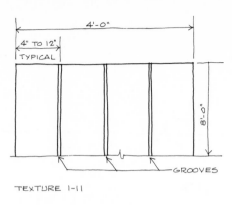

TEXTURE 1-11

ILL. 3

they are not. Aluminum is made to appear to be wood boards; plastic is cast to resemble random stone or slate. These cheap imitations of the real thing can only look like cheap imitations of the real thing. There are a number of advantages to these products, including the fact that they are maintenance free and in some cases cheaper than what they imitate. Be that as it may, we will not elaborate on these others. If you are eager to use them, it is easy enough to find information on their advantages and cost.

Exterior Wall Finishes

In choosing among the large number of exterior finishes available, you should consider color, pattern, material, texture, and direction of emphasis (either horizontal or vertical). In addition, there are the not so small considerations of price and ease of erection.

Horizontally applied siding comes in a number of styles. The two most popular are clapboards and beveled siding (Ill. 1). When siding is applied horizontally, the long horizontal shadows cast along the wall emphasize the length of the house. Had these same boards been applied vertically, the emphasis would have been on the height of the building. Clapboards are traditionally painted, but need not be. Beveled siding boards come in lengths up to 12'-0".

Vertically applied siding comes in tongue-and-groove boards and in board-and-batten patterns. Tongue-and-groove boards are manufactured to form a lock-and-key joint where they abut one another (Ill. 2). In the board-and-batten style the boards are usually wide and square-cut. Because they have a tendency to expand and contract depending on the weather, they cannot be laid tightly side by side. A small expansion joint is left between the boards, which is then covered up by the narrow batten strips (Ill. 2). Vertical siding can be painted, stained, or treated with a preservative and left to weather naturally.

Shingles are another category of exterior siding materials, although they are more difficult to install than either vertical or horizontal boards. They come in a variety of sizes, colors, and materials (from wood to asbestos). The most expensive are wooden hand-split shingles, which lend a rustic look to the house by their heavy texture. Factory-made cedar shingles are attractive and can be left in their natural state to weather. Asbestos and asphalt shingles are equally low in maintenance, and offer an array of colors.

Plywood exterior panels are becoming increasingly popular. They are easy to erect and because of their size require a good deal less work. An additional advantage is that the exterior plywood panel can be nailed directly to the studs thus eliminating the need for sheathing altogether. The panels come in widths of 4' and lengths of either 8', 9', or 10'.* If the exterior plywood panel is to be applied directly to the studs without sheathing, it must be a minimum of ½" thick (but should be ¾") to be able to act

* If one or more sides of the house is taller than the sheet of plywood siding is high, you may reconsider your decision to use plywood siding. Although the vertical joint between panels is easy to mask, the horizontal joint will be obvious. In addition, the horizontal joint may require metal flashing which might detract from the appearance of the wall.

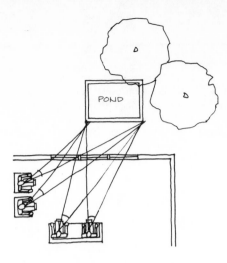

ILL. 4

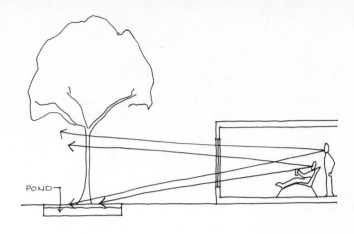

ILL. 5

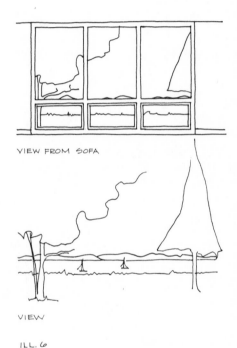

VIEW FROM SOFA

VIEW

ILL. 6

as structural bracing as well as finishing. There is a large selection of colors and patterns in plywood siding. The most popular are the board-and-batten style and a panel that has a vertical indentation every 12", which is called texture 1-11 (Ill. 3).

Before deciding on an exterior finish, check the literature in Sweet's Catalogue, the various construction magazines, the house and garden periodicals, and the folders at the lumberyard. There is a wealth of advertising literature on exterior siding.

WINDOWS

Among the most important criteria in selecting windows for the house are their size and placement. First determine what you wish to look out at (or conversely, what you wish to avoid seeing). Next determine the placement of furniture in the room. Be sure that you plan the windows so that they are placed between the sitting areas and the outside view (Ill. 4). Be careful that the window is big enough and low enough so that when you are sitting you can see more than the sky; also make sure it extends high enough so that, standing, you can see out as well (Ill. 5). If you want to allow light into the room but do not wish to look into the parking lot next door, you can purposely place windows high on the wall. Although these factors may seem obvious, they are the errors most often made in house design. Window types are detailed in Inset I.

Another common and difficult to avoid error is the design of the separation mullions between the glazed areas of the windows. One of the authors has a summer house with a view onto Long Island Sound. The view is simple, composed of a line at the end of the back yard, where the dropoff to the beach occurs, the horizon line of the water, and a misty, thin gray line for the hills of Connecticut some twenty miles away. The living room boasts 15' of windows facing the view. Unfortunately, when a person is seated on the sofa that faces the Sound, his view is bisected by the horizontal mullion of the window which coincides with the horizon line of the water. The result is frustrating, to say the least (Ill. 6).

If you have a good eye, go a step further and "frame" the view as if it were a painting (Ill. 7). The great master, Le Corbusier, framed a rural scene in his residence at Poissy, France. From the

Completing
the Exterior

127

INSET I / WINDOW FRAMES

The various window frames are named for the method by which they may be opened or closed—the single exception being the fixed window, which cannot be opened. The movable members of the window frame are referred to as its sash. The fixed perimeter members are its frame. The various members of the window sash are identified below.

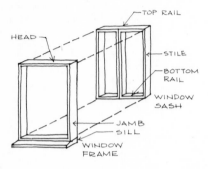

Casement window: The sash of this window is rectangular. The window is hinged and is usually positioned to swing out.

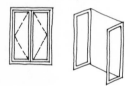

Projected window: Similar to the casement but does not employ the hinge device to open and close. The projected window usually opens by swinging out and sliding across.

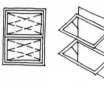

Awning window: Is hinged at the top and opens horizontally. The windows project outward, offering some rain protection when open.

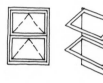

Hopper window: The same as the awning window except that it is hinged at the bottom.

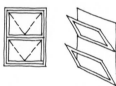

Sliding window: The window frames are set on tracks that slide past each other when the window is opened. Most sliding windows are designed with a spring action under the tracks to facilitate the removal of the sash from the frame for easy cleaning.

Double-hung window: Similar to the sliding window in that the window is mounted on a set of tracks. The windows, in this case, move up and down on the tracks and a counterbalance system is used to support the weight of the sash and to hold it in place.

Sliding glass doors: Similar to sliding windows only on a larger scale, these windows are designed for people to pass through (see Ill. 13, page 132).

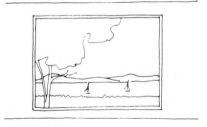

ILL. 7

upper deck one looks over the courtyard of the second floor, and through a square-cut opening in the unusually high roof-garden wall what one sees appears to be a painting, as organized and as composed as a Cézanne watercolor. Le Corbusier could have eliminated this high wall entirely, and opened the deck to the view of the entire countryside. In doing so he would have missed the opportunity to highlight the most exquisite heart of the valley.

Most of us wish to capitalize on a view if it is really worthwhile. You may fantasize about waking up in a high, turret-like bedroom with walls made of glass, surrounded by trees and filtered sunlight. Be sure to temper your fantasies with the realities of climate and the knowledge of our finite supply of fossil fuels. Glass is an excellent conductor of heat: into the house in summer, and out of it in winter. Replacing the lost Btuh (heat energy) costs money, and good ecological planning requires us to be discriminating in the size and location of glazed wall areas. There are a number of products on

Our Perma-Shield windows are even easier.

All exterior surfaces* of Perma-Shield windows are protected by a sheath of rigid vinyl, over a wood core. So you enjoy all the benefits of window beauty and weathertightness without traditional window bother. All Perma-Shield windows come in white. In addition, Perma-Shield casement and awning windows are also available in a new Terratone color—a rich, warm earth tone that blends beautifully with almost any home exterior—wood, brick, stone, masonry, etc.

* Except the sash on Perma-Shield Narroline® windows.

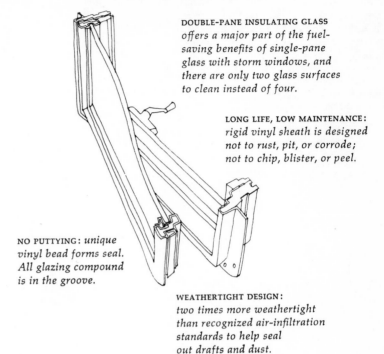

NO STICKING: *treated wood is stable and a natural insulator. Designed for easy operation.*

DOUBLE-PANE INSULATING GLASS *offers a major part of the fuel-saving benefits of single-pane glass with storm windows, and there are only two glass surfaces to clean instead of four.*

LONG LIFE, LOW MAINTENANCE: *rigid vinyl sheath is designed not to rust, pit, or corrode; not to chip, blister, or peel.*

NO PUTTYING: *unique vinyl bead forms seal. All glazing compound is in the groove.*

WEATHERTIGHT DESIGN: *two times more weathertight than recognized air-infiltration standards to help seal out drafts and dust.*

ILL. 8

the market that are designed to limit the amount of heat loss through glazed areas. These products are presented in detail in Chapter 13, Inset II, and their insulating values are discussed in Inset III. Remember that although these windows represent a decided improvement over the use of ordinary plate glass, they in no way have the insulating capacity of a well-insulated wall section. In addition, hermetically sealed glass is expensive.

Residential windows come in three basic materials: wood, plastic-coated wood, and metal. The plain wooden windows (made of Ponderosa pine) are the most commonly used. Wood is a very fine insulator, and so the wooden windows are weathertight as well as handsome. The only disadvantage to this moderately expensive frame is that it must be maintained. A redwood frame may be stained and creosoted with the rest of the house, or it may be painted. The stock pine windows, however, are usually painted, but can be left untreated on the interior. In most climates the trim (exterior side of the window frames) will need treatment only once every four or five years. Houses that

are located near salt water will require more frequent care.

Some wooden windows are manufactured with the exposed wood sections sealed with a rigid vinyl covering. In addition to eliminating "sticking" windows, the vinyl ends the need to paint the frame and sash. Although these windows are higher in price than the plain wood frames, the extra cost might be justified in some climates. As of this writing, the vinyl covering comes in white or earth tone only (Ill. 8).

Metal windows do not require painting. They also do not have the tendency of wood windows to swell with moisture in summer and stick in their frames. Metal windows, on the debit side, offer poor resistance to heat transfer and cause condensation problems. The heat transfer factor alone might persuade the northern climate buyer to stay away from the metal sash. Metal windows come in aluminum, steel, and stainless steel. The metal frame may be left untreated or given an etched or lacquered finish. Special vinyl coatings or anodized finishes may be given to the metal to further protect and beautify it, but these finishes add to the cost of the frames.

Completing
the Exterior

129

Table of Sizes

Perma-Shield® Casement

Color: White or Terratone vinyl.

Glazing: double-pane insulating glass.

Options: removable Perma-Fit® rigid vinyl grilles; Perma-Clean® Screens.

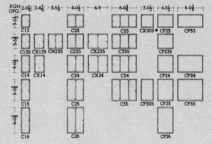

*"Egress" unit, hand operated, furnished without roto operator.

Wood Casement

Exterior: Factory-primed.

Glazing: double-pane insulating glass or vision-tested single glazing.

Options: removable Perma-Fit rigid vinyl grilles; Perma-Clean Screens, storm panels. Also picture window combinations.

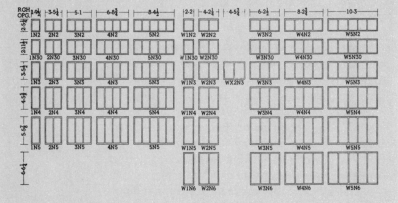

Perma-Shield® Gliding Doors

Color: White vinyl.

Glazing: double-pane insulating safety glass.

Options: Perma-Clean Screens.

Arrow indicates direction panel opens, as viewed from exterior.

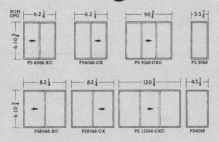

For all units, consult your dealer for information on using double-pane insulating glass over 4000' altitude.

ILL. 9

Although some steel windows are equipped with special polyvinyl chloride corrosion-resistant coatings, most will have to be painted to keep the corrosion-prone metal from deteriorating. Stainless steel windows are being used increasingly for commercial buildings, but are not available at this writing for residential use.

When you purchase a window from the lumberyard or from a local representative of one of the major window manufacturers, you will be buying the entire frame (the perimeter of the window) and sash (the movable part of the window) complete with glazing and hardware. The window will be ready to install; all you have to do is provide the rough opening in the wall. The manufacturer's literature will include all the available stock sizes and types (Ill. 9). (Be sure to check that the frame thickness conforms to the thickness of your wall.) In addition, there will be a number of options to choose from besides size, style, and material. You can purchase the window with single glazing, that is, one single sheet of glass in the frame. Another alternative is the hermetically sealed window, which features two thin sheets of glass separated by an airtight space. This sandwich panel offers greater resistance to heat transfer than does the singly glazed window. The manufacturer might offer a triply glazed window, which contains the hermetically sealed window and an additional single sheet of glass installed as a storm sash. This panel can be removed in the summer and replaced with a screen section if desired. If you are going to build in a cold climate, the triple glazing makes a great deal of economic sense.

Since the exterior siding and window treatment is crucial to the exterior appearance of the house, we suggest that you draw a detailed large-scale elevation of at least one side of the house. Draw in the walls of the house and the shape of the roof, but leave out the windows and the exterior siding. Next lay a layer of very thin tracing paper over the elevation and draw in the windows (the style and dimensions taken from the manufacturer's literature). When you are satisfied with the windows, lay another sheet of paper over the windows and draw in the siding you are considering. If you are thinking about horizontal siding, be sure you have made some choice about corner detailing. See page 297, Illustrations 14 and 15, for corner detailing. If you use a vertical corner board it will affect the elevation considerably, maybe positively. This is

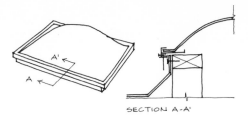

SECTION A-A'

ILL. 10

your decision. Another potential trouble spot is in the use of plywood exterior walls. The horizontal joint will be visible. Draw that line across the face of the elevation and see if you can live with it.

Skylights

Skylights, originally used to light the interior space of factories, are becoming more popular for residential use. The skylight allows for the dramatic introduction of light into any room in the house. A skylight may be constructed by simply framing glass between the rafters or roof joists. This kind of skylight, although inexpensive, is difficult to waterproof. Care must be taken to properly construct the skylight so that water is shed from it and does not puddle in the corners where it can leak. A prefabricated skylight, shaped like a plastic dome, is easy to install and is usually leak-proof. The bubbles come in many sizes and can be installed without difficulty. These units come complete and are designed to shed water. All that must be provided is the rough opening. In addition, there are skylights that can be opened for ventilation and varieties that have built-in ventilation fans. Check the manufacturer's literature for sizes, shapes, and cost (Ill. 10).

DOORS

Doors, like windows, can be classified by the way they are opened, the materials they are constructed from, and/or their design.

Doors may be either hinged, folding, sliding, overhead, or accordion-pleated. The hinged door is most commonly used as the front door of the residence and as the door separating rooms. The

Primed Wood Gliding Doors

Pre-Finished Wood Gliding Doors

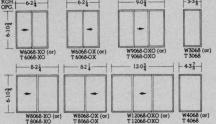

Glazing: double-pane insulating safety glass.

Options: Perma-Clean®Screens.

Arrow indicates direction panel opens, as viewed from exterior.

Prefix "W" indicates primed wood. "T" indicates pre-finished in Terratone color.

Perma-Shield® Gliding Windows

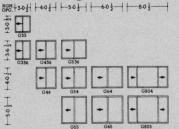

Color: White vinyl.

Glazing: double-pane insulating glass.

Options: Perma-Clean Screens.

Arrow indicates direction panel opens, as viewed from exterior.

Perma-Shield® Narroline® Double-Hung

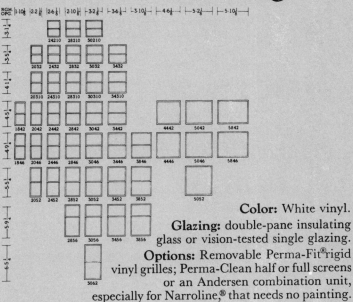

Color: White vinyl.

Glazing: double-pane insulating glass or vision-tested single glazing.

Options: Removable Perma-Fit®rigid vinyl grilles; Perma-Clean half or full screens or an Andersen combination unit, especially for Narroline,® that needs no painting.

ILL. 9

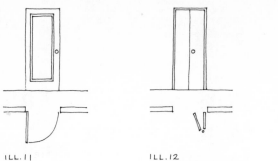

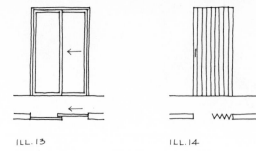

ILL. 11 ILL. 12 ILL. 13 ILL. 14

outside door is usually solid-core, consisting of solid wood covered with a wood veneer. The interior hinged doors will most likely be hollow-core, consisting of an interior of honeycombed wood strips covered by a veneer of plywood. The paneled door, seen in older homes, consists of a thin solid piece of plywood framed by heavier members at the top, bottom, and sides (Ill. 11).

Folding doors are often used for closets because they permit a large opening to be exposed while using a minimal amount of floor space. Each door has a hinge in the center and slides on a track (Ill. 12).

Sliding doors are also often used for closets. The doors do not take any room from the space they are opening into and, therefore, are preferred to folding doors if space is at a premium. They are hung from a metal track, which is screwed into the upper frame. The double doors are arranged on a track so that they slide past one another. Glass sliding doors are used extensively between a living space and a patio (Ill. 13).

Accordion folding doors are not often seen in residences, but are very useful if cleverly designed. The accordion door is similar to the folding door but the sections are very small. The door can be used to temporarily divide spaces or to open them up as one large room. For example, a children's sleeping wing might have one large space organized into two or three sleeping areas, a study area, and a play area. Accordion doors can be used to close off one or more of these sections at a time if privacy is desired. Many living-dining-family rooms consist of one open space. When two people are entertaining their friends at the same time, the area can be divided so that each group has privacy (Ill. 14).

Although doors can be obtained in a variety of materials, wooden doors are the most commonly used in residential architecture. Doors for interior purposes, such as closet doors, do come in metal and in vinyl-coated aluminum varieties,

but we do not recommend their use because the metal is too thin and flimsy. One good bang can change its shape or mar its appearance.

Most doors are 6'-8" high and come in a variety of standard widths. The front door is usually 3'-0" wide and 1¾" thick. The doors that separate rooms are 2'-6" wide and 1⅜" thick. It is not unusual to design the door to the bathroom at 2'-0" wide, but it is not recommended since the opening is too small.

Doors, both interior and exterior, are sold "pre-hung," which means that the door frame and hinges are preassembled. These doors, although more expensive, save a good deal of labor. They are particularly advantageous for exterior doors, because they come weatherproofed which is a tricky operation to do yourself.

Garage Doors

The most commonly used garage door is the overhead type composed of several hinged sections that roll up to the ceiling on tracks. The doors may be operated manually or by a remote-control device so that the door can be opened without your having to leave the car. The doors come in heights of 6'-6" and 7'-0" and are usually 1⅜" thick. A single-car garage may be equipped with a door that is 8' or 9' wide. Double doors are 16'-0" wide. As in window frames and interior doors, we prefer the wood varieties to the metal ones (Ill. 15).

ROOFING

Roofing materials come in two major categories depending on the slope of the roof. Built-up roofing is most generally used for flat and low-sloped roofs. This type of roofing provides watertight protection for the roof that does not drain rain water and snow quickly. Pitched

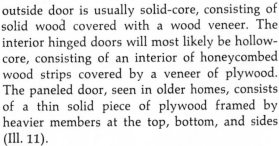

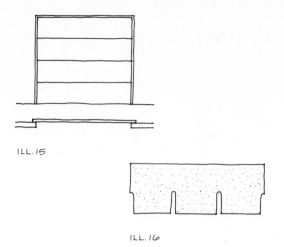

ILL. 15

ILL. 16

roofs, on the other hand, shed water and snow quickly, and a scale-like protection is all that is required.

We will begin the discussion with the sloped roof using wood shingles. Wood shingles and shakes are an extremely attractive roof finish. The shingles, be they cypress, redwood, or cedar, machine-finished or hand-split,* provide natural water resistance with their own resins and oils. Shingles are graded in no. 1 and no. 2 categories. They are cut in standard lengths of 16″, 18″, or 24″ and come in random widths for the purposes of design texture. The shingles come tapered and in a variety of thicknesses. Thickness determines how the shingles are laid, since they are overlapped one on the other. Usually one bundle of shingles will cover 100 square feet of roof. The disadvantages of the material are that it is combustible and relatively expensive. There are, however, some roofing systems using wood shingles that have been given a high fire-resistance rating. Such systems consist of a pressure-treated wood shingle applied over the roof deck covered with a plastic-coated steel foil.

Asphalt shingles come either in strip form† (Ill. 16) or as individual shingles. The shingles are composed of felt (rag, wood, or mineral fiber) that has been saturated with asphalt and coated on one side with granules for color and texture. The strips come in 12″ × 36″ pieces that are scored to look like individual shingles. Strip shingles are laid over asphalt-saturated felt and have a high fire-resistance rating.

* Split shingles, more commonly known as shakes, are sawed from hardwood. Because they vary considerably in thickness, width, and even in color, a shake roof or wall adds a good deal of texture and character to a house.

† The strips make the roof installation much simpler than it would be using individual shingles.

Asphalt cement shingles are highly resistant to fire, rot, and decay. They are composed of asbestos fibers and Portland cement with ceramic granules added for color and weather-proofing. The shingles are often textured and colored to make them look like wood or slate. This type of material is applied over a layer of roof felt for roofs with at least a 5 in 12 slope. For less steep slopes two layers of felt are required with a layer of hot-mopped asphalt between them. The shingles are brittle and must be nailed through pre-punched holes.

Metal shingles, including aluminum, are obtainable in textures that imitate wood, or in highly glazed enamel colors. They too are applied over roofing felts.

Roofing tiles, popular in Europe, are not commonly used here, because of their excessive weight (which necessitates structuring the house to accommodate the roofing material) and their high cost. The tiles consist of baked clay and come unglazed in a variety of orange-red or green-gray shades. They also come in brightly glazed shades.

Flat or low-sloped roofs require watertight roofing commonly known as bituminous substances. In built-up roofing, layers of felt and bitumen are alternated to form a seamless, waterproof, flexible membrane that protects the roof from water. The bitumens keep the felt watertight, and the felts provide support for the bitumens, which would otherwise crack under the heat of the sun.

The bitumens consist of either asphalt, which is a by-product of the distillation of petroleum, or coal tar, which is a by-product in the manufacturing of steel. The roofing felts (also used in conjunction with the tiles and shingles listed above) consist of asbestos, glass fiber, or rag saturated with asphalt, the latter being the least expensive and most commonly used.

Saturated felts are used in conjunction with shingles. They are composed of dry felts that have been saturated with asphalt or coal tar. It is important to be mindful that the rolled roofing used under the shingles or strips should have a low vapor resistance. This means that vapor easily passes through on its way up and out of the house, but that water, in the form of rain or snow, cannot penetrate the felt. (For further clarification see page 154.)

Steep roofs finished with wood shingles often do not require felt at all because of the fortunate tendency of the shingles to quickly shed water. The lower five or six rows of shingles

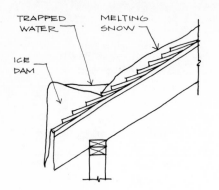

ILL. 17

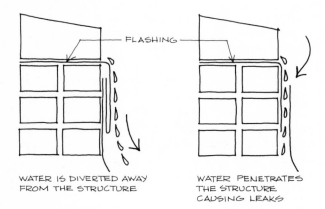

WATER IS DIVERTED AWAY
FROM THE STRUCTURE

WATER PENETRATES
THE STRUCTURE
CAUSING LEAKS

ILL. 18

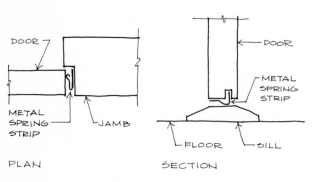

PLAN

SECTION

ILL. 19

FLASHING

Flashing consists of long thin sections of sheet metal or flexible sections of a waterproof membrane material that are placed where two different building materials are juxtaposed to prevent water from entering the joint. The flashing material is laid over the gap between the two materials so that a driving rain cannot penetrate, having been diverted away from the structure (Ill. 18). Common locations that will require careful flashing details are at roof ridges and valleys, at the point where the chimney meets the roof, at window and door openings, and where the roof is penetrated by pipes, vents, skylights, etc.

WEATHER STRIPPING

Wood, metal, and other materials have a tendency to expand in warm or moist weather and to contract in colder, drier air. This presents an interesting dichotomy when it comes to doors and to the infiltration of cold air in winter. In the summer the moisture in the air tends to swell a wooden door so that it might occasionally stick in its frame. On the other hand, in the winter, when we would prefer an airtight joint between the door and its frame, the door shrinks, causing a gap that allows cold air to infiltrate. This problem is easily rectified by installing metal spring strips around the doors to prevent infiltration (Ill. 19). The bent piece of metal is tensioned so that it is "open" in the winter when the gap is the widest, and it is "closed" in summer when under pressure from the door pressing against the frame.

COMPLETING
THE EXTERIOR OF THE
SAMPLE HOUSE

Many of the aesthetic decisions for the sample house were made while the house was still in schematic stages. For instance, upon inspection of the rough model, the Harris-Banks's decided on a vertical siding in a natural wood color. The long vertical lines created by this type of siding would emphasize the verticality of the house.

should, however, receive the protection of some roofing paper to prevent what is called the "ice dam effect" (Ill. 17). The ice dam is created by an accumulation of melting snow at the periphery of the roof a few days after a snowfall. The snow slides to the edge of the roof and is melting. The temperatures fall and the melting snow turns to ice. If more snow should fall, this ice dam will prevent the new accumulation from sliding off the roof. When this second layer begins to melt, the water will be backed up behind the dam and may make its way through the shingles to the sheathing.

The local lumberyard had samples of siding and after some deliberation they chose ¾″ thick western cedar (common) tongue-and-groove boards.

The next problem to be tackled was that of the windows and doors. As far as operability is concerned, the couple had no preference for one type of window over another. They were concerned, however, that the windows be well-proportioned, looking good on the exterior of the house as well as in each individual room.

Beginning with the kitchen, the window on the north wall was limited to a 3′-0″ width to conform to the built-in table and the cabinetwork on either side of it. An additional limitation to the placement of the window was the height of the table which would be 30″ from the floor. The window selected from the manufacturer's literature was a sliding window, 3′-6½″ tall and 3′-0½″ wide. This window (and all that followed) was finished in an earth-tone vinyl on the exterior of the frame and was doubly glazed, with an additional storm sash.

A sliding glass door was selected for the dining room to afford visibility to the view, allow maximum light penetration, and ease passage to the patio. The door specified was 8′-2¼″ wide and 6′-10¾″ high.

The type, size, and placement of the windows in the living room turned out to be most problematic. After long debate the couple selected a complex of windows that had three panels of fixed glass with three panels of awning windows directly below. The panels came in widths of either 3′-5½″ or 4′-1½″. The couple wanted the windows to fill the southern wall as much as possible from the western end to the beginning of the bookcases (Ill. 20). They had to allow for two mullions (each 4″ wide) between the windows. Were they to use the 4′-1½″ window width, the total length of the window wall would come to 13′-0½″, much too long for the available space (which was 11′-6″ long). They selected the 3′-5½″ window. The awning panel was 2′-1⅛″ high and was set 9″ above the floor (to leave room for the baseboard heaters that would most likely be placed directly under the windows). A 2″ wide mullion separated the awning window from the fixed window which was 4′-8⅛″ high. The vertical distance from the floor to the top of the window frame was 7′-8¼″, just perfect to clear the ceiling of the second-floor balcony.

These windows were most adequate as far as

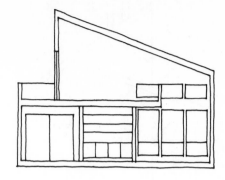

ILL. 20

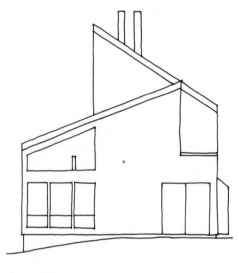

ILL. 21

access to the view was concerned. However, the couple had originally envisioned windows covering the entire southern wall of the living room with glass reaching as far as the ceiling. The Harris-Banks's considered placing a fixed panel of glass in the shape of a trapezoid above the already selected prefabricated windows. They were careful to draw the window so as to avoid the floor structure of the second-floor balcony (Ill. 21). This scheme was rejected for a number of reasons. First, the size of the glass pane would make its cost prohibitive. Second, the size and position of the panel might allow too much heat gain in the summer, and the panel, being fixed, would not allow for proper ventilation of this heat. Third, the railing of the second-floor balcony would butt into the glass and would look awkward.

Next the couple explored the possibility of using three awning panels on top of the three fixed panels. The awnings would solve the ventilation problems and would also limit the heat

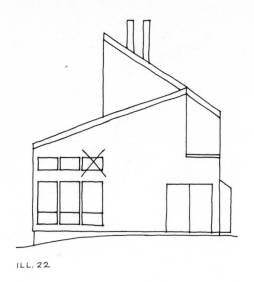

ILL. 22

gain. The solution shown in Illustration 22 was rejected because the upper-right-hand awning interfered with the floor structure of the second-floor balcony. The windows were raised to clear the structure (Ill. 20). This solution was likewise rejected because of the awkwardness of the upper-left-hand awning panel—a window which would give a knee-high view of the outside world. The panel was eliminated; the two remaining panels were specified to be 2'-5⅛" high.

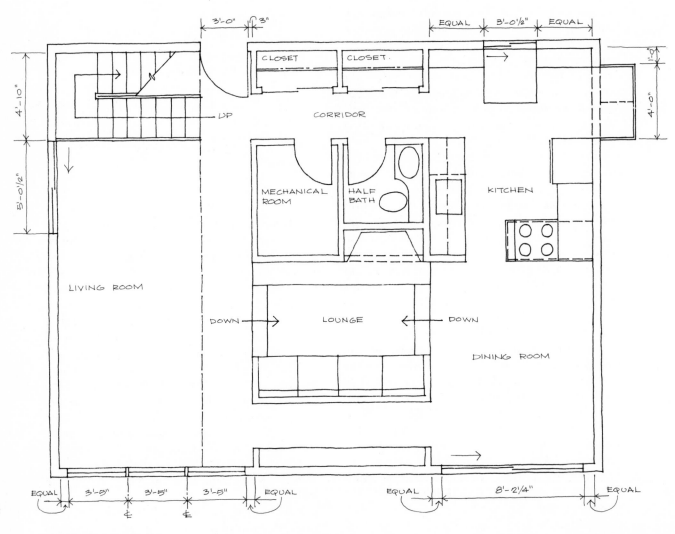

FIRST FLOOR PLAN

ILL. 23

A similar procedure was followed for the remaining windows and doors of the house. The final decisions are depicted in Illustrations 23–29.

The roofing was specified as 250-pound asphalt shingles with self-sealing tabs. (These shingles are designed to seal themselves together in the heat of the sun.) The color selected for the shingles was a deep warm brown.

The greenhouse was selected from the catalogue at a downtown nursery.

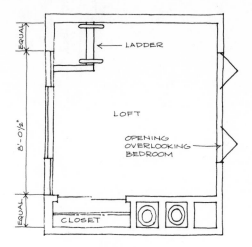

LOFT PLAN   ILL. 25

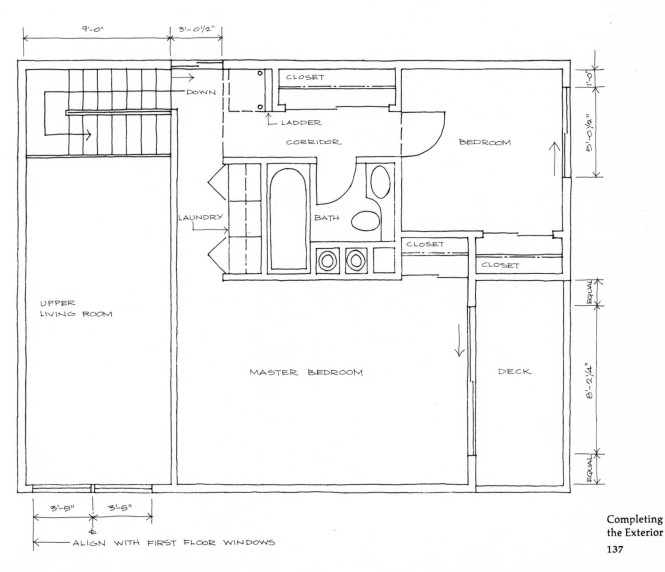

SECOND FLOOR PLAN

ILL. 24

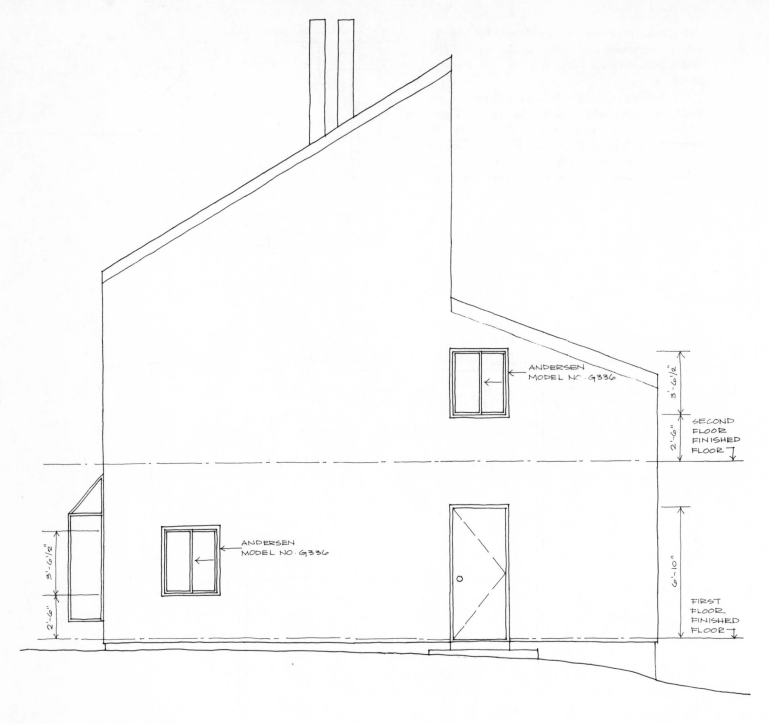

ANDERSEN
MODEL NO. G336

3'-6 1/2"

2'-6"

SECOND
FLOOR
FINISHED
FLOOR

ANDERSEN
MODEL NO. G336

3'-6 1/2"

2'-6"

6'-10"

FIRST
FLOOR
FINISHED
FLOOR

NORTH ELEVATION

ILL. 26

Design
Development
138

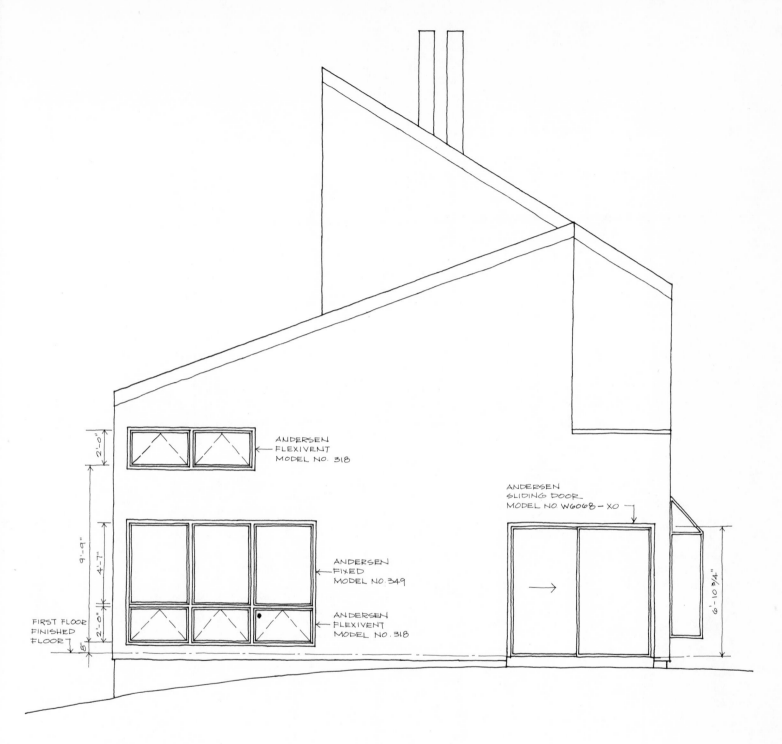

2'-0"

ANDERSEN
FLEXIVENT
MODEL NO. 318

ANDERSEN
SLIDING DOOR
MODEL NO. W6068 - XO

9'-9"

4'-7"

ANDERSEN
FIXED
MODEL NO. 349

6'-10 3/4"

FIRST FLOOR
FINISHED
FLOOR

2'-0"

ANDERSEN
FLEXIVENT
MODEL NO. 318

8"

SOUTH ELEVATION

ILL. 27

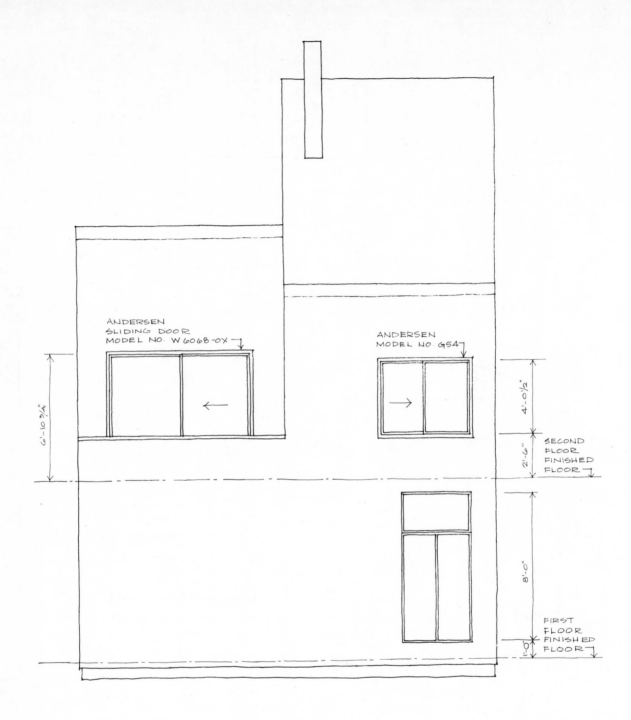

ANDERSEN
SLIDING DOOR
MODEL NO. W 6068-OX

ANDERSEN
MODEL NO. G54

6'-10 3/4"

4'-0 1/2"

2'-6"

SECOND
FLOOR
FINISHED
FLOOR

8'-0"

FIRST
FLOOR
FINISHED
FLOOR

1'-0"

EAST ELEVATION

ILL. 28

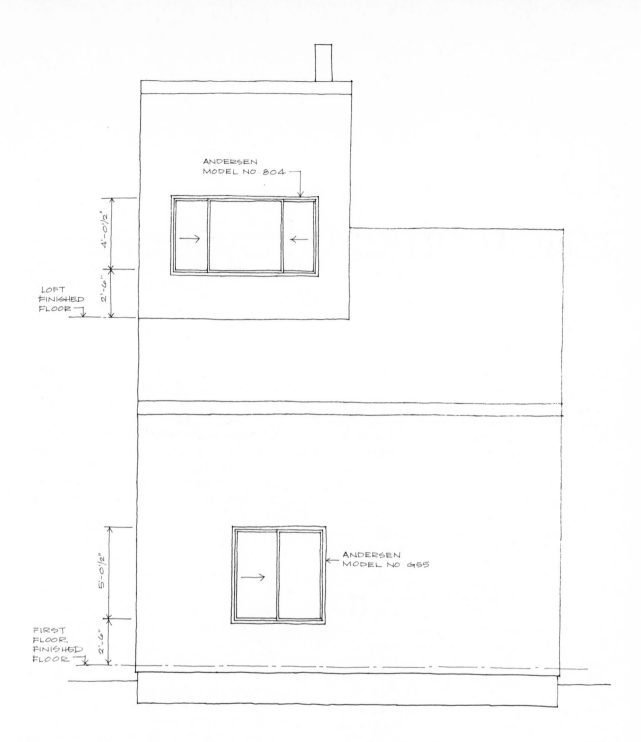

ANDERSEN
MODEL NO. 804

4'-0½"

2'-6"

LOFT
FINISHED
FLOOR

5'-0½"

2'-6"

ANDERSEN
MODEL NO G55

FIRST
FLOOR
FINISHED
FLOOR

WEST   ELEVATION

ILL. 29

13
Environmental Systems

It should be obvious that human beings were not adequately made to occupy most areas of this planet. The furry creatures that inhabit the earth with us seem to be better equipped to handle the climate. Perhaps humans were designed to occupy only a thin band of land circling the earth just so many miles from the equator. Whether to his credit or not, man's need to explore and his ability to adapt have led him to other, harsher, climates. Environmental engineering (however primitive) came into being with these migrations. Unless you live in some shangri-la, or are unusually rugged, you will have to confront the problem of environmental control. Before installing an elaborate central heating-cooling-humidity-control system or, at the other extreme, before building four fireplaces and laying in wood for the winter, it is a good idea to study just why our bodies seem to need such complex and expensive support systems to stay comfortable.

All living things and all machines need fuel in order to operate. In the case of the human body, starches, proteins, and fats are burned to produce energy and body heat. This heat must be expelled from the system to ensure that the other life-support systems are operating optimally. Heat loss is regulated by the blood vessels passing through the skin which expand to allow more heat to be lost and constrict to slow down the process.

The crux of this intricate system is that although heat must be lost from the body so that the organism can live, this loss must be care-fully controlled so that the body's temperature remains more or less the same all the time. The body can adapt to a wide range of temperatures (given adequate clothing) but is "comfortable" only when the surrounding air is within a relatively narrow range of temperatures. A house heating and cooling system does not warm or cool the body; the mechanical system allows the body to lose its heat at a regular rate by keeping the ambient air temperature at about 70 degrees.

HEAT LOSS

A building's heating system must supply heat to raise the temperature of a room to the desired level. At this point, ideally, the heating system should go off and stay off. This is never the case, however, since heat is constantly being lost to the outside. In order for a house's mechanical system to maintain a constant comfortable temperature inside, it must replace the amount of heat (measured in Btu's*) being lost to the outside. The amount of heat loss is dependent on four factors: 1. the difference between the interior temperature and that outside, 2. the amount of surface (walls, roofs, etc.) in contact

* A Btu, British thermal unit, is a measure of the quantity of heat. One Btu is the amount of heat necessary to raise the temperature of one pound of water one degree F, from 59°F to 60°F. Heat loss is measured in Btuh, the amount of Btu's lost per hour through a wall or window.

with the outside, 3. the materials used in the construction of the exterior walls, and 4. the amount of infiltration of cold air due to loose fits in the window and door frames.

It is not difficult to calculate the amount of heat loss from a building during any particular hour, although the arithmetic does tend to be tedious. The heat loss is determined by multiplying the *number of degree days* accumulated for the day by the *rate of heat loss*. The number of degree days (often used to estimate seasonal fuel usage) is the difference between the average temperature for the day and the desired interior temperature. The rate of heat loss is determined by analyzing the surface materials of the house.

The materials used in construction of the exterior walls and roof are of primary concern in economical heat design. Some materials transfer heat better than others. Metals are an example of excellent heat conductors and for this reason are used for pots and pans. Conversely, a material's ability to resist the transfer of heat from one surface to another makes it valuable as an insulator. Solid wood resists the transfer of heat. Even more valuable for its heat transfer resistance is air that is trapped in tiny pockets between blown or woven glass (fiberglass) or plastics (urethane, Styrofoam, etc.; Inset I).

The composition of a wall is rated as to its ability to resist the transfer of heat. This is known as its U factor.* A wall of a wood-frame house constructed of studs, siding, sheathing, and gypsum-board interior finish would have a U factor of .32. See Inset III. If 2″ of batt insulation (consisting of blown material) were placed between the studs, the U factor would decrease to .10. Were the insulation 4″ thick, the U factor would be .08. This suggests that the well-insulated wall (with the lower U factor) has four times the insulation value of the plain wall (Inset III, Table III-B).

Of greater importance than the materials used in the walls and the amount of insulation in them is the number and sizes of penetrations made in the walls for windows and doors. In addition, the quality of the window and door frames, the type of glass, and the direction they face are crucial to the design of the heating and

cooling systems. The amount of heat lost through a sheet of glass is many times greater than the heat lost through even a minimally insulated wall. In fact, 14 times more heat is lost per square foot through a single sheet of glass than through a well-insulated wall. The heat loss can be reduced by using a specially made thermal window unit, which consists of two (and sometimes three) sheets of glass separated by hermetically sealed air spaces (Inset II). This reduces the heat loss of the simple sheet in half, but it is still ten times more than a wall section. Windows, therefore, should be planned carefully.

A further argument against the indiscriminate use of glass and placement of windows is the infiltration of air into the building through the window frames. The cold air forced into the house by the wind must be heated. It is a good idea to determine the direction of the wind and try to avoid placing the windows and doors on that side of the house (see Chapter 2).

The point of the preceding explanations is to drive home the fact that good environmental design (the most economical use of fuel for the delivery of comfort) begins with the design of the house itself. The determination of the heating system (wood stove, forced air, hot-water heat) and the choice of the fuel are entirely secondary to the careful planning of the house's materials, orientation, and window and door openings. An elaborate heating system, of course, can generate and distribute enough heat to offset even enormous heat losses in a poorly designed and constructed house. The cost of the system, and the fuel that it consumes, however, is an avoidable financial burden. Instructions for heat-loss calculations can be found in Inset III.

HEATING AND COOLING SYSTEMS

When an engineer speaks of mechanically conditioned air, he or she is referring to air that has been heated or cooled, humidified or dehumidified, filtered or exchanged with fresh air, in such a way as to provide an interior environment that is both comfortable and healthy. Hospitals, schools, and theaters require elaborate and sophisticated conditioning systems to meet comfort and code requirements. Residences, on the

* The U factor is the overall coefficient of heat transfer. A wall with a U factor of .3 means that $\frac{3}{10}$ of a Btu will be transferred through the wall to the outdoors every hour for every 1 degree of temperature difference between the outside and the inside per square foot of wall area.

INSET I / INSULATION

There are many variations on the theme of insulation; only one factor remains constant. If the climate you live in requires you to provide mechanically produced heating or cooling, you should use insulating materials to hold that heated or cooled air inside. All surfaces that come in contact with the outside should be insulated. This includes walls, roofs (or ceilings), basement walls (if the basement is to be used as a living space), and the floor with a crawl space beneath it.

There are a large number of commercial products on the market sold as insulation. These products can be divided into two major categories: those that work as "mass" insulations (that rely on the ability of trapped air to resist the transfer of heat) and the reflective types (those that rely on the ability of the material to reflect heat back toward the source). Some marketed products combine both qualities. Insulation material is rated for its conductance resistance (R). The higher the rating, the better the material as an insulator.

The "mass" insulations are usually lightweight substances that are blown or foamed to trap millions of tiny air bubbles. These dead air spaces, which are noncontinuous, serve to resist the conduction of heat from one surface to the other. Mass insulation comes in a number of forms and thicknesses. Batt, or blanket insulation, the most popular type used in residences, is flexible and is sold in blankets or rolls about 15" wide. These strips are designed to fit in between the stud spaces, and come in thicknesses of either 2" or 3⅝". Blanket insulation consists of either mineral wools (made of silicates of calcium and aluminum), rock wools (made of limestone or other natural rock), slag wool (made from the by-products of the blast furnace), or glass wools (made from silica, limestone, etc.). The puffed material is secured between two layers of semiflexible material (such as paper) to form batts, which are either stapled or taped to the studs. Some batts come with vapor barriers attached for condensation control (refer to page 156 of this chapter). The batts with the barriers are designed to be placed with the vapor protection facing toward the inside, that is, the warm side of the wall.

Loose-fill insulation is primarily used on buildings that have already been constructed. The loose particles, or granules, are poured or blown into the cavity of the wall. This type of insulation is valuable in renovation work.

Rigid insulation is manufactured in varying thicknesses (½" to 6") and materials and can be used on walls, built-up roofs, as perimeter insulation (to insulate a concrete slab), or as a combination sheathing-insulating material. Most rigid boards manufactured today are made of Styrofoam and urethane. Other products include vegetable fiberboards consisting of compressed cane, wood, or other organic fiber, rigid cork board, which is compressed and baked cork (up to 6" thick), foam glass, which is aerated glass (in boards 2" thick), and

BLANKET

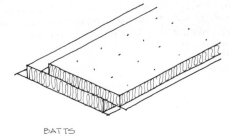

BATTS

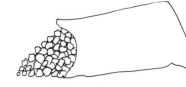

LOOSE FILL

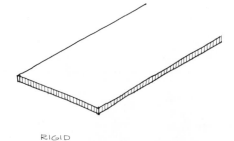

RIGID

fibrous glass, which is blown and compressed with a binder and covered with kraft paper.

The reflective insulations are based on the principle that the surface of a highly polished and shiny substance (usually aluminum foil backed with a heavy paper) will reflect up to 90 percent of the radiant heat. The system must have an air space of at least ¾" (and up to 4") in front of the reflective material for it to work. Very often the foil is double-sided and has an air space on both sides, which increases its insulating value. Multiple layers of reflective insulation are packages of two or three layers of reflective material with ¾" air spaces between them. Very often the reflective properties of aluminum foil and its additional property of being an excellent vapor barrier are combined when the foil is attached to a blanket-type insulation. This foil works to reflect the heat from the interior of the house back into the house. The illustration shows the various kinds of insulation and how they work. The table shows the various kinds' comparative resistance (R) factors.

TABLE I-A: RESISTANCE (R VALUES) OF INSULATING MATERIALS

(This table is primarily for the purpose of demonstrating the comparative values of different insulating materials and not necessarily for the purposes of calculating heat loss. Table III-B in Inset III lists the composite U values for walls and roofs and has been designed for heat-loss calculations.)

	R
Air spaces:	
without reflective material, ¾" to 4"	.92
one-side reflective material	2.17
aluminum foil both sides	2.64
Batts and blankets: all materials	
2" thick	7.64
3⅝" thick	13.41
Loose fill:	
rock, mineral, or glass, 3⅝" thick	12.08
Fiberboards:	
vegetable, 1" thick	2.64
glass, 1" thick	4.00
Insulation-board sheathing:	2.06
Concrete block (cinder):	
8" thick	1.66

Because glass loses heat at such a rapid rate, a great deal of research has gone into producing a window that limits the heat lost from a building without obstructing visibility. The result of this research has led to the production of a double-glazed window unit that is mass-marketed under a number of trade names. Essentially, the unit contains two thicknesses of sheet glass separated by an air space. The space between the glass is dehydrated to remove moisture and then sealed. The drying out of the air in the space prevents the development of condensate (water droplets) which would obstruct visibility through the glass. The sheets of glass can be sealed in one of two ways: by fusing two pieces of glass at the edges, or by using metal spacers and epoxy to hermetically seal the ends. See Illustration 6, page 152.

The air space between the glass varies from ½″ to ³⁄₁₆″; the two sheets of glass are usually of the same thickness (¼″ or less). Double-glazed glass will not cut visibility. However, the substitution of tinted glass will reduce glare and limit the amount of radiant heat entering the building in the summer.

Many manufacturers include a third sheet of glass, a storm sash, on the window. Yet another method of insulating glass surfaces is to provide insulated shutters which may be closed at night. Since these shutters can be constructed with rigid insulation, they can provide a significant reduction in the U value of even the best double-glazed window.

other hand, require only the simplest of equipment to accomplish the same goals. House heating and cooling systems offer a number of options that tend to confuse the novice and make the planning of the systems seem unnecessarily complex. Basically there are four choices you will have to make: 1. the fuel that is to be utilized, 2. the means by which the fuel is converted to heat or cold, 3. the means by which it is distributed through the building, and 4. the way in which it enters the room and is circulated through it. To simplify matters for the purpose of this book we will discuss only a few of the many options. Further discussion and design material can be found in the Bibliography.

Household conditioning systems can be broken down into three major categories based on their distribution methods.

1. The direct heating method, which uses individual electric units in each room. In this system the fuel line, a single electric wire, connects to the heating unit (or combined heating-cooling unit) and provides conditioning for that room only.

2. The forced-air system, in which air is heated (or cooled) at a centrally located area and is distributed through ducts to each room. The air returns through the ducts to the furnace or cooling unit and is reprocessed.

3. The hydronic (hot-water) system is exclusively a heating system in which water is the medium that carries the heat to the individual rooms of the house. The water is heated centrally and is distributed through hot-water pipes to radiators, baseboards, or convectors.

There are advantages and disadvantages to all of these systems. The direct electric system provides even and clean heating and cooling. It is the simplest and the least expensive to install. There is no boiler or furnace, nor are there ducts or pipes, making a mechanical equipment room unnecessary. These advantages are often offset by the high cost of the fuel.

Oil and gas are comparatively cheaper than electricity in some parts of the United States and therefore more popular. The forced-air system is a bit less expensive to install and operate than the hydronic system. The major advantage is that it can carry cool air in summer as well as hot air in winter, making it the preferred system where the house is to be mechanically cooled as well as heated. Another advantage of the air system is that the room air is constantly being changed and filtered. This is of particular importance for people with allergies, or in spaces where odors or fumes are likely to cause discomfort. The major disadvantage of this system lies in the large ductwork required for the air distribution. These ducts are difficult to hide in floors and walls. Hydronic systems, on the other hand, require only very small pipes for the distribution of hot water.

A solar heating system collects the sun's heat and can produce either hot water or air, making it compatible with either hydronic or forced-air systems. There are three basic problems associated with the use of the sun as a heat source. The first is its intermittent nature. At night and on cloudy days, when it is most needed, it is not available. A large storage system is required to accumulate heat for these periods. The second problem is the requirement that large sloped areas of the house face south. This often comes

INSET III / CALCULATION OF HEAT LOSS

(Calculate separately for each room. Use Table III-A for calculations.)

1. Determine the gross wall area that is exposed to the outside or to unheated spaces (such as the garage or attic). The exposed walls of closets adjacent to livable rooms must be taken into consideration as well.
   Gross wall area = length of wall × height.

2. Measure windows and doors and determine the total area of glass per room, and the total area of doors going to the outside (or unheated spaces).
   Measurements for windows are taken from the outside of the sash. Doors are measured by the size of the actual door.

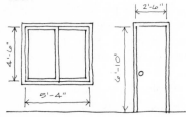

3. Determine net wall area exposed to the outside. Net wall area = gross wall area − total window and door area (for the room).

4. Determine ceiling area if the space above is unheated. (If there are heated rooms above, this step can be omitted.) Ceiling area = length of room × width.

5. Determine floor area if exposed to unheated space (basement or crawl space below).

6. Determine room volume (= length × width × height).

7. Using Table III-B (Heat-Loss [U] Factors) determine U factors for walls, windows, ceilings, and floors exposed to the outside.

8. Determine design temperature difference using Table III-C. The design temperature difference is equal to the difference between the desired indoor temperature (usually 70°F) and the usual low temperature for the area where the house is to be built. The lowest temperature ever recorded for the area is not the one used in this calculation since this low temperature occurs only rarely. (When the temperature of the air dips below the design outdoor temperature, the house temperature drops only a few degrees, which is considered tolerable since it happens infrequently.) Table III-C records outdoor design temperatures for different parts of the United States.

9. Calculate area × U factor for each room component (walls, windows, doors, ceilings, and floors).

10. Determine infiltration factor for window type using Table III-D.

11. Calculate room volume × infiltration factor.

12. Determine total heat loss per room by adding the area × U factors and the volume × infiltration factor; multiply this total by the design temperature difference.

13. Add total heat loads of each room to determine total house heating loss.

TABLE III-A: HEAT-LOSS CALCULATIONS

Room	Length of exposed wall	Height of room	Gross wall area (sq. ft.)		Windows #1	#2	Door	Walls	Floor	Ceiling			× Temp. diff.	Room heat loss
				Net area (A; sq. ft.)							Vol. (V; cu. ft.)			
				U*							F†			
				A × U							V × F			
				Net area							Vol.			
				U							F			
				A × U							V × F			
				Net area							Vol.			
				U							F			
				A × U							V × F			
				Net area							Vol.			
				U							F			
				A × U							V × F			
				Net area							Vol.			
				U							F			
				A × U							V × F			

TABLE III-B: HEAT-LOSS (U) FACTORS

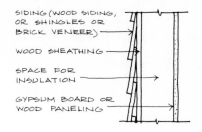

SIDING (WOOD SIDING, OR SHINGLES OR BRICK VENEER)
WOOD SHEATHING
SPACE FOR INSULATION
GYPSUM BOARD OR WOOD PANELING

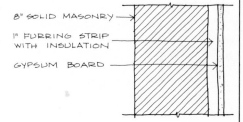

8" SOLID MASONRY
1" FURRING STRIP WITH INSULATION
GYPSUM BOARD

			U Factor
Glass	Single sheet	by itself	1.13
		with storm sash	.56
	Double glazed	¼" air space	.61
		½" air space	.55
	Double glazed with storm sash	¼" air space	.46
	(3 sheets of glass)	½" air space	.38
Doors	1" thick		.64
	1½" thick		.50
Wood-Frame Walls	Noninsulated (lath and plaster)	wood siding, no sheathing	.33
		wood siding, paper, sheathing	.25
		asbestos shingles, paper, sheathing	.29
	Insulated	with 1" bat or blanket	.14
		with 2"	.10
		with 3" or more	.08
Brick Walls	8" solid wall	interior unfinished	.50
		plaster directly on masonry	.46
		with 1" furring space filled with insulation + ⅜" gypsum board	.20
Poured Concrete	6" thick	unfinished	.80
	8"	unfinished	.70
	10"	unfinished	.20
	6", 8", or 10"	finished with 1" furring space insulated + ⅜" gypsum board	.17
Ceilings	(unheated attic space above)	gypsum-board ceiling, no floor, no insulation	.78
		same as above with 4" flexible insulation	.07
		+ subfloor	.06
Flat Roofs	Wood roof deck 2" thick	no ceiling, no insulation	.34
		no ceiling, with 2" rigid insulation above deck	.12
		any ceiling, 2" air space insulation	.08
Pitched Roofs	Asphalt or wood shingles on wood sheathing	undersides of joists open, no insulation	.53
		3⅝" insulation between rafters and gypsum ceiling	.06
		1½" wood deck, no ceiling 2" rigid roof insulation, wood shingles	.12
Wood Floors	(over exposed space, hardwood floor on subfloor)	no insulation	.39
		3⅝" flexible insulation	.06
		1" rigid insulation board	.13
Concrete Floors	6" thick	no insulation	.47
Wood Floors	(over enclosed, unheated space, finish floor, subfloor)	no insulation	.15
		3⅝" insulation	.04
		½" rigid insulation	.09

ALABAMA
Birmingham 15
Mobile 20
Montgomery 15

ALASKA
Anchorage –30
Fairbanks –60

ARIZONA
Flagstaff –10
Phoenix 25
Tucson 25
Yuma 30

ARKANSAS
Fort Smith 10
Little Rock 15

CALIFORNIA
Fresno 25
Los Angeles 35
Oakland 30
Sacramento 25
San Diego 35
San Francisco 35

COLORADO
Denver –10
Grand Junction 0
Pueblo –15

CONNECTICUT
Hartford –5
New Haven 0

DELAWARE
Wilmington 5

DISTRICT OF COLUMBIA
Washington 10

FLORIDA
Jacksonville 25
Miami 40
Pensacola 25
Tampa 30

GEORGIA
Atlanta 15
Savannah 20

IDAHO
Boise 0
Lewiston 0

ILLINOIS
Chicago –10
Peoria –10
Springfield –10

INDIANA
Fort Wayne –5
Indianapolis –5

IOWA
Des Moines –15
Dubuque –15
Mason City –20
Sioux City –15

KANSAS
Dodge City –5
Topeka –5
Wichita 0

KENTUCKY
Louisville 0

LOUISIANA
New Orleans 30

MAINE
Portland –15

MARYLAND
Baltimore 10

MASSACHUSETTS
Boston 0
Nantucket 0
Springfield –10
Worcester –10

MICHIGAN
Battle Creek –5
Detroit 0
Flint –5
Grand Rapids –5
Lansing –5
Sault St. Marie –20

MINNESOTA
Minneapolis –20
St. Paul –20

MISSISSIPPI
Vicksburg 20

MISSOURI
Kansas City 0
St. Louis 0

MONTANA
Billings –20
Butte –35
Helena –25
Miles City –25

NEBRASKA
Lincoln –10
Omaha –10

NEVADA
Las Vegas 20
Reno 0

NEW HAMPSHIRE
Concord –15
Manchester –10

NEW JERSEY
Atlantic City 10
Newark 5
Trenton 5

NEW MEXICO
Albuquerque 5
Roswell 5

NEW YORK
Albany –10
Binghamton –10
Buffalo –5
Massena –20
New York 5
Rochester –5
Syracuse –10

NORTH CAROLINA
Asheville 10
Charlotte 15
Greensboro 10
Wilmington 20

NORTH DAKOTA
Bismarck –30
Fargo –30

OHIO
Akron –5
Cincinnati 0
Cleveland 0
Columbus 0
Dayton 0
Toledo –5

OKLAHOMA
Oklahoma City 5
Tulsa 5

OREGON
Baker –10
Eugene 15
Portland 15
Salem 15

PENNSYLVANIA
Harrisburg 5
Philadelphia 5
Pittsburgh 0
Scranton –5

RHODE ISLAND
Providence 0

SOUTH CAROLINA
Charleston 20
Columbia 15

SOUTH DAKOTA
Huron –25
Rapid City –15

TENNESSEE
Chattanooga 10
Memphis 10
Nashville 5

TEXAS
Amarillo 0
Austin 20
Corpus Christi 30
Dallas 15
El Paso 15
Fort Worth 15
Galveston 30
Houston 25
Port Arthur 25
San Antonio 20

UTAH
Salt Lake City 0

VERMONT
Burlington –20

VIRGINIA
Norfolk 20
Richmond 10
Roanoke 10

WASHINGTON
Seattle 20
Spokane –5

WEST VIRGINIA
Elkins –5
Parkersburg 0

WISCONSIN
Green Bay –15
Madison –15
Milwaukee –10

WYOMING
Cheyenne –15
Laramie –15

TABLE III-D: INFILTRATION FACTORS FOR WINDOWS AND DOORS

Rooms with windows and doors	No weather stripping, no storm sash	With weather stripping or storm sash
on 1 side only	.018	.012
on 2 sides	.027	.018
on 3 or 4 sides	.036	.027

INSET IV / ZONED HEATING

When you zone the heating in a house, you are dividing it into two or more separate heating areas. At any one time all the zones can be set at the same temperature. If you prefer, however, to heat one part of the house at one temperature and the other at a setting that is higher or lower, you will have the potential to do so. Each zone is controlled by a separate thermostat, but all zones are connected to the same heat-producing source, the boiler. If one part of the house is hardly ever used, it can be zoned separately and shut off.*

In a very small house (three or four rooms) it makes sense to consider the house as one heating zone. In a larger house it might be more practical to divide the house into two or more sections and

* If the area in question has plumbing lines, the heat should be turned off only if the pipes have been properly drained. The water left in the pipes might freeze, expand, and burst. If the pipes are not drained the thermostat should be set at a minimum of about 50°F.

consider each section as one heating zone. The bedroom area, if not used much during the day, can have its thermostat set so that the temperature in this area is low in daytime and higher at night. The living areas might be set so that the reverse occurs.

When designing the zoned system, the entire heat loss for the house is calculated, and then the calculations for each zone are made. Remember that heat lost through the walls, windows, and roof must be replaced mechanically by the heating system.

in conflict with orientation to the view, existing site conditions, and interior space relationships. The third problem is cost. Since no solar heating system can produce all of the heat necessary to warm a house, a back-up or conventional furnace, boiler, or stove is still required.

There is, however, a very inexpensive way to utilize the sun for heating. All southern windows on a house can be thought of as solar collectors. The principle is called the "greenhouse effect." All hot bodies, like the sun, emit high-intensity short-wave radiation which easily passes through glazed surfaces. When it hits interior surfaces, it can heat them to a few degrees above room temperature. The surfaces emit low-energy long-wave radiation which will not pass back out through the windows but has the potential to heat the space. In a climate like New York City's, each square foot of unshaded south glazing can collect between 1,000 and 1,300 Btu's per day depending on the glazed surface (see Inset II) on the coldest day of the year. Many houses have incorporated large greenhouse-type spaces to trap the heat and heavy masonry wall or floor surfaces behind them to store and radiate this heat. These areas not only become heat sources but give a new spatial dimension to the house design.

Hot-Water System: The Series Loop

The hydronic series-loop baseboard system is the one most commonly used in small houses. The system consists of one pipe that carries hot water from the boiler through each of the baseboards around the perimeter of the house. The hot-water-carrying pipe circles the house and returns to the boiler (Ill. 1). Since the pipe goes through all of the baseboards in its loop about the house, the system can be adjusted or modulated only slightly in the individual rooms with dampers. The water is at its hottest when it leaves the boiler and is a few degrees cooler at the end of its loop (having lost much of its heat to the rooms in its travels). A single thermostat controls the room temperature for all the rooms in the series. For flexibility of temperature settings, the house can be separated into zones as described in Inset IV. If the house is to be zoned separately (which is recommended for a large house, since the loop can only travel so far and still maintain its efficiency), two separate loops can be designed, each having its own thermostat but sharing the boiler (Ill. 2).

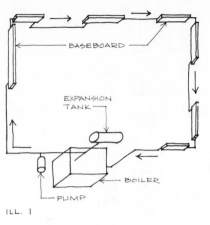

ILL. 1

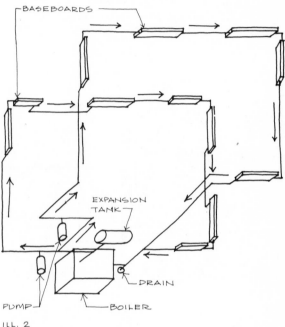

ILL. 2

Gas or oil are commonly burned in a cast-iron or steel boiler of water tube design (Ill. 3). Electric burners, which take up less space, or solar collectors, which can supplement the conventional fossil-fuel boiler, may be used to heat the water that is to be distributed through a series loop. Aside from the water-heating device, boiler, burner, or solar collector, the system uses a water main (a single water pipe designed in a loop), a number of fittings to join the pipe segments together, baseboard units, a thermostat to regulate the heat, a pump to push the water through the circuit, and an air-cushion tank (an expansion tank) to take care of the greater volume of water in the circuit.*

* When water is heated it expands. Provision must be made within the system for the extra water volume. A pocket of air is trapped in the expansion tank, which serves as a cushion for the expanded water. The extra volume of water compresses the trapped air.

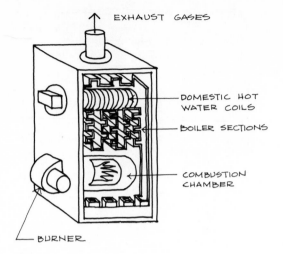

EXHAUST GASES

DOMESTIC HOT WATER COILS

BOILER SECTIONS

COMBUSTION CHAMBER

BURNER

ILL. 3

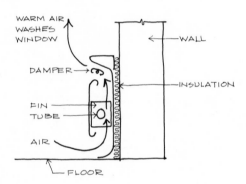

WARM AIR WASHES WINDOW

WALL

DAMPER

INSULATION

FIN TUBE

AIR

FLOOR

ILL. 4

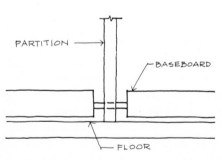

PARTITION

BASEBOARD

FLOOR

ILL. 5

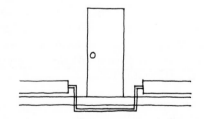

ILL. 6

TABLE A: MAXIMUM RECOMMENDED LOOP OR CIRCUIT CAPACITIES USING BASEBOARDS

	Heat loss per circuit	Tube (pipe) size
Copper-tube baseboard	15,000	½"
	35,000	¾"
	75,000	1"
	130,000	1¼"
Steel-pipe baseboard	18,000	½"
	40,000	¾"
	72,000	1"
Cast-iron baseboard	40,000	¾"

SERIES LOOP: SYSTEM DESIGN

1. Calculate the heat loss for each room and for the whole house (Inset III).

2. Divide the house into separate zones (Inset IV). Calculate the heat loss for each zone. Try, if possible, to keep the zones equal in heat loss.

3. Use Table A to determine baseboard tubing size for each circuit. The table will also give you the pipe size for the circuit, since the pipe between the baseboards will be the same size as the tubing that runs within the units. If you have more than one loop, the main line (the pipe that leaves the boiler before branching off into two or more circuits) also can be determined by using Table A. In this case consider the total house heat loss.

4. Determine the location of the boiler and the water heater, if there is to be a separate water heater (Chapter 14, see Inset II). Choose a location where the piping runs will be shortest.

5. Draw a layout of the piping systems. The system is more effective when the heat outlets (the baseboard units) are under the windows and/or along the exterior walls (Ill. 4).* The tubing can run through a partition if the baseboards in the rooms butt into it (Ill. 5). The tubing must be taken below the surface of the floor to clear doors and sliding glass doors (Ill. 6). Include expansion joints (see page 320).

6. Select the baseboards. You must have manufacturer's literature in order to select baseboards, since you need the actual rating for each linear foot of baseboard. (This will differ from one manufacturer to another.) See the sample

* When the baseboards are placed under the windows, air circulates in a convection current. Cooler air enters below the baseboard, is heated by circulating around the heated tubes and fins of the unit, and rises across the expanse of glass, so as to bathe the cold surfaces of the windows with warm air.

in Illustration 7. In order to use the literature in the sample, you will have to know the water flow in gallons per minute (gpm) and the water design temperature.* The water flow in gpm can be calculated by dividing the heat loss (Btuh) for the circuit by 10,000. (Since most manufacturer's literature usually gives two selections, one for 1 gpm and the other for 4 gpm, use the 4 gpm rating only when the flow is known to be equal to or greater than 4 gpm, otherwise the 1 gpm column should be used.)

The design temperature, for our purposes, will be 200°F. This selection is made for the sake of simplicity, and because it is most commonly used for residences.

When you have the baseboard (b.b.) rating, you can calculate the length of the baseboard for each room by using the following formula:

$$\text{The length of the b.b. per room} = \frac{\text{room heat loss (Btuh)}}{\text{rating of the b.b.}}$$

If you don't have enough baseboard length to fit in the room, choose a higher-rated unit for that particular room. The baseboard with the higher rating has fins that are more closely spaced so that more heat is radiated than in a lower-rated unit.

7. Determine how much pipe will be required: Measure the scaled drawings of the piping layout. Remember that the pipe not only runs horizontally, but also turns into a vertical position when it ducks under doorways and rises to the second floor.

8. Select the boiler. The capacity of the unit (its net output) should exceed the maximum heat loss by 15 percent. If the boiler is to have a tankless coil for the production of domestic hot water (see pages 318 and 319) the unit must be larger. One rule of thumb recommends that you double the capacity of the boiler for a tankless heater. The size of the coil depends on the number of people who live in the house. A 3 gpm coil will be adequate for four people. The larger the coil, the more heat it draws.† If you

are planning an expansion to the house, consider a larger boiler. When using the manufacturer's figures (Table B) use the I-B-R net rating.*

9. Select a pump. Many residential boilers now come equipped with pumps that are sized to provide the gpm required. If you order a boiler without a pump consider using a 112 HP pump. This size pump should be more than ample to counter the resistance in the pipes of a four-bedroom house using a series loop. If your house is smaller, the 112 HP pump will distribute the heat a little faster. Select the pump to fit the tubing size of the main line (i.e., a 1″ tube would require a 1″ pump).

10. Select the air cushion tank (expansion tank). This item, like the pump, is often included in the boiler package. If it is not, allow one gallon of tank size to every 5,000 Btuh of heat loss for the house.

Forced-Air System

The forced-air system operates by circulating conditioned air throughout the house. The advantage of this kind of system over the hydronic method of heating is that, in addition to heating, the same ducts can be used to cool, ventilate, humidify, dehumidify, and clean the air by removing dust, cooking and smoking odors, and allergenic substances. The air is conditioned at a central location, is distributed through ducts to each room of the house, and is released through outlets (registers in the walls or floor) into the space. An additional register in the room (or in the corridor outside the room) draws in the used air and returns it to the conditioning plant. This process is referred to as the conditioning cycle.

Of primary consideration is the location of the conditioning plant and the method of distribution. The furnace may be located in the basement, crawl space, attic, or a utility room on the ground floor of the house. You have a great deal of flexibility in locating the furnace since the manufacturers have designed the components to fit almost any shaped space. The unit comes in the highboy variety, which stands upright and releases air from the top (designed to be used in a basement with a distribution system under the

* Water design temperature is the average temperature of the water leaving the boiler and the water returning to it. As the water runs through all of the baseboards in the circuit, it loses its heat to the rooms. The water returning to the boiler is often 20 degrees cooler than the water that leaves the boiler.

† In the design of the boiler with tankless heater some engineers suggest that a minimum boiler of 100,000 Btu must be supplied for a 2 gpm coil, 150,000 Btu for a 3 gpm coil. The use of a storage tank in conjunction with the coil will draw less heat from the boiler during peak water needs and will deliver more domestic hot water. (See pages 318 and 319.)

* The I-B-R rating is established from standards set by the Hydronics Institute, once known as the Institute for Boilers and Radiators (IBR). This rating is used because it accounts for the likely heat loss through the pipes.

I-B-R APPROVED HOT WATER RATINGS

(BTU per hr. per linear ft. with 65° entering air)

ELEMENT	WATER FLOW	PRESSURE DROP*	HOT WATER RATINGS (BTU/hr.)									
			160°	170°	180°	190°	200°	210°	215°	220°	230°	240°
No. 30-75 Baseboard with E-75 element: ¾" nominal copper tubing, 2⅝" x 2⅛" x .009" aluminum fins bent to 2¼" x 2⅛", 55 fins/ft.	1 gpm	47	450	510	580	640	710	770	810	840	910	970
	4 gpm	525	480	540	610	680	750	810	860	890	960	1030

NOTE: Ratings are for element installed as per drawing below, with damper open, with expansion cradles. Ratings are based on active finned length (3" less than overall length) and include 15% heating effect factor. Use 4 gpm ratings only when flow is known to be equal to or greater than 4 gpm; otherwise 1 gpm ratings must be used.

DIMENSIONAL AND INSTALLATION DATA

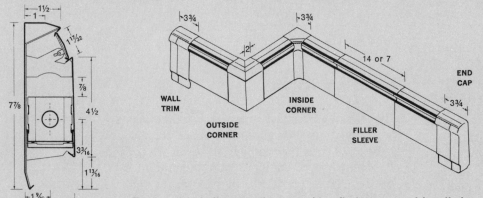

Baseboard and all accessories serve either flush or recessed installation.

ILL. 7

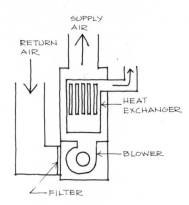

UPFLOW - HIGHBOY FURNACE

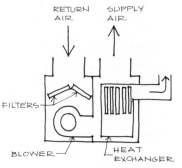

UPFLOW - LOWBOY FURNACE

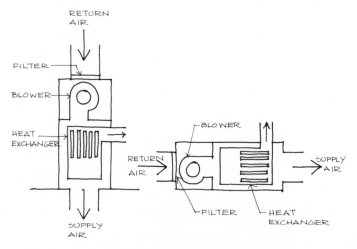

COUNTERFLOW FURNACE   HORIZONTAL FLOW FURNACE

ILL. 8

joists of the first floor or in a utility space with the distribution system in the ceiling of the first floor), the counter flow system, which stands upright and releases air at the bottom (designed for a utility room on the first floor with distribution lines in the crawl space below), and the horizontal furnace, which can be placed in the crawl space in an attic (Ill. 8).

The most common residential distribution systems include the *trunk system*, which is a central plenum adjoining the furnace with small feeder lines coming off it; the *radial system*, with all ducts radiating out of the central location and leading directly to the outlet registers; and the *perimeter loop*, which combines the radial concept with a loop system that surrounds the perimeter of the house. The latter system is used primarily in a slab on grade (a concrete floor that rests directly on the earth). The circulating warm air through the perimeter loop warms the concrete slab. A fourth system that is gaining in popularity is the *crawl-space plenum*, in which the crawl space of the house

Design
Development

152

is insulated and heated. At the periphery of the crawl space (under the windows of the first floor) there are registers which emit air to the living space. This system heats the floor under the living space and the rooms as well. Illustration 9 shows the various distribution systems.

The components of any air-handling system include the furnace, the cooling unit, the humidifier (dehumidifier), filter, fan, cooling coils, ductwork, and the registers. The system can be composed of items or can be purchased as a package containing most of the components in a single unit. The packaged systems might contain all of the cooling items in one unit and the furnace as part of another. Both units utilize the same ductwork. There are units that combine the heating and cooling functions, in which the heating is fueled by gas (or oil) and the cooling is electrically powered.

CONDENSATION CONTROL

Four characteristics of water and water vapor should be understood before attacking the problem of condensation control.

1. Water vapor is held in the air depending on the temperature of the air. Warm air is capable of holding more water than cold air.
2. Water vapor (like heat) tends to move from a place where it is in concentration to a place where there is less concentration.
3. Water vapor condenses (turns into visible droplets of water) when it comes in contact with a cold surface. The air surrounding a cool surface has less ability to hold water vapor and so the vapor condenses into droplets.
4. Water is highly corrosive, and to a greater or lesser degree will decompose most natural substances (including wood) sooner or later.

In winter the air inside the house is dry unless humidity is added to it. This is done inadvertently when we take a shower or boil water. Humidity can be added mechanically by a humidifier to keep throat and nose mucous membranes from drying out, and to keep house plants alive. Because there is more moisture inside the house (being held by the heated air) than there is outside, a relative vapor pressure builds up inside, forcing the vapor outward. In its path outward through the walls of the house the vapor reaches a cold point where it condenses into visible droplets.

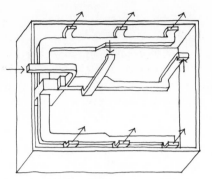

TRUNK SYSTEM

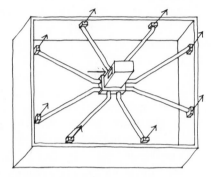

RADIAL DUCT SYSTEM

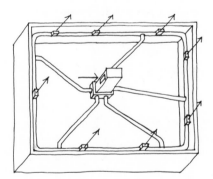

PERIMETER LOOP SYSTEM

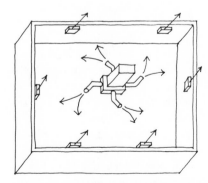

CRAWL SPACE PLENUM SYSTEM

ILL. 9

In older, uninsulated houses the difference in temperature between the inside surface and the outside is not so great. The vapor has a chance to escape the wall completely before it reaches that crucial cold temperature (known as its dew point). Usually it turns to water at just the point between the outside siding and the exterior paint, causing the paint to peel. In well-insulated houses without vapor barriers or with insufficient vapor protection, condensation problems are crucial. The thermal insulation inhibits the flow of heat but does not stop the flow of water through the wall. The temperature within the wall on opposite sides of the insulation varies considerably. Therefore, when the vapor moves out through the insulation it encounters cold air and cold surfaces somewhere in the middle of the wall (usually in the middle of the insulation). The vapor becomes water and stays trapped inside the wall, sometimes even forming ice crystals. The water will quickly decompose most insulation materials, and even if it doesn't, the weight of the water and ice causes the batts of insulation to become detached from the wall and fall to the bottom of the cavity. Condensation control in well-insulated houses is a problem that deserves a great deal of consideration.

Vapor Barriers

There are quite a few vapor barriers on the market, most of them either plastic or foil. The most important thing about the barrier is that it be continuous without so much as a microscopic hole or tear. The weight of the material must be equal to the job. A heavier membrane would be required if concrete is to be poured over it than if it were to be used on the inside of a wall. Polyethylene sheeting is most often used.

Many kinds of batt and blanket insulation come with vapor barriers preattached to the thermal insulation. These materials have proved to be effective as condensation-control devices depending on the care with which they have been installed. The vapor barrier must be stapled tightly to the studs to completely encase the cavity. Experts prefer polyethylene sheeting to vapor barriers attached to the batts because the sheeting covers the entire stud area in one continuous piece and allows visual inspection of the insulation and vapor barrier before proceeding with drywall installation.

OTHER MOISTURE PROBLEMS

Moisture, as we have learned, is capable of causing structural damage by decomposing wood. It is, therefore, of utmost importance to keep cellars, basements, crawl spaces, and attics dry.* In the case of crawl spaces, moisture often rises from the ground into the crawl space during periods of heavy rain. Surface water will also enter the space from the outside during peak rainy seasons. To prevent the concentration of this damaging moisture some precautions must be taken in the original design of the house.

1. The earth must slope down and away from the house, carrying surface water away.
2. The crawl space should be protected from moisture by a vapor barrier on the ground.
3. The foundation walls should be penetrated with vents so that moisture will not be trapped in the crawl space.
4. A vapor barrier should be installed under the floor above the crawl space, between the insulation and the subfloor.

Water Control in Basements

Basements usually have the most trouble with condensation in summer during muggy weather. The earth under the concrete basement floor is comparatively cool, causing the floor of the basement to be a cold surface. The hot air is laden with moisture and condenses when it comes in contact with the cooler surfaces of the floor and walls. This problem is difficult to control. If the surface of the concrete is rough and porous, the moisture will sink in and not cause a wetness problem. If, however, the floor is dense and smoothly finished, the tightly knit grains of concrete form a vapor barrier of sorts and the water collects on the slab. A plastic membrane does not seem to help much whether it is placed above or below the slab.

To keep moisture from rising up into the basement, 6" of coarse gravel should be placed over the compacted earth before the slab is poured. Water will not rise through the gravel unless under pressure. As around houses built over crawl spaces, the ground should slope down, and ventilation should be provided.

* Moisture in the crawl space and basement encourages wood-chewing insects such as termites.

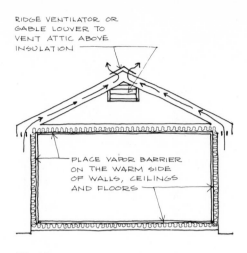

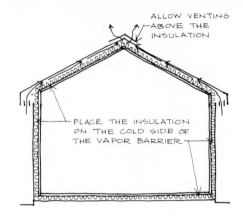

ILL. 10

Water Control Under the Roof

On the roof, as in the basement floor, there are two sources of water: one from the rain above, and the other from the vapor seeking to escape the house. In houses with good protection from rain penetration and no vapor barrier, the vapor moves upward through the thermal insulation and the sheathing and condenses against the roofing paper, through which droplets cannot pass. This causes dampness in the structural lumber and potential decay of the sheathing. In houses with inadequate flooring and adequate vapor protection, the reverse occurs but in such cases the water collects in the insulation. One of the best ways to reduce or eliminate the chances of water damage in attics or in the space between the rafters and the finished roof is by the proper ventilation of this space. The various ways of ventilating the roof structure are shown in Illustration 10. The ventilation, in essence, provides a stream of outside air to remove trapped moisture, before it is allowed to do any damage.

DESIGNING THE HEATING SYSTEM FOR THE SAMPLE HOUSE

The heating system for the sample house will be a simple two-zone series loop and can be de-

signed by following the directions on pages 150 and 151. We first calculate the heat loss for the house (Inset III) and on the basis of this information select the boiler. Next, the house is divided into two heating zones. In this case, the first floor comprises zone 1; the second and third floors constitute zone 2.

1. Calculate the heat loss for each room and the entire house (Ill. 11).   Btuh

First Floor:	living room	15,210
	lounge	728
	dining room	3,192
	kitchen	9,152
	hall and core	728
Second Floor:	master bedroom	6,230
	child's bedroom	3,718
	hall and core	1,650
Third Floor:	loft	4,512
Total House Loss:		45,120

2. Select the boiler. We must decide at this point on the domestic hot-water system, the hot water to be used exclusively for washing and bathing. Suppose we decide on a tankless coil which will be integrated with the boiler that supplies the hot water for heating. Check the Malibu M-100 (Table B), an oil-fired cast-iron boiler. The M-100 has an I-B-R net output of 95,700 Btuh. (We have adopted the rule of thumb that doubles the capacity of the boiler for a tankless heater.) This boiler has a 3 gpm tankless coil.

ILLUSTRATION 11: HEAT-LOSS CALCULATIONS

Room	Length of exposed wall	Height of room	Gross wall area (sq. ft.)		Windows #1	#2	Door	Walls	Floor	Ceiling			× Temp. diff.	Room heat loss
Living room	46'-0"	13', 15'	644	Net area (A; sq. ft.)	74	25	18	527	265	230	Vol. (V; cu. ft.)	3,968	65°	15,210
				· U*	.38	.38	.50	.08	.04	.12	F†	.027		
				A × U	28	10	9	42	10.6	27.6	V × F	107		
Lounge	10'	8'	80	Net area	—	—	—	80	120	—	Vol.	960	65°	728
				U				.08	.04		F	—		
				A × U				6.4	4.8		V × F			
Dining room	21'	8'	168	Net area	56	—	—	112	110	46	Vol.	880	65°	3,192
				U	.38			.08	.04	.08	F	.012		
				A × U	21			9	4.4	3.7	V × F	11		
Kitchen	21'	8'	168	Net area	10.5	87	—	133	110	—	Vol.	880	65°	9,152
				U	.38	1.13		.08	.04		F	.027		
				A × U	4	98		10.6	4.4		V × F	23.8		
Core and hall	10'	8'	80	Net area	—	—	—	80	120	—	Vol.	960	65°	728
				U				.08	.04		F	—		
				A × U		—		6.4	4.8		V × F			
Master bedroom	29'-6"	12', 9'	402	Net area	56	—	—	346	—	207	Vol.	1,863	65°	6,230
				U	.38			.08		.12	F	.012		
				A × U	21			27.7		24.8	V × F	22.4		
Child's room	26'-6"	varies	252	Net area	20	—	—	232	—	138	Vol.	1,200	65°	3,718
				U	.38			.08		.12	F	.012		
				A × U	7.6			18.6		16.6	V × F	14.4		
Core and hall	13'	8'	104	Net area	9	—	—	95	—	—	Vol.	1,196	65°	1,650
				U	.38			.08			F	.012		
				A × U	3.4			7.6			V × F	14.4		
Loft	43'	varies	387	Net area	32	—	—	355	—	138	Vol.	1,035	65°	4,512
				U	.38			.08		.12	F	.012		
				A × U	12			28.4		16.6	V × F	12.4		
				Net area							Vol.			
				U							F			
				A × U							V × F			

Total house heat loss: 45,120.
*U = Heat-loss factor; see Table III-B.
†F = Infiltration factor; see Table III-D.

		Hot water				Steam				I-B-R chimney size		
Model number	I-B-R burner capacity (gph)	Gross I-B-R output (Btuh)	Net I-B-R output (Btuh)	Net rating water (sq. ft.)	Tank-less heater capacity (gpm)	Gross I-B-R output (Btuh)	Net I-B-R output (Btuh)	Net rating steam (sq. ft.)	Tank-less heater capacity (gpm)	Rectan-gular (inches)	Inside diam-eter (inches)	Height (feet)
M-100	1.00	110,000	95,700	640	3	110,000	82,500	345	3	8 × 8	6	15
M-120	1.20	126,000	109,600	730	3½	126,000	94,500	395	3½	8 × 8	7	15
M-150	1.50	164,000	142,600	950	4	164,000	123,000	515	4	8 × 8	7	15
M-200	2.00	219,000	190,400	1270	5	219,000	164,300	685	5	8 × 8	8	15
M-250	2.50	275,000	239,100	1395	6	275,000	206,300	860	6	8 × 12	8	15

3. Divide the house into zones.

Heat loss per zone: zone 1, approximately 29,000 Btuh; zone 2, approximately 16,000 Btuh.

Determine the tubing size: use Table A to determine the baseboard tubing size. We will use ¾″ copper tubing for each circuit since the circuits are each less than 35,000 Btuh. We will use 1″ copper tubing for the main pipe leaving the boiler since it carries the total 45,120 Btuh.

4. The equipment is located in the service core on the first floor.

5. The piping layout is shown in Illustration 12.

6. The pump is included in the boiler.

7. The baseboards are selected as follows, using the manufacturer's literature from Illustration 7. Three-quarter-inch tubing is selected. To use the literature we must check to see if the gpm flow in each circuit is greater or less than 4.

Zone 1: gpm = heat loss/10,000 = 2.9
Zone 2: gpm = heat loss/10,000 = 1.6

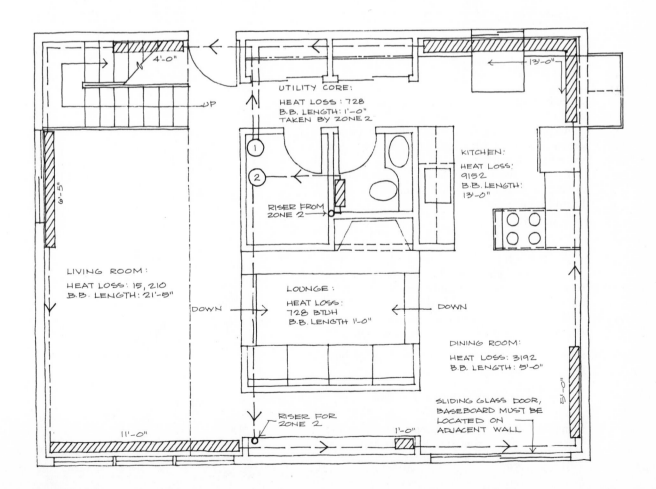

LIVING ROOM:
HEAT LOSS: 15,210
B.B. LENGTH: 21'-5"

UTILITY CORE:
HEAT LOSS: 728
B.B. LENGTH: 1'-0"
TAKEN BY ZONE 2

KITCHEN:
HEAT LOSS: 9152
B.B. LENGTH: 13'-0"

RISER FROM ZONE 2

LOUNGE:
HEAT LOSS: 728 BTUH
B.B. LENGTH 1'-0"

DINING ROOM:
HEAT LOSS: 3192
B.B. LENGTH: 5'-0"

SLIDING GLASS DOOR, BASEBOARD MUST BE LOCATED ON ADJACENT WALL

RISER FOR ZONE 2

UP   DOWN   DOWN

FIRST FLOOR HEATING LAYOUT
ILL. 12

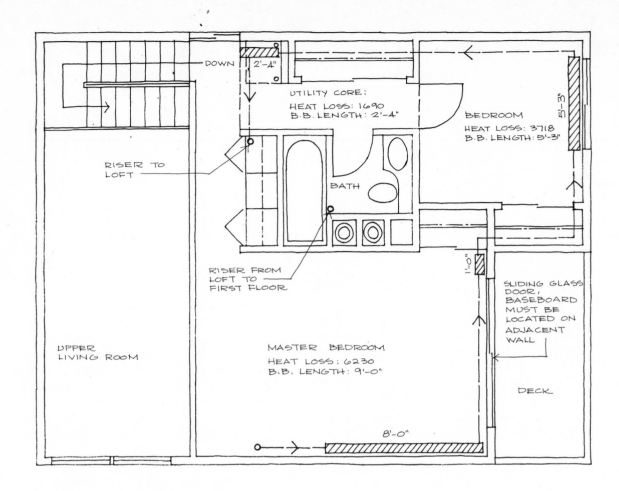

SECOND FLOOR HEATING LAYOUT

Since both are less than 4, use 1 gpm designation on the manufacturer's literature.

Assume the hot-water temperature to be 200 degrees. Select a baseboard rating of 710 from the table in Illustration 7.

To select the baseboard for the living room, divide the heat loss for that room by the baseboard rating.

$$\frac{15,210}{710} = 21.4' \ (21'\text{-}5'') \text{ of baseboard}$$

We divide the required baseboard length into three separate pieces so that we can cover the entire room. The baseboards are located under the windows and adjacent to the door (Ill. 12). We follow the same procedure to determine the baseboard lengths for all of the other rooms (Ill. 12).

8. Select the air cushion tank: 5,000 Btuh of heat loss per gallon of tank.

$$\frac{45,120}{5,000} = 10 \text{ gallon air cushion tank}$$

9. Required tubing: zone 1, about 100 linear feet
zone 2, about 100 linear feet

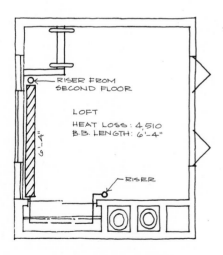

LOFT HEATING LAYOUT

ILL. 12

14
Plumbing System

Although the definition of shelter does not include running water or sanitary sewage disposal as essential elements to supporting life, it would be a rare person who would choose (or be allowed by health and building codes) to live without them. In this chapter we attempt to demystify plumbing by examining the various components that make up the system.

When we open a faucet and water comes out, we hardly ever question where this water comes from, how it gets there, and where it goes once we are through. All we know is that it is there when we need it and it conveniently vanishes when we don't. The cycle of bringing water in, through, and out of a house breaks down into three basic phases. The starting point is the source of water, be it a municipal water main, a private well, or some other source. Next there must be a distribution system inside the house, which makes the water accessible to the various fixtures and faucets in the building. Finally, the used water and any waste have to be drained and disposed of by means of a sewage disposal facility.

Before moving ahead to further explain the components of a plumbing system, we feel a few words of caution and advice are in order. Even though the plumbing required for a house is relatively simple to understand, its actual design and installation are far from easy or rewarding tasks. To begin with, you will find that plumbing, contrary to carpentry, is hidden within the walls of the house. No one will ever admire it. They will merely assume it is there

and will be highly inconvenienced when it does not operate properly. (Has anyone ever praised a house for the efficiency of its plumbing?) In addition to causing inconvenience, faulty plumbing installations can be a health hazard to you and your family. To add injury to insult, most pipes are heavy and cumbersome to handle, and the connection work necessary to join many of them is tricky. A word for the "tool freak." The tools necessary for plumbing work are rarely used for any other type of work. Finally, in most communities a license is mandatory to do plumbing work. In conclusion, we believe it wiser (although not cheaper) to hire a professional to do your plumbing.

In the event that the above paragraph is not a sufficient deterrent, we include this chapter on basic plumbing. Even if you do hire a plumber, it is helpful to have an understanding of how the system operates and what materials can and should be used. One way or another be sure to consult all codes and building officials before proceeding to do any aspect of the design or installation of the system.

GETTING WATER TO THE HOUSE

All water comes from precipitation, which later becomes surface water (streams and lakes) or underground water. Urban areas use rivers and lakes as their sources of water (although some

The factors affecting pump selection are the type of well (shallow or deep) and the quantity of water the well can supply (number of gallons per minute). The well driller carries a portable pump with which to determine the well's capacity.

Shallow-well pumps available are the piston, rotary, shallow-well jet, and the reciprocating pump. The reciprocating pump is not usually recommended and is rarely used at present. Piston pumps are motorized versions of the old-fashioned lift pump. The advantages of rotary and shallow-well jets are continuous action and having only one moving part. They are the ones most commonly used.

Deep-well pumps range from jet and turbine pumps to submersible ones. Turbine pumps are generally employed in high-capacity work. Jet pumps are quite popular for residential work. Because the entire pump system sits above ground (either over the well or in the house), jet pumps have the advantage of being easily accessible. The ease of accessibility, however, is tied to the problem of sound. Because of their surface location, their operation can be heard. Submersible pumps, on the other hand, are completely sunken in the well (even the motor) and are becoming quite popular in residential installations. They can bring water up from greater depths than the jets can, and they are completely silent in operation. However, submersible pumps are more expensive than jet pumps, and so is the repair work.

urban areas use deep wells). Before it is ready for use, however, the water is purified at a treatment plant. Later it is piped to the municipalities by means of a series of mains. Rural areas, on the other hand, have no access to such public water sources and rely completely on private ones such as wells and cisterns (sometimes even springs if they run close to the house).

If you are building in an urban or suburban area where there are municipal mains, your job is greatly simplified. All that needs to be done is to hook up to the main. The local code will dictate the requirements concerning the hookup, depth of trenches, and any other criteria. Most communities will require that a professional licensed plumber make at least the final hookup to the main.

There is more work to be done however in rural areas, where wells or cisterns provide the water. A cistern operates by collecting rain water on the roof of the house and leading it to a storage tank. The collected water is later pumped for distribution through the building. Cisterns are primarily employed in areas where rainfall is abundant and drilling for a well is either impossible or very costly.

Wells are by far the most popular type of private water source. There are two basic types: shallow (dug) wells and deep wells. Shallow wells are generally no more than 50′ deep and rely mostly on water filtered from rain. This type of well is acceptable in open country where the water table is high. Its main disadvantages are the possibility of dryness during times of drought, surface pollution by organic matter and bacteria, and an unpleasant taste and odor, also due to surface organic matter. Deep wells are more reliable than shallow ones and are often the only ones allowed by code. They may be over 100′ in depth and are constructed by means of a drilling rig.* Because of the machinery involved in their installation, there is little choice but to hire a well driller. He can, in addition to drilling your well, provide you with valuable information regarding successful well depths in your area and assist you in the selection of a pump (Inset I). Make sure to have the local health department test the well water for purity, color, and taste.† You can also have the water tested for hardness, a high mineral content that can line the inside of the pipes, water heaters, and boiler tubes, eventually clogging them. A water softener can be installed, if desired, to prevent clogging from taking place. The water may also have a high iron content. Such water is perfectly safe to drink; however, the iron makes the water red-brown (rust) when it is exposed to air. There are a number of filtering devices that eliminate this problem.

Regardless of the type of well you are using, one factor remains constant—its location. Wells should be placed at the high end of the property and a sufficient distance away from any sewage disposal fields (your own, a neighbor's, or a future neighbor's) to avoid contamination of the water supply. Most likely one of the requirements you will have to meet is a submission of the proposed site plan to the building or health authorities, indicating the house, well, and sewage disposal location.

It is common for localities to have specific dimensional relationships for supply and dis-

---

* There are two types of well-drilling rigs: the pounder and the rotary. The rotary is faster than the pounder but may sometimes seal off small veins of water.
† Although there are water-testing kits, we feel that you should have the health department test for bacterial contamination.

posal systems and the property lines. The well's depth and the percolation value of the soil will determine the necessary distance from your own sewage disposal system (or your neighbor's). Although in some areas it may be as close as 50', a common separating distance for a well is 100' from the property line, the house, or the road. No distance is too great for separation from your septic tank, cesspool, or effluent disposal field. The health department's regulations will be more stringent in areas that are swampy, land-filled, or on a rock shelf. Before drilling anything, or even before buying property, it is wise to consult the building and health departments as to the feasibility of a well on that property. One family we know bought a lovely and large house site on a salt-water marsh. They could not build on the land, however, because there was no way of accommodating sewage disposal and a well on the same three-quarter-acre site.

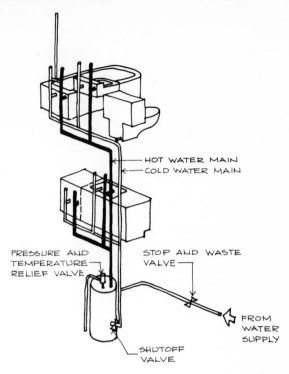

HOT WATER MAIN
COLD WATER MAIN
PRESSURE AND TEMPERATURE RELIEF VALVE
STOP AND WASTE VALVE
FROM WATER SUPPLY
SHUTOFF VALVE

ILL. 1

GETTING WATER TO THE FIXTURES

The primary function of the water-supply system is to make water available to the various fixtures in the house. It consists of a water-supply main, a water heater, hot and cold water pipes, valves, air chambers, and a meter (pumps and storage tanks are required for private systems).

It is impossible for water to gently flow through the pipes and into the fixtures; it has to be pushed there. For municipal mains the necessary pressure is generated by gravity (reservoirs are situated at high altitudes or in water towers). In private systems the problem is trickier. Where cisterns are used, the water pressure is obtained by means of a circulating pump. In well systems the joint effort of a well pump and a storage tank supply the pressure. The pump pulls the water out of the well and into the tank. Once there the compressed air in the tank pushes the water out of the tank and into the supply main (Inset I).

The water-supply main (pipe bringing the water from the source to the house) is a very important component of the system since any problems in the main could potentially cut off the water supply. Care must be taken in the design and installation of this pipe, particularly in cold climates. To prevent any danger of freez-

ing, which would cause the pipes to burst, the supply main must be located well below the frost line. Local ordinances will indicate the depth of frost penetration in your area. (The National Building Code specifies a minimum of 1' *below* the frost line.)

Upon entering the building, the supply main (like a tree) branches out to reach the fixtures and supply them with hot and cold water service. Any special provision, such as water softening treatment or the installation of a water meter, occurs at this point, before the main has been subdivided. Afterward, the main supply line is divided into a hot and a cold water main. The hot water main is connected to an electric, oil, gas, or solar powered water heater, where the water is brought up to a higher temperature (Inset II). (Houses using hydronic heating may utilize the boiler as the heating medium.) Once the water is heated, the pressure in the pipes directs it to each fixture branch pipe by means of intermediary branch lines and risers (Ill. 1). These lines become invisible by snaking through walls, floors, and ceilings.*

* Another approach to the standard hot water system is to provide a continued hot water circulation by returning it back to the water heater. The purpose of recirculating the unused water is to prevent it from cooling off while standing in the pipes near the faucet. Instead, it flows back into the heater, allowing the fixture branch pipe to receive new hot water upon demand. This system is more expensive.

A water heater is a heat transfer mechanism by which cold water is brought up to a higher temperature. The heat can be generated electrically, or by means of·oil or gas firing. Houses with hydronic heating systems may use their boilers as the heat source.*

Solar collectors offer another method for heating water. There are many systems commercially available which will supply between 40 and 100 percent of a house's requirements. The extra components of a solar system involve south-facing collectors of between 50 and 100 square feet in area, circulating lines, a storage tank, a pump, and connections to tap into the conventionally powered hot water heater. The angle of the collector is calculated by adding 5 degrees to the latitude (number of degrees above the equator) of your house.

Besides the difference in the method of heat generation, water heaters can be of the tank or tankless type. Tankless heaters are utilized on small compact houses. Tank-type heaters, on the other hand, are employed to have a large amount of water quickly available and assure a better supply of hot water at all times. Another advantage of tank-type heaters is that the size of the heater itself may be reduced because there is always a supply of water in the tank.

SIZING A TANK-TYPE HEATER

The size of the water heater needed varies according to the hot water used per person per day. Water consumption per person may range from 20 to 100 gallons per day (gpd). These variations take into account the use of water-consuming appliances such as dishwashers and washing machines. For our calculations, we'll use a comfortable 100 gpd, projecting the use of a dishwasher and washing machine. You should keep in mind, however, a few tips which will reduce your hot water requirements. Use spray-type faucets and short or insulated runs of pipe. In addition, washing machines, dishwashers, and other water-consuming appliances should be run at peak capacity. By following these suggestions, you can reduce the 100 gpd per person figure by two-thirds.

To calculate the size of the heater, a few points must be kept in mind. First, it has been estimated that the peak hot water demand in residences occurs within a four-hour period. This maximum hourly demand however only represents about one-seventh of the total daily demand. Second, a tank large enough to hold $\frac{1}{5}$ of the daily hot water requirements is recommended. Keep in mind that the figure representing the total tank capacity is deceiving, since when more than 70 percent of the tank's volume is drawn, the water starts to cool. For this reason, the tank's total capacity is multiplied by a factor of .70 in order to arrive at a net capacity (in other words, to find out how much hot water it will realistically supply).

The calculations follow. Let's assume a family of five.

1. Determine the total daily hot water requirement: 5 people × 100 gpd per person = 500 gpd total demand.

2. Determine the maximum hourly demand: 500 gpd (total demand) × $\frac{1}{7}$ (maximum hourly demand factor) = 71.4.

3. Find out the amount of water needed to satisfy the four-hour peak load: 71.4 (maximum hourly demand) × 4 = 285.6 gallons.

4. The tank's capacity should be one-fifth the total daily requirement: 500 gpd (total daily requirement) × $\frac{1}{5}$ = 100 gallons.

5. Determine the tank's net volume: 100 gallons (total volume) × .70 = 70 gallons.

6. Since the water needed to satisfy the four-hour peak load is 285.6 gallons and the net capacity of the tank is 70 gallons, there are still 215.6 gallons of water (285.6 − 70) that the water heater must heat.

7. To find out the heater's hourly output, divide 4 (peak hours) into 215.6 gallons of water which remain to be heated:

$$\frac{215.6 \text{ gallons}}{4 \text{ peak hours}} = 53.9 \text{ gallons per hour (gph)}.$$

In order to satisfy the house's hot water requirements, the water heater in the example must be able to produce 54 gallons of hot water per hour.

* This particular type of water heater can be of the internal or the external type: internal is where the heating mechanism is literally immersed in the boiler; external is where it sits outside the boiler but receives hot water from the boiler as the heating medium.

The cold water system, on the other hand, bypasses the water heater. Like the hot water, it branches out into intermediary pipes, risers, and fixture branch pipes until each fixture is reached.

An integral part of the cold and hot water-supply systems are the valves provided for the regulation of the water. A faucet is a type of valve that can be gradually opened or closed to get the desired quantity of water flow. Other valves are designed exclusively to completely close off the flow or completely open it to full capacity. Shutoff valves such as these are installed throughout the system to isolate sections and facilitate repairs. For instance, a shutoff valve is provided in the water-supply main before it branches out into hot and cold water mains. They are also installed at each fixture branch pipe and horizontal branches leading to the kitchen and bath.

Valves are also instrumental in the drainage of the water-supply system. Houses situated in cold climates need to have their water-supply system totally emptied if they are to remain unheated for a period of time. Otherwise, freezing water inside the pipes can cause severe damage to the system. To facilitate drainage, all the horizontal branch pipes are pitched toward one or more drain valves. (Pipe hangers can be used to adjust pipes to the correct pitch.)

Water pipes can be noisy. You probably have

had the experience of hearing a loud bang (water hammer) while quickly closing a faucet. This is caused by the water pressure and can be corrected by means of an air chamber. Don't be misled by the fancy name. An air chamber is merely an extra run of pipe (which looks like an amateur plumber's mistake) located at each fixture. The extra length of pipe tends to absorb the air cushion into the water (Ill. 2).

Air chambers depend on the continuing inflow of air bubbles trapped in the water for their efficient operation. A device called a petcock may be installed in the air chamber to recharge it with air. In addition to air chambers, there are mechanical shock absorbers, which provide a more sophisticated and efficient solution to the problem of water hammer.

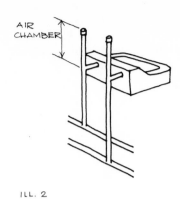

ILL. 2

Supply-Pipe Materials

Pipes are available in a wide range of materials, each with a different degree of corrosion resistance, method of connection, cost, and acceptability by the various codes. Materials range from plain or galvanized steel to wrought or cast iron, brass, copper, and even plastic. To further complicate matters, the selection of one material alone does not solve all your problems. Codes sometimes specify one material for the water-supply system, another one for the drainage system, or for a particular section of either system. Occasionally they stipulate that certain materials may not be used at all. What might prove to be a very good choice for water-supply pipes might not be so efficient for drainage or vice-versa. In essence, the problem is not simple. We have tried to narrow down the choices by rating the materials in terms of performance against corrosion and ease of installation. (Needless to say, if the code says otherwise, it wins.)

There are many ways of joining pipes: threading, soldering, brazing, caulking, and mechanical. The two most commonly used methods are threading and soldering. Threading is a tedious and difficult job, involving cutting a length of pipe, fitting a threader into the pipe, turning it until enough thread has been cut, screwing the pipe into the fitting, and applying a compound. A solder joint, on the other hand, only involves cutting, slipping on the fitting, and soldering the connection. An entire assembly of pipes can be set without turning any of the parts. Although neither one of the two can be considered elementary procedures,

soldering is easier than threading. This is very important when you consider how many connections you'll have to make. Ferrous pipes (steel and iron) as well as brass require threaded connections.

In terms of corrosion resistance, copper and plastic rate better than plain or galvanized steel, iron, or brass.* Plastic piping is becoming more widely available. Its great ease of installation, low cost, and light weight make it a very attractive choice. Because of its newness, however, many codes do not permit its use. In addition, at the date of this publication some controversy still exists in reference to its potential carcinogenic toxicity.† It is for this reason that we do not recommend its use for the water-*supply* system.

Copper is a very popular choice and the one we recommend in particular for the water-supply system. It is not subject to attack by acids or corrosion. Because it requires solder joints rather than threading, it is relatively simple to assemble. It is more expensive than either ferrous or plastic piping, but it is cheaper than brass. In addition, it is widely accepted by building codes.

* Red brass is an exception, offering excellent corrosion resistance. It is alloyed with copper and although it is almost pure copper, it is correctly called brass.
† Polyvinyl chloride (PVC) pipe uses as its base vinyl chloride, which in gas form is believed to account for the high incidence of liver cancer among workers in the plastic industry who have inhaled it. In May 1973 the United States Food and Drug Administration banned the use of PVC in liquor bottles; PVC was believed to be migrating into the liquor. In August 1975 the FDA banned the use of PVC plastic food packages. The prohibition applied to the plastic used in rigid or semirigid form. Presently, the FDA is exploring the possibility of whether water pipes made of PVC may also pose a health risk.

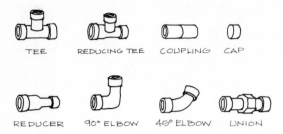

TEE REDUCING TEE COUPLING CAP

REDUCER 90° ELBOW 45° ELBOW UNION

ILL. 3

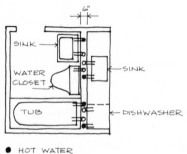

SINK

WATER CLOSET

SINK

TUB

DISHWASHER

● HOT WATER
○ COLD WATER

ILL. 4

Pipe Sizing

The sizes of pipes vary according to their function within the system and the amount of water they must carry. The principle is well illustrated in the structure of a tree: the further away from the trunk, the smaller the branch. A branch pipe leading water to a sink carries less water than the main that supplies the entire bathroom and is, therefore, smaller in diameter.

We could explain in detail the method of calculation necessary to arrive at the dimension of each pipe. This approach is rarely used for the design of a small house. Often codes meticulously outline the dimensional requirements. If so, the better for you; you will have one less variable to worry about. Otherwise the problem is all yours.

Pipe sizes not only vary according to their function but also according to the materials used. We have compiled a list of the most common sizes used for supply copper tubing in residential work. A word of advice: Do not make these sizes any smaller unless you want to hear humming in the pipes. Making them larger won't hurt.

Supply main—1″
Hot and cold water mains—1″
Intermediary branches—¾″
Branches to each fixture—½″

Pipe Fittings

In their run through the house, pipes have to change direction, branch into other pipes, reduce large pipes into smaller ones, and so on, while at the same time permitting the uninterrupted flow of water. Pipe fittings are provided for this purpose. They can be soldered, threaded, or specially designed as in the case of plastic or cast-iron piping. It all depends on the material you are using. Copper piping is connected by means of soldered fittings (Ill. 3).

How to Map Out the Water-Supply System

1. Take a look at the preliminary plans of your house and examine the locations of the bathrooms, kitchen, laundry, and any other facility requiring plumbing. Are they efficiently arranged? Can they be moved closer? Can they share a "wet" wall by being back to back? by being stacked?

   It should be evident at this point why grouping fixtures together facilitates the design and installation of a plumbing system. The closer the fixtures, the shorter the runs and, therefore, the less work and expense. Keep in mind that with the exception of basements (where pipes can run freely) pipes run inside walls, floors, and ceilings. The path of the pipes has to be integrated with these structural elements. (See page 306, Inset II.)

2. Indicate all the fixtures in the plan and provide each one of them with a hot and cold water-supply pipe (as required). You can indicate the pipes as circles in the wall next to the fixture (Ill. 4).

3. Determine the location of the water heater. (If a boiler is used instead of a water heater, its location has already been established in the design of the heating system.) Keep in mind the point of entry of the water-supply main. Try to keep the run between the supply main and the heater reasonably short.

4. If any water treatment equipment is being installed, establish its location, preferably close to the point of entry of the water-supply line.

5. Establish the shortest route that the hot and cold water pipes must travel in order to reach the supply main and the water heater. In order to do this, examine the available walls, floors, and ceilings through which the pipes can run. Consider the structural elements within the walls and floors (studs, joists, etc.). Make sure that the pipes work with them rather than disrupt them. Try to keep pipes parallel to the walls rather than angular to them.

GETTING RID OF THE WATER: DRAINAGE

The used water together with any waste it has collected has to be led out of the house and into a disposal system (be it a municipal sewer main or a private sewage system). This is the function of a drainage system. In addition to getting rid of the waste, the drainage system has to provide an exhaust for harmful and smelly gases generated by the waste. Two interlocking networks are provided for this purpose. The first is a network of pipes that carries all waste from each fixture to the sewage disposal system. The second is a venting system that allows gas to be exhausted to the outside while letting air in (Ill. 5).

The drainage system operates in a very similar fashion to the water supply. Waste from the fixture drains to the waste pipe and is discharged into an intermediary branch line, which picks up waste from those fixtures located on the same floor or area. In order to reach the basement, the waste is channeled to a vertical pipe (soil stack) that runs the full height of the building (from the basement to the roof). The purpose of the soil stack is to receive the waste from all intermediary lines and transfer it to the house drain, which is the link between the drainage and the disposal system (Ill. 5). The soil stack carries both solid and liquid waste. In large installations or where the distance between some fixtures and the soil stack is too great, a secondary stack called a waste stack is provided (Ill. 6). The waste stack as opposed to the soil stack only carries liquid waste generated from sinks, tubs, etc. Solid matter from toilets drains into the soil stack.

Unlike the water-supply system, which functions by means of pressure, the drainage system must rely completely on gravity. For this reason, all waste pipes are either vertical or have a

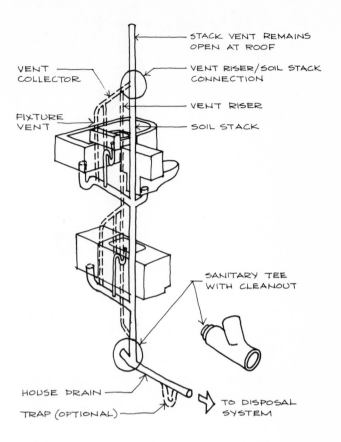

STACK VENT REMAINS OPEN AT ROOF

VENT COLLECTOR

VENT RISER/SOIL STACK CONNECTION

VENT RISER

FIXTURE VENT

SOIL STACK

SANITARY TEE WITH CLEANOUT

HOUSE DRAIN

TRAP (OPTIONAL)

TO DISPOSAL SYSTEM

ILL. 5

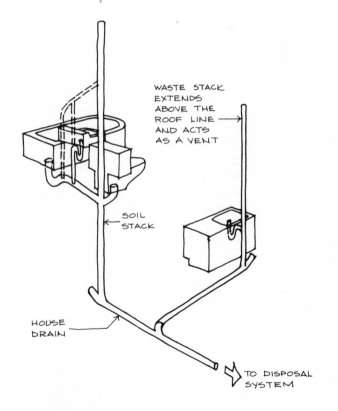

WASTE STACK EXTENDS ABOVE THE ROOF LINE AND ACTS AS A VENT

SOIL STACK

HOUSE DRAIN

TO DISPOSAL SYSTEM

ILL. 6

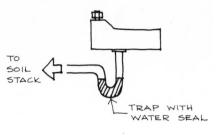

TO
SOIL
STACK

TRAP WITH
WATER SEAL

ILL. 7

downward pitch and are of large cross-sectional area (to prevent solid matter from accumulating and clogging the pipes).

The venting system is an integral part of the drainage system. To begin with, the soil stack, which is the main artery for drainage, becomes the "lungs" for the vents. It can serve this twofold purpose by merely remaining open at the roof (Ill. 5). This opening allows air into the soil stack (referred to as the stack vent once it extends over the highest fixture) at the same time that gases are exhausted, preventing suction and gas accumulation in the pipes.

Although the soil stack is the main source of air, it is difficult for the air to find its way to all the fixtures unless each is provided with a branch vent. Branch vents are pipes carrying nothing but air that lead from each fixture to a vent collector. In compact installations, the collector hooks up to a vent riser. The connection between the vent riser and the soil stack occurs above the level of the highest fixtures, where the soil stack becomes the stack vent (Ill. 5). In large installations or where distances between the vent riser and the soil stack are too great, the riser is led directly to the roof, becoming a direct ventilation source—it is common in houses for each bathroom and the kitchen sink to have a separate vent (Ill. 6).

Allowing for air intake and exhaust alone is not enough to prevent gases from entering the house. For further protection, traps are provided at each fixture. A trap is the U-shaped pipe you always see under sinks. Every fixture has a trap but most of them are hidden in walls, floors, or in the fixtures themselves. The trap does exactly as it says—it traps water in the U. The water acts as a seal against gas penetration (Ill. 7).

Venting is very important to the efficient functioning of the traps. With no air in the drainage system, suction (siphonage) can occur. Siphon action can draw the water out of the trap, breaking the seal and leaving an open path for gases to penetrate the building.

Maintenance devices such as cleanouts also have to be included in the drainage system. Cleanouts are openings in the pipe that give access to the interior of the system and prove of great value in the event of clogging or other problems. The number of cleanouts varies according to the complexity of the piping network, or as required by code. A cleanout plug, however, is always required at the bottom of the soil stack—before it turns into the house drain (Ill. 5).

Other components such as a house trap and a separate fresh air intake are sometimes included. The house trap (a trap in the house drain) has been the source of controversy. There are those who feel that although it provides added insurance against gas penetration from the disposal system, it could interfere with the efficient outflow of waste. The National Plumbing Code does not require house traps. Other codes do. Check your code to see what it has to say. A fresh air inlet is usually included whenever a house trap is provided, and omitted otherwise. Its purpose is to allow fresh air into the system.

Drainage-Pipe Materials

The criteria for the selection of drainage pipes are slightly different from those for supply pipes. Like supply pipes, drainage piping has to handle problems of corrosion and facilitate installation. It does not, however, have to sustain the pressure that supply pipes do or be affected by toxicity considerations. Instead, it must allow for easy flow of sometimes bulky waste. Due to the lack of pressure, its walls can be thinner. Because of the waste, its diameter should be larger. When you are buying drainage pipe specify it as such. The thinner-walled piping will be a bit cheaper and lighter than that used for supply lines.

Copper, plastic, and cast iron are the three most widely used materials for drainage piping. Many codes specify cast iron as the only acceptable material. Cast iron costs less than copper. The technique for connecting cast-iron piping, however, is rather complicated (at least, more so than soldering).* In addition, its weight is staggering. Copper tubing has been widely used for

* There is a new joining system for cast-iron piping on the market. These no-hub couplings consist of a plastic section protected by a thin metal ring. Although this system is easier to install than the traditional connections, its use may be limited by code.

drainage systems. Its essential characteristics have already been described on page 163. Plastic piping is an economical and work-saving option. Although many codes do not accept plastic in the water-supply system, they allow its use for drainage lines. Plastic is good against corrosion, lightweight, and quite simple to install. Unless the code requires otherwise, we recommend plastic tubing for the drainage lines.

Pipe Sizing

Because they carry waste in addition to water, drainage pipes are larger in diameter than water-supply pipes. In addition, the system operates 100 percent on gravity. The area of the pipes has to be ample enough to prevent any waste from getting stuck and clogging the system. On the other hand, too large a pipe is not desirable since the liquid will run off leaving solid matter behind.

As in the case of the supply lines, the size of the pipes is relative to their function within the network. Obviously, a pipe draining a sink will be smaller than one carrying waste out of a toilet.

Following is a list of widely used dimensions for copper and plastic tubing in residential work. These dimensions are merely indicators; always check your code first.

DRAINAGE PIPES

	Copper	Plastic
House drain	4″	4″
Soil stack	4″	4″
Drains in kitchen	2″	2″
Drains in toilet	4″	4″
Sink and bathtubs	1½″	1½″

VENTING PIPES

All vents	2″	2″

Pipe Fittings

The type of fitting in the drainage system varies from that of the supply system because its function is different. Fittings are needed not only to connect the different branches within the network but, more important, to permit maximum ease of flow of the sewage out of the building.

To prevent any waste from being trapped while turning, connections between branches and the main stack are gentle curves rather than sharp angles. (Angles are generally greater than

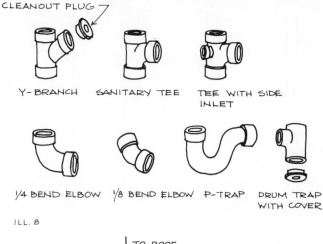

CLEANOUT PLUG

Y-BRANCH   SANITARY TEE   TEE WITH SIDE INLET

¼ BEND ELBOW   ⅛ BEND ELBOW   P-TRAP   DRUM TRAP WITH COVER

ILL. 8

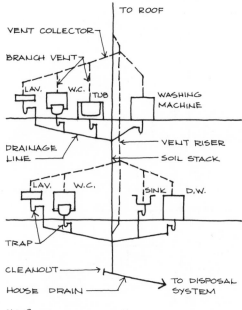

TO ROOF

VENT COLLECTOR

BRANCH VENT

LAV.   W.C.   TUB   WASHING MACHINE

DRAINAGE LINE   VENT RISER

SOIL STACK

LAV.   W.C.   SINK   D.W.

TRAP

CLEANOUT

HOUSE DRAIN   TO DISPOSAL SYSTEM

ILL. 9

45 degrees with the horizontal. Ninety-degree angles are not permitted.) In addition, the fittings are designed with no protrusions on their inside diameter (Ill. 8).

How to Map Out the Drainage System

By now you should have a preliminary plan indicating the location of all the bathroom, kitchen, and laundry fixtures. This plan should also include the hot and cold water-supply requirements.

1. Before doing any further work on the plan, draw a riser diagram—an elevation/section view of the fixtures that allows you to visualize all the components necessary in the drainage system (drains, vents, stacks, etc.). This diagram also serves as a checking device at the end of the planning stage (Ill. 9).

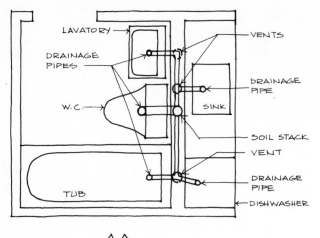

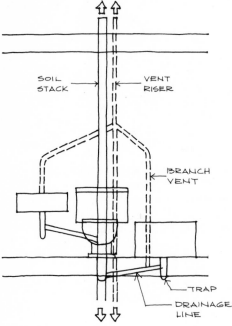

ILL. 10

2. Provide each fixture with a drainage pipe. Remember that drainage pipes generally run in the floors (Ill. 10).

3. Provide each fixture with a vent. Vents are usually within the wall (Ill. 10).

4. Establish the best location for the soil stack. Keep in mind that all branches must feed to this stack and that it must run vertically through the entire house. Check for available walls where it can run (Ill. 10).

5. Draw branch lines indicating the best and shortest run for each branch drain to the soil stack. Try to keep bends to a minimum (Ill. 10).

6. Draw the path of the vents to the soil stack or individual vent stack as required (Ill. 10).

7. The path of the house drain cannot be decided upon until the location of the disposal system has been determined. Once this is done the house

drain run will be simply that which connects the soil stack with the house sewer.

THE DISPOSAL SYSTEM

Waste coming out of the building must be disposed of in a manner appropriate with health standards. Should your house be located in an area where sewage mains are available, your job is essentially reading codes and contacting authorities. If a main is not available, you will have to decide on a type of disposal system. In either case, one criterion remains unchanged. Because of the health hazard involved in the installation of inadequate sewage disposal facilities, regulations concerning their design and installation are very strict.

Connections to a public disposal system (municipal sewer main) are generally required to be made by a licensed plumber or other authorized individual. The depth of the trenches, pitch of the pipe, length of the run, maximum number of bends, and type of material will be specified in the code. Be certain to follow these regulations.

When no sewage main is available, you have no choice but to provide your own disposal system. The purpose of a sewage disposal system is to take all waste from the house and break it down through bacterial action until it is rendered harmless and can be absorbed by the surrounding soil. Septic tanks and cesspools are the most commonly used systems, although new ones are being devised every day.*

Cesspools are large tanks (generally of precast concrete) with perforated walls (Ill. 11). The house sewer empties the sewage directly into the cesspool, where it is later absorbed by a layer of gravel and the soil adjacent to the openings. Because the sewage goes directly from the house to the cesspool and into the soil, there's little opportunity for the waste to thoroughly break down and be rendered harmless. A further disadvantage of cesspools is that the earth around them often becomes saturated and clogs the openings, creating the need for a second cesspool.

* There is a new Swedish-made device called a composting toilet, which handles all wastes from a house. By using this toilet, you could completely eliminate the need for a septic system.

Septic tanks are preferred over cesspools since they offer a greater breakdown of sewage. A septic tank system contains a sealed-joint pipe (house sewer), which carries all sewage from the house to the tank. (Its material and size are usually specified by code. A 4" cast-iron pipe is the most widely used.) Once in the septic tank, sewage is isolated from the air, allowing bacterial action to take place. Solids are broken down into liquids, gas, and sludge. Gas sifts back along the house sewer and out the soil stack. The sludge settles in the bottom of the tank, requiring periodic cleaning. The liquid flows out through another pipe (effluent sewer) and into a distribution box, where the effluent is distributed to various parts of the effluent field. Once there, it is absorbed into the surrounding soil (Ill. 12).

A grease trap is an optional element in the sewage disposal system, consisting of a small tank into which the kitchen waste empties before getting a chance to enter the house sewer. Its purpose is to prevent grease and oil generated in the kitchen from entering the system and clogging the lines thus retarding bacterial action.

Septic tanks of steel and precast concrete are available commercially. You can pour a concrete tank yourself. Consider, however, saving your energy for more creative tasks. Tanks made out of steel are generally cheaper than concrete ones. On the other hand, concrete tanks last longer and are more widely used. Check your code before deciding on the material. It might make up your mind for you.

It is important that the septic tank be of appropriate size. Too much sludge can otherwise accumulate, creating a backflow of sewage into the house. The house's occupancy determines the size of the tank. (Don't forget to take expansion plans into account.) Obviously, the larger the tank, the less frequently cleaning is required. Again check your local codes. They will most likely indicate the minimum sizes allowed. Table A gives an indication of the sizes most commonly specified.

The effluent disposal field also needs to be designed. Here is where the liquid flowing from the septic tank is rendered harmless by contact with air and is absorbed by the soil. There are three basic types of effluent fields: a subsoil system of drainage tiles, leaching cesspools, and sand filters. The selection is based on the code, the soil type, and the topography of the site.

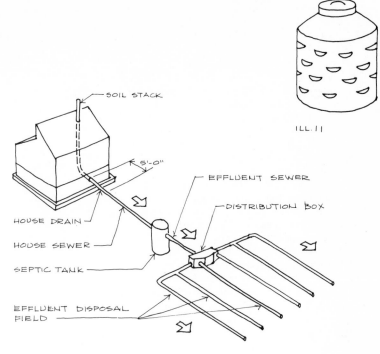

ILL. 11

ILL. 12

TABLE A: SEPTIC TANK CAPACITIES

Maximum number of persons	Capacity of tank (gallons)
4	500
6	600
8	750
10	900

Subsoil systems are preferred over the other two because they provide a better environment for effluent purification due to their location close to the surface of the soil. They are applicable to most soil types with the exception of impervious soils, where sand filters, although more expensive, are required. The system consists of a series of open-jointed, perforated clay drainage tiles sitting on a bed of gravel. The joints are covered with tarpaper to prevent clogging by particles of earth and rock. Size requirements for subsoil drainage fields and cesspools vary depending on the rate of absorbency of the soil (percolation). See Inset III.

Leaching cesspools are probably the cheapest of the three. Because of their depth, they cannot be installed in areas with a high water table. (The bottom of the cesspool should be at least 2'

The size of the effluent field is relative to the occupancy of the house and the absorbency of the soil: the larger the house, the larger the field; the less absorbent the soil, the larger the field.

To find out the absorption rate (percolation) of the soil, dig a pit approximately 1' wide and 1' long and about 2' deep. (Make sure that the test pit is at the proposed site for the effluent field.) Fill it with water and let it seep into the soil. Don't give the soil a chance to dry. Again pour water; this time, however, measure the amount you're pouring (about 4"). Time how long it takes for the water to be absorbed and divide it by the quantity of water (in inches) to get the time of absorbency per inch drop.

If you are planning a subsoil drainage field, Table III-A will give you the number of lineal feet of field required. If you are using cesspools, Table III-B will provide the number and area of cesspools required. Remember that these tables are merely to give you an idea of the area you will need depending on the type of effluent field you choose to use. Before actually designing your system, however, get a copy of regulations from the local building or health authorities.

TABLE III-A: LINEAL FEET REQUIRED FOR SUBSOIL DRAINAGE FIELDS

Occupancy	Time required for 1" of water to drop (minutes)		
	0–3	3–5	5–30
1–4	100'	150'	250'
5–9	200'	350'	700'
10–14	340'	500'	1,000'

TABLE III-B: REQUIRED NUMBER AND SIZES OF CESSPOOLS (CP'S)

	Time required for 1" of water to drop (minutes)								
	0–3			3–5			5–30		
Occupancy	No. of cp's	Diameter	Depth	No. of cp's	Diameter	Depth	No. of cp's	Diameter	Depth
1–4	1	5'-0"	5'-0"	1	6'-0"	6'-0"	2	5'-0"	5'-0"
5–9	1	6'-0"	6'-0"	2	6'-0"	6'-0"	2	8'-0"	7'-0"
10–14	1	8'-0"	6'-0"	2	8'-0"	6'-0"	2	10'-0"	8'-0"

TABLE B: TYPE OF EFFLUENT FIELD

Soil type	Subsoil drainage	Cesspool	Sand filter
Very absorptive	can use	can use	cannot use
Absorptive	can use	can use	cannot use
Impervious	cannot use	cannot use	can use
Water table	high	low	very high
Space requirements	large	small	large

above the water table or as required by code.) This type of cesspool is suitable where the soil is absorbent and the water table is low and is particularly effective in steep slopes or in tight pieces of property where a subsoil system could not be installed. See Table B (Ill. 13).

The location of the sewage disposal system is more often than not dictated by code. Minimum distances need to be observed between the house and the tank, effluent field, well, and property lines (Ill. 14). As we mentioned earlier, you will probably have to submit a proposed site plan to the local authorities showing the relationship between the house, well, and sewage disposal system. If it should happen that the area where you are building has no building code or other authority, contact the health department. They will inform you of any state regulations in effect.

While locating the site for the tank and effluent field, make sure to select ground that slopes away from the house as well as away from the well. Remember, all drainage should be downhill from the water supply (Ill. 15).

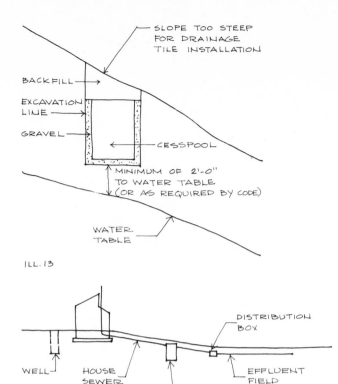

SLOPE TOO STEEP
FOR DRAINAGE
TILE INSTALLATION

BACKFILL

EXCAVATION
LINE

GRAVEL

CESSPOOL

MINIMUM OF 2'-0"
TO WATER TABLE
(OR AS REQUIRED BY CODE)

WATER
TABLE

ILL. 13

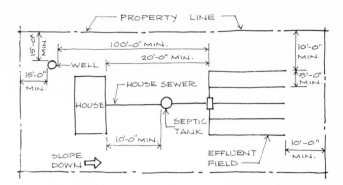

PROPERTY LINE

15'-0" MIN.

WELL

100'-0" MIN.

20'-0" MIN.

HOUSE SEWER

HOUSE

15'-0" MIN.

10'-0" MIN.

5'-0" MIN.

SEPTIC TANK

SLOPE DOWN

10'-0" MIN.

EFFLUENT FIELD

10'-0" MIN.

MINIMUM DISTANCE REQUIREMENTS FROM A
SAMPLE STATE DEPARTMENT OF HEALTH
REGULATIONS (WILL VARY WITH TOWN OR STATE)

ILL. 14

DISTRIBUTION BOX

WELL

HOUSE SEWER

SEPTIC TANK

EFFLUENT FIELD

ILL. 15

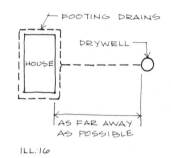

FOOTING DRAINS

DRYWELL

HOUSE

AS FAR AWAY
AS POSSIBLE

ILL. 16

STORM DRAINAGE

The easiest way to get rid of storm water is to let it be absorbed by the ground. If you have a high absorptive soil such as sand or gravel, you have little to worry about. A simple splash pan at the foot of a leader will divert the water sufficiently away from the house. If you have clay soil or a high water table, you have a problem which requires the design of a complex drainage system.

Storm drainage systems can range from a pipe leading to a gravel-filled box, to a drywell, all depending on the rate of absorbency of the soil. Impervious soils will require the installation of footing drains. They may be porous cylindrical clay pipes (without hubs) or perforated plastic pipes that are placed all around the base of the foundation. (See Chapter 20.) Their function is to collect excess water adjacent to the foundation walls and lead it elsewhere (to a drywell, storm sewer, or above ground) for distribution, thus reducing the possibility of basement-wall leakage (Ill. 16). (See page 253, Ill. 34.) The end of this pipe should be kept free at all times to avoid backups.

Keep in mind that regardless of the type of soil you're dealing with, the grade directly adjacent to the house should be sloped away from it to prevent water accumulation problems.

A drywell is a deep, large excavation filled with crushed stone, gravel, broken masonry, or other material, into which storm water is led by pipes coming from the house for distribution to the surrounding soil. The top of the drywell should be below the frost line, its location far enough away from the house to prevent water seeping into the soil from creating pressure against the foundation walls.

A common problem with drywells is that in periods of heavy rain, the surrounding soil becomes saturated with water. When the drywell fills up, the water has nowhere to go and it backs up into the cellar. An option to using a drywell is to allow the footing drains to flow by gravity and come out above ground (Ill. 17). On very flat sites where the pipe cannot come out above ground the footing drain can be brought into the cellar and emptied out in a "well" in the cellar floor. This "well" is simply a pit filled with soil with a sump pump in it, which pumps the water out (Ill. 18).

Plumbing
System

171

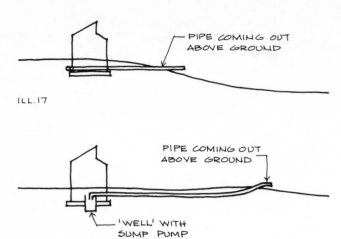

ILL. 17

PIPE COMING OUT
ABOVE GROUND

PIPE COMING OUT
ABOVE GROUND

'WELL' WITH
SUMP PUMP

ILL. 18

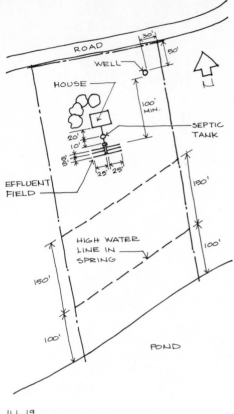

ILL. 19

DESIGNING THE PLUMBING SYSTEM FOR THE SAMPLE HOUSE

The water for the sample house will be supplied by a well equipped with a jet pump. We chose a jet pump over a submersible pump because the site is large enough so that noise is not a problem and jet pumps are generally lower in cost. Because the soil is absorbent, the sewage disposal system will consist of a septic tank, distribution box, and a subsoil disposal field. The local code prohibits the use of plastic pipe for the water-supply system, but allows its use for drainage. We will therefore use copper piping for the water supply and plastic for the drainage system. Although the house is heated by a hydronic system, we are going to install a water heater to ensure a sufficient amount of hot water at all times (and resolve the problem of running the boiler during the summer months).

1. Sizing the water heater (tank type):
   Gallons/ person/ day: 100 gpd
   Number of people: 4 (presently 3, but we are assuming growth)
   Total demand: 4 people × 100 gpd = 400 gpd
   Maximum hourly demand: 400 gpd × $\frac{1}{7}$ = 57 gallons
   Water needed to satisfy hourly peak load: 4 hrs. × 57 gal. = 228 gallons.
   Tank's total capacity: 400 gpd × $\frac{1}{5}$ = 80 gallons
   Tank's net volume: 80 gallons × .7 = 56 gallons
   Peak load (228 gallons) — tank's net capacity (56 gallons) = 172 gallons
   172 gallons ÷ 4-hour load = 43 gallons per hour

The water heater must be able to produce a minimum of 43 gallons of hot water an hour.

2. Sizing the septic tank: Looking at Table A, we choose a septic tank with a capacity of 500 gallons. Before finalizing the decision, we look at the local building code, which in turn refers us to the state's health department recommendations. For an occupancy of four people, the health department requires a 750-gallon tank.

3. Sizing the effluent field: Because the soil is absorptive and we have sufficient land, we have selected a subsoil drainage field to dispose of the effluent. After conducting a percolation test, we find out that it takes about three minutes for the water to be absorbed. Looking at Table III-A, we find that we need approximately 150 lineal feet of field. Again we check the code. It refers us to the state's health department regulations. Their recommendation for our occupancy and soil type is also 150 lineal feet.

4. With the water heater, septic tank, and effluent field sized, we proceed to draw a site plan indicating the location of the well and the sewage disposal system. Since the local code's plumbing section is strongly related to the state's health department regulations, we start by referring to both. The restrictions are as follows:

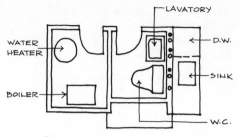

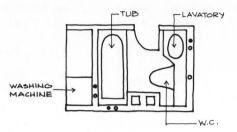

WATER HEATER

BOILER

LAVATORY

D.W.

SINK

W.C.

FIRST FLOOR

TUB

LAVATORY

WASHING MACHINE

W.C.

SECOND FLOOR

● HOT WATER
○ COLD WATER

ILL. 20

- The effluent disposal field must be a minimum of 150′ from a pond or a lake.
- The well must be a minimum of 15′ from any property line and a minimum of 100′ away from the effluent field.
- The septic tank can be no closer than 10′ to the house.
- The effluent field has to be a minimum of 10′ away from any property line and 20′ from the house.
- The effluent field trenches need to be at least 5′ from each other.

Taking note of all the above criteria, we are ready to draw the site plan. Illustration 19 shows the site plan for the house.

5. All fixtures are located in the first- and second-floor plans. Each one is provided with hot and cold water pipes as needed (Ill. 20).

   We locate the hot water heater as projected in the boiler room.

6. By drawing a section through the utility core, we try to determine which is the best route for the hot and cold water lines to travel (Ill. 21).

   Pipes may be exposed in the boiler room, but we want to conceal them from the other rooms by snaking them through walls and floors.

   Pipe sizes will be as follows:
   Hot and cold water mains—1″
   Intermediary branches—¾″
   Branch to each fixture—½″

7. With the water-supply system reasonably worked out, we move on to design the drainage system.

   First, we draw a riser diagram to study all the necessary components in the system and indicate the pipe sizes (Ill. 22).

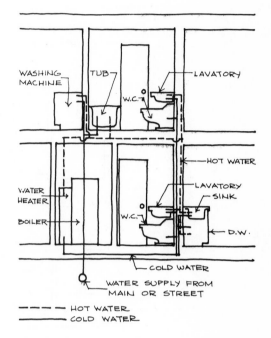

WASHING MACHINE

TUB

LAVATORY

W.C.

HOT WATER

WATER HEATER

LAVATORY
SINK

BOILER

W.C.

D.W.

COLD WATER

WATER SUPPLY FROM MAIN OR STREET

------- HOT WATER
——— COLD WATER

ILL. 21

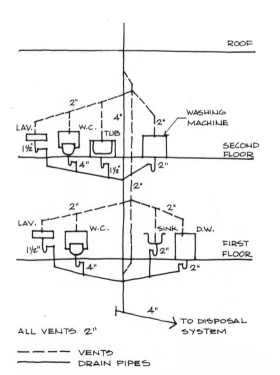

ROOF

LAV.
W.C.
TUB
WASHING MACHINE
SECOND FLOOR

LAV.
W.C.
SINK
D.W.
FIRST FLOOR

TO DISPOSAL SYSTEM

ALL VENTS 2″

------- VENTS
——— DRAIN PIPES

ILL. 22

Plumbing System

173

8. We now provide each fixture in the plan with a drainage pipe. (For the sake of clarity, we will not show the supply pipes; Ill. 23.)

With the drainage pipes indicated, we must decide the best location for the soil stack. It seems most logical to place it directly behind the toilet for ease of waste outflow and because the wall running vertically for two floors provides a perfect location for the pipe to run within.

9. The location of the soil stack, however, seems to pose a problem on the second floor, where the drains from the tub and washing machine must travel a long distance to reach it. For this reason, we provide a waste stack to carry the waste of the tub and washer (Ill. 24).

10. At this point the riser diagram is adjusted accordingly (Ill. 25).

11. Our last step is to take the plans that show the drainage pipes and locate the areas where branch vents should be provided (Ill. 26).

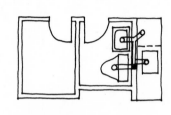

FIRST FLOOR

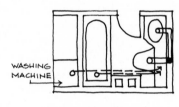

SECOND FLOOR

○ DRAINS
● SOIL STACK

ILL. 23

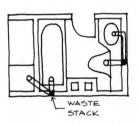

WASTE STACK

ILL. 24

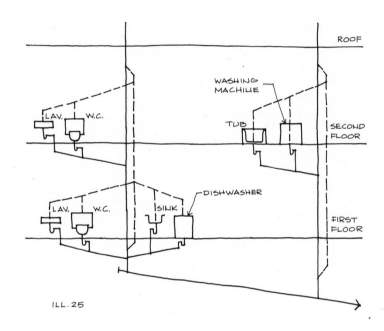

ILL. 25

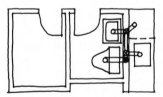

FIRST FLOOR

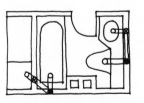

SECOND FLOOR

◉ VENTS

ILL. 26

15
Electrical System

Whenever electric power is cut off because of a hurricane, snow storm, or generator failure, we come to the realization once again of our enormous degree of dependence on electricity. It is not unusual in some areas of the country to be presented with an uncooked Thanksgiving turkey because a snow storm knocked down the power lines and the oven is electrically operated. Worse yet, making a simple cup of coffee or opening up a can may become difficult tasks. After the massive blackout of the 1960's, one of our friends who owns an all-electric house in New York City said that he found himself with a house that offered "a roof over his head and cold water."

This invisible source of power that simplifies our jobs, saves our muscles, provides us with heat, lights our homes, and is instrumental to our entertainment is a highly complex subject. We do not (and cannot) claim to be experts in this field. What we attempt to do in this chapter is to give you an understanding of the basic criteria involved in the design of your house's electrical system.

Although it would be unfair to say that electrical work is difficult, we can rightfully say that it is potentially hazardous. A faulty electrical installation could be the cause of fire or personal injury. For this reason, we discourage anyone (other than a licensed electrician) from doing his own electrical work. We are not alone in our advice. There are numerous areas in which the building code will not allow you to do your own electrical work. Furthermore, some insurance companies may charge you higher rates when they find out that you were your own electrician.

A reasonable solution to your involvement in electrical work could be to hire an electrician to handle the overall job, while working yourself as one of his helpers. Such an arrangement will give you the assurance that a qualified professional is in charge of the job while still allowing you to continue as an integral part of the house-building crew.

THE CORE COMPONENTS

Electrical Circuits

The moment you turn on a lamp, you're triggering an intricate series of events. Electrical energy, composed of moving particles called electrons, starts flowing from the generator (at your local power company) to the lamp via a system of wires. The flow of electrons (current) from the source by way of the wires to the lamp constitutes a simple electrical circuit (Ill. 1).

This circuit may be compared to the water-supply cycle in a plumbing system, except for one important difference. While in a plumbing system, the water comes from the source through the pipes to the fixtures and is later drained and disposed of, in an electrical circuit two terminals are needed to induce the current flow. The reason for this is that electrons are

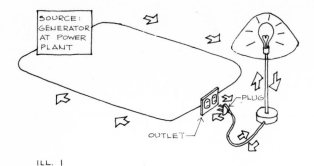

ILL. 1

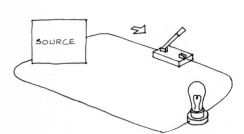

ILL. 2

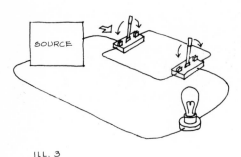

ILL. 3

negatively charged particles that flow because they have a higher positive electric charge at one terminal than the other. The circuit therefore starts at the source, goes to the appliance where the power is consumed, and ends at the source (Ill. 1).

Switches

The switching device you used to turn the lamp on is designed to open or close the circuit. When the switch is in the off position, the magnetic field is destroyed and the circuit remains open. No current is allowed to flow through and the light will be out. When the switch is in the on position, the reverse takes place (Ill. 2).

Switches vary in their complexity. There are instances in which you may want to turn on the light at one location and turn it off at another. A three-way switch, designed to open or close the circuit in two different ways, can do this (Ill. 3). Four-way switches are also available.

Outlets

Outlets are those devices within the circuit where electric power becomes available. They include receptacles, ceiling outlets, and sockets among others. In the simple circuit previously described, the lamp becomes part of the circuit by being plugged into a receptacle. It draws power from the circuit via the receptacle by contact with the wires in the plug. The receptacle itself consumes no current. Receptacles are most commonly seen in duplex form, that is, with provision to accommodate two plugs (Inset I).

THE UNITS OF MEASURE

Approximately every month, you receive an electric bill stating the number of kilowatts (or thousand watts) consumed by the house's electrical system. The charge is based on a rate per kilowatt-hour. If you take a look at the appliances you presently own, you will see that they are also rated in watts; a lightbulb may be 30, 60, or 100 watts, a toaster 1,200 watts, and a radio 150 watts. This rating means that these appliances need that specific number of watts to operate properly. For instance, if a T.V. set is rated at 400 watts and is receiving considerably less, the picture may not be able to spread the full area of the screen.

Watts are a measure of the electric power flowing through a circuit at a given time. They are a function of the current flowing in the circuit (measured in amps) and the push needed to get the current from the source to the appliance (measured in volts). Watts = Amps × Volts or $W = I \times V$. For example, let's say you have a washing machine requiring 700 watts and 115 volts to operate. You will need $W = V \times I$, or $W \div V = I$; $700 \div 115 = 6.08$ amps for the washing machine to function properly.

The location of the house will determine the voltage it receives, be it 115/230, 120/240, or

125/250.* The amperage, on the other hand, is dependent on the service entrance that you request from the power company. Therefore, to satisfy the house's electrical requirements, you must determine the amount of electrical power (watts) you need and divide it into the available voltage to get the desired amperage capacity (Inset II).

The service entrance is the place where the cables from the power company enter the house for distribution to the various circuits. The incoming power (or entrance capacity) from these wires has to be sufficient to feed all the house's fixtures and appliances with an adequate amount of electrical energy and allow room for

* To find out the exact voltage in your area check with your power company. All areas, however, are subject to periodic minor voltage variations as a result of changes in current demand.

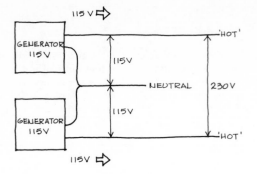

ILL. 4

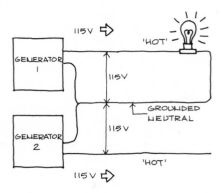

ILL. 5

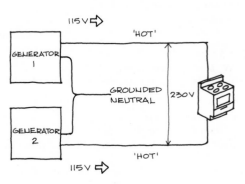

ILL. 6

small, making it next to impossible to run the units unless most of the appliances including the lights were turned off. He failed to realize that a house built in the early 1900's had very few electrical requirements (probably only the lights). His was a long, hot summer until he raised enough cash to pay for a larger entrance.

THREE-WIRE SYSTEM

The electrical needs of contemporary houses range from a clock, requiring 2 to 8 watts, to an electric range, which may consume up to 14,000. Because the variation is so great, a three-wire system has been devised. With this system, two different voltages are made available: one relatively low voltage (115, 120, or 125) for devices using little power and a higher one (230, 240, or 250) for high-wattage appliances.

The operation of a three-wire system is not difficult. The cables from the power company are brought into the house and connected to a single meter. They are then brought into the service entrance panel for distribution to the various circuits. Either voltage is obtained at the service entrance. The three incoming wires are generally black, red, and white. The black and red wires are called "hot" wires; the white one is the "neutral." (Don't be misled by the "hot" and "neutral" terminology; they're all equally dangerous.) The hot wires are each connected to a 115 volt generator, while the white neutral is connected to both generators (Ill. 4).* When the wires in a circuit are connected to the neutral and one hot wire, they are hooked up to *one* generator. The voltage being supplied is 115 V + 0 V = 115 V (Ill. 5). When the circuit is connected to both hot wires, each of which is connected in turn to a separate generator, the resulting voltage is 115 V + 115 V = 230 V (Ill. 6). Devices in the circuit connected to either hot wire and the neutral will receive 115 volts while those connected to both hot wires will receive 230 volts. Either voltage can be obtained according to the need of the appliance or circuit. Circuits handling the heavy wattage equipment will most likely require 230 volts while those supplying lamps and other small appliances will need only 115 volts.

* We are isolating 115 voltage as our example throughout.

growth. Should the entrance capacity be too small, it could mean you will not be able to install large power-consuming appliances or expand the building later on.

A good friend of ours bought a lovely old house in Philadelphia. Everything was fine until summer, when he decided to buy air-conditioning units for his windows. He soon discovered that the building's Old World charm did not permit the installation of air-conditioning units. The service entrance capacity was too

SAFETY DEVICES

Overcurrent Protection: Fuses and Circuit Breakers

At times we may inadvertently overload a circuit by connecting too many appliances and fixtures to it. Such an accidental overload will increase the heat in the wires and thus the possibility of fire. Safety devices—either fuses or circuit breakers—should be provided to limit the amperes to a predetermined number, in the same manner that safety valves keep in check the pressure and temperature in a plumbing system.

You are undoubtedly familiar with the location of the fuse box in your house or apartment. Most likely you have replaced a blown fuse at one time or another. A fuse consists of a short length of metal wire with a low resistance to heat (melting point). As long as the current flowing through the circuit is of a predetermined amperage, the metal in the fuse will carry it with no problem. The moment the amperage exceeds that specific level, the metal will melt because of the heat generated by the excess amperage breaking the circuit. Whenever you try to draw more power from a circuit than it can deliver (for example, if you turn on the stereo, a color T.V., a blower, an air conditioner, a typewriter, an iron, and all the lights on one circuit at the same time), you will blow a fuse. Fuses are rated according to the maximum amount of amperage they can carry—15 A, 20 A, 30 A, and so on (Ill. 7).

Circuit breakers operate as a switch. Whenever more current flows than the breaker is designed for, it automatically opens up, breaking the circuit and stopping the current flow. Circuit breakers are preferred over fuses for new construction because, unlike fuses, they can be reset (Ill. 8).

Overvoltage Protection: Grounding

Grounding is the provision of an escape route for excess electrical power. When you install a lightning rod, its purpose is to direct the electric charge via a separate path away from the house to the surrounding earth (Ill. 9). Similarly, when you ground the electrical system, you are providing an alternate path by which excess

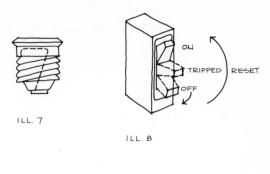

ILL. 7

ILL. 8

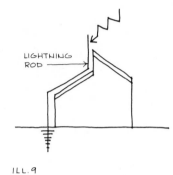

LIGHTNING ROD

ILL. 9

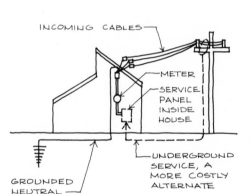

INCOMING CABLES

METER

SERVICE PANEL INSIDE HOUSE

UNDERGROUND SERVICE, A MORE COSTLY ALTERNATE

GROUNDED NEUTRAL

ILL. 10

electricity can be discharged. This is customarily done by connecting one of the wires in the system (the neutral) to the earth by means of a wire leading to the water pipe in the house or a metal rod driven in the ground (Ill. 10). The grounded neutral wire is never interrupted by a switch, fuse, circuit breaker, or any other device.

In addition to grounding the entire system, appliances requiring large electrical loads, such as ranges and water heaters, are also grounded. The reason for this is that a defective appliance can become accidentally grounded. In other words, the electricity-carrying equipment within the appliance (normally insulated from the casing) can accidentally come in contact with the casing, establishing an electrical circuit. The circuit is then an accidental ground. Should you touch the casing, you will become part of the

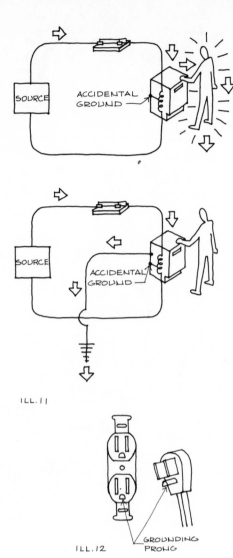

ILL. 11

ILL. 12

GROUNDING PRONG

circuit, carrying current through your body to the ground (Ill. 11).

To avoid this danger, codes specify that all special appliances (all devices with motors plus heavy electricity consumers, such as electric ranges, water heaters, clothes dryers, and bathroom heaters) be grounded by means of grounding-type receptacles (Ill. 12). These are similar to ordinary 115–125 volt receptacles except that they have provision for an additional circular prong. This third prong connects the appliance casing to the grounded wire in the system. Fixtures such as refrigerators, freezers, and dishwashers come equipped with a three-prong plug. Minor appliances like radios and irons that do not have such a plug can also be connected to three-prong receptacles, since they are designed for use with either plug.

In addition to system grounding and special-appliance grounding, the entire wiring system

(regardless of type) must be continually grounded. The purpose of this is to automatically ground fixtures when they are connected to the outlet. More on this follows in the section on wide types, pages 181 and 182.

Ground-Fault Protection: Ground-Fault Circuit Interrupters

To further protect you from the danger of shock or fire, ground-fault circuit interrupters (GFCI or GFI) should be included in your electrical system. A GFI is a device designed to open the circuit and stop the flow of current in the event of a ground fault. The latter may occur as the result of the accidental contact between a hot wire and grounded conduit, the armor of a cable, a grounding wire, or the casing of a motor or appliance. The current flowing as a result of a ground fault is often too small to blow a fuse or trip a circuit breaker, but is large enough to give you a shock or start a fire.

Although three-prong plugs and three-wire cords properly installed to grounding receptacles should reduce these dangers, the possibility remains that the cord or plug is defective. In addition, many tools and equipment still on the market are only available with two-prong plugs and two-wire cords.

Some GFI's available offer protection to an entire two-wire system,* whereas others only protect a single receptacle. Keep in mind that the GFI's amperage rating has to be the same as that of the circuit or receptacle it protects.

The National Electrical Code (NEC) requires among other things the installation of GFI's in all outdoor 115 V, 15 A and 20 A outlets and in all 15 A and 20 A receptacles in construction sites. In addition to those locations specified by code, it is wise to install GFI's in kitchens and bathrooms, where appliances are used close to grounded plumbing.† Most likely, future editions of the NEC will call for more widespread use of GFI's.

* A GFI will not protect a two-wire circuit that is part of a three-wire circuit with two hot wires sharing a common neutral.
† The neutral wire in the electrical system is grounded by connecting it to the earth via a wire leading to the water-supply pipe in the plumbing system. In the event of a ground-fault current, if you touch a faucet or another part of the plumbing system, you'll be completing the circuit from the ground fault to the plumbing through your body.

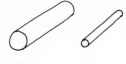

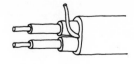

CONDUCTOR
INSULATED CASING
STRANDED WIRE

ILL. 13

NO. 00   NO. 8

ILL. 14

ILL. 15

TABLE A*

Wire size	Ampacity
14	15
12	20
10	30
8	40

*This table indicates the values as given by the NEC; check your local code for specific values.

THE WIRES

Wires are the path through which electric current travels. They consist of a copper conductor (aluminum and copper-clad aluminum are also available although not recommended) wrapped in an insulating layer of plastic compound or rubber (Ill. 13).

Wire Sizes: Ampacity

Wires offer resistance to the flow of current. The energy lost by this resistance translates itself into heat. The greater the current flow (amperage) in the wire, the greater the resistance encountered and therefore the greater the heat that is generated. As the heat increases, the chances of the wire breaking down and consequently the possibility of fire increases. For this reason, it is extremely important to limit the amount of amperage that a wire can carry.

The ampacity, or current-carrying capacity, of a wire is dependent on its size. The larger the wire, the more amperage it can carry with less resistance. A most peculiar aspect of wire sizing leading to much confusion is the fact that the smaller the circumference of the wire, the larger the number it is assigned. For example, size 00 wire is approximately ⅜" in diameter, while size 8 wire is only about ⅛" (Ill. 14). (This size represents the diameter of the copper conductor and does not include the casing around the wire.) Wire sizes range from large ones, size 0000 (4/0), which is about ½" in diameter to minuscule ones, size 40. Table A lists the ampacity of some commonly used copper wires in residential work.

According to the NEC, a wire is not rated exclusively according to its ampacity, but also according to the rating of the fuse or circuit breaker protecting the circuit. For instance, a no. 12 wire rated for an ampacity of 20 amps will be rated for that capacity *only* if the circuit it serves is protected by a 20 amp fuse or circuit breaker. Should the circuit have only a 15 amp fuse or breaker, the wire's ampacity will be reduced to 15 amps.

Wire Types

For ease of installation, two or three wires are grouped together to form a cable. Two-wire cables have one white neutral and one black hot wire. Three-wire cables have one white neutral and one black and one red hot wire.

The two most commonly used types of cables for residential work are nonmetallic sheathed cable and flexible armored cable, each with a different cost, type of installation, and acceptability by code. Conduit (both rigid and thin-walled) is yet another alternative but is usually not required for new residential construction (unless there is a very strict code or it is to be used for surface wiring or some other special condition).

Nonmetallic sheathed cable, generally referred to by its trade name, Romex (Rx), is available in type NM for use in dry locations and type NMC for damp (although not permanently wet) locations. This cable is cheaper than armored cable and is easy to install, requiring no special tools. Type NM consists of two or three wires covered with a fire- and moisture-resistant material. Type NMC has both wires imbedded in solid plastic. An additional insulated wire is also present for grounding purposes. This wire is carried from outlet to outlet to provide a continuous ground. Although nonmetallic sheathed cable is very popular, some codes do not allow its use, favoring armored cable instead (Ill. 15).

Flexible armored cable (usually referred to by its trade name, Bx) is most commonly available for residential work in type ACT. This type

Electrical System

181

ILL. 16   ILL. 17

consists of two wires covered with a spiral layer of tough paper. The wires in turn are covered by a spiral galvanized steel armor. Like nonmetallic sheathed cable, it uses an uninsulated copper wire for grounding. The metal casing is grounded to every metal box or cabinet (see page 332, Inset II). Many codes prefer this type over nonmetallic sheathed cable because it offers greater protection against accidental grounds. It is, however, more difficult to install and generally more expensive (Ill. 16).

Neither nonmetallic sheathed cable nor armored cable is suitable for underground installation. Check your local code for recommendations on cables to be installed in such special conditions.

A few words on cable sizes. The size of a cable is referred to first by the size of the wire, say 12, then by the number of wires. For example, a 12–3 cable will be one with three number-12 wires. A 12–3 cable with ground will have in addition a grounding strip.

Conduit is still another wiring method which, although not generally used for new residential construction, deserves special attention. Conduit is essentially a steel pipe. Wires are not already in the conduit, they are pulled through once the conduit has been installed. Metal conduit is available in rigid or thin-walled forms. It is difficult to install, not necessarily because of cutting and connection work but because it is difficult to bend. It is, however, a very safe wiring system generally required for large jobs, surface wiring of old installations, and certain other special conditions (Ill. 17).

PLANNING THE ELECTRICAL INSTALLATION

Before beginning to plan your electrical system, it is wise to contact the local power company. Find out how much work the company's men will do in connection with the service entry. It usually varies with the company. Also find out any particular requirements as to where the service cables should enter the building. Sometimes problems with cables going over other property, highways, etc., may determine the specific location of the service entrance. The company will probably send a representative over to check the location of your house and study any problems in your installation. They can also be very helpful in orienting you to local codes and regulations.

The next very important step is to become thoroughly familiar with your local electrical code. Most likely, unless you are building in a heavily built-up area such as New York City, which has its own, quite strict code, you'll be required to follow the National Electrical Code. Many localities have adopted the NEC as their guideline for construction. Others have amended it to incorporate local conditions.

A few words about the NEC. The primary goal of this code is safety. We point this out for two reasons. The first is to emphasize that not following the code will lead to an unsafe installation, making any deviation an unwise (and often illegal) move. The second is to point out that its requirements are those needed for *minimum* safe conditions. In other words, improving on minimum recommendations by providing larger service entrances and wire sizes and more circuits than required will give you a better installation with more room for expansion. Keep in mind that the use of electricity has increased drastically in the past and will probably continue to do so in the future.

Another recommended although not essential step to include before designing the system is to contact the company that will provide you with fire insurance. Find out if any variation in the methods, materials, or design you are planning might make a difference in future insurance rates. For example, does the fact that you are doing your own electrical work imply that your fire insurance rate might be higher than if you had hired an electrician? Will the use of armored cable (even if not required by code) bring you a lower rate in the end? With these facts in mind, and a little arithmetic, a number of decisions (with regard to the materials you select and whether or not you will do the electrical work) can be made.

Once these three steps are out of the way, sit down with a copy of the building code nearby and start designing the electrical system.

Determine the Size of the Service Entrance

Sizing the service entrance is the first and a very important step in the design process. The 1975 NEC specifies a minimum service entrance of 100 amps and three-wire service for a single-family house of five or more circuits. (You will learn later on in this chapter that a house would have to be quite small to require fewer than five circuits.) While the NEC deals with minimum safety requirements, it does not take into account possible expansion of the house. It seems wiser, instead, to plan a service entrance with sufficient capacity for future growth, particularly if you consider that it is much cheaper to install a large service entrance while constructing the house than to do it later on. Some codes already require a minimum service entrance of 200 amps. We recommend a service of no less than 150 amps and preferably 200 amps (Inset II). If you are planning to have electric heat, the minimum service will have to be 200 amps.

Determine an Adequate Number of Circuits

Houses are not designed with one single circuit for a number of excellent reasons such as avoiding being left in the dark should you blow your one and only fuse. Instead, outlets are grouped together into various circuits, each protected with its own fuse or circuit breaker. In addition, equipping the house with many circuits decreases the possibility of overloading any one of them.

Your local code will indicate the minimum number of circuits that may be installed. The controlling criterion is generally based on the floor area of the house. There are three types of circuits: the general (or lighting) circuit, the small-appliance circuit, and the special circuit.

The general circuit includes not only permanently installed devices such as ceiling fixtures, but also receptacles for floor and table lamps and other minor appliances like radios and vacuum cleaners. The figure used for estimating the total load of the general circuit according to the NEC is 3 watts per square foot of floor area. The calculation to arrive at the number of general circuits is as follows: A house that is 2,500 square feet will require 2,500 × 3 watts, or 7,500 watts, total load to be carried by the general circuit. If the house is wired with no. 12 wire having an ampacity rating of 20 amps and a voltage of 115 volts, the load-carrying capacity of the wire will be: $W = I \times V$, or $20 \times 115 = 2,300$ watts.* In order to find out how many circuits are needed to successfully deliver the required 7,500 watts, divide the total watt load (7,500) into the wattage that a no. 12 wire can carry (2,300). It follows that $7,500 \div 2,300 = 3.26$ required circuits. As it is not possible to install a fraction of a circuit, four circuits will be provided instead. Keep in mind that the code is dealing with minimum safety figures. Together with their 3 watts per square foot requirement, the NEC makes a recommendation (not a requirement) to install one circuit per 500 square feet of total floor area. Using this figure instead will give you five circuits for the same 2,500 square foot house. Going one step further and providing one circuit per 400 square feet will give you greater flexibility and make allowance for future needs. According to that figure, the same house will be equipped with 6.2, or rather 7 circuits.

Although the NEC indicates no limit on the number of outlets that can be installed in any one general circuit, it is good practice to supply no more than eight outlets per circuit. Your local code may have a different guideline.

General circuits cannot handle the heavy loads required by small appliances such as toasters, blenders, and coffee makers. Although not permanently installed, these appliances need a tremendous amount of electric energy for their operation. Have you noticed how the lights dim when you turn on the toaster? That indicates that the circuit does not have as much power as needed. Small-appliance circuits are designed to handle such loads. These circuits are strictly for portable appliances; no permanent appliances or lighting outlets may be installed to them.

The NEC calls for a minimum of two small-appliance circuits, each equipped with no. 12 wires and protected by a 20 amp fuse or circuit breaker. (Each of these circuits will have a capacity of 20 amps × 115 volts, or 2,300 watts.) When installing the outlets, it is wise to connect alternate outlets to alternate circuits. In other words, if you have four small-appliance

* We recommend no. 12–20 ampacity wire as the minimum wire size for general circuits.

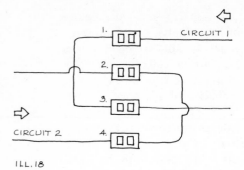

CIRCUIT 1

CIRCUIT 2

ILL. 18

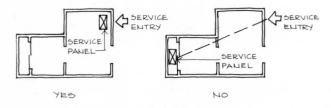

SERVICE ENTRY

SERVICE PANEL

YES

SERVICE ENTRY

SERVICE PANEL

NO

ILL. 19

and any other area requiring them. Finally draw the location of the entrance service cables.

To obtain a workable set of electrical plans, the following components have to be located:

- the service panel
- the wall outlets
- the ceiling outlets
- switches
- small-appliance outlets
- special-appliance outlets
- the circuits

LOCATE THE SERVICE PANEL EQUIPMENT: The controlling criterion in this decision is the position of the entrance cables. The service panel* should be very close to the point of entry of the conductors. The reason for this is that until they arrive at the main lugs or disconnect switch (in the service panel), the service entrance cables are without overcurrent protection. As a fire and safety precaution, the length of unprotected conductor must be kept to a minimum. The maximum allowable distance varies with different codes and sometimes is not even specified. In any case, make sure that the lengths of unprotected conductors are kept in accordance with the NEC.

In addition, the service panel should be easily accessible and have sufficient working space around it. It should not be located over cabinets or appliances making it difficult to reach in case of an emergency. Areas that are highly combustible, like closets, should be avoided (Ill. 19).

LOCATE THE WALL RECEPTACLES: First check your local code. It sometimes indicates the maximum distance requirements between receptacles. The NEC calls for wall receptacles to be no more than 12' apart so that no fixture or appliance will be more than 6' from an outlet. Few appliances or fixtures, however, come with 6' long cords, so you should consider placing the receptacles closer together. Provide enough receptacles to allow for flexibility of furniture and appliance arrangement. You may otherwise find yourself using an extension cord every time you change your favorite reading spot. Extension cords, in addition to being a hassle, are unsafe and unsightly (Ill. 20).

At this point also include any weatherproof

outlets in a row, connect the first and the third to one circuit and the second and fourth to the other, further reducing the possibility of an overload (Ill. 18). Check your local code for its specific requirements.

Although not required by some codes, it is good practice in most new installations to provide separate circuits for permanently installed appliances requiring heavy power loads such as electric ranges, water heaters, dishwashers, clothes dryers, or any appliance with a power rating over 1,000 watts or any permanently connected motor with a rating of ⅛ horsepower or more (for an oil burner, furnace blower, water pump, etc.). These circuits will be either 115 volts or 230 volts depending on the appliance rating. Wiring of a sufficient amperage should be designed for each—30, 40, 50 amp, or as required.

Drawing the Electrical Plans

Get hold of your house plans and trace onto a clean sheet of tracing paper the walls and partitions of the house, including all openings for doors and windows. In addition, make sure to draw the location of all special appliances in the kitchen, laundry room, workshop, utility room,

* The service panel is essentially a flat metal box with circuit breakers.

receptacles you might want to have in the exterior of the building. Make sure to provide them with ground-fault circuit interrupters.

LOCATE THE CEILING OUTLETS: Lighting techniques in themselves are a complex subject, which unfortunately we do not have enough space to discuss in detail. Probably the best approach to the lighting problem is to study the types of activities that are to take place in a room or area. Is the room going to be lit by means of floor or wall lamps or from an overhead source? Would one light source, centrally located, be sufficient or do you need more lights to obtain proper illumination levels? Do you want a central outlet or would you rather highlight an area or element in the room such as a fireplace? By answering some of these questions you can determine how many (if any) ceiling outlets you need (Ill. 21).

LOCATE THE SWITCHES: Examine each room or area and determine whether it requires switching from one or more than one location. Stairs, for example, should have a three-way switch at either end of the run. Walk through the plans and try to visualize how you would go about turning the various lights on and off. Imagine the different ways in which the house will be traveled. For example, make sure that you do not need to walk halfway through the house to turn on your foyer light when you come in. Also consider the possibility of having one or more wall outlets connected to a switch. This way, if the living room is lit exclusively by floor and table lamps, you do not have to run all around the room to turn them on and off; you can instead control them from a single switch. Always place switches on the latch side of door openings. Check that each of your ceiling outlets is controlled by a switch.

To indicate which outlets are connected to which switches, draw a dotted line between the outlet and the proper switch. In addition, indicate whether it is a one-pole, three-, or four-way switch (Ill. 22).

LOCATE THE SPECIAL CIRCUITS: Kitchens, laundry rooms, workshops, utility rooms, etc., all deserve careful attention due to the concentration of appliances requiring special circuits. All such appliances should be shown in your drawing to remind yourself of the special outlets you need to provide. Give each one an outlet, noting next to it the exact power requirements (Ill. 23).

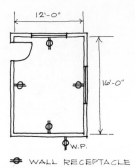

⊖ WALL RECEPTACLE

ILL. 20

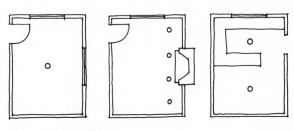

○ CEILING OUTLETS

ILL. 21

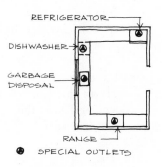

↭ SWITCHES

ILL. 22

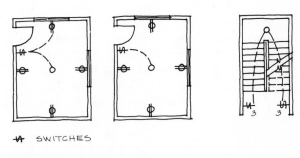

REFRIGERATOR

DISHWASHER

GARBAGE DISPOSAL

RANGE

◉ SPECIAL OUTLETS

ILL. 23

Electrical System
185

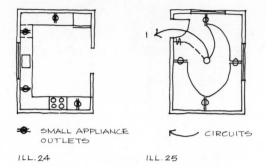

SMALL APPLIANCE OUTLETS   CIRCUITS

ILL. 24   ILL. 25

LOCATE THE SMALL-APPLIANCE OUT-LETS: Provide above-the-counter outlets in the kitchen and laundry room to service portable appliances such as blenders, coffee makers, irons, etc. (Ill. 24).

INDICATE THE CIRCUITS: With a solid line connect the various outlets which are to be installed in one circuit. Keep in mind their maximum capacity; for example, 15 A, 115 V circuit has a maximum capacity of 1,725 watts. If the appliances to be installed in any one circuit exceed the circuit's capacity, split it up into two or more circuits as needed. Check yourself by adding up the power required by each of these appliances for its operation and comparing it against the circuit's maximum capacity.

Splitting up circuits will not only prevent overloading but will give you usable outlets in each room should one of the circuits go dead. Provide the refrigerator and the freezer with one circuit each. When they share a circuit with other appliances, you run the risk of being stuck with a lot of spoiled food if something in the circuit goes wrong and causes the circuit breaker to trip.

Once the circuits are established, each one is given a number. The drawing of the room with all the outlets, switches, and circuitry included should look something like Illustration 25.

LOCATE MISCELLANEOUS DEVICES: It is at this point that the location of doorbells, the intercom system, and any other special electrical devices should be included.

DESIGNING THE ELECTRICAL SYSTEM FOR THE SAMPLE HOUSE

1. Before starting the design of the sample house's electrical system, we take a look at the local code.

It requires a minimum service entrance capacity of 200 amps and a three-wire system. Because the house is so small and the number of appliances in it far from extraordinary, we decide that such an entrance capacity will not only satisfy our present needs but also allow for future growth.

2. Our next step is to determine the adequate number of circuits.

GENERAL CIRCUITS: To find out the total load in the general circuit, we multiply the house's total square footage times 3 watts per square foot (as required by code): 1,368 square feet × 3 watts per square foot = 4,104 watts. The minimum wire size allowed by code is no. 12 wire, which has an ampacity rating of 20 A. The available voltage is 115/230 V. When we use no. 12 wire in a circuit, it will provide us with 115 V × 20 A = 2,300 watts total power. If the total load is 4,104 watts and the wire can give us only 2,300 watts, we need 4,104 ÷ 2,300 = 1.78, or 2 general circuits.

To double-check, we look again at the code and find that it requires a minimum of one circuit for every 500 square feet of space. To satisfy this requirement, we divide the total square footage of the house into 500 square feet: 1,368 sq. ft. = 2.7, or 3 circuits.

We go one step further and provide the house with four general circuits to further reduce the chance of overloading any one circuit.

SMALL-APPLIANCE CIRCUITS: The code calls for a minimum of two small-appliance circuits fed by no. 10 wires and protected by 30 A circuit breakers.

SPECIAL-APPLIANCE CIRCUITS: Although not required by code, we will provide a separate circuit each for the special appliances (boiler, hot water heater, dishwasher, washer, dryer, and range).

3. Before starting to draw the electrical plans, we determine the wire sizes needed for special appliances. Amperage = Wattage divided by Voltage (I = W ÷ V). See table on facing page.

4. We start drawing the electrical plans by locating the service entrance panel directly adjacent to the point of entry of the conductors from the power company. The panel will be inside one of the wall cabinets, easily accessible from the kitchen and entry spaces.

5. The next step is to locate the wall outlets. We check the local code to see if there are any restrictions concerning the minimum distance between wall outlets. There are no restrictions, so the wall outlets are located by keeping furniture and appliances in mind (Ill. 26).

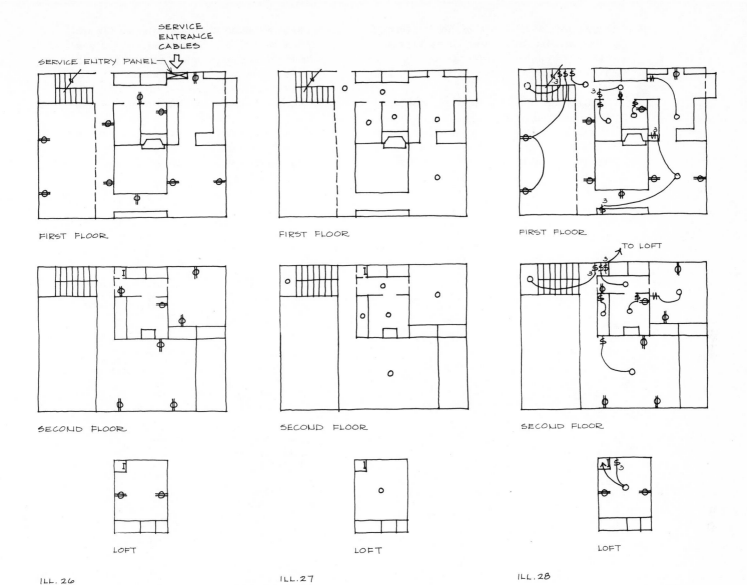

SERVICE
ENTRANCE
CABLES

SERVICE ENTRY PANEL

FIRST FLOOR

FIRST FLOOR

FIRST FLOOR

TO LOFT

SECOND FLOOR

SECOND FLOOR

SECOND FLOOR

LOFT

LOFT

LOFT

ILL. 26

ILL. 27

ILL. 28

6. The ceiling outlets are placed, keeping in mind the various functions which are to take place within each room or area. We decide to provide overhead lights everywhere with the exception of the living room and the lounge, which will be lit by floor and table lamps (Ill. 27).

7. By combining the wall and ceiling outlets into one drawing, we can readily visualize whether we want wall outlets as well as ceiling outlets to be controlled by a switching device.

The location of the various switches is established and a line drawn connecting each switch to the wall or ceiling outlet or outlets it controls.

Switches that are controlled from more than one location, like the ones for the stairs, study loft, and dining room, are labeled accordingly (Ill. 28).

Appliance	Wattage	Amps	Wire size
Dishwasher	$1,000 \div 115 =$	8.7	14*
Range	$14,000 \div 230 =$	60.8	4
Water heater	$5,000 \div 230 =$	21.7	10
Dryer	$6,000 \div 230 =$	26.0	10
Washing machine	$800 \div 115 =$	6.9	14*
Boiler	$500 \div 115 =$	4.4	14*
Refrigerator	$300 \div 115 =$	2.5	14*

* We will equip the washing machine and boiler with no. 12 wire since it is the minimum allowed by code.

Electrical
System
187

8. The next step involves establishing the general circuits. According to our calculations, the house should have a minimum of four general circuits, each with a maximum of eight wall or ceiling outlets.

Taking a close look at a set of plans showing both the wall and ceiling outlets, we try to connect them into circuits. One of the most important things to keep in mind is splitting circuits, so that each room is serviced by more than one circuit (Ill. 29).

9. Finally, we indicate the location of all the special-appliance outlets. Next to each of these we indicate the appliance rating. Each of these appliances will be fed by a single circuit.

Small-appliance outlets are provided above the kitchen counters and the circuitry is indicated.

One weatherproof outlet is located on the exterior of the building (Ill. 30).

10. The final electrical plans for the sample house are shown in Illustration 31.

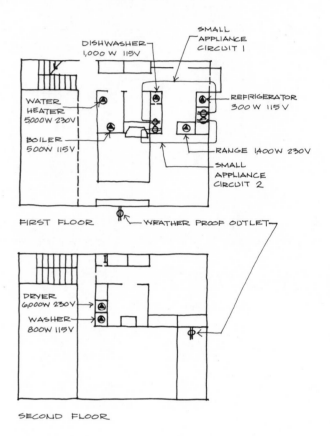

GENERAL CIRCUIT 1

GENERAL CIRCUIT 2

FIRST FLOOR

GENERAL CIRCUIT 3

SECOND FLOOR

GENERAL CIRCUIT 4

LOFT

ILL. 29

DISHWASHER 1,000 W 115V

SMALL APPLIANCE CIRCUIT 1

WATER HEATER 5,000W 230V

REFRIGERATOR 300 W 115 V

BOILER 500W 115V

RANGE 1400W 230V

SMALL APPLIANCE CIRCUIT 2

FIRST FLOOR   WEATHER PROOF OUTLET

DRYER 6,000W 230V

WASHER 800W 115V

SECOND FLOOR

ILL. 30

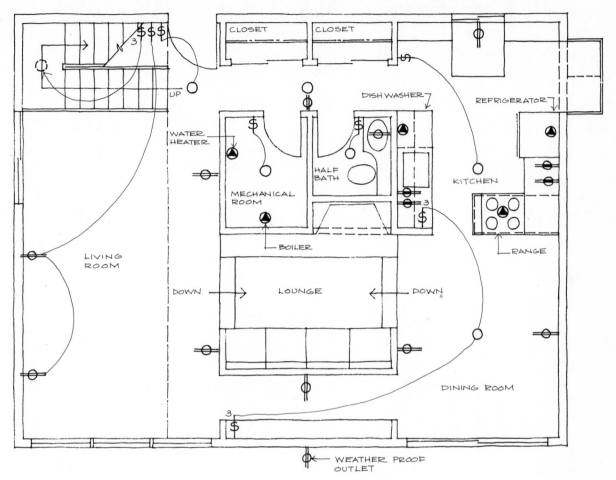

CLOSET　　CLOSET

UP

WATER
HEATER

MECHANICAL
ROOM

BOILER

LIVING
ROOM

DOWN　　LOUNGE　　DOWN

HALF
BATH

DISH WASHER

KITCHEN

REFRIGERATOR

RANGE

DINING ROOM

WEATHER PROOF
OUTLET

FIRST FLOOR PLAN

ILL. 31

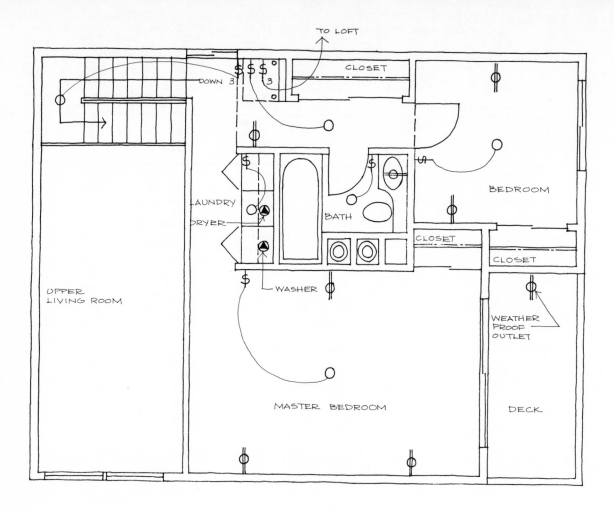

SECOND FLOOR PLAN

ILL. 31

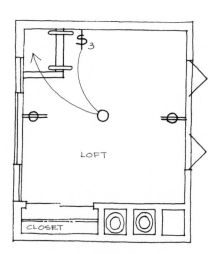

LOFT PLAN

16
Fireplace, Chimney, and Stair Design

FIREPLACES AND CHIMNEYS

Over the centuries fireplaces have often functioned as the only heat source for buildings. Not only were they important as heat generators, but fireplaces also provided the facilities for cooking. Heat from the fireplace was critical to the warmth and welfare of the building's inhabitants, making its efficient design and operation very important. Fireplace design was continually developed and improved until the turn of the century, when it evolved into a primitive form of central heating. By providing a better distribution of heat, the central heating concept rendered the fireplace obsolete.

Although the use of a fireplace as the sole heating medium has become extremely rare (perhaps with the exception of summer cottages or buildings in warm climates that make occasional use of the fireplace on cool evenings), fireplaces continue to be incorporated in contemporary house plans, regardless of the sophistication of the central heating system (Inset I).

Whether or not a fireplace satisfies a functional or aesthetic need, its efficient design and operation are still important. Fireplaces, like the sun, emit heat through radiation. The fire transmits heat directly to the surrounding objects. These objects in turn heat the air adjacent to them. New England settlers located their fireplaces at the center of the house, where maximum heat could reach the residents and the chimney heat could be retained (Ill. 1). The advent of central heating freed the fireplace from its primary responsibility as a heat source and allowed the house builder to place the fireplace wherever he desired.

While a fireplace may take various external forms or be placed in different locations, the basic principles regulating its successful functioning remain the same. A word of advice: The proper design of a fireplace is not simple. It took masons repeated errors to arrive at the adequate proportions and requirements for a safe and smokeless fireplace. We do not recommend that a beginner get involved in tricky design solutions unless he has a thorough understanding of the principles behind fireplace design. If he does not, he may find himself with a great-looking fireplace that smokes him out of the room.

Fireplace Design

Traditionally, fireplaces have been built out of masonry. The beauty of such fireplaces is closely tied with the professional skills of the mason. We've come to admire them not only for their appearance and warmth but also for the craftsmanship and effort involved in their construction. Not everyone, however, can become a skilled mason overnight or afford to hire one. New solutions to the problem of fireplace design and construction have brought about the development of a wide range of prefabricated fireplaces, available commercially from a variety of manufacturers.

There are two basic models. One is a free-

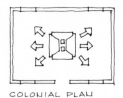
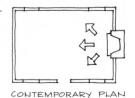

COLONIAL PLAN   CONTEMPORARY PLAN

ILL. 1

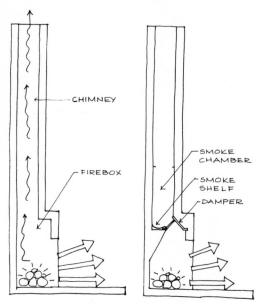

CHIMNEY

FIREBOX

SMOKE CHAMBER

SMOKE SHELF

DAMPER

ILL. 2

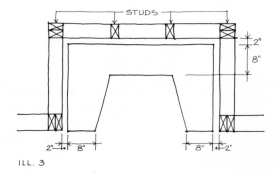

STUDS

2"

8"

2" 8"   8" 2"

ILL. 3

standing decorative unit requiring only minimal installation; it is complete in itself. The second model provides you with "the works"—that is, all the interior apparatus of the fireplace. This model is later finished in a number of different materials. Whether you are building your own masonry fireplace from scratch, installing an ornamental fireplace, or encasing a prebuilt unit, it is helpful to understand the mechanisms that make them work.

There are two essential components in a fireplace: a firebox, which holds the fuel (wood) while combustion takes place, and a chimney, which exhausts smoke and combustion gases (Ill. 2). In addition to these, a fireplace incorporates other elements that refine its operation, such as a damper, a smoke shelf, and a smoke chamber (Ill. 2).

THE FIREBOX: The firebox is the place where the fire burns. Its walls receive the most intense heat and should therefore be made of heat-resistant materials such as firebrick or insulated steel. Prefabricated units are built completely out of steel. The walls of the firebox when made out of masonry must be thick enough to protect combustible building materials, such as the wood structure of floors and walls, from being damaged. Masonry walls should be at least 8" thick, or as required by code. In addition, a minimum of a 2" air space must be left between the brick and the wood-framing members (Ill. 3). Manufacturers of prefabricated fireplaces claim, in some cases, that the insulating value of the walls of their product is enough to make such clearance unnecessary (zero-clearance units). If you are purchasing such a fireplace, check with the local codes and building authorities as to the acceptability of this approach.

To aid radiation, the firebox has angled walls. Both side walls open out toward the room (Ill.

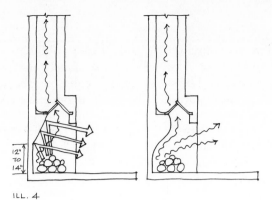

ILL. 4

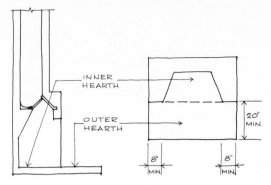

ILL. 5

3). The back wall is built vertically to a height of 12″ to 16″ and is then sloped forward toward the damper (Ill. 4). It should not be built as a curve, since it might tend to push smoke into the room rather than allow its passage to the chimney (Ill. 4).

The firebox floor is called the hearth. The inner hearth is that part that actually holds the burning fuel. It is constructed out of the same materials as the other walls of the firebox—that is, firebrick or some other heat-resistant material. The outer hearth protects the floor in front of the fireplace from heat and sparks. It must be of noncombustible materials such as brick or stone. For further protection from sparks and heat, the outer hearth should extend at least 20″ in front of the fireplace opening and project a minimum of 8″ on either side (Ill. 5).

Inevitably, ashes accumulate in the hearth. To solve this maintenance problem, an ash pit (although not essential) is commonly provided. Ashes are collected by means of an opening in the hearth into a fireproof compartment placed below the firebox. This compartment is equipped with a cleanout door for periodic cleaning (Ill. 6).

THE CHIMNEY: The chimney is the shaft through which hot gases and smoke are exhausted to the outside. The hot gases in the flue are lighter than the cold air outside. They therefore rise, displacing the cold air above, thus providing natural air circulation (updraft) in the chimney (Ill. 7). To prevent the possibility of downdraft, it is important that the chimney extend a minimum of 2′ over the highest peak in a sloping roof and 3′ over flat roofs (Ill. 8).

The flue must run as straight as possible. A pronounced offset in a chimney can become an obstacle for easy passage of gases to the outside, by allowing the accumulation of soot and ashes, which might eventually block up the

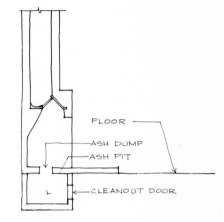

ILL. 6

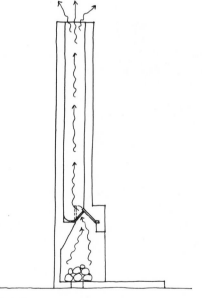

ILL. 7

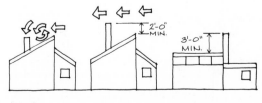

ILL. 8

Fireplace, Chimney, and Stair Design

193

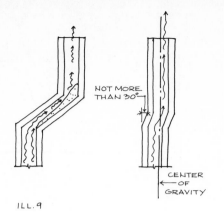

ILL. 9

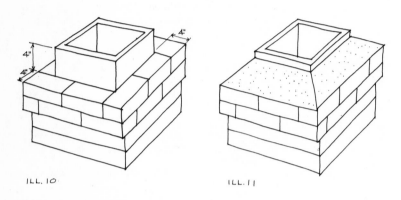

ILL. 10   ILL. 11

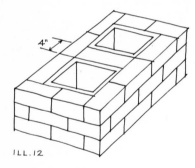

ILL. 12

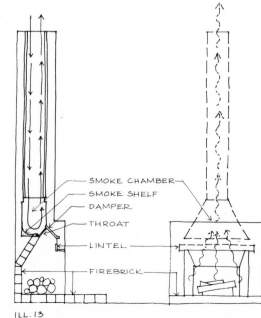

SMOKE CHAMBER
SMOKE SHELF
DAMPER
THROAT
LINTEL
FIREBRICK

ILL. 13

chimney entirely. (It's also easier to build a straight flue.) If an offset is absolutely necessary, it should be such that the center of gravity of the upper portion falls within the opening of the lower portion (Ill. 9).

Chimneys have traditionally been constructed out of common brick (see Chapter 7). This type of brick cannot withstand the hot gases that will rise up the chimney. For this reason, the inside of the chimney or flue is lined with fire clay or insulated steel. No other material such as plaster should be substituted. Plaster cannot withstand such high temperatures and will crack, leaving the brick exposed and becoming a fire hazard. Flue lining comes in 2' sections that are inserted in the brickwork as it is being erected. The brick walls surrounding the flue should be no less than 4" thick, or as required by code.

The flue extends approximately 4" over the top of the chimney (Ill. 10). A sloping cement topping is applied to prevent rain and snow from falling in and further decrease the possibility of downdraft (Ill. 11). If there are two or more fireplaces, each must have its own flue separated by a minimum of 4" of brick, or as required by code to prevent seepage of smoke from one fireplace down into the other (Ill. 12).

Prefabricated chimney sections are also available for installation with fireplace units.

THE SMOKE CHAMBER, SMOKE SHELF, AND DAMPER: The firebox and the chimney are connected by a slot-like opening called the throat. It is at this point that a damper followed by a smoke shelf and a smoke chamber are provided to help direct the smoke and combustion gases out of the chimney to the outside (Ill. 13).

A damper is a metal door used to regulate the draft in the chimney. With the aid of the damper, the throat can be completely opened or closed, preventing heat loss from the room when the fireplace is not in use and keeping insects out of the house during summer. The damper extends the full width of the fireplace opening and is installed approximately 6" to 8" above the lintel, which is the piece of metal that allows masonry to span the fireplace opening.

To prevent downdrafts from the outside from interfering with updrafts carrying smoke and gases, a smoke shelf is provided. Its function is to bounce downdrafts back up the chimney. The smoke shelf runs the full length of the throat.

Its depth ranges from 6″ to 12″ according to the depth of the fireplace. In masonry fireplaces the smoke shelf is built out of brick, stone, or other material and made concave with mortar. (A special mixture of firebrick mortar is used throughout the fireplace and chimney construction. See Chapter 24 for further information on this type of mortar.) Prebuilt fireplaces have the smoke shelf already built in.

The smoke chamber is the space above the smoke shelf that acts as a funnel for smoke and gas. It slants from the firebox walls toward the chimney, correcting the length gap between the two while squeezing gases out to the flue.

Masonry Fireplaces

If you decide to attempt the construction of a masonry fireplace from scratch, Tables A and B will aid you in its proper design.* Masons and engineers have evolved these recommendations after years of practical experience. Table A provides you with the width : depth : height ratios, while Table B helps you to determine adequate flue sizes. We should note that there may be slight variations from these tables depending on the geographical location of your property. Wind patterns and other characteristics may affect the draft. Check your local code. If any special provision is required, it will indicate the procedure to follow.

The proportional requirements of a fireplace originate with the width of the firebox opening (Ill. 14). All other dimensions for height, depth, etc., are relative to this width. While studying these tables, keep in mind a couple of general points. The higher you make the opening, the greater the risk of a smoky fireplace. The wider the fireplace opening, the deeper the firebox should be. Shallow fireplace openings radiate more heat than deep ones, but hold less wood. A minimum firebox depth of 18″ is recommended to prevent the danger of burning wood falling out of the firebox onto the surrounding floor. The damper should be placed as far forward as possible to permit greater depth for the smoke shelf. Another important consideration is the

* Another approach to fireplace design is outlined by Vrest Orton in his book *The Forgotten Art of Building a Good Fireplace* (Dublin, New Hampshire: Yankee, Inc., 1974).

TABLE A: FIREPLACE DIMENSIONS (IN INCHES)

Width (W)	24 to 84
Height (H)	2/3 to 3/4 W
Depth (D)	1/2 to 2/3 H — 16 to 24 recommended for coal / 18 to 24 recommended for wood
Flue (effective area)	1/8 W × H for unlined flue / 1/10 W × H for rectangular lining / 1/12 W × H for circular lining
Throat (area)	5/4 to 3/2 in addition to flue area
Throat (width)	3″ minimum to 4½″ maximum

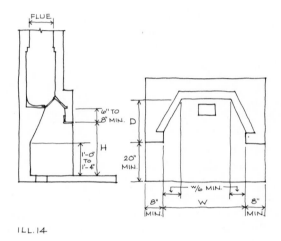

ILL. 14

TABLE B: RECOMMENDED FLUE SIZES (IN INCHES)

| Fireplace width | Rectangular flues | | | Equivalent round | |
	Nominal or outside dimension	Inside dimension	Effective area	Inside diameter	Effective area
24	8½ × 8½	7¼ × 7¼	41	8	50.3
30 to 34	8½ × 13	7 × 11½	70	10	78.54
36 to 44	13 × 13	11¼ × 11¼	99	12	113.0
46 to 56	13 × 18	11¼ × 6¼	156	15	176.7
58 to 68	18 × 18	15¾ × 5¾	195	18	254.4
70 to 84	20 × 24	17 × 21	278	22	380.13

size of the flue. To allow for good exhaust of smoke and gases, make sure to provide an adequate-sized flue. If the size you need is not available, get the larger size—never the smaller one.

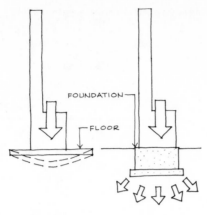

FOUNDATION

FLOOR

ILL. 15

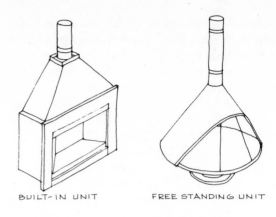

BUILT-IN UNIT

FREE STANDING UNIT

ILL. 16

Here are a sample set of fireplace design calculations. Let's assume a 36″ wide fireplace. According to Table A, the height will be H = ¾ W, or ¾ × 36″ = 27″. Using the same table, we find that the depth is D = ⅔ H, or ⅔ × 27″ = 18″. Since we are using a rectangular flue, we find that the minimum flue area should be equivalent to 1/10 W × H, or 1/10 × 36″ × 27″ = 97.2 sq. in. To double-check, we refer to Table B and find that for a 36″ to 44″ wide fireplace, a 13″ × 13″ flue with an effective area of 99 square inches is recommended. Going back to Table A, we see that the throat should be ¼ to ½ larger than the flue area, making it anywhere between 125″ and 150″. The throat width can range between 3″ and 4½″.

FOUNDATIONS: Visualize for a moment the construction of a masonry fireplace. Brick is laid over brick, or stone over stone all the way up to the tip of the chimney. It should be clear to you that the fireplace and the chimney combined are probably too heavy for a simple floor to carry without failing structurally. For this reason, masonry fireplaces are provided with their own foundations independent from those of the rest of the building. This foundation will resolve the masonry load evenly to the ground without disturbing the other building components (Ill. 15).

The criteria for the design of fireplace foundations are the same as that for the rest of the building. In cold climates, they are set a minimum of 1′ below the frost line (or as indicated by code). They should not, however, be less than 18″ deep. In addition, the foundation should overlap the fireplace by a minimum of 6″ all around.

Prefabricated Fireplaces

For those of you whose masonry abilities are either poor or nonexistent, there is an easier approach to fireplace construction—the prefabricated fireplace. These units are commercially available and come in a great variety of sizes and models, most of them approved by building codes. Prefabricated fireplaces combine three very important assets to the amateur home builder: ease of installation, relatively low cost, and guaranteed performance (if correctly installed). They come in two types: built-in or free-standing (Ill. 16).

If you decide to purchase a prebuilt fireplace and chimney unit, make sure that it is approved by the Underwriters Laboratory (UL) or the International Conference of Building Officials (ICBO). Fireplaces and chimneys approved by either of these two organizations will most likely be approved by local codes.

BUILT-IN UNITS: While built-in units require more work than free-standing ones, they offer greater flexibility of placement and design. They give you the choice of integrating the fireplace within the building just as if it were built from scratch. Built-in units are purchased complete with all the necessary components including the chimney. They are constructed of multiple layers of metal walls separated by either an air space or insulating material. These units are positioned against a wall and can be recessed into the wall or projected into the room. Later they are encased in brick, stone, or any number of finishing materials.

An additional advantage of a built-in fireplace is its light weight. Because the metal unit is lighter than masonry fireplaces, in many instances foundations are not necessary. (Check with the unit's manufacturer for recommendations.) For example, if you frame a built-in unit into a wall and merely face it with drywall, most likely a foundation will not be required. On the other hand, if the fireplace is projected into the room and is totally encased in brick, a foundation will probably be in order.

HEAT CIRCULATORS: Built-in units are also available in a modified version called heat circulators. Heat circulators are designed to provide more efficient heat distribution by drawing in cold air, warming it, and releasing it back to the room by means of grills (Ill. 17). A standard fireplace, on the other hand, draws cold air from the room and warms it by radiation and convection; much of the warm air, however, is lost through the chimney.

The air inlets can be located to draw air from the room or from the outside; each location has its advantages and disadvantages. While it is usually desirable to draw outside air into the fireplace, in very cold climates the outside air may be so cold that it is impossible for the circulator to sufficiently warm it. Indoor grills, however, are sometimes a problem in tightly constructed and heavily weather-stripped houses, where the amount of air required for combustion may not be replaced in time, creating a vacuum and the danger of smoke backing into the room.

FREE-STANDING UNITS: Free-standing fireplaces are by far the easiest to install and the least expensive of the three. They require no special foundation or framing, only a noncombustible floor covering, an opening for the chimney, and, if installed very close to walls, heat shields (to protect the walls). Because they stand free, they radiate more heat and can heat a room quite rapidly. They are small enough to fit in areas where large fireplaces would be impractical. Some models, however, may not meet local code requirements. Check your code.

STAIRS

Like so many aspects of house construction that we have touched on, there are quite a number of ways in which to design and build stairs. Illus-

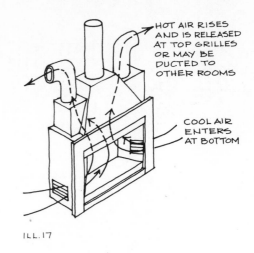

HOT AIR RISES AND IS RELEASED AT TOP GRILLES OR MAY BE DUCTED TO OTHER ROOMS

COOL AIR ENTERS AT BOTTOM

ILL. 17

tration 18 shows some of the most basic stair types in plan and elevation. A simply designed staircase is relatively easy to construct out of wood. A more complex stair, such as a spiral staircase, requires trickier construction techniques. Fortunately, in most areas spiral stairs may be purchased prefabricated. (Keep in mind, however, that many codes do not allow spiral staircases as primary stairs.)

The type of stair you choose will have to do with its location within the house and whether or not you want it to become a prominent part of the space. A stair may be an inconspicuous, merely functional element or an important part of the house design. The latter is well illustrated by the ornate staircases of Victorian times. Whichever approach you choose to take, the fact remains that the primary purpose of a stair is a functional one. For this reason, there are very specific requirements that its design must meet. These criteria together with the relative complexity of the construction techniques needed to build an ornate stair will largely determine your design.

Functional and Safety Requirements

Stairways are defined by code as "stepped footways" with treads and risers (Ill. 19). The stair is designed with the average human stride in mind, which is considered to be 24" long. This stride is broken down into the vertical component of the riser and the horizontal component of the tread. Codes generally specify the size range and desirable ratio of treads and risers. For example, when referring to buildings of public assembly such as schools, many codes

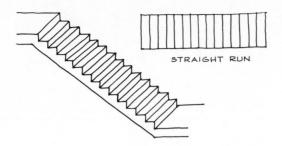

STRAIGHT RUN

TABLE C

Straight-run stair

Height, floor-to-floor	No. of risers	Riser	Tread	Length
8'-0"	13	7.38"	10¼"	10'-3"
8'-6"	14	7.29"	10½"	11'-4½"
9'-0"	15	7.20"	10½"	12'-3"
9'-6"	16	7.13"	10¾"	13'-5¼"
10'-0"	17	7.06"	11"	14'-8"
10'-6"	18	7.00"	11"	15'-7"
11'-0"	19	6.95"	11"	16'-6"

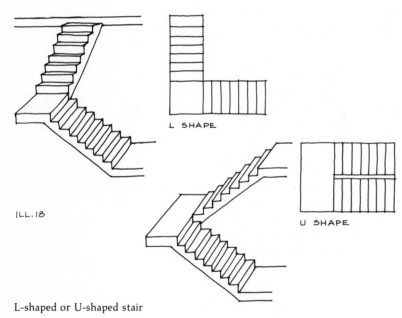

L SHAPE

U SHAPE

ILL. 18

L-shaped or U-shaped stair

Height, floor-to-floor	No. of risers	Riser	Tread	No. of risers	Length L₁	No. of risers	L₂
8'-0"	13	7.38"	10¼"	7	5'-1½" + W	6	4'-3¼" + W
8'-6"	14	7.29"	10½"	7	5'-3" + W	7	5'-3" + W
9'-0"	15	7.20"	10½"	8	6'-1½" + W	7	5'-3" + W
9'-6"	16	7.13"	10¾"	8	6'-3¼" + W	8	6'-3¼" + W
10'-0"	17	7.06"	11"	9	7'-4" + W	8	6'-5" + W
10'-6"	18	7.00"	11"	9	7'-4" + W	9	7'-4" + W
11'-0"	19	6.95"	11"	10	8'-3" + W	9	7'-4" + W

recommend a 7¼" riser and do not allow it to exceed 7¾". The depth of the tread is likewise limited to a minimum of 9½".

There is more room for variation in the case of houses. Riser heights may vary from as little as 6" to as much as 9". Similarly, tread depth can range anywhere between 8" and 13½". The Federal Housing Administration, for example, will accept a maximum riser height of 8¼" and a tread as narrow as 9". A comfortable riser height, however, is approximately 7". The 6" riser would generally be used for exterior stairs, while 9" may be acceptable for stairs leading to an attic.

For reasons of safety, it is very important that all treads in a stairway are of the same depth and that all risers are precisely the same height. A person going up or down a stair assumes, after the first few steps, that the remaining steps are the same. When this is not the case, the person may trip and fall, injuring himself.

Stair Design

The design of stairs starts with calculating the floor-to-floor distance that they travel and converting that figure into inches. This number is next divided by a riser height of about 7". If the quotient is an even number, you will have determined the number of risers. More likely, the quotient will be a mixed number such as 14½. Since you cannot have half a riser, you have to manipulate your figures so that the riser height is approximately 7" (but not more than 8¼") and the *number* of risers is a whole number. Once you have determined the number of risers, the tread width can be selected by using one of the following rules of thumb:

$$\text{Tread} \times \text{Riser} = 70 \text{ to } 75$$
$$\text{Riser} + \text{Tread} = 17" \text{ to } 17\frac{1}{2}"$$

Table C will help you design some of the most commonly used stairs without all these calculations.

In addition to selecting the tread and riser ratios, there are other determinants that go into the design of the stair. The *run* of the stair is the distance between landings. Since a very long run is both tiring and unsafe, the code will not permit you to run the stair straight up in one direction for an unlimited distance. Check your local code. If the run is longer than the code permits, or if convenience dictates that the run be divided, landings must be designed between the separate runs. These landings should be as wide and as long as the width of the stairs. In calculating the number of risers the landing is considered as a single tread.

Another consideration to keep in mind is the width of the stair. Although a 3′-0″ wide stair might be wide enough for you to climb, it might be impossible to move large pieces of furniture or appliances up the stairs to the upper floor of the house. Straight-run staircases with unlimited headroom do not pose much of a problem in transporting furniture, but a U-shaped or spiral stair might cause difficulties when the furniture has to be turned (in order to change direction) (Ill. 20). A width of about 4′-0″ is required in order to bring a large triple dresser up a U-shaped stair.

Exterior stairs are less steep and have wider treads than interior stairs because they are exposed to such possible hazards as ice and rain. The maximum recommended riser is 6″ and the minimum tread depth 12″. The rise of the stair (total vertical height between landings) should not exceed 5′-0″ (Ill. 21).

An important design feature on each tread is a small projection at its end called the nosing. The nosing provides space for the heel of the foot when a person is descending the stair, and allows ample toe space for the person ascending. Stairs are considered unsafe and illegal if the nosing is omitted. A nosing of 1″ to 2″ is all that is required (Ill. 22).

Wood-Stair Construction Techniques

The structural components of a stair are the treads, the risers, and the stringers. The stringer is the main support for the stair and its major framing member. It is the stringer that spans between landings and carries the weight of the treads and risers. At the top of the run the stringer is secured to header joists and at the bottom to a kick plate (Ill. 23). The risers and treads act as mini-beams giving the stair rigidity. When stairs are enclosed between two walls, the stringers are supported by the wall framing.

Stair construction methods vary according to the way in which the risers and treads are fitted to the stringer. The most painstaking technique is the one called housed stringer (Ill. 24). The

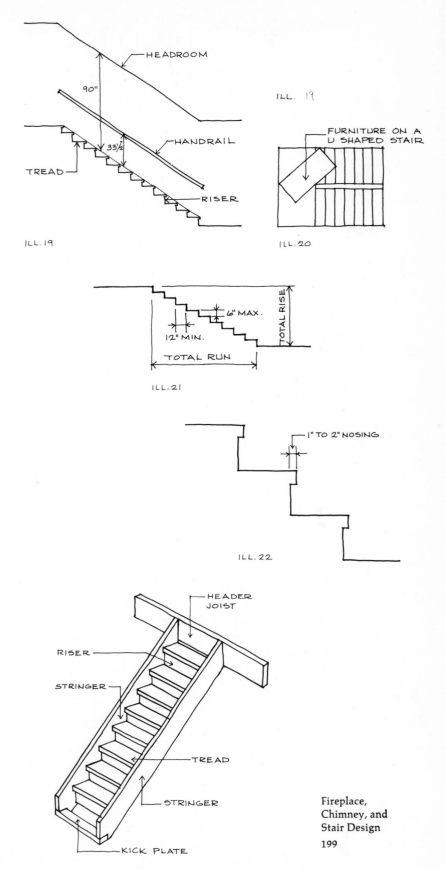

Fireplace, Chimney, and Stair Design
199

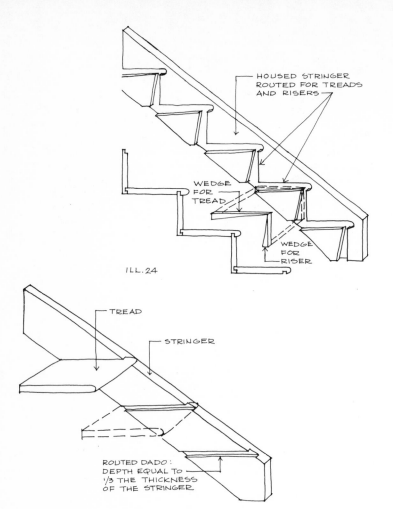

HOUSED STRINGER
ROUTED FOR TREADS
AND RISERS

WEDGE
FOR
TREAD

WEDGE
FOR
RISER

ILL. 24

TREAD

STRINGER

ROUTED DADO:
DEPTH EQUAL TO
⅓ THE THICKNESS
OF THE STRINGER

ILL. 25

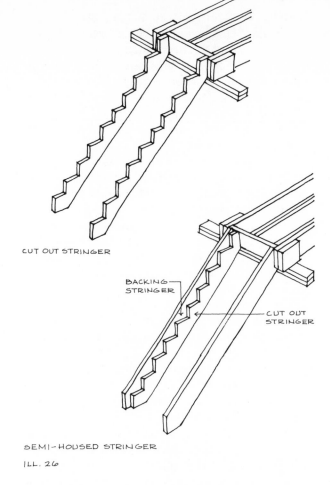

CUT OUT STRINGER

BACKING
STRINGER

CUT OUT
STRINGER

SEMI-HOUSED STRINGER

ILL. 26

housed stringer has routed (gouged-out) grooves into which the risers and treads are fit. Although this stair is the strongest and least likely to squeak when trod upon, the routing of the grooves presents special problems. Since this operation would take forever if done by hand, it is usually executed with the aid of a metal template and an electric router—two pieces of equipment you will not be able to put your hands on readily.

The routed stringer can be purchased custom fabricated from a stair builder. The shop will cut and route the stringers for you in compliance with your specifications. Furthermore, if you are interested in minimizing your own work, the stair builder will sell you the risers and treads, rails, newels, and balusters. If you want to skip the carpentry involved in stair building altogether, the shop will assemble the stair on location for a bit more than the cost of the parts. Find the stair builder under "Stairs" in the Yellow Pages. The open riser stair also uses a routed groove. This stringer could be constructed at home or at a shop (Ill. 25).

For the amateur carpenter, we recommend two other construction techniques that require no routing: the cutout and the semi-housed stringer (Ill. 26). In the standard cutout stringer stair, the stringers (usually three of them if the stair is over 3'-0" wide, one on either side and a third section in the middle) are measured and cut in a stepped pattern. The treads and risers are positioned to rest on the cutout shelves provided for them. The treads and risers for these stairs may be purchased precut and prefinished from the lumberyard or can be cut from standard clear 2" lumber.

The standard cutout stair is often used as a service stair because of its simplicity and ease of construction. Its uses, however, need not be limited to such servile functions. If constructed tightly or if finished with carpeting or another interesting material, it could serve quite nicely as a main staircase. The semi-housed stringer stair is a variation of the cutout stair. It uses the cutout stringer for support of the riser and treads, but backs it up with a solid piece of lumber.

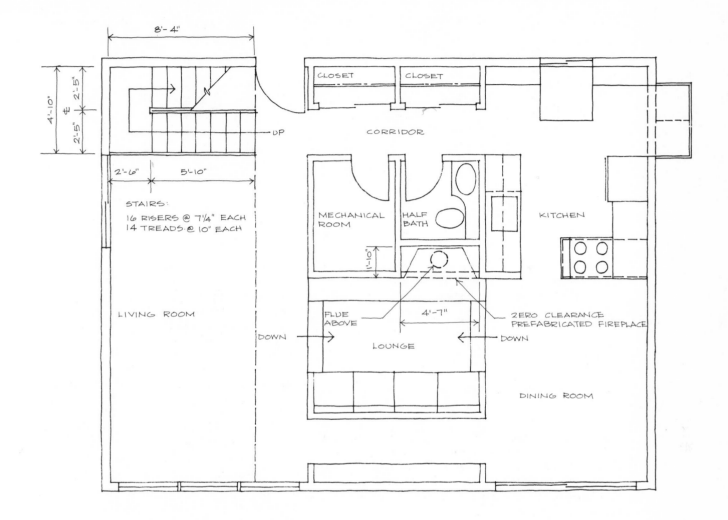

FIRST FLOOR PLAN

ILL. 27

DESIGNING THE FIREPLACE AND STAIRS FOR THE SAMPLE HOUSE

Fireplace

1. We have decided to use a prefabricated unit that will fit inside an opening provided for it in the core. Because the core is so tight, we select a zero-clearance unit approved by both the UL and local code. Its dimensions are 1'-10" deep by 4'-7" wide (Ill. 27).

2. The unit is light enough so as not to require foundations. By eliminating the need for foundations, we solve the problem of the fireplace foundation being too close to the pier foundations.

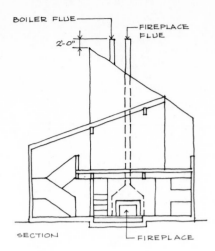

ILL. 28

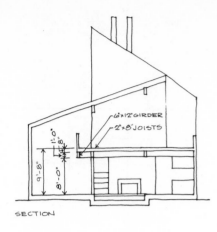

ILL. 29

3. A prefabricated chimney will be used in conjunction with the fireplace. It will extend a minimum of 2′ over the highest peak in the roof (Ill. 28).

Stairs

1. We start by calculating the floor-to-floor distance. According to our figures, the distance is 9′-8″ (Ill. 29).

2. Looking at Table C for U-shaped stairs, we see that there is no entry for 9′-8″ stairs. We will have to calculate the riser and tread sizes. Total height floor to floor = 9′-8″. Desirable riser height is 7″. We divide 7″ into 9′-8″ to get the number of risers.

$$\frac{9'\text{-}8''}{7''} = 16.6 \text{ risers}$$

Since we cannot have 16 risers of 7″ and 1 short riser of 4″ (.6 of 7″ = 4″), we will distribute the 4″ into each of the other 16.

$$\frac{4''}{16''} = .25'' = \frac{1}{4}''$$

Therefore each riser will be 7¼″ high.
To find the width of the treads we use the rule of thumb:

riser + tread = 17″ to 17½″
7¼″ + tread = 17″ to 17½″
tread = 17.5″ − 7.25″ = 10″ (approx.)

The stairs will have 14 treads each 10″ wide and 16 risers at 7¼″.
To check, multiply 7¼″ × 16 = 116″ = 9′-8″.

3. The next step is to determine W, the width of the stair. (The depth of the landing is equal to the width of the stair.) We want the edge of the stair to line up with the core wall. For this to happen, the total width of the stair (both runs) will have to equal the depth of the closet plus the width of the entry hallway. Going back to the plan, we do a few calculations. The depth of the closet is 2′-0″ in addition to a 4″ partition; the total depth of the closet is 2′-4″. The hallway is 2′-6″ wide. The combined width is therefore 4′-10″. Each run will be 2′-5″ wide. This width presents no problem in terms of bringing furniture up since one side of the stairs is open to the living room.

4. Having determined the width, we can find the total length of the stair. The landing should be approximately the same depth as the stairs are wide; in this case it would be 2′-6″. We have 7 treads in each run; every tread is 10″ wide. It follows that 10″ × 7 treads = 70″ = 5′-10″.

tread length = 5′-10″
landing = 2′-6″
total length of run = 8′-4″

5. It's a good idea to double-check the length of the stair against the total living room width to see if there is enough room for the front door (Ill. 27). The total width is 12′-0″. The outside wall is 6″ thick and one-half of the closet partition is 2″. The remaining clear space is 12′-0″ − 8″ = 11′-4″. The length of the stair is 8′-4″. It follows that 11′-4″ − 8′-4″ = 3′-0″. We will have enough room to install a 2′-6″ door.

17
Interior Finishes and Hardware

A vast range of materials qualify as interior finishes. Walls can be plastered, painted, paneled, or covered with mirrors, burlap, or plastic laminate. Similarly, floors can be covered with anything from brick to rubber. A ceiling can be acoustically treated, surfaced with plaster, or finished with wood. In essence, what we are saying is that when it comes to finishing materials almost anything goes. Of course, most of us will have to take into account cost, ease of installation, and functional criteria such as maintenance.

When you select a finish for a part of the house, you must consider the type of activity which will take place in that area and determine the suitability of the material for that use. Many materials that are suitable for one select use might fail if subjected to other punishment. More than one home owner has carpeted his kitchen with indoor-outdoor carpet only to discover that although the carpet is tough, it is also extremely vulnerable to stains.

Our discussion of finishes is limited to what we consider the bare essentials. New products are constantly being introduced, each with its virtues and problems. We strongly suggest that you consult Sweet's Catalogue, which can be found in the nearest library. It is an excellent source of information on any new building product (Inset I).

PLASTER

Traditionally, walls and ceilings have been finished with lath and plaster. Although plaster provides a beautiful texture for both interior and exterior surfaces, it has one important drawback: it is very difficult to apply. A few years back one of our friends was involved in renovating a loft in New York City. He comes from a long line of masons and he himself has had quite a bit of construction experience but unfortunately not in plastering. Our friend assumed that because he was handy and had access to good tools and good teachers, his chances of success were good. After spending an entire day on a 6' by 8' wall, he realized not only that the wall was terribly sloppy but that there was more plaster on the floor than on the wall. The following day he returned the tools and purchased gypsum board.

We don't intend to discredit plaster; as a matter of fact we're very partial to it. However, plastering is best left to the professional.

GYPSUM BOARD

The alternate to plaster is gypsum board (also known as Sheetrock, one of its trade names).

Sweet's Catalogue compiles the product literature of a vast number of building product manufacturers. Unfortunately, not all manufacturers advertise in Sweet's—causing the catalogue to fall short of being a complete building product encyclopedia. Sweet's is updated on a yearly basis, thus assuring current information. It is composed of several volumes, which have a classification guide (finishes, appliances, etc.) and are indexed both by products and by manufacturers. For example, if you are interested in researching the material on wood flooring, look under "Flooring–wood" and it will list the volume and booklet number where you can find the information.

A new service offered by Sweet's is the Buy Line, a toll-free number you can call to find out the telephone number of the sales representative you want to reach. All you have to do is tell the operator the name of the manufacturer and the product line in question.

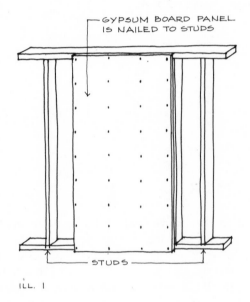

GYPSUM BOARD PANEL IS NAILED TO STUDS

STUDS

ILL. 1

Gypsum board, like plaster, is used for walls and ceilings. Gypsum board is a sandwich panel manufactured from powdered gypsum mixed with water and other ingredients which are shaped to form a wide, flat panel. This panel is then covered on both sides with a tough, durable paper. The resulting product is both dense and durable and is resistant to fire and noise. Gypsum board is installed by nailing the panels to the structural studs. The joints between the panels are concealed with tape and spackle to create a smooth seamless wall. The taping and spackling of the joints is a rather tedious job. Chapter 29 describes the technique in detail (Ill. 1).

Unlike plaster, it cannot, if desired, be left without an applied finish. Because of the joint work between the panels, gypsum board has to be covered with paint, wall coverings, tile, or other applied finish.

The main advantage of gypsum board over plaster is its relative ease and quickness of installation, both of which make it very appealing to the amateur home builder. It comes in 4' wide sheets (corresponding to the 12" and 16" spacing of joists and studs). The lengths vary from 6' to 16', although it is very difficult to purchase gypsum board in anything other than 8' lengths. The thicknesses range from ¼" to ⅝". Standard (½" thick) gypsum board is the most commonly used for residential construction.

There are a few different types of gypsum board to meet special requirements. For example, standard gypsum board cannot be installed in areas subject to wetness or on the exterior of buildings. Special moisture-resistant boards are available for use in such areas, for example, bathrooms and kitchens. Another type of board is the backer board, intended for use as a backing material where a double layer of gypsum-board wall or ceiling is called for.* It is also used in areas that are to be covered with acoustical tile. The backer board is cheaper than the standard board. Its surface, however, will not take applied finishes such as paint or wallpaper. For walls at the perimeter of the house, back foil board may be used. It has insulating foil on one side and is installed on walls with an exterior exposure.

Gypsum board comes with different edge conditions to suit various functions. The edges can be square, beveled, V-shaped, round, or tongue and groove. The square-edge board is the most widely used. The edges may also be tapered to provide a smoother and stronger joint (Ill. 2).

Where different pieces of board meet to form an outside corner, a bead is installed. Beads are

* For the walls of the mechanical room if they need a high fire-rated wall.

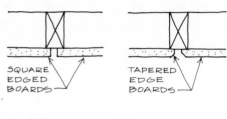

ILL. 2

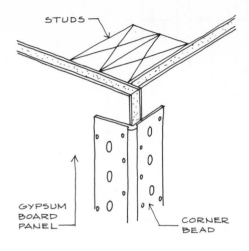

ILL. 3

metal angles that can be nailed at the corners, giving you a right angle (Ill. 3).

WOOD

Wood is an excellent material for walls and ceilings and especially for floors. Because wood is considerably more expensive than gypsum board or plaster, it is used selectively. It is durable, very attractive, and requires relatively little maintenance. It is easy to install, requiring the same carpentry skills used throughout the framing of the house. The pieces are nailed directly to the framing members.

There is a great variety of woods available for finish work. Your choice is dependent on the surface being treated—that is, whether you are applying it to a wall, a floor, or a ceiling. (See Chapter 7 for a more detailed discussion of wood.)

Walls

Wood can be applied to walls as single wood boards or large plywood panels. The advantage of the wood board over the plywood sheet is its rich texture, which is difficult to match in a highly manufactured product such as plywood. Boards are easier to install in areas with many openings, since they are easier to cut than large sheets. In addition, they give you greater design flexibility. For example, you may install the boards vertically or diagonally. You may use one or more types of wood to achieve various patterns, or you may even decide to use different size boards to add further interest (Ill. 4).

Plywood panels do not offer such versatility.

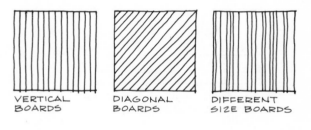

ILL. 4

The advantage of plywood for the amateur is that the installation of the panels is quicker than that of single boards (unless you have a surface with a multitude of openings and notches). Plywood panels are available in interior and exterior grades. They are generally 4' wide and vary in length (8' panels are the most commonly used). Another advantage of plywood is its availability in a variety of exotic woods. Plywood is constructed of a number of thin veneers of scrap wood held together by glue. The outer face of the panel is covered with a paper-thin slice of fine wood. Because of the thinness of this surface veneer, expensive and rare woods can be used at small expense.

You must be aware while buying plywood paneling that not everything that looks like wood is necessarily so. Some of the wood look-alikes are plywood panels covered with wood-grain printed vinyl. Although the vinyl surface is durable, it does not offer the richness of

Interior Finishes
and Hardware
205

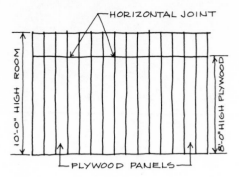

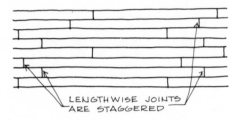

ILL. 5

LENGTHWISE JOINTS
ARE STAGGERED

ILL. 6

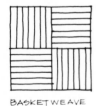

BLOCK   BASKETWEAVE

ILL. 8

surface textures. Texture 111 is perhaps the most popular.

One problem with plywood paneling is the horizontal joint. Because boards come in lengths of generally no more than 12', there is a joining problem if the wall surface is any higher than the maximum length of the panel (Ill. 5). If you are planning to use plywood paneling, it may be a good idea to inquire about the lengths that the panel comes in while you are still in the design stages.

Floors

Wood floors have traditionally been constructed out of hardwood because of its durability and better resistance to wear and tear. Oak has always been and still is a favorite for flooring, although maple, birch, beech, and pecan are also used, among others. Many turn-of-the-century buildings exhibit beautiful oak floors that not only are still in excellent condition but will most likely last for a long time to come.

Wood flooring falls into several types: strip, plank, block, and parquet.

STRIP FLOORING: Strip flooring is one of the most commonly used wood floors. It consists of wood strips ranging in width from 1½" to 2½" and is about 1" to 2" thick. The length depends on the available pieces. These strips are blind nailed to the subfloor in tongue-and-groove fashion every 10" to 12". The lengthwise joints are staggered (Ill. 6).

PLANK FLOORING: Plank flooring is made up of wood planks of varying widths. Some may be as narrow as 4" or less and others as wide as 12" (Ill. 7). Some wood plank systems presently available may be applied to the subfloor by means of mastic or adhesive or may be blind nailed. Check Sweet's Catalogue.

BLOCK AND PARQUET FLOORING: This type of floor has traditionally been more difficult to construct than either strip or plank flooring. Parquet floors, in particular, required a painstaking amount of work. Thin pieces of hardwood were cut and secured to the subfloor piece by piece, forming an intricate design. (Victorian houses exhibit some of the most extravagant parquet floors.) Fortunately, parquet blocks are presently available, which may be

wood. The reason for its popularity is its low cost. If you can't afford real wood veneer paneling, you'd be better off sticking to gypsum board and paint.

A very interesting alternative to interior plywood paneling is using exterior plywood panels inside the house. They are tough and durable since they are designed for outside use, are reasonably priced, and provide you with a pleasant texture. These panels are available in several

applied as easily as vinyl asbestos tile. These parquet blocks come in sizes ranging anywhere from 6″ × 6″ to 19″ × 19″ squares, with a large range of patterns and types of woods available (Ill. 8). The blocks are applied in mastic directly to wood or concrete subfloors.* Ornamental borders and moldings are also available. It is not unusual to apply such flooring on walls.

Ceilings

Wood ceilings may be approached in many ways depending on the time and effort you are willing to invest. The simplest solution is to leave the structure exposed. Another approach is to cover the structure with a layer of wood strips or planks nailed to the underside of the joists.

CERAMIC TILE

The heading of ceramic tile covers a vast range of tile types, the most familiar being the glazed tile used on bathroom floors and walls. Ceramic tile is made out of clay that has been fired in a kiln at very high temperatures. It is an excellent material as far as maintenance is concerned since it is water resistant and nearly impossible to stain. Its color does not fade and it is hard, tough, and durable. The tiles themselves are very easy to clean. The grout between them, however, can be a cleaning problem if the wrong type is used. Care must be taken to select the right grout for the job—for example, kitchen applications should have grout that is not adversely affected by kitchen grease.

There are two problems with ceramic tile. The first is its cost; it is more expensive than resilient floors. The second is in its installation. Tiles are set with adhesive or cement mortar to the wall or subfloor surface. While the placing of the tile on the mortar or adhesive bed is easy, the trimming required to get around openings and fittings (all the piping around the bathroom sink) can be a problem. Unless you have mastered the art of tile cutting, you may spend a lot

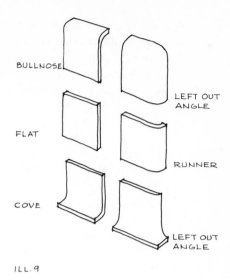

ILL. 9

of time piecing together the remains of shattered tiles.

Ceramic tile is available glazed and unglazed. Glazed tile is the one most commonly seen in bathrooms, kitchens, and other wet locations. It has a face of ceramic material fused onto the body of the tile, which may be glossy, semimatte, matte, or crystalline. These tiles are available in 4¼″ × 4¼″ and 1″ × 1″ squares (mosaic tiles). Various trimming tiles are available for edge and cove conditions (Ill. 9).

Unglazed tile is hard and dense. Its color is that of clay itself. This type of tile is used primarily for floors and walks. Examples of unglazed tile include quarry tile and pavers. They are larger than glazed tile, the smallest size being approximately 6″ × 6″. They are also available in a variety of shapes (hexagons, diamonds, etc.). Unglazed tile is used in heavily traveled areas requiring frequent cleaning such as foyers, kitchens, dining rooms, and decks, where an attractive and easy-to-clean surface is desired.

RESILIENT FLOORING

Resilient flooring materials are thin coverings made of various combinations of resins, plasticizers, and fibers in addition to other components. The composition is formed under heat and pressure. This type of flooring is applied to the subfloor with mastic cements and is available in tile or sheet form. Although resilient

* It is inadvisable to apply wood flooring directly to a concrete slab or grade. Changing moisture conditions may damage the floor by causing the wood to swell and buckle.

flooring is not as durable or as easy to maintain as ceramic tile, it is easier to install and lower in cost. In addition, a resilient floor is more comfortable underfoot and reduces noise. The types of resilient flooring available include vinyl, vinyl asbestos, rubber, and linoleum. The tiles are generally 9″ × 9″ or 12″ × 12″ squares. The sheets range in width from 36″ to 72″.

The installation of this type of flooring varies with the location of the floor (above or below grade) and the material of the subfloor (wood or concrete). Because the material is adversely affected by moisture conditions, the selection of resilient floor and the adhesive must be carefully researched. Consult your dealer for recommendations.

Linoleum has excellent resistance to grease and abrasion. It performs poorly, however, when too much water or alkali detergents are used on it. The constant use of water and strong detergents removes the oil content in the linoleum and causes it to become hard, brittle, and subject to tearing.

Vinyl is very resilient and is highly resistant to abrasion. It is durable and performs well under grease, alkali, and water conditions. Its cost, however, is rather high compared to other resilient floors.

Vinyl asbestos tile (VAT) is relatively easy to maintain, offering good grease, alkali, and abrasion resistance. It has poor resilience and is subject to indentation. It costs less than vinyl flooring and is available in a vast number of colors and patterns.

Rubber is durable, resilient, and easily cleaned, and offers good resistance to water. It performs well against grease, alkali detergents, and abrasion. Of all the resilient floors, it is probably the softest and quietest.

STONE

Stone is a beautiful material all around. Types of stone used for flooring include limestone, granite, slate, and marble. Stone floors are suitable where a durable and attractive material is required. Keep in mind, however, that stone is easily stained. Another important consideration is its weight. Although the stone used for flooring is cut into slabs of approximately 1″ in thickness, it still manages to add up to a substantial weight. Before selecting this material, make sure that the floor system can take the load of the stone flooring.

There are two major disadvantages to the use of stone: its tough installation and its high cost. Stone like ceramic tile is easy to lay on the mortar bed. Cutting the stone to fit, however, is a tough and precise job.

BRICK

Brick floors and walls are always interesting additions to the house texture. Many a renovator has spent long and painful hours chipping away at the plastered walls to get at the brick-bearing wall beneath. The result is well worth the effort. Types of bricks are discussed in Chapter 7; installation methods in Chapter 20.

Beware of one problem with brick floors: Don't use too porous a brick such as common brick. It is not very durable and will produce a chalky dust as it wears down. Paving brick is a much better choice. With brick as with stone, be cautious of the heavy loads you are applying to the floor system. Make sure you've provided for this in your structural design.

ACOUSTICAL TILE

We include this material with a degree of reluctance since we don't feel that acoustical tile has a place in residential work. The kind of noise conditions present in commercial and industrial installations are rarely present in houses. You may, however, be a musician or a music lover who is designing a room in which to practice or listen to your favorite pieces. Perhaps one of your kids is a member of a band and rehearsals take place in your house. Here's a place where acoustical tiles can come in handy.

These tiles are available in many textures, sizes (12″ × 12″, 16″ × 16″, 24″ × 48″), and noise reduction coefficients (NRC). They are difficult to clean but can be easily painted. For residential use the tiles are usually mounted on walls and ceilings with adhesive.

APPLIED FINISHES

Paint

Of the applied finishes, paint is by far the most popular. This should come as no surprise since paint is cheapest and easiest to apply. Paints have been developed and improved in the last few years to cover a vast range of applications. It would be impractical to list all the paints presently available. The list would be excessively long and, because new products are constantly being developed, would soon become obsolete. Your best bet is to contact the paint manufacturers directly or visit a paint store. They have a wealth of information available and can help you select the best paint for the specific job.

A year ago one of the authors was involved in the renovation of a firehouse. Needless to say, some of the painting involved was rather specialized. Many of the surfaces to be painted (for example, the walls of the apparatus room, where the fire engines are washed) were subject to unusual conditions. The paint had to be both durable and highly water resistant. After consulting the manufacturer, the author was surprised to learn that a number of products in a wide range of colors and finishes could be used.

Paints are essentially divided into two types: latex (water-based paints) and alkyds (oil-based). Latex paints are preferred to alkyds because of their ease of application, quick drying time, little odor, and easy cleanup (with soap and water). They are available in different finishes: flat, satin (eggshell), semigloss, and glossy. The choice of finishes is dependent on the usage of the surface. For example, in a kitchen, where you may be scrubbing down walls periodically, a semigloss or glossy finish will stand up better than a flat one. Flat finishes tend to show marks if abrasive cleansers are used. Keep in mind, however, that the glossier the paint, the more imperfections the surface will show.

Alkyd paints are no longer the hassle they used to be in the past. The new ones are easy to handle. Many of them are advertised as dripless because of their heavier consistency. Alkyds generally take longer to dry than latex paints and have more of a smell. They are available in the same colors and finishes as latex. Their main advantage over latex paints is their better performance under heavy scrubbing and their tendency not to absorb dirt. This makes oil-based paint a popular choice in kitchens, bathrooms, on window sills, etc.

Both latex and alkyd paints have corresponding primer-sealers. Priming the surface before painting is necessary when the surface is being painted for the first time. The purpose of the primer-sealer is to penetrate and seal the pores of the material and make it ready to receive paint. Primers go on easily and are quick-drying; one coat is usually sufficient. The exceptions are instances where the surface is extremely porous, as for example concrete block.

There is a wealth of paints designed for special applications, such as epoxy enamels for use on surfaces requiring a particularly tough finish; aluminum paints used to inhibit rust; masonry paint specifically designed for use on extremely porous surfaces; and deck and floor enamels. The best approach for any problem surface is to consult the paint dealer. He will be eager to offer recommendations. But beware if you are dealing with an outfit having an obviously small selection. The salesman might say that the paint type you want doesn't exist just to sell you something else.

CLEAR FINISHES

These products are designed to protect and preserve wood surfaces from soiling and decay without radically changing their appearance. They all, however, regardless of their claim of being clear, tend to deepen the wood color and accentuate the grain.

Lacquer is composed of resins, plasticizers, and a solvent. Of the clear finishes, it is the one that least affects the natural tone of the wood while at the same time offering a tough and durable finish. Lacquer's quick drying rate makes it difficult to apply with a brush. It is generally sprayed onto the surface. A satin finish could be obtained by rubbing the lacquer once it dries.

Shellac is available in several different types, including clear and orange. It acts as a sealer for new wood, protecting it from stains and dirt. Clear shellac doesn't vary the color too much. Orange shellac does exactly that, adds an orange tint to the wood's surface. One of the contractors we've dealt with gave us a tip on the uses of orange shellac. He suggested that before painting a wood surface and even before priming it, you cover all the knots and imperfections with orange shellac to make sure that the imperfections will not show through the paint. The sealer and the paint are later applied. We've tried with our woodwork and it has worked.

Varnish is a good finish to use in areas where wood is subject to heavy soiling and will require periodic washing. Although it is available in flat, semigloss, and glossy finish, varnish has a tendency to be on the shiny side. It also adds a yellowish tint to the wood. The biggest problem with varnish is that it scratches easily and it is difficult to touch up. For this reason, it is advisable to cover it with a coat of paste wax.

Polyurethane offers perhaps the best protection for hardwood, particularly floors. It is rugged and long-wearing with outstanding abrasion resistance. Because it seals the surface, it has good resistance to household materials such as water, alcohol, and grease. The finish may be glossy or satin. Be careful not to apply polyurethane on softwoods. This type of wood has a tendency to absorb many coats of polyurethane before a workable finish is obtained. The results are much better when it is used on hardwoods.

Oil stains provide the most natural wood finish. These, unlike water and varnish stains, are easy to apply, only involving brushing on and wiping down. There are two types—clear and opaque. Clear stains penetrate the wood deeper than opaque ones and allow the grain to show through while only slightly changing the color. Opaque stains both change the surface color and darken the grain. With stains as with varnish, a coat of paste wax will protect the surface from scratching.

FINISH HARDWARE

Finish hardware refers mainly to locks, latches, and hinges. Because these devices are a visible and integral part of the building (as opposed to rough hardware, which is hidden), it is important to select them not only for their operating characteristics but also for their appearance. Take a trip to the library and look at Sweet's Catalogue. In it you'll find more design variations for visible hardware than you'll know what to do with. After flipping pages and becoming familiar with what is available in the market, visit your supplier and find out what he carries or can get for you.

Hinges

Doors swing on hinges in order to open or close. A hinge is made up of two leaves, which are joined together by a pin. They are available in several types (Ill. 10). Some hinges are completely concealed, others are totally exposed, and there are still others in which only the pin is visible (butt hinges). A mortised hinge is one in which the leaves are notched into the wood. When the leaves are visible, it is called a surface hinge.

Wrought steel, brass, bronze, and stainless steel are some of the materials in which hinges are available. Stainless steel provides the most durable, strong, and corrosion-resistant hinge at a relatively high price.

In terms of size, hinges vary from 2" to 6". The size is relative to the weight and the thickness of the door (see Table A). Hinges are generally mounted on doors 5" from the head and 10" from the floor. Should a third hinge be necessary, it is placed at the center point between the top and bottom one (Ill. 11).

TABLE A: HINGE GUIDE

Door thickness	Door width	Minimum hinge height
⅞" or 1"	any	2½"
1⅛"	to 36"	3"
1⅜"	to 36"	3½"
1⅜"	over 36"	4"
1¾"	to 41"	4½"
1¾"	over 41"	4½" heavy*
1¾" to 2¼"	any	5" heavy*

*To be used for heavy doors of high-frequency or unusual stress.

Locks and Latches

Locks and latches are used to hold doors in place and provide security. When a door is closed, the latch automatically slides into position. The locking device is called a bolt. It may be manually operated (dead bolt) or be set automatically (latch bolt). Locks and latches are often combined into one unit.

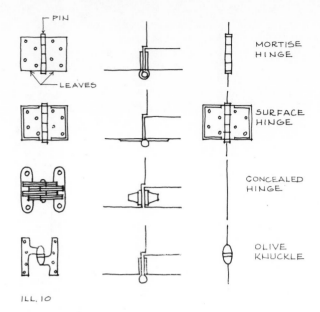

ILL. 10

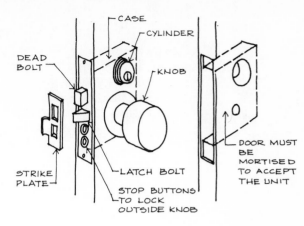

ILL. 12

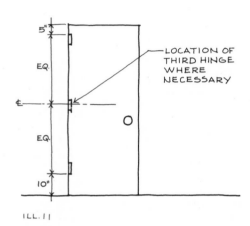

ILL. 11

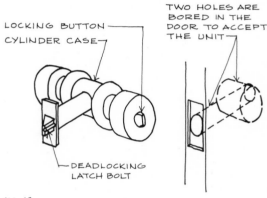

ILL. 13

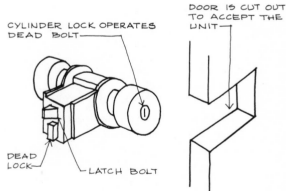

ILL. 14

The most common locks and latches used in residential construction are of the mortised and bored-in type. ("Mortised" and "bored-in" refer to the method of installation.) In the mortise type, the unit is concealed in the edge of the door. Its installation involves carving a hole in the core of the door, into which the unit will fit (Ill. 12). The bored-in type (whether cylindrical or tubular) is easier to install, only requiring the boring of two holes (Ill. 13). One other type of lock and latch deserves mention—the unit lock. This lock is very simple to install, only requiring a notch or cutout in the door. The unit is merely slipped into the notch (Ill. 14). In addition, unit locks are factory assembled, eliminating much fussing on the job. Mortise-type integral locks and latches may also be purchased factory assembled (Ill. 15).

Lock and latch mechanisms vary according to the functions they must serve within the house. For example, the lock and latch combination

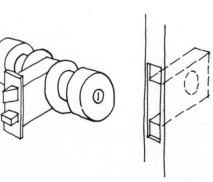

ILL. 15

Interior Finishes
and Hardware
211

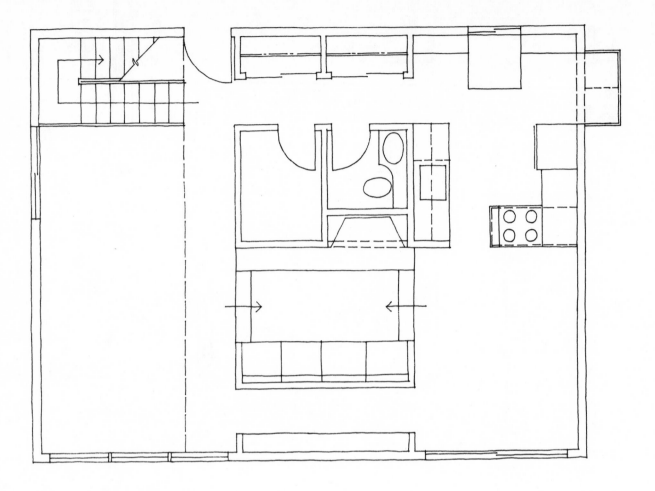

used in a bedroom or bathroom door is not the same as that used for a closet door. While the one for the bedroom or bathroom will need a latch bolt operated by a knob from either side and should be able to be locked or unlocked by a push button or a turn from the inside, the closet will only need a latch bolt that is operable at all times by a knob on either side. Care must be taken to select the right mechanism for the specific job.

Locks and latches are available in a wide range of materials including stainless steel, brass, bronze, and aluminum. The visible components such as knobs and lever handles may be obtained in a variety of finishes and designs ranging from bright to satin and from contemporary to traditional.

DESIGNING THE INTERIOR FINISHES FOR THE SAMPLE HOUSE

1. We start with the selection of wall finishes. In order to keep costs and labor to a minimum, all walls are going to be finished with gypsum board and paint. Satin-finish latex paint will be used throughout with the exception of the kitchen, which will receive satin-finish alkyd enamel. For maintenance reasons the bathroom walls are to be covered with ceramic tile.

2. The floors are next (Ill. 16). Ease of maintenance is the key to the flooring for the kitchen and entrance hallway. Quarry tile will probably be the best solution to these heavily used areas, providing both an attractive and easy to clean

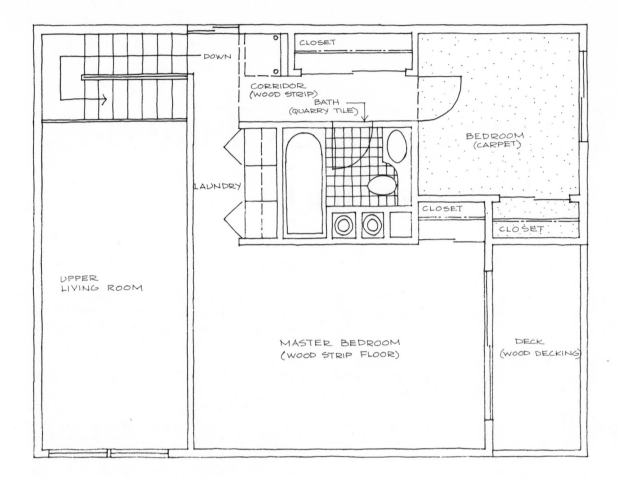

SECOND FLOOR PLAN

floor. We will also use quarry tile for the powder room and bathroom floors, while the boiler room is to be covered with vinyl asbestos tile. A warm and soft floor is desired in the lounge, small bedroom, and loft, so we will cover them with wall-to-wall carpeting.

All the remaining areas of the house including the living room, dining room, and connecting hallways will be of wood strip flooring with a polyurethane finish. The master bedroom's deck will be protected with built-up roofing covered with wood planks on nailing strips.

3. The plank-and-beam roof structure will remain exposed and the wood protected with an oil stain. All the flat ceiling areas including the kitchen, bath, powder room, boiler room, lounge, and dining room will have the ceilings finished with gypsum board and paint to match the walls.

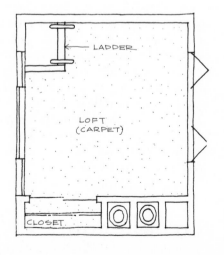

ILL. 16   LOFT PLAN

Interior Finishes
and Hardware

18
Building Codes, Take-offs, and Financing

This chapter serves as a catchall for all the information required to build a house that does not directly pertain to its design or construction.

The first part of the chapter discusses building codes.

This discussion is followed by a materials take-off section, which perhaps constitutes the most tedious but important aspect of the paper work required to build your house. In this section you will find instructions for calculating the probable construction cost. These calculations are detailed and depend on your knowledge of the quantities of materials needed and their cost on the local market.

In the financing section, you will profit from the authors' visits to a number of local banks and lending institutions. Although this material in no way constitutes the definitive work on the subject, it should offer an adequate introduction to the intricacies of the financial scene.

Finally, the brief section on building permits introduces you to the inevitabilities of the building and health departments. Hopefully, you will be prepared to meet their demands.

The chapter concludes with a section on design development. When you have completed these final steps, you will be able to commence construction. Good luck!

BUILDING CODES

Although it would be foolish to list the criteria in any one state's building code (they vary from state to state and town to town), there are some items which seem to be general to all codes. Many communities have adopted what is called a performance code as their construction guideline. This means that you must meet certain general requirements for construction, rather than following exact standards for structure, electricity, plumbing, heating, etc. Although much in the code may seem worthless at first glance, this type of code offers a great deal of flexibility to the designer. Only those parts of the code that pertain to safety requirements for evacuation in case of fire and for sanitary safety are explicit. Other municipalities abide by codes that specifically tell you what their requirements are down to the size of every pipe. Generally, the more rural the area, the less strict the code will be.

1. Every habitable room must have a window. This includes all bedrooms, living and dining rooms, family rooms, etc. Some codes permit unwindowed kitchens and bathrooms if proper mechanical ventilation is provided.

2. A minimum ceiling height is specified for habitable spaces, usually at least 7'-6" (except in areas with sloping roofs). Bathrooms, kitchenettes, corridors, and recreation rooms might have a minimum of 7'-0"

3. The total height of the building is restricted. There are areas in which a one-family home of frame construction will under no circumstances be allowed to exceed two or two and a half stories (the half-story being the attic, which may be habitable).

4. There are often a number of restrictions regarding staircases. In most areas a narrow winding stair will be allowed only as a *second* stair between floors. The primary stair will have to be a certain width and not be too steep or too shallow.

5. Because of the combustibility of most house-building materials, some building departments have rigid codes regarding the prevention of fire and its spread to other structures. These codes vary considerably from municipality to municipality, but must be checked. Some common requirements are:

   A certain distance must be kept between structures on different pieces of property and between structures even if on the same piece of property. Sometimes this distance can be lessened by making the walls of the structures of a higher fire rating.

   The materials permissible for the roofing and other areas of the house are sometimes regulated by needing a fire rating.

   There are restrictions regarding mechanical rooms. The floor of the room might have to be of a noncombustible material (such as concrete) or, if not noncombustible, be protected by a top layer of noncombustible material. The walls and ceilings around the equipment will most likely have to be of a much higher fire rating than the other walls of the house. In some areas there might even be a requirement that the heat-producing equipment be a certain minimum number of feet from the walls and ceiling. (An automobile is likely to be considered a heat-producing piece of equipment. Be sure to read the code regarding garages.)

   Be sure to see if the code requires firestops in the stud walls. These are wood strips between the studs that will prevent flames and hot air from moving upward within the wall. (Some areas require that firestopping be placed no more than one story apart. In platform-frame construction, the floor platform acts as an adequate divider and no firestopping is required.) Firestopping will be required in most cases between the joists at the places where they are supported. These solid wooden bridges prevent the horizontal movement of fire and hot gases within the floor.

   The code will regulate the use of fire-resistant structural, mechanical, and finishing materials. Codes are often very strict with plastics since some plastics are highly combustible. Before using material that is not strictly traditional (that is, brick for the fireplace), check with the building department or consult the codes. If the inspector does not allow it, it might have to be ripped out and replaced.

6. The codes on plumbing are very specific and must be read in full. In some cases you will be required to use public water if there is a public water supply within 100'. Plumbing and sanitary disposal codes vary considerably depending on the community.

7. Heating and electrical equipment must be designed with such safety devices as shutoff valves and heat regulators.

8. Chimneys and fireplaces will have a fixed set of codes that must be adhered to. The height of the chimney above the roof will be determined by code. A separate set of codes governs the size, type, location, and support of fuel tanks.

9. Some municipalities will not permit you to do certain parts of the work on your own, and these restrictions will not necessarily be contained in the code itself. Further investigation on your part may be required. Again, it is valuable to make a friend at the building department. Although many of these individuals are severely overworked and may not have the time for your questions, there will probably be at least one kindhearted person who will deal with you patiently. Remember to keep your questions to a minimum and try to obtain the answers from a reliable source.

Caution: This is merely a rundown of some of the information usually found in building codes. Read yours carefully!

MATERIALS TAKE-OFF

The first step in translating a set of drawings into a building is to do a materials take-off. Plans and elevations must be translated into lists of materials to be purchased. To do a take-off you must patiently sit down with a pencil, a scale, paper, and a complete set of drawings. The materials that are called for in the drawings are carefully recorded and a contingency of 5 to 10 percent added to be on the safe side.

A materials take-off will also help you to assess whether or not it is feasible to contract out parts of the work. Let two or three contractors give you the prices on different stages of the job. You can then estimate whether the price of labor is sufficient to make the investment of your own time and labor worthwhile. Keep in mind that contractors, unlike the one-time builder, buy in bulk. They can purchase at lower prices, which may sometimes offset the cost of labor.

Your materials supplier may be of great help to you while doing the take-off. Suppliers have many rules of thumb that can come in handy. As a matter of fact, it is not unusual for a supplier to do the take-off. The idea behind it is, of course, that you'll give him your business in return.

In this section, we attempt to give you a basic outline to work from. For the sake of clarity, we've organized the material to correspond to the chapters in Part Three. (A professional estimator will most likely use a different format.) There are a number of miscellaneous items that will vary with the house itself. You must include these in your own estimate.

Site Preparation

Site preparation is difficult to estimate because site conditions vary greatly. You may be building on a flat lot or on one with a steep slope; the excavation may involve bedrock or sandy soil. The cost and effort involved in the site work will vary as much as the site itself.

Another problem with site preparation is the fact that the work requires the utilization of specialized equipment. Renting a backhoe automatically involves hiring an operator to handle it. It is difficult to rent a level because its delicate mechanism requires meticulous care.

For these reasons, site work is a part of the construction process that is easier to delegate to the professionals. Get a few estimates from different contractors and compare their prices with the cost of renting a backhoe, hiring an operator, and renting a level.

Here are a few words of advice on contracting out site work (or for that matter any part of construction). Once a piece of equipment is on your property, get the operator to do everything that needs to be done with that equipment. For example, if you rent a backhoe, make sure not only that the basement or crawl-space excavation is done, but also that the trenches are dug, the tree stumps removed, the cavity for the septic tank excavated, and so on. Every time that the equipment has to be brought back to the site, you pay dearly for it.

A second important point is not to hire the contractor on an hourly basis. Assuming that you are getting the maximum hourly performance in return for your pay, unexpected problems may arise to cause delays. When you are paying by the hour, the delay becomes your problem. Conversely, when you pay a lump sum, the delay becomes the contractor's headache.

Foundations

POURED: The materials cost in poured foundations is taken up mostly by the cost of the concrete and the lumber for, or the rental of, formwork. The cost of ready-mix concrete may vary with the conditions on your property. For example, if it is difficult for the ready-mix truck to pour into your formwork, the cost will obviously go up. You may also be charged extra if the distance between the plant and the construction site is great. Check to find out which days of the week the company will deliver. Compare them with your own building schedule and see whether they are compatible. Delivery on unscheduled days may not be possible or may involve an extra charge.

Ready-mix concrete is sold by the cubic yard. The procedure used to estimate the amounts of concrete in cubic yards is described on page 72, Inset V.

CONCRETE-BLOCK WALLS: The number of blocks that will fit into one square foot of wall will vary with the type of block you are using. Table A lists the number of blocks in 100 square feet of wall area for some of the most commonly used sizes. If the type of block you're using is not included, ask your supplier for the estimated number of blocks per square foot for that specific type. Blocks (like bricks) are sold by the unit; you can purchase one or one thousand.

The amount of mortar needed will vary with the thickness of the joint. Table B outlines how much mortar you'll need for ⅜" joints.

Floor System

To do an accurate take-off of the floor system, you must closely refer to your structural plans. While doing the quantity estimates, don't forget to take into account lapping of wood members at joints. Wood is sold by the linear foot or the board foot. The figures you will arrive at working directly from the plans will be in linear feet; if your supplier deals in board feet, use the conversion method described in detail on page 68, Inset III.

T A B L E   A

Concrete-block type	Number of blocks per 100 square feet	Cubic feet of mortar per 100 square feet
8″ × 16″	112.5	6.0
8″ × 12″	150.0	7.0
4″ × 16″	225.0	9.5

T A B L E   B

Brick type	Number of bricks per 100 square feet	Cubic feet of mortar per 100 square feet for ⅜″ joints
3¾″ × 2¼″ × 8″	655	5.8
3¾″ × 2¾″ × 8″	551	5.0
4″ × 2²/₃″ × 8″	675	5.5
4″ × 4″ × 8″	450	4.2

T A B L E   C

	Item	Unit
Footings	lumber for forms (boards)	linear foot, or board foot (see page 66, Inset I, and page 68, Inset III)
	lumber for stakes	linear foot, or board foot
	ready-mix concrete	cubic yards (see page 72, Inset V)
	nails (common)	pound
	reinforcing bars	linear foot
Poured foundation walls	prefab forms (rental)	
	HOME-MADE FORMS:	
	plywood	square foot
	lumber (boards)	linear foot
	wall ties and spreader	linear foot
	nails	pound
	concrete nails	pound
	form oil	gallon
	anchor bolts, nuts, and washers	each
	reinforcing bars	linear foot
Concrete-block walls	CONCRETE BLOCKS:	
	type 1	square foot (or number of units)
	type 2	square foot (or number of units)
	type 3	square foot (or number of units)
	MORTAR:	
	lime	bag (see Table B)
	sand	cubic foot (see Table B)
	cement	bag (see Table B)
	anchor bolts	each
	reinforcing bars	linear foot
Waterproofing	black asphalt, tar, pitch	gallon
	felt	square foot
	drainage tile	linear foot
	gravel	cubic yard

Quantity × unit price = total.

Item	Unit
sill	linear foot
JOISTS:	
size 1	linear foot
size 2	linear foot
size 3	linear foot
cross bridging	linear foot
BEAMS:	
size 1	linear foot
size 2	linear foot
size 3	linear foot
girders	linear foot
plywood subfloor	square foot
termite shields	linear foot
sill sealer	linear foot
bolt nuts (to fit over anchor bolts)	each
galvanized nails	pound
timber connectors (if required)	each
joist hangers (if required)	each

Quantity × unit price = total.

Walls and Columns

The procedure to follow to estimate walls and columns is the same as that for floors. This time keep in mind that the height of walls and columns varies with the floor-to-ceiling distance.

A rule of thumb commonly used to calculate the number of studs is to provide one stud per linear foot of wall. This number is multiplied by the height of the wall to obtain the total linear feet. The other method is simply to count them off the plan. Consider throwing in a little more lumber to account for the extra studs needed to frame around windows and doors.

While calculating the square footage of sheathing, start by figuring out the total square footage of wall including the openings for windows and doors. Then deduct the area of these openings. Some of those pieces of sheathing such as the ones cut out to make room for doors may be reused.

Item	Unit
studs	linear foot
headers	linear foot
plates	linear foot
sheathing	square foot
insulation	square foot
vapor barrier	square foot
building paper	square foot
galvanized nails	pound

Quantity × unit price = total.

Where walls are made out of masonry instead of wood, they are handled in a manner similar to that described for concrete-block foundation walls. The type of brick, block, or stone will change the number of units you'll get per square foot. Refer to Table A.

Item	Unit
BRICK, BLOCK, OR STONE:	
type 1	square foot (or number of units)
type 2	square foot (or number of units)
type 3	square foot (or number of units)
MORTAR:	
lime	bag
sand	cubic foot
cement	bag
reinforcing bars	linear foot
insulation	square foot
vapor barrier	square foot
metal ties (for masonry facing on stud walls)	each

Quantity × unit price = total.

Roofs

Roofs are treated in a manner similar to floors and walls.

Item	Unit
RAFTERS:	
size 1	linear foot
size 2	linear foot
size 3	linear foot
BEAMS:	
size 1	linear foot
size 2	linear foot
size 3	linear foot
girders	linear foot
sheathing	square foot
insulation	square foot
building paper	square foot
vapor barrier	square foot
galvanized nails	pound
flashing	linear foot

(Roofing materials are included in the section on Closing In.)
Quantity × unit price = total.

Stairs

It is difficult to provide a guideline for stair take-off since the design of stairs varies greatly. Many portions of a stair are available ready-made or the entire stair may be purchased pre-fabricated and merely installed. You will have to make provision for your particular stair design in the take-off.

Item	Unit
stringer	linear foot
TREAD:	
wood	linear foot
stone	square foot
riser (if required)	linear foot
handrail	linear foot
newels	linear foot
balusters (if required)	linear foot

Quantity × unit price = total.

Closing In

Item	Unit
WINDOWS:	
type 1	each
type 2	each
type 3	each
type 4	each
type 5	each
DOORS:	
type 1	each
type 2	each
type 3	each
type 4	each
LOCKSETS:	
type 1	each
type 2	each
type 3	each
skylights	each
OVERHANGS AND CORNICES:	
fascia	linear foot
soffit	square foot
lookouts	linear foot
frieze	linear foot
louver grill	each
SIDING:	
plywood panels	square (1 square = 100 square feet)
vertical	linear foot
horizontal	linear foot
shingles	square
ROOFING:	
shingles	square
ridge cap	linear foot

Item	Unit
rake edge	linear foot
drip edge	linear foot
BUILT-UP ROOFING:	
felt	square foot
asphalt	gallon
gravel	cubic yard
flashing	linear foot
leaders	linear foot
gutters	linear foot
fittings	each

Quantity × unit price = total.

Fireplaces and Chimneys

Before doing the take-off for fireplaces and chimneys, make sure that you have included the foundation work necessary for them in the foundation take-off.

Item	Unit
BRICK, BLOCK, OR STONE:	square foot (or number of units)
facing brick	square foot
firebrick	square foot
MORTAR:	
cement	bag
lime	bag
sand	cubic foot
concrete (for hearth base)	cubic yard
reinforcing bars	linear foot
plywood (for formwork)	square foot
ash pit unit	each
fire clay collar	each
flue lining	linear foot
metal shields	square foot
damper	each
lintel	each
grout	bag
flashing	linear foot
insulating material	square foot
waterproof paper	square foot
caulking	tube

Quantity × unit price = total.

Mechanical Systems

It is very difficult to estimate the quantities required for the mechanical installations. Although the major components such as fixtures, boilers, switches, and outlets could easily be recorded from the plans, the lengths of cable, piping, or ductwork are hard to calculate. The twists and turns a pipe might need to travel between two fixtures are tough to pinpoint. Because of this problem, general contractors, more often than not, give their mechanical plans to their supplier. The supplier does the material take-off in return for a sale. A wealth of applicable rules of thumb has been developed over years of experience.

Plumbers and electricians have done so many installations that without much difficulty they can estimate the quantities from your drawings—if they are being hired to do the job. Otherwise, the problem is all yours.

If you are doing business with a particular supplier, don't hesitate to approach him to see whether he's willing to do the take-off. If he won't, you have no choice but to attempt to do it yourself and hope that your calculations are reasonably accurate.

PLUMBING: Riser diagrams come in handy to estimate the length of pipe and the number of fittings you may require. Study them carefully together with your plans while doing the take-off.

Item	Unit
PIPING:	
drainage	linear foot
venting	linear foot
disposal	linear foot
SUPPLY:	
aboveground	linear foot
underground	linear foot
pipe adapter (if required)	each
fittings	each
valves	each
drains	each
FAUCETS:	
indoor	each
outdoor	each
septic tank	each
distribution box	each
EFFLUENT FIELD:	
tile	linear foot
cesspool	each
drywell	each

Item	Unit
water heater	each
water treatment equipment	each
grease trap (optional)	each
well pump	each
FIXTURES:	
bathtub (with fittings)	each
shower (with fittings)	each
lavatory (with fittings)	each
sink (with fittings)	each
water closet	each
MISCELLANEOUS:	
pipe hangers	each
roofing nails	pound
putty	quart
insulation (if required)	square foot
solder compound (for copper pipes)	spool
flux (for copper piping)	can
oakum (for cast-iron piping)	coil
solvent (for plastic piping)	can

Quantity × unit price = total.

HEATING: Many of the materials required for a hydronic heating system are similar to those used for plumbing.

Item	Unit
Hydronic heating	
piping	linear foot
valves	each
fittings	each
baseboard units	linear foot
thermostats	each
boiler	each
smoke pipe	linear foot
Forced-air system	
furnace	each
smoke pipe	linear foot
supply-air registers	each
return-air grills	each
pipes	linear foot
ducts	linear foot
fittings	each
thermostats	each
volume dampers	each

Quantity × unit price = total.

ELECTRICITY: The calculation of switches, outlets, doorbells, intercoms, etc., is very simple. They are counted right off the plans. Estimating the length of cable, however, is trickier. Perhaps it is best handled by showing your plans to the electrical supplier. Most likely he can estimate from the house's square footage and the amount of electrical work you plan to do approximately the length of cable you'll need. Electrical cable is sold in coils 250' in length.

Item	Unit
CABLE:	
type 1	linear foot
type 2	linear foot
DEVICES:	
standard duplex outlets	each
high-voltage outlets	each
weatherproof receptacles	each
lighting outlets	each
SWITCHES:	
two-way	each
three-way	each
four-way	each
front doorbell	each
intercom	each
service panel	each
BOXES:	
switch boxes	each
outlet boxes	each
junction boxes	each
FASTENING METHODS:	
box hanger	each
straps	each
cable connectors	each
finish plates	each

Quantity × unit price = total.

Interior Finishes

	Item	Unit
Gypsum board	panels	each
	backer board panels	each
	joint tape	linear foot
	joint compound	gallon
	annular ring nails	pound
Wood-strip flooring	wood strips	linear foot
	plywood or particle board underlayment	square foot
	flooring nails	pound
	building paper	square foot
	baseboard	linear foot
	molding	linear foot
Resilient tile	resilient tile	square foot
	adhesive	gallon
	baseboard	linear foot
Carpeting	carpet	square yards
	padding	square yards
	nailing strips	linear foot
	nails	pound
Ceramic tile	ceramic tile	square foot
	adhesive	gallon
	grout	bag
	silicone grout sealer	tube
Applied finishes	PAINT	
	type 1	gallon
	type 2	gallon
	type 3	gallon
	PRIMER SEALER	
	type 1	gallon
	type 2	gallon
	type 3	gallon
	wallpaper	
	wallpaper	square foot
	adhesive	gallon
	acoustical tile	
	tile	square foot
	adhesive	gallon

Quantity × unit price = total.

FINANCING

We do not in any way purport to be experts in the area of financing. We, therefore, direct you to those who can readily inform you on the ins and outs of the local money market, your friendly neighborhood bankers. Information on the financing of your home is easy to obtain; financing is not. Although most of the banks in and near your area will be glad to talk to you about the house you plan to build, not all of them will be eager to finance the project. We attempt here to present an introduction to the subject of owner-built financing and to explain some of the procedures and hazards you may face.

When a person walks into a bank and requests a mortgage (Inset I) on a house he has seen in the neighborhood and wishes to buy, the bank makes a decision on whether to provide him with a loan to finance the purchase based on the following criteria:

People usually purchase houses with money borrowed from banks in the form of mortgage loans. A mortgage loan is a collateral loan in which the house and property are put up as security in case the borrower defaults on his payments. If the payments are not met, the lending institution forecloses on the property (gains title to it) and, usually, resells it to the highest bidder. From the amount of sale the bank pays itself the money it is owed, pays any workmen who have liens (unpaid debts) against the property, and if anything is left, pays the former owner the remainder. Foreclosing on a house is not common, so don't let that fear loom heavy over your head. It costs banks a lot of money and time to foreclose on a house, and they are usually very considerate about overdue monthly payments. If for some reason you cannot keep up with the payments on the house, the bank will probably encourage you to sell the house yourself, and will allow you the time to get a fair price. Most foreclosures made today are on deserted property.

The majority of mortgage loans are amortized. In an amortized loan you borrow the principal (the amount of money the bank lends you) but pay back principal and interest.

Let us say that you are going to borrow $10,000 from the bank. This is the amount of the loan—the principal. The rate of interest, let us say, is 10 percent. The term, or duration of the loan, is twenty years.

An amortized loan is paid back in equal monthly payments: 20 years × 12 months = 240 payments.

The interest on the loan is more difficult to compute. Every month you will pay the same amount to the bank. Part of that amount will be paying back the principal, and part will be paying back the interest. The interest on the loan is computed on the basis of how much is left to pay back on the principal. In the first year you will pay the bank mostly interest and very little principal. The next year's amount of interest will be calculated on the amount of principal left. The second year (although you will be paying the same amount each month) more of that money will be credited toward principal and less of it will be interest. Each year you are buying back proportionately more of your house from the bank.

Added to the monthly payment will be the tax bill. Most banks prefer to collect the taxes and make the payments for you annually or semiannually rather than have you pay the tax collector directly.

In addition to simple amortized loans made by banks there are special benefits for veterans and specially insured FHA mortgages, which may reduce the rate of interest or allow you to borrow a higher percentage of the purchase price.

A word about points. During some years, when money is very tight, banks make you pay a premium for the privilege of borrowing money from them. Points are percentage points above and beyond the rate of interest. They can be a whole or half or less of a percentage point. For instance, if you are borrowing $10,000 the bank might make you give them an advance of 1 percent, or $100, before it would lend you any money.

1. The bank has the money available and wishes to lend it out on mortgage loans.

2. The bank knows the area, has determined that the neighborhood is in good shape, and that the investment is a sound one.

3. The bank will determine the worth of the house and land. The bank is not likely to lend 100 percent of the value of the property. In fact, the government will not permit the lender to do so. Most banks have their own formulas for determining the percentage of the purchase that they will finance. For instance, some banks demand that the borrower supply 25 percent of the asking price and the bank will provide the remaining 75 percent. The lender is eager for the investor to have as large a piece of the pie as possible. This way the investor will not run out on his debt, or let the collateral (the house) run down.

   If the house and the land cost less than the bank's appraisal, the lenders might still stick to the maximum of 75 percent of the purchase price. (Although it does not concern us directly, some banks will lend a higher percentage for newer homes and a lower percentage for older houses. For example, they might only lend up to two-thirds of the purchase price on a house more than forty years old.)

4. The bank knows the prospective borrower. It will investigate his or her earning potential to determine whether the borrower will be able to keep up with the mortgage payments. It will set a maximum on how much it will lend based on how much it feels the borrower will be able to afford to pay in monthly payments. For example, some banks will double the yearly salaries of the working adults in the family* and will set that figure as a maximum loan. For instance, if the husband and wife each earn $10,000 (yearly total of $20,000) the bank might fix a maximum of $40,000 for the loan, even if the house costs much more than that.

   It is irrelevant that the cost of the house (and its appraised value) is $80,000, and that 75 percent of that is $60,000. Mitigating circumstances, such as an inheritance or large holdings in the

---

* Many laws have recently been passed to end discrimination by the banks on the basis of race, religion, color, sex, or age. Be sure to check into the new legislation if you are having trouble. For instance, at one time the banks would only extend a mortgage based on the earning power of the man, even if his wife worked full time and earned as much as he did. This is no longer permitted. The banks must consider the income of the wife just as they consider the husband's income, even if she is of child-bearing age.

stock market, may swing the bank in favor of making the larger loan, but under ordinary circumstances, the bank will set a maximum on how much it will lend based on how much it feels the potential debtor will be able to repay.

5. There is one more factor that may or may not be the policy of the banks in your area, and that is the setting of a maximum loan. One bank in New York State will not lend any individual who is purchasing a home for himself more than $50,000, no matter what his earning power or the value of the property.

When you are building your own house, although all of the above conditions still hold true, more rules are added to the game. For instance, since the bank cannot look at the house to see its worth, it will have to evaluate the house plans and specifications carefully to determine the value of the finished product. Secondly, savings banks (the major home mortgagers) are not allowed to give construction loans to anyone unless the land is owned free and clear.

Before a savings bank will consider your application, you must be the owner of the property. The bank is not permitted by law to extend a loan to you on unimproved land (land without a house on it). It will, however, be able to extend a construction loan based on the cost of the house plus the cost of the property once the land is in the possession of the builder. There is a catch to all of this. Let us say that the estimated cost of the entire project is $40,000; the land cost $15,000. You have $10,000 in your savings account. The bank has looked over your plans and is willing to give you a construction loan of $30,000. All would seem well, but the bank will not approve the loan until you have purchased the property. You still need an additional $5,000 to buy it.

This additional amount can be obtained in one of three ways: 1. You can borrow it from a member of your family and promise to return it when the bank gives you your construction loan. 2. You can borrow the amount from a commercial bank. This loan must be a signature loan and not a collateral loan. (If the collateral for the loan is the property itself, you will not have free and clear title to it and the savings bank cannot give you a mortgage on it.) 3. The most popular means of financing the land purchase is through the seller. The land owner himself might lend you the money for the purchase of the land by asking you to make a down-

payment (in this case $10,000) on the signing of the contract, and pay the remaining amount ($5,000) in installments over a few months or years. The purchaser receives use of the property on the signing of the contract and receives the deed to it when the installments are completed.

This type of private loan is not a primary collateral loan with the property put up as security against default. If you are seeking a construction mortgage from a savings bank, the seller must agree that his financing of the land purchase is in the form of a secondary or subordinate mortgage. In other words, if the house or partially constructed house is foreclosed (that is, you find that you are unable to make the payments and the bank takes over the property) the primary mortgage holder, the bank, gets paid first, and the subordinate lender, the original land owner, gets paid after the bank's debt is satisfied.

There is another catch to borrowing money on a house you intend to build yourself. Most banks are a bit leery of lending to people who intend to either build a house themselves, or to G.C.* the job, unless that person has considerable experience in the trade. They explain that often the layman who is serving as his own general contractor is not able to schedule the job properly. This causes a number of potential problems. One cited is that the job often takes longer than is necessary and that the work might extend past the loan period (usually three months to a year). The second potential problem is that things get done out of sequence. The walls are lathed and plastered before the building inspector gets to check the electricity. Or worse, something that should be in the wall is left out. Surely these are extreme cases, but they must occur often enough to frighten the banks. An additional problem is that the owner-builder might be tempted to purchase items that were not in his original specifications but that he feels like adding once construction is under way. These items might include paneled doors instead of hollow flush doors, or better floor tile, or more expensive windows. In such a case the bank may have extended more than half its funds when the house is only one-third built. Thus, the banks are leery of extending a loan to a build-it-yourselfer equal to the percentage they would make available to someone who

* Administrate all aspects of construction without actually doing the labor.

wants to purchase an already standing home of equal value.

The banks' prejudice seems to be based on a collective bad experience. Be that as it may, it is difficult to argue with them, especially if you are not an experienced house builder. Be prepared for the bank to offer to finance only 50 or 60 percent of the finished cost. You may, however, need less money than would a professional general contractor since you are going to do most of the work yourself and he has to pay for labor.

An additional catch to the land and house financing game is the way the bank plans to authorize the construction payments, once having approved the construction loan. First of all, you will receive no money in advance. The bank will write you a check for 25 percent of the amount it has agreed to lend you only after 25 percent of the house has been built. When you have completed a sizable portion of the work, the bank inspector will come around to determine if enough work has been completed to warrant your first payment.

By the way, this same procedure is followed in commercial construction. The contractor has a schedule of payments. When about one-fourth of the work is finished, he will call the architect on the job to inspect that portion of the work. If the architect is satisfied that the work the contractor has said he has done is completed, he will authorize the owner to pay the contractor the percentage of the fee due him. The contractor does not get paid in advance and has to arrange credit with his subcontractors and material suppliers.

Where you will get the money for the first few loads of materials is considered your problem and not the bank's. It is possible to arrange personal credit at the lumberyard and with other local suppliers if you are established in the area and have a good credit rating locally.

Most banks will make four payments: 1. 25 percent after 25 percent of the work is completed; 2. 25 percent after half of the job is completed; 3. 40 percent when all the work is completed; and 4. 10 percent after the certificate of occupancy has been issued.

The Procedure

Although the bank or lending company personnel will be extremely helpful to you, it is important that you come to them with some basic knowledge about what you want, how much it will cost, and the feasibility of your plans. It is wise to observe the following general guidelines:

1. Have the plans and specifications ready. You will have to leave a copy with the lending institution, so be prepared to do so. If you have done a materials and labor take-off, be prepared to give the bank your estimate of the cost of the project.

2. The bank will be interested in you, what you do for a living, and how much you earn. If you are going to do most, if not all, of the labor yourself they will be interested in your former experience.

3. The bank will also want to know about the land. Bring along a copy of the survey of the land if you have one. For your own sake as well as the bank's, you should have some idea of how much you will have to pay in real estate taxes to the municipality once the house has been built. Do not be misled by the low property taxes on the land itself. Unimproved land is taxed at a very low rate for the most part. A new house on the same parcel of land can easily quadruple the real estate taxes. Remember that each community taxes itself differently. For example, two houses of equal size may be taxed differently, depending on the block where they are located. Try to get an estimate from the tax assessor. He will not be able to give you an exact figure, but at least he can give you a general idea of what your taxes will be.

The bank will be anxious to ascertain that you own the property free and clear. You will need a title search to prove that the people selling the land really own it; that there are no liens or claims against the land by workmen or other people who have not been paid by some previous owner; and that all of the boundaries are correct and there are no easements on the land that you are not aware of.

Your lawyer should arrange the title search for you (for that matter, he should arrange for the purchase of the property). You are also advised to purchase title insurance on the property, which guarantees that the title to the land is clear.

FILING PERMITS

Every community has its own rules and regulations regarding permits to build and building inspections. Some are extremely stringent, others are more lax in their attitudes. For the most part, the health department and the building department are out to protect you, your neighbors, and the environment. If they give you a hard time, try to keep this in mind. Below is a brief outline of the requirements for one semisuburban, semirural township. The neighboring township has very different requirements and, no doubt, so will yours. Make a visit to the health and building departments before finalizing your plans (especially if there may be sewage disposal problems). Ask them precisely for a list of permits and insurance certificates that you may need. Question them as to the number of visits and tours of inspection that will be made, how to contact the inspectors, and what they will expect to find on their tour.

Be aware that the cost of the building permit might be a percentage of the anticipated cost of construction or it might be based on the size of land being covered or the volume of the structures. (The size of the house and the probable cost of construction will most likely be the basis for the real estate evaluation yet to come.)

Sample Community's Procedure for Filing and Inspections

BEFORE FILING

1. You will need a preliminary o.k. from the building department regarding the sanitary disposal system.
2. You will need a preliminary o.k. from the local planning board as to the zoning requirements and water drainage.
3. You may require a preliminary o.k. from a community board on the aesthetic design of the house, or have to demonstrate that the design conforms with the character of the neighborhood.

FOR FILING

Approach the building department with the following:

1. Preliminary o.k. from the health department and the planning board.
2. Two sets of plans (if your house is over 1,500 square feet, these plans must bear the stamp of a registered architect or engineer).
3. A blank check for the permit fee, which will be based on the number of square feet of the proposed building.

DURING CONSTRUCTION

If everything proceeds smoothly and all work is done properly so as not to require multiple visits by the building inspector, a minimum of three inspections will be made.

1. The foundation inspection is made after the concrete is poured and before the waterproofing and backfilling.
2. The rough carpentry inspection is done after all the structural framing is completed, sheathing installed, rough plumbing and electricity done, in fact, everything that goes in before the wallboard is installed to cover the stud spaces.
3. The final inspection is made to check the plumbing, electricity, etc.

IN ADDITION

1. You will need a visit from the board of fire underwriters, who must be contacted separately. In this community you cannot get a C.O. (certificate of occupancy) without certification from the board of fire underwriters attesting to the safety of the electrical installation. (You probably will need this certificate to get fire insurance on the house as well.)
2. The health department will want to look at the cesspools.
3. The planning board will be concerned with the water drainage from your site onto your neighbors'.
4. The tax assessor will take particular interest in your house and land. Expect a visit.

PART THREE: CONSTRUCTION

An Introduction to Construction

You are now on the threshold of what could be one of the most gratifying experiences of your life. The path, however is fraught with potential frustrations, disappointments, and construction accidents. To hold these to a minimum (or eliminate them completely) we offer the following advice. The list is compiled by the experts, who have been through it all. Happily, you can profit from their mistakes. Study the list and memorize it. It may save you much time and anxiety, and perhaps your life.

1. The evening before plunging into a day's work, pore over the construction plans of the job ahead of you. Familiarize yourself with the details and be sure that you understand what is required in each step of the procedure. If you have any questions, call an experienced friend, build a model of the questionable area, or consult your reference books for a solution. Don't expect the problem to resolve itself the next day. It probably won't. At best you will be wasting valuable daylight hours pondering, at worst you may have to rip out half a day's work to remedy a mistake.

2. Make sure you have all the materials and tools you will need for the day's work. It is frustrating to have to stop work to search for a missing item. At such a time the temptation is great to substitute an inferior or ill-suited item for the one you are missing—a bad construction practice.

3. Be sure you have read and provided for all the safety admonitions in this book and in the instruction booklets of all power tools. Remind yourself that people lose fingers by removing safety guards, and their lives by ignoring grounding rules.

4. Never drink on the job or work when you are intoxicated. A high can make you feel like you are superman or superwoman—that you can work longer, harder, and faster than you ever worked before. This is the best way we know to hurt yourself. Besides, in the morning you will probably judge the work to be sloppy.

5. Don't work where or when it is too dark to see.

6. Don't work when you are exhausted or dizzy from the heat. Aside from the fact that it is dangerous to use hand or power tools or to climb ladders when you are not super-alert, it will also ruin you for the next day's work.

7. Keep work areas clean. It is very easy to slip on accumulated debris and sawdust. Often the wind sweeps unattached materials and debris onto the heads of workers and passersby.

8. Don't use power equipment in wet or damp areas. Keep tools stored in dry, safe places when not in use.

9. Use safety glasses when using power saws. Do not wear loose clothing, necklaces, or long hair that might get caught in the machinery.

19
Site Preparation

You have already considered all the alternatives involved in your house design. The variables have been evaluated and both the house and site plan are now ready. Construction is about to begin.

LAYING OUT THE BUILDING

Laying out the building on the property is the first step in the construction process—a very important step. We cannot overemphasize this, since any error made at this point will interfere with every succeeding job. Inaccuracies in the measurements of the building walls or the angles at corners will manifest themselves in all other construction work. In addition, mistakes relating to the location of the house on the property, such as being too close to a property line or violating any code restriction, will eventually cost you time and money to rectify.

There are various methods of laying out. One is with the use of a transit. This method, although the most accurate, requires learning all aspects of operating a transit. We have chosen instead the layout square method. It provides the degree of accuracy necessary for a small building and it is very simple. This method requires both the use of a layout square and a builder's level.

MATERIALS

The materials and tools required for laying out are not particularly difficult to come by or sophisticated to operate. As a matter of fact, many of them you can easily construct.

You will need the following materials:

- 2" × 2" stakes approximately 2'-0" to 4'-0" long
- 2" × 4" stakes approximately 3'-0" to 4'-0" long
- 1" × 6" boards approximately 4'-0" to 10'-0" long
- Eightpenny nails (8d)
- A mason line
- Weights (bricks will do)

(Some of these materials will be employed in the construction of tools such as the layout square.)

TOOLS

Two types of tools are needed: tools necessary for laying out and those used for excavation.

The following is a list of layout tools. For a description of each tool and explanation of its use, refer to the Glossary of Tools at the end of the book.

- Layout square (see Inset II)
- Plumb line with plumb bob
- Carpenter's, or spirit, level

A number of skills must be mastered in order to successfully lay out a building.

First and most obvious is measuring. Taking accurate measurements is essential. We are certainly not going to give you an explanation of how to measure. We trust you have done it at some time or another. This time, be accurate.

A second skill is the construction and use of the layout square. Both these procedures are described in Inset II.

In addition to measuring and using the layout square, you must learn one basic operation of the builder's level. Select the location where the readings will be taken and firmly set up the tripod. Work the points well into the ground. The tripod head should be adjusted until it appears to be level. Place the builder's level on the tripod head, screwing it firmly. Level the instrument with the use of the four leveling screws (Ill. I-1). The bubble should be lined up with the marking. Once the bubble is centered, turn the telescope 90 degrees until it sits over the other set of leveling screws and level it again. Check leveling over each pair of screws. The in-strument is level when you can turn it completely around without disturbing the bubble. You are now ready to start sighting. Make sure not to bump into or touch the tripod.

When you look through the telescope, you will see two lines intersecting at right angles, known as cross hairs (Ill. I-2). An assistant, holding the rod, will be standing at the point you want to get a reading on, holding the folding rule perfectly vertical (check by using the carpenter's level). The bottom of the rule should be resting on the ground. Rotate the level until you see the desired point. Focus the image. The cross hairs will intersect the rule at one specified height—that's the reading. To take readings on other points, keep the level fixed in its original location. Sight the new points by rotating the level.

Other skills such as hammering, driving stakes, pulling nails, sawing wood, and so on, will also be employed in the layout process. They are tasks we have all done at some time or another. We strongly advise that whenever using any skills, whether they are old or new to you, you follow all safety measures and manufacturer's directions; exercise good judgment and, above all, be careful.

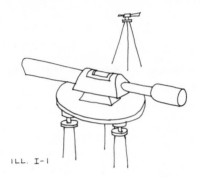

ILL. I-1

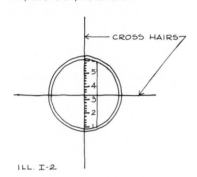

CROSS HAIRS

ILL. I-2

- Line level
- Claw hammer
- Hatchet
- Crosscut saw
- 6'-0" and 100'-0" metallic tapemeasures
- Builder's level
- Folding rule

The remaining tools are for excavation:

- Shovel
- Pick

You could, of course, do all the required excavation by means of a pick and shovel. However, excavating is an exhausting, time-consuming, and tedious project. Unless you are either totally unable to finance it, or completely committed in principle to doing everything yourself, it seems more logical to hire a bulldozer or power shovel with an operator for leveling and excavating. Let him dig the footings and trenches. You in turn can save your energy for more creative tasks. If you still have your heart set on doing some excavation, don't worry. There's enough hard trimming of edges that will remain to be done. A few suggestions about excavating by hand. Always remember to pick the soil loose before shoveling and try to mix excavation with other tasks. Build your excavation ability gradually. A day of heavy shoveling could turn into a week in bed with aching muscles.

LOCATING THE BUILDING CORNERS AND CLEARING THE SITE

You should now have a reasonable idea of the materials and tools necessary for laying out the house. We must point out once again that the process itself is not difficult. The accuracy of your work, however, is essential to the successful outcome of the building. If precise measurement is something that you are notoriously not proficient at, we suggest you subcontract this facet of the building process to a competent professional.

INSET II / HOW TO CONSTRUCT A LAYOUT SQUARE

A layout square is essentially a gigantic 90-degree wood triangle. In order to build it, you need three perfectly straight wood boards approximately 1" × 4" or 1" × 6" and 10'-0" to 12'-0" in length. Take two boards and carefully square off the ends. Make a lap joint at one end. This is done by making identical notches at the end of each board to half the depth of the wood. The pieces are then fitted together and nailed, screwed, or glued to each other. Then proceed as follows (Ill. II-1):

- Take board 1, measure 6'-0" along it, and mark it.
- Take board 2, measure 8'-0", and mark it.
- Take board 3, measure 10'-0", and mark it.
- Place board 1 on the ground.
- Place board 2 on top of board 1, joining the lapped ends.
- Place board 3 on top of boards 1 and 2, joining the 6'-0" and 8'-0" markings.
- Fasten with nails.

- Notch at point P to allow for the dimension of the corner stake.

To use the layout square, place one of its legs directly under the stretched mason's line. The notched end fits around the stake. Check for perfect alignment by means of a plumb bob. The adjacent leg will indicate where the next line should be located to obtain a right-angled corner (Ill. II-2).

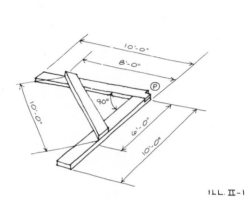

ILL. II-1

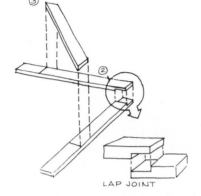

LAP JOINT

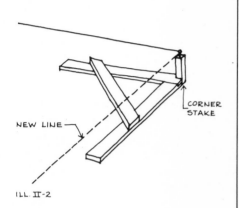

NEW LINE

CORNER STAKE

ILL. II-2

The surveyor* handed you a plot plan. In addition, he should have placed short stakes in the earth indicating the exact corners of your property. The various criteria affecting the siting of the house have been considered (Chapter 3) and you have drawn a site plan. Before you start clearing the site, you should post a grading, building permit, or any other required license needed to start work on your property on a tree close to the street or road. Even though it is desirable to maintain as much of the existing plant growth on the property as possible some clearing of bushes or underbrush from the building site will be necessary. Clean the site of any roots, stumps, and tree limbs and remove any debris such as rocks or blocks of wood. Be sure to remove any underground wood, which may eventually cause termite problems.

The approximate building site should be located by taking rough measurements from the property line. Be particularly careful about clearing this area. Check for any electric wire or conduit that might have remained underground from a previous electric power connection. Make sure any old installation is dead. It is also advisable to check with the local building authorities for any old plumbing, gas, or sewer lines that were once part of some now demolished structure that might still be underground. They should be properly capped with the required devices. If the topsoil is of good quality, remove it with a bulldozer for later use in landscaping.

When the site is gently sloping, such as our sample site, creating a level platform at the approximate location of the house is not necessary. If the site has a steep slope, you will need to have the bulldozer operator level off a platform at the estimated building area.

The surveyor's corner stakes come in handy to establish the exact location of the house. Each one of these stakes has a nail or tack at the top

* A surveyor measures land parcels, sets boundaries, and draws up the required site maps.

Site Preparation

231

(approximately at the center), which marks the corners of your property. Stretch a mason's line tightly between the stakes which indicate the front corners of the property. (If they are too low or too hard to see, drive your own stakes a small distance away from his.) Using the front lot line as a guide, the front building line can be found by measuring back into the property the desired distance for the front yard, in our case 120'-0". Our sample house is located parallel to the front lot line. Therefore, with the use of a layout square (see Inset II) we take measurements 120'-0" away from the lot line and at right angles to it. These measurements are taken at two different points along the front lot line and a stake is driven at each (Ill. 1). Make sure that the stakes are carefully pointed—that is, all cuts are at even lengths; otherwise the stakes will twist (Ill. 2).

The next step is to establish the first corner. Measure along the front building line the appropriate distance from the lot line for a side yard. We measure 100'-0". Corner 1 has now been located. Drive a stake at this point (Ill. 3). Starting at corner 1, measure along the front building line the length of the front of the house. We measure 32'-0" and locate corner 2. Again drive a stake at this corner. Check by measuring the opposite side yard to see if that number matches the required footage in the site plan (Ill. 4).

Once the two front corners of the house have been found, we use a layout square to find corners 3 and 4. Place one leg of the square directly underneath line 1–2. The adjacent leg will indicate the perpendicular. Measure along this line about 6'-0" longer than the side dimension of the house. Drive in stake 1A (Ill. 5). Stretch a mason's line between points 1 and 1A. Starting at point 1, measure 24'-0" to find corner 3 and drive a stake (Ill. 6). Repeat this procedure to find the corner 4 (Ills. 7 and 8).

The accuracy of the corners should be checked by measuring the lengths of diagonals 1–4 and 2–3. The diagonals of a perfect rectangle are always equal; should there be any discrepancy, readjust the lines accordingly by repeating the above procedure (Ill. 9).

Make sure to double-check all measurements of the front, side, and rear yards, in addition to checking the lengths of the front, side, and back walls. Don't forget that all other construction is to be based on these first steps! If your house plan is not a simple rectangle, measure off any wings using the lines already established.

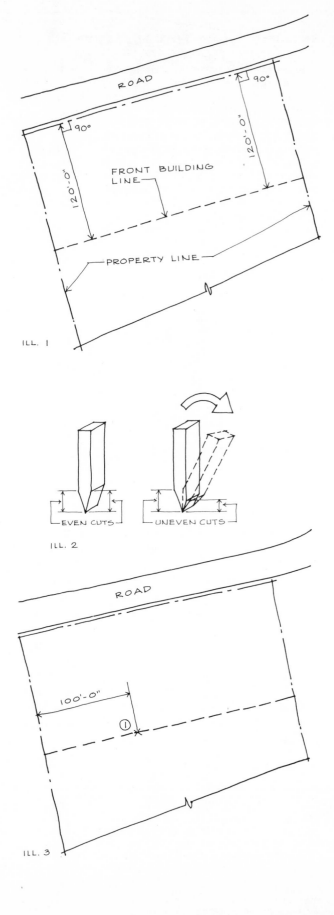

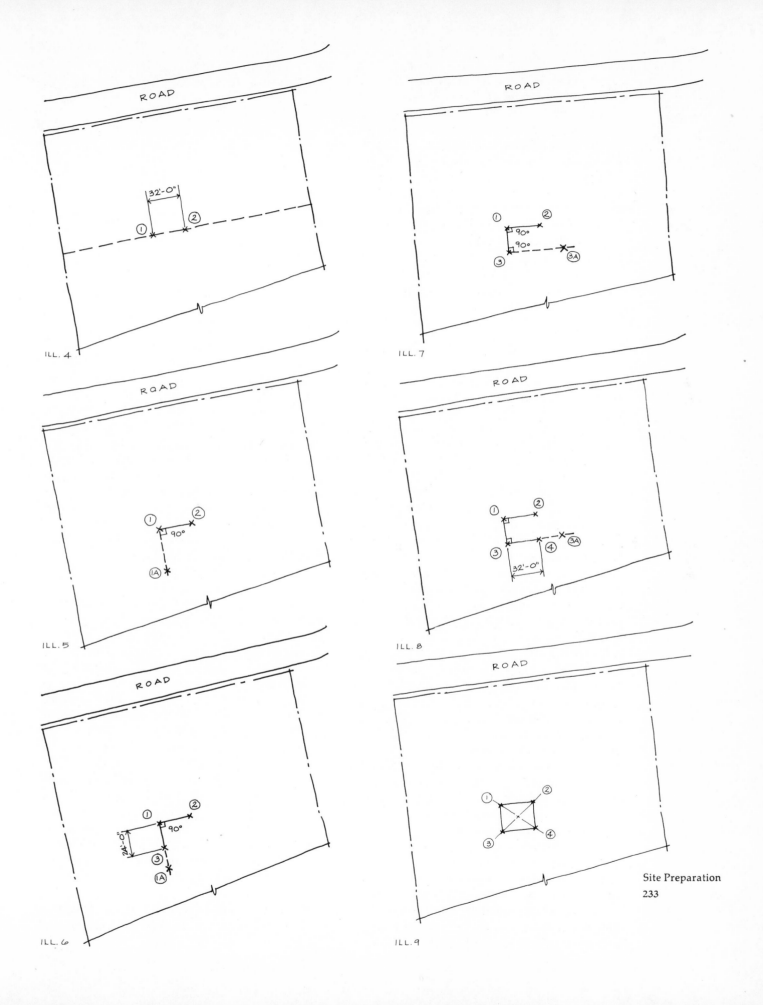

ROAD

32'-0"

① ②

ILL. 4

ROAD

① ②
90°
90°
③ ③A

ILL. 7

ROAD

① ②
90°

①A

ILL. 5

ROAD

① ②

③ ④ ③A
32'-0"

ILL. 8

ROAD

① ②
90°
24'-0"
③
①A

ILL. 6

ROAD

① ②

③ ④

ILL. 9

Site Preparation
233

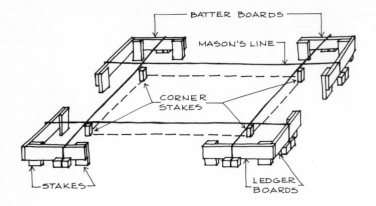

BATTER BOARDS

MASON'S LINE

CORNER STAKES

STAKES

LEDGER BOARDS

ILL. 10

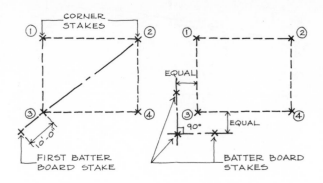

CORNER STAKES

① ② ① ②

EQUAL

③ ④ ③ ④

90°

10'-0"

FIRST BATTER BOARD STAKE

BATTER BOARD STAKES

EQUAL

ILL. 11

ERECTING BATTER BOARDS

We now have four stakes precisely located at the house corners. In our excavations for footings and foundations these stakes will inevitably be in the way and most likely be lost. Remember that footings protrude a minimum of 4" outward from the wall of the house (albeit underground) and that in addition to allowing for the footing projection, we need to allow room in which to construct the footing forms. The excavation should be at least 2' greater than the perimeter of the house. In order to remove the corner stakes prior to construction and still provide for easy location of the corner points, we erect batter boards. These boards frame the corners of the house but stand 4' to 10' back from them, depending on the depth of the excavation (Ill. 10).

Erecting batter boards is a very simple procedure. The verbal explanation, however, tends to be somewhat confusing. We suggest that you refer closely to Illustration 11. For the sample house we have decided to locate the batter boards approximately 6' outside the building lines. The first batter board stake is located directly in line with the building line diagonal. The distance away from the building corner stake should be about 10'. The second and third stakes are driven at right angles to the first, making sure that they are parallel to the building line. They should be located past the building corner, as shown in Illustration 11. We are now almost ready to nail the ledger boards to the stakes. Before doing this, the elevation of the top of the foundation wall must be determined.

Batter boards are useful not only to maintain the building corners but also to act as guides in establishing the height above grade of the foundation wall. In general practice, this is done by choosing the building corner that falls on the highest elevation and adding to its elevation the required height above grade for the top of the foundation wall (Ill. 12). (This height is generally 1' above grade, but may vary according to geographical location or local codes.)

The builder's level is used in conjunction with the batter boards to establish the correct elevation of the foundation wall at all building corners (Inset I). Place the level at a high point on the site from which you can see all batter board stakes. Locate the instrument and take a rod reading at the corner stake representing the highest elevation. In our case it is corner stake 4 (Ills. 12 and 13). This reading indicates the length of the rule beneath the site line. At corner stake 4 the reading from the cross hairs to grade is 5'-0". The top of the foundation wall is to be located at 1'-0" above grade. The difference between the reading (5'-0") and the height of the foundation wall above grade (1'-0") will be the number we use to locate the elevation at all other corners (4'-0"). Mark the dimension 1'-0" on the first stake, turn the level and take a reading at corner stake 3. A 6' reading indicates that it is 6'-0" to grade. The difference between 6'-0" and 4'-0" gives the correct height of the top of the foundation wall above grade. Make a mark on the stake at a point 4'-0" beneath the sight line (which will be approximately 2'-0" above the earth).

This procedure is repeated at all remaining corners (Ill. 14). The batter board ledgers are

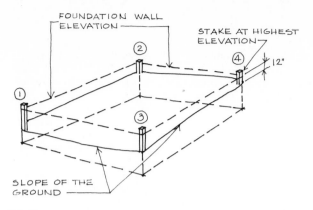

FOUNDATION WALL ELEVATION

STAKE AT HIGHEST ELEVATION

12"

SLOPE OF THE GROUND

ILL. 12

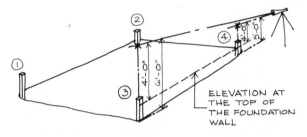

ELEVATION AT THE TOP OF THE FOUNDATION WALL

ILL. 13

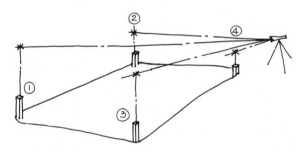

ILL. 14

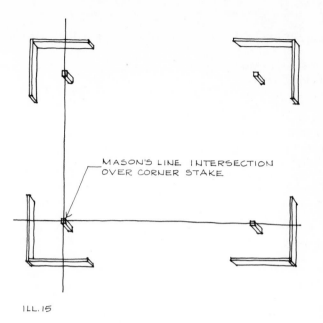

MASON'S LINE INTERSECTION OVER CORNER STAKE

ILL. 15

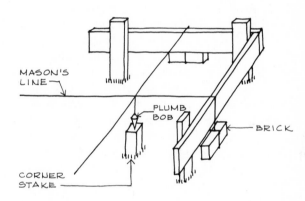

MASON'S LINE

PLUMB BOB

BRICK

CORNER STAKE

ILL. 16

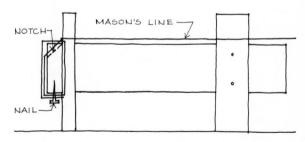

NOTCH

MASON'S LINE

NAIL

ILL. 17

then nailed to the stakes with the tops flush with the elevation mark. With the aid of a carpenter's level, check the top of the ledger boards, making sure that they are level.

Locating the building lines on the batter boards is done by stretching a mason's line between batter boards at right angles to each other (Ill. 15). The mason's lines are kept in place by attaching them to bricks (Ill. 16). The lines are adjusted with a plumb bob until they intersect directly over the tack on the corner stake (Ill. 16). Mark the location of the mason's line along the batter board and cut a notch on it. Place the line on the notch, wrapping it around the ledger board a few times and tie it to a nail (Ill. 17). Check the line for levelness by using a line level. The corner building stakes can now be removed.

Site Preparation
235

A few tips on the excavation of sewage trenches and septic tank holes.

The depth for the septic tank hole is important. It should provide a downward pitch from the house sewer to the tank of 1 percent minimum and preferably 2 percent; that is, ⅛" per foot, or ¼" per foot. Otherwise sewage material might get stuck, clogging the pipe. (The pitch should not exceed ¼" per foot. A steeper pitch makes the liquids flow too fast to carry along the solids.) You don't have to worry much about the frost line. Bacterial action tends to keep the temperature above freezing.

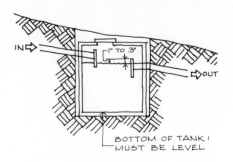

It is important that the bottom of the tank be level, since the outlet pipe is approximately 1" to 3" lower than the inlet pipe. Any slope at the bottom of the tank can alter this relationship causing backflow of sewage (left).

The trenches holding the pipes from the tank to the distribution box should be deep enough to seal the pipe and at approximately the same pitch as those mentioned earlier. Make sure to check your local codes. They are usually very specific as to the septic tank, sewage trenches, and disposal field requirements. (Refer to Chapter 26 for more information on septic tank and sewage trenches.)

Once the building lines have been located, you can mark off the distance along the batter boards to the excavation lines. You should excavate at least 3' out from the actual building lines to allow yourself room to work on the foundations (Ill. 18). Cut notches at this point too, and transfer the mason's line from the building line to the excavation line notch. Using a plumb bob, drive a stake directly under the intersection of the stretched excavation lines. This locates the excavation corners. Remove all lines from the batter boards. You are ready to start the main building excavation.

Note: If you have chosen to build your house on piers, the procedure for locating them is described in Chapter 20.

LOCATING THE UTILITIES

Before proceeding with the excavation, the location of the utilities should be staked out. This way utility trenches can be dug at the same time as the house excavation. If your house is in a municipality that has sewage and water-supply systems, your job is greatly simplified. Once you find out where the connections to the sewer and water main are, all that remains to be done is to find out the required depth for the excavation of the trenches (similarly with the gas and electrical connections). See Inset III.

The house sewer (the pipe bringing sewage out of the house) comes out of the basement or crawl space, or under the basement floor if there are appliances or a boiler room in the cellar (see

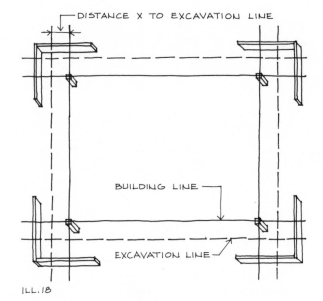

ILL. 18

Chapter 26). Connections to municipal sewers are usually fairly deep because of sewer lines running under the street. Check the local code for regulations. It will probably include details of the procedure to be followed in laying out the sewer line. Local codes generally require the actual connection to the street to be made by an authorized contractor or sewer authorities. Make sure to obtain a copy of the code before work starts. Guesswork can cost you lots of time and money.

The water-supply line must be brought into the house below the frost line (depth to which the ground will freeze). Generally you will be required to lay the supply pipe at a specified depth given to you by the local codes. Water-supply lines are usually let into the house through the basement wall, well below the frost line, and then up through the floor at a distance inward from the walls to prevent freezing. If the crawl space is unheated, insulation must be provided.

Other utilities such as gas and electricity also have to be located. If gas is available in your area, connection to the main will probably have to be done by a gas company representative. Find out from the gas company where the gas main is and how deep the trench should be. As for electricity, chances are that it will be coming through overhead cables. If this is not the case, find out the location of the connection to the power source and the necessary trench depth.

When your house is located in an area without any utilities, you must provide your own. In the case of our sample house, we need a septic tank and a well. The first step is to stake out the location of the septic tank and well on the site (see Chapter 26).

First let's consider the septic tank. Once the size and type have been selected, find out from the manufacturer the dimensions and weight of the tank. You need the size to establish the dimensions of the excavation and the weight to figure out how to lower it into position (sometimes a manufacturer does this). Stake out the four corners indicating the area to be excavated. Refer to Inset II for tips.

For the well, there's not much you can do other than to hire a well driller. He will provide you with information regarding pump selection and freezing protection methods that have been successful in that area. It is advisable to drill the well before beginning construction in the event that the first drill is unsuccessful and the well has to be relocated to a different spot. In addition, water availability is important during the construction process to mix mortar, concrete, etc.

Gas will most likely be unavailable in most suburban and rural areas. Electric power will have to be brought onto the site with an overhead or underground connection and installed by a licensed electrician.

EXCAVATION

You can now instruct the bulldozer or power shovel operator to start excavating. In cold areas the depth below grade of the footing depends on the frost line (see page 120, Inset I). The ground expands when it freezes causing foundations that are not secured by footings placed below the frost line to move, thus damaging the house. Local codes or building authorities can tell you the depth of the frost line in your particular area.

The main house excavation can be handled by either a bulldozer or a power shovel. Because power shovels have various attachments (such as a backhoe), they can do a more accurate job than bulldozers. This means in return less trimming and hand work for you to do. In addition, they can excavate trenches.

A word on safety. When trimming trenches by hand, installing pipes, or doing any work involving digging, try to keep the following things in mind. Earth is often unpredictable. Sometimes a bank that looks safe will cave in on you. A few warning signs to look for are cracks along the surface of the earth on top of the trenches, or earth trickling down a bank. Your best bet is to brace the excavation with boards placed vertically along the bank of the trench. In addition, throw any excavated material way back. Don't pile it close to the trenches. If you decide not to use bracing, at least slope the banks as much as possible, particularly on loose soil. Finally, it's not a good idea to let excavations stand idle for days. Install all work that goes in the excavations promptly. Rain or wind can set off a slide.

20 Foundations

In this chapter we gradually work our way out of the ground and into areas where the building progress can be more easily appreciated. Chances are that some minor excavation work still remains to be done. The bulk of the excavation, however, should be complete since the next job is building the foundations. It is at this stage that the construction work starts to literally look up. Foundation building is not an easy task. Remember that the rest of the house must sit on these foundations. It is most important to measure and build them accurately to ensure the house a good solid base.

MATERIALS

The materials will vary according to the type of foundation to be built. Since poured concrete footings are common to all foundation types, we will start with a list of the materials needed for the footings. They are:

- 2″ × 8″, 2″ × 10″, or 2″ × 12″ footing forms, depending on the footing size; length to suit
- 2″ × 2″ or 2″ × 4″ stakes; length to suit
- Ready-mixed concrete (if mixing your own, see Inset II; for directions on estimating quantities, see page 72, Inset V).
- Nails
- ½″ or ¾″ diameter deformed (non-smooth) reinforcing steel bars (or as required by code)

The formwork for cast-in-place walls will require:

- Prefabricated all-metal or wood-metal forms, or
- Homemade forms: ¾″ plywood, 2 × 4's, wall ties and spreaders
- Nails
- Concrete nails
- Form oil
- Anchor bolts, nuts, and washers (½″ thick and 12″ to 18″ long)
- Reinforcing steel bars (same as for footings)

For concrete-block walls, you will need:

- Concrete blocks (stretchers, corners, and a few sash blocks)
- Mortar (see Inset III)
- Anchor bolts (same as above)
- Horizontal joint steel reinforcement (for stack bond walls)

In addition, if you are building a full basement of either wall type you will need:

- Electric conduit, outlets, and switch boxes
- Pipes for the plumbing system

(Refer to the chapters on plumbing and electricity for further information.)

The materials needed for waterproofing the foundation walls are:

- Tar or black asphalt
- Builder's felt (if installing membrane waterproofing)
- Drainage tile or perforated black plastic pipe
- Tarpaper
- Gravel or crushed stone

INSET I / BASIC SKILLS

In foundation construction as in most other building processes, accurate measuring and leveling of all work is essential to the successful outcome of the building. Other skills that need to be mastered are:

Mixing mortar (Inset III).

Building forms, unless you are planning to rent them (Insets IV and V).

Laying concrete block (Insets VII, VIII, and IX).

Mixing concrete, if you are not able to use ready-mix concrete (Inset II).

INSET II / HOW TO MIX CONCRETE

Concrete can be hand or power mixed. Hand mixing involves lots of work and muscle if you are dealing with large quantities. Whenever you are mixing more than 1 cubic yard, you are better off using a concrete mixer.

Proportions of concrete ingredients (for trial batch): (You are advised to consult the supplier for his suggestions on the correct proportions for your specific use.)

1. For foundation walls that need not be watertight (for crawl spaces)

   • 6 gallons of water (We assume that the sand is moderately damp. If the sand is wet use less water.)
   • 1 bag of cement
   • 2½ to 3 cubic feet of sand

   • approximately 4 cubic feet of stone aggregate (no piece larger than 1½″)

2. For foundations that must be watertight (for example, a basement wall)

   • 5 to 5½ gallons of water (assuming moderately damp sand)
   • 1 bag of cement
   • 2 to 2½ cubic feet of sand
   • 3 cubic feet of stone (no piece larger than 1½″)

Hand mixing: To mix concrete, you need a large watertight platform or a narrow mixing box. The platform should be no smaller than 10′ × 10′ with tight joints. It should also be well supported and level. Place the measured amount of sand on the platform and spread it out evenly. On the sand, spread the correct quantity of cement. Turn the sand and cement with a shovel until they are of a uniform color. To this mixture, add the coarse aggregate. Mix the three ingredients until the aggregate is well distributed. The water is now added by forming a depression in the center of the dry ingredients. Turn the materials as the water is being added. Continue mixing until all the ingredients are thoroughly combined.

Power mixing: A power mixer is a large drum with blades inside, which rotates to mix the contents. You can rent a power mixer at a building supply store. Place all the materials in piles close to the mixer. Start by putting a little water (about 10 percent of the water you must use) in the mixer. While the drum is rotating, gradually add a small amount of each of the ingredients, including the rest of the water.

INSET III / HOW TO MIX MORTAR

Mortar is a mixture of cement, lime, sand, and water. There are various types of mortar with different material contents such as straight-lime or straight-cement mortar. A very popular type is known as masonry cement mortar. This is a mixture of masonry cement, which is manufactured for mixing *only* with sand and water, thus minimizing the variables in the mixing process.

The recommended proportions for mixtures vary with the function of the masonry; for example, mortar mixtures to be used for foundation walls vary from those for nonbearing partition walls. This is the reason why you should always consult the recommendations made by organizations such as the Portland Cement Association or your local building code (which in many instances is very specific about the mortar proportions for various localities). The most widely used proportions are one part of masonry cement to three parts of sand (1:3). If you are using Portland cement, the proportions become one part Portland cement to one-fourth part hydrated lime to three parts sand (1:¼:3).

The water recommendation is trickier. Water increases the workability of a mixture but decreases its strength. The water content should not be such that the mortar slides off the trowel when picked up, or falls off the ends of the brick when laid up. The consistency of the final mixture should not be too soft or too stiff. (You are better off if it is a bit too stiff rather than too wet.)

Mortar can be mixed by hand or with a mixer. The power mixer will save you time and effort, so if possible rent or borrow one. When using a power mixer, start by adding a little water to the drum. Next, add about a third of the sand; then add all the cement (and lime if required). While the machine turns, keep adding the rest of the sand and water until the right consistency is obtained. Once all the ingredients are in, keep mixing for a few more minutes (about three minutes). The total mixing time should come up to about five minutes.

If you can't get hold of a mixer (or choose not to use one), you can mix the mortar by hand using a hoe. Start by placing approximately half of the sand in the metal mortar box and lay over it all the cement (and lime if required). Add the rest of the sand and mix these dry ingredients until even in color. (Make sure all the ingredients are mixed together thoroughly.) Water is added by making an indentation in the center of the pile of dry ingredients, pouring water into it (a hose is very useful), and mixing until the desired plasticity is obtained.

Mortar must be constantly mixed fresh. If it is more than two or three hours old (depending on the weather) it becomes hard to handle and must be discarded. If it begins to stiffen before that, a bit of water may be added.

TOOLS

The tools required for foundation work are quite varied. Many of them have already been used for site preparation. In addition, masonry and carpentry tools will be required. The tools needed will depend on whether you are pouring the foundations or building them out of concrete block. The following is a list of tools common to both techniques. (Tool descriptions are found in the Glossary of Tools.)

- Plumb bob
- Carpenter's level
- Mason's line
- Sledge hammer (choose the size you can best handle) to drive the stakes
- Claw hammer
- Windable chalk line
- Wooden rule
- 50'-0" retractable metal tape
- Hand or electric saw (if power is available on the site; see the Glossary of Tools)
- Long-handled shovel (for small excavations)
- Pointed trowel
- Hoe or garden rake (for spreading concrete inside footing forms)
- T-angle
- Framing square (preferably steel, 16" × 24")
- Screed board

For poured concrete foundations, you will also need:

- Flat hoe or spade (to work the sides of the concrete form)
- Paint roller with tray (for applying oil to forms)
- Wheelbarrow (to transport concrete)
- Wrecking bars (for prying forms apart)
- Hand float (to level the top of the foundation walls)

Concrete-block foundations require:

- Mortar board
- Metal tub (to mix mortar)
- Story or course pole
- Straightedge or long spirit level
- Brick hammer
- Brick set
- Mason's corner (also called clip or cut nail)
- Joining tool

PROCEDURE

Foundation work starts by re-establishing the building lines on the batter boards. This is done

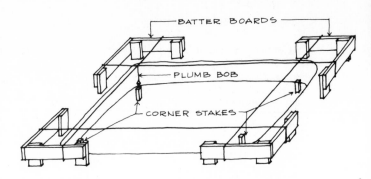

ILL. 1

by replacing the mason's line in the grooves cut in the batter boards. A plumb bob is dropped at their intersection to locate the building corner (which is also the foundation wall corner), and a stake is driven at that exact location as a marker (Ill. 1). When all the corners are located, the house dimensions are checked against the distances between the stakes to make sure everything is still as accurate as when originally measured prior to excavation. The next step is to locate and build the footing formwork.

Building the Footing Forms—Outside Perimeter

Footing forms can be trenches dug on the soil or built-up wood forms. Pouring footings in a trench is possible if the soil is firm and capable of holding a sharp cut. In loose soils, such as sands, gravel, etc., this method cannot be used. The advantage of trench forms is the savings on carpentry work. A major drawback is the difficulty in leveling the earth bed of the trench. If the bottom of the trench is not level, the footing will not be level. The time saved by not erecting formwork is spent in the leveling process. For this reason, we recommend wood forms (Ill. 2).

The stakes just driven represent the corners of the foundation walls. Footings, however, project a distance outside these walls, and their location also has to be established. The building corner stakes are used as reference points. Our sample house has foundation walls that are 8" thick and 4'-0" high resting on 8" high and 16" wide footings (Ill. 3). From one corner stake (we'll call it stake A), measure the distance that the footing projects outward from the foundation walls, that is, 4", and add to this dimension

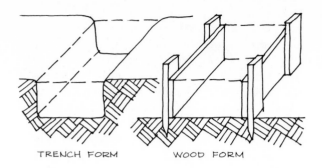

TRENCH FORM   WOOD FORM

ILL. 2

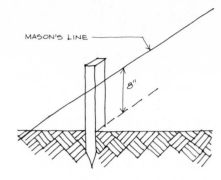

MASON'S LINE

8"

ILL. 5

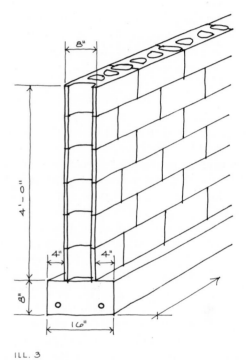

8"

4'-0"

4"   4"

8"

16"

ILL. 3

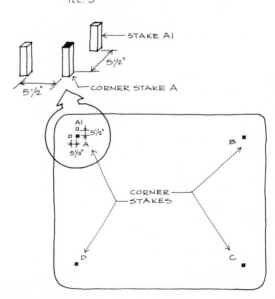

STAKE A1

5½"

5½"

CORNER STAKE A

A1
5½"
A
5½"

CORNER STAKES

B

D   C

ILL. 4

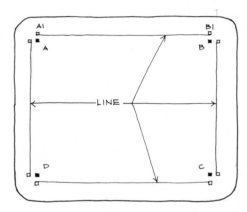

A1   B1

A   B

LINE

D   C

ILL. 6

the thickness of the form board you are using,
that is, 1½" (a 2" board is actually 1½" thick).
Be sure to make this measurement (5½") in
both outward directions at each corner and
drive a stake at each (Ill. 4). Repeat this procedure at all corners. Follow this step by marking
the height of the footing on one of the outside
stakes, that is, 8", and securing one end of the
line to that level (Ill. 5). Repeat this at a second
stake (stake B) and stretch the line tightly between them, making sure to check for levelness
with a line level. Continue this process until all
stakes are joined, delineating the perimeter of
the footings (Ill. 6). Intermediate stakes are then
driven a fraction of an inch away from the
stretched line (Ill. 7). These stakes should be
spaced no more than 2½' to 3' apart. (Concrete
is heavy. It is better to have an overstructured
form than one that collapses during the pour.)
When all stakes are driven, the mason's line can
be removed.

It is time to nail the form boards to the
stakes. (Make sure that the top of the board is

Locating the Intermediate Piers

Your floor-framing plan will most likely require intermediate girders to carry a portion of the house loads. These girders sit on piers, which in turn sit on footing pads. These interior footing pads are now located using the corner building stakes. Our sample house requires two piers, which are to be constructed of double rows of concrete blocks, measuring 16″ by 16″. The center line of pier A is located 12′-0″ from the outside of one foundation wall (*not* the footing that we just measured!) and 12′-0″ from the other, as shown on plan (Ill. 10). Start with the original *building corner stakes* and stretch a line between them. Measure along this line the distance to the pier edges. In our case, we measure along the north wall of the house (Ill. 11, line AB) first 11′-4″ (12′-0″ − 8″ = 11′-4″) to locate point 1 and then 10′-0″ to locate point 2. A stake is driven at each of these points and the procedure repeated along the south wall (line CD). The opposing stakes are connected with a mason's line, thus locating one edge of each pier (Ill. 12). In order to find the corners, we measure the perpendicular distance, that is, 11′-4″, along both side walls (lines AC and BD). Stakes 5 and 6 are driven and connected with a line. The intersection of both sets of lines establishes the pier corners. Drive a stake at each intersection (Ill. 13). The footing pads project 8″ on all sides. To locate the footing corner, follow the procedure outlined earlier for continuous footings. You need only to find one corner since pier footings are square. (These forms can be ready ahead of time and dropped into place.) If you are digging trenches instead of building forms, you need to locate all four footing pad corners and excavate to the required depth.

Building the Footing Forms—Inside Perimeter

Now that the piers have been located and marked, the next step is to build the inside perimeter forms. To find the exact location of the inside footing form, measure the width of the footing, that is, 16″, and add to this dimension the thickness of the form material, 1½″. Measure in from the outside perimeter forms 17½″ and drive a stake where the side and end measurements intersect (Ill. 14). The steps that follow are similar to those described earlier for

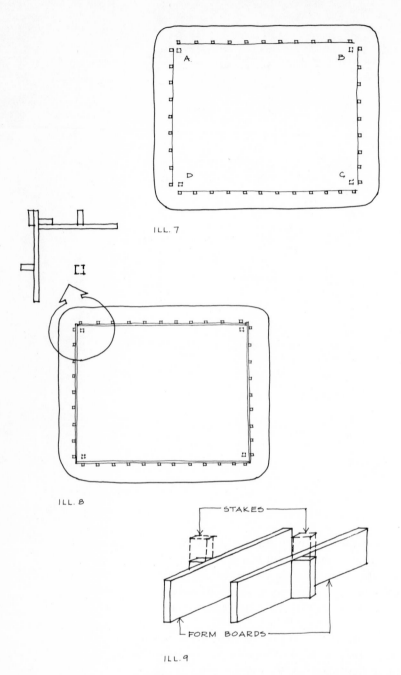

ILL. 7

ILL. 8

STAKES

FORM BOARDS

ILL. 9

in line with the previously marked height.) Nail one form board to the inside of the end stake and fasten the other end to an intermediate stake. Check the top of the form board for levelness with the carpenter's level. Butt a second board against the first and repeat the same procedure. All the remaining boards are attached in this fashion until the outside perimeter is completed (Ill. 8). Again check for levelness. Once all the boards are nailed, cut the stake tops flush with the top of the forms. This is done to facilitate the leveling of the top of the footing when the concrete is poured (Ill. 9).

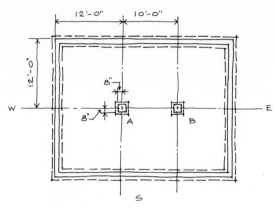

ILL. 10

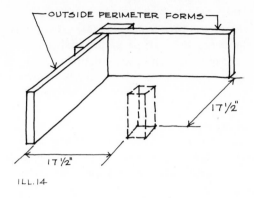

ILL. 14

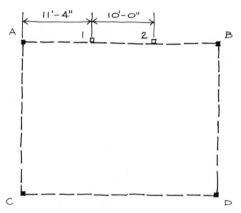

ILL. 11

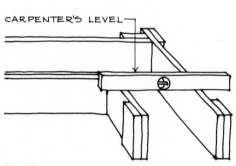

ILL. 15

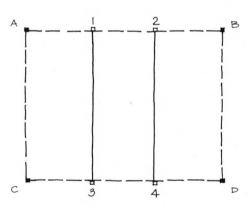

ILL. 12

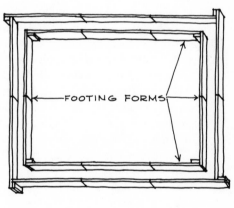

FOOTING FORMS

ILL. 16

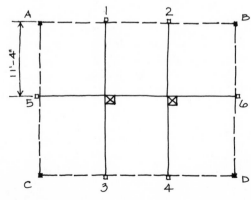

ILL. 13

exterior perimeter formwork. Measure and mark the footing height at an end stake, stretch a line between two corner stakes, locate intermediate stakes, and nail the boards. Using a carpenter's level, make sure that the inner and outer perimeter forms are level with one another (Ill. 15). The final product should look like a rectangular doughnut (Ill. 16).

Foundations

243

Preparing to Pour

There are two remaining tasks before pouring the concrete: first, preparing of the ground surface to receive the concrete, and second, placing steel reinforcement bars in the formwork or trench. (These procedures must be done in exactly that order. Once the steel bars are in place it is impossible to successfully prepare the ground.) Steel reinforcement bars are not always used for house footings. Unless specifically required by the local building code, footing reinforcement is optional. We recommend its use, however, as reinforcement provides insurance against settling problems.

Immediately before pouring the concrete, wet the base of the footing forms with a garden hose. Be sure not to overwater the forms and see to it that there are no remaining puddles when the concrete is poured. We wet down the soil bed (or, for that matter, any surfaces that come in contact with wet concrete or cement) to prevent the dry soil from absorbing the moisture in the concrete which will cause it to lose strength. Tamp (press) the earth down firmly with a square shovel and wet again.

Reinforcing bars are usually placed in the lower half of the footing. They must be held up in some way at their final position (2″ from the bottom of the trench) until the concrete is poured. This temporary support may take a variety of forms. The most professional support is a small metal device called a chair (Ill. 17). A more primitive way of accomplishing the same end is to support the bars on small, thin pieces of masonry such as concrete block or brick. The recommended diameter of reinforcing bars is ½″, unless otherwise specified by local codes. When you have to join two lengths of reinforcement, the bars should overlap about 20″ (40 times the diameter of the bar). It is crucial that the bars are solidly joined where they overlap. Tie them securely together with wire (Ill. 18).

You are now ready to pour. Find out whether the work must be inspected by a building official before pouring. When planning the date of the pour, keep two things in mind. First, you will not be able to continue with the foundation work for a couple of days after the footing is poured. The mixture needs sufficient time to set before the foundation walls can be started. Second, plan to pour in weather that is neither too hot nor too cold, since extreme temperatures can alter the setting process of concrete. (Build-

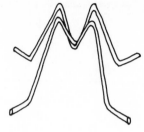

ILL. 17

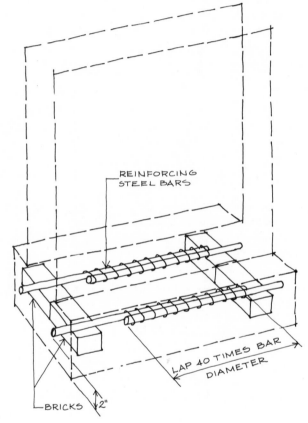

REINFORCING STEEL BARS

LAP 40 TIMES BAR DIAMETER

BRICKS 2″

ILL. 18

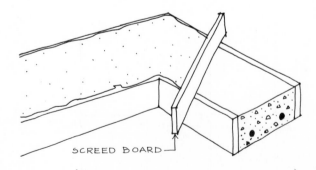

SCREED BOARD

ILL. 19

ing authorities can actually stop you from pouring in freezing temperatures.) Once these two factors have been taken into account, you can call the ready-mix company and have them deliver the quantity and quality of concrete needed.

While close to a phone, make a few more calls, this time to friends. Get them to volunteer their help during the pour since plenty of extra hands will be welcome. Now for a few tips on concrete pouring: Have all the formwork ready before the truck arrives. Should the forms be located in such a way that the truck cannot reach them all, have one or two wheelbarrows, planks, and the friends you just recruited at hand. The truck can deliver the concrete mix to a wheelbarrow (don't overload it!) that will in turn travel over the planks. The concrete can be poured from the wheelbarrow into the forms before it sets. While your friends "work" the concrete that has just been poured, you can go back for another load. "Working" concrete is the term used to describe the process of helping the mixture compact itself and preventing pockets or voids from forming. With the aid of a flat hoe or a spade, move the mixture at the center of the forms (the sides can be handled by lightly tapping the forms with a hammer). Be careful not to work the concrete excessively since this will tend to separate the materials within the mixture. (Some ready-mix companies have a pumper, which hooks onto a concrete truck and has a long hose that can deliver concrete up to 50' or more away from the truck.)

It is important that the concrete be evenly distributed within the forms. This is done by pouring the mixture at several points and spreading it to where it is needed with a garden rake or a hoe. (Professional concrete laborers, wearing knee-high boots, actually climb into the formwork with the wet concrete and push the stuff around with shovels. Of course, this is only required for a larger mass of concrete than a house footing.) Work the concrete into the forms by using a pointed trowel, moving it around to fill any depressions and get rid of any excess. To help the mixture flow into gaps and compact itself, tap the sides of the forms lightly with a hammer. The concrete at the top of the footing is leveled with a screed board (this can be any straight piece of wood that is longer than the footing is wide). With a person positioned on either side of the footing, move the board along the top of the form (Ill. 19).

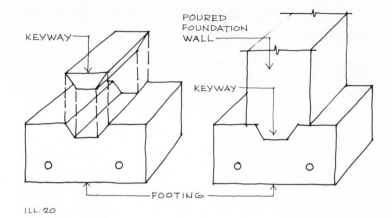

ILL. 20

If you are building the foundation walls out of poured-in-place concrete, you will have to provide a tie between the footing and the wall. There are many ways to do this, the most popular being the keyway method. A keyway is a 2" × 4" tapered wooden board that is inserted on top of the footing (Ill. 20). To hold it in place, it is attached to straps running along the top of the forms. (Don't forget to oil the keyway for ease of removal.) Once the concrete is dry and the keyway removed, the remaining cavity becomes a concrete tie to the foundation wall.

If you are planning to build the foundation walls out of concrete block instead of poured concrete, use vertical reinforcing bars in the footing as a tie to the wall above in place of the keyway. These bars are placed at regular intervals (usually 2'-0", but they vary according to code). The steel is inserted in the footing forms while the concrete is still plastic.

Erecting the Foundation Walls

The stage is ready for erecting the foundation walls. Begin by re-establishing the building lines. Drop a plumb at their intersection and mark the corner with chalk. From this point on, the erection process varies depending on whether you're building a poured-in-place or a concrete-block wall.

POURED-IN-PLACE WALLS: The main concern in poured-in-place walls is the formwork. The choice boils down to renting prefabricated metal (or metal-wood) forms or building lumber ones from scratch (Inset IV). If prefabricated forms are available for rent in your area, check the comparative economics. Chances are that renting prefabricated forms will be cheaper.

INSET IV / FORMS

Forms are made up of three basic components. The studs make up the framework in which to support the retaining walls or sheathing, which shapes the concrete (Ill. IV-1). The frame is kept in place, stiffened, and aligned by a system of horizontal and diagonal braces. Both form layers are held together by a system of wire ties and the correct spacing maintained by horizontal wood members called spreaders. Wire ties may also act as spreaders (right).

Forms may be continuous, layered, or sectional. Continuous forms are custom made to the requirements of the house. The lumber can be reused but the forms themselves have to be totally rebuilt. Layer forms are used when lumber is expensive. They can be sectional or continuous but

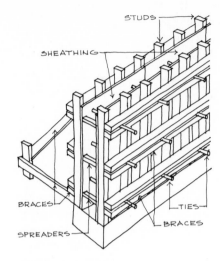

they only extend to a predetermined height and must be taken off and reinstalled at a higher level after the first pour. A second pour then takes place. Needless to say, this procedure is more time consuming.

Sectional forms are the most practical and the ones we recommend (Ill. 21). They consist of a series of panels that are either built independently of the rest of the construction process or rented. Once the site is ready, they are installed. They can be built to any height or width and can be stacked to different heights, that is, 2'-0" × 4'-0" sections can make up an 8'-0" wall. These sections contain all the basic form components—studs, sheathing, notches for wire ties, and spreaders.

INSET V / TYPE OF LUMBER FOR FORMS

Use green lumber or lumber that is only partly kiln-dried. The reason for this is that kiln-dried lumber tends to absorb the water content in the concrete, not only altering the makeup of the mixture, but also causing the forms to swell and eventually warp. In the event that kiln-dried wood has to be used, make sure to wet it thoroughly before pouring the concrete.

Prefabricated systems come with all the necessary components for erection. The erection process in itself is similar to that required with homemade forms.

If you are constructing the formwork, assemble ¾" plywood and sufficient 2 × 4's and build a series of sections or panels (Insets IV and V). These panels are generally 2'-0" or 4'-0" wide (Ill. 21). Smaller ones are easier to handle. Check the plan for the length of the foundation wall and determine the number of panels needed. Most likely, you will need a few odd-sized ones. Since plywood comes in 4'-0" widths, building 4'-0" panels involves less cutting. They can be constructed to a specific height requirement or simply stacked; with 4'-0" panels you can construct an 8'-0" high wall. The panels can be built while the footing sets.

The erection process is little affected by whether you use prefabricated or homemade forms. Give special attention to corner forms since they are the most vulnerable to failure. One way to resolve the corner problem is to build the inside and outside forms in such a way

that the ends of standard inside and outside panels line up when continued on from the corner pieces (Ill. 22). Prefabricated panel systems take this problem into account and resolve it in a number of different ways that are built into the total design. Before beginning erecting formwork, grease the inside face of the form

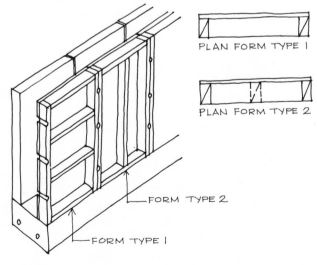

ILL. 21

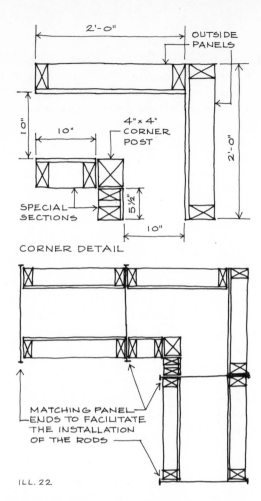

CORNER DETAIL

ILL. 22

MATCHING PANEL
ENDS TO FACILITATE
THE INSTALLATION
OF THE RODS

with oil. A paint roller and tray make the oil application easier.

The object of oiling the inside of forms is to prevent water absorption and facilitate form removal. Waterproofing the wood prevents it from absorbing the water in the concrete, which in turn could cause swelling and buckling of the forms. This thin coat of oil also stops the concrete from entering the wood pores and therefore adhering to it.

Start the erection of formwork by snapping a chalk line on the footing, delineating the outer edge of the foundation walls. Nail the outside corner sections together and install them (with the plywood face flush with the chalk line) by nailing the bottom plate to the footings using concrete nails. If you are using homemade forms, brace them temporarily. On the other hand, if you are working with a prefab system, brace it by locking the sections together with keys and wedges provided for this purpose. Repeat this procedure at all corners and erect the intermediate panels. Next, set up the inside forms following the procedure already described, making certain that the plywood face is flush with the chalk line. Place the tie rods

through the notches in the form and tighten them. Check periodically that the forms are plumb.

If you are building a house with a basement, you will need window openings, doors, electric conduits and outlets, water and gas pipes, switch boxes, etc., in addition to a place for girders to rest on. With a crawl space, you don't need as many items. You will, however, still need window openings for ventilation, access door openings, and girder seats to support the structure above. These openings have to be integrated into the foundation wall formwork, before pouring.

You might, in a building supply house, be able to get hold of prefabricated steel window and door frames that are designed for nailing to the inside of the wall forms. Otherwise, you have to build lumber frames. Window and door frames are essentially four-sided boxes. A small tapered piece of wood (keystrip) is attached to the outside of these boxes. This keystrip can be attached to the frame in two ways. The first (with the wider side of the strip touching the frame's surface) will be removed together with the frame, thus providing a recess in the concrete into which a sash can be dropped (Ill. 23). The second (with the narrow face of the strip touching the frame's surface) will remain in the concrete wall and serve as a nailing strip for the finished frame (Ill. 24). Another approach is to

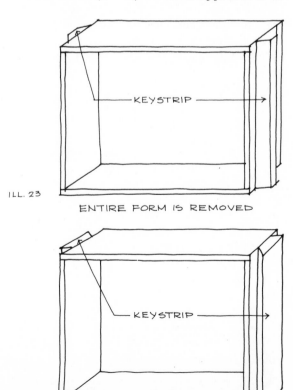

ILL. 23

ENTIRE FORM IS REMOVED

ILL. 24

FORM IS REMOVED BUT KEYSTRIP
REMAINS AS NAILING STRIP

Foundations
247

use the finished door or window frames. In order to provide a connection to the wall to keep these frames in place a keystrip is attached to the outside of the frame. Filler strips are also used if the frames are not thick enough to go through the full thickness of the foundation wall.

The forms for girder seats offer slightly different problems. The girder form need only be a three-sided box (since the top of the girder projects above the top of the foundation wall) and does not perforate the foundation wall completely. In order to give the girder sufficient bearing surface on the wall, the form must project a minimum of 4" into the thickness of the foundation wall. Care must be taken in determining the height along the wall at which the girder form is installed. This height must not only allow for the depth of the girder but also take into account that it projects 1½" (or sometimes 3") above the top of the foundation wall in order to be flush with the sill. Allow an extra ½" along both sides and the end of the form to provide some room for play (Ill. 25).

A few pointers on frame building. First, the dimensions of the opening, or pocket, will be those of the outside of the frame or box. Second, make sure that the frames for openings that go through the wall are wide enough so that they fit snugly within the foundation wall forms.

Before starting to pour, make sure all formwork is plumb and level. Concrete must not be dropped from a height of more than 3' or 4', which might cause the aggregate to separate.

For drops greater than this, use a chute and be careful that the concrete falls directly onto concrete and doesn't bounce off from the form wall (which can also separate the aggregate). Make sure to pour all the concrete in one day. This will not only be cheaper (since bringing a ready-mix truck two days in a row will definitely be no bargain) but will also spare you the problem of break lines (construction joints) between pours. Once you are finished pouring and working the concrete, level the top of the foundation walls with a screed board. While the concrete is still plastic, insert the anchor bolts approximately 4'-0" apart. (Make sure that the anchor bolts are located where they will not later interfere with the placement of the joists [check the framing plan] and that they project a sufficient amount over the top of the wall to clear the sill.)

When the concrete sets (24–48 hours in average conditions), remove the forms. (Wrecking bars come in handy at this point.) The ties should be broken off from the outside wall since they would otherwise interfere with the application of waterproofing. The inside ties need only be removed if you are planning a basement.

The intermediate piers may be constructed according to the directions on pages 252 and 253. Remember, when constructing this formwork the top of the piers will most likely have to be a few inches lower than the top of the foundation wall. The girder, as you recall, is lowered into a pocket in the wall. Therefore, the top of the intermediate pier must be that many inches lower than the top of the foundation wall so that the girder may rest on it (Ill. 26).

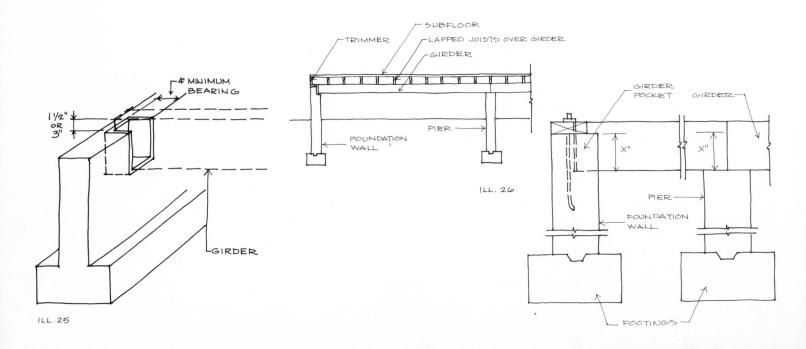

INSET VI / MEMBRANE WATERPROOFING

Membrane waterproofing is a sandwiching of layers of bituminous materials such as tar, pitch, and asphalt, and fabric-type materials such as builder's felt. The application of membrane waterproofing starts by making a concrete slope joint between the outside surface at the bottom of the foundation wall and the top edge of the footing (Ill. VI-1). This slope helps to minimize the danger of leakage through the joint between the footing and the foundation wall. Once the concrete slope is completed, a coat of asphalt (tar or pitch) is applied to the exterior surface of the wall (from the very top of the wall to the bot-

tom of the footing). The first layer of felt is then installed (membrane waterproofing can have two, three, or more layers, depending on the wetness of the soil), starting near the bottom of the wall and making sure to lap it over the footing projection. Asphalt (tar or pitch) is applied over the felt and a second layer of felt applied. Always make sure that there is enough lapping between layers of felt so as to provide two *full* layers of felt over the block. This process is repeated until the entire wall is covered. A final layer of tar is applied over the entire wall at the end (right).

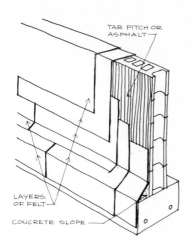

INSET VII / HOW TO CUT CONCRETE BLOCK

Sometimes you will need a block of less than the standard size and you will have to cut. Two tools are used for cutting block, a brick set and a brick hammer. Place the

block on a surface that is not too hard and make the first blow to score the desired spot on the solid side of the block. The second blow is normally the last one for an

experienced mason; a beginner, however, will probably need to score a few more blows before the block is cut.

Waterproofing should be applied next. In order to have a reasonably smooth surface on which to apply waterproofing, the tie holes must be filled with grout. Keep in mind that unnecessary projections can perforate the waterproofing and defeat the purpose of all your hard work. Unless located in very wet soils or required by local codes, poured concrete walls usually need only the application of black asphalt waterproofing (it can either be troweled or brushed on) on the exterior wall surface. In wetter soils the application of membrane waterproofing will be necessary (Inset VI).

CONCRETE-BLOCK WALLS: The alternate to poured concrete foundation walls is concrete block. Laying concrete block is tedious, heavy work. It is therefore very important to work efficiently so as not to waste your efforts. Organize your materials so that they are at arm's reach. Make sure you always have a small supply of blocks close by. Position the mortar board (Inset VIII) at a convenient height. Most important, when you bend to pick up a block, bend your knees, keeping your spine straight. You'll be sore for a few days but won't run the

risk of a herniated disk! You should not only try to save on muscle, but also on errors. Drawing an elevation of the block wall to scale might prove helpful for the beginner. This drawing will carefully outline the number of courses needed to reach the required wall height and indicate any openings within the walls such as doors, windows, and vents.

Construction begins by re-establishing the building corners and snapping a chalk line between them on the footing as a guide to locate the first block course. In order to visualize any shifting or cutting that might be needed, set the blocks without mortar all around the footing. As you are doing this, keep in mind that the joint thickness is approximately ⅜". Most likely, you will find that some blocks need to be cut (Inset VII). Reposition the blocks until they successfully fit the wall length and mark the joint location on the footing with chalk. Then remove the blocks, leaving only the chalk mark behind.

We are now ready for the serious business of erecting the wall (Inset VIII). First and most important is to carefully place the corner blocks.

Foundations

249

Start by learning to use the trowel. Grasp it firmly, palm and thumb up. The muscles that you will be using to spread the mortar are those in your forearm. If after the first day's work, your forearm is sore, you are holding the trowel correctly. Place a small amount of mortar from the mixture onto the mortar board without overloading it. Lift the board from the ground by prying it up with a trowel and carry it over to the work area.

The first course of block will be set directly over the footing and should rest on a full bed of mortar to ensure complete bonding. The second course will be set over block and, instead of laying it in a full bed, you will lay it in a face shell bedding. This means that you apply mortar only to both edges of the block, leaving the core voids and webs undisturbed (below). Blocks must be bonded to each other not only by horizontal but also by vertical mortar joints. Applying mortar to the vertical edges is referred to as buttering.

A few words on "throwing" mortar. With the trowel held upward, lift a quantity of mortar (make sure that your thumb is up so you can turn the trowel over). When you are over the block, slowly invert the trowel from an upward to a downward position. Place the mortar in a cylindrical shape along both edges of the block. Next, pick up a buttered block (some masons prefer also to butter the side of the previously laid block), remembering to keep the thick-webbed side facing up, and lower it into position pushing both downward and forward into the mortar bed (below). (Don't be surprised if the mortar falls out when you pick up the block. It generally happens the first couple of times. Eventually you'll get the hang of applying the mortar at the right pressure.) The top of the block should be level with the mason's line. Should the block be much too high over the line either you

placed too much mortar or the mixture is too stiff. On the other hand, if the mixture gives too quickly and the block sinks in, the cause will most likely be too much water. After a few blocks have been placed, use a level as a straightedge to ensure correct alignment of the block. In addition, check for plumbness and levelness. The excess mortar squeezed out the sides should be cut off (upward motion).

The last step in laying block is the tooling of the joints. This means compressing the mortar squeezed out of the joints tightly back into the joints and taking off the excess. Since tooling is not only for appearance but also for weathertightness, we recommend the concave joint. This joint is not only the most simple one to do, but also one of the best for weathertightness. Simply press the convex side of the joining tool against the mortar. This will give you a concave joint (below).

FACE SHELL BEDDING

FULL BEDDING

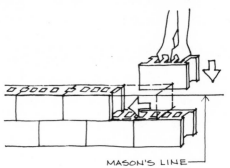

MASON'S LINE

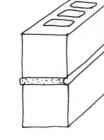

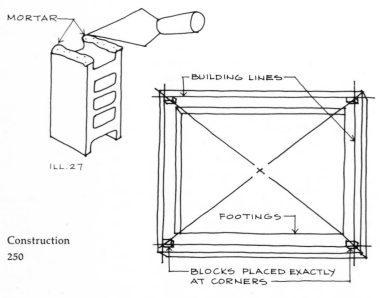

MORTAR

ILL. 27

BUILDING LINES

FOOTINGS

BLOCKS PLACED EXACTLY AT CORNERS

ILL. 28

It's essential that these blocks be positioned correctly since they will act as a guide for the remaining wall construction. Lay a full mortar bed at the footing corners (Inset III). Take one concrete block, stand it on end, and apply mortar to the end surface (Ill. 27). Picking it up by the webs, set it on the mortar bed. To ensure levelness, place a carpenter's level over the block and tap the block lightly with the trowel handle until the level's bubble is centered. Also see to it that the block is plumb and that it is directly at the building corner. Lay the remaining corner blocks in the same manner. To check for squareness, measure the diagonal distances between corner blocks. They should be equal. Otherwise adjust the corners accordingly. Most likely, relocating a corner block that might not be directly under the string intersection will be the solution (Ill. 28).

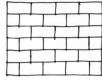
The second stage of construction is to build up the corners of the wall by laying three or four courses of block in half lap (Inset IX). With the aid of a carpenter's level, make sure that the corners are plumb, level, and aligned. A story or course pole* might come in handy to check whether the top of the masonry courses are at the planned height. If they don't line up, the joints might have become excessively thick or thin. Every built-up corner must be the same height. Once all corners are ready, the side walls are constructed with the aid of both a mason's line and the chalk line already drawn on the footing. Secure the mason's line to one built-up corner with a clip attached to the block (be careful that it is not attached to the mortar joint) and stretch it tightly between two of them (Ill. 29). This line serves as a guide to leveling the top edge of the block. (If the line is left overnight, watch out for sagging due to moisture.) How to handle the block for placement on the line is gradually worked out by each individual. A good start, however, is to tip the block toward you, so that you can see the edge of the block below. This way you can line it up with the new block by eye.

The last course should be either of solid concrete block or regular block with the cavities filled with concrete. To prevent the concrete being poured in the cores from falling all the way to the footing, a piece of metal lath is placed two courses before the last. Anchor bolts (tying the foundation wall to the house structure above ground) are inserted in the filled block cores at approximately every 4', while the concrete is still plastic. They extend down into the wall about the depth of two courses of block and sufficiently above the top course to go completely through the sill (Ill. 30).

* A story pole is a straight piece of wood used to check or transfer key dimensions easily.

Like poured concrete foundation walls, concrete-block walls require openings to accommodate windows, doors, vents, girders, etc. The best approach, as already mentioned, is to plan the location of these openings before the actual construction begins by means of a scaled drawing. This advance planning will save you considerable block cutting (which is not easy). Essentially, this means that both the heights and widths of all openings should occur in places that are multiples of eight (assuming that you are using an 8″ × 8″ × 16″ concrete block). The

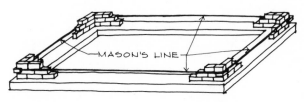

MASON'S LINE

ILL. 29

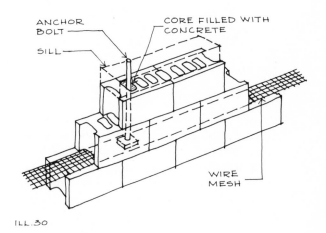

ANCHOR BOLT

SILL

CORE FILLED WITH CONCRETE

WIRE MESH

ILL. 30

Foundations
251

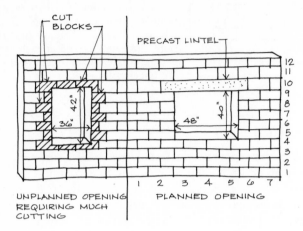

ILL. 31

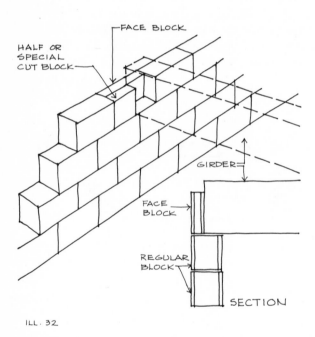

ILL. 32

One additional problem is the framing of the girder into the foundation wall. The girder pocket can be easily provided by using a facer block (which is only 4″ wide) and a half or special-cut block to fit around the girder and make the wall solid (Ill. 32). Since the girder transfers such a heavy load to the wall at that particular point, it is important that the cores of all the blocks under the girder be filled with concrete.

Waterproofing should be applied once the wall is completed. Concrete-block walls offer more leakage problems than poured concrete ones. While a layer of black asphalt is sufficient for a poured concrete wall in average conditions, membrane waterproofing is recommended for concrete-block walls (Inset VI).

PIER FOUNDATIONS: You might have chosen to build your house entirely on piers. In this case, locate the piers and footing pads as described earlier. Once their location is established the procedure varies depending on whether the piers are built of poured concrete or concrete block.

When casting concrete piers, both the footing pad and the pier itself are cast at the same time. The formwork for the pads incorporates that of the piers. These forms can be prepared ahead of time and installed when the pier locations are established. If you are using steel reinforcement, build the footing forms first, install them in place, prepare the ground, and *then* locate the reinforcing bars. The steel should be running in both directions at right angles to each other and no less than 2″ from the bottom of the footing. Once these are in place, build the pier form on top of the footing form and place the pier's reinforcement. (Stick four vertical bars in the ground and connect them with horizontal bars at approximately 1′ intervals.) Don't forget to prepare the ground surface for pouring before placing the steel. Once the concrete is poured, insert the anchor bolts (Ill. 33 and page 255, Ill. 2).

Concrete-block piers are easier to erect. The footing pads are poured. While the concrete is still plastic, four reinforcing bars are placed. Once it sets, a double row of blocks is constructed over the footing (the reinforcing bars go through the cores in the block). The blocks are set in a full bed of mortar (the sides with the small openings facing up). After laying a row,

windows, doors, and vents themselves should be multiples of 8″ to fit these openings (Ill. 31).

There are various methods in which to bridge the gap left above the openings. The easiest one is to use precast concrete lintels, which are available where you buy the blocks. Precast concrete sills are also available. Keep in mind that the blocks at either side of the openings should be of the sash or jamb type. These blocks are already designed to accommodate window and door jambs and sashes and will considerably facilitate the installation of the finished frames.

check for levelness before proceeding to the next course. Make sure all piers are at the same height. Place the anchor bolt and fill all the cores with concrete.

Backfilling

The next step to complete the foundation work is backfilling. Before backfilling the excavation, however, the drainage tile should be installed. It lies directly adjacent to the bottom of the footing and follows the perimeter of the house until it is eventually connected to a storm sewer, drywell, or other means of water disposal (see Chapters 14 and 26). The tile should slope approximately ¼″ or ½″ per 10′-0″ of distance. Tiles are placed end to end, leaving only a small gap between them to allow the water to seep in. The gap is covered with tarpaper to avoid clogging by small stones and silt. Gravel or crushed stone is placed all around the tile. Perforated black plastic pipe may be used in place of drainage tiles (Ill. 34).

You are now ready to backfill the excavation. Here are a few pointers. If you are dealing with high basement walls, make sure to brace them properly before backfilling. Increased earth pressure against a tall unbraced wall could conceivably knock it down. As a matter of fact, you can save yourself some work by simply waiting until the first-floor framing is in place before filling the excavation. Crawl spaces are not so much of a problem because of their lower walls. In any event, be careful. In addition to avoiding tumbling walls, be cautious not to damage the waterproofing you've just applied. One final word: Don't make the mistake of backfilling the excavation with an expansive soil such as clay.

If you are building the house in termite country, once the foundation work and backfilling have been completed, spray the entire area with a termite protection compound. (See page 257, Inset I.)

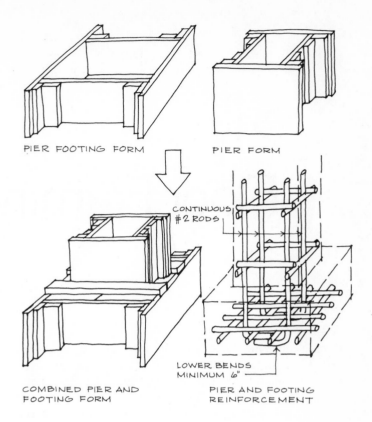

PIER FOOTING FORM   PIER FORM

CONTINUOUS #2 RODS

COMBINED PIER AND FOOTING FORM   PIER AND FOOTING REINFORCEMENT

LOWER BENDS MINIMUM 6″

ILL. 33

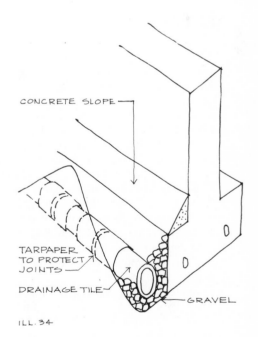

CONCRETE SLOPE

TARPAPER TO PROTECT JOINTS

DRAINAGE TILE

GRAVEL

ILL. 34

21
Floor Framing

Having completed the foundations, we are now ready to begin building the house proper. In platform-frame construction, the first step is building the floor system.* For this part of the operation you will need the following materials:

MATERIALS

- 2″ × 6″ lumber (preferably creosote-treated) for the sills. Order enough lumber to go around the house's periphery twice. The lumber will inevitably have a considerable number of defects and a good part of it will be rejected or cut away.
- Nails—6d (sixpenny), 8d, 10d, 12d, and 16d.
- Insect protection (see Inset I).
- Sill sealer: 1″ × 50′-0″ roll of fiberglass, approximately 6″ wide. Calculate the periphery of the house and add about 10 percent more.
- Bolt nuts: to fit over the anchor bolts.
- Joists: specified dimensions and the number will be shown in the framing plan. Buy at least 20 percent more in case of damaged or warped lumber.
- 1¼″ × 4″ rough sawn lumber for the cross bridging.
- Plyscore for the subfloor (⅝″ thick): Calculate the square foot coverage of the first floor. There is very little waste in plywood, but be sure to order enough 4′ × 8′ sheets to cover the floor.
- Timber connectors and joist hangers where needed.

* As mentioned earlier, we are not going to detail the pouring of the concrete-slab floor.

TOOLS

- Claw head hammer (It's not a bad idea to have two or more around, in case a friend decides to help.)
- Crosscut saw (or a portable power saw if you have a power source at the site)
- Framing square and/or combination square
- Tapemeasure
- Scratch awl (or a few dark pencils with a knife to sharpen them)
- Drill with ¾″ bits
- Wrench
- Carpenter's level
- Hacksaw
- Chalk-line reel

These same tools will be used for most of the construction work on the house.

THE GIRDERS

In the previous chapter, on the construction of the foundations, we framed a pocket for the end of the girder. The pocket should be 1″ wider than the girder, and should have a minimum bearing surface of 4″. The ½″ clearance on either side of the girder provides the essential space for ventilating the wooden member so that moisture can escape. A small piece of roofing membrane (pick up some scrap pieces of rolled roofing from the lumberyard) is put on the bearing part of the pocket for the absorption of moisture (Ill. 1).*

The built-up girder (very often substituted for the solid sections specified in Chapter 8) is made up of a number of pieces of 2″ lumber stock that are nailed together. One of the reasons that the built-up girder is often chosen over a solid piece of lumber is that the joints over the intermediary supports may be staggered, reducing deflection by constructing a continuous span rather than a series of simple spans between supports (Ill. 2). Be sure that all of the cuts are "square." This can be done with the help of the framing square or combination square.

Line up the first three pieces of wood, sandwiching the shorter piece in between the longer ones. Nail the individual sections of the built-up girder together using 10d nails. Continue nailing on one side and, when complete, turn the "sandwich" over and nail the other side. It is important to nail the sections together so that the girder acts structurally as one unit (Ill. 3).

When both ends of the girder span are lying in their respective pockets, check to see that the girder is level, using the carpenter's level. Corrections may be made (if you are only off by a few fractions of an inch) by wedging wood chips between the girder and its support on the side that is low. When completed, the girder should be level (or should have a slight camber upward) and should project at least 1½″ above the foundation wall. The girder need not be attached in any way to the pockets of the foundation wall but may or may not be bolted to the intermediary supports. The connection between the girder and its intermediary supports may be made as shown in Illustration 2. The joists and floor that will be nailed to it will provide additional stability.

THE PLATFORM FLOOR

The empty stage—the foundation walls and the in-place girder—is now ready for the construction of the platform floor (Ill. 4). Before you are a copy of the floor framing plan (another copy should be at home neatly tucked into a drawer, since framing plans often get lost or damaged

* Many contractors simply cement the areas around the girder.

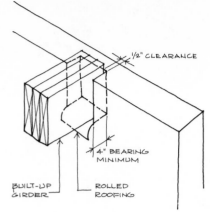

½″ CLEARANCE

4″ BEARING MINIMUM

BUILT-UP GIRDER

ROLLED ROOFING

ILL. 1

STAGGERED JOINTS

1. FILL APPROPRIATE VOIDS OF CEMENT BLOCK WITH MORTAR.
2. SINK 1½″ STEEL STRAPS INTO CONCRETE. ALLOW TO SET.
3. CONSTRUCT AND POSITION GIRDER.
4. DRILL HOLES THROUGH STRAP, GIRDER AND LAG BOLT.

ILL. 2

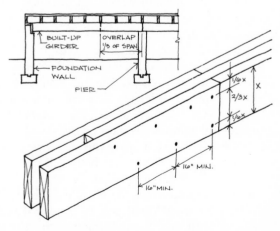

BUILT-UP GIRDER

OVERLAP ⅓ OF SPAN

FOUNDATION WALL

PIER

⅙ x

⅔ x

⅙ x

X

16″ MIN.

16″ MIN.

Floor Framing

255

ILL. 3

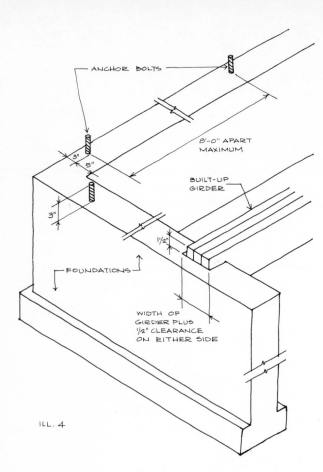

ANCHOR BOLTS

8'-0" APART MAXIMUM

BUILT-UP GIRDER

3"

5"

3"

1½"

FOUNDATIONS

WIDTH OF GIRDER PLUS ½" CLEARANCE ON EITHER SIDE

ILL. 4

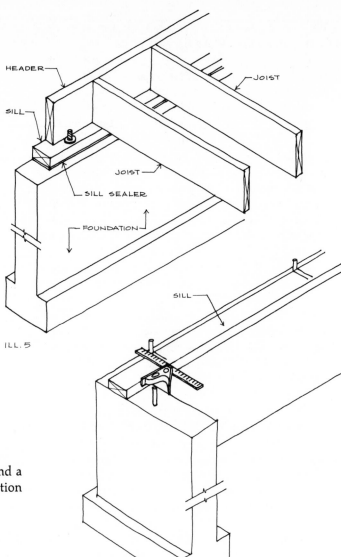

HEADER

JOIST

SILL

SILL SEALER

JOIST

FOUNDATION

ILL. 5

SILL

ILL. 6

on the site), a pile of lumber for the joists, and a boxful of nails. The first step is the construction of the mud sill. Refer to Illustration 5.

The Sill

The sill is the wood section that is bolted to the foundation wall. The floor joists span between the sill and the girder. We must first cut the sill and make the necessary holes for the bolts, after which we remove the sections, apply sill sealer, replace the sills, and fasten the bolts.

Choose straight, clean, long pieces of 2″ × 6″ lumber for the sills. Beginning at the corner of the foundation wall, lay the sill alongside the anchor bolts in order to mark their exact location on the lumber. Place the combination square's handle on the side of the wood away from the bolts and transfer the marks as shown in Illustration 6. The anchor bolts will not be in perfect line with one another. Be sure to measure the distance from the outside of the foundation wall to each bolt and measure that same distance onto the lumber being used for the sill (Ill. 7). Remove the sill section to the sawhorses

and drill ¾″ diameter holes at the points marked. (Although the bolts are only ½″ in diameter, we drill a slightly larger hole to compensate for possible miscalculations.)

At the point where the sill interferes with the 1½″ projection of the girder above the level of the foundation wall the sill must be notched. This can be most easily accomplished by arranging to have a joint in the continuous sill at the point where the pocket falls. This way the notch can be cut at the end of one of the sections only. An alternative is to saber cut the sill to the depth of the pocket and strike with a chisel. The piece will fall out (Ill. 8).

Slip the section over the bolt tops and measure the next sill section, being sure to butt the

Most areas in the United States are subject to termite infestation. To prevent the invasion of these wood-eating insects:

1. Use pressure-treated sills, which resist insect damage and also protect against wet- and dry-rot damage. (Alternately, use redwood heartwood or cedar heartwood.)

2. In the past termite shields were used extensively, but since the shield is one of the first elements to be installed after the foundation, it is subject to damages that tend to reduce its effectiveness. In theory, a termite or other insect would not be able to negotiate an undamaged termite shield. A series of dents or irregularities in the shield, however, would serve as a pathway for these wood-chewers. In recent years the FHA has approved chemical soil treatments, which provide positive treatment against termites by making the soil adjacent to the building inhospitable to insect life. The chemicals used are chlordane or dieldrin, which are the more powerful relatives of DDT and should be handled only by experts (dieldrin is closely related to nerve gas).*

3. In areas where termites are not a major problem the careful installation of a termite shield may be considered as a form of insect insurance.

* Do not store these chemicals where children or animals will have access to them. Because the chemicals are soon washed deep into the soil, once in the ground they shouldn't be a menace to children or pets.

---

next section squarely against the last. Work around the foundation wall until all the sill sections are completed. When this feat is accomplished, mark each sill section and its corresponding location on the foundation wall, so that the replacement of the sections will be easy. Remove the sill sections.

Position the termite shields, if you are going to use them (Inset I). Apply the roll of sill sealer to the top of the foundation wall. (Snip or puncture the holes for the bolts.) This material, normally 1″ thick, will compress to approximately ⅛″ or less when installed. The sill sealer will protect against insects, air infiltration, and dust. Reposition the precut, predrilled sill sections. Choose an extremely level piece of lumber as a straightedge (or use an aluminum one).

Rest one end of the straightedge on the girder and the other on the sill. Place the carpenter's level on the span. Check to see that the girder and the sills lie on or close to the same plane. If major corrections are to be made, now is the time to make them. (Because the girder will have a slight camber, and the sill sealer is not yet compressed, it is impossible to completely check for levelness at this time. More precise leveling of the floor is done after the joists and subfloor are added.) Apply the nuts and washers to the bolts and tighten. Check the levelness of the sill carefully. (Accommodations can be made to raise portions of the sill slightly in order to level it by loosening the bolts and wedging wood scraps under the sill. The gaps left by the wedges should be grouted.)

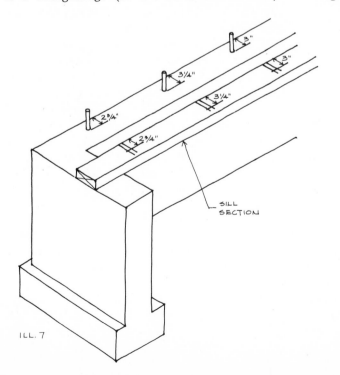

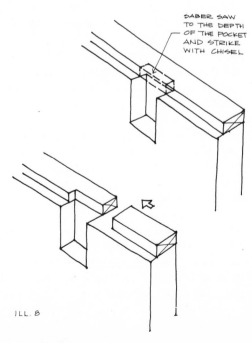

Floor Framing
257

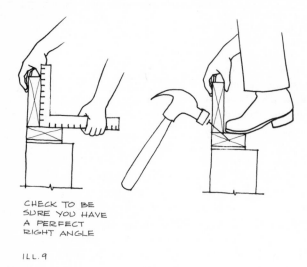

CHECK TO BE SURE YOU HAVE A PERFECT RIGHT ANGLE

ILL. 9

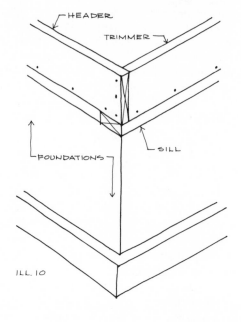

ILL. 10

Headers and Trimmers

Joist headers and trimmers (illustrated above) in conjunction with the sill enclose the platform floor. They are constructed of lumber of the same dimensions as the joists themselves so that the entire unit ends up flush. The subfloor is nailed to these surfaces.

Working flush with the exterior edge of the sill, toe-nail (Inset II) the header to the sill every 16″ using 12d nails (Ill. 9). Make sure that the sill and the headers are at right angles before nailing. Check for special details, such as a cantilever, which would eliminate the need for a header in that location, before completing the work. When the sill turns a corner, be sure to nail the headers to each other as shown in Illustration 10.

Marking Off the Joists

The perimeter is complete, the girders are in place, and now we must locate the joists. Study the floor framing plan carefully. The method that we will be discussing is for the lap joint of the joists over the girder (see Ill. 11, page 83).

Most plans call for joists spaced 16″ on center, but occasionally they are spaced at 12″ or 24″ intervals. Whatever the required spacing, it is simplest to first make a template (story pole) of the spacing on a straight piece of lumber and then transfer the markings from the template to the headers and the girder. To make the story pole, first measure the exact demarcations with a tape or rule. Using a combination square (or a framing square) draw lines across the width of the template perpendicular to the edge. (The most convenient length for the template would be about 8′.) The template will have evenly spaced markings 16″ (12″ or 24″) apart on it. It will be used when you have a clear run of joists without interruption. If you have a special condition, such as the doubling of the joist for a partition or to frame an opening (refer back to Chapter 8, page 84), you can mark these special conditions with a different-colored pencil (Ill. 11).

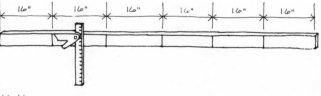

ILL. 11

Marking the Header

To mark the header, measure 15¼″ from the corner where the header meets the trimmer, along the header. Then, lay the template on the sill along the header and transfer the 16″ demarcations onto the header. The reason that we first measured a 15¼″ spacing is in anticipation of the installation of the subfloor. The subfloor material comes in 4′ × 8′ sheets. We want the end of the sheet to lie on the center line of the joist (Ills. 12 and 13). Use the combination square as an aid in transferring the marks. On the side of the mark closest to the header draw an "X." This X mark is a convention used by carpenters to indicate on which side of the mark the joist is to lie.

The template may be used along the rest of the header, marking off the 16″ demarcations. There will most likely be some framing details, such as openings for stairs and the doubling of joists under partitions and bathtubs, that will interfere with this even line of joists. Check the framing plan. Mark the exact location of any additional joists onto the header. Transfer the mark, if you wish, onto the template using a contrasting-colored pencil. Be sure to draw an X indicating on which side of the line the joist is to be placed. Be sure to write the word "start" on the end of the template nearest to the trimmer, so that you will not be confused as to which end of the template is the beginning and which is the end when you start to mark the girder.

To mark the girder, transfer the marks from the template to the girder. When marking the adjacent row of joists (that go from the girder to the *other* foundation wall) remember that we are using a *lap joint* over the girder. The joists will not lie in exactly the same places as on the first foundation wall (Ill. 14).

PLACING THE JOISTS

Select the joist lumber. If the joist is to lap over the girder, the exact length is not important as long as the end laps no more than 8″ over the girder.* (The squareness of the cut is not crucial either; that is the advantage of this joint.) If the joist is to butt up against the girder, it must be measured and cut precisely to the necessary

---

* When cutting the joists or any other members that must be cut in multiples, be sure to cut only one or two pieces first to make sure that they fit.

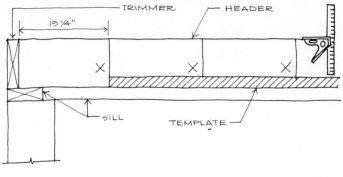

ILL. 12

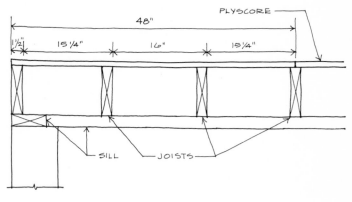

ILL. 13

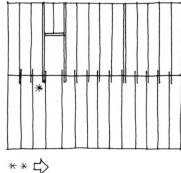

*NOTE: IF THE FRAMING PLAN SPECIFIES JOISTS SPACED 16" O.C., KEEP IN MIND THAT THIS IS A MINIMUM SPACING, YOU COULD ALWAYS MAKE THE SPACING SMALLER THAN 16" O.C., IN ONE OR TWO CASES WHERE IT IS CONVENIENT. WHEN IN DOUBT, THROW IN AN EXTRA JOIST FOR INSURANCE, YOU'LL SLEEP BETTER AT NIGHT. (DOUBLE UP JOISTS UNDER TUBS.)

** ⇨

JOIST LOCATION SHIFTS THE WIDTH OF THE JOISTS

ILL. 14

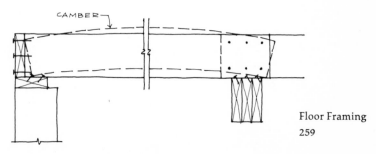

Floor Framing

259

ILL. 15

length. Set the joist on the sill and on the girder. If the joist has a slight camber (desirable) set it with the convex side up (Ill. 15). The weight of the floor will rectify the camber. Make sure that the joist sits squarely in the "box" created for it by the sill and the header. Nail the joist to the header with three 20d nails. Be sure that the joist is right on the line that was so painstakingly marked with the combination square to ensure its being perpendicular to the sill. Recheck with the framing square before nailing.

Framing an Opening

Before constructing the opening for a stair or fireplace, remeasure to ascertain that you will be building it in the exact location specified in the plans. Install the inside set of trimmers first, exactly as you would ordinary joists. Mark the locations of the four header joists on the trimmers. (There will be outside and inside trimmers.) Cut the header joists to size, and install the outside headers. Finally, install the outside trimmers. The stability of the entire system depends on the accuracy of your measurements and on the squareness of the joints (Ill. 16).

If the length of the opening is not running parallel to the line of the joists, care should be taken to beef up the nailing at the junction of the headers and the trimmers. If the opening is particularly long (over 10 feet), you may want to triple the header and triple the trimmer (Ill. 17).

Bridging and Flooring

Although cross bridging (Chapter 8, Ills. 24 and 25) is more economical of materials than solid bridging, it is less economical of labor. In cross bridging the cutting and temporary nailing are done before the subflooring is applied; the final nailing, however, must wait until the subfloor is completed. This is difficult to do in a crawl space.

Solid bridging is constructed before the subfloor. Measure and cut each piece of bridging so that it exactly fits the joist space. Stagger the blocking to simplify nailing. Be sure to align the tops of the joists (Ill. 17).

Plywood subflooring 5/8" thick is laid with the grain of the outer piles at right angles to the joists. Subflooring is nailed with 10d nails to each joist every 6" along the edges of the panel and every 10" for the intermediate joists.

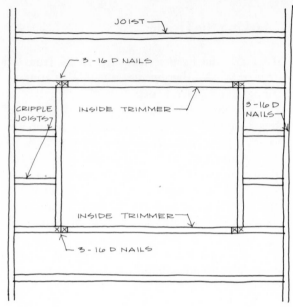

STEP 1

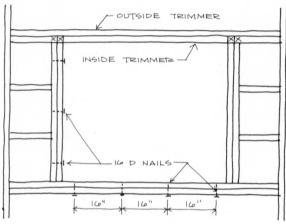

STEP 2

NOTE: LEAVE OUT THE JOISTS ADJACENT TO THE OPENING, UNTIL THE OPENING HAS BEEN FRAMED. OTHERWISE THERE WILL BE NO ROOM TO SWING A HAMMER.

ILL. 16

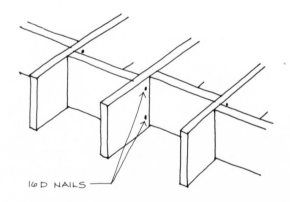

ILL. 17

22
Wall Framing

Having just completed the floor, you are apt to look at your work and feel that all you have to show for your herculean efforts is an outdoor stage. Take heart! When the walls are erected, you will feel as if you have accomplished a great deal.

The platform floor should be cleared of all debris and swept as clean as possible since this is now to be the work surface. Also, sawdust and splinters interfere with the chalk lines that must be drawn on the floor. Now is the time to transfer the first-floor plan of the house onto the rough floor. Dimensions can be measured off at full scale, and the accuracy of the plans can be checked. At this time it is still possible to move around the partitions and change the sizes of the rooms. Sometimes it is easier to get a feeling for the room size when you are looking at the chalk lines on the floor.

MATERIALS

Wall sections are constructed primarily of 2 × 4 stud stock. Most lumberyards stock lumber that is stamped "stud" at the end. Usually this lumber is of slightly poorer quality than the joist or beam material. No. 2 (construction) or no. 3 (standard) grade lumber is adequate for the studs, which will receive only compressive loads for the most part. No. 1 (select) graded lumber should be used for the horizontal supporting members, such as beams and joists, since the sections will be put under bending stresses and therefore must be stronger. Basically, you will need:

- 2 × 4's for the studs and plates. Walls are usually designed to make the most efficient use of the stud section (which is sold in increments of 2'). Figure on using an 8' long stud from floor to ceiling. To determine the number of studs, simply assume that, with waste and imperfect lumber, you will need a stud for every foot of wall and partition. The 2 × 4 plates can be ordered by tripling the number of feet in the periphery of the house and adding 15 percent. Be sure the stock is marked "dry" and not "grn" (green).
- 4 × 8 sheathing (or if you will be using plywood siding as both the sheathing and finished wall, you will need those panels now). Lumberyards sell the 4 × 8 sheathing panels as "sheathing plywood" or "sheathing board." Some sheathing material is made of fiberboard, which has some insulating value. This insulation by itself might be adequate for southern climates but will most likely not have enough heat-transfer resistance to act as an insulation in northern climates.
- Window and door headers, as required.
- Nails—6d, 8d, 10d, 16d.

PROCEDURE

Transferring the Plans to the Platform

Take your long tape, the spool of chalk line, and the house plans and start measuring the exterior wall. Choose one side of the house and measure inward 3½" for the width of the sole plate. (Remember that the actual depth of a 2 × 4 is 3½".) Snap a chalk line along the exterior wall at the 3½" line (line A on Ill. 1). Do the same for the adjacent exterior wall (line B) and for the other exterior walls. Locate the first major parti-

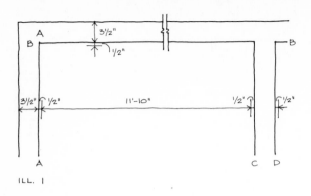

ILL. 1

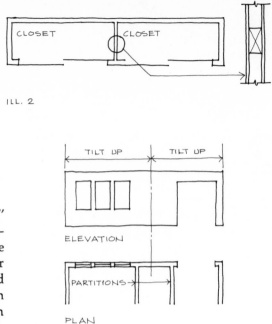

ILL. 2

ILL. 3

tions (an exterior wall is called a "wall," whereas an interior wall is referred to as a "partition"). Measure the actual dimension of the room (let us say 11'-10") and add ½" each for the wallboard on the exterior wall *and* the board (whether gypsum board or wood paneling) on the partition, so that the real dimension between sole plates is the dimension of the room plus 1". Snap line C and 3½" beyond it snap line D.* These represent the exact locations of the sole plate for the partition. Be careful in laying out the sole plate locations. There may be some partitions that need to be wider than the usual 2 × 4 stud width to accommodate pipes in the wall of a bathroom or built-in bookshelves. In such cases the stud sizes might be 2 × 6 or even 2 × 8. For some minor partitions, such as in the short stub walls between closets, 1 × 2 studs (or 2 × 4 studs set sideways) may be used to make the walls thinner (Ill. 2).

Lay out the house in this way measuring off all of the major room partitions before dealing with the minor ones. After having traversed the platform with your tapemeasure, you will know whether the dimensions on the plans are completely accurate. This is the way to check to see if the openings in the floor made for fireplaces and stairways are in exactly the right places. Should there be some error in their placement, it is easier to move the partitions slightly than it is to change the opening that has already been framed. If you move anything be sure to make the changes on the plans for the floors above and in the mechanical plans.

* This book is designed especially for the novice. Understand that once you become familiar with what you are doing, you will learn techniques that will save you labor. For instance, the practiced carpenter will not snap two chalk lines to position the partition plates. He will snap the single line and then mark an X on the side of the line on which the plate will be positioned. We recommend the double chalk lines to simplify the mathematics and to help the novice visualize the room sizes.

Construction
262

Cutting the Plates

You are now ready to cut the plates. Before actually choosing the lumber for the plates, decide how many wall sections will be constructed on the floor to be tilted up into place and the length of each section. On commercial jobs whole walls are often made and lifted by workers with the aid of cranes. On your house it might be advisable to build the walls in smaller sections so that two or three workers can lift them into place.* If so, you should determine where the section breaks will be. Be sure to organize the breaks in the wall sections so that they will not fall in the middle of a window or door, but between openings (Ill. 3). Also, avoid making a division where partitions will butt up against the wall.

Cut the sole plate and lay it between the

* Not every carpenter chooses to prefabricate the walls and then tilt them into place. Practiced carpenters very often will shortcut the process by laying out the three plates simultaneously (two on top, one on the bottom), nailing the sole plate solidly to the floor, and then nailing the studs to the double plates at the top only, leaving the bottom ends free. When this assemblage is completed, it is lifted onto the sole plate and the free ends of the studs are toe-nailed to the sole plate. We deem this operation to be more difficult for the novice than the one described here, but it might be tried by the more experienced builder.

exterior edge of the platform and the chalk lines—lines A and B previously drawn (Ill. 1). Tack the plates down at each end so that they will not slip off their exact locations. (Tacking is temporary nailing. The nails should not be driven down flush with the board. Leave enough nail showing so that the tacks can easily be removed.)

A word about corner posts. There are a number of ways of handling corners, each with its advantages. We suggest that you assemble the wall sections first, raise them into position, and then build up the corner posts by joining the sections and adding blocking as shown in Illustration 4. Keep in mind that there will be sheathing on these sections, which will cover the corner post and help tie the adjacent sections to each other.*

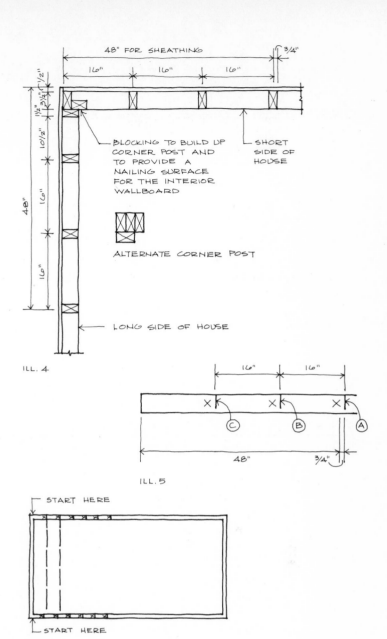

Laying Out the Location of the Studs

To position the sheathing and studs, start with one of the long walls of the house. Begin with the corner and measure 48″ (the width of a sheet of plywood sheathing) out from the corner along one of the walls. Add ¾″ to the 48″ width of a sheet of plywood to make 48¾″. (The sheathing must be centered on the stud, which is 1½″ wide, in order for it to have a nailing surface. This accounts for the ¾″, which is the width of the stud divided by two.) Mark the plate with a blue pencil. (You are going to have so many marks on the plates and studs that it might be wise to keep your pockets filled with a few different-colored pencils. This way the various markings will not look alike.)† This mark represents the first piece of 4′-0″ sheathing and the remaining half of a stud. From that blue mark, measure back (toward the corner again) 16″ and then back another 16″, marks a, b, and c, respectively, on Illustration 5. This locates the studs. Place an X on the side of the blue mark

* The other varieties of corner posts, many of which are preferred by practiced carpenters, are built, erected, and attached to the platform before the walls are constructed. Again, we believe that the tilt-up method is easier for the novice to master, but show the alternate corner post in Illustration 4.
† If you can manage to mark two pieces of lumber at once it is helpful to lay the 2 × 4 section that is to be used as one of the top plates adjacent to the sole plate and mark both of them.

closest to the corner. This is where the stud will be positioned.

To position the next series of studs, measure from mark "a" along the wall and mark the plate at 16″ intervals, regardless of where the openings fall. (Make sure that the plate is continuous around the periphery of the house, even under doors and sliding glass doors. The plates will be cut away after the completed wall sections are positioned.) Having completed the stud markings on the first long side of the house, cross over to the other long side and mark the studs there as well.

Begin the markings on the same end of the house you began with for the first long wall so that the studs on the parallel sides of the house line up (Ill. 6). When the long walls are com-

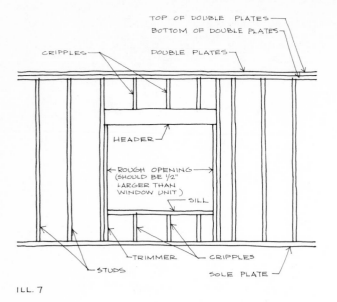

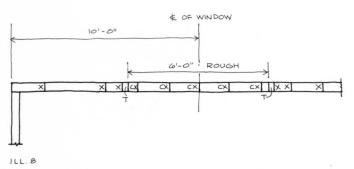

ILL. 7

ILL. 8

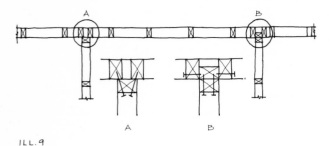

ILL. 9

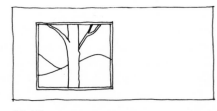

ILL. 10

is a stud 48" from the corner to nail the sheathing to (Ill. 4).

Laying Out the Wall Openings

You are now ready to accommodate the doors, windows, and partitions that butt the wall (Ill. 7). Take out the red pencil and locate the rough window openings. The architectural plans will designate these rough openings in one of two ways. The designer might have given you the exact rough opening. If so, your work is simple. On the other hand, if the designer indicated the dimension of the center line of the window only (Ill. 8), you will have to measure from the corner of the building to the center line. Find out the needed *rough* opening for the window (it will be on the manufacturer's literature, or if you have the window in your possession you can measure it), divide that figure in half, and measure the halves on either side of the center line.

Draw a red line to indicate the rough opening, and a "t" on the side of the red lines outward from the rough opening (Ill. 8). Draw another set of red lines 1½" out from the first set of red lines to position the studs. You can get rid of the regular studs drawn in blue pencil if they are not exactly where you will need them, or if they are superfluous. The X's marking the studs for the rough opening should be joined by a "c" to indicate that they are cripples (Ill. 8).

Special provisions should be made where the partitions abut the walls. (They should be clearly marked right there on the platform floor.) The sturdiest accommodation is made by adding two or more studs as shown in Illustration 9. It is essential that the partitions have sturdy nailing surfaces. The marks indicating the future location of the partitions should be made in red.

After the house and all its rough openings are transferred to the sole plates, rest, and rethink your work. Perhaps it was a mistake to put the large picture window facing the elm tree. Put a chair on the platform floor and sit in front of the opening marked for a window. You probably didn't realize that the elm tree would completely bisect the view (Ill. 10). Would it make more aesthetic sense to move the window over a few feet? Redraw the elevations. Do they look o.k.? It is still not too late to make radical modifications in the placement of the windows and doors. One advantage of being your own

pleted, mark the end walls. Follow the same beginning procedure. Mark 48" from the corner of the house plus ¾" and then mark back 16", and again, 16". The distance between the first and second studs will be short (only 10½", see Ill. 4) but the sheathing will eventually cover and join the entire corner. When you get to the other end of that short wall, be sure that there

builder is that you won't charge yourself extra for making last-minute changes.

Assembling the Wall Sections

You will now need a piece of lumber the same dimensions and length as the sole plate. This will be the top plate. The studs will be nailed between the two. All of the markings on the sole plate must be transferred to the top plate.

Transfer all the marks (both red and blue) to the top plate. Remove the tacks from the sole plate and move both top and sole plates to a level part of the platform. Cut the regular studs to size if they require cutting. Hopefully the wall has been designed so that standard-size studs can be used without cutting. The ends of the machine-cut studs are precision cut to be true to square. If you are doing your own cutting you must be careful to cut the ends at right angles.

To simplify the procedure of measuring off the vertical dimensions for the placement of the header and sill it is advised that you construct a master pole—a separate piece of lumber on which the vertical dimensions are clearly marked. The critical dimensions are then transferred from the master pole to the studs.

Constructing the Wall Sections

To make the master pole, choose a very straight piece of 2 × 4 or 1 × 4. Mark the 1½″ for the top of the sole plate from one end of the pole (Ill. 11, a). Mark the distance to the bottom of the rough opening (b). Mark the top of the rough opening (c) and the bottom of the double plate (d). The sill should be marked and so should the top of the header (e and f).

Position the full-length studs as indicated by the blue marks and nail top and bottom to the plates (with two 16d nails as shown in Illustration 12). Be especially careful to square the studs that frame the window openings. Using the master pole, measure and cut 2 × 4's for the trimmers and nail these pieces to the sole plate and to the adjacent studs. Measure the distance between the trimmers and cut the sill, using the master pole for the vertical distance. The sill is then positioned and nailed to the trimmers. Measure the header lumber and assemble the header (Inset I). Position the header on top of

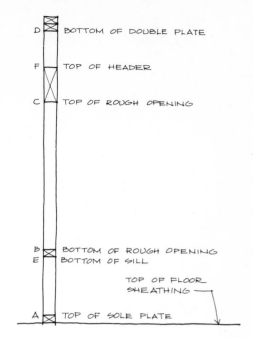

D — BOTTOM OF DOUBLE PLATE

F — TOP OF HEADER

C — TOP OF ROUGH OPENING

B — BOTTOM OF ROUGH OPENING
E — BOTTOM OF SILL

TOP OF FLOOR SHEATHING —

A — TOP OF SOLE PLATE

ILL. 11

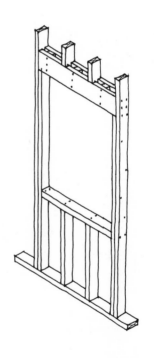

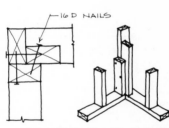

16 D NAILS

INTERSECTION OF WALL SECTIONS AT A CORNER

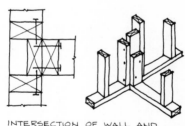

INTERSECTION OF WALL AND PARTITIONS

DOUBLE PLATE OVER CORNER POST

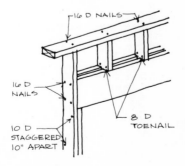

16 D NAILS

16 D NAILS

10 D STAGGERED 10″ APART

8 D TOENAIL

ILL. 12

There are many openings in the walls of a house—for windows, doors, pass-throughs, and so on. Since most exterior walls are load-bearing, some provision has to be made for the transfer of loads over and around these openings. The double plates help to transfer the load to the studs. But in the case of the crippled studs over an opening, they end over the window. The window frame and the glass are in no way strong enough to take on the load of the roof, or the second floor and the roof. This becomes even more critical over large openings such as those for garage doors, bay windows, or sliding glass doors. The header, which is framed over the window opening, acts as a beam to transfer the loads to the trimmer studs. The header can be made up of beam material (4 × 6's, or 4 × 8's) but it is more economical to build up this piece out of 2″ material (2 × 6's or 2 × 8's). To do this place the two pieces of header on edge. Since each piece is 1½″ thick, a ½″ piece of plywood scrap or ⅜″ Sheetrock scraps are nailed in between as blocking to bring the composite width up to the width of the 3½″ studs and trimmers (right). Very often the distance between the header and the double plates is too short to justify the placement of cripple studs. In such cases the space is completely blocked in and filled with a solid piece of wood. The length of the header is equal to the rough opening plus the width of the trimmers.

Recommended Header Sizes

Rough opening	If supporting floor above and roof above that	If supporting roof above
3′-0″	2 × 4	2 × 4
3′-6″	2 × 6	2 × 4
4′-0″ to 6′-0″	2 × 6	2 × 6
6′-0″ to 8′-0″	2 × 8	2 × 8
8′-0″ to 10′-0″	2 × 12	2 × 10
10′-0″ to 12′-0″	2 × 14	2 × 14

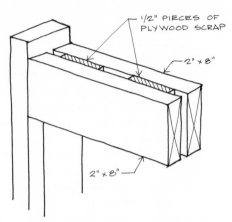

1/2" PIECES OF PLYWOOD SCRAP

2" × 8"

2" × 8"

NOTE: IT IS A GOOD IDEA TO USE OVERSIZED HEADERS THAT GO FROM THE TOP OF THE WINDOW TO THE PLATES. THIS AVOIDS THE CONSTRUCTION OF CRIPPLES ABOVE THE HEADER.

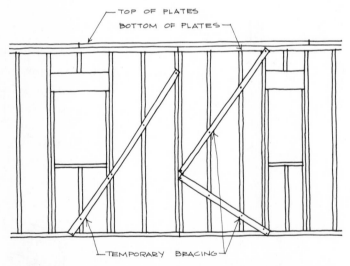

TOP OF PLATES

BOTTOM OF PLATES

TEMPORARY BRACING

NOTE: POSTPONE THE PLACING OF THE TOP OF THE TWO UPPER PLATES UNTIL THE PARTITIONS ARE COMPLETE. THIS WAY THE TOP PLATE CAN OVERLAP THE PARTITION AND THE WALL.

ILL. 13

the trimmer and nail to the trimmers and the adjacent studs. Measure and cut the crippled studs for the top and bottom of the rough opening and nail into place. Check for squareness with the framing square. If square, tack 1 × 4 temporary bracing across the studs on the diagonal (Ill. 13). Make sure that all parts of the assembly are nailed securely, using the nailing details in Illustration 12.

Raise the wall into position utilizing as many hands as are available. Be sure that the sole plate is located exactly on the chalk line. With a few temporary nails, nail the sole plate to the platform floor, and brace it with 2 × 4's as shown in Illustration 14. Before the wall sections are secured permanently, they will have to be plumbed. This is best accomplished after all of the wall sections are completed.

Assembling the Corners

When all of the sections are completed and temporarily braced, the corners are plumbed and nailed permanently. Illustration 4 shows the organization of the corner. One piece of wall section should come flush with the outside of the platform. The other, intersecting section should butt up against it. A third stud length should be cut and positioned between them, as shown. This stud not only stabilizes the corner, but also provides a nailing surface for the interior wallboard.

The walls can be plumbed with a plumb bob or with a carpenter's level. The short carpenter's level should be used in conjunction with a long straightedge so that the full height of the wall can be checked. Often there is a slight warp in the stud, and the straightedge does not lie flat on the surface of the wall. To rectify this problem attach blocks to the ends of the straightedge so that the middle section of the straightedge can stand an inch or so off the wall (Ill. 15). Adjust the braces until the section is plumb.

When all the wall sections are plumb, and the corners nailed firmly together, nail the top plate of the double plates (Ill. 13) onto the assembled-in-place walls and partitions. Be sure to use the top of the two plates to span the breaks between sections and to connect the partitions to the walls.

Once the walls are leveled and joined by the top plate, the sole plate should be nailed securely to the platform. Be sure to nail the plate into the joists beneath the subfloor! The line of the joists can be found by looking for the nail

pattern on the floor. It is important to nail the sole plate to the joists and not merely to the subfloor. Make sure there are at least two nails from the plate to each joist. If you feel that the wall is moving as you nail, you know that the braces are not secure enough.

The Sheathing

The plywood used for sheathing is usually specified at ½" thick. The 4 × 8 sheets are nailed to the studs using 6d nails, either vertically or horizontally. Alternatives to plywood are fiberboard or diagonally applied boards. Diagonal boards are seldom used because they require more work and diagonal corner braces. Fiberboard comes in ½" thick sheets 4' × 8' and larger. Ask the lumberyard for specific nailing instructions. Fiberboard is not a substitute for plywood. The finished exterior wall cannot be nailed directly onto the fiberboard, and special roofing nails most often have to be used to attach the fiberboard sheathing to the studs. Unless you have corner braces (which is not likely if you have followed this book exclusively), you must substitute plywood sheathing panels for the fiberboard in the corners. This plywood should be applied vertically.

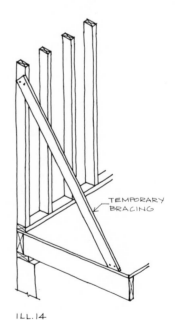

TEMPORARY BRACING

ILL. 14

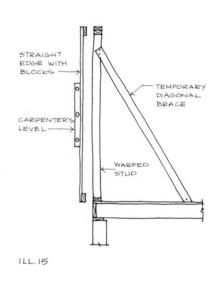

STRAIGHT EDGE WITH BLOCKS

TEMPORARY DIAGONAL BRACE

CARPENTER'S LEVEL

WARPED STUD

ILL. 15

23
Roof Framing and Roofing

Roof framing is exacting work. Here again, measurements must be accurate to the fraction of an inch. Before leaving for the construction site to begin work, be sure to review all of the framing plans. Order the lumber as needed, being sure that the lengths, grade, and type of wood is delivered as specified.

MATERIALS

The tools for this part of the operation are listed on page 254. The following materials will be required. Additional equipment may be needed for special types of roofs.

• Ceiling joists, 2″ stock: As per the dimensions required in the ceiling plan. Estimate quantities similarly to the floor joists.
• Rafter stock: Check the framing plans for the required dimensions. To determine the length of the rafter stock, use a framing square to make a scaled drawing of the rafter. Use the side of the square where the inch is divided into twelve parts. This way you can assume that each $1/12$ is an inch and that twelve $1/12$'s are a foot. Set the framing square on a piece of paper and mark the total run on the blade (the longer arm of the square). Draw a line from that point to the intersection of the blade and tongue (the short leg of the framing square). Draw a line up the tongue to the total rise of the roof. Be sure that your measurements are totally accurate. Lift the square off the paper and draw the hypotenuse of the triangle. The

length of the hypotenuse minus $3/4$″ (for half the thickness of the ridge) is the line length of the rafter. Add to this figure the length of the overhang and about 9″ for cuts off the ends (Ill. 1).

An alternate way of determining the line length of the rafter is to use the following formula:

$$\frac{\text{line}}{\text{length}} = \left[\frac{\sqrt{12^2 + \text{the pitch per foot}^2}}{12} \times \text{run} \right] - 3/4''$$

Add to this figure the overhang, and about 9″ to 12″ for cutting.

For the number of rafters required, multiply the length of the roof (the ridge length) $\times$ $3/4$ (for 16″ o.c. spacing; for 24″ o.c. spacing use $1/2$) and add 1 for the end rafter.* Double this figure for the rafters on the other side of the ridge. Always add at least 10 percent for errors, omissions, and waste.

• Plywood sheathing: Use the following table for thicknesses.

| | Thickness of plywood | |
Rafter spacing	Asphalt or wood shingles	Asbestos-cement
16″ o.c.	use $5/16$″ plywood	use $1/2$″ plywood
24″ o.c.	use $3/8$″ plywood	use $5/8$″ plywood

To estimate the number of plywood panels required, multiply 2 $\times$ (the length of the rafter + overhang) $\times$ the length of ridge. In the case of plywood roof sheathing, you need only order

* Count the rafters on the framing plan for plank-and-beam construction.

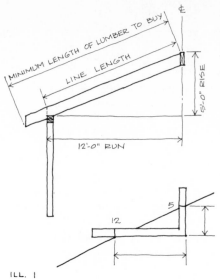

RISE:
TOP OF PLATES TO TOP
OF RAFTER- RIDGE
INTERSECTION

RUN:
FROM OUTSIDE
SUPPORT TO CENTER
LINE OF RIDGE

LINE LENGTH:
THE HYPOTENUSE OF
THE TRIANGLE MADE
BY THE RISE AND
RUN, MINUS ONE
HALF THE WIDTH OF
THE RIDGE

ILL. 1

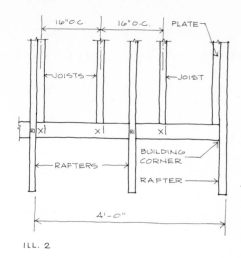

ILL. 2

about 5 percent over the calculated amount required since there is little waste.

- Ridge stock, 2″ thick. For the depth of the ridge, add 2″ to the depth of the rafters as determined by the design. The length of the ridge is the length of the long walls + the gable overhang, if there is to be one.
- Nails: 3d, 4d, 8d, 10d.
- Wood shingles: Estimate 4 bundles (1,000 shingles) for every 100 square feet of roof and 3 pounds of nails for 100 square feet. Asphalt strip shingles: 3 bundles per 100 square feet.
- Metal roof flashing: As required.
- Flexible roof flashing and cement: If required.

FRAMING

The gable and the shed roof are constructed similarly. We will detail the construction of the simple gable roof; you can modify these instructions to apply to the shed roof. The plank-and-beam roof is composed of similar but heavier sections than the raftered-gable roof. The construction procedure is similar except that a crane might be required to raise the ridge beam. Remember that the connections for plank-and-beam construction must be made with anchors and not with nails. Consult Chapter 9, Roof Design, for connection details.

Laying Out the Rafters (and Ceiling Joists) on the Plates

The top plates of the exterior walls and interior load-bearing partitions must be carefully mea-

ILL. 3

sured and marked to receive the rafters and ceiling joists (Ill. 2). Make sure that the ceiling joists rest directly over the studs below (unless, of course, the spacing is different). If there are no ceiling joists in the design, arrange for the rafters to be placed directly over the wall studs. Consult the framing plan and measure off the location of the joists and rafters directly onto the top plate, using the method outlined on page 258 for floor framing. Make sure that all of the joists and rafters are laid out on the opposite exterior wall (and partitions) before proceeding further.

Position the ceiling joists and toe-nail them to the plates using 8d nails (Ill. 3). If there is an intermediary support (such as a partition) between the two exterior walls, plan to use an overlapping or butt joint as shown in Chapter 8, Illustration 22.

INSET I / PREPARING THE RAFTER STOCK FOR CUTTING

Before laying out the cuts on the rafter stock, check the figures on the framing plan to determine if the mathematics are correct. You will need the following figures: 1. The slope of the roof, that is, the unit rise to the run, as expressed in the ratios 5:12, 8:12, or the exact rise and run dimensions; and 2. the line length of the rafter as expressed in feet and inches (Ill. I-1 and Ill. 1). This figure can be determined from your calculations and large-scale drawings made as directed in Chapter 9, Roof Design (pages 94–5), or from methods described in the materials list of this chapter. Actually, more than one method should be used to ensure accuracy.

Next choose a very straight and clean piece of rafter stock. Before cutting all of the rafters, make a pattern, test it on the roof, adjust it if necessary, and then cut all of the other rafters from this pattern.

To lay out the rafter, measure off the rise on the tongue (short end) and the run on the blade (long end) of the framing square. Since these dimensions will be referred to again and again, it is a good idea to hold them by applying tape at these exact points on the framing square or by using clips manufactured for this purpose.

Study Illustration I-1. The line length of the rafter is a mathematical length that will be used to determine the distance from the ridge cut to the bird's mouth cut, which will serve as the seat for the rafter on the plates of the wall. Position the rafter so that the crown (bow) of the camber will be the top of the rafter.

1. Position the framing square (as directed in Ill. I-2) on point 1 and draw the ridge cut line.

2. From point 1, along the top of the ridge, measure the line length of the rafter (Ill. I-3). This will give you point 2.

3. Position the tongue mark (in this case 5) on point 2, and move the square until the 12 mark on the blade rests on the

top of the rafter stock in the position illustrated in I-3. Draw a line down along the outside of the tongue, from point 2; this will be the vertical cut line for the bird's mouth.

4. Invert the square. Lay it as shown in Illustration I-4 and measure off 3½". This is the final cut of the bird's mouth, representing the width (3½") of the plates.

5. Measure off the overhang as designed and draw the line for the overhang cut.

THE SHED ROOF RAFTER

The shed roof rafter (Ill. I-5) has two bird's mouth cuts. The design span of the rafter and the line length are the same. To lay out this kind of rafter, follow steps 1 through 5.

6. Position the framing square as shown (Ill. I-6) for top end bird's mouth.

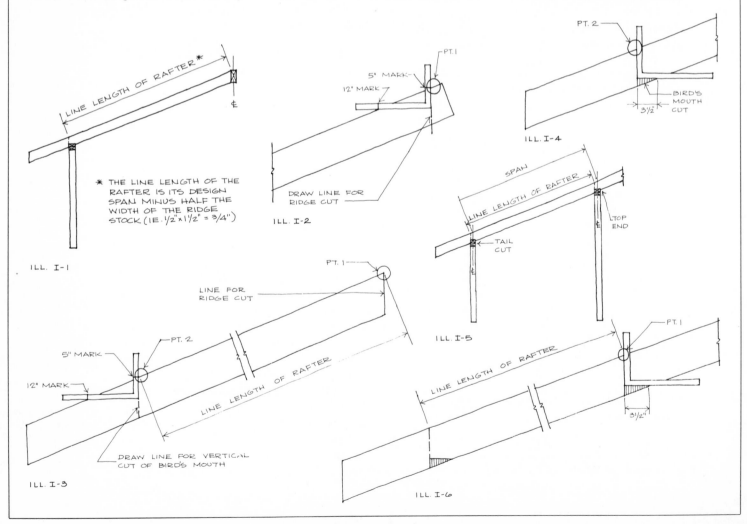

The Ridge

The first step in constructing the roof is to select the ridge stock.* Although this piece of lumber serves little structural purpose, it should be as straight as possible. The rafters that will butt against it are cut exactly to fit, and too much of a warp or camber in the ridge stock will throw off the assembly.

Before installing the ridge, set the ridge section alongside the plates and lay out the rafter spacing on the ridge by transferring the marking directly from the plates. Make sure that the ridge pieces (if you need more than one to make up the full length of the roof) are joined to each other at the point of intersection with two rafters (Ill. 4). Next, move the ridge section to the center of the building and rest it across the ceiling joists directly below where it will be when in its final position as the ridge. Cut five pieces of rafter stock as outlined in Inset I. Do not cut more than these few pieces until the rafters are tested for accuracy. The first four pieces will serve as testers and will be nailed temporarily in place to the ridge section. If these prove to be correct, the remaining piece will serve as a pattern from which the others can be traced and then cut. At first glance this procedure might seem overly cautious. On the other hand, such caution is warranted by the fact that many errors are possible. The rafters need to be cut at exactly the correct angle and length, and lumber is too expensive to waste.

Although it is possible to raise the roof by yourself using bracing and makeshift scaffolding, it is much easier to work with one or two helpers. Beginning at one gable end, nail a rafter to the plate. (You will most likely need the help of one friend for this operation. If no one is available, erect some sort of scaffolding out of boards and sawhorses to hold the other end of the rafter in position while you nail its lower end to the plate.) Temporarily nail the rafter to the plate by hammering the nails down so that

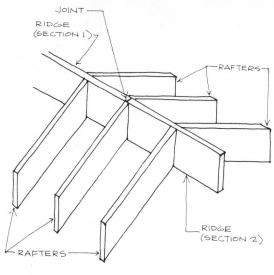

ILL. 4

the nailheads can be withdrawn easily. Nail the second rafter to the opposite plate as your friend holds the two rafters in place at their intersection with the ridge. Lift one end of the ridge section, and while someone else supports the other end (here is where the third set of hands is helpful), temporarily nail the rafters to it. Shift the scaffolding so that it now supports the free end of the ridge. Move down about six rafter spacings and nail the two remaining rafters temporarily in place. The assembly should now be plumbed and braced. (The ridge section should be level.) Measure the vertical distance from the ceiling joists to the ridge section, making sure that this dimension conforms to the one on your framing elevation drawing. If all seems to be in order, it is now time to cut the remaining rafters (Ill. 5).

Nail the intervening rafters in place following the above procedure of first toe-nailing the rafter to the plate and then to the ridge section. Alternate the installation of the rafters so that only two or three rafters are nailed into place on one side of the ridge before you move to the other side and install the other half of the rafter pairs. Nail a 2 × 4 as bracing to the top of the rafters (Ill. 6). This will not only help to keep the framing straight until it is completed, but will also serve to keep it sturdy. Since you will be climbing over the framing, and may be leaning on it for support, bracing the framing is not meaningless work.

Nail the rafters to their adjoining ceiling joists (Ill. 2). When the roof is complete, drop a

---

* In plank-and-beam construction the ridge beam is supported by walls or columns and not by the rafters. Therefore, the ridge beam must be installed first, before the rafters. Connections are illustrated on page 100, Ill. 10. You may have to use a crane to lift the ridge beam into place. If the lengths are short, you may be able to use people power. The rafters are either cut with bird's mouths, as described later in this chapter, or are cut off straight. The rafters are connected to the ridge as illustrated on page 100, Ill. 10.

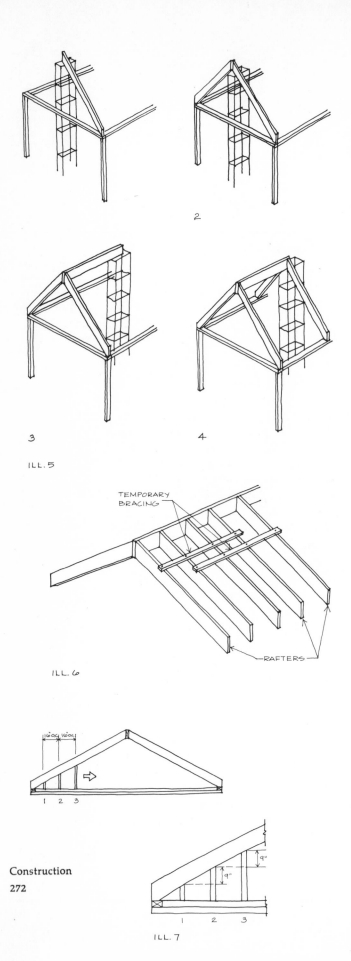

2

3 4

ILL. 5

TEMPORARY
BRACING

RAFTERS

ILL. 6

ILL. 7

plumb line at either gable end to ensure that the end gables are straight.

Completing the Gable Wall Section

Lay out the stud spacing at the gable ends at 16" o.c. If there is to be a window or vent opening, lay out the trimmers as well, following the directions outlined in Chapter 21, page 258. Hold a piece of stud stock at the first stud space (Ill. 7) and mark the angle at which it intersects the end rafter. Repeat at each stud spacing. Cut the studs and nail them in place. (Care should be taken not to force the gable end studs into place. The pressure might distort the end rafter.) Not all of the sections need to be custom fit as described. The distance between the first and the second studs will be standard. If the second stud is 9" longer than the first, then the third stud will be 9" longer than the second, and so forth. The studs can then be laid out on the ground and cut in pairs. The window or vent opening is framed similarly to a conventional opening, as described in Chapter 22, page 264.

Gable Overhang

Many roofs have a broad gable overhang (Ill. 8). This type of roof must be framed slightly differently than the one outlined above. As we discussed previously in reference to the statics of cantilevers, the backup for the cantilever should be three times as long as the cantilevered portion. The roof is framed as shown in Illustration 9. If the overhang is 2'-0", the backup portion should be about 6'-0". This means that the end rafter and the second rafter are eliminated from the original framing of the roof, and the ridge extends the length of the overhang. The rafters are installed as directed in the section above, but starting with the fourth rafter spacing instead of the gable end. The gable wall is then constructed independently, having its own top plate. The top plate should be flush with the bottom of the rafter.

Roof Openings

Roof openings may be framed by measuring and cutting the rafters before installation, or by erecting the roof framing first without consider-

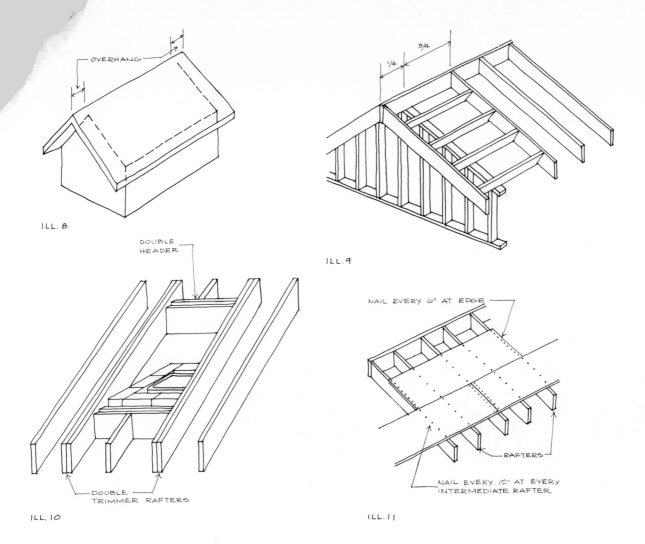

OVERHANG

ILL. 8

3/4

1/4

ILL. 9

DOUBLE HEADER

DOUBLE TRIMMER RAFTERS

ILL. 10

NAIL EVERY 6" AT EDGE

RAFTERS

NAIL EVERY 12" AT EVERY INTERMEDIATE RAFTER

ILL. 11

ation of the openings and then cutting and framing the opening in much the same fashion as outlined for floor openings in Chapter 21, page 260. The second method is advisable for most small openings, especially for the novice carpenter. The waste of material is compensated for by the simplicity of framing the roof without having to worry about additional details (Ill. 10). Before cutting any openings be sure that you drop a plumb line down to the house below to ensure that the hole you are framing is directly above the item (for example, the chimney) you are framing. Before making cuts in the rafters, nail temporary bracing to them so that they will not collapse as soon as they become "cripples."

Use a straightedge to make sure that all of the rafters lie on an even plane. Use a taut line to check that the rafter ends (at the exterior walls) end in a straight line. If there is to be a fascia piece at the end of the rafters, plan for it.

Roof Sheathing*

The most commonly used sheathing is plywood, which provides a nailing surface for the roofing material and also serves to stiffen the roof framing. Plywood is installed with its long side perpendicular to the run of the rafters. Start applying the plywood sheathing on the lower part of the roof and work your way up to the ridge, cutting the boards where needed. As in floor sheathing, the panels should be applied in an alternating pattern as shown in Illustration 11. See the materials list, page 268, for thicknesses.

When installing sheathing, as in all other roof work, be very careful! Don't leave loose plywood on the roof. The wind or gravity might cause it to fall. A neighbor who is a careful and

* In the case of plank-and-beam construction the sheathing consists of tongue-and-groove planks. Be sure to install the tongue pointing up (as illustrated on page 99, Ill. 4) so that water will not penetrate the roof.

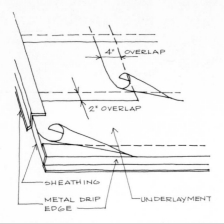

4" OVERLAP

2" OVERLAP

SHEATHING

METAL DRIP EDGE

UNDERLAYMENT

ILL. 12

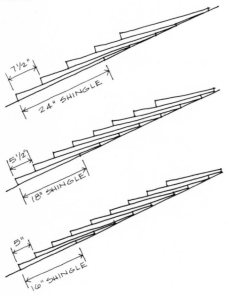

7½"

24" SHINGLE

5½"

18" SHINGLE

5"

16" SHINGLE

ROOF SLOPE GREATER THAN 5:12

ILL. 13

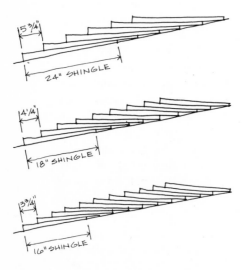

5¾"

24" SHINGLE

4¼"

18" SHINGLE

3¾"

16" SHINGLE

ROOF SLOPE LESS THAN 5:12

ILL. 14

cautious workman temporarily lost the use of his right hand after a fall from a roof. Apparently he stepped on a piece of plywood that he assumed was secured to the framing. In actuality, the carpenter was storing the plywood on the roof until he could use it. The plywood and our friend fell together, the plywood barely missing the man. As an additional safety precaution, scaffolding should be erected at the periphery of the house to facilitate the nailing of the lower row of sheathing. The scaffolding can be moved around the house as the work progresses.

ROOFING

Immediately after the sheathing is applied and completed, a permanent or temporary protection of the sheathing should be provided. If the roof is to be shingled in wood, and the shingling is to be accomplished right away, no roofing protection is required, although one is sometimes provided along the eaves of the roof. However, if the roof is to be finished with a manufactured product, such as asbestos shingles, it must be protected with roofing paper, and that operation should take place immediately.

Prepare the sheathing for the paper by making sure that 1. there are no nailheads of splinters projecting, 2. the sheathing is perfectly dry, 3. the sheathing surface is clean and free of dirt and sawdust, and 4. knotholes are repaired by nailing metal flashing material over them.

Underlayment

Roofing underlayment consists of asphalt-saturated felt or a similar material. The material comes in rolls 36″ wide and 72′ or 144′ long. The paper is laid in long horizontal rows beginning with one layer parallel to the edge of the roof, and working the layers up to the ridge. The horizontal joints should overlap about 2″ (Ill. 12); the overlap when one roll ends and another begins should be 4″ (Ill. 12). Two people are usually required for the job. The underlayment is stapled to the sheathing every 12″ and along the edges of the roof. Lap the felt over the ridge. A drip edge (purchased prefabricated) should be installed under the felt at the bottom edge of the roof and over the felt at the side edge (Ill. 12). Install all flashing as directed in Inset II.

Installing Wood Shingles

Wood-shingled roofs do not usually require an underlayment of saturated felt. As a matter of fact, such an underlayment is generally not recommended because it might hinder the movement of moisture out of the house. (The felt is usually as vaporproof as it is waterproof.) However, a 4' to 6' strip of saturated felt might be used at the lower border of the roof as "flashing" to prevent water from entering the house due to the phenomenon known as "ice damming" (see Chapter 12, page 134).

The type of wood shingle selected and the amount of overlap depend on the slope of the roof. (The steeper the roof, the quicker snow and rain will be shed, and the fewer layers of protective shingles are needed.) If the slope is more than 5:12, follow the exposure pattern in Illustration 13. If the slope is less than 5:12, follow the pattern in Illustration 14.

Chimney flashing (Inset II) is coordinated with the laying up of the shingles and the masonry. Nailing must be done with rust-resistant, hot-dipped, zinc-coated nails. Threaded nails are preferred. For 16" and 18" shingles, 3d nails are recommended; for 24" shingles, 4d nails. (Carpenters often use a shingler's hatchet for cutting wood shingles. This item is not necessarily required, as a piece of plywood used as a straightedge and a hammer are almost as good.) Only two nails are placed in each shingle. Shingles are nailed 1¼" over the point of overlap with another shingle underneath (Ill. 15) and about 1" from the edges.

Begin at the eaves. Extend the first shingle about ¼" beyond the gable end, and ¼" over the eaves as a drip cap. Double the first layer of shingles. Space the shingles ¼" apart to allow for the swelling and expansion of the wood. For reasons of appearance and watertightness, be sure that the vertical joints in successive rows of shingles are staggered. Three courses should not line up (Ill. 16). It is important that the lines be kept straight and parallel with one another and the lines of the roof. Snap chalk lines across the sheathing as guidelines for each course of shingles. A helpful trick is to nail a long 1 × 2 under where the next row of shingles will be. Lay the shingles in a row on the board and hammer them in (Ill. 17).

For the ridge, specially made ridge units may be purchased to cap the house (Ill. 18). Alternatively, shingles the width of the exposed shingle

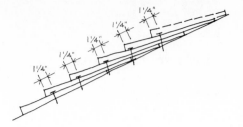

ILL. 15

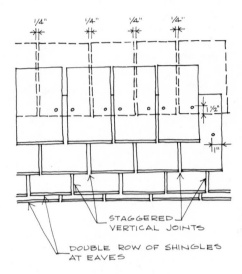

STAGGERED VERTICAL JOINTS

DOUBLE ROW OF SHINGLES AT EAVES

ILL. 16

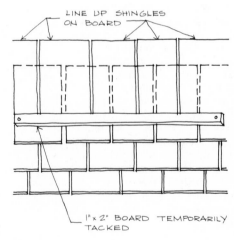

LINE UP SHINGLES ON BOARD

1" × 2" BOARD TEMPORARILY TACKED

ILL. 17

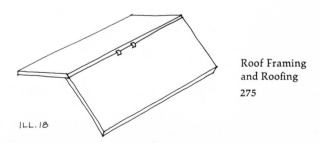

Roof Framing and Roofing

ILL. 18

A very important aspect of the building is flashing. Flashing, as mentioned in Chapter 12, Completing the Exterior, must be placed between the intersection of two different materials, at the juxtaposition of two planes, or at any crucial area where moisture penetration may occur.

Flashing material may be metal, such as copper (formerly the most popular choice but now quite expensive) or aluminum. It may also be made of a flexible material, such as heavy roofing paper.

FLASHING AROUND THE CHIMNEY

Flashing around the chimney is particularly difficult because the chimney and the house frame are structured to be discontinuous. There is likely to be some settling of the structural frame of the house, which will create gaps between the chimney and the roof. Therefore, two overlapping layers of flashing are used to prevent the penetration of water while allowing for the independence of chimney from roof. One is attached to the roof itself, and the other is integrated into the construction of the chimney. The overlapping of the layers allows for some movement.

The bottom section of the flashing is constructed of 90-pound mineral-surfaced roofing paper. It is called the base flashing and is cemented to the roof. First the shingles are applied up the roof until they reach the bottom of the chimney penetration (Ill. II-1). The roofing paper is cut for the bottom section as shown in Illustration II-2. The flashing should extend about 10″ up the chimney and 10″ along the roof. Cut the four pieces of roofing and cement securely to the roof as well as to each other. The flashing must be applied in the following order so that no rain can penetrate as water travels down the roof: bottom, sides, then top.

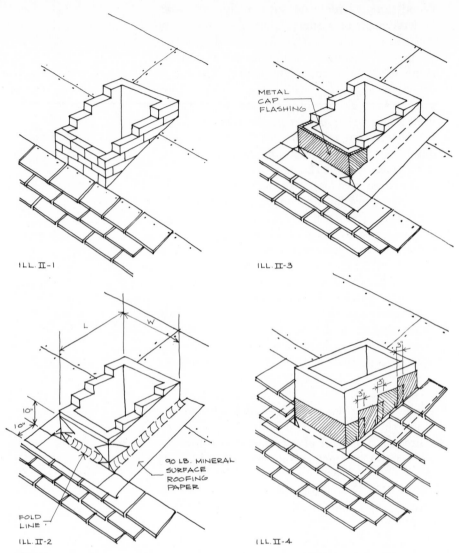

ILL. II-1

ILL. II-2

ILL. II-3

ILL. II-4

The flashing that is attached to the chimney is cap flashing, made up of metal flashing material that is set into the joints between the masonry when the bricks are being laid. The first of the pieces applied is the lower section. It is cut the width of the chimney plus enough more to wrap around the corners. The material is set ½″ into the mortar joint and overlaps the base flashing (Ill. II-3). The side pieces must be stepped

---

section (5¾″ for 24″ long shingles, and so on, according to the sizes given in Illustrations 13 and 14) and the length of the shingle may be used. Follow the pattern in Illustration 19 for laying the ridge shingles.

Installing Asphalt Strip Shingles

Asphalt strip shingles are very easy and quick to install. The most common shingle is the

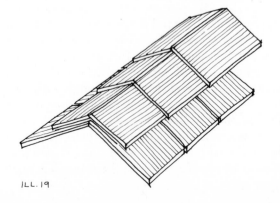

ILL. 19

up the chimney in shorter pieces to conform to the slope of the roof (Ill. II-4). The back of the chimney presents a special problem because it provides a pocket for water and snow accumulation. For this reason, a small cricket or gable is built to keep snow and water from collecting. It is covered with flashing and carried under the shingles and cap flashing (Ill. II-5).

FLASHING AROUND VENTS

Use one piece of sleeve flashing to cover the vent pipe. The sleeve should lap 2" over the vent and flare a minimum of 6" at the base. Use cleats to hold the flashing sleeve in place (Ill. II-6).

FLASHING AT THE RIDGE

Flashing at the ridge can be exposed or concealed. We suggest that you use the concealed flashing for aesthetic reasons. Use 16 ounce copper, .019" aluminum, 26 gauge stainless, or 24 gauge galvanized steel material. Use 10" lengths of flashing material and lap 4". Shingles are applied up to the point where they reach the ridge. The flashing is applied and nailed over the shingles into the sheathing. Special ridge shingles are installed in an alternating pattern as shown (Ill. II-7).

ROOF EDGE FLASHING

The edge of the roof, over the cornice, must be protected from a driving rain. The material to be used is the same as that used for ridge flashing. Details are shown in Illustration II-8. If a gutter is to be installed, see details in Illustration II-9.

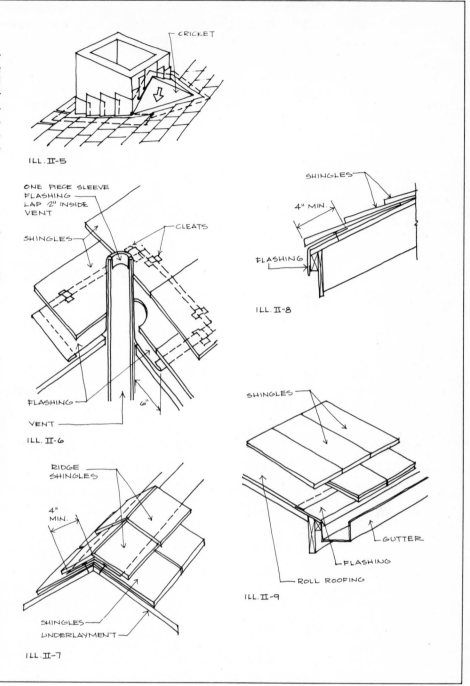

ILL. II-5

ILL. II-6

ILL. II-7

ILL. II-8

ILL. II-9

square-butt strip that is 16" long and 12" wide and has three "tabs" (phony shingles) with two cutouts between the tabs. With this type of shingle 5" of the strip is left exposed to the weather. The strips are sold twenty-seven to a bundle. Three bundles will cover 100 square feet of roof.

Asphalt strip shingles require a full underlayment of saturated felt, which is applied as directed in the section on underlayment above. Drip edges of 26-gauge galvanized steel are applied at the eaves and at the rake. Install all flashing (Inset II).

The strips are applied in long horizontal lines. Chalk lines are snapped to keep the rows straight and parallel. (Begin the work by snapping one line for each course. As you get more proficient you will need only one line for every three courses.) Use 1¼" galvanized nails with barbed shanks and large heads. The shingle manufacturer will most likely recommend the type of nails that will best do the job. Nail

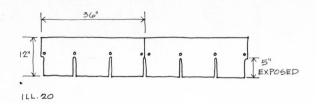

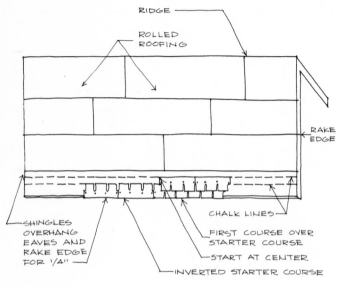

RIDGE

ROLLED ROOFING

RAKE EDGE

SHINGLES OVERHANG EAVES AND RAKE EDGE FOR 1/4"

CHALK LINES

FIRST COURSE OVER STARTER COURSE

START AT CENTER

INVERTED STARTER COURSE

ILL. 21

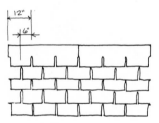

HALF-BREAK POINTS

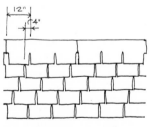

THIRD BREAK POINTS

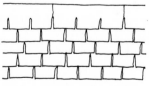

RANDOM SPACING

ILL. 22

according to the nailing pattern in Illustration 20. Cut strips with a linoleum knife.

To begin, start at the eaves somewhere in the center between the gable ends, and work outward in horizontal lines. Lay a starter strip, which is nothing more than a layer of strip shingles applied upside down, or a special strip sold for the purpose. (A layer of wood shingles under the starter course is sometimes used. The wood shingles are laid with ½" projecting past the eaves to prevent water from getting under the asphalt strips.) The starter strip is designed to close up the gaps made by the cutouts in the strip shingle at the eaves. Lay this starter strip so that it barely covers the drip edge (Ill. 21).

There are three major patterns that can be followed in laying shingles (Ill. 22). Adhere carefully to the pattern chosen and check often to be sure that the lines are straight. Use individual 10" wide shingles at the ridge. Fold them over the ridge and lay them one over the other (Ill. 23) so that the nailing is covered.

Gutters and Downspouts

Gutters and downspouts compose the water-divergence system of the roof. The gutters are trough-like canals that are attached to the eaves of the roof and divert the rain water to downspouts, which channel the water to the ground. The excess water might be deposited directly onto the grass or some paved area or might be taken down into a drywell (Chapter 14). See Illustration 24.

Gutters are made of either wood, galvanized metal, or aluminum and come prefabricated and shaped. Wood gutters are installed after the roof sheathing is applied and before the roof is shingled. The gutter is nailed directly to the fascia using galvanized nails. Be sure that the wood gutter is primed before it is erected. Roof gutters are set so that there is a slight incline toward the downspout, but not one that is visible to the naked eye. The downspouts, usually made of metal, are connected to the gutters at some point where they will be least obvious. A hole is made in the gutter at the point of intersection and the sheet-metal sleeve (for the downspout) is fitted inside (Ill. 25).

Galvanized iron and aluminum gutters and downspouts are designed so that the component parts fit easily together. Instructions on connecting the various parts will come with the system.

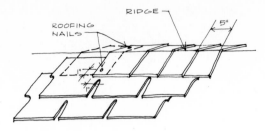

ILL. 23

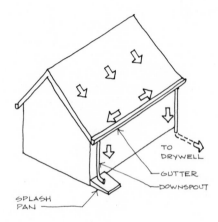

ILL. 24

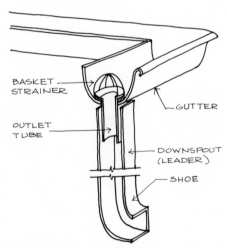

ILL. 25

24
Fireplace, Chimney, and Stairs

FIREPLACES AND CHIMNEYS

After worrying about every other aspect of the house construction, you'll most likely look at the fireplace project with a sigh of relief. On the other hand, you may be so tired at this point that you are seriously thinking of hiring a mason. Should your energy and will power still be running strong, here are the steps required to get the fireplace and the chimney built.

Materials

The necessary materials are:

- Common bricks (for fireplace and chimney construction)
- Firebricks (for firebox and throat construction)
- Mortar (see Chapter 20)
- Firebrick mortar: The recommended proportions for firebrick mortar are nine parts mortar sand, three parts Portland cement, one part fire clay, with enough water to obtain a rather stiff mixture (9:3:1).
- Concrete (see Chapter 20)
- Lightweight concrete block (8" × 8" × 16")
- Ash-pit unit or ash-pit door and dump
- Fire clay collar (for furnace flue smoke pipe)
- Flue lining
- Insulating material (for installation between chimney and wood framing)
- Metal shields
- Plywood (for construction of formwork)
- ½" reinforcing steel bars
- Damper
- Lintel
- Metal flashing
- Waterproof paper
- Caulking and mastic
- Facing brick, stone, or other material
- Prebuilt fireplace unit (if you are skipping the difficult and skilled labor of building the fireplace from scratch)

Tools

The tools required for this enterprise are as follows:

- Trowel
- Joining tool
- Brick set
- Brick hammer
- Mixing hoe or garden hoe
- Mason's corner (also called clip or cut nail)
- Mason's line
- Mortar board
- Metal tub
- 4'-0" mason's level

A description of these tools is found in the Glossary of Tools. In addition, you'll need assorted carpentry tools for cutting, leveling, nailing, etc.

Fireplace, chimney, and stair construction require careful measuring and leveling. Skills such as cutting, nailing, and so on, will also be employed. In addition, fire-place and chimney construction involve mastering other skills such as:

• Mixing mortar—see page 239, Inset III.

• Laying concrete block/brick—see pages 249, 250, and 251, Insets VII, VIII, and IX.
• Mixing concrete—see page 239, Inset II.
• Applying flashing—see page 276, Inset II.

Construction of a Traditional Masonry Fireplace

FOUNDATIONS: The construction of a traditional masonry fireplace and chimney starts with the foundations. (In many instances, the construction of a prefabricated unit may also involve foundation work, particularly if the unit is to be encased in masonry.) Fireplace foundations are erected in the same manner and at the same time as those for the rest of the house. The first step is to locate the fireplace in relationship to the building, followed by the excavation, erection of the footing formwork, placement of the reinforcing bars, pouring the concrete, and finally the erection of the walls themselves. Foundation walls can be constructed out of poured concrete or concrete block. It seems most logical to build them out of the same material as the foundation walls for the rest of the house. A detailed explanation of the processes required for siting and building the fireplace foundations can be found in Chapters 19 and 20.

The form the foundations will take is most likely a large rectangle (Ill. 1). (This, of course, may vary with the fireplace design itself.) To give added strength to the firebox, two inner walls are erected, which slice the rectangle into three parts (Ill. 2). The center cavity becomes the ash dump. The outer two house vertical reinforcing bars (approximately ½" in diameter), which are imbedded in the footing and extend the full height of the fireplace. These are provided to increase the overall strength of the masonry work.

As the walls are erected, provision must be made in them for openings as required by the fireplace design. For example, if the fireplace includes an ash pit, an ash-pit cleanout door has to be installed. This door is usually placed close to the basement floor. The cleanout door is usually located two to three courses above floor

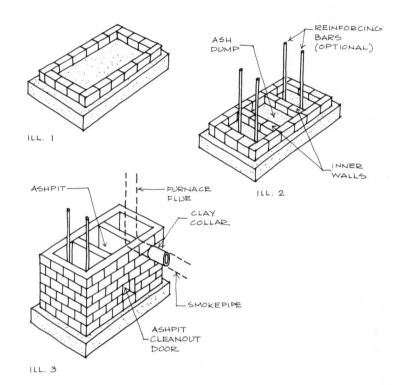

ILL. 1

ILL. 2

REINFORCING BARS (OPTIONAL)

ASH DUMP

INNER WALLS

ILL. 3

ASHPIT

FURNACE FLUE

CLAY COLLAR

SMOKEPIPE

ASHPIT CLEANOUT DOOR

level to provide more storage for ashes, and because a door placed too close to the floor rusts more quickly. In houses with crawl spaces, or where a cleanout door in the basement is inconvenient, it can be installed to be accessible from the outside (Ill. 3). Other openings are sometimes required, for instance when the furnace flue and the fireplace flue share the same chimney. (Fire laws prohibit the fireplace and furnace from sharing the same flue.) The smoke pipe coming from the furnace punctures the foundation walls by means of a clay collar. It then connects to a separate clay tile flue, which makes its way up to the chimney (Ill. 3 and Inset II).*

* You may want to include a spare flue that could later be used for a wood stove in another room.

A cylindrical clay section, or collar, is installed in the fireplace foundation wall to serve as the connection between the furnace smoke pipe and the inside of the fireplace. Once inside the fireplace structure, the smoke pipe becomes a flue that continues up through the fireplace into the chimney and provides exhaust for furnace smoke and gases. The furnace flue is built in sections simultaneously with the masonry walls. The procedure is similar to that of the fireplace flue. It is important to keep the collar flush with the inside of the fireplace walls. A projecting collar could block the passage of smoke and gases into the flue and therefore to the outside (right).

The furnace flue too must be supported

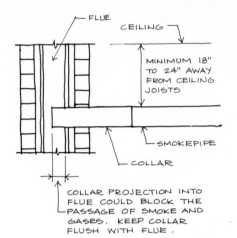

FLUE
CEILING
MINIMUM 18" TO 24" AWAY FROM CEILING JOISTS
SMOKEPIPE
COLLAR
COLLAR PROJECTION INTO FLUE COULD BLOCK THE PASSAGE OF SMOKE AND GASES. KEEP COLLAR FLUSH WITH FLUE.

at the foundations. This is done by filling the cavity underneath it with concrete blocks.

Caution must be taken that the furnace smoke pipe is not too close to the woodwork. Minimum clearances are usually specified by code. If the code does not include minimum distances, make sure that the smoke pipe is not less than 18" and preferably 24" away from the ceiling joists and 6" away from any other woodwork. For additional protection, install a metal shield between the woodwork and the smoke pipe (left).

The foundation walls are brought out of the ground and up to joist level (Ill. 4). At this point, you can switch the masonry from concrete block to brick (or stone) if the bulk of the fireplace is to be exposed. If your fireplace is totally hidden by the house structure, you can simply construct it out of block and finish those parts that are exposed, such as the front of the firebox, with your choice of finishing materials. It all depends on your particular fireplace design.

THE HEARTH: You must now provide formwork in which to pour the subhearth. For the front of the subhearth, a piece of plywood is cantilevered between the front wall of the fireplace foundation and the floor framing members (Ill. 4). The back hearth has the plywood anchored to the walls themselves. In order to have a surface on which the plywood can rest, a shelf is created in the wall by projecting out a row of bricks (Ill. 4).

With the formwork in place and before pouring the concrete, a wood box is installed where the ash dump is later to be located. Make sure that the outside dimensions of the box are those of the ash dump. Similarly, if a furnace flue is coming up from the basement, install it. Lay a grid of ½" steel reinforcing bars a minimum of 6" apart as explained in Chapter 20, page 244 (Ill. 4). You can now pour the concrete mixture. (See page 239, Inset II.)

The location of the hearth may vary with the design of the fireplace, and with it the location

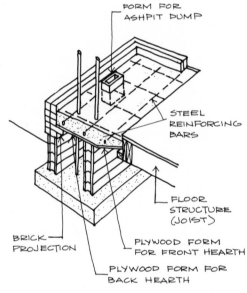

FORM FOR ASHPIT DUMP
STEEL REINFORCING BARS
FLOOR STRUCTURE (JOIST)
BRICK PROJECTION
PLYWOOD FORM FOR FRONT HEARTH
PLYWOOD FORM FOR BACK HEARTH

ILL. 4

of the formwork. If the hearth is raised over the floor, the foundation walls should extend above the floor joists and the formwork should be installed at the appropriate level. If the hearth is to be flush with the finished floor, make sure to pour the concrete only to such a level that when the firebrick and the front hearth finishing material are applied, they are flush with the floor (Ill. 5). Allow at least 6" of concrete for the subhearth (½" for mortar), in addition to the thickness of the finishing material.

While the concrete is hardening, lay a few

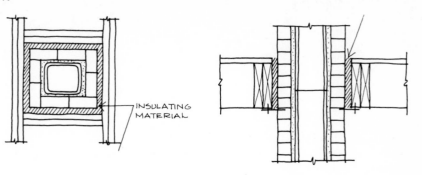
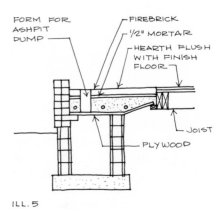

FORM FOR ASHPIT DUMP

FIREBRICK

1/2″ MORTAR

HEARTH FLUSH WITH FINISH FLOOR

JOIST

PLYWOOD

ILL. 5

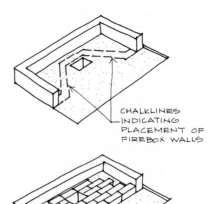

CHALKLINES INDICATING PLACEMENT OF FIREBOX WALLS

ILL. 6

courses of masonry in the outer wall. Make sure to keep these walls a minimum of 2″ (or as required by code) away from the house structure (walls and floors) as an insulating measure (Inset III). Those walls that are later to be faced with another material such as brick or stone should be provided with ties in the mortar joints with which to anchor the facing (Ill. 10). Once the concrete has set, start laying firebrick (the finish surface for the front hearth may be laid now or later on). Firebrick only covers that area of the hearth where the firebox is to be built. Therefore, before laying the firebrick, it is a good idea to chalk in guidelines indicating the placement of the firebox walls. With this done, mix a batch of firebrick mortar (see proportions in materials list, page 280) to bond the firebrick to the subhearth (Ill. 6).* Any irregularities in the concrete subhearth surface can be evened out with the mortar. To protect the firebrick from being damaged by dropping mortar later on, cover it with a layer of sand.

Once the concrete has dried, remove any form material that is still accessible. Don't forget, before moving on to your next task, to cut a hole in the plywood form below the ash dump to allow ashes to fall through.

THE FIREBOX: Because of its sloping and angled walls, the construction of the firebox is

Fireplace, Chimney, and Stairs

283

* To save themselves the trouble of mixing two different batches, masons often use firebrick mortar for the entire fireplace and chimney construction.

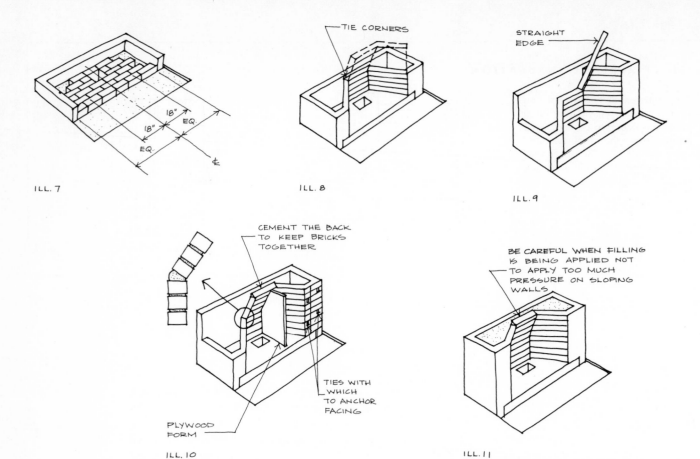

ILL. 7

ILL. 8 — TIE CORNERS

ILL. 9 — STRAIGHT EDGE

ILL. 10 — CEMENT THE BACK TO KEEP BRICKS TOGETHER — TIES WITH WHICH TO ANCHOR FACING — PLYWOOD FORM

ILL. 11 — BE CAREFUL WHEN FILLING IS BEING APPLIED NOT TO APPLY TOO MUCH PRESSURE ON SLOPING WALLS

rather tricky. Firebox walls can be erected simultaneously with the outside walls or after the outside walls have been brought to the height of the damper.

Start by chalk-marking the firebox walls on the hearth. Since the damper rests directly on these walls, it is important to have the damper sitting there, right next to you, for reference during the entire process (Ill. 12). Determine the center line of the firebox opening and measure to each side one-half the length of the damper (Ill. 7). For example, if the damper is 3′ long, you measure 18″ to either side. This will give you the location of the firebox walls.

The back and side walls of the firebox are laid straight and plumb to approximately 12″ to 16″, as indicated in your design. (Here, too, you must use firebrick mortar applied in thin layers of about ⅛″ to ¼″ thick.) Use ties at the corners where the three walls meet. Before building the sloping wall section, continue laying the side walls, this time with no mortar. In order to meet the angle of the back sloping wall, the brickwork on the side walls will require cutting (Ill. 8). To find out exactly where the bricks should be cut, place a straightedge at the top of the back wall and against the side wall (Ill. 9). Move the straightedge along the side wall until you obtain the angle called for in your design, and chalk-mark it on the brick. Because the courses have been laid dry, the bricks can be taken apart and cut at the required angle. They can now be laid permanently in place with mortar.

Once the two side walls are ready, erect the back wall. To build the sloped back wall of the firebox, cut a piece of plywood to the proper shape for your specifications. This plywood can be placed inside the firebox as you lay each course of bricks to ensure that the slope of the back wall is correct (Ill. 10). The first course of brick over the straight piece of wall is laid over a wedge-shaped mortar joint (Ill. 10). To give the wall added strength, plaster its back with mortar.

When the firebox is completed, fill in the space left between the outer walls and the firebox walls with broken bricks and pieces of masonry to allow for firebox wall expansion (Ill. 11). Care must be taken while doing this not to put undue pressure on the firebox's vertical sloping wall. A sudden excessive weight may cause this wall to collapse.

Construction
284

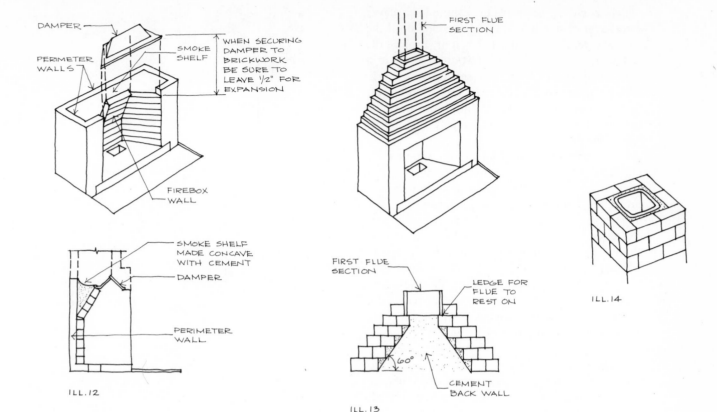

DAMPER

PERIMETER WALLS

SMOKE SHELF

WHEN SECURING DAMPER TO BRICKWORK BE SURE TO LEAVE ½" FOR EXPANSION

FIREBOX WALL

FIRST FLUE SECTION

SMOKE SHELF MADE CONCAVE WITH CEMENT

DAMPER

PERIMETER WALL

ILL. 12

FIRST FLUE SECTION

LEDGE FOR FLUE TO REST ON

60°

CEMENT BACK WALL

ILL. 13

ILL. 14

THE DAMPER: With the firebox walls erected, the damper is set in place. You can, if you want, mortar it to the brick it rests on, but this is not necessary. Make sure to leave a space of at least ½" between the ends of the damper and the brickwork. The damper is subject to intense heat, which may cause it to expand. If there's not sufficient clearance between the masonry and the damper, the expanding metal will push against the brickwork, causing it to crack (Ill. 12).

After the damper is in place, it is a good idea to protect this clearance from accidentally dropped mortar by placing a few bricks or a piece of metal temporarily over the joint as a protective device.

THE SMOKE SHELF: The smoke shelf is created by the installation of the damper and the filling of the space between the perimeter walls of the fireplace and the firebox walls. To improve its efficiency, make the smoke shelf concave with cement (Ill. 12).

THE SMOKE CHAMBER: The masonry work is corbeled to bridge the gap between the di-

mensions of the outer walls of the fireplace and those of the chimney. Corbeling is the stepping in of bricks for a few courses, until the smoke chamber narrows down to the flue size (Ill. 13). This process is somewhat tricky because you're corbeling from three directions—the front and the two side walls (Ill. 13). The walls should corbel quickly (with a minimum number of courses) to increase the funneling action of the chamber.

The next to the last course of brick should provide a ledge for the flue to rest on (Ill. 13). For minimum interference with the passage of exhaust from the chamber out the flue, smooth all the interior surfaces of the chamber by plastering the sides with mortar.

THE CHIMNEY: Cement the first section of flue tile for the chimney on the ledge provided for it at the top of the chamber. Completely encase the flue by laying bricks around it and fill any space left between the brick and the flue tile with grout (Ill. 14). The sections of flue lining should be cemented close and flush with each other. Their joints should be thoroughly filled and have no projections on the inside, which could cause soot to accumulate. Layer after layer of flue is laid in this fashion until the chimney reaches the desired height. Project the last course or two of bricks out to provide a water drip. Extend the last section of flue 4″ above the last course of brick. Trowel in mortar to seal over the brickwork and form an angle between the top of the brick and 1″ below the top of the flue (Ill. 15).

If downdrafts are a problem, you might erect masonry pillars at the corners of the chimney once the sloping mortar bed is laid. These pillars project to approximately four courses over the flue projection. A stone is then laid over and cemented to the pillars. Be sure that the stone is slightly pitched so it can shed water properly (Ill. 16).

When chimneys run for long distances unsupported, extra reinforcement is provided by placing steel bars at each corner of the flue, between the flue and the brick (Ill. 17).*

THE FACING: Generally masons prefer to apply the facing once all other parts of the fireplace and chimney have been completed. Facing brick, stones, or tiles can be used. The facing material is anchored to the fireplace by means of anchors or ties already provided in the rough brickwork. A metal lintel is placed at the appropriate height (6″ to 8″ below the damper) to bridge the masonry facing across. It should have a minimum bearing of 3″ on each masonry wall.

If the front hearth has not already been laid, now is the time to do so.

WEATHERPROOFING THE FIREPLACE AND CHIMNEY: In fireplace and chimney construction, as in every other aspect of building, it is very important to keep water from leaking into the structure (see Chapter 12, page 133). When a fireplace is located on the exterior of a building, all the joints between the masonry work and the building structure should be thoroughly waterproofed. Apply waterproof paper at every joint where the masonry butts against

* In addition, the chimney can be anchored to the building frame by placing an iron strap around the flue and reinforcing rods, and tying it to the building structure (Ill. 17). The problem with anchoring the chimney to the building frame is that in the event of differential settlement in the foundations, the chimney may induce stresses in the building frame that could cause structural problems. We do not recommend it.

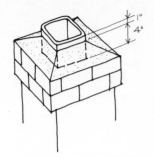

ILL. 15

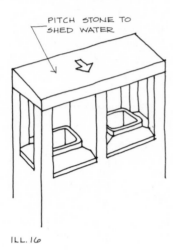

PITCH STONE TO SHED WATER

ILL. 16

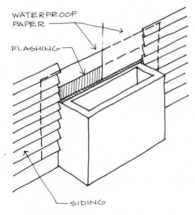

ILL. 17

WATERPROOF PAPER

FLASHING

SIDING

ILL. 18

the framing members. Seal the joint further by applying caulking compound (Ill. 18).

It is important to waterproof not only the joints between the building and the fireplace, but also any other exposed fireplace surface—particularly those lying perpendicular to the angle of water and snowfall, since they are the most subject to leakage. To divert water away from these surfaces, install metal flashing. Place the flashing underneath the exterior wall finish and cover it with a layer of waterproof paper (Ill. 18). The piece of flashing that fits into the brickwork is mortared to the joint and sealed with mastic.

The chimney also requires careful flashing. A detailed discussion of chimney flashing can be found on pages 276 and 277, Inset II.

Installation of a Prefabricated Fireplace Unit

Manufacturers of prefabricated fireplaces generally provide you with lots of literature and instructions on the installation and maintenance of their product. Follow them carefully.

When foundations are necessary, the installation of a prefabricated fireplace unit, like that of a traditional fireplace, starts with the foundation work. Use the procedure described earlier in the chapter. Prefabricated units may come with or without a hearth. Those units that come complete with a hearth only require to be anchored onto the foundation walls. Hearthless units involve the pouring of a hearth onto the foundation walls before the unit can be installed. The hearth pouring process is similar to that for a traditional fireplace.

When foundations are not needed, simply position the fireplace on the rough floor. To find the precise placement, drop a plumb bob from the place where the chimney punctures the roof and any other floor level. Make sure that the location of the chimney on the roof corresponds to the location of the chimney opening in the fireplace unit. Before framing in or encasing the unit, erect the chimney. Chimney installation has to be handled by two persons: one to hold the section and the other to lock it in place. Install the first section of chimney over the fireplace unit (Ill. 19). Follow the manufacturer's instructions to lock it into place. Proceed to install the intermediate sections in the same fashion until the top section extends through

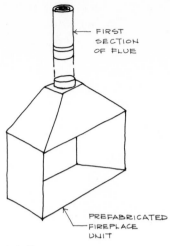

FIRST SECTION OF FLUE

PREFABRICATED FIREPLACE UNIT

ILL. 19

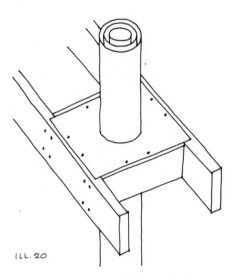

ILL. 20

the roof. Note that flues are slender vertical elements requiring support to prevent them from buckling under their own weight. Install the chimney support boxes where the chimney passes through the ceiling into the attic. In multistory houses provide firestops as the chimney punctures each floor (Ill. 20).

Once the chimney is above the roof, close the leftover opening and apply flashing on top of it. Fit the flashing over the flue and nail it to the roof frame. Roofing is applied to cover the flashing except for the lower flange. This one laps over the roofing instead, to divert water away from the structure (Ill. 21). The remaining components of the chimney are locked into place. A storm collar is inserted in the flue over the flash-

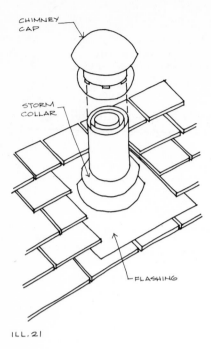

ILL. 21

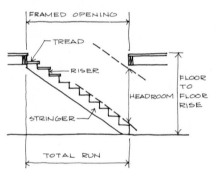

ILL. 22

ing and the joint sealed with waterproof mastic. If there is a chimney cap, it is now attached (Ill. 21).

The fireplace unit is now framed or encased according to your design. The last step is to apply the finishing material for the front hearth.

Installation of a Ready-to-Use Fireplace Unit

This is the easiest type of fireplace to install. All that needs to be done is to provide a fire-resistant material (firebrick, stone, etc.) on which the fireplace can rest, which will protect the floor from the intense heat. When walls are too close to the fireplace, it is wise to also protect them from the excessive heat with metal shields.

The chimney sections are built in the same manner described for prebuilt units.

STAIRS

Stair carpentry is advanced work, and a well-constructed staircase is the pride of the master craftsman. The stair consists of stringers, treads, risers, and handrails (Ill. 22). If you are going to build stairs, here is how to do it.

Materials

The materials required for stair construction will change with the stair design. For a standard wood stair, you'll need the following:

• 2″ × 8″ or 2″ × 10″ lumber for the stringer
• ¾″ lumber for the risers
• 1⅛″ hardwood, or vertical grain softwood, for treads
• 8d and 16d nails
• Newels, balusters, and handrail sections
• Masking tape
• Plastic wood

Tools

In addition to basic carpentry tools, you'll need the following:

• A story pole (see page 258)
• Framing square
• Router (as required)

Construction

LAYING OUT THE STRINGER: The stringer is the main support for the stair and is its major framing member. The procedure for its layout is similar for all types of stairs. The stringers will be joined to the frame of the house at the double header (or trimmer) in the opening framed for it on the second floor. (Review pages 199 and 200.)

You should have a fair idea as to the number of treads and risers required in the stair, the run of the stair, its pitch, etc. (See pages 197–9.) Before transferring these dimensions to the stringer, it is enormously helpful to construct a story pole, a carpenter's aid, shown in Illustration 23.

Position a piece of 1″ × 4″ or similar lumber vertically on the first floor and mark off the location of the second floor on it. Remember that the exact stair height is to be from finished floor to finished floor. If both the second and first floors are rough floors, and if they will be receiving the same thickness of finishing material, then the rough-to-rough height as measured should be the same as the finished floor difference. If one of the floors is already finished and the other is not, or if one of the floors is to receive a finish of greater thickness than the other, make sure to compensate for this difference. Remember that the riser heights must be equal for a safe stair, and even small discrepancies can throw the stair off.

Check to see if the calculated riser height is correct for the actually measured floor-to-floor height by measuring the riser height up the pole (Ill. 23). If the last riser does not come out *exactly* right, recalculate the riser height and try again. The discrepancy might be caused by the settling of the second floor rather than by a mathematical error. Be that as it may, all of the riser spaces must be equal.

The lumber for the stringer should be 2″ × 8‴′s or, preferably, 2″ × 10‴′s, since there must be at least 4″ of lumber left after the cuts are made (Ill. 24). The length of the lumber can be measured from the large-scale drawing or can be calculated knowing the rise and the run of the stair. (The stringer is the hypotenuse of a right triangle and can be determined by using the formula $rise^2 + run^2 = stringer^2$.) Choose a piece of lumber at least 1′ longer than the required stringer.

Take a framing square and measure the exact riser height on its short leg. Use the dimension determined from the exercise with the story pole. You can put a piece of masking tape on the exact point on the square or you can mark the spot with a snap clothespin (the type with a spring). Next measure the tread length on the longer leg of the square. This distance does not include the nosing. Again, put a piece of tape or clothespin at that point. Beginning a few inches from what will be the top of the stringer (it is for this reason that we are using a piece of lumber longer than the needed stringer length; it is easy to cut off excess wood, but impossible to add to the length of the stringer) position the framing square as shown in Illustration 24 and trace the outline of the triangle onto the stringer. Move the square over and continue down the stringer, until the proper number of risers and treads are measured off.

To finish laying out the stringer, the exact

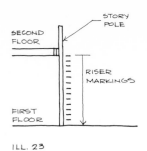

ILL. 23

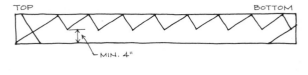

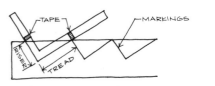

ILL. 24

thickness of the tread material must be known. Once the tread has been positioned above the bottom riser, its height will include the tread thickness and it will be greater than the other risers. This must be compensated for in the stringer by reducing the bottom riser by the thickness of the tread. (Riser height minus tread thickness equals height of bottom riser as measured on the stringer.) Likewise, the top riser must be increased by the thickness of the tread. Tread material is usually 1⅛″ hardwood or vertical grain softwood.

To complete the stringer, make a right-angle cut underneath the lowest riser, one at the end of the lowest riser, and one at the end of the uppermost tread (Ill. 25).

Carefully cut out the stringer with a saw. The two remaining stringers can be marked by laying the completed stringer on the next piece of lumber and tracing the first onto the second.

In assembling the stair the free-standing stringers are nailed to the floor below and to the header above using 16d nails. If the stair is to be positioned against a wall, the stringer can be nailed through the wall into the studs.

Cut the treads from 1⅛″ stock and the risers from ¾″ stock. The width of the tread includes

Fireplace,
Chimney,
and Stairs

289

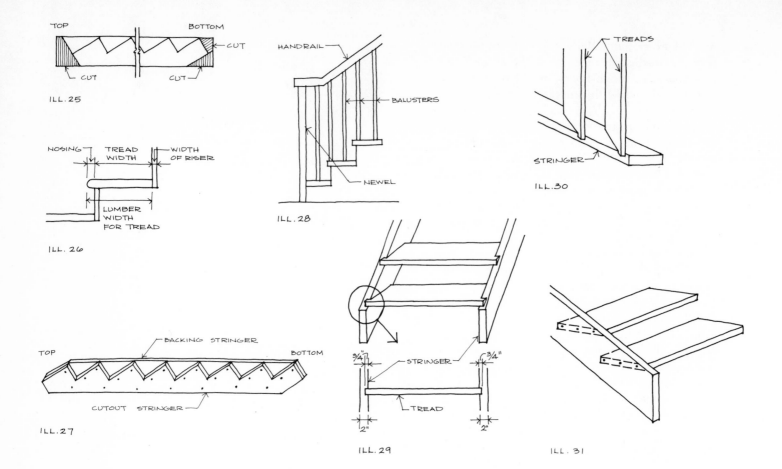

ILL. 25

ILL. 26

ILL. 27

ILL. 28

ILL. 29

ILL. 30

ILL. 31

the nosing, minus the thickness of the riser material (Ill. 26). Risers and treads are installed as shown in Illustration 26 and fastened with 8d nails.

For the semi-housed stair, a backing stringer is nailed to the cutout stringer on either side of the stair (Ill. 27).

To complete the stair, factory-made parts may be purchased. Many kinds of decorative first steps, newels (the end post at the bottom of the stair), balusters (the supports for the hand-rail), and handrail sections are available and can be chosen from a catalogue at the lumberyard (Ill. 28). Simple handrails and balusters can be built using stock lumber.

FRAMING AN OPEN RISER STAIR: A very simple, yet attractive, stair does not have risers. The stringers (only two) are laid out as described above, using the story pole for accuracy, and the framing square. In this case, however, the exact thickness of the tread must be marked off on the stringer. In addition, the length of the tread and its exact position on the stringer must be located. Be sure to keep all the dimensions equal. That is, the distance from

the top of the stringer to the beginning of the tread must always be equal to guarantee a safe and attractive staircase. The stringers, as men-tioned previously, can be laid out and fabricated for you by a professional stair builder. Other-wise you can do the work yourself by using a saw and chisel or router. The pockets for the treads must be cut out equally. It is wise to use 2" lumber or thicker for the stringers so that there is enough room for the groove to be at least ¾" deep (Ill. 29).

The treads are cut and finished exactly to size and are placed in one side of the stringer, which is laid on its side on a flat surface. The treads should be glued in place (Ill. 30). Hopefully, the fit will be tight. When the treads on one of the stringers are in place, the second stringer should be positioned and tapped into place. (Make sure that all of the treads fit properly before apply-ing glue on this side.) When the stair is com-pleted, the treads can be further secured by nail-ing through the stringers into the treads (Ill. 31). The nail holes should be sunk and can be covered with plastic wood or dowel heads. The completed stair is then nailed top and bottom into position.

25 Closing In

Closing in is the process of sealing the building from the outside. It is done to protect the interior and allow construction to take place even in bad weather. Now is the time to install windows and doors, erect the siding, and block any other openings. Although closing in involves tedious and repetitious work, it is exciting in that for the first time a finished building begins to emerge.

TOOLS

The tools required for this stage are essentially the same ones you've used throughout the framing stages. An additional tool you need is a caulking gun in which to place tubes of caulking compound. You may also need a hatchet, if you are installing wood shingles, and a nail set.

MATERIALS

- Kraft paper
- Window and door units
- Siding
- Nails
- Locksets

To finish the overhangs you'll need wood boards for:

- A fascia
- Ledger boards
- Lookouts
- Plywood for the soffit
- Screens or ventilation louvers

APPLYING THE KRAFT PAPER

Before most finishing work* can take place, you must apply kraft paper over the sheathing. Kraft paper is applied in horizontal layers. It comes in 48" wide rolls and is marked with a white line, which serves as a guide for overlapping the layers (Ill. 1).

The application of kraft paper is a two-person job. Starting at one of the building corners, the bottom layer of paper is applied. While one person unrolls the paper, the other one staples or nails it (approximately every 8"). Make sure that the paper is going straight. When you come to an opening, cut the paper with a matte knife.

INSTALLATION OF WINDOWS AND DOORS

Door and window installation is made easier by planning ahead. Be sure as you are framing in the rough openings that they are level. Although this advice may seem redundant, it is not unusual to find yourself with rough openings that are not plumb. Such an opening will in turn throw the windows and doors out of level,

* Plywood siding does not require kraft paper.

The skills required for finish work are not much different from those required for rough carpentry. Leveling, cutting, planing, nailing, and so on, are all needed in the erection of siding, the installation of windows and doors, and the closing in of overhangs. Perhaps the only difference is that extra care must be taken while in the finishing stages that all work is neatly and carefully done. Although sloppy workmanship is a problem in any stage of construction, in the finishing stages it becomes more visible.

There's one skill you may need at this stage that has not been described before—cutting wood shingles. Scribe the shingle with an awl where the cut is to be made. (When you get the hang of it most likely you can just "eye" the cut and eliminate the need for scribing.) Hold the shingle firmly, perpendicular to a strong surface, and cut it lengthwise with a hatchet.

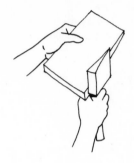

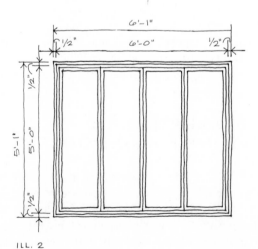

ILL. 1

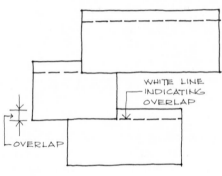

ILL. 2

making their installation trickier. Both windows and doors are heavy objects; any unnecessary fussing to get them perfectly straight can become a tiring enterprise.

Another item to keep in mind while framing in the openings, is to allow for sufficient clearance so that window and door units can easily fit. A space approximately ½" all around is usually enough to give you installation leeway. For example, if a window is 5'-0" × 6'-0", the rough openings should be 5'-1" × 6'-1" (Ill. 2). Manufacturers often outline recommended clearances.

Be aware as you are doing the installation that walls have depth and so do window and door frames. Consider the depth of the siding and the interior finish and place the units accordingly (Ill. 3). If the frames are too deep and project far into the room, you may find yourself having to cut them down to fit. On the other hand, if they are too shallow, you're also in trouble (Ill. 3).

When preparing to install the windows and doors, make sure that you have a helper. Two people are needed to lift the window in place. Once in place, one person holds the unit in the rough opening while the other one levels and nails it. (Use aluminum or galvanized casing nails spaced every 16" on center.)

Windows

Window units come complete with frame, outside trim, and hardware. (Check to see that they

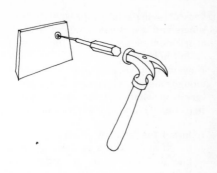
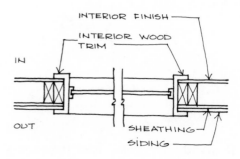

ILL. 3

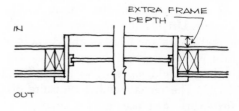

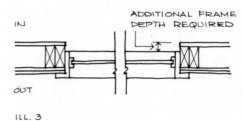

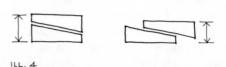

ILL. 4

come with a drip cap; otherwise you have to install one after the window is in place.) Start by double-checking the size of the unit against that of the rough opening and make sure they correspond. Most windows require ½″ space on each side and ¾″ above the head for plumbing and leveling. From the outside of the building, lift the window unit onto the rough opening. Since it's easier to work from a secure floor than hanging from a ladder, one person holds the window in place while the other goes inside to level and nail it. Check at the sill to see that the window is level and that the space at the top between the frame and the rough opening is not too great. If everything checks, tack the unit in place. By tacking we mean leaving the nail out about ¼″ or so. Tack the unit at the top, sill, and both sides. Once the window is tacked, open and close it to make sure it's working properly. Again check the sill for levelness. If all is well, drive the nails in (Inset II). To prevent heat loss and drafts, any space left between the window unit and the rough opening is stuffed with insulation.

If the window unit isn't level, a little moving around is in order. Shims are used to level the window. (They are any kind of scrap wood that is wedged under the sill until the window is level.) Wood shingle scraps are particularly good for use as shims because they slope. Using two shingles with slopes in opposite directions, you can arrive at various thicknesses (Ill. 4). With the window level, tack and nail it as previously described. Make sure, however, to nail through the shims into the rough opening.

Closing In
293

Lockset manufacturers provide instruction sheets and a template to guide you in the installation. Some doors come with pre-drilled holes to accommodate the locksets. They make your job one step easier. Although the installation of a lockset may vary somewhat with the lockset type, the steps usually required are as follows.

1. Install the latch by inserting it into the bored hole. With a pencil, mark its outline and remove it. In order for the latch to be flush with the door, chisel out the area where the latch is to be installed. Insert the latch in place and tighten the screws (Ill. III-1).

2. The strike plate is installed next. The template will give you directions on how to find the location of the strike plate's screws. With a pencil, mark this spot on the door jamb. Drill the latch bolt hole. Place the strike plate on its proper location by matching the center line of the screw holes with the one you've drawn on the jamb. Draw the strike plate's outline, remove it, and chisel out the outlined area so that the strike plate will be flush with the door jamb. Install the strike plate by fastening the screws (Ill. III-2).

3. Finally, insert the knob that has a spindle into the latch and push it against the door. The other knob is installed by placing it on the spindle of the first. This knob, too, is pushed against the door and firmly tightened with screws (Ill. III-3).

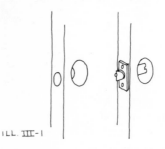

ILL. III-1

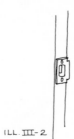

ILL. III-2

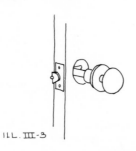

ILL. III-3

Doors

Doors come already prehung. This is a great advantage over the old process of constructing the frame, hinging the door, weather stripping, and so on, particularly for the amateur builder. It saves you time and meticulous work.

The procedure to follow for the installation of a door unit is essentially the same as for a window. Lift the door in place and check it for plumbness on the hinge side. Keep in mind that the sill should be flush with the finish floor. When the door is plumb, tack it in place. Check that it closes well. Make sure to nail the door to the rough opening through the jambs and shims. Do not nail through the doorstop. Install the lockset (Inset III).

INSTALLATION OF SIDING

An important aspect of the application of siding is to use the right nails. Corrosion-resistant, galvanized, stainless steel, or other nails made of similar metals will not bleed and spot the siding's surface. These nails, however, will probably cost more but they are worth it. In terms of shape, the nails used for siding are usually thin and have a flat head (box nails). The reason why thin nails are used is to reduce the chance of the wood splitting. You must be careful, however, to drive them only to the wood's surface. Driving the nails too hard could show hammer blows and increase the chances of crushing the wood.

Bevel siding should lap no less than 1″ and preferably 2″. The recommended exposure distances (exposure distance is the amount of siding left exposed to the weather) are 4″ for 6″ siding, 8″ for 10″ siding, 10″ for 12″ siding, and so on (Ill. 5). Both from the standpoint of weather resistance and appearance, the exposure distance is changed and adjusted to meet the fixed dimensions of windows and doors (Ill. 6). The procedure used to determine how much the recommended exposure distance has to be adjusted to meet these dimensions is not difficult. Let's say that you are using 8″ siding and the window height is 55″. The number of courses needed between the top and the bottom of the window is found by dividing 6″—the recommended exposure distance for 8″ siding—into 55″—the height of the window (Ill. 7). You need $55 \div 6 = 9\frac{1}{6}$, or nine courses. To find out precisely the exposure the siding must be to get nine courses, divide 55″ (the window height)

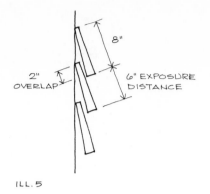

ILL. 5

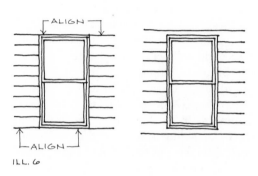

ILL. 6

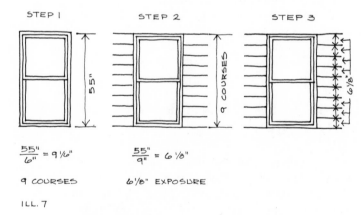

ILL. 7

STEP 1   STEP 2   STEP 3

$$\frac{55"}{6"} = 9\frac{1}{6}"$$

9 COURSES

$$\frac{55"}{9"} = 6\frac{1}{8}"$$

6⅛" EXPOSURE

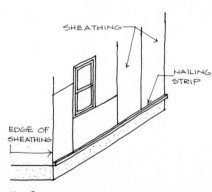

ILL. 8

ILL. 9

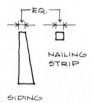

ILL. 10

by 9 (the number of courses). You need $55 \div 9$ = approximately 6⅛" exposure for each course of siding to meet the window flush at either end.

The exposure for siding located between the window sill and the foundation wall should also be adjusted. You may, otherwise, find yourself with two noticeably different siding exposures or a very narrow end course within the same wall (Ill. 8). For example, if the distance between the bottom of the window sill and the top of the foundation wall is 31", you need $31 \div 6 = 5\frac{1}{6}$ courses between the two. To arrive at the necessary exposure for the right number of courses divide 31" by 5 and you get 6.2", or $6\frac{3}{16}$", which is only slightly over what the exposure will be for siding above the sill and therefore the difference will be hardly noticeable.

Although siding can be installed by one person alone, it is easier to handle with two. The erection of siding starts by securing a nailing strip to the bottom edge of the sheathing (Ill. 9). This strip should be equal in thickness to the "top" thickness of the siding (Ill. 10). Make sure that the nailing strip is level all around the house. At either end of the wall, measure up from the nailing strip the dimension of the siding and snap a chalk line (Ill. 11). Using the chalk line as a guide, position the board and nail it on the studs at approximately every 16" on center. When you're through with the first board, simply butt up the next board against the one you've just nailed.

Once the first row of siding is complete, measure up from the top of the first row, the exposure distance for the second row (Ill. 12). Snap a chalk line and locate the board. Nail the second row in the same manner as the first. This time, however, make sure that you're nailing up far enough along the siding to clear the lower course (Ill. 13). The remaining courses are installed in the same manner.

Closing In

295

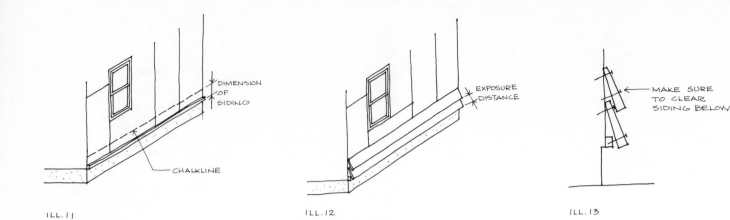

ILL. 11   ILL. 12   ILL. 13

To fit around windows and doors, butt the siding up against the frames. If you think you may have a waterproofing problem, leave a ¼" space between the siding and the frame and fill it with caulking.

Here are a few general points to remember while installing siding: Try to minimize joints. Joints are the point of least resistance to weather. The fewer the joints, the more weathertight the wall will be. To minimize joints, use longer sections of siding under windows, over doors, and whenever there is a long uninterrupted stretch of wall. Save the smaller pieces for areas in between openings. Keep in mind that these joints should occur over the studs and should be staggered between courses. For further protection against moisture penetration, dip or brush the ends of the siding in a water repellent preservative before nailing in place. In addition, check that all the ends are perfectly square. Joints must be good and tight, otherwise water may find its way in. Whenever cutting the board is necessary, cut it with a table saw, a radial-arm saw, or a miter box to ensure a square end.

Corners

There are two corner conditions you have to worry about—inside and outside corners. Outside corners are easier and can be handled in a number of ways. The two most popular ones are mitering and butting against a wood strip.

Mitered corners involve cutting both corner boards at an angle that will form a 90 degree corner when butted against each other (Ill. 14). Miters have a tendency to come apart, so add extra nails around the miter joint from both sides.

Another way to handle outside corners is by using a nailing strip. This type of joint involves nailing two vertical wood strips at the corner of the building; this will serve as a surface against which both pieces of siding can butt (Ill. 15).

Interior corners are trickier. Mitering doesn't work in this type of corner. One solution is to place a nailing strip in the corner and butt up both surfaces of siding against it (Ill. 16). Another, more difficult joint involves taking one piece of siding and butting it right up to the sheathing (Ill. 17). The other side is cut to fit the first. This is done by holding the siding in place against the one you've just nailed and scribing it at the proper angle. Cut the siding at this angle and nail in place (Ill. 17).

INSTALLATION OF SHINGLES

The installation of shingles is more time consuming and difficult than that of siding because they are smaller, irregular in shape, and have to be applied one by one. There are several things you should be aware of before installing shingles. Shingles come in varying widths. Try to spread the widths out evenly so that you don't get a concentration of narrow shingles at one end and wide ones at the other (Ill. 18). The maximum recommended exposure for shingles is ½" less than one-half its length. For example, a 16" shingle has an exposure of 7½", an 18" shingle an exposure of 8½", etc. As with siding, shingle joints are the areas of least resistance to weather. For this reason, the joints should be staggered so that no two courses have joints overlapping any closer than 1½" (Ill. 19).

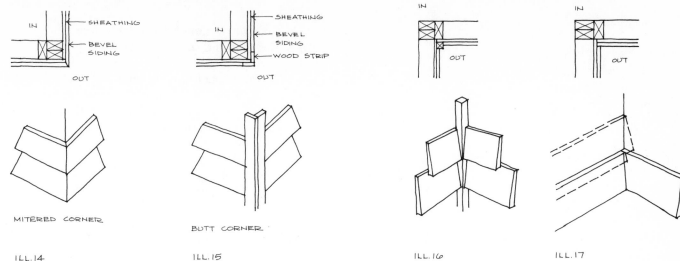

SHEATHING
BEVEL SIDING
IN
OUT

SHEATHING
BEVEL SIDING
WOOD STRIP
IN
OUT

IN
OUT

IN
OUT

MITERED CORNER

BUTT CORNER

ILL. 14   ILL. 15   ILL. 16   ILL. 17

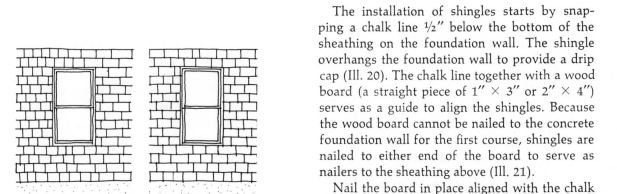

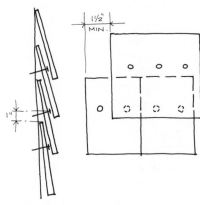

ILL. 18

1½" MIN.
1"

ILL. 19

The installation of shingles starts by snapping a chalk line ½" below the bottom of the sheathing on the foundation wall. The shingle overhangs the foundation wall to provide a drip cap (Ill. 20). The chalk line together with a wood board (a straight piece of 1" × 3" or 2" × 4") serves as a guide to align the shingles. Because the wood board cannot be nailed to the concrete foundation wall for the first course, shingles are nailed to either end of the board to serve as nailers to the sheathing above (Ill. 21).

Nail the board in place aligned with the chalk line. The first row of shingles is located using the wood board as a guide (Ill. 22). The reason for using the bottom of the shingle as a measuring point rather than the top is that shingles may vary slightly in length. Since the bottom is the part that remains visible, that's the part that should be carefully aligned. Use two nails for shingles 8" wide or less and three nails for wider shingles (Ill. 23). Once the shingles are nailed, remove the board and reset it until the first course is complete.

A second layer of shingles is applied directly over the first course. With the double course finished, start the second course by measuring up from the bottom of the shingle the distance it is to be left exposed—that is, 7½" for 16" shingles. Snap a chalk line. Again align the wood board with the chalk line and nail it directly to the sheathing. Rest each shingle on the top of the board and nail it in place. Make sure when you drive in the nails, that you do so about 1" clear of the course below (refer to Ill. 19). The following courses are laid in the same manner.

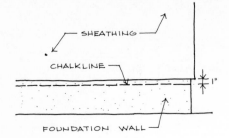

ILL. 20

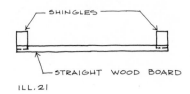

ILL. 21

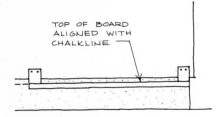

ILL. 22

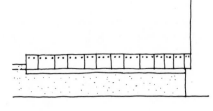

ILL. 23

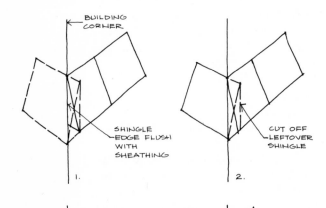

ILL. 24

The space that should be left between shingles varies with the amount of moisture present in the wood. If the wood is new and damp, you can butt them against each other. If it's old, leave a space of ⅛″ to ¼″ to allow for expansion under moist conditions. Generally, the cheaper the grade of shingle, the drier it is and the more it will expand. When shingles meet windows and doors, merely butt the ends to meet the frame, leaving enough expansion clearance depending on the moisture content of the shingle.

Corners

Both exterior and interior corners are handled in essentially the same manner. For an exterior corner, nail one shingle flush with the corner edge of the sheathing. The shingle meeting it from the other side will overlap this one. Nail the overlapping shingle. The excess wood is cut off with a hatchet (Ill. 24). Laps should be alternated in each course.

Interior corners are handled in the same way. The only difference is that instead of nailing the second shingle and cutting it in place, it is held in place and scribed. It is then cut and nailed in place.

VERTICAL TONGUE-AND-GROOVE SIDING

In order to provide a good nailing surface for the boards, the plywood sheathing underneath vertical siding should be thicker than that used for horizontal applications (approximately ⅝″ to ¾″). In horizontally applied siding, the boards are nailed to the studs every 16″ on center. This is not the case with vertical siding, and hence the thicker plywood.

Start the siding application at one of the building corners. Position the board plumb against and aligned with the sheathing. The bottom of the board should overlap the foundation wall approximately ½″ to provide a drip cap. Check to be sure that the board is perfectly vertical. Start nailing from the top of the board. The nails should be located as close to the groove as possible (Ill. 25). Another row of nails is then driven at the tongue side, which will be hidden from view (Ill. 25). Insert the second board into the groove of the first and nail it,

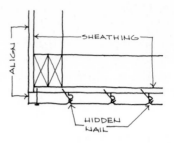

ILL. 25

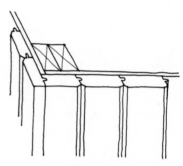

LAPPED CORNER

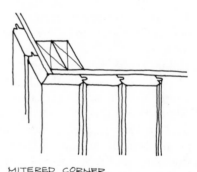

MITERED CORNER

ILL. 26

this time, however, only at the tongue; the other edge is held secure by the groove (Ill. 25).

To fit over an opening, allow a ¼" gap between the board and the door or window frame. Leave a gap at the sides, although it may be narrower. Fill them with caulking.

Corners

The corner conditions, both exterior and interior, are most easily handled by lapping boards. You will have to cut the board lengthwise (Ill. 26). Exterior corners may also be mitered.

PLYWOOD PANEL SIDING

Plywood siding is very popular because it is easier and faster to apply than any other type of siding. Because the panels come in 4' widths, their application is not vastly different from that of sheathing. These panels may be applied directly over studs or over sheathing. Panels installed directly over studs should have a minimum thickness of ½" to ¾".

Panel application over sheathing begins by snapping vertical chalk lines from the building corner every 16" on center. These lines will serve as a guide for nailing the paneling over the studs. Pick up the first panel and position it in one corner of the building. Make sure it is plumb against the sheathing. Nail it in place approximately 4" to 6" on center at the perimeter and 8" to 12" at intermediate studs (Ill. 27). The next panel is either butted or inserted into the edge of the first, depending on whether the edges are square, shiplap, or tongue and groove. Butt joints are protected with a batten strip (Ill. 28). Nail it in place in the same fashion as the first. Siding applied without sheathing is nailed directly to the studs.

If a horizontal joint is necessary, flash it well to protect against moisture penetration (Ill. 29). Some panel manufacturers have joining devices specifically designed to protect horizontal joints in their panels. For extra protection against moisture penetration, you can treat the edges with water repellent.

A space of approximately ¹⁄₁₆" should be left between the panel and window and door frames. This opening is later caulked.

BRICK VENEER

When a wall is finished with brick veneer, the foundation should be slightly modified to carry the weight of the brick (Ill. 30). A ledge of approximately 5" is designed into the foundation wall for the brickwork to rest on.

The brickwork itself is laid in the same manner already described on page 250, Inset VIII. To provide a good bond between the stud wall and the bricks, corrosion-resistant metal ties are nailed to the studs and later inserted in the mortar joint between courses. They are spaced approximately 32" apart horizontally and 16" vertically to work into the brick courses (Ill. 30).

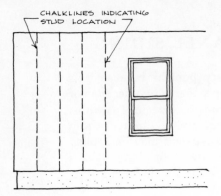

CHALKLINES INDICATING
STUD LOCATION

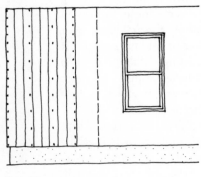

ILL. 27

SHEATHING

PLYWOOD
PANEL

BATTEN

ILL. 28

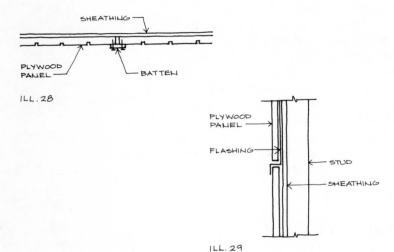

PLYWOOD
PANEL

FLASHING

STUD

SHEATHING

ILL. 29

A space of about 1" is left between the sheathing and the brick to allow for ease of construction. Be careful not to drip mortar in this space (Ill. 30).

Weep holes to dispose of excess moisture should be provided in the brickwork every 4'-0" on center. You can do this by eliminating the mortar from a vertical joint. The first brick course below the bottom of the sheathing should be flashed. The flashing laps under the building paper (Ill. 30).

FINISHING THE OVERHANGS

There are two basic types of overhang, or cornice, conditions—the flush, or simple, cornice and the rafter overhang, which can be opened or closed (Ill. 31).

Flush and Open Overhang

Both the sheathing and building paper should have been notched to fit around the rafters. The rest of the installation consists of laying out, beveling, notching, and nailing on the frieze (Ill. 31).

In the case of open overhangs, cut the frieze to fit between rafters (Ill. 32). For flush cornices cut the frieze to span between the building's corners. Level the pieces, tack them in place, and nail them. The joints should be smooth and square for a tight fit.

Boxed-In Overhang

A boxed-in or closed overhang requires more work. This type completely hides the rafters with a fascia and a soffit.

Start by leveling across between the rafter overhang to the wall (Ill. 33). Do this at both ends of the overhang and snap a chalk line (Ill. 33). Nail, aligned with this line, a ledger, or nailing strip (Ill. 34). Lay out and cut the lookouts. Set them in place, level, and nail them. (First nail to the rafter and then toe-nail to the lookout ledger.) The lookouts can be also installed in the framing stage and nailed directly to the rafters and studs.

The next step is to cut out the plywood soffit. Openings should be provided in the soffit for ventilation. These openings are protected with a screen to prevent insects from flying into the building. Ventilation louvers are also available, which only require installation into the openings. With the soffit cut out and ready, nail it to the bottom of the lookouts, making sure it's level.

The fascia is installed next. It is nailed directly to the ends of the rafters and lookout (Ill. 31). The fascia should extend about 1" below the soffit to provide a drip edge. The top is beveled to meet the roof slope. A frieze is later installed under the soffit (Ill. 31).

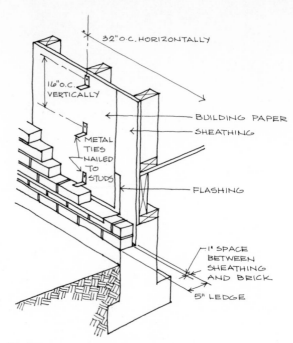

32" O.C. HORIZONTALLY

16" O.C. VERTICALLY

BUILDING PAPER

SHEATHING

METAL TIES NAILED TO STUDS

FLASHING

1" SPACE BETWEEN SHEATHING AND BRICK

5" LEDGE

ILL. 30

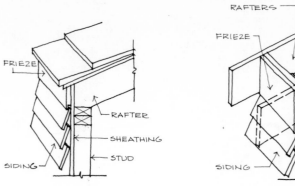

FRIEZE

RAFTER

SHEATHING

STUD

SIDING

FLUSH/SIMPLE CORNICE

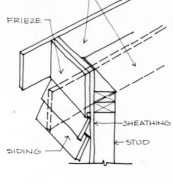

RAFTERS

FRIEZE

SHEATHING

STUD

SIDING

OPEN OVERHANG

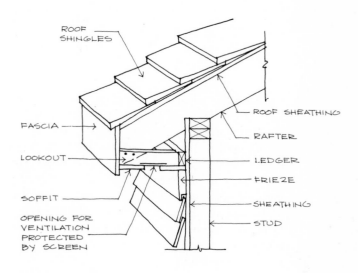

ROOF SHINGLES

ROOF SHEATHING

FASCIA

RAFTER

LOOKOUT

LEDGER

FRIEZE

SOFFIT

SHEATHING

OPENING FOR VENTILATION PROTECTED BY SCREEN

STUD

BOX/CLOSED CORNICE

ILL. 31

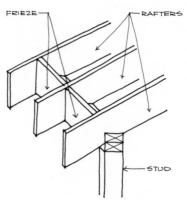

FRIEZE

RAFTERS

STUD

ILL. 32

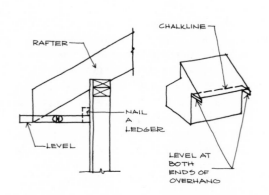

RAFTER

CHALKLINE

NAIL A LEDGER

LEVEL

LEVEL AT BOTH ENDS OF OVERHANG

ILL. 33

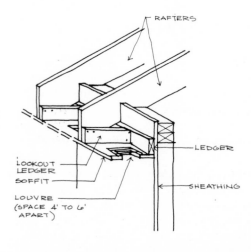

RAFTERS

LEDGER

LOOKOUT LEDGER

SOFFIT

SHEATHING

LOUVRE (SPACE 4' TO 6' APART)

ILL. 34

Closing In
301

26
Plumbing

Unlike other aspects of building, the plumbing installation does not follow a rigid pattern. The most important aspect of the system is its proper design (and of course a very thorough understanding of what you are doing). You must become proficient at the basic techniques involved for measuring, cutting, and joining the pipes, and also become familiar with the various fittings available. You must be aware of how the pipes are integrated into the house structure without weakening it in any way. In this chapter we will describe plumbing procedures, advise you on where to start the installation, and teach you how to organize the pipe assembly. The specific steps to be taken after these basic ones are a function of your particular house design.

MATERIALS

The materials necessary to install the plumbing system are relative to the plumbing design. What follows is a basic outline of the materials you may need.

Drainage and disposal system materials:

- Piping for drainage, venting, and disposal (plastic, copper, or cast iron)
- Pipe adapter (if required) to change lines from one material to another, for example, plastic to metal
- Fittings: couplings, elbows, sanitary tees, Y-branches, etc.
- Reducing tees

- Cleanout plugs
- Floor drains (if required)
- Roof flashing
- Drainage tile (or perforated black plastic pipe)

Water supply system materials:

- Copper piping: Type K flexible copper tubing for underground installation and Type L flexible copper tubing for above-ground installation
- Pressure and temperature relief valve
- Outside water faucets (freeze-proof if you live in a cold climate)
- Valves and fittings, as needed: shutoff valves, unions, tees, etc.

Materials required to aid in the installation of the system:

- Pipe hangers
- Roofing nails
- Steel wool or emery cloth
- Rags
- Plumber's putty
- Pipe insulation (where needed)
- Solder compound (for copper piping)
- Oakum (where cast-iron pipe is used)
- Solvent (for joining plastic pipe)

In addition to the above, you will also need:

- A well pump
- A water heater
- A distribution box (optional)
- A grease trap (optional)
- A septic tank (if needed)
- A drywell (optional)

TOOLS

The tools needed for plumbing installation vary with the pipe material you are using. Regardless of materials, however, you will need the following carpentry tools for cutting the woodwork (refer to the Glossary of Tools for further details).

- Reciprocating saw
- Wood chisel
- Carpenter's level
- Plumb bob
- Tape
- Folding ruler

In addition to these tools, you should have an adjustable wrench or a wrench set for tightening nuts when installing the fixtures. A ladder is also handy, since a lot of the plumbing work takes place in the ceiling and other hard-to-reach places. If you want to avoid a lot of bending, use a workbench instead of the floor to assemble the pipes.

The tools required for the assembly of copper piping are:

- Propane gas torch
- Hacksaw or tubing cutter
- Conduit bender
- Round file
- Wire brush
- Vise
- Jig

Cast-iron piping requires the following tools:

- Hacksaw
- Cold chisel
- Sledge hammer
- Yarning iron (if using hubbed pipes)
- Putty knife

If lead joints are required in the cast-iron pipes, you will also need:

- Caulking iron (both the inside and outside type)
- Blowtorch or plumber's furnace
- Melting pot
- Iron ladle

Following is a list of tools needed for the installation of plastic pipes:

- Hacksaw and jig
- Pocketknife or round file

- Bristle brush (make sure it is a natural bristle brush, otherwise the chemicals in the compound might affect it)

INSTALLATION OF PIPES

The plumbing installation takes place in two stages: the rough stage, when all the pipes and fittings are located and assembled, and the finish stage, when the fixtures are installed.

Roughing In

With the aid of your plans, indicating the precise location of the fixtures, together with a piece of chalk, pencil, or crayon, measure and mark on the building platform all the places where the fixtures, their drains, hot and cold water lines, and the soil stack puncture the floors and walls (Ill. 1). Once this is done, proceed to make room for the pipes by cutting the woodwork as required (Inset II). Areas are cut out for each pipe according to its installation priority. That is, main stacks and supply mains will be installed before branch pipes. Only drill or notch enough woodwork at a time to handle the specific pipe run you're installing. If you cut the woodwork for the entire plumbing system at one time, inaccuracies between the original layout and the actual pipe assembly might get you in trouble.

The installation of the drainage system is slightly more complex than that for the water supply. For this reason, we will discuss it first. In addition, the drainage system can also serve as a guide to the installation of the water-supply network.

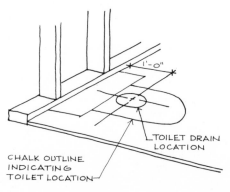

CHALK OUTLINE INDICATING TOILET LOCATION

TOILET DRAIN LOCATION

ILL. I

The skills necessary for plumbing work are many and varied. They include aspects of carpentry such as cutting, notching, and drilling woodwork, together with the nitty gritty of plumbing itself such as cutting, joining, and supporting pipes. Other skills such as leveling and measuring are as important to plumbing as to most other building operations.

The following is a discussion of the essential skills in plumbing work. You might need to master all or perhaps only a few of them. It all depends on your particular plumbing design.

HOW TO MEASURE PIPING

Measure the face-to-face distance the pipe must travel between fittings. To this distance add the depth that the pipe must travel into each fitting. (Make sure to add this quantity to both ends.) Let's say that the distance between fittings is 11″ and the distance the pipe will go into each fitting is ½″. The total required length of pipe will be 12″ (Ill. I-1).

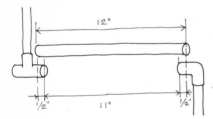

ILL. I-1

HOW TO CUT AND JOIN PIPE

The method of cutting and joining pipes varies with each material. Regardless of material, however, make a few practice cuts and joints before going ahead to the actual installation to get the hang of the material.

Cast-iron pipe: Joining cast-iron pipe may vary with the local code requirements. Most codes no longer require leaded joints, which are cumbersome and difficult to do. Just in case, however, we include a description of leaded joints.

Cast-iron pipe is most widely available in the hub and spigot type. It consists of a section of pipe with one end having a larger diameter than the other. The larger diameter end is called the hub. The opposite end has a slight ridge and is called the spigot. These ends are designed to fit inside each other. The hub is always located at the end facing up (receiving the

flow of the drainage). The spigot end fits inside the hub of the section underneath (Ill. 1-2).

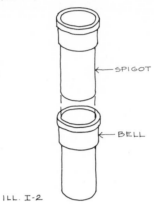

ILL. I-2

Cuts in cast-iron pipe are made by means of a cold chisel or a hacksaw, depending on the thickness of the pipe. (There are two thicknesses of cast-iron pipe, a heavy one for exterior use and a lighter one for interior use.) Chalk-mark the length to which the pipe must be cut. Place a piece of wood on the floor and lay the pipe over it. If the pipe is lightweight, use a hacksaw to make a shallow cut all around the pipe. Tap the pipe with a hammer until it breaks. A hacksaw won't work when using heavy pipe. Instead, score the pipe at the chalk line with a cold chisel. The first cut should be a light one all around. Then continue chiseling progressively harder until the pipe breaks (Ill. I-3).

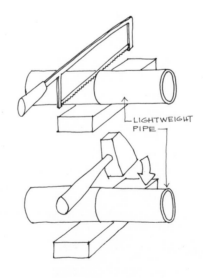

LIGHTWEIGHT PIPE

ILL. I-3

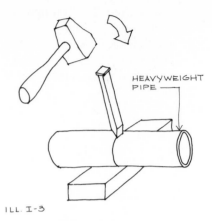

HEAVYWEIGHT PIPE

ILL. I-3

Joining the pipe starts by fitting two sections together. Place the spigot of the upper section on the hub of the lower one (make sure the upper section is centered in the hub of the lower one). With the aid of a yarning iron, pack oakum in the leftover space between the hub and the spigot. Tightly pack the oakum to about 1″ from the top of the hub. Here is where the difference in code requirements comes in. Should the code allow use of a joint compound, this 1″ space is filled with the compound. A putty knife comes in handy for applying the compound. If joint compound is not allowed, lead is used instead (Ill I-4).

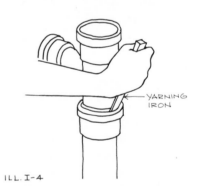

YARNING IRON

ILL. I-4

Leaded joints involve melting the lead and pouring it into the leftover space in the hub. Using a plumber's furnace (a blowtorch that shoots flame upward) or a blowtorch, melt the lead in a melting pot. Once it is molten, scoop the lead with a ladle out of the pot and into the hub (over the oakum) until it comes a little above the top of the hub. Pour it slowly all around the joint. When the lead is cooled, it should spread against both surfaces of the hub. This is done by gently tapping with a caulking tool. To pack lead against the pipe, use a caulking tool (Ill. I-5).

LADLE TO POUR LEAD

CAULKING TOOL

ILL. I-5

Pouring the lead becomes more difficult when you are doing a horizontal joint; this is where a joint runner comes in handy. A joint runner is a piece of asbestos pipe with a clamp at one end. It is attached against the open bell to prevent lead from pouring out. There is a little opening at the top of the runner into which to pour the lead. The runner is removed after the lead has cooled and any surplus lead is cut off. The joint is completed by tapping with a caulking tool as already described (Ill. I-6).

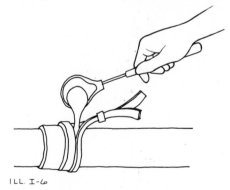

ILL. I-6

By now you should be able to understand why we recommend using a pipe material other than cast iron whenever allowed; not only is the cutting and joining

work difficult but the pipes are heavy and cumbersome. Following are a few tips on doing cast-iron joints: Protect your hands while in the leading process by using heavy-duty rubber gloves. Keep your feet out of the way as you are pouring in case hot lead falls onto the floor. Also, make sure to heat the ladle before scooping out the lead. A cold ladle may explode when coming in contact with hot lead.

Copper tubing: Copper is considerably easier to cut and join than cast iron. To cut copper tubing, chalk-mark the desired length. Copper can be cut with a hacksaw and a jig or with a pipe cutter. Regardless of the method, the important thing is to get a square cut. If you are using a pipe cutter, place the pipe on a vise and the cutting blade of the cutter on the chalk mark. Rotate the cutter around the pipe at the same time that you are tightening the cutter's handle (Ill. I-7). The cut pipe is likely to have burrs, which must be removed with a file.

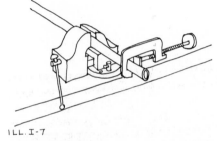

ILL. I-7

Before the pipe can be soldered, its ends as well as the inside of the fitting must be cleaned with steel wool. It is wise at this point to check for any dents in the pipe. Remember that the pipe must be perfectly round if the joint is to be successful. With a brush, apply a coat of flux to the inside of the fitting and the outside of the pipe you have just cleaned. The fitting is then slipped on and turned a few times in order to spread the flux evenly all around. Any excess flux should be removed.

The soldering process starts by heating the fitting with a torch. When hot, solder is applied to the edge of the fitting all around the joint, sealing it. (Capillary action allows the melted solder to penetrate into the space between the pipe and the fitting.) Remove the heat after the connection has been filled. Wipe away any surplus solder. (Be careful not to burn yourself.) While the solder joint is cooling, prevent the solder seal from being broken by making sure that the pipe and fitting are not moved.

Plastic piping: Plastic is by far the easiest material to cut and join. Cutting plastic pipe can be done with a hacksaw, a hand-

saw, a power saw, and sometimes even a pocketknife. (Make sure that the saw is fine-toothed.) Here again, a square cut is important. This can be easily done by using a jig. Once cut, any burrs in this pipe should be removed with a file or pocketknife.

Plastic pipe is joined by means of solvent. Before it can be applied, however, the inside of the fitting and the outside of the pipe should be cleaned with emery cloth. The solvent is then applied on both the outside of the pipe and the inside of the fitting with a bristle brush, covering the entire area which makes up the joint. It is important to get the correct solvent for the type of plastic pipe you are using. The easiest way to avoid confusion is to purchase the solvent at the same time as the pipe. Slip the fitting onto the pipe as far as it should go. Press it against the pipe, and turn it (about a quarter of a turn) to ensure the even distribution of the solvent (Ill. I-8). Hold the joint together for a few seconds and then remove any excess solvent. Do not move the joint until it has had sufficient time to set.

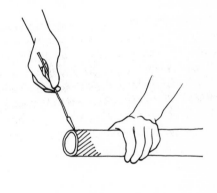

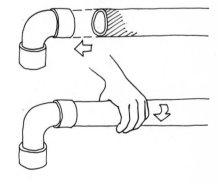

ILL. I-8

Compare this procedure with that for copper or cast-iron piping and the reason why plastic pipe is gaining in popularity becomes obvious.

The piping network weaves its way through the structure of the house and is supported by it. It is essential that the structural strength of the frame not be diminished by the holes cut in its members. Cutting away at the house frame to make room for the pipes must not alter the load-carrying capacity of the frame. Nobody wants a sagging floor or, worse yet, a collapsed one.

Here are a few pointers to keep in mind.

• When drilling holes or cutting notches through the studs or joists, the cut should never exceed one-quarter of the total depth of the member (below).

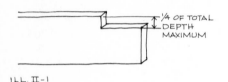

¼ OF TOTAL DEPTH MAXIMUM

ILL. II-1

• Holes drilled through joists should be centered between the top and the bottom face of the joists (above, right).

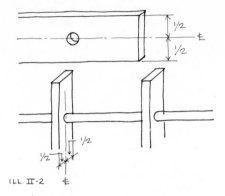

ILL. II-2

• Never cut joists at the center of their span. That is the point where they are carrying the maximum stress and therefore where they need the most material. Instead, keep the cuts in areas close to the supports (below).

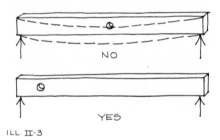

NO

YES

ILL. II-3

• If a large notch is absolutely necessary in a joist, beef up the joist with additional wood (below).

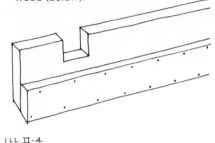

ILL. II-4

• A steel plate can be added to the side of a notched stud to add to its strength (below).

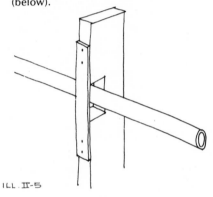

ILL. II-5

Drainage

The soil stack and the building drain are the two main components of the drainage system; therefore the installation network starts with these two pipes. All other branch piping will follow.

The location of the building drain will vary with the design of the house and so will its installation. A house with a basement can have its building drain running underneath the floor slab (if it has fixtures in the basement) or hung from the ceiling (if it does not), or it can use a combination of both. A home with a crawl space might hang the building drain from the structure beneath the first floor in the crawl space (Ill. 2). Actually, you could bury it in the ground, but this means a lot of unnecessary digging for its initial installation and in case of repairs later on.

In addition, the building drain location varies depending on the disposal facility it connects to,

in other words, a municipal sewer or a private disposal system. This is due to the different depths at which these facilities may be located. In general, municipal sewer connections are deeper than those for private disposal facilities, thus requiring lower connections and a lower placement of the building drain (Ill. 2).

Whether you have a basement or a crawl space, the first step in the installation of the drainage system is to cut a hole (as marked in chalk) where the soil stack penetrates the first floor (or the highest floor in which the house has a bathroom) and another one for the water closet drain. (Water closets should drain directly into the soil stack.) Take a sanitary tee and an elbow and position them together. Hold them temporarily in place with braces directly underneath the two openings provided as shown in Illustration 3. The procedure which follows varies slightly depending on whether your house has a basement or a crawl space.

If it has a basement, drop a plumb bob (accu-

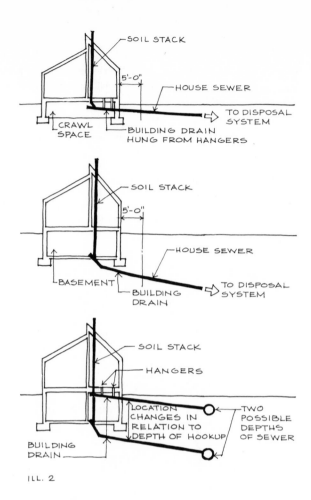

ILL. 2

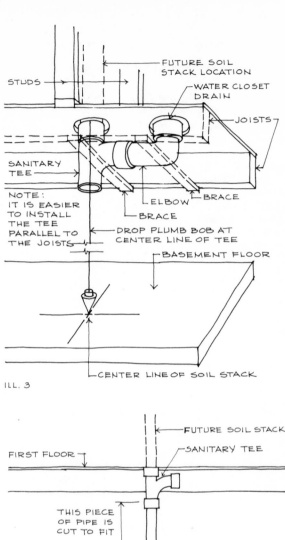

ILL. 3

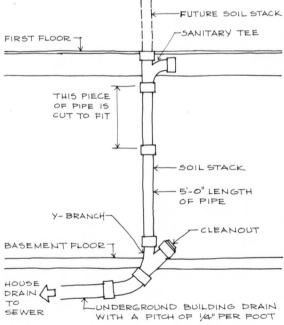

ILL. 4

rately centered on the tee) to the floor below and mark the exact location where the soil stack will fall on the basement floor (Ill. 3). (If the house has a bathroom on a higher floor, start at the top and repeat this procedure until you get to the first floor.) A line between this point and that where the building drain exits to become the house sewer gives you the location of the building drain. Start to lay the building drain (whether cast iron or plastic) at the point where it exits from the basement to a spot directly underneath the soil stack (already marked). You will probably have to cut the last pipe to fit the required length of run (Inset I). Assemble the pipes on the floor or bench before placing them in position. Join the pipe segments as required by the type of material you are using (cast iron or plastic) to the corresponding fittings (Inset I). Always make a test, dry run installation to check the assembly before joining the pipes. Don't forget that the building drain should have a minimum rise of ¼″ per foot (or as required by

code). Make sure to install a cleanout (a sanitary Y-branch with a cleanout plug) where the soil stack and the building drain come together. When the entire house drain has been assembled, check with a level to make sure that there is at least ¼″ drop per foot and that the sanitary Y is directly in line with the soil stack position on the first floor (Ill. 4). At this stage, it is a

Pipes are heavy slender elements that have to span large distances. To prevent their buckling and sagging, supports are provided. The strength of the pipe is relative to its material. That is, copper and plastic tubing require closer supports than cast iron. When a pipe is traveling horizontally through a wall, the support is provided by studs (right). Similarly, when a pipe travels vertically support is sometimes provided by plates (right). At other times the run does not occur within the structure (as may

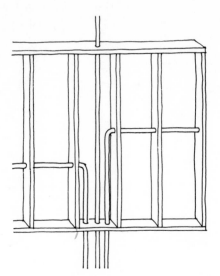

be the case in the basement ceiling) and pipe hangers and other clamping devices must be used.

Horizontal pipes should be supported at least every 10'. A closer spacing of 6' to 8' is required for ½" or smaller diameter sizes. Vertical runs of 1" pipe need to be supported at every floor. The plumbing supplier can provide you with additional information regarding the spacing of supports for the specific type you are using and the various supports available.

---

good idea to provide a basement drain and any necessary branch lines to basement fixtures.

Should your house have a crawl space instead of a basement, determine the shortest path the house drain may follow to connect with the house sewer, and lay the building drain as already explained. It will hang from the first-floor structure by means of pipe hangers (Ill. 5 and Inset III).

After checking that the sanitary Y is plumb and directly underneath the location of the soil stack, start assembling the soil stack from the bottom up. The first run of vertical pipe is connected to the sanitary Y (cleanout). If the material of the house drain is different from that of the soil stack—for example, if it changes from cast iron to copper—you will have to first provide an adapter. Otherwise, continue upward with the stack until it reaches the point where it connects to the first-floor sanitary tee; some pipe cutting will be required (Ill. 4). The tee can have one or more side outlets, depending on the number of branch lines it must receive (Ill. 6). Our sample house calls for a sanitary tee with one side opening (to receive the line carrying waste from the dishwasher). The sanitary-tee connection between the toilet and the soil stack, which had previously been temporarily held in place, can now be joined to the soil stack.

The soil stack continues its run to the roof by joining successive lengths of pipe. Once it

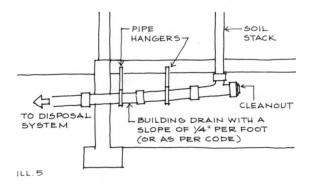

reaches the roof, it should extend at least 6" beyond it and be carefully flashed. (See Chapters 12 and 23.) On its way to the roof, branch pipes connect into the soil stack as required by the design of the drainage system (Ill. 7). In the case of our sample house, we have to connect a branch line slightly above the one already provided for the first-floor water closet. This line carries waste from the kitchen and bathroom sinks to the soil stack. Whenever the soil stack is brought up to a level where branch waste lines occur, they should be connected to the soil stack before it is built up any further (Ill. 6). The branch lines are located by measuring, cutting, and joining pipes until they follow the path required between the fixture drains (as indicated by the chalk mark) and the soil stack. These runs will sometimes occur inside a wall (as in the case of sinks) and other times under-

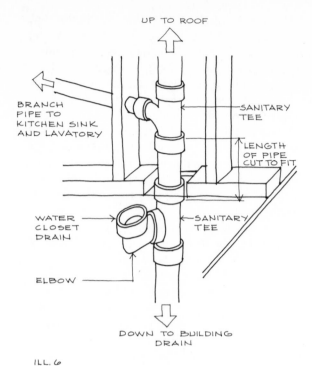

UP TO ROOF

BRANCH PIPE TO KITCHEN SINK AND LAVATORY

SANITARY TEE

LENGTH OF PIPE CUT TO FIT

WATER CLOSET DRAIN

SANITARY TEE

ELBOW

DOWN TO BUILDING DRAIN

ILL. 6

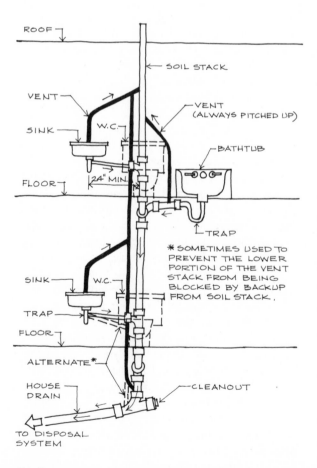

ROOF

SOIL STACK

VENT

VENT (ALWAYS PITCHED UP)

SINK

W.C.

BATHTUB

FLOOR

24" MIN.

TRAP

* SOMETIMES USED TO PREVENT THE LOWER PORTION OF THE VENT STACK FROM BEING BLOCKED BY BACKUP FROM SOIL STACK.

SINK

W.C.

TRAP

FLOOR

ALTERNATE *

HOUSE DRAIN

CLEANOUT

TO DISPOSAL SYSTEM

ILL. 7

neath the floor (as in the case of bathtubs and water closets). To allow for free passage of waste, avoid sharp bends. Make sure that every fixture is supplied with a trap. Double-check all horizontal drain lines to be certain that they are pitching at a minimum of ¼" per foot (or as required by code).

In our sample house, we found it necessary to have a waste stack in addition to the soil stack to accept the waste from the bathtub and the washing machine (since they are both too far from the soil stack). The assembly of this waste stack is similar to that described for the soil stack. Upon reaching the crawl space, it too must be connected to the building drain and cleanout provided.

VENTS: The venting network is an integral part of the drainage system and it is installed at the same time. Because they function by gravity, drainage lines pitch down toward the soil stack. Instead of letting these lines terminate at the level of the fixture trap, they are extended upward above the trap and are hooked to a vent riser. When continuation of the fixture drain pipe upward is impossible, a vent line is connected to a branch line as close to the fixture as possible (Ill. 7). The connection between the drainage line and the vent is done with a tee and generally occurs inside the walls. A horizontal vent branch is then installed to join the various fixture vents. Horizontal vents should always pitch up toward the vent stack to prevent waste in the drainage lines from entering the vents (Ill. 7). The vent branch is then connected to a vent riser. Its path through the house is parallel to that of the soil stack, until it is either connected to the soil stack (above the level of the highest fixture) or continues its run directly to and through the roof (Ill. 7). The vent lines for a particular area should be installed at the same time as the drainage lines.

When the drainage and venting systems have been installed and until such time as the fixtures are hooked up, debris must be prevented from entering the pipes. This can be done by plugging up all the pipe outlets temporarily with rags. Another reason for plugging the pipe outlets is to prevent poisonous gases from the house sewer from backing up into the house, once the house sewer is connected to the town sewer. In addition, check for any unused openings in the tees or other connections. If there are any, plug them up with a cap and nipple.

Water Supply

The water-supply main brings the water from the well or municipal main to the house. It sits at the bottom of a trench, which must be located at least 1' beneath the frost line to prevent the pipe from freezing (check your local code). The trench slopes the necessary amount to bridge the well or main and the point of entry of the pipe to the house. Care must be taken while backfilling the trench that no rocks are thrown over the supply main, possibly damaging the pipe. For additional protection against damage to the pipe resulting from vehicles or planting above it, make the trench a minimum of 3' deep. (Refer to Chapter 19 for trench excavation details.)

If you are hooking up to a water main, the code will probably require a licensed plumber to make the connection. Codes are more lenient, however, when connecting to a well. The method of connection will vary with the type of pump and the manufacturer. Should the pump not be provided with instructions on how to hook up the water-supply line, get directions from the supplier. Once the connection to the water supply has been made, the lengths of pipe are laid solidly at the bottom of the trench and joined as required by the materials you are using; in other words, copper pipe will require solder connections. (Flexible copper tubing comes in 60' coils, requiring few connections.)

The techniques involved in installing the water-supply system are essentially those employed in installing the drainage system. The fixture placement is already known and the drainage pipes can serve as guides for the location of the hot and cold water-supply lines. The steps required for aligning and erecting the supply-pipe assembly are similar to those for the drainage pipes (of course, the actual connection work will vary with the pipe material).

The supply main punctures the foundation wall at a point beneath the frost line. (In cold climates the basement crawl space, through which the pipe must travel, must be kept above freezing to prevent the water inside the pipe from freezing.) If an opening has not already been provided in the foundation wall, drill one with a masonry bit and drill. You are better off, however, if you provided an opening while building the foundation (see Chapter 20). Be careful to thoroughly caulk (not cement) the hole where the supply main comes in to avoid the danger of leakage.

With the supply line inside the house, the first step is to install a shutoff (stop and waste) valve and a faucet. These two items are important in case of a plumbing emergency and for draining the system later on as needed. The valve shuts off the water supply, while the faucet lets out any water already in the pipes (Ill. 8). If the source of water is a municipal main, leave room for the later installation of a water meter. Get in touch with the local authorities to find out how much room is required. Install a short run of pipe to where the meter is later to be placed.

The installation continues by placing the water heater in its proper location. Afterward the water-supply main is split in two with the aid of a tee (Ill. 9). One branch is connected to the water heater and becomes the hot water main. The hookup of the water lines to the water heater starts by connecting a cold water line (by means of a union) to the water heater (Ill. 9). Before connecting the union, install a shutoff valve (Ill. 9). You will otherwise not be able to stop the water flow into the heater in the event of a breakdown or a necessary repair. The next, very important step is to provide the water heater with a temperature and relief valve (unless the heater comes already equipped with one). The relief valve is a safety measure against an explosion of the water heater (or boiler) due to a buildup of pressure. In addition to being connected to the heater, this valve is joined to a ½" pipe directed toward the floor. The purpose of the pipe is to release any excess water and steam. It must be directed down toward the floor to prevent anyone from getting hit by a discharge of high-pressure hot water (Ill. 10). The last pipe to be connected to the water heater (again by means of a union) is the one that receives the heated water from the heater and takes it to the fixtures, the hot water main (Ill. 9).

With the hot and cold water mains ready, the next step is to branch them out to the various fixtures they service. To plot the routes the pipes must take, use the same techniques employed in the drainage system. Make sure to run cold water branch pipes to service one or more outside faucets. If you are in a cold climate, they must be of the freeze-proof type. These faucets will supply you with the water you'll need for gardening, washing the car, and hosing down the kids on a hot summer day. Once again take a look at the location of the fixtures the branch pipes have to service and re-evaluate the route

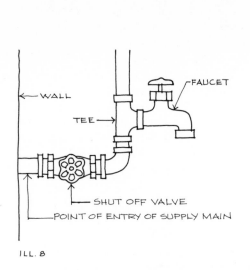

ILL. 8

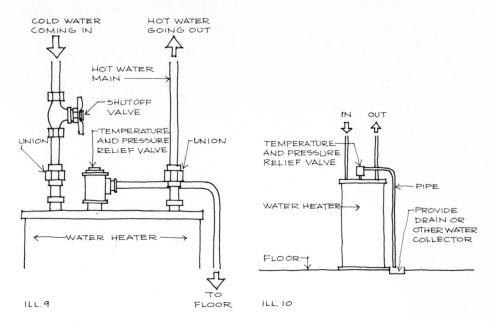

ILL. 9

ILL. 10

they must take, making sure it is the easiest way to get them there (minimizing bends and cutting). Cut out all required woodwork to make room for the pipes (Inset II). Remember that pipes have to be properly secured within the structure of the house (Inset III). In addition, be aware that there is a limit to how much woodwork you can cut without damaging the house structurally (Inset II).

Here are a few things to keep in mind while installing the hot and cold water-supply pipes.

- Hot and cold water pipes run side by side approximately 8″ apart. Where the pipes must cross, be certain that they are still an adequate distance apart (Ill. 11).
- Always provide a shutoff valve at each fixture supply line to facilitate repairs. It is also a good idea to provide each branch pipe leading to a kitchen, bathroom, or laundry room with a shutoff valve. This can prove helpful in the event that the water has to be cut off from an entire area at one time; it avoids having to go around closing each individual fixture valve.
- Don't forget to pitch all horizontal branch pipes down toward the stop and waste valve you have already installed at the lowest point in the system. Drainage of the system may otherwise be impossible.
- Hot water supply pipes are usually located to the left of the fixtures (looking at the fixtures head on).
- Air chambers must be installed above each supply pipe. This is easily done by installing a tee at the top of the vertical supply pipe. A capped length of pipe approximately 12″ in length is installed at the top of the tee and becomes the air chamber (Ill. 12).

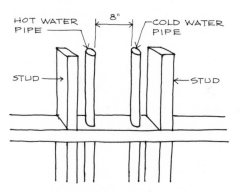

ILL. 11

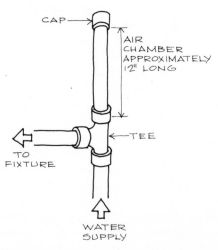

ILL. 12

Plumbing
311

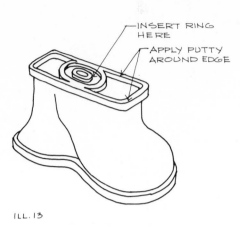

INSERT RING HERE

APPLY PUTTY AROUND EDGE

ILL. 13

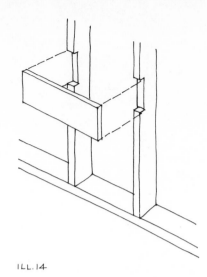

ILL. 14

Finish Installation

The finish installation takes place once all wall, floor, and ceiling finishes are up. It consists of hooking up the fixtures (water closets, tubs, lavatories, sinks, etc.) to the plumbing system. The installation of the fixture varies with both the fixture and its manufacturer. As a general rule, manufacturers supply detailed instructions and recommendations for the installation of their products. Get all the literature and help that you can from them. They're probably the best available source.

Here are a few items to keep in mind while doing the finish installation.

WATER CLOSETS: Most likely you'll have a toilet with a separate tank and bowl. To make a watertight seal between the bowl and the floor, turn the bowl upside down and apply putty to the outside rim. Then place a ring (rubber, putty, or wax designed for this purpose) around the drainage opening. Turn the bowl rightside up and move it slightly until you position it over the flange bolts. Tighten the nuts carefully. Don't overtighten them; you might crack the bowl. You can now install the tank over the bowl as per the manufacturer's instructions (Ill. 13).

SINKS AND LAVATORIES: Unless it rests on a cabinet or pedestal, the sink or lavatory is hung from the wall. In order to do this, a 1″ × 6″ piece of wood is nailed to the studs approximately the length of the sink. Before the wall finish is applied, notch the studs to provide for the thickness of the wood (Ill. 14).

TUBS: Keep in mind that the floor of the tub should slope toward the drain.

CONNECTIONS: For typical hookups of fixtures to water-supply and drainage system refer to Illustration 15.

INSTALLING A SEPTIC TANK SYSTEM

Installation of a sewage disposal system involves not only laying out the pipes and the septic tank but also excavating the trenches. For the sake of simplicity, the excavation of both the trenches and the hole for the septic tank should occur simultaneously with that of the house. (You will otherwise have to bring all the excavation equipment to the site twice.) Chapter 19 discusses trench and septic tank excavation.

With the trenches ready, the first pipe to be laid is the house sewer. (The trench for the house sewer should be deep enough to take a 4″ or 6″ diameter pipe. Check with the local code for specific regulations.) Pipe of the bell and spigot type with a built-in sealer (cast iron, asbestos cement, or bituminous pressed fiber) is generally employed for the house sewer. Lay the pipe firmly at the bottom of the trench, always pointing the bell in the direction of the foundation. The house sewer should pitch ¼″ per foot (or as required by code) toward the septic tank. Bends in the pipe should be avoided since they are usually not allowed by code.

The house sewer is then connected to the distribution box (if one is included in the de-

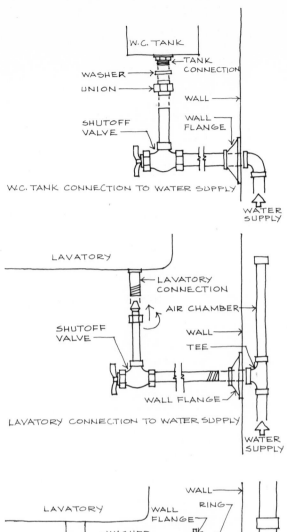

W.C. TANK

TANK CONNECTION

WASHER

UNION

WALL

SHUTOFF VALVE

WALL FLANGE

W.C. TANK CONNECTION TO WATER SUPPLY

WATER SUPPLY

LAVATORY

LAVATORY CONNECTION

AIR CHAMBER

SHUTOFF VALVE

WALL

TEE

WALL FLANGE

LAVATORY CONNECTION TO WATER SUPPLY

WATER SUPPLY

WALL

LAVATORY

WALL FLANGE

RING

WASHER

UNION

WASHER

TEE

WASHER

TRAP

TRAP CLEANOUT

DRAINAGE

LAVATORY CONNECTION TO DRAINAGE

ILL. 15

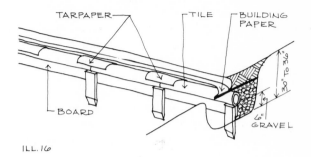

TARPAPER

TILE

BUILDING PAPER

BOARD

30" TO 36"

6" GRAVEL

ILL. 16

sign) and continues on in the same fashion as already described to connect to the septic tank. A description of the procedure to follow for installing a septic tank can be found on page 170, Inset III. A few tips on septic tank installation: Once the tank has been lowered into place, fill it partially with water. If the tank is left empty, any increase in ground water level due to rain will push the tank upward even after it has been covered with earth. The top of the tank should be at least 2' below the finished grade, or as specified by code.

The next job is the installation of the effluent field. Before doing any work, check your code. Since cesspools, septic tanks, and effluent fields contain disease-carrying bacteria that have the potential of polluting clean water sources, the codes are quite specific in their requirements, outlining everything from trench lengths, widths, distances, and methods of laying the pipe to the pipe material. The trenches for the effluent tile are generally deeper than those for the house sewer since approximately 6" of gravel is put at the bottom of the trench before the pipe is laid. The function of the gravel is to increase the absorbency of the soil. To provide an even base for the tile to sit on, lay a piece of board over the gravel before placing the tile. This board should also make it easier to establish an even downward pitch (usually ¼" in 6').

The tiles are then placed over the board with enough gravel built up on each side to help keep them in place. The spacing between the tiles is approximately ¼" to ½". This space is covered with a layer of tarpaper (enough to cover the space) to prevent soil and stones from clogging it up. Another layer of gravel is then applied over the tiles. To prevent earth from filtering down through the gravel, a layer of building paper or straw is applied over the gravel. The remainder of the trench is backfilled with earth. Place a piece of flat stone at the end of the tile run to prevent excessive discharge in that direction (Ill. 16).

The overall depth of these trenches usually never exceeds 3', and their run no more than 100' in length. The minimum distance between trenches is generally 6'. Check your code for special recommendations.

INSTALLING A STORM DRAINAGE SYSTEM

A storm drainage system is necessary in areas that have impervious soil. Such a system starts with the installation of footing drains around the perimeter of the foundation. The installation of these pipes takes place at the same time as the foundation work. Refer to Chapter 20 for details. In addition to the collection of underground water, rain water from the roof is collected by means of gutters and leaders. The steps necessary for their installation are outlined in Chapter 23.

Both the pipes coming from the roof (leaders) and those coming from the footing drains are joined underground to form a single pipe, which will discharge this water elsewhere on the property or to a municipal storm sewer. This pipe is usually tight-joint bituminous clay fiber or black perforated plastic. You might find that if you are hooking up to a municipal storm sewer main the code requires a plumber or other authorized individual to do the connection.

Where a storm sewer is not available, the drainage piping may be fed to a drywell. (See page 171 for information regarding drywells.)

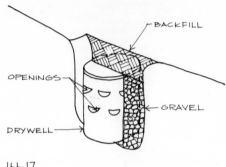

ILL. 17

Caution must be taken that the water table is lower than the bottom of the drywell. The ground will otherwise not be able to absorb the water. Prefabricated concrete cylinders with perforated walls are available commercially for use at drywells. (They are also used as cesspools.) Their installation consists of digging a hole of the proper dimension (according to the size of the drywell) and lowering the cylinder into place. Gravel should be placed all around the outside of the drywell to improve water absorption. Make sure to locate the drywell far away (at least 50'-0") from the house to prevent backflow of water (Ill. 17).

27
Heating

Provision for the design of one simple heating system has been described in detail in Chapter 13, Environmental Systems. This system, the simple series loop, uses hot water as the heat distribution system. The installation of this system is outlined first. The forced hot air system, although not described in Chapter 13 because the process is slightly more complicated, is very easy to install. We have included instructions for the installation of hot air distribution equipment since many manufacturers will design the system for the do-it-yourself installer without charge if he agrees to buy the component parts from them. The forced hot air system can be installed following the directions in the second part of this chapter. (The manufacturer of the system will include instructions for its installation on request.)

Both of these systems are described very basically, without referring to sophisticated equipment that can be used in conjunction with the basic machinery. For instance, the forced hot air system is often used in conjunction with air cooling. Although we acknowledge that an air cooling system is more or less essential in the southern part of the United States, we have not included instructions for its design and installation. Other literature will have to be consulted if air cooling is desired. A number of devices, such as electronic air cleaners, have been similarly omitted.

INSTALLING THE HOT WATER SYSTEM

Five procedures are involved in installing a hot water system. First, the boiler and its paraphernalia are installed. Second, the connection to the fuel supply is made. Third, the baseboards are assembled and temporarily placed in their final locations so that holes can be drilled through the subfloor. Fourth, the hot water pipes are run from the boiler to the baseboards and connections are made between boiler and household plumbing (if domestic hot water is to be heated by the boiler). Last, the baseboards are permanently installed after finished walls and floors are completed.

Before assembling any part of the system be sure that you understand the workings of each component and that you have all of the necessary parts and safety control devices. In addition, see that no parts have been damaged in shipment. Most of the tools and skills required for installing this type of heating system have been outlined in Chapter 26 under the headings for the installation of copper piping.

Materials

- Copper tubing: The sizes outlined in the design drawings. Always order about 5 percent more than the lengths measured off the drawings

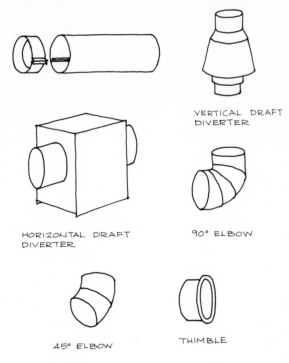

VERTICAL DRAFT
DIVERTER

HORIZONTAL DRAFT
DIVERTER

90° ELBOW

45° ELBOW

THIMBLE

ILL. 1

(which even when drawn to scale are not completely accurate). In addition, extra pipe length will be required where fittings have to be made.
• Elbows, air vents, etc., as required.
• Flexible connectors used as expansion joints.
• Baseboard units, as designed.
• All equipment required for installation of boiler (Inset I).
• Smoke pipe.

The Boiler

All boiler manufacturers make their products a little differently. Some build in many of the components and in addition preconnect much of the wiring.* Others ship the boiler in parts and expect you to piece it together and connect all the wiring. Be that as it may, detailed instructions for assembling of the equipment will be shipped with it. Although we cannot detail all of the different boilers available, we can define the functions of the parts so that you can better understand the manufacturer's instructions (Inset I).

* In choosing the boiler, ease of installation is a feature to look for.

The Fuel Supply

Oil tanks can be installed either inside the house (in the basement or crawl space) or outside. If installed indoors, the tank must be at least 7′ away from the boiler according to most codes. Check your local codes carefully for controls and guidelines. The most popular size domestic tank has a 275 gallon capacity and is 64″ × 42″ × 27″. There are different models of this size tank depending on how the tank is to be positioned.

Four pipes lead out of the fuel tank. On one end are the fuel filler pipe, which leads outside of the house for the periodic fillings from the oil delivery truck, and the vent line. Unless dictated otherwise by code, run the pipes as directly as possible to the outside, using black iron pipes with malleable iron fittings at least 2″ in diameter for the feeder line, and 1¼″ for the vent line. Be careful in making the pipe connection. Oil can dissolve ordinary pipe compound. Special oil-line compound must be used for this purpose. To be sure that the compound does not inadvertently get into the oil pipes, apply compound to the first three or four threads of the male end of the connection, using a small paint brush, and then tighten the fitting to close.

The lines (sometimes there is only a single line from the tank to the boiler; other boiler models have a supply and a return) leading from the fuel tank to the boiler are of copper, usually ½″ in diameter (check the specifications of the selected boiler) and having flare-fitting connections.

When installing the boiler, be careful when moving the unit to its location. Be sure that the floor surface on which it will sit is strong enough for its weight and is level. If not, make the required corrections. Some models are equipped with self-leveling devices.

Installing the Smoke Pipe

The smoke pipe leading from the boiler to the outside must be airtight to ensure that there are no leaks of toxic or unpleasant fumes into the house. In addition to airtightness, be careful that the pipe rises slightly in its horizontal run. The pipe, although light in weight, must be supported properly.

Lay out the pieces of pipe on the floor in the order that you will need them (Ill. 1). Make sure that the crimped end of the smoke pipe faces the chimney (Ill. 8). You will need the properly adjusted elbow sections to make the required turns.

If the smoke pipe is to be installed into a chimney flue, take the last piece of the run and install it in the chimney thimble, forcing the crimped end all the way in. Return to the furnace and assemble the run. If you must, shorten the last section as required and use a draw-band* to make the final connection. Use wire to support the smoke pipe at every turn and at every other pipe section. See instructions for joining round pipe in the latter part of this chapter, page 322.

The Prefabricated Flue

If you do not have a masonry chimney, and do not plan to have one, a prefabricated flue is an excellent and economical way to dispose of the waste gas from the boiler. The flue can be purchased at most home supply stores completely prefabricated with assembly instructions included. Be sure, however, to check the local codes to see if this solution is permitted, and if so, what restrictions are placed on it.

Locating the Baseboard Units

Before installing the hot water tubing, it is a good idea to determine the exact location of the baseboards even though these units will not be installed until later.

1. Unpack the units and place them in the rooms in their anticipated locations. Most likely the units are designed to sit under the windows if not along the entire length of the exterior walls.

2. Set the baseboards in the rooms as per the design. Remember that the as yet uninstalled wall will be about ½" thick, and allow for it. Approximate the thickness of the finished flooring. Cut the scrap blocking to estimated thickness and set baseboards at finished floor height.

3. Slip on all fittings and connections and temporarily assemble all end panels and accessories (Ill. 2).

4. Determine the location of the supply and return risers. At either end of the assembly, at the point

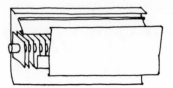

CONVECTOR PANEL ASSEMBLY

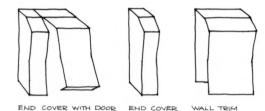

END COVER WITH DOOR   END COVER   WALL TRIM

OUTSIDE CORNER   INSIDE CORNER   SPLICE PLATES

ILL. 2

where the risers should come through the floor, drill exploratory holes to make sure you are clear of the joists. If the assembly coincides with the joists, the baseboard units on the floors above can be shifted a few inches to clear the structure. In the case of a corner baseboard installation, the baseboard can be cut slightly or a flexible connection can be arranged. The exploratory hole is drilled with ¼" bit from above in the center of the projected pipe. The hole is inspected by going down to the floor below. (Actually you will know from the feel of the drill whether you have penetrated a joist.)

5. Next enlarge on the exploratory holes to accommodate the size of the actual risers. Metal expands as it is heated, and the entire system is expected to move somewhat depending on the temperature of the water circulating in the pipes. To accommodate this movement, oval holes—larger than the risers themselves—are cut through the floor. Drill a hole not larger than 1¼" and enlarge it lengthwise with a keyhole saw. For up to 25' of baseboard the long end of the oval should be 1½". If the length of baseboard assembled in the room exceeds 25', add another ⅛" to the hole for each additional 10' of baseboard length.

* A draw-band is a thin strip of sheet metal used to tighten and cover the joint, available where smoke pipe is sold.

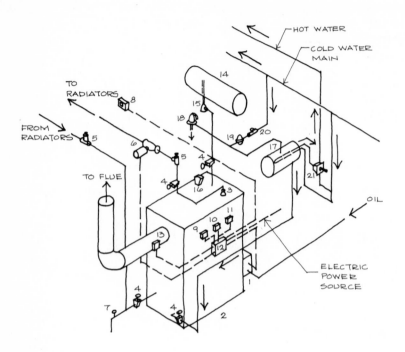

4. *The gate valve* (placed here and at other critical locations) allows for the shutting off of a section of the system for repairs, without having to close down the entire system to drain it of water.

5. *The flow control valves* work in conjunction with the circulating pump. When the pump stops (controlled by the thermostat) these valves close, preventing hot water from rising and circulating through the system by the force of gravity.

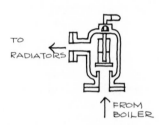

5   FLOW CONTROL VALVE

6. *The circulating pump* is a centrifugal pump controlled by the house thermostat. It turns on whenever heat is called for. The water flow in small, simple systems is for the most part powered by natural gravity. A pump is used mostly to counter the friction encountered by the water flowing through the pipes.

    The water returns from the radiators and baseboards through another flow control valve. A gate valve is positioned in the return pipe before its juncture with the boiler.

1. In *the oil burner* the oil is first changed from a liquid to a vapor by means of a device called an atomizer. The atomizer breaks the liquid into small globules. Air is then blown into the burner and is mixed with the oil, preparing it for combustion in the lower portion of the burner. Ignition takes place by means of an electric arc.

2. What is called *the boiler* is actually a combustion chamber. Water is circulated above the flames and heat is transferred to the circulating water. On its journey through the rest of the house the boiler water must first pass through the air-control fitting.

3. *The boiler air-control fitting* prohibits air, which often accumulates in the boiler, from entering the distribution system. This fitting prevents air from leaving with the heated water, diverting the excess air to the tank air control fitting, which expels it to the air cushion tank.

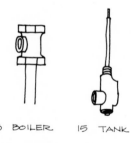

3 BOILER   15 TANK

AIR CONTROL FITTINGS

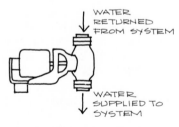

6 CIRCULATING PUMP

7. A *drain* is included since this is the lowest point in the water circulation system and drainage is most easily accomplished here.

8. The circulation of the water is controlled by the *thermostat,* which turns both the circulating pump and the oil burner on and off by means of electrical connections.

   In addition to the above, there are a number of control devices that are an integral part of the system.

9. *The low limit control* turns on the oil burner when the boiler water falls below a chosen temperature.

10. *The high limit control* turns off the burner before a particular (preset) high temperature is exceeded.

11. *The reverse acting control,* not always included, stops the circulating pump when the water in the boiler is not hot enough.

12. *The juncture box and relays* control the other controlling devices.

13. *The stack control device* turns the burner off in case the fuel has not ignited. This control is placed in the smoke stack itself and is heat sensitive. It monitors the heat in the stack. In the event that the burner fails to ignite, no hot fumes will pass through the stack. The cold stack triggers the mechanism that automatically shuts off the fuel supply to the burner.

14. Because water expands when it is heated, there is a varying amount of pressure in the system at any one time. This pressure is controlled by *the air expansion tank* which cushions the water with a pillow of air on the top of the tank.

15. The pipe leading to the expansion tank contains a *tank air-control fitting* and a *gate valve.*

16. An additional control, *the temperature and pressure gauge,* mounted on the boiler, allows one to monitor the boiler pressure and temperature.

DOMESTIC HOT WATER

Domestic hot water—that water used for washing dishes and taking showers—may or may not be an integral part of the heating system. In the case of a detached system, the hot water used for washing and so on is produced in a separate water heater powered most likely by electricity or gas. In the case of an integrated system (combining the domestic hot water system with the heating system) water for washing is either produced in a tankless heater (often buried within the boiler itself) and distributed directly through the pipes to the taps, or is produced in the tankless heater and stored in a separate insulated tank.

In the case of the tankless heater without storage facilities the system operates as follows:

17. *The tankless heater* may or may not be buried within the boiler itself. Boiler water flows from the combustion chamber to the tankless heater coils, which are intertwined with coils from the domestic hot water system. Heat from one water system to the other is thus transferred without water flowing from one system into the other.

18. *A pressure-relief valve* lets water out of the pipes in case the pressure exceeds 30 psi.

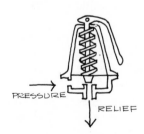

18 PRESSURE RELIEF VALVE

19. *The pressure-reducing valve* attached to the cold water inlet opens when the pressure in the system drops below 12 psi and automatically fills the system with water.

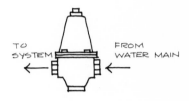

19 PRESSURE REDUCING VALVE

20. *The check valve* is an emergency valve that operates in case the pressure-relief valve and the pressure-reducing valve should fail. This prevents the boiler from excessively pressuring the domestic hot water system, which would no doubt damage the system.

21. *The tempering valve* automatically mixes the cold water with the hot water by mechanical thermostat. Cold water must be mixed with the hot water leaving the tankless heater so that scalding water does not circulate to the taps.

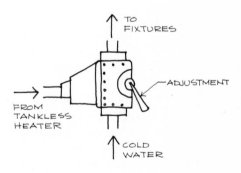

21 TEMPERING VALVE FOR DOMESTIC HOT WATER

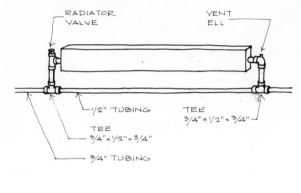

ILL. 3

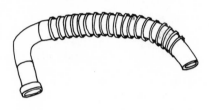

ILL. 5

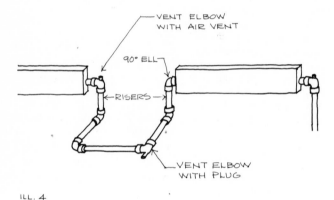

ILL. 4

Installing the Hot Water Pipe

Install the pipe system, making all connections permanent except those to the baseboards. If there is more than one loop to the system, that entire loop should be completed before another is started. Begin at the supply end and assemble the pipe lengths according to plan. Assemble each connection and be sure that it is watertight before going to the next connection. Support the pipe every 10' or 12' as you progress.

Since all of the connections are to be made from rigid copper tubing, directions for cutting the pipe connecting it, and running it through the walls and across the floors are essentially the same as the instructions for the hot water lines in the plumbing chapter, pages 304 and 305.

In the series loop installation, the water main is intersected with baseboards. The system is very unsophisticated in that the heat in any

one room cannot be shut off or in any way modulated (therefore, no valves). This situation may be modified somewhat by installing a bypass pipe, which allows you to completely close off a room in the system (Ill. 3).

Hot water pipe will expand and contract. (Copper tubing can expand as much as 1½" per 100' of run.) To accommodate this expansion without placing stress on the pipe you can construct expansion joints from elbows as shown in Illustration 4. It is much simpler, however, to use flexible connectors, which not only take care of expansion but reduce vibrations, eliminate soldered connections, and compensate for errors in measurements. The flexible pipe is made up of ring-like corrugations of copper, allowing the pipe to bend (Ill. 5).

Installing the Baseboard Units

Remove the baseboard units to a safe place and store until the walls and floors are in place. When they are completed, install the baseboards.

The baseboard units are designed to be attached to the walls and rest on the finished floor. In case thick carpeting is anticipated (but not yet installed) the baseboards will have to be mounted slightly higher on the wall. To accommodate carpeting, rest the units on the floor and draw a horizontal line about 1½" above the top of the unit. A piece of lumber can be rested under the unit to facilitate the installation of the baseboards at this slight elevation.

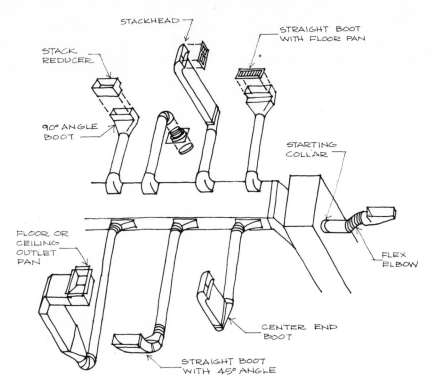

STACKHEAD

STRAIGHT BOOT
WITH FLOOR PAN

STACK
REDUCER

90° ANGLE
BOOT

STARTING
COLLAR

FLOOR OR
CEILING
OUTLET
PAN

FLEX
ELBOW

CENTER END
BOOT

STRAIGHT BOOT
WITH 45° ANGLE

ILL. 6

To install the baseboards, remove the innards from the units—that is, the heating elements (the fins) and the front panels—and nail the rear panels to the wall. Use a punch to start the holes, and always nail the panels to the studs. (These can be located by tapping the walls with a small hammer and listening for a solid thunk.) Replace the heating elements, and reassemble units.

Install the air vent elbows at the *return* end of the baseboard. (You will not need to install valves for baseboards in a series loop.)

The assembly now can be permanently joined. Solder the various components together, removing them if possible from the floor to an elevated working area. Soldering instructions for rigid copper conduit can be found on page 305.

INSTALLING THE FORCED HOT AIR SYSTEM

You should have a good idea about the layout of the duct distribution system and the location of the furnace.

Tools

Screwdrivers	Ruler
Hammer	Tape
Tin snips	Wood chisels
Hand or electric drill	Carpenter's square
Hand brace and auger bits	Hacksaw
	Wrenches
Keyhole saw	Level
	Flashlight

Materials

The materials required for the ductwork depend on your plan. Illustration 6 shows all of the potential component parts of the system. You will not, of course, need all of these items. The installation procedure is as follows:

1. Install the furnace.
2. Assemble the pipes and ducts.
3. Install the return-air runs.
4. Install the supply-air runs.
5. Install the smoke pipe.
6. Connect the fuel supply and the controls.
7. Install the supply-air registers and return-air grills.

Heating

321

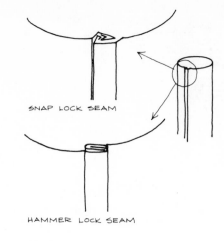

SNAP LOCK SEAM

HAMMER LOCK SEAM

ILL. 7

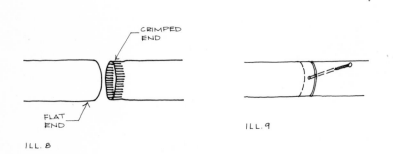

CRIMPED END

FLAT END

ILL. 8

ILL. 9

Installing the Furnace

All furnaces must be installed following the manufacturer's directions enclosed with the item. The leveling of the unit and the connections to the fuel lines are similar to those outlined in this chapter in the section on boilers (page 316).

Assembling the Pipes and Ducts

There is no precise sequence of steps to follow in installing the ducts. It is, however, a good idea to review your plans to determine if a supply line is to cross the return line or another supply line. If so, it makes good sense to install the upper one (one closest to the ceiling) first.

CUTTING AND ASSEMBLING ROUND PIPE: All ductwork is shipped flat and will have to be assembled. The pipe will either have a snap lock or a hammer-lock seam. The snap lock is joined by pressing the tongue on one edge into the slot on the other. The seam will

snap closed. The hammer-lock seam will require hammering to get the seam to close. Place the pipe around a piece of 2 × 4 and gently hammer the seam closed (Ill. 7).

CONNECTING ROUND PIPE: Round ductwork comes with one end flat and the other end crimped. To join the pipe, fit the crimped end of one pipe section into the flat end of another (Ill. 8). The crimped end should always face away from the furnace. Push the ends together for a tight fit. Use sheet-metal screws to secure the joints. Drill two holes through the joint and secure the screws. Round pipe should be supported every 10' or so (Ill. 9).

SHORTENING PIPE SECTIONS: Measure the exact length of the required section onto a section that has not yet been rounded. (It is easier to cut the pipe when it is still flat.) Always cut off the plain end and not the crimped end. Open pipe can be cut with tin snips. (If the edge seam gets crushed in the process, renew it by prying it open with a screwdriver.)

CUTTING AND ASSEMBLING RECTANGULAR DUCTWORK: Large sections of rectangular duct are used as main line plenums.* Rectangular or round duct can be used off of the central plenum.

JOINING LARGE DUCTWORK: Most ductwork comes with S-shaped connectors on the long sides. The two short sides are bent back. Push the sections together, joining the S seams on the long sides (Ill. 10). Slip drive clips over the two shorter ends. To install the clips bend one end tab inward. Start the clip upward and, if required, tap it upward with a hammer. When in position, bend the top tab down (Ill. 11). Ducts should be supported with hangers every 5'.

To shorten rectangular duct, measure and cut the section before the long seams have been joined. First assemble all of the regulation length ductwork, and then measure and cut the last piece. Cut the plain end and not the end with the S clip. It will be necessary to reshape the short sides so that they will join with the

---

* A plenum is a space, generally above the ceiling, that is used to conduct the flow of air. It is more often used as the return for spent air, but is also used at the beginning of the supply air system.

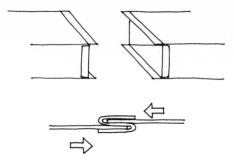

ILL. 10

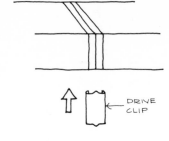

DRIVE CLIP

ILL. 11

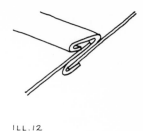

ILL. 12

regular sections. Cut 1″ into the sides and bend the short end backward to receive the drive clip.

JOINING SMALL RECTANGULAR DUCT-WORK: This type of ductwork is most often used as wall stack because it is designed to fit neatly in between the studs. It is joined with snap locks. Fit the snap end of one section into the shaped end of the next section and push gently but firmly together (Ill. 12).

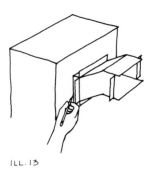

ILL. 13

MAKING OPENINGS IN THE SHEET METAL: When one duct meets another, an opening must be made in the larger one to accommodate a connection. Make a template by placing a sheet of paper on the opening of the smaller duct or fitting and tracing its size. Transfer the required opening onto the sheet metal of the larger duct. Take a sharp-edged tool (or a screwdriver) and with the help of a hammer, drive a hole or a rip in the center of the required opening. Now, you can use the tin snips or a fine-toothed saw to complete the opening.

Installing the Return-Air Runs

Return runs are installed prior to the supply ducts since the return ducts are often positioned directly below the floor joists and above the supply ducts.

There are a variety of ways of installing the return-air run, depending on the furnace and the distribution system. Some systems do not have return-air ducts but draw the air from the surrounding area. This is especially true for installations where the furnace is in a utility room on the main floor of the house.

For those systems with return-air ducts an

opening must be cut in the plenum chamber of the furnace. Having first determined the exact location of this opening, position an offset take-off collar at that location (Ill. 13). (Clear the floor joists or any other combustible material by at least an inch or two.) Trace the size of the collar onto the plenum chamber. Some systems may require more than one collar. Trace all collars before making cuts. To facilitate the cutting you might consider removing the plenum from the furnace. Cut the holes and position the collars in the openings. The collars are secured to the plenum by bending back the tabs. It is unwise to secure a grill directly to the plenum chamber of the furnace. First place a take-off collar on the plenum and then attach the grill to the collar.

Return-air plenums can be constructed using the already existing stud and joist spaces. The areas between the studs and between the joists make ideal plenums if they are closed off properly. The areas between the studs are bounded on the short sides by the studs and on the long sides by wallboard. These long, vertical spaces make ideal vertical ducts. Holes must be cut in

Heating

323

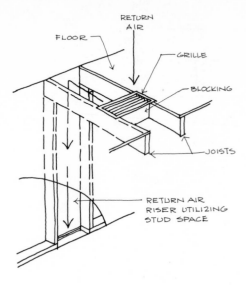

RETURN AIR

FLOOR

GRILLE

BLOCKING

JOISTS

RETURN AIR RISER UTILIZING STUD SPACE

ILL. 14

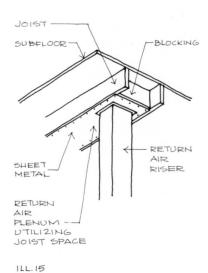

JOIST

SUBFLOOR

BLOCKING

SHEET METAL

RETURN AIR RISER

RETURN AIR PLENUM UTILIZING JOIST SPACE

ILL. 15

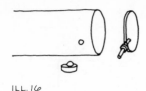

ILL. 16

Larger return-air ducts will not hurt the system, but ones smaller than required might cause vibrations and inefficient distribution. The sheet metal can be nailed directly to the structural wood.

Installing the Supply-Air Runs

Although it is permissible to run the return air in unlined stud spaces, vertical supply ducts in the walls must consist of sheet metal. You want these ducts to be relatively airtight so that the heated air is not lost through cracks. Build up the sheet-metal ductwork as per plan starting from the furnace and working outward to the registers. Remember that the snap end of the small ductwork points to the furnace. Holes cut to accommodate the ductwork should be larger than the ducts.

The supply-air plenum at the furnace must be assembled and installed according to the directions supplied with the unit itself. Make all the openings and install the take-off collars before permanently installing the plenum to the furnace (Ill. 13).

Install a volume damper in each run of duct (Ill. 16), which can control the flow of air. Place it where it will be accessible. Supply runs through unheated spaces should be insulated. Blanket insulation material sold in 1″ or 2″ thick rolls for this purpose is easy to install, and may be purchased at the building supply store.

Installing the Smoke Pipe

Instructions are the same as those reviewed in the hot water heating section in the first part of this chapter.

Connecting the Fuel Supply and Controls

Instructions for installing the fuel supply should come with the furnace. In addition, fol-

the floors and walls to connect the stud spaces to each other. Be sure to block up that portion of the stud spaces above or below the part used as a plenum (Ill. 14).

For the horizontal return ducts, the space between the joists can be used if the bottom section is enclosed with sheet metal (Ill. 15). This situation is viable only if the duct runs parallel to the line of the joists. If not, a regular sheet-metal duct must be used below the joists as the return-air plenum. Holes in the floor must be cut carefully and fully blocked. Cut holes at least as large as the required return duct size.

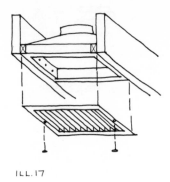

ILL. 17

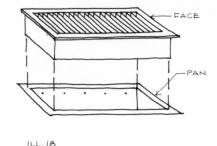

FACE

PAN

ILL. 18

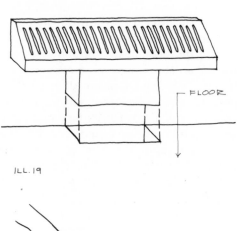

FLOOR

ILL. 19

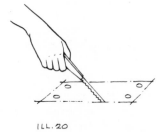

ILL. 20

low instructions and warnings on the connection of the oil-supply system detailed in the beginning of this chapter. Wiring instructions should be followed carefully. If you are not sure about what you are doing, call in an electrician.

Completing the System

Registers and grills cannot be installed until the walls and floor are completed. This may be accomplished in one of two ways. When installing the walls and floors, special attention may be paid to cutting the holes for the registers and grills *before* nailing the material to the studs and joists. The alternative is installing the floors and walls, marking the location of the registers and grills, and then cutting through the material. The latter solution may be easier for the beginner because it simplifies the process of applying drywall and flooring material. This solution should certainly be adopted for the floor registers so that the subfloor and finished floor can be cut simultaneously.

If the walls, ceilings, and floors are completed without providing register and grill openings, they may be cut as follows.

Cutting the Openings in the Walls and Floors

There are a number of different kinds of supply registers, and each variety requires a different kind of cut. The rectangular ceiling register (Ill. 17) requires a square hole between the joists. The round ceiling register requires a round hole cut in the ceiling. Floor registers (Ill. 18) require a rectangular hole made through the subfloor and finished floor large enough to fit the pan snugly. The perimeter baseboard register (Ill. 19) requires a floor opening cut flush against the wall. The return-air grills are installed in rectangular cuts in the floor. The opening for the grill is the same size as the shoulders on the underside of the grill.

To cut the opening in the floor, drill four holes (1″ in diameter), one in each corner of the opening and use a keyhole saw to complete the opening (Ill. 20).

Heating
325

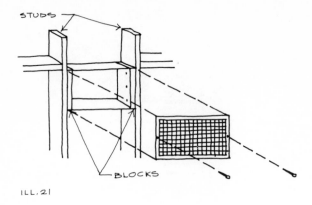

STUDS

BLOCKS

ILL. 21

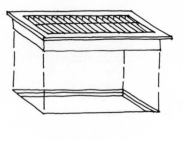

ILL. 22

If the register is to be located in the wall it must be positioned between the studs (Ill. 21). This opening must also be lined up with the joists in the floor below (or above if your plan calls for an above supply) to allow for the supply duct from the basement. (If the walls of the house are already enclosed, cut the hole for the register as required. For cutting gypsum board, use a fine-tooth saw and cut continuously around the outline. Since gypsum board is heavy and brittle, hold on to the piece you are cutting so that the pressure will not break the blade.)

Installing the Air Supply Registers

Floor registers consist of two parts, a face and a pan. Slip the pan in the hole cut for it and nail through its sides into the opening edges. Slip the register face into the pan (Ill. 18).

Perimeter baseboard registers have a register extension, which fits into a hole cut for it. The back plate is nailed to the wall behind it. The register face is then attached (Ill. 19).

Rectangular ceiling registers have a face and a boot. The boot is designed to fit snugly into the cut hole. Wood blocks are nailed to the joists on each side, and the boot is nailed to the blocks. The face is slipped into the boot and is secured with screws (Ill. 17).

Wall registers attach to boxes called stackheads. The wall opening must be the same dimensions as the stackhead. Wood blocks cut to the required width are nailed to the adjoining studs and the stackhead is secured to them. The register face is positioned on the stackhead and screwed to it (Ill. 21).

Return-air grills fit directly into the openings cut for them. When the grill is in place on the floor, the flanges rest on the periphery of the opening (Ill. 22).

Wall grills fit between the stud spaces. The grill is supported by wood blocks nailed to the studs. The grill is attached to the blocks with screws.

The system may now be fired up and tested. Dampers should be adjusted to obtain desired air flow.

28
Electricity

The electrical installation work involves great care. Whenever you are working on the system, caution must be taken that the wires are dead. All connection work must be meticulously and accurately done to avoid short circuits or malfunctionings. Code requirements and recommendations should be strictly followed. If there's any question in your mind as to the installation of the system, don't improvise—hire an electrician instead!

MATERIALS

You'll need the following materials:

- Cable: two- and three-wire
- Standard duplex outlets
- High-voltage outlets
- Weatherproof receptacles
- Lighting outlets
- Switches: two-, three-, and four-way (as needed)
- Service panel
- Boxes: switch, outlet, and junction boxes
- Box hangers
- Cable connectors
- Straps
- Finish plates

TOOLS

Here are some of the most widely used electrical tools:

- Long-nosed pliers
- Electrician's pliers
- Electrician's multipurpose wiring tool
- Electrician's screwdrivers
- Standard ¼" screwdriver
- Pocketknife
- Hacksaw
- Drill or brace and bit
- Metallic tapemeasure
- Yankee push drill
- Doorbell and low-voltage battery (for testing the circuits)
- Soldering iron
- Cable reaper
- Compass saw
- Adjustable wrenches

ELECTRICAL INSTALLATION

The service panel may be installed before, after, or at the same time as the interior wiring. Whichever option you choose, we advise that the installation of the panel be done by an experienced electrician. There are very good reasons for this recommendation. Not all service panels are similar in design. As the designs vary, so do the steps necessary for proper installation. It is near impossible for us to include step-by-step instructions on how to install the panel without knowing which type you are using.

Aside from this problem, the installation work itself is tricky. Its efficient operation, however, is essential to that of the rest of the sys-

CUTTING CABLE

The procedure varies with the type of cable. We will discuss nonmetallic sheathed cable and armored cable.

Nonmetallic sheathed cable: This type of cable can be stripped with a knife. Slit the outer covering, being careful not to damage the insulation of the wires inside. Once a slit is started on the outer cover, you can pull it off as far as you want with a pair of pliers. A cable ripper can be used instead when type NM cable is used. It will save you some time. For type NMC cable only a knife is needed (Ill. I-1).

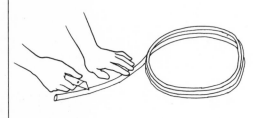

ILL. I-1

Armored cable: Armored cable is more difficult to cut than nonmetallic sheathed cable. With a fine-toothed saw, start a diagonal cut on the cable where the armor is to be removed (Ill. I-2). Be careful as you are sawing the armor not to damage the wire insulation or the bare grounding strip inside. This takes quite a bit of practice so do a few trial cuts before starting

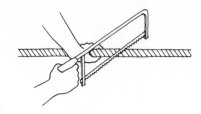

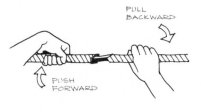

PULL BACKWARD

PUSH FORWARD

ILL. I-2

on the real thing. Put down the saw and, grabbing the cable with one hand at either side of the cut, twist the cable against the spiral until the armor breaks off (Ill. I-2).

To prevent the sharp edge of the cut armor from damaging the insulation of the wires, a bushing is installed. A bushing is a small cylinder with one side having rounded edges. It is made out of a tough fiber with a high insulating value (Ill. I-3). The bushing is slipped between the armor and the wires. Make sure that the grounding wire is bent back over the outside of the armor (Ill. I-3).

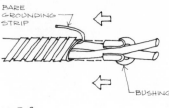

BARE GROUNDING STRIP

BUSHING

ILL. I-3

It is very important that a bushing is provided; otherwise the danger of damaging the wires and a consequent short circuit or ground is increased. No inspector will approve an installation without bushings.

SPLICING THE WIRE

To splice is to join together two or three wires in such a manner that the resulting wire remains as strong mechanically, as good a conductor electrically, and as well insulated as a continuous piece of wire. The first step to make a splice is to remove the insulation from the wire. You can do this with a pocketknife (being careful not to damage the conductor) in the same manner in which you sharpen a pencil. The insulation should decrease smoothly toward the conductor. It should not be a right-angle cut (Ill. I-4). Make sure that there are no traces of insulation left on the wire.

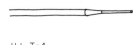

ILL. I-4

tem. A mistake in the installation of the service panel could become a hazard for the entire system. Don't take any chances; hire a qualified professional for this operation. As a matter of fact, many electrical contracting companies allow the service panel installation to be performed by only the most experienced electricians on the work force.

Like plumbing, electrical work takes place during both rough and finish stages of construction. Roughing in takes place while the house frame is still exposed. The finish work occurs after all wall and floor finishes are in place. The steps involved in an electrical installation are:

Roughing In

- Installing the service panel
- Locating and installing the boxes
- Stringing the cable to the various boxes
- Connecting the cable to the box
- Grounding the cable to the box

PIGTAIL SPLICE

ILL. I-5

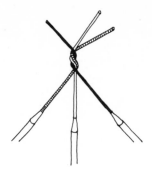

BUNCH SPLICE

ILL. I-7

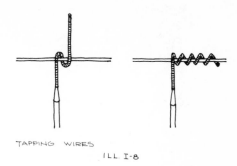

TAPPING WIRES

ILL. I-8

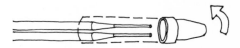

SOLDERLESS CONNECTOR

ILL. I-9

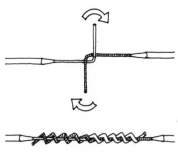

WESTERN UNION SPLICE

ILL. I-6

There are instances in which three wires are joined together and a slightly more complex version of the pigtail called the bunch splice is used (Ill. I-7). For tapping the wires the joint in Illustration I-8 is usually done.

When the wires have been joined mechanically, flux is applied over the splice. Be careful to apply the type of flux that is used for electrical purposes such as nonacid resin. Check with your supplier. Hold the wire splice with a pair of pliers and heat it with a soldering iron until the solder melts on contact. Push the solder inward to provide enough solder for a good bond. Make sure that the splice is well soldered on all sides.

After the solder has hardened and cooled, tape the entire splice over with rubber tape (then plastic tape).* Wrap the

---

* Plastic, vinyl, and friction tape have no acceptable insulating qualities.

---

tape spirally to completely cover the splice and overlap the wire insulation. The proper application of tape is very important since it provides the insulating jacket for the splice.

Solderless splices are easier to do than soldered ones. Unfortunately, they cannot be used in places where the splice is under stress. Some codes do not allow their use at all. They do save considerable time and aggravation, so use them whenever allowed.

A solderless splice connector consists of a small insulated cap, which is screwed onto the ends of the wire. Only enough wire is stripped to fit into the connector. The wires are placed side by side and screwed onto the cap (Ill. I-9). Be careful not to leave any bare wire exposed.

The splice can be soldered or solderless. Soldered splices start by mechanically joining the wires. This can be done in a couple of different ways. The most common one is the pigtail splice, which joins two wires (Ill. I-5). This type, however, is only recommended for joints that will not be under strain. Areas under tension should have the Western Union splice instead (Ill. I-6).

- Stripping 1" of insulation off the wires
- Testing the circuits
- Inspection

Finish Work

- Wiring the various devices
- Installing the finish plates
- Final hookup at the service panel
- Final inspection
- Permanent hookup to the power line

Here are a few pointers to remember while doing the installation:

- Always make sure that all power is turned off before doing any work.
- Electrical cables are color-coded to simplify their installation. Always connect white wires to white wires and black wires to black wires. (Exceptions to this rule are described on pages 333–4.)
- White wires are connected to chrome screws. Black wires are connected to brass screws.
- Two-way switches are connected to black wires not white ones. (See pages 333–4 for exceptions.)

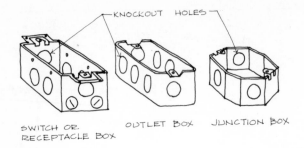

KNOCKOUT HOLES

SWITCH OR
RECEPTACLE BOX   OUTLET BOX   JUNCTION BOX

ILL. 1

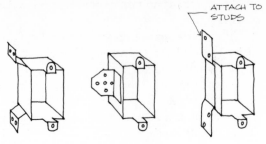

ATTACH TO
STUDS

BOXES WITH BUILT-IN HANGERS

Roughing In

The code requires all the connection between the cables and the devices (switches and outlets) and all wire splicing to take place inside approved boxes. This is to reduce the possibility of fire or shock brought about by a defective connection left unprotected inside a wall. (A few sparks could ignite accumulated dirt collected inside the wall cavity.) The roughing-in stage starts by locating and installing all the boxes for switches and outlets as indicated in the plan. There are many boxes available to satisfy a number of different conditions. The most common ones are rectangular and octagonal (Ill. 1).

Octagonal or square boxes are used to house outlets. They come in various sizes, with 4" square being the most widely used size. This size allows enough room to work on the connection and to comfortably house the device. Avoid working with small boxes. They will not only make the installation work more difficult but will hardly leave sufficient room to house the wiring and the device. (See square-inch requirements in the code.)

Rectangular boxes are generally used for switching devices. These boxes can be "hooked" together to form a larger box when necessary.

Cables enter the boxes through knockout holes (Ill. 1). Knockouts are sections of metal that can be opened by tapping with a screwdriver and a hammer. The piece of metal is then twisted loose with a pair of pliers. Each box is equipped with more knockouts than required to accommodate various installation conditions. It is important to remove *only* those knockouts necessary for the connection work. Don't leave an unused knockout open. If you pull one open by mistake, close it with a closure washer.

Most boxes are attached to the woodwork by

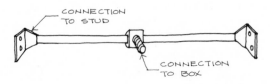

CONNECTION
TO STUD

CONNECTION
TO BOX

BOX HANGER

ILL. 2

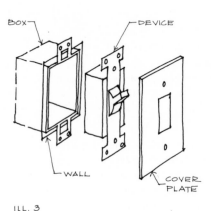

BOX   DEVICE

WALL   COVER
PLATE

ILL. 3

means of hangers (Ill. 2). Some boxes (usually switch boxes) come equipped with mounting brackets. While you're mounting the boxes, keep in mind that the outside edge of the box should be flush with the finish wall surface (Ill. 3). Adjust the mounting accordingly.

It is helpful to know the heights commonly used for installation of boxes. Those used to house floor outlets are usually 12" to 14" above the floor. Over-the-counter outlets are generally placed at approximately 36" above the floor. Switches are 48" high. Outlets and switches to satisfy special conditions should be placed accordingly.

With all the boxes in place, the next step is to string the cable to the various boxes according to the circuitry designed. (The 115 volt circuit is customarily strung before the 230 volt circuit.) Electrical cables, like plumbing pipes, snake through and around the house structure. (It is a good idea to keep the path of the electrical cables and the plumbing pipes separate from each other to avoid problems should leaks develop in the pipes.) Holes are drilled in the studs, joists, and plates to allow their passage. (Their diameter should be slightly larger than that of the cable.) To minimize interference with the building's structural capacity, keep in mind the tips for drilling outlined on page 306, Inset II.

To prevent the cables from sagging and causing possible damage, they must be secured to the woodwork by means of straps or staples (Ill. 4). There are staples specifically designed for use with armored cable, making the installation work considerably easier. (Care should be taken to use the right type of staples for the type of cable you are using; you may otherwise damage the cable.) Check your code for the required spacing of the cable supports. Illustration 5 shows a few alternate ways in which to run the cables in relationship to the house structure. Avoid sharp bends.

A few tips on stringing cable. Cable comes wound in big rolls. Only unwind as much cable from the roll as you will need to make a run between one set of boxes. When too much cable is unwound at a time, it tends to twist, making the stringing job more difficult. Begin by stringing the cable from the service panel (or projected location of the service panel) to each outlet box along a particular circuit. To avoid a mixup later on, tag all circuits at the service panel end. Leave 4' to 6' of cable behind for later installation to the panel. Once you get to the box, cut the cable (Inset I) allowing about 1½' extra length for both the incoming and the outgoing cable. Strip about 8" of cover from the cable, leaving the wire exposed. Remove two knockout plates from the box and carefully connect the cable to the box (Inset II).

To provide a continuous ground, the cable is grounded at each box. The grounding procedure varies with the code. Generally, however, if you are using nonmetallic sheathed cable, the uninsulated grounding strip in the cable (of both the incoming and the outgoing cable) is fastened

ILL. 4

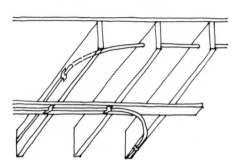

ILL. 5

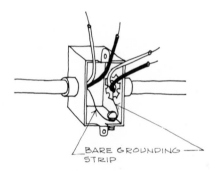

BARE GROUNDING STRIP

ILL. 6

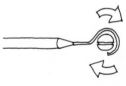

ILL. 7

with a screw to an unused hole in the box (Ill. 6). Make sure that the wire is wrapped around the screw in such a manner that when you tighten the screw, you will wind the wire (Ill. 7). This screw should be used for no purpose other than for grounding. The other end of the grounding wire will later on be connected to the neutral strap in the service panel. If you are using armored cable, the grounding will be accomplished together with the connection of the cable to the box (Inset II).

The last step in the roughing-in process is to

Cable connectors are used to fasten the cable to the outlet boxes (Ill. II-1). The type of connector varies to accommodate different conditions—for example, straight-run and right-angled connections (Ill. II-1). They are installed by slipping the connector over the end of the cable. The screws (on the connector) are then tightened. Before inserting the connector through the knockout in the box, remove the lock nut. Once in the box, fasten the lock nut and connector tightly to each other—and therefore the box (Ill. II-2). Some boxes come with built-in clamps, eliminating the need for connectors (Ill. II-3).

When installing connectors to armored cable, be sure to push the cable into the connector as far as it will go to prevent the bushing from falling out of place. The bare grounding strip should be *in* the connector. This way when you tighten the screws on the connector to anchor it to the cable, the grounding wire will be squeezed. It should not lie loose. This is very important in order to obtain a good continuous ground.

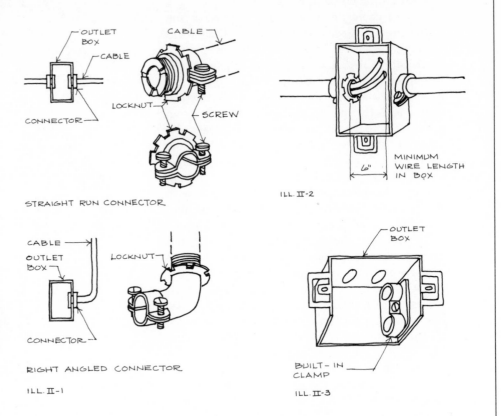

STRAIGHT RUN CONNECTOR

ILL. II-2

RIGHT ANGLED CONNECTOR

ILL. II-1

BUILT-IN CLAMP

ILL. II-3

strip about 1" of insulation at the end of the wires (Inset I). These ends will be connected to the devices during the finishing stage. Before moving on to the next box, bend the wires back into the box to keep them out of the way. Repeat the same procedure at every box in the circuit.

Once all the circuits have been installed, the electrician will install the service panel (if he has not done so already). In order to complete the roughing-in stage, you must check over the work you've done for any mistakes. A few tests are performed to check for short circuits, proper current flow, and good circuit ground. Make sure before you do any of these tests that the power has *not* been connected at the service panel. The testing device consists of a doorbell or buzzer and a low-voltage battery, some wire, and alligator clips. Remember to check all circuits separately and to take all tests at the last box in the circuit.

To check for short circuits (two wires coming in contact accidentally) connect the doorbell and battery together with wire, placing the alligator clips at the end of the wire. Connect one wire from the test device to the white wire in the box and the other to the black wire. If the bell does not ring, the circuit is fine. If the bell rings, it's an indication that a short circuit exists somewhere in the circuit which needs fixing (Ill. 8).

To check for proper current flow, take the doorbell and battery apart. This time connect the battery wires to the white and black cables at the service panel that correspond to the circuit you are testing. Go to the last box in the circuit and connect the wires of the doorbell to those of the box. If the current is flowing properly, the bell will ring (Ill. 9).

Note: To check the lighting circuits, you must first twist together the wires at each switch box to create a "switch on" condition in the circuit. The circuit will otherwise be open.

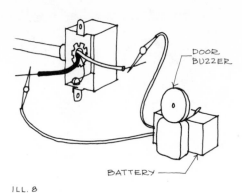

ILL. 8

DOOR BUZZER

BATTERY

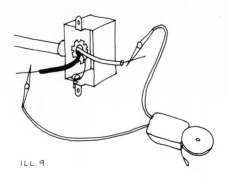

ILL. 9

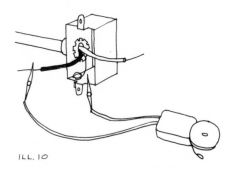

ILL. 10

To check for good circuit ground, connect the battery to the black wire and the grounding wire in the service panel. Again go to the last box in the circuit and connect one bell wire to the black wire in the box and the other one to the metal box itself. If the ground is good, the bell will ring (Ill. 10).

You are now ready to call the inspector and have him check over your wiring for approval.

Finish Work

With the rough work checked and inspected and the finishes up, you can start to install the devices (receptacles, fixtures, and switches) to the wires in the boxes.

Most devices are connected to the wires by means of two sets of terminal screws, a brass and a chrome set. The black wires are attached to the brass screws and the white wires to the chrome screws (Ill. 11). With a pair of small-nosed pliers (you can wrap the jaws with tape to prevent damaging the wire) make a loop in the end of the wire and place it around the screw. Do this in such a way that when you tighten the screw, you're winding the wire; never the opposite (Ill. 7). Make sure that all bare wire is wound in the screw. No bare wire should be left exposed. It can cause shorts. Should you have more bare wire than you need to go around the screws, trim it off.

Two-way switches have only brass screws. This is a reminder that only black wires are connected to them. The two leftover white wires are connected to each other with a soldered or solderless connection (Ill. 12). An exception to

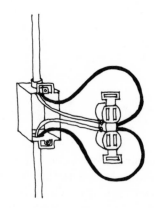

ILL. 11

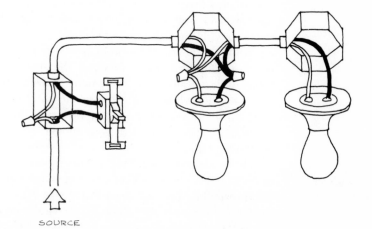

SOURCE

ILL. 12

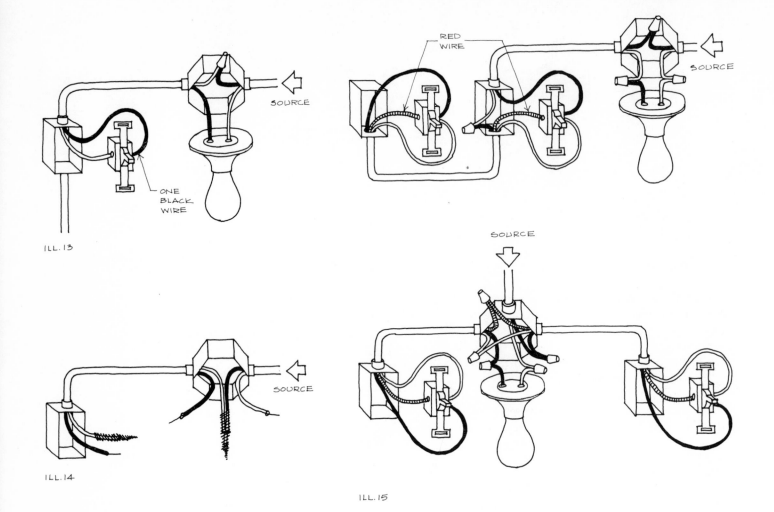

SOURCE

RED
WIRE

SOURCE

ONE
BLACK
WIRE

ILL. 13

SOURCE

SOURCE

ILL. 14

ILL. 15

this rule occurs when a two-way switch is located at the end of a circuit. Whenever you have this condition, you will find yourself with only one black wire with which to effect the connection instead of the two you need (Ill. 13). To solve this problem, the National Electrical Code allows you in this particular case to connect a black and a white wire together, providing you with the two wires needed.

While in the roughing-in stages, if you have such a condition, twist together the incoming black wire at the outlet the switch controls with the outgoing white wire going to the switch (Ill. 14). Tape the end of the white wire with black tape as a reminder that it is no longer a "neutral" wire (Ill. 14).

Three-way switches have a pair of brass terminals and a single darker one called the common terminal. You will need three-wire cable to make these connections. The black wire is connected to the common terminal while the red and white wires are connected to the remaining terminals (Ill. 15). Here again, tape the end of the white wire with black tape.

A tip on device installation. To avoid working in cramped quarters, pull the wires out of the box. Once the device has been installed, push them back into the box, making sure that no strains are being induced on the connections or splices.

A number of devices are available to simplify the finish wiring. Generally, they are more expensive than the ones we've already described. You can check with your local supplier to see what he has available. Also check with your local code to see if their use is allowed. The two most common ones are the back-wired and the push-in types.

In back-wired devices, the bare wires are inserted in the back of the device. Once inside, the wire is sandwiched between two plates, which when pushed together grip the wire to make

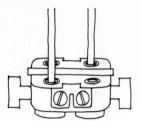

ILL. 16

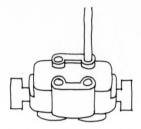

ILL. 17

contact. This is done by tightening two screws located at the side of the receptacles (Ill. 16). This device also has a stripping guide to measure the quantity of wire which needs to be bared.

The push-in type also has holes in the back that are matched to the wire sizes.* When the

* Some electricians do not recommend this device.

bare wire ends are pushed into the holes, a spring mechanism makes the connection and holds the wire in place. Whenever it is necessary to release this mechanism, it can be done by pushing a knife into a slot labeled for this purpose (Ill. 17).

Once the device has been connected to the wires and pushed back into the box, the cover plate is installed. The finish work for that device is completed (Ill. 3).

29
Interior Finishes

Applying the finishes is practically the last step in the long process of house building. By now you may be so happy that the building is nearing completion that the time employed in the finish application may seem to go unnoticed. On the other hand, you may be so overexposed to construction work that any fussing with the finishes will become a hassle.

Remember that finishes are the most visible of all your work. Don't become impatient and let them become sloppy in order to gain time. It would be a shame to let your previous hard work be covered by a less-than-perfect job. Take heart! You're close to the end of your project.

MATERIALS

The materials necessary for the various finishing jobs include:

For the Application of Insulation and Vapor Barrier

Blanket insulation
Bulk insulation
Polyurethane sheets (where needed)

For the Application of Gypsum Board

Gypsum-board panels
Backer boards (where required)

Joint tape (calculate 75' of tape per 200 sq. ft. of surface)
Ready-mix joint compound (approximately 1 gallon per 200 sq. ft.)
Annular ring nails (1 lb. of nails per 200 sq. ft.)

Use the following size nails for the installation of gypsum-board panels:
1⅛" nails for ¼" board
1¼" nails for ⅜" board
1⅜" nails for ½" and ⅝" board
For installation over backer boards use 2¼" cement-coated nails. Estimate approximately 2 lbs. per 200 sq. ft. of surface.

For the Application of Wood Strip Floors

Wood strips	Nails
Plywood or particle board underlayment	Building paper
	Baseboard and molding

For the Application of Resilient Tile

Tile
Adhesive (unless tile is self-adhesive)
Baseboard

For the Installation of Carpeting

Nailing strips
Padding
Carpet

For the Installation of Ceramic Tile

Tile   Grout
Adhesive   Silicone grout sealer

TOOLS

Here is a list of tools you'll need to install the various finishes:

Insulation and Vapor Barrier

Stapler
Knife

Gypsum Board

Plumb bob   Wall scrapers (in 4",
Hammer (with slightly   6", and 10" widths)
round edges)   for applying compound
Pocketknife or   Sandpaper
utility knife   Ladder
Rule or steel tape   Approved respirator
Keyhole saw   Pencil

Wood-Strip Flooring

Saw   Nail set (if using
Hammer or nailer   hammer)
Chalk

Resilient Tile

Utility knife
Notched trowel

Carpeting

Roller   Stapler
Matte knife   Tapemeasure

Ceramic Tile

Notched trowel   Tile or glass cutter
Squeegee or sponge   Nippers
Carpenter's level   File
Jointer
(or something with a
rounded handle)

INSTALLING THE INSULATION AND VAPOR BARRIER

Before the application of finishes can take place, all perimeter walls, floors, and ceilings should be provided with insulation and vapor barriers as called for in the house design. Many types of blanket insulation come complete with a vapor barrier. Others do not. The latter must be covered with a layer of polyurethane.

The application of blanket insulation is simple. Unfortunately, however, some people are bothered by the fibers and complain of itching. If you have this problem, wearing a long-sleeved shirt helps. Starting at one corner of the walls, measure and cut the blanket insulation to the proper length. Staple one side of the insulation to the stud. The spacing between staples should be very close. Once the full length is in place, grab the opposite edge and stretch it well. This side can now be stapled to the stud. With both edges stapled, the top and bottom edges are secured to the floor and ceiling members. It is very important that the insulation be continuous. Don't skimp on joints or edges. It's preferable to overlap or have extra insulation at the ends than to leave gaps.

Whenever openings have to be provided to accommodate outlet boxes or other fixtures, cut them out with a utility knife. Cut a hole of the appropriate size in the backing, trying to penetrate as much as possible into the insulation material.

If the insulation you're using doesn't come with a vapor barrier, you must install a polyurethane sheet over the entire area being insulated. This has become a very popular method of condensation control, its main advantage being fewer joints and therefore fewer areas of possible moisture penetration.

To prevent air leakage through cracks in the framing, stuff bulk insulation in the spaces left between window and door frames and the studs. In addition, stuff bulk insulation against any space left between the header and sill plate and the subflooring in all perimeter walls. Be careful not to pack these spaces too tightly. It may cause the window to stick and the insulation becomes less effective (since its effectiveness depends on dead air spaces).

Basement ceilings, crawl spaces, and attics are similarly insulated, the difference being that the insulation strips are stapled to the bottom of the

HOW TO CUT GYPSUM BOARD

Mark the panel where it must be cut and place a straightedge on the mark. With a sharp knife, score the surface paper trying to press hard enough to cut into the gypsum core. Be careful to cut slowly; a quick cut could get out of control and you'll wind up slicing your hand instead of the panel. Bend the board backward until you break the core. Slice the back paper with a knife and smooth the edges.

HOW TO CUT RESILIENT TILE

Score with a utility knife and snap it at the score mark.

HOW TO CUT CERAMIC TILE

There are different opinions as to which is the best way of cutting ceramic tile. Some people prefer to use a tile cutter; others prefer glass cutters. A tile cutter can be rented or loaned where you buy the tile and firsthand instructions obtained from the dealer.

If you are using a glass cutter, the idea is to score the tile as you would glass and snap it. Because ceramic tile is tougher than glass, you'll need extra help to snap it. Set the tile on an edge and step on the part that you're not using on the installation. The cut edge is then smoothed with a file.

There are instances where you need other than a straight cut such as when you have to fit tile around a pipe. Nippers, which are essentially tile scissors, are used for this. Hold the glazed side up and, starting at one edge, make very small cuts until you get the desired shape. Smooth the edges with a file.

When a hole is located at the center of a tile, your best bet is to cut the tile in half and using the nippers cut out the hole in each half.

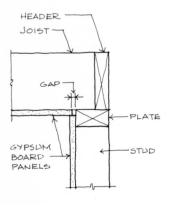

GAP AT PANEL INTERSECTION CAN BE COVERED WITH WALL PANEL

ILL. 1

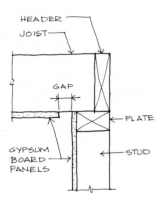

GAP AT INTERSECTION TOO LARGE

ceiling joists rather than the studs and that ceilings get thicker insulation (usually 6" as opposed to 3½" for floors).

INSTALLING GYPSUM-BOARD PANELS

The installation of gypsum board, although not difficult, requires lots of muscle and tender care.

The muscle is needed because gypsum panels are heavy (a ½" panel weighs about 2 pounds per square foot, making a 4' × 8' panel 64 pounds). The care is needed because the seams must be "invisible." For both these reasons make sure to have at least one or two other people on hand while installing the drywall, together with ample time to spend on your jointwork.

Some brands of joint compound contain asbestos fiber. Since there's no way of finding out whether your brand contains it or not, it is wise to wear an approved respirator while sanding the joints. The consequences of inhaling asbestos fiber into your respiratory system could prove quite frightening.

The erection of the gypsum board starts with the ceiling panels both because it's harder to install the ceiling than the walls, and because sloppy connections between the ceiling panels and the wall framing can be corrected while installing the wall panels. Of course, this does not mean leaving a 2" gap between the ceiling panels and the walls (Ill. 1).

Start by checking to see that the corner of the ceiling where you plan to begin is square. If it's out of square, take measurements between the center of the joists (where one edge of the panel is to be nailed) and the top plate to find out the angle at which the panel should be cut. Transfer these dimensions to the panel and cut it to fit

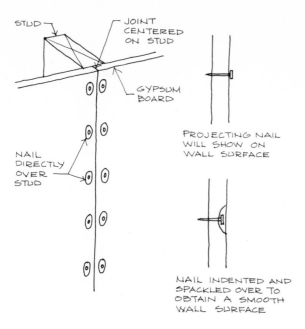

STUD

JOINT CENTERED ON STUD

GYPSUM BOARD

NAIL DIRECTLY OVER STUD

PROJECTING NAIL WILL SHOW ON WALL SURFACE

NAIL INDENTED AND SPACKLED OVER TO OBTAIN A SMOOTH WALL SURFACE

ILL. 2

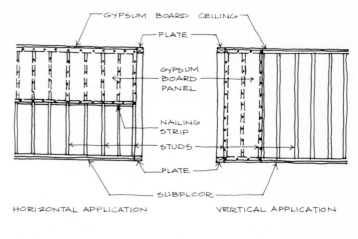

GYPSUM BOARD CEILING

PLATE

GYPSUM BOARD PANEL

NAILING STRIP

STUDS

PLATE

SUBFLOOR

HORIZONTAL APPLICATION   VERTICAL APPLICATION

ILL. 3

the corner (Inset I). With the panel cut, you're ready to lift it in place. Butt the panel against the wall. As one person holds one side, nail the other one to the underside of the joists at approximately every 6", using annular ring nails to prevent them from popping out.* Remember that all joints must be centered over wood. Hammer the nails a little below the surface of the panel. The idea is to be able to cover the indentation with spackle in order to obtain a smooth finish at the end. Projecting nailheads will otherwise stick out on the surface (Ill. 2). The remainder of the ceiling panels are installed similarly, making sure the edges butt against each other.†

Once the ceiling is complete, the wall panels are erected. Any small inaccuracies that have been left at the edges of the ceiling panels can now be covered. Begin the installation at one corner. The first step is to ensure that the corner is plumb. Cut the panel to match the corner where necessary.

---

* Some builders put a nailing strip on the ceiling perpendicular to the ceiling joists. This strapping can be adjusted in the event that a joist has more crown than the ones next to it.
† Butt joints at the ceiling are very difficult to finish. One way of avoiding them is to use sheets of gypsum board that are as long as the room is wide. You will, of course, have to enlist some extra help to handle such large sheets but it may be well worth it.

Gypsum board may be installed either vertically or horizontally. Because the jointwork is difficult, it is wise to apply the panels in whichever manner will result in fewer joints. (Horizontal applications usually result in fewer seams.) Avoid vertical joints at the top of doors and the top or bottom of windows.

For horizontal applications, start by installing the top panel. (There's no way you can do this without the aid of another person.) Butt the panel up against the ceiling and nail it every 6" (Ill. 3). The lower board is then cut to fit the floor. Any gaps or inaccuracies left between the panels and the subfloor are covered by the baseboard.

For vertical installations, check the corner for plumbness and cut the panel as needed. Butt the panel well against the corner and nail it in place (Ill. 3).

Openings must be provided in the panels to allow for outlets, switches, etc. Determine the exact location of the opening and mark it on the face of the panel. Poke holes at the corners of the projected opening with a knife, and with the aid of a keyhole saw, cut out the remainder.

Tape and Spackle

Taping and spackling involve meticulous work. One of our friends, an experienced carpenter and all-around builder, just completed an extension to his house. Whereas doing the foundation, carpentry, roofing, heating, and electrical work did not bother him, he complained at the prospect of having to fuss with taping and

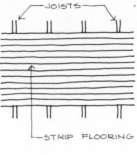

JOISTS

STRIP FLOORING

ILL. 4

spackling. He nailed the gypsum panels in place but brought in a "pro" to do the jointwork.

While we don't think that taping and spackling are impossible for the amateur to handle, we must make you aware that it is the type of job that requires good, neat workmanship and lots of patience.

You'll be wise to minimize the sanding of the joints by applying the tape and joint compound carefully. Although mistakes can be partially fixed by sanding, they cannot be totally corrected. In addition, you don't want to take the chance of having tons of dust potentially containing asbestos fiber floating all over the place. Be sure, in any case, to wear a respirator approved by the U.S. Bureau of Mines. An alternate to sanding the joints is to even them out with a sponge before they dry.

Before beginning the tape and spackling, install corner beads at all outside corners. Cut them out to the required lengths and nail in place at all corners.

There's no particular order in which the jointwork has to take place. Each joint, however, should be completely done before moving on to the next one. Once the joint compound dries, it becomes tough to work with. With a scraper, apply 4" of compound over the joint. Start at one end and move all the way to the other. Try to do this in as long and even a stroke as you can. Short strokes give you a rough surface which is hard to smooth out later on.

Once the first layer of compound is applied, take the roll of tape and center it over the joint. (Soaking the tape in water before application is sometimes helpful.) Hold the tape with one hand while with the other hand you press the tape with the scraper into the compound. The tape shouldn't wrinkle. Where wrinkles appear, lift the tape to a spot before the wrinkles begin and apply the tape over again. Sometimes the

tape starts to slant away from the joint. Cut it out and start a new strip. It should be directly over the joint.

The next step is to cover the tape with another layer of compound. It should be a thin, smooth layer. Leave the compound until it has thoroughly dried (approximately twenty-four hours). Irregularities can be sanded smooth. Make sure to cover all exposed nailheads and exposed corner beads with compound. After sanding the irregularities at all joints, apply another coat of compound—this time, however, with a wider scraper (6"). The idea is to spread the compound beyond the first strip. Allow the second coat to dry, and sand again.

A fourth layer of compound is applied. The strip should be much wider (about 10") than the previous ones, thinner, and very evenly applied. Once again, give it time to dry. Sand over all the joints and nail spots. The wall is now ready to receive the primer.

INSTALLING THE FLOORING

Floors are the finish surface installed last, to prevent their being damaged during the application of other finishes. In addition, the finish floor cannot be applied until the end since the baseboard running around the bottom of the wall rests on it. Before installing any type of flooring make sure that the subfloor is well nailed, level, and clean.

Wood Strip Flooring

A layer of building paper is customarily laid over the subfloor as the first step in the installation of strip flooring. The building paper prevents dust from passing through to the joists. It's a good idea to snap chalk lines over the building paper indicating the location of the joists below.

Strip flooring is installed at right angles to the floor joists (Ill. 4). The strips are matched and grooved on both sides and at either end to provide an easy fit. Keep in mind that wood expands and contracts with the amount of moisture present in the air. Enough room (approximately ½") should be allowed between the

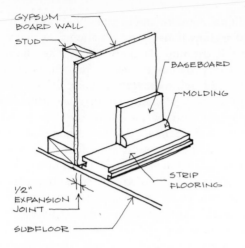

ILL. 5

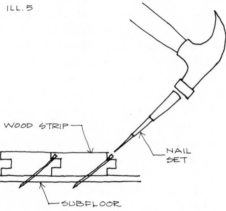

ILL. 6

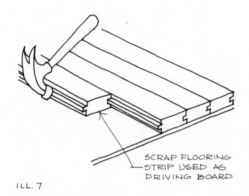

ILL. 7

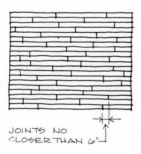

ILL. 8

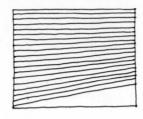

ILL. 9

strips and the wall for this movement to take place. The strips will otherwise buckle, damaging the floor.

Lay the first strip about ½″ from the edge of the wall, placing the groove side toward the wall (Ill. 5). Nail through the top (face nail) into the subfloor and the joist below. A nailer, or nailing gun, can be rented to install strip flooring. A word of caution: Although this tool speeds up the installation process, you must be particularly careful while using it. More than one highly experienced carpenter has put a nail through his finger by not using a nailer properly. If you don't feel confident with it, stick to a hammer and a nail set.

Use flooring nails of sufficient length. They are designed with blunt ends and square or rectangular shanks to crush the wood rather than split it. Don't worry about the nails showing, they'll later be covered by the baseboard. Once one side of the strip is face-nailed, nail the other edge through the tongue at an angle. Use a nail set to avoid crushing the tongue (Ill. 6). Hook the groove side of the second strip to the tongue of the first. These strips should be driven tightly against each other. You can do this by using a piece of scrap flooring as a driving board (Ill. 7).

The remaining strips are installed in the same manner. You may have to cut the last strip lengthwise to fit the room. Here again a gap of ½″ should be left to allow for expansion. Joints between the butt ends of the strip and the wall are not that critical since most of the expansion and contraction occurs along the width rather than the length. Keep a few things in mind. Butt joints should be staggered, with joints no closer than 6″ from each other (Ill. 8). In addition, be particularly careful that the boards are straight. If they are not aligned, you'll have a problem when you reach the other wall (Ill. 9).

Interior Finishes

341

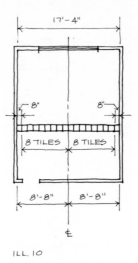

ILL. 10

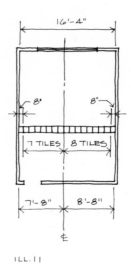

ILL. 11

Thresholds and saddles are nailed in place once the floor is completely laid. Door trims can also be fitted to the floor. The baseboard is the last of the trimming to be installed. It is usually made up of a 1″ × 2″ or 1″ × 4″ piece of wood and a quarter-round molding. The molding is nailed to the floor, not the baseboard. Its purpose is to cover any cracks between the baseboard and the floor due to unevenness (Ill. 5).

Resilient Tile

Resilient tile, unlike wood strip flooring, does not add to the strength of the floor. For this reason, when resilient tile is applied, it needs an additional underlayment of ½″ plywood to avoid springy floors.*

Install the underlayment using ring shanked nails every 6″ on center at the edges of the panels and approximately 12″ on center at the intermediate joists. Any indentations in the underlayment should be filled with a type of plaster used to level floors. Check with your supplier. Joints between underlayment sections should also be filled. The reason for doing this is that the type of tile used for residential installation is not too thick. Defects in the underlayment could show through and eventually damage the tile itself.

For a really high-quality job, apply adhesive to the plywood underlayment and put down over it a layer of saturated felt. Once dry, apply adhesive to the felt and install the tiles. The saturated felt helps to smooth out any irregularities in the underlayment.

One way of applying tile is to start at one corner of the room and work your way into the other. A better way is to find the center line of the room and determine how many tiles need to be installed at either side. For example, a room that is 17′-4″ wide will require eight full (1′ × 1′) tiles to both the right and the left of the center line. The edge tile at both ends of the room will be 8″ (Ill. 10). The same system is used for the length. The center line can be adjusted slightly to accommodate various conditions. For instance, if the room was 16′-4″, the edge tile would be a skimpy 2″. By moving the center line to 7′-8″ and 8′-8″ the edge tile can become 8″ (Ill. 11).

If the type of tile you are using is self-adhesive, be careful. Once it's laid down it is quite difficult to lift. When the adhesive is separate, follow the instructions on the can. Adhesive application should be done with a notched trowel.

Start laying the tile by applying adhesive up to one of the center lines. Allow the adhesive to set to the proper dryness. Line up the tile with the line and press it firmly against the adhesive. The following tile is butted tightly against the first. The remaining tiles are similarly installed. Don't try to push tiles into place once you've laid them. Lift and relocate them instead. When all the tiles are laid, the baseboard is installed.

* Most resilient tile adhesives are not compatible with particle board.

Carpeting

Although the installation of carpeting is not a difficult job, there are a few tips and tools that can make it a lot easier. Buy padding that is not too thick for the type of carpeting you're using. The best advice can be given to you by your supplier. One of the authors recently carpeted her daughter's room. The reason for carpeting was to soften the child's falls as she learned how to walk. She bought the thickest available padding, although the carpet itself was of flat commercial stock. After a long day spent on the installation, the baby's room had a very soft, but rather undulating floor.

One useful item to have is a roller. Carpet installers always use this device to flatten out and stretch the carpet. Try to rent or borrow one.

Start the carpet installation by nailing in place all the nailing strips. These are wood strips with nails set on them facing up at an angle (Ill. 12). The carpet is fastened to the floor by anchoring it to these nails. Nail the strips all around the edges of the area to be carpeted. The nails should point toward the wall (Ill. 12). Cut the padding to fit the area inside the nailing strip and staple it to the subfloor. The floor is now ready to receive the carpet.

Carpeting comes in rolls. If possible, cut it down to size in an area large enough to give you room to maneuver. Make sure that the carpet size you are cutting is at least 1' larger all around than needed. Once it's cut, roll it in as close to the position where it will be installed as possible. A roller comes in handy at this point for flattening out the carpeting. (Always remember as you are installing the carpet to work it out from the center of the room toward the edges to avoid bubbles.)

Working on parallel sides, hook up the carpet to the nailing strip at the midpoints (Ill. 13). This is done by pulling the carpet away from its center toward the edges and pushing it down to hook into the nails. Go over to the side directly opposite the one you've just attached and do the same. Do this on all sides. Make sure there are no ripples.

Once all edges of the carpet are attached to the floor at their midpoints, go back and fasten the remainder of the perimeter. Starting at the midpoint, work toward the corners (Ill. 14). When the entire perimeter is fastened to the

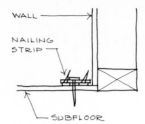

WALL

NAILING STRIP

SUBFLOOR

ILL. 12

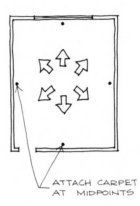

ATTACH CARPET AT MIDPOINTS

ILL. 13

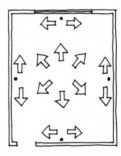

WORKING FROM THE MIDPOINTS TOWARDS THE CORNER ATTACH THE REST OF THE PERIMETER

ILL. 14

floor, take a sharp matte knife and slice the extra carpet. Lay the matte knife almost flat and let it run on the floor.

Ceramic Tile

In the past, the installation of ceramic tile involved lots of time and fancy work. Tiles were imbedded in cement, which was evenly applied over metal lath. With the development of adhesives, the job has been greatly simplified. All that is required is to spread the adhesive over the surface (with a notched trowel) and set the tiles in place. The best recommendation on the type of adhesive to use will come from your supplier. Directions for use are on the can.

While applying the tile, keep in mind the adhesive's drying time. If you apply too much at a time, it may be too dry by the time you're ready to set the tile.

The application for walls and floors is not vastly different. The walls, however, should be done first. (Walls located in moist areas should be backed by either waterproof plywood or moisture-resistant gypsum panels.) Ceramic tile, like resilient tile, should be centered on the wall. You may otherwise wind up with very narrow edge tiles which aside from looking awkward are quite difficult to cut (Inset I). (Cutting tile to less than half its width is not easy.) To center the tile on the wall or floor, use the procedure outlined previously for resilient tile.

Begin the installation of ceramic tile by setting up a vertical guideline. (You can use the center line you've already drawn to calculate the tile location.) Make sure that the line is plumb. A wood strip is nailed over the line. (Without the wood strip the line would disappear when you apply the adhesive.) Check to see that the floor is level and start the application of the cove tile. Apply the tile in rows, using the level cove tile and the wood strip as guides. The rows of tile should be checked frequently with a carpenter's level.

Tiles are set by pressing them firmly against the adhesive. (A slight twisting motion helps to adhere them to the surface.) Butt the tiles against each other. Every so often, go back over a few rows and tap them down with a wood board to make sure they're all on the same plane. Allow tiles to set as recommended by the adhesive manufacturer.

Now is the time to grout the joints. Grout is the material used to fill the joints between the tiles. It comes in a couple of types, the most popular being a powder, which when mixed with water forms a thick paste. Before applying the grout, make sure that all the joints are free of adhesive. With the aid of a squeegee (some people prefer a trowel), pack the grout well into all the joints, going over them a few times. Wipe off excessive grout. Let the grout set for ten or twenty minutes and tool the joints. You can use a tooling joint or any gadget with a rounded handle (including a stick).

When all the joints have been tooled, wipe clean the film of dry grout with a damp (not wet) sponge. Don't let the grout dry completely before removing the excess. Once it dries, it is quite tough to remove. Most likely, you'll have to wipe off the tile several times before its completely removed. Polish the clean tiles with a dry cloth. To waterproof the grout, spray a silicone grout sealer over the joints.

GLOSSARY OF TOOLS

BIBLIOGRAPHY

INDEX

Glossary of Tools

We now enter the wonderful world of tools, where the question "Do I really need all this junk?" crops up often. The answer is inevitably "yes." There is nothing so frustrating as building up enthusiasm and energy to pursue a particular task and discovering, after you have completed the time-consuming preliminaries, that you do not have the crucial tool for the job.

There are two schools of thought on the subject of purchasing tools. One school suggests that you buy them as you need them. The other maintains that you buy a large assortment of tools so you will be prepared for any job. The home handyperson, who putters around on Saturday morning repairing screen doors, is safe in following the advice of the first school. He has time to drive to town in search of a Phillips screwdriver. The house builder, on the other hand, should not subscribe to this tool-buying theory. His battalion of tools should be there, in good repair, so that he can devote all of his time to building.

Some people, of course, are gadget crazy. They will rush out and buy a set of twenty-five screwdrivers or an expensive and sophisticated power tool whether they need it or not. We are not recommending this course either. We suggest that you purchase a minimum supply of carpenter's hand tools (with a few extra hammers in case someone begs you to let them help) and three or four power tools (if power is available where you are working). Many of the items that will be required can be rented.

BIT BRACE: For use with drill, screwdriver, or reamer bits.

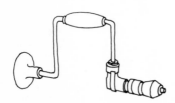

BLOWTORCH: Used to melt lead. Requires white gasoline as a fuel and should be carefully handled because of the high temperatures generated; *see also* PROPANE TORCH.

BRICK HAMMER (masonry tool): A brick hammer has a curved chisel-like edge on one side and a hammer on the other. It is generally used as a chisel for smaller cuts or to clean the face of bricks.

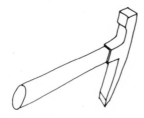

BRICK SET (masonry tool): A brick set is essentially a wide chisel used, together with a hand sledge-type hammer, to cut brick.

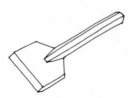

BRISTLE BRUSH (plumbing tool): Used to apply joining compound for plastic pipe. Use only natural bristles; the chemicals in the compound might affect a synthetic bristle brush.

C-CLAMPS: Used for finish carpentry work. Will hold glued connections secure while setting and generally required for finer cabinet or furniture work.

CABLE REAPER (electric tool): To slit cover when using nonmetallic sheathed cable.

CAULKING GUN: Used to apply caulking beads and various glue compounds, which are available in matching application tubes.

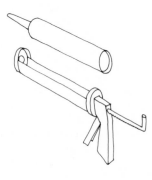

CAULKING IRON (inside and outside types): Used to spread lead into the pipe and hub. It resembles a bent chisel-like tool.

CHALK-LINE REEL: Used for layout work of partitions and other plan information to be transferred to the platform floor. As the line is unreeled, it is automatically passed over blue chalk. One end of the line is secured to the end of the line to be struck. The other end is held by the bearer. The cord is lifted slightly off the floor and snapped abruptly so that the line strikes the marking surface, depositing chalk residue in a perfectly straight line.

CHISEL, WOOD: Used to cut away wood, to form joints or connections. The following sizes are needed for general use: 3/8", 1/2", 3/4", and 1 1/4". A soft-face hammer or mallet should always be used to drive the chisel, especially when making deep cuts.

COLD CHISELS: Used for accurate scoring of masonry or metal. Do not use wood chisels for this purpose. Popular sizes for this tool are 1/2", 3/4", and 1".

COMBINATION SQUARE: Used for squaring and for checking for 90-degree angles. Can be adjusted to other angles as well.

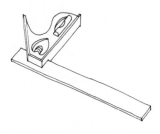

CONDUIT BENDER: Used for bending conduit (electrical) and small copper tubing. It is used with a lever arm (generally a piece of steel piping). Instructions for its use are included with the tool.

CROSSCUT SAW: For cutting across the grain of wood. It is made of flexible tempered steel. The teeth are very small with sharp points. It varies as to the number of points per inch. We recommend 8 points per inch since it will be needed for rough work. It is available in various blade lengths.

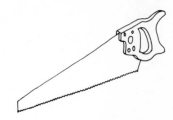

ELECTRICIAN'S PLIERS: For gripping lock nuts, cutting wires, and splicing.

ELECTRICIAN'S WIRING TOOL (multipurpose): Cuts and trims wires, attaches terminals, etc.

FILE, ROUND: Used to smooth concave surfaces, for example, the removal of burrs inside a cut pipe.

FRAMING SQUARE: Used extensively in measuring off the notched cuts for stairs and in laying out rafters. Approximately 22" × 16". Instructions come with the item.

347

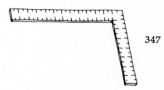

HACKSAW: For cutting through metal.

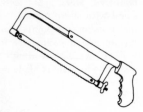

HAMMER, BELL: A curved-claw hammer with a bell face. It is available in a number of sizes depending on weight, from 7 to 20 ounces. Remember that a heavier hammer used correctly will drive a nail with fewer strokes than a light hammer. On the other hand, if you can't lift it, you won't use it.

HAND FLOAT: Used to level off wet concrete.

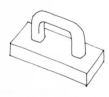

HATCHET: Basically an axe, with a hammer head at one end and a triangular blade for pulling nails. Its most common use is for pointing stakes. It can also be used in lieu of a claw hammer for driving and pulling nails.

IRON LADLE: Used to scoop molten lead from a melting pot, and to pour the lead into the required pipe joints.

JIG: Used in conjunction with a hacksaw to ensure a square cut. A necessary device for the proper threading of pipes.

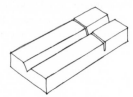

JOINTER: The jointer is required to press mortar between the joints. It is S-shaped and round on one side. One of medium thickness is recommended.

KEYHOLE SAW: Used for fine sawing and for cutting in hard-to-get places.

LAYOUT SQUARE: Basically, a gigantic wood 90-degree triangle, used to lay out right-angled corners. One side is placed directly beneath a taut mason's line. The adjacent side will indicate the location of the second line needed to form the corner.

LEVEL, CARPENTER'S: The carpenter's level is made of either aluminum, wood, or a lightweight metal. It is indispensable in determining perfect straightness. The question is whether to buy the standard 24" long level, or one of greater length (4' or 6'). The advantage of the greater length is the ability to check the levelness of things that are more than 2' apart without the need for a straightedge.

LINE LEVEL: Consists of a small, thin cylindrical tool equipped with a glass tube and hooks. It can be hooked to a line to determine its horizontality.

LONG-NOSED PLIERS: Used for looping wire ends.

MASON'S LINE: Heavy cord used to strike a level line for coursing of block- and brickwork. The line is secured to the work with heavy cut nails or a mason's corner.

MELTING POT: Used with a propane torch or a blowtorch to serve as a container for melted lead.

METAL TUB: Used to mix mortar and small amounts of concrete.

MORTAR BOARD: A mortar board is a piece of thick plywood (¾" to 1") cut to about 30" by 30". It is used to carry a small quantity of mortar to where you are working. (If the size proves to be unwieldy, make it smaller. Remember, this tray has to be lifted together with a load of mortar.)

NAIL SET: Used to set nailheads (finish) below the level of the wood surface.

NIPPERS: Used to cut tile or form difficult shapes.

NOTCHED TROWEL: Used to apply flooring glue in the proper quantity and thickness for maximum adhesion.

PHILLIPS SCREWDRIVERS: Sizes 1, 2, and 3 are recommended. Used with screws of that name. Star-shaped head ensures a very positive grip.

PICK: A long, thin, pointed metal tool used in conjunction with a shovel to loosen the soil prior to excavation.

PLIERS: Used to hold nuts while tightening bolt assemblies and for other light attachments. *See also* ELECTRICIAN'S PLIERS, LONG-NOSED PLIERS.

PLUMB BOB: Used in conjunction with a line, the plumb bob falls free to a perfect vertical. The plumb bob is weighted and has one pointed end. With the help of gravity, the plumb line is used to check for verticality.

PORTABLE POWER SAW: A 7" or 8" diameter blade saw (the size of the saw is determined by the largest blade it will take) is preferred. However, it makes no sense at all to buy a powerful portable saw that you can't lift. Buy the lightest saw that will cut through 1½" thicknesses. If in doubt as to whether you will tire quickly, rent the power model for the weekend. Before buying any power tools, be sure you have electricity at the site.

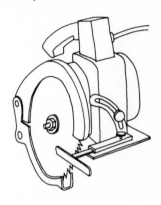

PROPANE TORCH: Used for soldering pipes together and for melting lead. Carefully follow the manufacturer's directions. *See also* BLOWTORCH.

PUSH SCREWDRIVER: Used for starting screw holes, light drilling, and mounting outlets on wood framing.

PUTTY KNIFE: Used to pack joint compound in pipes, to apply glazing putty for windows, and sometimes to apply caulking.

349

RECIPROCATING SAW: Used for cutting internal openings, rough and finish cutting, commonly called an all-purpose saw that can be used to cut wood, metal, and masonry. *See also* PORTABLE POWER SAW.

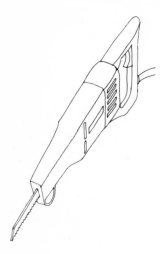

RULE, CARPENTER'S: The carpenter's folding rule comes in the standard length of 6'. It is available in 8' lengths as well.

SAWS: *See* CROSSCUT SAW, HACKSAW, KEYHOLE SAW, PORTABLE POWER SAW, RECIPROCATING SAW.

SCRATCH AWL: Used to scratch lines on lumber, mark and start holes for screws or nails. A handy little device that, unlike a pencil, never loses its point.

SCREWDRIVERS: You will need a few good-quality screwdrivers in a variety of sizes ranging from 3" to 8". *See also* PHILLIPS SCREWDRIVER, PUSH SCREWDRIVER.

SHOVEL: A long-handled scoop used for excavation.

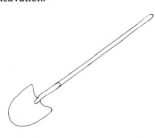

SLEDGE HAMMERS: Available in various weights for use with such tools as the cold chisel for cutting or shaping metal or stone. Heavy, long-handled sledges are used extensively in demolition and other heavy construction chores.

SOLDERING IRON: May be electric or used in conjunction with a propane torch for making finished soldered connections. Keep the tip sharpened and silvered for optimal use. Use acid flux in conjunction with solder to ensure permanent connections.

SQUARES: *See* FRAMING SQUARE, LAYOUT SQUARE, COMBINATION SQUARE.

SQUEEGEE: Used to apply grout to floor and wall tile. Used in conjunction with a sponge for application and cleaning.

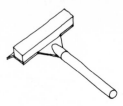

STAPLER GUN: Universal tool used to make quick attachments such as insulation, construction paper, flexible flashing, etc. In heavyweight models may be used for nailing of sheathing and other siding materials.

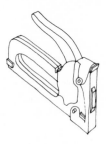

TAPE RULE: If you get a long one (50') make sure it winds back quickly. Get a carpenter's tape with 16" (32", etc.) clearly called out; you will be using it to mark off joists and studs. The 6' and 8' models come in round casing and are retractable. The longer ones (up to 100') come equipped with a small hand crank for closing.

TILE CUTTER: A device for the accurate cutting of tile. It can be rented at a nominal fee at the tile supply store.

TIN SNIPS: Used to cut sheet metal. The longer the snip, the easier it will be to cut heavy-gauge metal. If you must cut radii, use a curved tin snip for this purpose.

TRANSIT, BUILDER'S (DUMPY LEVEL): The builder's transit is a combination of a spirit level and a telescope that sits on a circular base. It is used in conjunction with a tripod to which it is attached. For leveling purposes, it has four leveling screws. The transit can be rotated completely around its base.

TROWELS: The large trowel is the most used tool in the mason's kit. Choose a good one (preferably one of well-tempered steel) since it takes a lot of abuse. The metal end of the trowel is used for picking up, throwing, spreading, and cutting off mortar. The wooden handle is used to rap the brick into position. The small trowel is used for buttering the ends of the brick—that is, the placing of mortar on the short ends of the brick so that the vertical joints between the bricks are closed.

VISE (plumbing): Used in conjunction with a pipe cutter, it is a clamping mechanism that holds the pipe in place while you're cutting it.

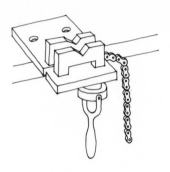

VISE (carpentry): Used to hold wood assemblies for cutting or gluing purposes. Extensively used in fine cabinet work with clamps and glue.

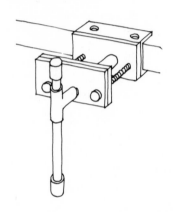

WIRE BRUSH: Used to scale rusty metal parts prior to fabrication.

WRECKING BARS (ripping bars): Used to pry forms apart and for general demolition purposes.

WRENCHES (plumbing):
ADJUSTABLE: For small hex fittings and lag bolts.

ADJUSTABLE SPUD: For large hex-shaped parts.

STILLSON: For gripping pipe and round fittings.

YARNING IRON: Required to pack oakum into the hub of the pipe (if using hubbed pipes). It is essentially a chisel-shaped tool.

351

Bibliography

Anderson, L. O. *Wood Frame House Construction*. Los Angeles: Craftman Book Company of America, 1971.

Bazinski, Stanley, Jr. *Carpentry in Residential Construction*. Englewood Cliffs, N.J.: Prentice-Hall.

Blackburn, Graham. *Illustrated Housebuilding*. Woodstock, N.Y.: The Outlook Press, 1974.

Boudreau, Eugene. *Buying Country Land*. New York: Macmillan, 1973.

Browne, Dan. *The House-Building Book*. New York: McGraw-Hill, 1974.

Callendar, John Hancock. *Time-Savers Standards: A Handbook of Architectural Design*. New York: McGraw-Hill, 1966.

Ching, Francis D. K. *Building Construction Illustrated*. New York: Van Nostrand Reinhold, 1975.

Dalzell, Ralph J. *Simplified Concrete Masonry: Planning and Building*. New York: McGraw-Hill, 1972.

Dalzell, Ralph J., and Townsend, Gilbert. *Brick Laying: Skill and Practice*. Chicago: American Technical Society, 1954.

Daniels, George. *Home Guide to Plumbing, Heating, and Airconditioning*. New York: Barnes and Noble Book, Division of Harper & Row, 1967.

Daniels, George. *How to Be Your Own Electrician*. New York: Harper & Row, 1973.

Day, Richard. *The Practical Handbook of Concrete and Masonry*. New York: Arco Publishing Co., 1969.

Dazettel, Louis M. *Audel Masons and Builders Library*. 2 vols. Indianapolis, Ind.: Theodore Audel and Co.

Demske, Richard. *Plumbing*. New York: Grosset and Dunlap, 1975.

Dietz, Albert G. H. *Dwelling House Construction*. Cambridge, Mass: MIT Press, 1971.

Harris, W. S. *Modern Hydronic Heating: Design, Installation, Service*. Columbus, Ohio: North American Heating and Air-Conditioning Wholesalers Association, 1974.

Higson, James D. *The Higson Home-Builder's Guide*. Los Angeles: Nash Publishing, 1972.

Kern, Ken. *The Owner-Built Home: A How-to-do-it Book*. New York: Charles Scribner, 1975.

Landsmann, Leanna. *Painting and Wallpapering*. New York: Grosset Good Life Books, 1975.

McGuiness, William J., and Stein, Benjamin. *Mechanical and Electrical Equipment for Buildings*. New York: John Wiley and Sons, 1971.

Neal, Charles D. *Do-It-Yourself House-Building, Step-by-Step*. New York: Macmillan, 1973.

Olivieri, Joseph B. *How to Design Heating-Cooling Comfort Systems*. Birmingham, Mich.: Business News Publishing Co., 1973.

Oravetz, Jules, Sr. *Audel Plumbers and Pipe Fitters Library: Materials, Tools Calculations*. 2 vols. Indianapolis, Ind.: Theodore Audel and Co., 1967.

Orton, Vrest. *The Forgotten Art of Building a Good Fireplace*. Dublin, N.H.: Yankee, Inc., 1974.

Parker, Harry; Gay, Charles M.; and Macguire, John W. *Materials and Methods of Architectural Construction*. New York: John Wiley and Sons, 1958.

Putnum, Robert. *Concrete Block Construction*. 3d ed. Chicago: American Technical Society, 1973.

Ramsey, Charles G., and Sleeper, Harold R. *Architectural Graphic Standards*. 6th ed. New York: John Wiley and Sons, 1970.

Randall, Frank A., Jr., and Panarese, William C. *Concrete Masonry Handbook for Architects, Engineers and Builders*. Portland Cement Association, 1976.

Richter, H. P. *Practical Electrical Wiring*. 9th ed. New York: McGraw-Hill, 1972.

Schuler, Stanley. *The Wall Book*. New York: M. Evans and Co., 1974.

Sears, Roebuck and Co. *How to Install Central Heating and Cooling.* Philadelphia: Sears, Roebuck and Co.

————. *How to Install Hydronic Heating.* Philadelphia: Sears, Roebuck and Co.

————. *Simplified Electrical Wiring: A Handbook of Planning, Installing, Expanding and Modernizing.* Philadelphia: Sears, Roebuck and Co.

Smith, Ronald C. *Principles and Practices of Light Construction.* Englewood Cliffs, N.J.: Prentice-Hall, 1970.

Sunset Books and Magazines' Editors. *How to Plan and Build Your Fireplace.* Menlo Park, Calif.: Lane Books, 1973.

Ulrey, Harry F. *Audel Building, Construction and Design.* Indianapolis, Ind.: Theodore Audel and Co., 1970.

————. *Audel Carpenters and Builders Library.* Vol. 3. Indianapolis, Ind.: Theodore Audel and Co., 1970.

————. *Audel Carpenters and Builders Library: Layouts—Foundations—Framing.* Indianapolis, Ind.: Theodore Audel and Co., 1970.

United States Navy, Bureau of Navy Personnel. *Basic Construction Techniques for Houses and Small Buildings, Simply Explained.* New York: Dover Publications, 1972.

Wagner, Allis H. *Modern Carpentry.* South Holland, Ill.: Goodheart-Willcox Co., 1973.

Watson, Don. *Construction Materials and Processes.* New York: McGraw-Hill, 1972.

Wilson, Douglas J. *Practical House Carpentry: Simplified Methods for Building.* New York: McGraw-Hill, 1973.

Wilson, John, and Warner, S. O. *Simplified Roof Framing.* New York: McGraw-Hill, 1927, 1948.

Index

A NOTE ABOUT THE AUTHORS

Lupe DiDonno and Phyllis Sperling are both distinguished young architects, both graduates of Pratt Institute School of Architecture. Lupe DiDonno's professional background includes graduate training at Pratt, several years' experience in architectural firms, lecturing at New York City Community College, and her current partnership with her husband in DiDonno Associates, Architects. Phyllis Sperling holds a masters degree from Columbia's School of Architecture and Planning and was an architectural designer and architectural representative for the construction of the Health Sciences Center at Stonybrook. Since 1975 she has been teaching design and construction at New York City Community College. Both authors have had work exhibited in the "Women in American Architecture" show at the Brooklyn Museum. Both are members of the American Institute of Architects and are practicing architects in New York City.

A NOTE ABOUT THE TYPE

The text of this book was set in a film version of Palatino, a type face designed by the noted German typographer Hermann Zapf. Named after Giovanbattista Palatino, a writing master of Renaissance Italy, Palatino was the first of Zapf's type faces to be introduced to America. The first designs for the face were made in 1948, and the fonts for the complete face were issued between 1950 and 1952. Like all Zapf-designed type faces, Palatino is beautifully balanced and exceedingly readable.

The book was composed by American Book-Stratford Press, Brattleboro, Vermont. It was printed by Murray Printing Company, Forge Village, Massachusetts, and bound by The Book Press, Brattleboro, Vermont.

Design by Margaret M. Wagner